RESTRAINING RAGE

WILLIAM V. HARRIS

Restraining Rage

The Ideology of Anger Control
in Classical Antiquity

HARVARD UNIVERSITY PRESS

Cambridge, Massachusetts, and London, England

2001

Library of Congress Cataloging-in-Publication Data

Harris, William V. (William Vernon)
Restraining rage : the ideology of anger control in
classical antiquity / William V. Harris.
p.   cm.
Includes bibliographical references (p.)and index.
ISBN 0-674-00618-6 (cloth : alk. paper)
1. Anger—Greece—History.   2. Anger—Rome—History.
3. Civilization, Classical.
I. Title.

BF575.A5 H346   2002
152.4′7′0938—dc21   2001047076

To Silvana Patriarca

Contents

III. Intimate Rage

IV. Anger and the Invention of Psychic Health

Acknowledgements

In exploring classical anger, and in writing about what I think that I found out, I have been helped by a rather large number of people—which is no doubt an index of how slow I have been, as well as of the widespread interest the subject arouses. I especially wish to thank those who made comments or raised objections after lectures which I gave about anger at Rome, Pisa, Leiden, Heidelberg, Oxford, New Haven, Chapel Hill, Durham (Duke), Boulder (University of Colorado), San Francisco (at a meeting of the Society for Biblical Literature), Seattle (University of Washington) and Vancouver (University of British Columbia).

But it was particularly at Cambridge, where I gave the Gray Lectures on this subject in 1998, that I previously put these wares on display. I offer my warmest thanks to the Faculty Board of Classics there, to my hosts at St. John's College (where my godfather, John Thorpe, was an undergraduate some seven decades ago), and to all my Cambridge friends and acquaintances, above all to Malcolm Schofield (who is emphatically not to be held responsible for my philosophical opinions).

Later in 1998 I also benefited greatly from being a fellow of the National Humanities Center in North Carolina, and I thank all who made that possible and helped me during my stay there, especially the director of the center, W. Robert Connor. It is hard to think of any individual who has done more for humanistic scholarship in America in the past fifteen years than he has. Whether this book should be included among his good deeds, others will judge.

Three friends who could probably write better books about anger control have improved this work so much that I cannot help implicating them, even though I am sure that they will still see many faults in it: the psychologist Carol Dweck and the Hellenists Suzanne Said and Deborah Steiner. All three are by nature judicious critics, and wherever I have failed to follow their advice I shall probably regret it.

Debbie Steiner suggested that I should indicate more explicitly why I have emphasized some texts rather than others which might seem to be equally relevant, such as oratorical invective and the poetry of abuse (not that these are altogether ignored). Selecting the evidence to bring forward is, obviously, the perennial worry of every cultural and social historian. In this case it is enough to say that the main subject of the book is a specific theme—the reasons why the Greeks and Romans were so concerned to limit the action of certain kinds of anger. My desire to answer this question has been the guiding principle in selecting the evidence to present and discuss.

I should also like to thank for particular *beneficia* Evangelos Alexiou, Melissa Barden Dowling, Mary Beard, Glen Bowersock, Susanna Braund, Caroline Bynum, Alan Cameron, Andrew Carriker, Angelos Chaniotis, S. J. D. Cohen, H. G. Edinger, Jon Elster, Andrea Giardina, Tom Harrison, Keith Hopkins, Christopher Jones, Umberto Laffi, Myles McDonnell, Glenn Most, Silvana Patriarca, Catherine Peyroux, Saundra Schwartz, Seth Schwartz, David Sedley, Miranda Spieler and Yan Zelener.

It is a deplorable contemporary habit to pepper works of scholarship with the first-person pronoun. This book is about the Greeks and Romans, not about me. Which is not to claim a false objectivity, but simply to recognize that literary genres differ and have their respective (though not unalterable) rules. There is a boundary between the scholar and the subject, and it should be treated with respect. Anyone who wishes to know how my choice of subject or my conclusions may have been affected by personal experience is asked to wait patiently for my autobiography. As to whether it has been therapeutic to write a book about anger, the answer is yes, but only to a modest degree.

One other preliminary: I have made my own translations of most of the ancient authors quoted here, while freely plundering phrases from others. When it has seemed necessary, I have sacrificed flow and idiom in favour of accuracy. In the case of Homer, however, I experienced especial awe and self-doubt, and I have made heavy use—though with some misgivings and alterations—of the fine recent versions of both the *Iliad* and the *Odyssey* by Robert Fagles.

Abbreviations

The names of ancient writers and their works are abbreviated, when they are abbreviated, according to standard practices. In case of obscurity, see the Liddell, Scott & Jones *Greek-English Lexicon,* the *Oxford Latin Dictionary,* or the *Oxford Classical Dictionary.* I use angle brackets in translated quotations to enclose words not in the original which have been supplied to make acceptable English; square brackets enclose extra information.

ANRW	*Aufstieg und Niedergang der Römischen Welt,* ed. H. Temporini (Berlin & New York, 1972–)
Audollent	A. Audollent, *Defixionum tabellae* (Paris, 1904)
CC-SL	*Corpus Christianorm, Series Latina*
CIL	*Corpus Inscriptionum Latinarum*
C.Iust.	*Codex Iustinianus*
CMG	*Corpus Medicorum Graecorum*
C.P.Lat.	*Corpus Papyrorum Latinarum,* ed. R. Cavenaile
CSEL	*Corpus Scriptorum Ecclesiasticorum latinorum*
C.Th.	*Codex Theodosianus*
Dig.	*Digesta*
D-K	H. Diels & W. Kranz, *Die Fragmente der Vorsokratiker* (8th ed., Berlin, 1956)
EAA	*Enciclopedia dell'arte antica*
FGrH	*Die Fragmente der griechischen Historiker,* ed. F. Jacoby
FIRA	*Fontes Iuris Romani Anteiustiniani,* ed. S. Riccobono et al.
IGRR	*Inscriptiones Graecae ad Res Romanas Pertinentes,* ed. R. Cagnat
ILS	*Inscriptiones Latinae Selectae,* ed. H. Dessau
LFE	*Lexikon der frühgriechischen Epos,* ed. B. Snell

LIMC	*Lexicon Iconographicum Mythologiae Classicae*
L-S	A. A. Long & D. N. Sedley (eds.), *The Hellenistic Philosophers* (Cambridge, 1987)
LSJ	H. Liddell, R. Scott & H. S. Jones, *Greek-English Lexicon*
LTUR	*Lexicon Topographicum Urbis Romae*, ed. M. Steinby
P.Amh.	*The Amherst Papyri*, ed. B. P. Grenfell & A. S. Hunt
PG	*Patrologia Graeca*
PGM	*Papyri Graecae Magicae*, ed. K. Preisendanz
P.Herc.	Herculaneum Papyri, listed in M. Gigante (ed.), *Catalogo dei papiri ercolanesi* (Naples, 1979)
P.Hibeh	*The Hibeh Papyri*, ed. B. P. Grenfell et al.
PIR	*Prosopographia Imperii Romani*
PL	*Patrologia Latina*
P.Lond.	*Greek Papyri in the British Museum*, ed. F. G. Kenyon et al.
PMGF	*Poetarum Melicorum Graecorum Fragmenta*, ed. D. L. Page & M. Davies
P.Ross.Georg.	*Papyri russischer und georgischer Sammlungen*, ed. G. Zereteli et al.
RE	*Realencyclopädie der classischen Altertumswissenschaft*, ed. A. F. von Pauly, G. Wissowa & W. Kroll
RIC	*Roman Imperial Coinage*
SIG	*Sylloge Inscriptionum Graecarum*, ed. W. Dittenberger
SVF	*Stoicorum Veterum Fragmenta*, ed. H. von Arnim
TGF	*Tragicorum Graecorum Fragmenta*, ed. A. Nauck & B. Snell
TLL	*Thesaurus Linguae Latinae*

PART I

Approaches

CHAPTER 1

Striving for Anger Control

Lifelong therapy, that was the only way to deal with emotions such as anger if one wanted to come through "safe and sound." This was the grim advice of the Hellenized Roman philosopher Musonius Rufus, as it is transmitted by Plutarch in his essay on the restraint of anger.[1] In his hostility towards anger Musonius was far from being alone. Many men of letters in classical antiquity favoured its control or elimination.[2] Throughout the history of classical literature, from Homer and Hesiod to Libanius and Augustine, criticisms of anger make themselves heard. The theme first takes the form of direct advice in the verses of Sappho, and it appears to be remarkably persistent, even when one makes allowance for the fondness of the Greeks and Romans for topoi and familiar literary subject matter. Epic, lyric, tragedy, comedy, and satire—among other genres—all contribute. The great historians all seem to have views on the subject.

Philosophers, and others with philosophical interests, took up the theme, and from the fourth century B.C. they discussed it in numerous treatises about the emotions as well as, later, in monographs about anger itself. Two such monographs survive virtually intact, the younger Seneca's (probably written about 49 or 50 A.D.), and that of Plutarch

---

1. Musonius fr. XXXVI, from Plu. *De cohibenda ira* 2 (*Mor.* 453d).

2. Some have found the term *control* very vague in this context (e.g., Spelman 1989, 268), but with respect to emotions its normal meaning is clearly "diminution," "limiting."

(probably written about 100 A.D.); a third survives in part, the work of Philodemus of Gadara (written between about 70 and 40 B.C.), rather less than half of which has proved to be legible on a Herculaneum papyrus roll. Other works about the emotions, such as Cicero's *Tusculan Disputations* and Galen's essay *On the Diagnosis and Care of the Passions of the Soul* also gave anger plenty of space.[3]

At first, criticisms of anger were limited in scope, concentrating in particular on the reining in of extreme or unrelenting anger, and in classical Athens anger had not only its place but its defenders,[4] in particular Aristotle, who regarded *aorgēsia*, which means roughly "habitual absence of vigorous anger," as no better than irascibility. But eventually a number of voices—and not simply those of Stoics such as Musonius Rufus—came to advocate nothing less than an absolute moral prohibition of anger.

We might imagine a four-stage critical progression:

(1) reining in angry actions and speech,
(2) eliminating angry actions and speech,
(3) reining in angry feelings,[5]
(4) eliminating angry feelings.

But we must not make such a scheme too definite, for while statements in favour of (2), (3) and (4) took some time to appear in classical antiquity, (1) is still commonly the primary aim, even when the subject has been under discussion for many centuries. Even after the inven-

---

3. Here and in many other places in this book I have translated πάθος, *pathos,* as "passion." That is not very satisfactory, for several reasons: one being that in ordinary speech "passion" usually means "passionate enthusiasm," which does not fit the Greek word. Yet "emotion" is usually even less satisfactory as a translation of *pathos,* because "emotions" in English are often mild things such as nostalgia, whereas *pathē* are mostly strong (L-S I.419–420 is perhaps a little misleading about this). It is important to observe, however, that when Aristotle lists some typical *pathē* of the soul he includes—besides anger *(thumos),* fear, pity, joy, hate and affectionate love—*praotēs,* even temper, and *tharsos,* bravery or boldness (*De anima* i.1.403a17–18); and these are not exactly "passions."

4. But only a very inattentive reader could suppose with Lossau 1992, 60, that the literary tradition about anger was "very favourable" prior to Aristotle.

5. I should make it clear that when I refer to emotional "feelings" I do not mean to refer to some inner state that is independent of cognition.

tion of Stoicism, the majority of philosophers never truly endorsed objective (2), let alone (4). But removing anger, presumably in sense (4), became, ostensibly at least, a standard aim of Stoic and Stoicizing philosophers under the Roman Empire.

As we shall see, many ancient persons, from Homer onwards, showed themselves capable of distinguishing between feeling emotions and acting on those emotions. But it is worth remarking at once that the general supposition seems to have been that anger could not be hidden (we shall examine this matter in Chapter 3). If this hypothesis is correct, anger control will have been all the more desirable.

It was frequently assumed, however, that it was actually *possible* to rein in one's anger, that at least in this respect the individual was autonomous. The tension between this belief and the notion that strong emotions are irresistible external forces beyond our control forms an essential element in this study (see especially Chapter 15).[6] The predominance of the former idea, at least in post-archaic times (that is to say, after 500 B.C.), is I think one of the most characteristic features of classical culture. Greeks and Romans commonly believed that anger restraint was possible. Not that the story is simple: while Homer often treats strong emotions as coming from outside the individual, he also shows us characters mastering their emotions; some of the principal post-archaic words for angry emotions, in particular *orgē/orgizesthai*, refer to intense and hard-to-resist feelings (see Chapter 3), and even the most innocently optimistic Hellenistic and Roman philosophers often seem aware that almost everyone is sometimes *carried away* by some passion or other.

Parallel to the evolving morality of human anger was the development of ideas about the anger of the gods. At first this anger was simply part of existence, and if Homer thought that the anger of the gods was sometimes arbitrary or excessive, he kept silent about it. Divine anger fulfilled several essential functions throughout antiquity. It was not merely a projection of the anger of humans. It offered explanations of otherwise inexplicable facts and happenings, from ordinary natural

6. This dispute continues: cf. Elster 1999, 312–317 (but he underestimates the strength of the support for the view that emotions are under our control). It seems evident that both views are too extreme. For a philosophical discussion, see Adams 1985, who takes it for granted that "anger is rarely voluntary" (3).

events such as sicknesses and storms to the place of man in the cosmos (as in the myth of Zeus and Prometheus). It explained the gods', or an individual god's, disfavour towards a person or a collectivity of persons. It provided support for fundamental rules of conduct. And, not unimportant, it maintained respect for religious practitioners, from Apollo's priest Chryses (in Book I of the *Iliad*) onwards.

However, it gradually came to be supposed that passions or passionate extremes which were to be deplored in humans could not be felt by the gods, and we shall see philosophers, and others too, begin to assert that the gods were entirely immune from anger. This was to cause a serious intellectual difficulty for the Christians of patristic times, who had apparent authority that their god was sometimes angry; one reaction was Lactantius' surviving treatise *De ira dei (On the Anger of God)*, another was a contradiction of Scripture by Augustine.

This classical preoccupation with anger, widespread though sometimes oddly absent (for instance from Xenophon's *Cyropaedia*), will be amply documented in the chapters that follow. But we must without delay ask whether a preoccupation with anger was really a special characteristic of classical culture. After all, many other ages have produced literary works that are much concerned with the angry emotions. *The Song of Roland,* for instance, constantly speaks of certain kinds of anger:

> King Charles rides like fury . . .
> The French barons all spur furiously,
> They are all in a state of blind anger.[7]

So do many other works of mediaeval literature, and many Elizabethan plays:

> The fearful passage of their death-marked love,
>   and the continuance of their parents' rage,
> which, but their children's end, naught could remove,
>   is now the two hours' traffic of our stage.

Paradise Lost and *Jane Eyre* both have much to say about angry characters. So does *Crime and Punishment,* and so does Naguib Mahfouz's

7. Lines 1842–1845 (mostly as translated by G. J. Brault). For other references in this poem and many mediaeval parallels, see S. D. White 1998, 131–139.

Children of the Alley. Italian humanists wrote many pages on anger control.[8] Revenge, virtually throughout the history of European dramatic literature, has exercised irresistible attraction (on this theme John Kerrigan's *Revenge Tragedy* is required reading),[9] and in every act of revenge, however coldly executed, a state of anger reaches its climax.

Yet the Greek and Roman texts, taken as a body of writing, are rather different. The master texts of the entire culture, the staples of the educational system over many lands and many centuries, were the *Iliad,* the *Odyssey* and the *Aeneid.* In the first and last of these works, in particular, the effects of anger are very visibly under scrutiny, and the *Odyssey* is a tale of retribution tied to a tale about the anger of the god Poseidon. A number of other central intellectual figures of the classical world, among them Aristotle, and the most illustrious practitioners of some important literary genres—Aeschylus, Euripides, Cicero, Juvenal, Galen, simply to name a few highly disparate names—put forward teachings about anger. The main philosophical schools of the age, especially the Stoics, had much to say on the subject. And to a considerable extent these texts form a single tradition, in the sense that they respond to what had been written on the subject earlier.

It is not my purpose to argue that this concern was a unique feature of the classical world. The ancient attempt to control anger had its own distinct shape and development, but there may be quite close parallels in other cultures, for example in some of the more civilized parts of middle- and late-mediaeval Europe.[10] Since the argument of this book is that ancient attempts at anger control were responses to social and political conditions, it will be a comfort rather than the reverse if we find that similar conditions have produced similar responses in other times and places. Modern critiques of anger, however—in the United States, for instance, there was once a moralistic literature about anger[11]—may or may not have the same pervasive quality as the an-

8. Cf. Herlihy 1972, 130, 132.

9. Kerrigan 1996.

10. There is a growing literature on medieval ideas about anger: see especially Rosenwein (ed.) 1998; Casagrande & Vecchio 2000, 54–77 (simplistic). The wrathful in hell: Dante, *Inf.* vii.109–126, xxxi.72; in purgatory: *Purg.* xv–xvii.

11. See Stearns & Stearns 1986, chs. 3–4. These authors wrote that in classical antiquity anger "was not only acceptable but often desirable" (21).

cient critique, and in any case do not respond to conditions at all similar to those of the classical world.

Anger control is rather obviously a contemporary problem, though it is seldom seen as such except by psychiatrists. One of the latter has written that "the complicated clinical problems presented by anger and rage remain far and away the most confounding Gordian knot faced in the effective practice of psychotherapy."[12] Which may at least suggest that current discussion of the subject, which periodically "rediscovers" Aristotle or Seneca,[13] might benefit from Graeco-Roman experience. Exactly how, I shall suggest in Chapter 2 and in my conclusion. What we should think and do about anger, as individuals and as citizens, is an enormously difficult set of problems, and scientific psychology—in spite of the advantages it enjoys with respect to the Greeks and Romans—is not well situated to solve them all.[14]

What, incidentally, of the expression "Graeco-Roman"? Is it legitimate to ascribe a preoccupation with anger to both the Greeks and the Romans—terms which themselves have manifold connotations? Is it possible within one pair of covers to analyse the attempts at anger control of both Greeks and Romans, given all the differences between them? And in this age, when some historians have lost confidence in their ability to speak about large conglomerations of human beings at all?

Not only possible, but essential; we should not on this occasion attempt to treat the Greeks and Romans separately. There are naturally factors which mattered in the Greek world and never among the Romans, and vice versa. But there is a vital unity to the whole story. It would be absurd to write a book about Greek anger control which did not include philosophers and other writers of the Hellenistic age, and these texts in turn lead by a continuous path into the Roman Empire. On the other side, nothing that was written by Romans on this subject from the age of Livius Andronicus onwards can be interpreted without knowledge of what the Greeks had said before: most of the Romans we shall be considering knew parts of the Greek tradition very well. One

12. Diamond 1996, 7.

13. E.g., Schimmel 1979; Lazarus 1991, 217; Solomon 1993, 4–5.

14. Cf. Elster 1999, 48–50 (though he operates with a distinction between "wrath" and "anger" which I find unsustainable—see Chapter 2).

can maintain, if one so desires, that the Hellenism of the educated Romans—and it is the educated ones who are in question here—was almost always superficial, but even Juvenal and even the Roman jurists have to be read as the products of a Graeco-Roman tradition.

Why, then, was anger, or excessive anger, so much the target of criticism in classical antiquity? Why was controlling anger, or keeping it within limits, or eliminating it, thought to be so important? That is the central set of problems which this book is intended to solve. It is not enough to say simply that humans prefer a world in which people are not angry with them, for the Greek and Roman texts are too insistent to be explained by a watery quietism. What good results was the restraint or elimination of anger thought to produce, whether in public or private life or in the psyche? These will have to be anticipated results which appealed not only to philosophers but also to practical intellectuals such as Polybius and Cicero. In later chapters, several complementary ways of answering these questions will be explored. Convincing answers will have to be based on an analysis of the function of each relevant text—what effect was it intended to create? And they will also have to be historical, thus avoiding the mistake (which scholars have not always avoided) of supposing that the same set of ideas about anger and the control of anger was always current in antiquity.

A psychologist, unconsciously echoing an ancient view which we shall encounter in the next chapter, has offered the opinion that "with the rise of civilization, occasions when people needed to use anger-mobilized energy for physical defense and survival tactics became less and less common."[15] Which implies that the classical critics of anger were simply trying to perform the Herculean task of making morality keep up with evolution. No doubt this is largely true, but it is also terribly simplistic, and also optimistic in the sense that it implicitly underestimates the continuing need for defensive anger in "civilized" Greek and Roman society.

One of the few responses which scholars have offered to the classical concern with controlling anger has come from a student of Seneca's *De ira* who argued, in effect, that it was just the reaction of philoso-

15. Izard 1991, 243.

phy to life.[16] In her view the Greeks and Romans were in fact exceptionally irascible, and all philosophical schools reacted against this nasty reality.

This appears to be a reasonable line of thinking, but it is open to crippling objections. Do we know that "anger held a large place" in the lives of the Greeks and Romans, or even of sub-populations within these vast and heterogeneous totalities? We seem to have no means of establishing such a thing securely. And since there is no automatic reason *why* philosophers should have reacted against the level of irascibility that obtained among their contemporaries, the "reaction" hypothesis would in any case have little explanatory force. But it does not completely miss the target, for some Greeks—so it will be argued in Chapters 7 and 8—wanted to limit the action of anger because they thought that there was too much of it in the contemporary polis, or a danger of too much of it. Others, both Greeks and Romans, opposed what they saw as the excessive anger of monarchical rulers (Chapter 10).

We cannot know in a secure way whether the Greeks and Romans were highly irascible by modern standards, whatever those may be. Even if they sometimes seem irascible to us, it may only be because they were angered by different things. "A New Yorker," it has been remarked, "will become infuriated on standing in a queue the length of which would make a Muscovite grateful,"[17] and what characteristically brought out the ire of Greeks and Romans is one of the open questions before us. How in any case could you measure whether a society has much anger in it? It might be possible for a careful historian to compare levels of violent aggression in two or more nations, by reference to bellicosity, violent crime, domestic violence (including violence towards slaves), and violent amusements (such as gladiatorial games), but the results are likely to be very rough-and-ready. And anyway, violent aggression is not the same as anger.

The question whether "anger held a large place," in spite of its distressing vagueness, is nonetheless worth exploring, for apart from its

16. Fillion-Lahille 1984, 8–10.

17. Solomon 1984, 240. The observation is not accurate: New Yorkers wait quite stoically "on line"—after being rebuffed in their attempts to gain access without waiting their turn. But the general point is sound.

inherent interest it can teach us some of the difficulties of using the sources about the history of classical anger. What can in fact be admitted as evidence about actual real-world occurrences of anger?[18] Not in any case anecdotes about philosophers. Their irascibility became a topos,[19] having been minted, one might guess, very shortly after the first philosopher publicly suggested that anger needed to be kept under control. Equally unhelpful as a source of information about actual practice is the supposedly evil temper of Socrates' wife Xanthippe,[20] which probably started life as a joke (of which there were many) at the wise man's expense, this one being founded on the already ancient allegation that women were more prone to anger than men.[21] Periander, the ruler of Corinth, was liable twice over to be the subject of accusations of irascibility, once for being a tyrant, a second time for being a sage.[22] King Xerxes' legendary anger with the Hellespont tells us that many Greeks in fact despised a monarch who lost his temper in the wrong circumstances.[23] Nor would it help us at all to discover that Seneca's older brother Novatus, the addressee of the philosopher's *De ira,* was in fact irascible (there is in fact no solid reason to think so).[24]

At the same time, many of the stories about violence against slaves, which form part of the case for Graeco-Roman irascibility, while they are not free from literary influences, probably contain factual elements too. Here, in the region of contact between slaves and free,

18. This paragraph and the following one respond to the argumentation of Fillion-Lahille.

19. Some of the evidence is mentioned in Fillion-Lahille 1984, 8. Pyrrho: Diog.Laert. ix.66 and 68. Speusippus: Diog.Laert. iv.1.1. The theme is a favourite with Lucian: see Chapter 15. It was also a standard anecdote that an admired philosopher *restrained* his anger just in time: see Riginos 1976, 155–156 (where the case of Socrates could have been added: Sen. *De ira* i.15.3, iii.11.2).

20. She is cited by Fillion-Lahille (1984, 8). A story to this effect was already in circulation in the 380s (Xen. *Mem.* ii.2), and may indeed have had some basis in fact. Later allusions are numerous: Sen. *De const.* 18.5, Epictet. iv.5.3, Plu. *De cohibenda ira* 13 (*Mor.* 461d), Diog.Laert. ii.37, etc.

21. For this stereotype see Chapter 11. The discrepancy in the ages of Socrates and Xanthippe, great even by Athenian standards, may also have contributed.

22. Cited in Fillion-Lahille 1984, 9.

23. Ibid. (cf. Hdt. vii.35).

24. Ibid. *De ira* does not say that Novatus was irascible, and Sen. *Nat.Quaest.* ivA. *praef.* suggests otherwise.

was a great locus of classical anger.[25] On the day of a dinner party, the slaves forgot to buy bread: "Which of us," asks Plutarch, "[if he had been the owner] would not have made the walls fall down with shouts?"[26] That is not a question likely to have been asked by a well-brought-up person in the nineteenth or twentieth century. But violent outbursts of anger by master against slave were a daily occurrence in ancient households, and those slave-owners who were supposed to have restrained themselves were given credit for an exceptional achievement. The slaves, meanwhile, normally had to repress their anger but inevitably felt a great deal of it, as indeed the sources suggest.

The fantastic scenes of rage described in some of the ancient narratives we shall encounter in this book suggest something of the extreme behaviour which anger might lead to in antiquity. But virtually all these texts are either fictional in a straightforward sense or formed by the rhetorical/literary conventions which make some aspects of ancient "factual" narratives seem decidedly unfactual to modern minds. Here, for instance, is Galen:

> Once when I was still very young and pursuing this <psychological> self-training, I watched a man eagerly trying to open a door. When [the door failed to open], I saw him bite the key, kick the door, abuse the gods, glare wildly like a lunatic and all but foam at the mouth like a wild boar. When I saw this, I conceived such a hatred for anger [*thumos*] that I was never thereafter seen behaving in an unseemly manner because of it.[27]

But Galen's key-biter is apparently a fiction, for he himself reports elsewhere that the Stoic philosopher Chrysippus had written, some four centuries before, that when doors fail to open we "often" bite the key, and a similar observation was made before Galen by Philodemus.[28] It was a good way of suggesting the absurdity of the angry. Herodotus'

---

25. See Chapter 13.

26. Plu. *De cohibenda ira* 13 (*Mor.* 461d).

27. *De propriorum animi cuiuslibet affectuum dignotione et curatione* 4.5 De Boer.

28. *SVF* III.478; Phld. *De ira* fr. 8 Indelli. Fillion-Lahille 1984, 9, ignores the inevitable conclusion. Given the strong interest of New Comedy in both doors and anger, the origin was quite possibly a play.

tale about the killing by the Persian king Cambyses of the son of his courtier Prexaspes may or may not have a historical element in it, but it served admirably as a lesson about kings, Persians and uncontrolled rage.[29] It begins to appear that, what with fiction, topoi and truly abnormal cases, ordinary facts about ancient displays of anger are not so very easily identified. Not that we will want to underestimate the instructiveness of either fiction or topoi.

Sometimes, of course, we encounter authors who are themselves angry—in Graeco-Roman curse tablets, for example. Many hundreds of them survive, written between the sixth century B.C. and the end of antiquity.[30] Such curses were directed by individuals against individuals and took the form of a request to one or more divine beings.

> Lord gods Sukonaioi . . . , Lady goddess Syria Sukona . . . punish, show your wonderful power and direct your anger at whoever took <and> stole the necklace, at those who had any knowledge of it, at those who were accomplices, whether man or woman.[31]

> Malcius belonging to Nicona: <his> eyes, hands, fingers, arms, nails, hair, head, feet, thigh, belly, buttocks, navel, chest, nipples, neck, mouth, cheeks, teeth, lips, chin, eyes, forehead, eyebrows, shoulder blades, shoulders, sinews, bones, *merilas* [meaning unknown], belly, penis, shin: in these tablets I bind <his> income, profit and health.[32]

> Spirits under the earth and spirits wherever you may be . . . , since you take men's grievous passion [*thumos*] from their heart, take over the passion of Ariston which he has towards me, Soterianos also called

29. Hdt. iii.34–35 (quoted below, p. 230). The story was taken up by Sen. *De ira* iii.14.1–4.

30. The standard collection is still Audollent 1904. See also Jordan 1985. Gager 1992 provides a useful survey and guide to the bibliography. Such texts obviously take us, at least in most cases, well outside the upper social elite. To make a comparison with mediaeval cursing, see Little 1998.

31. Hellenistic, from Delos. Bruneau 1970, 649–655; Jordan 1985, no. 58; Versnel 1991, 66–68; Gager 1992, no. 88.

32. Undated, from Nomentum, near Rome. Audollent 1904, no. 135; Gager 1992, no. 80.

Limbaros, and his anger; and take away from him his strength and power and make him cold and speechless and breathless.[33]

As a psychological phenomenon, such texts are not easy to interpret. They often express venomous anger—also from time to time cold loathing, fear, envy and sexual passion. They are overt, in a sense, but also secret, hidden. There is, in short, no clarity as to whether they reflect an unusually angry culture or not.

It would even be possible to argue that parts at least of the Greek population were remarkably good at keeping anger under control. We may be a little sceptical of the claim, included by Thucydides in Pericles' Funeral Oration (ii.37.2), that Athenian citizens resisted temptations to get angry with each other, but at least the ideal was there (when it had emerged, and why, we shall discuss in Chapter 8). Is it not possible, after all, that the attempts of some Greeks to control their anger to some extent succeeded? In Thucydides, as was recently observed, Athenian crowds do not let their displeasure turn violent, and in Herodotus such a thing is extremely rare.[34] Anger was not always dominant in Greek society—in spite of the freedom which male members of the citizen body commonly enjoyed.[35] Neither in classical Greek cities, nor at Rome either, did civilians openly carry arms within the city,[36] for they did not expect that they might at any moment be assaulted or be compelled to fight. In certain limited periods, political street-fighting was common, and no one would want to exaggerate the tranquillity of street life in classical cities, but they seem to have done

33. Second or third century A.D., from Amathous, Cyprus. Audollent 1904, no. 22; Gager 1992, no. 45.

34. Herman 1994, 110. The exceptions are in Hdt. ix.5 (in wartime) and v.87 (a legend about women).

35. We shall return in Chapter 8 to the relationship between this freedom and anger.

36. Thuc. i.6 (it had not always been so; cf. Van Wees 1992, 30); for Rome under the Republic, see Nic.Dam., *FGrH* 90 F 130 sect. 81; cf. Nippel 1995, 55. Under the principate: *Dig.* xlviii.6.1–2 (the main legitimate reasons for possessing weapons were hunting and inter-city travel; but see also xlviii.6.11.2—and the reader should be warned that a new investigation of this matter is needed), SHA *Hadr.* 13. Lawrence Stone (1983, 22) pours cold water on the implications of the extent of weapon carrying (in England), while admitting (25) the effects of sword wearing; and we do not indeed know how much Greeks and Romans carried knives.

remarkably well in this respect, and almost always without anything like a modern thoroughness in policing.

In short, we cannot establish that the Greeks and Romans expressed, or felt, much more anger than we do, though we cannot exclude the possibility either.

What is clear, however, is that the Greeks and Romans *talked* and *wrote* a great deal about anger. This is not only a question of books about philosophy or therapy, not only a question about other works of literature into which their authors more or less deliberately introduced the subject. Anger discourse, in both languages, goes much further than that: it permeates the language of many Greek and Roman authors, from Homer onwards. This is true of the *Odyssey,* and it is true of Plutarch's lives; it is true of Herodotus, and it is true of Heliodorus. The Attic orators are constantly speaking of *orgē*-anger. Statistics about this are easier to compile for Latin authors than for Greek, the Latin vocabulary for anger being simpler. Livy, for example, uses the word *ira* 321 times and the verb *irascor* ("I am angry") 61 times, which makes it a leitmotif, in the strict sense of that expression, of his history. Petronius, to take another instance, though he uses all sorts of other words for anger-like emotions (including the unique *caldicerebrius,* "hot-brained," and *scabitudo,* "irritation"), has *ira, iracundia, iracundus* and *irascor* a total of 42 times in a short text (numbers, however, can hardly give an adequate notion of the pervasive role of anger in the surviving section of the *Satyrica*).[37] Few inveterate readers of Greek and Latin texts would doubt in any case that the vocabulary of anger came very easily to Greek and Roman pens.

Why? No doubt the incessant references of many classical authors to anger have a good deal of the conventional about them, which is not to deny that something akin to anger was felt or described. There is a parallel in modern psychiatric experience, reported long ago:

> For a good many years I have been interested in listening to patients' accounts of their emotions . . . I still listen with great interest to patients' statements along these lines, but not with the expectation of discovering what "emotions" he or she is really experiencing—rather with

37. For Livy, see D. W. Packard's concordance. For Petronius, that of J. Segebade & E. Lommatzsch. For the distinction between *ira* and *iracundia* see Chapter 3.

the hope of discovering in some measure the conventionalized scheme of symbols by which the patient tries to represent himself to himself and others. Not only are the words conventional symbols; the motor patterns of behavior are also conventionalized.[38]

The emotion-reporting language of the ancients, or at least their reports about anger, may similarly contain a large element of the conventional.[39] Which invites us to explain the origin of the conventions.

It seems a likely hypothesis that anger discourse takes up space in Greek and Roman minds because other concepts which we are accustomed to are absent. *Mood*, for instance: while it is possible to make statements in Greek and Latin about mood, we seldom, I think, find ourselves making use of this concept when we translate from the classical languages. But there is no easy answer here, for Aristotle and all the other classical authors who defined anger agreed, in effect, that it was an emotion with a specific object,[40] which is precisely what a mood is *not*.

The reason why anger bulks so large in ancient authors may rather have been that *depression* was largely absent. I am not suggesting that the Greeks and Romans suffered from depression while usually failing to identify it by any closely equivalent term; rather, that the frustrations of life, commonly recognized as a major source of modern depression, tended in antiquity to produce emotions akin to anger. The emotional state we know of as depression may have been less common.

To examine the Greek semantic cluster *athumia/dusthumia/ melancholia* in full would take us out of our way. The complications are considerable: *athumos* can certainly mean "despondent," for instance, but when the exact meaning of *athumia* is determinable, it seems to be "faintheartedness," something close to "lack of courage."[41] Nor was Greek *melancholia,* contrary to what is naturally and commonly as-

38. Whitehorn 1939, 263.
39. Many have noticed that ancient narrative writing tends to reduce motives to conventional simplicities; Tacitus, his cynicism notwithstanding, is a partial exception (cf. Syme 1958, 210).
40. See Chapter 3.
41. E.g., Hipp. *Airs* 16, Hdt. i.37, Pl. *Laws* v.731a, Xen. *Cyr.* iv.1.8, *Hist.* vi.2.24. The semantic assertions in this chapter are summary in nature; for more detail see Chapter 3.

sumed, the simple equivalent of "melancholy."[42] There were of course melancholy Greeks—and in *Black Sun* Julia Kristeva astutely identifies Homer's Bellerophon as the first one.[43] But what the Greeks and Romans meant by *melancholia* was usually a rather aggressive kind of madness. That, so they thought, was a common result of the predominance of "black bile."[44] Cicero says that the Latin equivalent was *furor,* "insane passion."[45] For the medical writer Caelius Aurelianus, *melancholia* is akin to *furor* or actually a form of it.[46]

None of this shows that one cannot express in the classical languages the thought that someone is depressed. The concept appears from time to time in modern translations of Greek and Latin books, and may not always be inexact.[47] Among the Greek terms which can border on meaning depression are *lupē,* "mental pain," and later on (from the first century B.C.) *akēdia,* the ancestor of mediaeval *accidie.* But it is probably symptomatic that the best description of depression in ancient literature, which is to be found in Seneca's *De tranquillitate animi,* is accompanied by an express admission that there is no name for this condition (the *opposite* of it would be Greek *euthumia* or Latin

---

42. Simon 1978, 228, assumes that it corresponds to melancholy, as does S. W. Jackson 1986.

43. On the basis of *Il.* vi.200–203. See Kristeva 1989, 7, and Rütten 1992, 57–61. Cf. Heiberg 1927, 3.

44. See Hipp. *Aphorisms* vi.56 ("with respect to melancholic conditions, the likely results are apoplexy of the whole body, convulsions, madness or blindness"); Men. *Samia* 563, *Shield* 306–307; Ps.-Aristot. *Probl.* xxx.1.954a21–27; Plin. *NH* xi.193; cf. Phld. *De ira* 4 (col. ix.37–41). See Flashar 1966, esp. 136; Kudlien 1967, 77–78. The account given by Toohey 1990, 143–147, is inaccurate.

45. *Tusc.Disp.* iii.11. He claims that it is often a consequence of anger *(iracundia)* or fear or resentment, using the usual proof by myth (Athamas, Alcmaeon, Ajax and Orestes are his examples).

46. *On Chronic Diseases* i.6 (this text is based on Soranus). Cicero and Vergil, he says (i.6.180), had used related expressions to refer to profound anger. Those who suffer from *melancholia* are always sad *(tristes),* but they have many other symptoms. Apparently, however, one could be considered *melancholikos* without suffering from the extreme conditions which black bile was thought to cause: Hipp. *Aphorisms* vi.23, Ps.-Aristot. *Probl.* xxx.1.953a10–15. See, further, Rütten 1992, 81–94.

47. Thus the *OLD* not unreasonably gives "depressed" as a meaning of *tristis* and "depress" as a meaning of *contristare,* but modern depression is characterized by obscure aetiology, and that feature is not very evident in classical writers.

tranquillitas).[48] Hence a certain gap remains, and that gap may have been full of anger-like emotions.

Before we can return to our central set of questions—what led the Greeks and Romans to strive so much to control anger—we must alert ourselves to two different positions from which anger-control texts may set out. Are they attempting to assert an accepted societal norm, or alternatively to improve on one? When the curtain rises on Greek history, there are of course norms of behaviour already in place. We shall often wish to distinguish between, on the one hand, what an anthropological study has called "the acquired conventions, norms or habits that dictate what emotion can be shown to whom and in which contexts,"[49] in this case, when anger can be shown and to whom and in which contexts; and on the other hand, non-conventional rules demanding, again with respect to anger, stricter standards of emotional control or behaviour. An example of the kind of text that echoes the accepted conventions is the second Juvenal (the one whose *persona* we encounter from Satire 10 onwards);[50] of the latter, any text, such as Seneca's *De ira,* that expresses absolute opposition to anger—which, however, also becomes a kind of convention.

A further aim of this study is to recreate some of the emotional content, specifically some of the anger content, of Greek and Roman history. In modern scholarly accounts of ancient history, which are mostly supervised by severe northern European ghosts, the affective life of the actors is kept quite strictly out of sight. Hardly anyone, apparently, wants to see "undisciplined squads of emotions"[51] complicating historical narrative or analysis. Occasional attempts to break this rule have not been enthusiastically received.[52] Christian Meier wrote a thought-

48. See esp. *De tranq. animi* i.15–17; uncertainty about what to call this affliction: i.4, ii.1. For the fact that some cultures do not recognize anything closely akin to "depression" see Marsella 1980.

49. Lutz & White 1986, 410.

50. For this distinction between successive *personae* in Juvenal's work see Chapter 9.

51. The phrase is from Eliot, *East Coker.*

52. For instance, Carlin Barton's *The Sorrows of the Ancient Romans* (1992). A notable study of social institutions which does something to recreate emotional atmosphere is David Cohen's *Law, Violence and Community in Classical Athens* (1995). D. S. Allen, *The World of Prometheus: The Politics of Punishing in Democratic Athens* (2000), is too narrowly focused to be able to give a convincing historical account of the evidence about anger which she considers.

provoking article about *Angst* and the early Greek state,[53] but I have seldom seen it cited and never seen it treated as a model. We are well accustomed to discussing interests as motive forces for behaviour, but are not so capable of describing the role of emotions.

In most of our scholarly literature about the classical world, political and religious change, for example—which might be expected to have aroused vigorous passions from time to time—seems to take place in a remarkably calm fashion. When the fifth-century Athenian Empire rises and falls, it generally seems to do so without arousing much strong emotion among its supporters or its enemies, who with some exceptions pursue their perceived interests in an unemotional way. The same could be said about the expansion of the Roman Empire. Even when the functioning of political life is the explicit subject, emotions are neglected: thus a useful book about *stasis* (civic strife) in classical Greece omits consideration of the rage which, as the sources attest, normally accompanied *stasis* conflicts.[54] Robert Burton would not have made the same mistake: "Look into our histories," he wrote, "and you shall almost meet with no other subject, but what a company of hare-brains have done in their rage."[55]

The religious history of antiquity has perhaps fared somewhat better. A solid tradition linking such disparate scholars as Nock *(Conversion)*, Dodds *(The Greeks and the Irrational)* and Simon Price has ensured that the emotional content of this history has received some attention. Yet even here, when for example the great conflict between Christianity and the old way of worshipping the gods was raging in the third and fourth centuries, historians sometimes give the impression that few deep emotions were involved.[56]

---

53. Meier 1986. Meier saw that Norbert Elias's *The Civilizing Process* could to some extent be applied to Greece (cf. Chapter 7), but he does not justify the centrality of *Angst* in his essay, which is in any case a sketch. For an interesting discussion of *phthonos* (envy) see Rakoczy 1996.

54. Gehrke 1985. The new *Cambridge History of Greek and Roman Political Thought* (2000) also offers some sadly limited readings of Greek authors.

55. *The Anatomy of Melancholy*, 6th ed. London, 1652; repr. New York, 1864, I:360.

56. The work of Peter Brown has taken us some way in the other direction. More typical is the approach of Drake 1996 to Christian intolerance towards non-Christians in the fourth century, which he thinks must have been either "political" or "theological" (6), without any thought that vengefulness, for instance, might have entered into the matter.

Naturally it is open to anyone to espouse a theory of historical materialism or a theory of rational choice which renders all feelings of anger, hatred, resentment, fear, greed, shame, patriotism, hero-worship, love, and religious awe into epiphenomena of little or no significance. And historians are for the most part likely to agree that political and even religious emotions are usually linked to perceived interests. Yet such emotions are felt, and we must not force them out of our histories if we wish to understand how and why people behaved as they did in the ancient world, in both public and private life. The greatest Greek historians, Thucydides and Polybius, are widely thought to have led the way towards minimizing the description of emotion in serious history-writing;[57] but they did so only in a relative way (many passages in Thucydides come to mind, and Polybius well knew how to describe the workings of anger) and, at least in Polybius' case, for confused reasons—was it decorum or was it accuracy that he thought was endangered?

In modern writing about the social and even political history of the Greeks and Romans, the emotions have begun to receive more attention. It is still possible to write at length about classical slavery without paying any attention either to the anger which frequently made itself felt between master and slave, in both directions, or to the occasional affection that existed. And there is, after all, plenty to say about slavery as a status and as an economic system without taking emotions into consideration. Yet a system which was based on fearsome punishments and on hopes of manumission necessarily had a large emotional component, and some writers now attempt to give this fact its due.[58] Recent monographs about Roman family life have also made some attempt to capture its emotional tone as it was experienced in the more articulate social classes.[59] It is an unadventurous kind of historian who withdraws because the story is a complex one or because it has sometimes been botched.[60]

57. Cf. Walbank 1972, 34–40.
58. Hopkins 1993 was a good beginning.
59. See in particular Treggiari 1991 and Dixon 1992. On the other hand Pomeroy 1997, 3, is "pessimistic about our ability to discover very much about the emotional experiences of the past [sic]," an attitude of undue timidity.
60. Saller 1994, 7, objects to the writing of Roman family history "in terms of

Novelists, not historians, know the exact details of their characters' emotions.[61] A cautious historian, writing about the ancient world or any other, certainly has ample reasons to steer clear of emotions, and of anger perhaps above all of them. Anger is so elusive. Most of it is commonplace or evanescent, or both. Sometimes, although anger is felt, the fact is not evident to anyone except the person who is angry— and in this study we shall have to be alert for anger that exists but is not displayed. Sometimes even the angry subject may be unaware that anger is at work. Of all kinds of anger, political anger is probably the least difficult for a historian to study[62] (and it may be that the clearest results of this study will lie in that field), but even the anger of a monarch or an assembly, or of one city against another, is commonly hard to describe and analyse.

Investigating specific emotions as a historical project was first suggested, some sixty years ago, by the fathers of *Annales* history, especially Lucien Febvre. The question which most interested Febvre was whether certain historical periods have been characterized by particular emotions or by a certain emotional tone.[63] But the question must have seemed too vague and too difficult,[64] and such inquiries never be-

---

trends in affection," but that is not quite the issue, which is whether to *include* emotions in history-writing. His arguments are two: behavioural patterns were complicated, and indicators of family affection are hard to understand cross-culturally. These are indeed real dangers (though Saller's examples are hardly formidable ones), but they are common to most historical enterprises. Demographic determinism is not an attractive alternative, especially when the demography is itself speculative.

61. Cf. *Zuleika Dobson,* ch. 11 beginning.

62. A. Kneppe's *Metus Temporum* (1994) is a recent attempt to write some "emotional history" of political life under the principate.

63. Febvre wrote an essay entitled "La sensibilité et l'histoire: Comment reconstituer la vie affective d'autrefois" (Febvre 1973 [1941], 12–26). Marc Bloch was sympathetic: Bloch 1961 [1939], I:72–75. R. G. Collingwood maintained a very different view: the "irrational elements [in the mind] are the subject-matter of psychology. They are . . . not parts of the historical process: sensation as distinct from thought, feelings as distinct from conceptions" (Collingwood 1946, 231, written in 1935).

64. Except that many have written about *acedia/accedie,* believed to be a mediaeval European emotion, something like sloth, which is thought to be absent from the modern world. In fact it was known in antiquity and under this name: ἀκήδεια or ἀκηδία already meant "listlessness" or something similar by the time of Cic. *Att.*

came very popular with *Annales* historians. Not that they have been entirely ignored;[65] and there is in many countries a large literature on national character which sometimes touches on such questions. For most historians, however, any work on historical emotions comes close to or belongs to the poorly regarded practice of psychohistory, and should be left well alone. Recent counter-examples have sometimes attracted attention but have not so far changed the pattern.[66] The fact that historians have been passing through a period of "epistemological hypochondria" (Geertz's phrase), makes it even more uncertain whether they will engage further with the hydra-headed history of the emotions.

Anthropologists have taken more interest in anger and the limitation of anger than historians have. All complex cultures have their own ways of expressing anger or anger-like emotion, their own rules about when and how far anger may be expressed, and also their ways of limiting its effects.[67] The comparative material is now quite extensive, though we suffer from the fact that most of it concerns what may be considered traditional anthropological populations (now an anthropology of British anger, that would be worth writing). But for a historian, illumination, or at least a good question, may come from anywhere, from learning about the Utkuhikhalingmiut Eskimoes of the Canadian Arctic, who severely disapprove of anger (except towards dogs), or about the apparently hot-tempered world of the Italian Re-

---

xii.45.1, though not, as some scholars say, earlier (see D. R. Shackleton Bailey ad loc.).

65. His challenge was picked up by J.-L. Flandrin in his study of the family under the ancien régime: Flandrin 1976, ch. 3. There is an interesting theoretical discussion of history and emotional climates in Barbu 1960, 43–68.

66. See Muir's *Mad Blood Stirring* (1993), a study of feuding in Friuli in the sixteenth century, and the essays contained in Rosenwein (ed.) 1998. For a pertinent study of feuding in nineteenth-century Corsica, see Wilson 1988. For an important discussion of another emotion, see Bynum 1997. An optimistic account of some recent work is to be found in P. N. Stearns 1993, 18–22. According to Elster, however, the field of historical psychology is at present "virtually non-existent" (1999, 405), a situation which in his opinion and mine badly needs rectifying.

67. For some anthropological studies of the handling of anger in various cultures see, for instance, G. G. Harris 1978 on the Kenyan Taita, and Heald 1989 on the Ugandan Gisu; and for a brief survey of such literature, see Heelas 1986, 253–255.

naissance city. How anthropology has influenced the study of anger, and how it might help us to answer questions about classical anger control, we shall consider in the next two chapters.

The subject of this study, however, is not anger but attempts at the control of anger. One book and one book only, as far as I know, has undertaken any similar task, and it concerns a modern nation: C. Z. and P. N. Stearns's *Anger: The Struggle for Emotional Control in America's History*.[68] The authors deserve honour among historians for their pioneering attempt to make sense out of texts, and out of an aspect of American life, that demand explanation.[69] Incomparably greater quantities of evidence are available to a historian who tries to describe the development of anger control in a modern country than to a historian of antiquity. But the social structures of the United States are so remote from those of antiquity that the usefulness of the Stearns's volume for this inquiry is necessarily limited.

Is this then a Foucaultian project? Neither its inspiration nor its methods come from that direction. The most relevant part of the philosopher's work is *Le souci de soi*, the third volume of his history of sexuality,[70] where he does indeed make a number of remarks about self-control which will require attention later in this study (in Chapters 5, 12 and 15). But in spite of his interest in the "self's relationship to itself," Foucault had little to say about the emotions, and his notion of self-control does not, as far as antiquity is concerned, go beyond sexual self-control. It is scarcely necessary to point out again that his notion of the freedom of classical man to create his own patterns of behaviour, to act as a "self-fashioning subject," is hopelessly flawed.[71] Yet that notion will haunt us, because the pursuit of self-mastery, though Foucault took no notice of the fact, comes in antiquity to require among other things the elimination or the control of anger.

---

68. For scholarly jostling around this project, see *Psychohistory Review* xviii (1989–1990), 293–318. The Stearns's book strangely makes no reference to Norbert Elias. For further work of theirs, see also P. N. Stearns 1992.

69. Notwithstanding the optimism which allows the authors to maintain that self-restraint of anger works quite well in the contemporary United States, in spite of the nation's fearful devotion to homicide (7.0 homicides per 100,000 inhabitants in 1997, versus, for instance, 1.9 in Canada).

70. Foucault 1986 [1984].

71. See the critique by Cohen & Saller 1994.

Finally, the term *ideology*. The term has been used in such a wide variety of ways[72] that one hesitates at this date to inject it into historical analysis. But used in the ordinary-language sense—a normative set or system of ideas, concerning in the first place political or social practices, or both (though of course some ideologies have a strong religious component), propagated in the interests of a class or group[73]—the term seems useful, indeed invaluable.[74] For it is indeed an evolving ideology that we are investigating—or so at least it will be argued in the following pages.

What *is* anger? It will rapidly emerge that there is fairly ample disagreement (Chapter 2). Whether anger should be thought of as a physiological reaction or as a "social construction" may seem little more than a false dilemma, but it is important to show that anger-like emotions vary from culture to culture, and that this is not inconsistent with current science, even though the latter sometimes insists on the physiological character of the emotions. We shall also see that the cross-cultural study of emotions has suffered very severely, until recently, from the failure of psychologists to absorb the fact that most of the human race uses terms for its emotions that normally lack exact equivalents in English. Recent anthropological work, however, beginning with Michelle Rosaldo, has shown the way towards a general realization that emotional terms in different languages may radically fail to correspond with each other. Here the contributions of Anna Wierzbicka are especially stimulating.

Other disagreements—as to whether, for example, anger is typically of short duration—are also of fundamental importance for the study of anger control. On this point, a number of ancient writers tell a

72. See, among many others, Thompson 1984; Claessen & Oosten 1996, 7–11; Schieffelin, Wooland & Kroskrity 1998.

73. Cf. Luhmann 1982, 97–100. My use of the term is intended to be moderate, neither restrictive nor latitudinarian (it is not therefore equivalent to the totality of ideas or values existing in a given society).

74. The discussion of this term in Ober 1989, 38–40, is not altogether satisfactory. If "ideology" is to mean anything, it must be distinguished from "feelings" and even from attitudes. Veyne 1976, 670–671, rightly underlines the essentially *justificatory* character of ideologies.

more coherent story than is usually told by contemporary psychology. Not that coherence about anger-like emotions is easy to obtain, since there is such a rich variety of them (and new mutations continue to appear). It will also be essential to consider modern ideas about the desirability on various grounds of limiting anger, or alternatively of letting it come out and express itself.

But the most vital preliminary—obvious, but often neglected—is to ask what the Greeks and Roman meant by the terms which they used for anger-like emotions (Chapter 3). The effects of Wierzbicka's work on our understanding of Greek and Latin anger discourse are likely to be crucial. It has long been realized that *mēnis*, the word used for the wrath of Achilles in the first line of the *Iliad,* does not correspond closely to English "anger"; the important point is that neither *cholos* nor *orgē* (the key word in ancient philosophizing about anger) nor *thumos* (these are the commonest Greek words which are habitually translated as "anger") mean precisely "anger" either. These are the names of anger-like emotions, of course, but the differences from English may be crucial. If, in particular, it turns out that *orgē* is a more passionate or more violent emotion than typical "anger," that will have a significant effect on our understanding of the classical discourse of anger control.

How can we find out what the Greeks and Romans thought and said on this subject? We must recognize at once that we are, generally speaking—not entirely—confined to the mental and psychological world of the social elites.[75] That is a largely insurmountable problem. As for what the written works of the educated are trying to tell us, the philosophical texts are complex, but at least the philosophers instruct us overtly. What is exceedingly difficult is the interpretation of texts and images that are not explicitly didactic. To meet this challenge, a historian has to consider each text according to the circumstances of

---

75. A recent study has reviewed the papyri in which the adolescents of Greek-speaking Egypt transcribed moralistic fables (Babrius was the favourite author). Extreme anger was frowned upon in these stories, not surprisingly (Legras 1996, 75–77, based on *P.Amh.* ii.26 = *C.P.Lat.* 40). Here we are outside the upper elite, but not among the poor. The desire to control the anger of powerful individuals spread quite widely, to judge from the kind of magical spell known as *thumokatochos*, e.g. *PGM* xiii, lines 251–252, and xxxvi, lines 35–68 (see Faraone, forthcoming).

its production, and that is going to take the whole of this book; we shall constantly be looking for our authors' imagined audiences. But some general hermeneutic principles are worth discussing first (Chapter 4).

It will already have occurred to many readers that anger control was part of a larger Greek and Roman project of emotional self-control or moderation. Chapter 5 will begin to develop this theme by attempting to show how anger control differed from other kinds of striving for self-control, and by speculating briefly about the wider ideology of self-control in the ancient world. Anger control as a doctrine had a longer and more intense history than attempts to control any other emotion, but there was a much wider pattern. Anger control was not merely part of a general desire to impose *sōphrosunē* (approximately "self-restraint") or *enkrateia* ("self-control")—for it had its own specific justifications; but if we pay attention to what created the wish for *sōphrosunē* and *enkrateia* we may find out more about the wish to control *orgē* and *ira*.

It is one of the main contentions of this book that many Greek intellectuals other than philosophers held views about the limitation of rage, and expressed them. But it was by and large philosophers, professional or, like Cicero, Seneca and Galen, amateur, who set out detailed and explicit views. (Not that there was ever a hermetic division between philosophers and general intellectual trends). It therefore seems advisable to describe these views (Chapter 6) before we fit them into their wider circumstances.[76] The main lines of division need to be set out, especially the line between the moderate moralists of various kinds who admitted the propriety of anger-like emotions on certain conditions, and those whom I shall call the "absolutists"—those, that is, who at least ostensibly disapproved of all *orgē* whatsoever. This was a characteristic Stoic view, though the Stoics had some forerunners (in Chapter 8 we shall encounter some unexpected evidence of that), and eventually the "absolutist" view was embraced by a number of those, such as Cicero, who were by no means orthodox Stoics.

All that having been said, we shall finally be ready to consider the

76. One purpose of this work is to show how philosophical developments can be driven by "external" as well as "internal" factors.

ideology of anger control with respect to society and the state (Chapters 7 to 11), the family and slaves (Chapters 12 and 13), and the individual (Chapters 14 and 15), taking into account not only the anger which was criticized but also the anger which was accepted or approved.

Anger-like passions are the central abstract theme in the *Iliad*, and the poet represented as disastrous Achilles' unwillingness to dampen down his rage, his *mēnis* or *cholos*, against Agamemnon. An epic-singer of 700 B.C. might have decided to include disastrous heroic rage in his composition for any of several reasons—because of tradition, perhaps, or simply because such anger could contribute to a powerful narrative. But if we think of the *Iliad* and other archaic Greek texts that were directed towards the control of anger in their original contexts, insofar as that is feasible, another possibility arises, that the texts in question were part of a struggle to create and foster polis government and the rule of law—"civil society" in the early-modern sense of that expression. It will be argued that some of our authors aimed at diffusing doctrines of restraint in a period in which Greek cities were developing stable political institutions and extending the use of fixed laws. In this period a substantial part of Greek discourse about anger functioned as a means of helping citizens to live together in the polis.

To set out the case in favour of this interpretation (Chapters 7 and 8) will require the careful examination of a set of texts ranging from Homer and Hesiod to Solon and eventually as far as Polybius and the monographs of Philodemus and Plutarch. We must consider the circumstances in which these texts were produced: what was the original audience, and what was the author's relationship to that audience? It will also be necessary to examine some possible counter-arguments about the meanings of texts and their authors' intentions. The purpose here, in any case, is to relate the texts about the control of anger to the historical process of state building and state consolidation.

In archaic times, in both Greece and Rome, powerful men had sometimes ignored with impunity such public authority as existed. With the growth of criminal and civil law between the seventh and fourth centuries B.C. in Athens, and between the fifth and first centuries B.C. in Rome, the authority of the state grew stronger. The belief spread that punishment inflicted by the state should for the most part take the place of privately inflicted physical vengeance. This meant that a lot of serious anger was now supposed to be expressed by means of formal procedures and under public surveillance.

Less is really known about how government came into being at Rome, because much of the process took place in an era when the Romans were not yet producing literary texts of their own that have survived. But questions about how citizens should live with each other continued to arise in later ages, and hence there is Roman discourse, too, about anger control (Chapter 9). It owes many of its peculiarities to the fact that it was often produced under an absolute or nearly absolute monarchy, and sometimes by men who were within the emperor's immediate sphere of activity—a dangerous if interesting place to be.

The fearsomely angry individual in Greek and Roman literature is often a king or emperor (Chapter 10), though he can be any kind of monarchical or quasi-monarchical ruler, including the governor of a Roman province. The anger of the ruler, and his subjects' ability to limit it, could sometimes be matters of considerable importance, life-and-death importance. The most intriguing part of this story, at least as far as it can be told from the surviving evidence, concerns Roman emperors and provincial governors. But from Homeric times onwards there is a continuous tradition. In spite of its repetitiveness, this tradition is worth studying. For one thing, it is not to be taken absolutely for granted that repetitive ancient texts were nothing but futile verbiage: there must, after all, have been some reason or other why it was thought worthwhile to compose such texts. And the figure of the furiously irate ruler contributed to the formation of the image of the angry man as it is to be found in all the main texts about anger from the fifth century B.C. onwards. Monstrous monarchs from Cambyses to Caligula could be instrumentalized to show that the effects of anger were appalling.

Anger, *cholos*, is offhandedly stigmatized in Homer as a vice of women, and this was a traditional Greek slander. Many men repeated that rage was typical of women, also of children and the weak in general (the economically weak or those in ill health), those, in other words, who did not have a full role to play in the body politic. Thus a negative character trait is attributed to the excluded, and their exclusion is implicitly justified. It may in fact be possible to explain this negative stereotype more precisely (see Chapter 11). The special negativity which attaches to women's anger finds many forms of expression (low humour, for instance, in Herodas 5), but it has a particular and serious point. The stereotype in question implies that there was simply no legitimate place for women's anger in the classical city. This was one part of the Greek, and especially Athenian, method of perpetuating a degree of female subordination which was high even by the standards of traditional society. Yet there were complications, in the first place because there were some unorthodox texts, such as Euripides' *Medea* and *Hecuba,* and in the second because there seems to have been a certain development in Graeco-Roman thinking about the anger of women, mainly in the period from Philodemus to Plutarch.

The previous discussion will lead to a more detailed account of anger within the family (Chapters 12 and 13)—the family, that is, in the sense of the Greek *oikos* or the Roman *familia,* which included the family's slaves. What could be more obvious than that blood relationships and marriages are spoiled by excessive anger? "This warrior irascibility of yours," Cicero asks sarcastically—he is addressing the Peripatetics, who thought that anger assisted courage—"when it has come back home, what is it like with your wife, children and slaves? Do you think that it's useful there too?"[77] The classical Greek family sometimes and in some places seems perilously close to being dysfunctional, and that obviously makes the discourse of anger control easier to comprehend, all the more so since in the classical world the economic and social functions of the family were more essential to human existence than they are often considered to be in the modern west.

We shall also try to find out when the less predictable kinds of anger control within the family began to gain some ground: the notion that husbands should restrain their anger towards wives, and fathers their anger towards their sons.

As for slavery, there were plenty of reasons for owners to be angry with their slaves, and vice versa. The owners were subject to pathetically little outside restraint: this was the extreme case of the "intensely personal nature of power in ancient society."[78] But slave-owners should restrain their anger towards their slaves, so it was commonly said. From

---

77. *Tusc.Disp.* iv.54.

78. Brown's phrase, 1992, 50. Burnyeat 1996, 3–6, sees that there was a connection between untrammelled personal power and the philosophy of anger control.

Theophrastus onwards, slave-owners were told that they should never punish slaves or others while they were angry, but wait until their anger had departed and punish coldly. The origins and the prudential logic of this approach to slave management will be investigated in Chapter 13. The slave-owners were subject to two conflicting imperatives: they had no intention of giving up harsh methods, and it would have been difficult for them to do so without imperilling the entire system, a system which was based on rationally administered brutality. At the same time, the more intelligent ones realized that they needed to be moderate, and also tried to retain the sometimes precarious dignity which was so essential to their authority over resentful and often alarmingly numerous slaves.

By the time of Aristotle, however, an entirely new type of reason had arisen for emotional self-control and in particular for the control of anger, namely psychic health (Chapters 14 and 15). But how did anger first come to be thought of as a suitable object of treatment or therapy, whatever those terms may mean in the context of classical Greece? A momentous change occurred in the cultural history of the Athenians in the last decades of the fifth century and the first decades of the fourth, spreading eventually to educated people all over the Greek world: a greatly increased interest in inner experience and in the well-being of the individual's soul. Introspection became more popular. This new preoccupation with what Plato called "the city within" led many to see anger, among other ills, as a failing of the individual as much as, or more than, a menace to society or to other people. It was also of course part of the inheritance of the Hellenistic philosophers.

This interest in inner experience, which lasted for the rest of antiquity (and has indeed in various forms lasted down to the present), is a historical phenomenon and deserves explanation (Chapter 15). But there were cures as well as a disease. What did Hellenistic and Roman thinkers propose to do about the psychic condition of the angry? What therapies did philosophy devise for the passions and in particular for the angry passions? Thinking about one's anger, keeping it within reasonable bounds (whatever they might seem to be), and justifying one's own anger to oneself became quite common activities among educated Greeks and Romans. How were they supposed to do it? We may be little inclined to think that the ancients practised psychotherapy, but that may be because the lay public still has a Freudian or neo-

Freudian image of what psychotherapy consists of. Meanwhile the contemporary psychotherapy of anger has taken quite other turns, which, as it happens, make the ancient remedies more relevant and easier to evaluate. These remedies vary from the fatuous to the extremely sensible, but in any case, in spite of the repetition of banalities, they have a history. It begins, I think, with music. It passes through many philosophical variations, both before and after Chrysippus wrote the first book devoted explicitly to the therapy of the passions. This history will require us to consider the role of the philosopher in Hellenistic and in Roman society, and the acceptance of philosophy as a guide to life— also the derision which philosophers sometimes incurred. It will also require us to explain the surprising popularity among Greek and Roman thinkers of the paradoxical or at least rather peculiar "absolutist" view that one should avoid anger altogether in all circumstances—if that is indeed what they meant.

A rival guide to life, Christianity, cast its shadow over the Roman Empire. It also offered teachings about anger, and this book would not be complete if it did not inspect them. Both the text (Matthew 5:22) and the implications of what Jesus said on the subject are open to dispute. Furthermore, as we have already noted, there seems to be a stark contradiction between what the sacred texts said about the anger of God and a powerful pagan intellectual tradition about divine impassibility. These matters will be examined in Chapter 16.

The overarching design, then, is to locate texts and images in society and, as far as possible, to explain. This is not a reductive attempt to explain works of literature and philosophy as mere responses to the imperatives of political or social life, but rather an attempt to explain processes of cultural history which included all of our anger control texts.[79] The aim is to trace the origins and significance of a particular theme without eliminating the autonomy of authors or of any particular kind of intellectual activity—but without exaggerating that autonomy either.

79. Cf. Bryant 1996, xi: "Art, morality, law, religion, philosophy, science: the point is not to 'reduce' these domains of intellectual and aesthetic praxis to more 'fundamental' pursuits, economic or political, as mere ideological reflexes of constellations of power and privilege, but to view each as a distinct form of life *integral* to wider patterns of social organization."

CHAPTER 2

Science and Feelings

It is not easy, as Freud observed, to deal scientifically with feelings.[1] But the modern science of psychology has attempted to grapple with the emotions in general and anger in particular. The emotions were already a subject of scholarly study in the early nineteenth century, and by the time Darwin wrote *The Expression of Emotions in Man and Animals* (1872) there was a considerable literature. Since the emergence of academic psychology in the generation after Darwin, this stream of writing has become a torrent, or rather a slow-moving, broad and muddy river.

The *Oxford English Dictionary* defines the substantive *anger* as follows: "the active feeling provoked against the agent; passion, rage; wrath, ire, hot displeasure."[2] With respect to "rage," the same dictionary gives as its principal meaning something narrower than anger, namely "*violent* anger, furious passion, usually as manifested in looks, words or action; a fit or access of such anger [my italics]"; that, generally speaking,

1. *Civilization and Its Discontents* (1961 [1930]), ch. 1. For a recent survey of scientific knowledge of the emotions, see Lewis & Haviland 1993; for a survey from a philosophical standpoint, Lyons 1980. For some conceptual problems about emotions, see esp. Griffiths 1997. There is a continuous stream of psychological work about anger, which can be traced through, e.g., Tangney et al. 1996 and Mikulincer 1998.

2. 1989 edition.

is the distinction between "anger" and "rage" observed in this book.[3] "Wrath" we may judge to be obsolescent, though it may still have some use for anger on a heroic or mock-heroic scale.

Then we possess a range of substantives for milder anger-like states, such as "indignation" (not very mild perhaps), "annoyance," "irritation" and "resentment." And in the colloquial language we possess a good healthy supply of adjectives meaning something like "angry," and a number of ways of saying something like "be angry with."

It is immediately obvious that all these terms are to a certain degree nebulous, which suggests that this and all other studies of anger should be on the alert for a full range of emotions in and around the semantic field of anger. But there should be some limits: this book is not, for example, intended to be a study either of violence or of angst. However, as we shall see, modern psychology has tended to err in the opposite direction, excluding from its studies of anger some emotional states which in fact there is no reason to exclude.

On a commonsense view, anger is a practically universal human experience—and indeed an experience shared by most other mammals too.[4] According to one anthropologist, anger and some other emotions are "panhuman,"[5] and a psychologist typically asserts that children in all cultures "are born with the capacity to experience basic emotions" such as anger.[6] And of course most languages in all parts of

3. Thus when William James challenged his readers to think of an anger-like emotion free of physical manifestations, which he thought an impossibility, he tendentiously wrote (James 1890, II:425) of rage, not anger—since *anger* without physical manifestations is an everyday experience.

4. Stoics, such as Seneca (*De ira* i.3.3–4), denied that any non-human animal felt anger (though earlier, i.1.6, he had assumed that they did), for "although *ira* is the enemy of reason, yet it only comes into being where there is a place for reason." Animals show *impetus, rabiem, feritatem, incursum*.

5. Gerber 1985, 159.

6. P. L. Harris 1989, 103. He argues (101–103) for the view that there are some basic universal emotions, "such as happiness, sadness and anger" (103). In his opinion, although there may indeed be emotions in one culture that have no obvious equivalents in another, "the existence of such emotions does not disprove, rather it presupposes the existence of a basic set, on whose foundations they are constructed" (ibid.). The notion that there exist a few basic emotions is a favourite with some psychologists, e.g. Johnson-Laird & Oatley 1989, Ekman 1992. According to Johnson-Laird &

the world have words for anger states and those who are experiencing them.[7] Ethnographic reports have sometimes described populations which supposedly do not feel anger, or do not express it, such as the Utkuhikhalingmiut Eskimoes or the Malaysian Chewong.[8] Such reports have understandably been greeted with scepticism in some quarters,[9] and might have been received even more sceptically if greater attention had been paid to the difference between feeling anger and expressing it, for the methods have not been invented that would allow an ethnographer to know that a given tribal population did not even *feel* angry emotions. Not that an occasional exception would necessarily matter very much.

In relatively recent times, mainly since 1980, anthropologists studying the emotions have been showing symptoms of concern about the difficulties involved in entering the conceptual worlds of their study populations,[10] and in feeling empathy with the emotions of other cultures. The realization that *liget*, the nearest concept to anger in the

---

Oatley (90) there are five "basic" human emotions—happiness, sadness, anger, fear, and disgust—these "should be universally accepted as discriminable categories of direct experience" (90), and all other emotions can be broken down into these five. Ekman (e.g., 1998, 367) also maintains (more plausibly) that there is a "universality of facial expressions" of emotion. Now it is obvious that there exist some virtually universal *types of* emotion, but a short list (in English!) of "basic" emotions is an *ignis fatuus* (cf. Ortony & Turner 1990; J. A. Russell 1991, 440–441; Wierzbicka 1994, 134— she calls this theory a form of "shallow universalism"). No more convincing is the generalization of Johnson-Laird & Oatley (ibid.) that emotions are a form of communication. For a useful survey of some anthropological opinions about universal emotions, see Lutz & White 1986, 410–411.

7. Cf. Boucher 1979, 175.

8. On the Utkuhikhalingmiut (Utku) Eskimoes, see Briggs 1970, who showed not that the Utku were never angry (apparently they took it out on their dogs), but that they intensely disapproved of anger-like emotions, something rather different. Another population apparently little troubled by anger are the timorous Chewong, concerning whom see Howell 1984, esp. 37, and Heelas 1984. Incidentally, these are (were) populations of a few dozen people each.

9. On the Tahitians and the Utku Eskimoes as apparent exceptions, see, e.g., Solomon 1984, 243–246.

10. See M. Z. Rosaldo 1980, a subtle and ground-breaking analysis of the anger-like *liget* emotion of a head-hunting population (which curiously assumes, however, that *Greek* words for anger must go straight into English [222]); Solomon 1984, Rosenberg 1990. For further bibliography see Wierzbicka 1994, 135.

lexicon of the head-hunting Ilongot in the Philippines does *not* correspond well to "anger" or to any other English term has had far-reaching consequences for the study of the emotions. Anthropology now
recognizes, for example, that what the Gisu people in Uganda mean
by *lirima,* the word in their language which apparently most nearly corresponds to "anger," may be something significantly different.[11] This is
a matter of fundamental importance, as the world of psychology gradually seems to be recognizing.[12] The best "state-of-the-question" known
to me is the work of Anna Wierzbicka.[13] She also makes the intriguing
suggestion that the "untranslatable" emotion terms of other languages
can be translated into a "natural semantic metalanguage." This means
that all statements about emotions in all languages are supposed to be
translatable into a sort of very basic English.[14] In any case, the general
point that emotion words commonly do not have exact translations in
other languages is now increasingly recognized.[15]

The same approach can be applied to German *Zorn,* French *colère,*
and comparable words in the 3,000 or more other natural languages

11. See Heald 1989. Lutz 1988, 157, to take another example, showed with great
skill that her study population, the Ifaluk in the western Carolines, had no single
term for anger but several different words for different kinds. See Wierzbicka 1994,
137, for a further attempt to characterize Ifaluk *song* ("justified anger," or perhaps
rather "anguished disapproval"). Another case: Goddard 1991.

12. Cf. Mesquita & Frijda 1992, 200. James (1890, II:485) already made the point
that "each race of men" has "found names for some shade of feeling which other
races have left undiscriminated," and that all sorts of groupings of emotions would be
valid.

13. Wierzbicka 1994; cf. 1992, esp. 119–179.

14. 1992, 135; 1994, 139–142. The key fallacy here is not so much the notion that
all or most languages possess equivalents of "good," "bad," "think," "feel," as that if a
statement about anger is reduced to the form "Because X did something bad, Y
wished to do something bad to X," the procedure eliminates precisely what is emotional (as distinct from, e.g., judicial).

15. See, for instance, W. I. Miller 1993, 98–99. For some research vitiated by a failure to realize this, see Sommers 1988, 27–29. In 1990 one could claim to be doing
"cross-cultural" research about the emotions without paying attention to the semantic problems (Matsumoto 1990); the semantic issue was still ignored by the contributors to Watson-Gegeo & White 1990 and by Hupka et al. 1996. The problem persists,
even in mainstream journals dealing with the emotions: e.g., Fischer, Manstead &
Rodriguez Mosquera 1999 still appear to believe that everyone in Europe thinks in
English.

which are said to exist or have left records. The study of classical emotions has been seriously impeded by our failure to realize, with a few noteworthy exceptions,[16] that the relevant Greek and Latin terminology is very unlikely to correspond neatly to modern English usage.

There is no need, however, to be transfixed by exaggerated doubt about our ability to understand the anger language of people who have left us as much explicit writing on the subject as have the Greeks and Romans. A modern scholar recognizes that Greek *aidōs* is not identical in meaning with its nearest English equivalent "shame,"[17] but does not for that reason despair of analysing its nuances.

There is a biological and neurological basis for believing in the virtual universality of at least some types of emotion, which has emerged more clearly in recent years and is a continuing subject of research. This seems to have led some psychologists to positions similar to that of William James, who notoriously theorized, more than a century ago, that emotions were nothing more than our perceptions of some of our own physiological states.[18] One recent author states, for instance, that "anger is a simple bodily response."[19] This sort of thing is more likely to be said about anger than about quieter emotions.[20]

A characteristic neurologist's judgement about emotions is that "although much remains unknown, the[ir] anatomy and chemistry . . . are within our grasp."[21] That was written in the 1980s, when many thought that the so-called limbic system of the brain—a term which has changed its definition from time to time[22]—functioned as the site of the human emotional system. "The importance of individual areas of the limbic forebrain in emotional functions remains," it was said, "indisputable,"[23] and a great deal was supposed to be known about how

16. Such as Adkins 1969.

17. D. L. Cairns 1993, 8–10.

18. James 1884.

19. Lewis 1993, 159, writing admittedly in the context of infant psychology. He says that anger "exists in all organisms" (165).

20. Solomon 1984, 242.

21. LeDoux 1987, 419 (he also gave a useful history of modern scientific thinking on the neurobiology of emotions, 420–424; for a longer survey, see Cacioppo et al. 1993).

22. LeDoux 1987, 424–425.

23. LeDoux 1987, 424. Not long ago, its functions were thought to be even wider than this: see Isaacson 1982; Buck 1988, 113–126.

the brain processes, and reacts to, emotional stimuli. But the neuro-science of that time did not strike all outsiders as having the emotions neatly tied up,[24] since—to mention only two aspects of the matter—the work in question concerned a very limited range of emotions and mainly animal, not human, subjects. Five years passed, and the limbic system lost some standing.[25] The scientist quoted above maintained by 1992 that the limbic theory was misleading,[26] and argued instead that the centre of the emotional action is the area of the brain known as the amygdala. The questions likely to interest a non-neurologist, such as what causes people to react with different emotions to similar stimuli, still seem to be quite a long way from clarification.[27]

But is anger "a simple bodily response," and would we know all about it if we really did understand its anatomy and chemistry? Historians and anthropologists are, on the contrary, likely to take it almost for granted—literary scholars even more so—that anger is in part a "social construction," in the sense that its modalities if not its very existence derive, in any society, from social structures and practices.[28] As a minimum, this doctrine holds that each human *learns* from others how to be angry, and (this is a different matter, clearly) when to be angry. A standard anthropological view has it that words describing emotions "derive their meanings from a broad range of understandings and practices."[29] A social-construction theory of the emotions may, however, be more or less strict or purist.[30]

24. Thus an informed psychiatrist wrote that "nothing . . . can be definitively said at this point about the chemistry of emotion" (Gaylin 1989, 55). According to a psychologist of anger, current science on the subject "is very much in its infancy" (Tafrate 1995, 113).

25. But see the very interesting work on the limbic system reported by Servan-Schreiber & Perlstein 1998.

26. LeDoux 1992, developed more fully in his book *The Emotional Brain* (1996, esp. 98–102).

27. Theories change, but optimism abides: see LeDoux 1996, 11.

28. See Armon-Jones 1986. For the literature about this theory, see Lynch 1990; Shaver, Wu & Schwartz 1992, 208–212; Oatley 1993a; Reddy 1997. On the mania for "social construction," see Hacking 1999, who, however, muddies the waters as far as emotions are concerned (18–19).

29. Lutz & White 1986, 417. Geertz had called emotions "cultural artifacts" (1973, 81).

30. Cf. Armon-Jones 1986, 37–39. A purist version is fairly easy to refute, an exercise which is undertaken by Reddy 1997 (see the comments at the end of his article

A classic exposition of the social-construction argument tells us that "the physiological reaction itself is virtually never sufficient to distinguish one emotion from another, even in a gross way." At present that is certainly true. Anger, the argument continues, is "*essentially* an interpretation," a view of its object, together with "consequent forms of behavior." "An emotion," furthermore, "is a system of concepts, beliefs, attitudes, and desires, virtually all of which are context-bound, historically developed, and culture-specific."[31]

Some of these assertions seem exaggerated. In most (though not all) cultures, the physiological symptoms of anger are so much a part of anger that without such symptoms the genuineness of the emotion may be called into question. In the future, it seems quite possible that the neurological basis of anger will be established in more detail. Conversely, it seems heavy-handed to say that an emotion *is* a system of concepts and so on, for it pre-empts the possibility that at least some emotions are broadly similar from culture to culture. Now no one, presumably, would deny that the stimuli which cause particular emotions vary from culture to culture, but that leaves us with the *possibility* that the essential experience of, say, anger-like emotions is somehow much the same almost everywhere.

It has been claimed that "an emotion is not primarily a physiological reaction *cum* sensations . . . A strong emotion may well have as its predictable secondary effects the bodily responses that James identified as primary, but this is neither necessary nor always the case." And it has further been claimed that long-term emotions do not necessarily include physiological reactions.[32] Not necessarily, perhaps, but very often. While it is true that anger is an experience of interpreting a situation in a certain way, it is misleading to say that it may or may not be accompanied by "characteristic physical sensations,"[33] for they are precisely *characteristic*. Nor can the neural reactions which can be presumed to go with all or almost cases of anger—even those which are long lasting—be ignored.

---

by S. Howell [342–343] and C. Lutz [345–346], though the latter misrepresents J. L. Austin's teaching about "performative utterances").

31. Solomon 1984, 249 (though this account is not especially recent, it is exceptionally lucid).

32. Ibid. 248, 249.

33. Ibid. 250.

Yet these are exaggerations of an essentially sound position, and what will lead to an understanding of the history of anger within a given culture is not the limbic system but an appreciation of the fact that anger is indeed judgemental,[34] and that the judgements it expresses are the product of culture as well as of nature.

However, scholars who propound a "social-construction" view of the emotions, besides revealing in some cases their inability to come to terms with the natural sciences, have often neglected to explain the needs which led the Greeks, for example, to "construct" anger or other emotions in this or that fashion. The most valuable attempts to do this, to establish why anger has had a particular character in a particular culture, have come from two directions: from studies of Homer and the so-called Homeric world, such as in particular the fine books of Redfield and Van Wees,[35] and from anthropologists, some of whom have tried to work out how family structures limit acceptable kinds of anger and hence "construct" the locally predominant conceptions of anger, for example in Samoa.[36] It happens in fact to be Samoan society that most famously indicates the difficulty of this sort of enterprise, since *Coming of Age in Samoa* (1928) led to the *querelle* set off by *Margaret Mead and Samoa: The Making and Unmaking of an Anthropological Myth*,[37] in which there was suddenly plenty of room for anger, both Samoan and Western.

There need in any case be no intellectual strain whatsoever in holding both that the biological nature of humans, not necessarily to be thought of as uniform in all ages and places, partly determines the character of our emotions, *and* that the emotions are *in part* socially constructed—in other words, that the form they take within particular cultures is determined *in part* by the system of values which prevails there.[38] Whether anger is "panhuman" or not is a false problem.

---

34. Ibid.; this was the prevailing view in antiquity, and it is the prevailing view of psychologists and humanistic scholars. In the late twentieth century a good deal of energy also went into discussing whether feeling anger and other emotions was a "cognitive" process. This rather futile debate (on which see Griffiths 1997, 2–3, 21) has not contributed anything directly to the subject of this book.

35. Redfield 1975/1994, Van Wees 1992.

36. Gerber 1985, 154–155.

37. Freeman 1983.

38. With the moderate position outlined here compare Gerber 1985, 121; Heelas 1984, 37–39; Heelas 1986, 257; Averill 1994, 79; Griffiths 1997, 138.

In an important sense it is not, because English is not a panhuman language; but it is obvious, too, that *anger-like* emotions are indeed panhuman.

The very range of feelings which may be described as anger makes anger extremely difficult to discuss systematically, and even psychologists' specialized works often duck the question of definition.[39] One could improve the *OED* definition as follows: "a vigorous, temporary, emotional condition in which the subject desires the object's harm, and/or desires to attack the object with words, because of some perceived failing." It is, however, vital to recognize that anger varies

(1) in intensity,[40] from homicidal mania to mere annoyance or irritation;

(2) in duration, since it is prone to disappear rapidly, or change its intensity, but in some forms may continue indefinitely;

(3) in openness, for it can be expressed at once (in a great variety of ways), or it can be kept more or less out of sight or bottled up;

(4) in consciousness—unconscious anger being a scarcely deniable phenomenon. The brain, in the words of a neurologist, "often

---

39. Such as Buck 1988. Averill 1982, 317, defines anger as "a conflictive emotion that, on the biological level, is related to aggressive systems and, even more important, to the capacities for cooperative social living, symbolization, and reflective self-awareness; that, on the psychological level, is aimed at the correction of some appraised wrong; and that, on the sociocultural level, functions to uphold accepted standards of conduct" (italics omitted). This is obviously not a definition in the ordinary sense at all, and the author recognizes (322) that it goes beyond "our ordinary concept" of anger. Here is another attempt by psychologists: anger is "a negative, phenomenological (or internal) feeling state associated with specific cognitive and perceptual distortions and deficiencies (e.g., misappraisals, errors, and attributions of blame, injustice, preventability, and/or intentionality), subjective labeling, physiological changes, and action tendencies to engage in socially constructed and reinforced organized behavioral scripts" (Kassinove & Sukhodolsky 1995, 7). Once again, scarcely a definition. This description has the merit of recognizing anger of considerable duration, but it is obviously tendentious in excluding well-founded anger: not all anger arises from distortions and deficiencies of the angry person. For an interesting but debatable attempt to define anger which unconsciously revives the Aristotelian notion of definition (which we shall be examining later), cf. Fehr & Baldwin 1996, 219–245.

40. On the complexities of this problem see Frijda et al. 1992.

processes emotions unconsciously and thereby hides them from our own mind's eye."[41]

And, to complicate matters, anger also varies

(5) in selfishness, since people are sometimes, if not very often, angry for reasons that do not serve their own ends (most death-penalty abolitionists, for example).

To complicate matters further still, conscious anger may vary

(6) in continuity, for "when we say that Smith is angry with Brown we need not be implying that Smith is now thinking of Brown . . . [he] may be asleep or attending to someone else."[42]

On the other hand, it would be better not to distinguish attacks of anger according to their degree of subjective "righteousness," as distinct from intensity, since it is almost a definitional quality of anger that it hears only one side.[43] "Righteous indignation" is commonly self-righteous indignation.[44]

And we have still not exhausted the varieties of anger. A psychologist can suppose, for example, that anger is felt only by individuals,[45] but historians commonly have to deal with anger which is felt by or at least attributed to groups, especially crowds.[46] Narratives of anger make still further distinctions: Cleitus and Alexander, for instance,

41. LeDoux 1987, 419. Ortony, Clore & Collins 1988, 176–178, maintained a similar view. But for Freud, what occurred in the unconscious could not be an emotion (Freud 1957 [1915], part III).

42. Hardie 1980, 95. Such passions may refer to "actual feelings, a thrill or a throb, and occurrent thoughts or to a temporary proneness to have an actual feeling or thought, and to behave in certain characteristic ways" (96). Cf. Stocker 1996, 23. This matter is handled much less well by Oakley 1992, 8–9.

43. "'I'll be judge, I'll be jury,' said cunning old Fury: 'I'll try the whole cause, and condemn you to death,'" *Alice in Wonderland*, ch. 3. More prosaically, a psychologist reports that the vast majority of those who are treated for irascibility "rigidly adhere to the correctness of their [own] behavior" (DiGiuseppe 1995, 134).

44. To take a phrase from S. J. James, *TLS* 8 May 1998, 14.

45. "The individual is the locus of emotion" (Kemper 1993, 41).

46. I do not claim that this list exhausts the variables. There is such a thing as resigned anger, for instance. We can distinguish displaced anger (kicking the office cat) from a more genuine kind of anger.

are represented as having whipped each other into a fury (but not all anger is like that). Quintus Cicero seems to have been easy to provoke to anger—but not all anger is felt by those who are irascible in character.

It is a strange or at least disappointing fact that when academic psychologists write about anger, they do not always take full account of this range of feelings.[47] Most of them appear to hold that anger is essentially episodic or short-lived;[48] it lasts no longer than a storm. Less! This convention goes back at least to Darwin.[49] A standard modern work informs us that "the typical episode of anger does not end abruptly, but merges into, or becomes mingled with, some other affective state,"[50] and entirely fails to take long-enduring anger into account. Is this because of an unconscious desire to keep anger within the range of things that can easily be examined by means of experiments, whereas the deep-seated and enduring anger of a spouse with a spouse, or of a neighbour with a neighbour, is a very awkward subject for research? The whole notion of reaching conclusions about emotions by stimulating volunteers in artificial environments has been subjected to criticism which psychologists would be well advised to confront.[51] Some of the best ancient writers about the emotions were in the habit, as we shall see, of relying on examples from Greek myth; this at least had the advantage that the stories had been judged psychologically credible, at some level, by generations of people. It is not clear

47. For a psychologist's view of these varieties see Lazarus 1991, 227–234. But the standard work on anger, Averill 1982, gives only a partial account. Greater complexity is acknowledged by Stoney & Engebretson 1994, 218–219.

48. See, for instance, Plutchik 1991, 84 (who argues this from proverbs—though the phrases he quotes are not in fact proverbs); Ekman 1992, 185; Tafrate 1995, 111 (but see Frijda et al. 1992, 67–68; Kassinove & Sukhodolsky 1995).

49. 1872, ch. 11.

50. Averill 1982, 204. He and B. M. Fridhandler report (ibid. 278) a study in which "only 10% of the subjects [who had been asked to report the most intense incident of anger they had experienced in the previous week] reported that their anger lasted more than three days [quite credible], *which seems to suggest an upper limit*" (my italics). This by no means follows. Averill is, however, one of those *most* alert to persisting states of anger (see 258–277).

51. See Elster 1999, 49–50.

that better results are to be obtained by questioning student volunteers in one's Psychology Department.[52]

Greeks and Romans occasionally wrote as if anger were essentially episodic or short-lived, as we shall see (long-lasting anger could be categorized as bitterness), but much more frequently, from the *Iliad* onwards, they show themselves to be well acquainted with *persisting* states of anger. This is in fact the nature of the great Homeric angers, which are anything but short-lived. Philodemus wrote that anger could not only last until death but also be passed on to one's children's children.[53] No ancient writer truly contested the existence of persisting anger, and no modern one should do so.

Contemporary academic psychologists are also unwilling to deal with political or social anger, partly (one supposes) because it is truly difficult to investigate, but also (one suspects) because it is not supposed to exist, least of all in the United States. There is one exception, but even that seems not to have made its way into the sanctum of academically investigatable subjects, namely feminist anger. By the 1980s many feminists had noticed the indispensable importance of anger to their cause, and the resulting debate will make an appearance in Chapter 11 below. For the moment, the point is simply that no historical inquiry into anger can possibly afford to neglect the rage which expresses itself in politics and society. For the purposes of historical study, we want to use a large net and make sure not to leave out any important variety of anger.

Ancients and moderns may also make different assumptions about anger and gender. Many Greek and Roman writers professed to believe that women were more prone to anger than men. In the modern world, by contrast, it is widely believed that women, although generally more emotional than men, are less irascible.[54] Academic psychologists

---

52. Twenty graduate students in psychology implicitly treated as a sample of the human race (and it is not as if the research concerned their natural emotions): Manstead & Tetlock 1989.

53. *De ira* 5 (col. xxx.15–24) ("some people are not only continually in a rage [*thumountai*], but are taken over by long-lasting and hard-to-cure fits of anger [*orgai*]").

54. W. D. Frost and J. R. Averill, in Averill 1982, 281.

have argued that in contemporary America women are more inclined to express their feelings of anger than men are, while men (obviously) are more inclined to be physically aggressive;[55] others have concluded that there is no substantial difference between women's irascibility and men's.[56] There is no likelihood that this question will be resolved, and no likelihood either that we can discover whether the classical stereotype was anything other than a misogynistic distortion.

What, then, is contemporary thinking about the control of anger? The answer is not simple, and there are great differences according to gender, and, even between Western countries, according to nationality. One authority has been courageous enough to set out "a partial list of the [modern American] rules and norms related to anger," a list which by reflecting, in a rough-and-ready fashion, the ambiguities and evasions of contemporary attitudes[57] has the important incidental effect of reminding us that ambiguities and evasions characterized popular thinking about anger in antiquity too.

Popular culture certainly seems to consider that while anger can be excessive it may also be legitimate to feel and express it, and even harmful not to express it. "Bottling it up" is held to be risky. This attitude is quite widespread in traditional societies, for instance in Alaska, Kenya and the Philippines.[58] Its modern version has some roots in one phase of Freudian psychology[59] (from 1895 to about 1926) during which the master held, roughly speaking, that emotions were safety-valve discharges of psychic tension, a point of view which he subsequently revised.[60] But modern "ventilationism" has other and older roots too, for similar doctrines were expounded by eighteenth-century

---

55. Stoney & Engebretson 1994, 218–219.

56. Frost & Averill, in Averill 1982, 281–316; Kring 2000.

57. Averill 1982, 324–325. For example: "A person has the right (duty) [but which?] to become angry at intentional wrong-doing, including an affront to one's honor, freedom, property, or other rights." "Anger should not be used as a tool to achieve selfish ends."

58. See Heelas 1986, 254. But here doubts may arise about the ability of the ethnographic project to report such matters correctly.

59. For the poorly informed assumption that Freudians are ventilationists, see for instance Stanford 1983, 3.

60. On the phases of Freudian thinking on this subject, see Rapaport 1953; Nichols & Zax 1977, 34–36. Freud 1955 [1895], esp. 201–202. Cf. Gaylin 1989, 82.

German medical writers such as Hieronymus Gaub, who wrote of anger as an emotion both destructive and therapeutic.[61] A ventilationist argument is already to be found in a pure form in the poetry of Blake ("A Poison Tree," part of *Songs of Experience* [1794]):

> I was angry with my friend:
> I told my wrath, my wrath did end.
> I was angry with my foe:
> I told it not, my wrath did grow.

D. H. Lawrence was another exponent. Indeed there lies behind modern attitudes a quite complicated history (still to be written) including, for example, an American trend, located by one study in the period from the 1890s to the 1950s, towards using rather than restraining anger—using it, that is, as a basis for competitiveness or moral indignation.[62] The ancient roots of ventilationism are, as we shall see, Aristotelian and Neoplatonist, but Aristotle's thinking on the subject is not generally ventilationist, and such ideas were of very limited importance in antiquity.

At all events, many modern psychiatrists and others are in principle against the repression of anger. This view is now formulated in a fairly sophisticated way, and not, for example, by reference to any facile belief in the benefits of what is natural. It is sometimes argued that constant repression of the "negative" emotions increases the likelihood of both psychological and medical troubles.[63] Another authority maintains that a large proportion of outbursts of anger take place within (quasi-) contractual relationships such as marriage which the parties may legitimately wish to renegotiate by this means.[64] Another says that

61. Hieronymus David Gaub, *Sermo academicus alter de regimine mentis* (Leiden, 1763), ch. 7, lists the harmful physical effects of suppressing anger. See further Rather 1965.

62. Stearns & Stearns 1986, esp. chs. 4 and 6. James already refers to "the calming effects of speaking out your mind when angry and having done with it" (1884, 198), not a thought likely to be framed in antiquity, because it was assumed that anger was likely to go beyond words to deeds.

63. See various contributions in Singer 1990; also Barraclough 1994, 94–100.

64. Oatley 1993b, 164. Cf. Novaco 1975, 4. But when the latter wrote (ibid.) that "the aim of clinical interventions for anger problems should not be to extinguish or eliminate anger categorically, but rather to work toward personal competence in its

anger is "basically a social construction, the function of which is to uphold accepted standards of conduct."[65] How this statement could be reconciled with the obvious link between anger and aggression, or with the spectacular number of murders and assaults committed in the last author's homeland (not to mention the gargantuan amount of simulated violence it produces), is obscure. Which is not to deny that "upholding accepted standards of conduct" can be *one* of the functions of expressing anger, especially perhaps in socially egalitarian societies in which other ways of upholding accepted standards of conduct are commonly ineffective, such as traditional Papua.[66]

Another argument is that some anger is adaptive.[67] Or that anger in general is.[68] This is taken to be a standard modern view.[69] A psychiatrist wrote not long ago that "although emotions can . . . be maladaptive in excess or in the wrong circumstances, their general [adaptive] utility is now accepted."[70] Such a theory is evidently thought to mean that those who show anger survive, prosper and reproduce themselves. This doctrine has some Aristotelian affinities, and it does not depend for its justification on equating anger with carefully calculated aggression. Nonetheless the theory may seem to be practically vacuous, since it cannot tell us which manifestations of emotions are adaptive or maladaptive, or why it might be a good idea for a particular person—or a whole community—to cooperate with the dimly perceived and slowly grinding wheels of biological evolution. It is not, however, part of my intention to evaluate such views until much later (Chapter 17). It is

---

regulation or management," he may have been hoping to reduce anger quite drastically—more, say, than Aristotle would have wished.

65. Averill 1990, 396. S. D. White, 1998, 145, takes a similar view of mediaeval anger.

66. A thought which easily occurs to the reader of E. L. Schieffelin's descriptions of Papuan anger (1983, 1985). For the view that anger is common in egalitarian societies, see also Myers on the Pintupi population of New Guinea (1988, 600).

67. About the adaptive functions of emotions, see recently Oatley 1993b, 162–164.

68. Izard 1983, 307.

69. Kemp & Strongman 1995, 405.

70. Nesse 1990, 264; but he soon has the good sense to retreat (267: "the tendency of hair to stand on end during terror is an atavistic remnant of a trait that probably no longer provides a selective advantage"). See also Plutchik 1980, and many other writings of the same author; Smith & Ellsworth 1985, 836.

enough to point out that anger was thought by some ancients, too, to be useful to those who expressed it, which makes it all the more necessary to find explanations for teaching that aimed at anger's control or elimination.

The high-water mark of psychologists' tolerance of anger now appears to be in the past.[71] The time has probably gone by in which one could write in a psychiatry journal that anger "has great constructive potential"[72]—though such a statement is far from being unintelligible. Even twenty years ago, exponents of cathartic therapy were decidedly on the defensive.[73] Irascibility is widely regarded by clinical psychologists as a condition which, at least above a certain level, needs treatment.[74]

Excessive anger is now generally held to contribute to physical ills as well.[75] What is commonly aimed for, however, is not the elimination of anger but its reduction or "management."[76] Since some recent work has suggested that even those who outwardly express moderate quantities of anger may be increasing their chances of suffering from coronary heart disease,[77] one wonders whether stricter self-control of anger will soon be advocated.

71. Kemp & Strongman 1995, 410. See also the bibliography of works which maintain that "the expression of anger results in well-being for the self and the relationship" given by Retzinger 1991, 47.

72. Rothenberg 1971–72, 454, continuing as follows: "despite the fact that anger and anxiety are highly related."

73. Of course it is one thing to express anger in the course of psychotherapy, another to express it in real life. Nichols & Zax 1977, 217, asserting that anger was "a particularly ripe subject for catharsis in psychotherapy," suggested that patients could not only "ventilate" their anger in therapy but also learn when and how to allow anger to emerge in everyday life. For current views about cathartic therapy see Chapter 15.

74. Deffenbacher, Demm & Brandon 1986; Kassinove 1995 (where, incidentally, the proposed definition of anger [7] is indefensible).

75. Leventhal & Patrick-Miller 1993, 367; Mittleman et al. 1995, Kawachi et al. 1996. See the balanced evaluations in Siegman & Smith 1994.

76. Deffenbacher 1994, esp. 267

77. Kawachi et al. 1996, 2094, where it is explained how anger was measured in the (male) subjects in question. The connection between rage and heart attacks was known to ancient doctors: see Galen, *De propriorum animi cuiuslibet affectuum dignotione et curatione* 4.6 De Boer.

In any case the importance of the "tolerant" attitude towards anger should not be exaggerated, since twentieth-century society and law have made only limited concessions to the psychologists' views. It is generally true that those who show in public that they are giving way to anger rapidly lose sympathy unless their anger is mild and carefully calibrated (aggressive reprisals against book reviewers are permitted).[78] Educated people seldom display anger in public, or even in semi-public. Raucous commotions in parliaments are not much of an exception. In some countries, particular circumstances—driving a car for instance—often lead to fleeting fits of ill temper. At the same time, indignation—while not what it was in the era of reform (let us say, *grosso modo,* 1830 to 1979)—can be encountered easily enough. This absence of anger is probably in large part a matter of decorum, our anger being kept quiet and out of sight because we realize that it is commonly counter-productive. Private anger is a different matter, but while anger is no doubt thriving within the family, here too decorum has its influence, and we take it for granted that definite limits should be imposed on serious expressions of anger and kindred emotions. To what extent this story of modern restraint applies to the mass of the population in any modern country is an open question. Designing and executing the research which would discover the answer would be extremely difficult. There can be little doubt, however, that amid contemporary hedonism the predominant code concerning anger is one of self-restraint.

There remains something of a contrast between contemporary culture and antiquity in this respect. People who believe in avoiding anger altogether are in modern times exceedingly rare (they are hardly to be found outside Buddhist monasteries),[79] whereas such a belief was quite common for many centuries of antiquity. In the contemporary world, the expression of anger is commonly regarded as a positive

---

78. Lutz 1988, 179, said that it was acceptable "in many sectors of the U.S. upper middle-class to be angry if someone smokes in your presence." Faulty fieldwork; censorious yes, angry no.

79. For the complete negativity of anger for a person seeking "full enlightenment for the sake of all beings," see Tenzin Gyatso [the fourteenth Dalai Lama], *The World of Tibetan Buddhism,* trans. G. T. Jinpa (Boston, 1995), 67–69, 77–83. Needless to say, Buddhist thinking on the subject is a great deal more complex than that.

event, even though the consequent dangers are clear, whereas in antiquity, though the uses of anger were widely recognized, it was subject to frequent criticism. Many ancients thought that there was nothing wrong with appropriate anger, but most of those who reflected on the matter held either that anger should be eliminated altogether or that it was important to keep it within limits; the emphasis in any case was more markedly on restraint. For semantic reasons which are about to appear in full force, this contrast between ancient and modern is less stark than it seems, but it is nonetheless real.

Although the claim that anger has "great constructive potential" is probably not now judged to be cogent by many, a similar proposition, to the effect that many great projects, and in particular many great reforms, would never have been carried through except on a swell of indignation and anger, is undeniable.[80] A Platonist might possibly have formulated such a thought in antiquity, employing the ambiguous concept *thumos,* but in general it would have been unappealing, partly because of the lack of interest in reform and partly, perhaps, just because of the angry emotions' bad or at least dubious repute.

80. Cf. Elster 1985 on Marx. Elster was obviously right to say that life without emotions would be colourless—but does that apply to anger? I return to the question in the last chapter.

CHAPTER 3

The Greek and Latin Terminology

There lies before us a complex Greek semantic landscape of anger.[1] To describe it in every detail is not necessary for the purposes of this study, but some of its important features must be pointed out, and the decidedly poorer resources of Latin in this area also require some comments. If we are going to understand the classical critique of anger, we shall have to understand precisely what it was that the critique was directed against. Fortunately the anger terminology of a number of authors has already been the subject of special study: this applies to Homer, Sophocles, Herodotus, Thucydides, Aristotle, and to the authors of the surviving Greek monographs concerning anger, Philodemus and Plutarch.[2] Nonetheless the most important point of all, the substantial difference between Greek *orgē* and "anger," has usually been missed.

---

1. There is no single publication which can be referred to for any kind of history of these terms and their cognates. See, however, Kleinknecht et al. 1968 [1954], as well as the works referred to in the following notes. J. H. H. Schmidt 1876–1886, III:551–572, collected much of the Greek material but treated it ahistorically. For the most part, I intentionally ignore etymology here, never having seen any evidence that Greek usage of these terms was influenced by notions of what their remote prehistoric roots may have meant (*cholos* may be an exception); not that Greeks were uninterested in etymologies (on *thumos*, for instance, see Pl. *Crat.* 419e).

2. See especially (on Homer) Considine 1966, Scully 1984, Considine 1985, Considine 1986, Muellner 1996; on Sophocles, Camerer 1936; on Herodotus, Edinger unpublished; on Thucydides, Huart 1968, 153–162; on Aristotle and Plutarch, Becchi 1990; on Philodemus, Indelli's commentary (1988).

We must note in passing that the semantic landscape referred to here is almost entirely a literary one, some distance removed, especially in Hellenistic and Roman times, from everyday Greek semantics. We are not of course devoid of sources written in everyday Greek of the classical period and in *koinē* (which do not in fact suggest any radical divergences in anger vocabulary), but there is an undeniable literariness and elitism about this study which cannot be avoided. In so saying, one simply recognizes that the history of popular culture in antiquity will always be in the highest degree fragmentary. We must also take note of the likelihood that the connotation of Greek and Latin terms for anger changed over time. It would be extremely perilous to assume that there was one constant meaning that was attached to *cholos* or to *orgē* or to *ira* in all ages.

The archaic Greek nouns for states of anger were *mēnis* and *cholos* (literally "bile").[3] The term *mēnis* is restricted in Homer to the wrath of gods or of the hero Achilles (who was of half-divine parentage) over perceived major offences,[4] which suggests that it meant something like "*irresistible* wrath."[5] Since, with *mēnis,* perceived major offences are at issue, it is normally lasting, and some have therefore supposed that duration is another definitional aspect of the term.[6] At all events, *cholos* is a wider term. Another archaic word close by was *kotos,* with the overtone "resentful anger."[7] Verbs included not only the close cognates of

3. LSJ, s.v. *orgē*, still states incorrectly that *thumos* was the Homeric term. On the early meaning of *thumos,* see Sullivan 1993.

4. In both epics the verb *mēniō* is also applied to the anger of other mortals of heroic rank, and in the *Odyssey* (xvii.14) even to a beggar (but a beggar who is Odysseus in disguise).

5. The lengthy analysis of Muellner 1996 leads him to the conclusion that it denotes "the cosmic sanction against tabu behavior" (133), though he is fair enough to admit (8) that some things which cause *mēnis* in epic do not seem to fit this interpretation. The proposed definition is very hypothetical (though I have no doubt he is right to say [ibid.] that *mēnis* is never used of anger aroused by a minor offence). It is to be noticed that he claims that Achilles' anger is "consistently" referred to as *mēnis* in the *Iliad* (1), whereas the poet sometimes refers to it as *cholos* (*Il.* i.192, 224, iv.513, and other references listed by *LFE* s.v. *mēnis,* col. 188). The lack of scholarly agreement on the exact nuances of *mēnis* in epic can be seen in this last-named article. It is clear, however, that *mēnis* is "dreadful, usually fatal, in its effects and so is to be feared and avoided by its object" (Considine 1986, 56). See now D. L. Cairns, forthcoming.

6. Schwyzer 1931, 213.

7. Cf. *LFE* s.v.

these nouns but also *ochthein, chōesthai,* and *meneainein,* each of which, however, has its own usage and fails to correspond exactly, as we shall not be surprised to learn, with "to be angry."[8] There is also *nemesan.* The richness of this vocabulary is striking;[9] much of it came into being, I suggest, at a time when "a man [or at least a hero—we must remember the poetic context] who has received an unpleasant stimulus from his environment"[10] was very likely to show uninhibited rage.

By the fifth century, in any case, *mēnis* and *cholos* and their cognate verbs had largely been replaced, though not in all poetic texts, by *orgē* and *thumos.* These latter words and their cognates had earlier referred to less determinate things than anger (*orgē* appears to have meant something like "temperament" or "disposition"), and they sometimes retained such meanings.[11] The earliest texts in which *orgē* denotes anger are fragments of Sappho: in particular the lines

> When *orgē* is spreading through your breast,
> it is best to keep your yapping tongue in check

8. Adkins 1969, 12–18. Passages in which *ochthēsas* (the commonest form of *ochthein*) probably or certainly means something like "distressed" and not, as often, "angered," include *Il.* i.517, xi.403; *Od.* v.298. See also Scully 1984, esp. 14. There should be one root notion, which is, I think, that of being acutely aware that serious harm is at hand, a situation to which a Homeric god or hero may react with either swift anger, an internal debate about whether to run away, or simply grim anticipation.

9. Cf. R. Laurenti, in his joint commentary with G. Indelli on Plu. *De cohibenda ira* (1988), pp. 7–11 (not to be accepted on all points, however).

10. Adkins 1969, 17.

11. On *orgē* as "temperament" or something similar: Kleinknecht et al. 1968 [1954], 382; Huart 1968, 156–158; the earliest instance is in Hes. *Works and Days* 304, on which cf. G. O. Hutchinson's note on Aesch. *Septem* 678. Clear fifth-century examples are in Hdt. vi.128.1, Hipp. *Airs* 5 and 24 (twice). For *orgai* as "disposition" or something similar, see Soph. *Ant.* 356, *Ajax* 639, Eur. *Troad.* 53. The word is used in this way several times in the early books of Thucydides, then in viii.83, but not in any definitely later prose text. In Aristophanes' *Wasps* 1030, "a sort of *orgē* of Heracles" is normally taken to mean something like "spirit," but perhaps anger was intended. The apparent suggestion of Allen 2000, 54, that *orgē* occasionally means "sexual desire" is entirely unfounded (it never seems to be affected by the verb *organ*); there is no "fundamental ambiguity" (118). The wide sense of *thumos* as "passion," "emotion," or the location of such things, does not need documenting here; see esp. Van Bennekom 1991, cols. 1080–1087; Sullivan 1993.

seem to be an instance.[12] But the first really clear instances appear in Theognis and in Pindar.[13] From the 450s they are fairly numerous, and from the 430s onwards in tragedy and the 410s onwards in prose it seems to have been old-fashioned to use the word to mean anything such as "temperament."

There are many nuances of anger in the literary language, as there must have been in the spoken language: in Herodotus, for instance, *cholos* (which, however, is a term he uses only three times) appears to mean an anger which "is retained and masked and is discharged at a later time, sometimes much later."[14] The words *nemesan* and *nemesis* continued to refer to a kind of anger approximately equivalent to "righteous indignation."[15] One may suspect that in the fifth century it was not easy to couple the idea of justice with human *orgē*.[16] Other groups of semantically related words seem generally somewhat milder than *orgē*, though quite vigorous enough to refer to emotions which give rise to violence—in particular *chalepotēs/chalepainein* and *aganaktein*. It is natural to say that if a person experiences *orgē* he will become very *chalepos*, hard to deal with;[17] *orgē* was intense.

In Hellenistic Greek *orgē* and *thumos* continued to be the principal nouns. The terms had never been synonymous, for in post-archaic Greek *thumos* had a double sense, meaning not only anger but also

12. Fr. 126 Diehl = 158 Voigt, from Plu. *De cohibenda ira* 7 (*Mor.* 456e). Some have doubted that Sappho used the word *orgē* in this text (e.g., Ringeltaube 1913, 33 n. 2); but it is to some extent guaranteed by the metre, and the canine metaphor, traceable to *Od.* xx.13–16 (cf. Cavallini 1984–85), supports this interpretation. In fr. 108 Diehl = 120 Voigt, where Sappho claims not to be παλίγκοτος, "resentful" or "revengeful," *orgē* might mean "temperament." In frr. 44A, line b8, and 103, line 4, Voigt "anger" is the most probable meaning.

13. Theognis 1223–1224: "nothing is more unjust than *orgē*." Pind. *Nem.* v. 32 (probably). Early instances in tragedy: Aesch. *Supp.* 187 (probably), *Ag.* 71 and 216 (probably), *Choeph.* 326 (probably), *Eum.* 981 (?), [Aesch.] *PV* 315 (in my opinion, but in this play *orgē* often means "temperament"—invariably so, according to Griffith 1977, 173); Soph. *Ant.* 766, *Trach.* 933, and often in *OT*. But it is partly a matter of genre and taste: Sophocles, Euripides and the author of the *PV* sometimes used *cholos* for "anger," whereas Aeschylus paradoxically had not done so.

14. Edinger, unpublished.

15. Cf. Burger 1991.

16. See Chapter 8.

17. E.g., Isocr. xv.31.

"the seat or agency of anger and zeal within the person."[18] Plato and Aristotle had notoriously used *thumos* to refer to a part or faculty of the soul which did other things besides get angry. The *thumos,* said Aristotle, is the capacity of the soul by which we feel affection.[19] Aristotle also distinguished between irrational *orgē*-anger and less irrational *thumos*-anger.[20]

When Hellenistic philosophers attempted to distinguish the two terms, their performance was mixed. The Stoics sensibly tended to derive their definition of *orgē* from Aristotle—a definition which we shall shortly examine—but they said less felicitously that *thumos* was *orgē* which was just beginning.[21] It may be slightly more natural to think of anger which sets in for the long term as *orgē* rather than *thumos,* whereas when it started out it was *orgē* or *thumos* indifferently, but this distinction is difficult to find in the texts. Philodemus in any case fails to convince when he claims to differentiate extreme *thumos* from more moderate *orgē,*[22] and in fact he was aware that in ordinary usage the kinds of anger these words referred to did not differ in intensity.[23] In the educated Attic Greek prose of the high Roman Empire, such as that of Plutarch, *orgē* and *thumos* can hardly be said to refer to different kinds of anger.[24]

18. Simon 1988, 82. This double meaning is illustrated by the story about Zeno and the slave in Diog.Laert. vii.23.

19. *philoumen, Pol.* vii.6.1327b41. On the ambiguity of *thumos* in Aristotle, see G. Indelli's commentary on Phld. *De ira,* p. 193.

20. See *Nic.Eth.* iii.8.1117a8.

21. Chrysippus, *SVF* III.395 (from Stobaeus), 396 (from Diog.Laert.), 397 (from Pseudo-Andronicus). That Chrysippus distinguished the two terms is confirmed by *SVF* II.886–887 (from Galen).

22. Phld. *De ira* 7 (col. xlv.33–37). It is true that the sentiment attributed to Chrysippus by Galen in *De placitis Hippocratis et Platonis* iii.1.25 could be read in that sense.

23. Phld. *De ira* 7, cols. xliii.41–xliv.5. Scholars have added their own confusions: e.g., Demosthenes xxiv.118 does not help us to distinguish the two terms. Indelli (on Phld. loc. cit.) is mistaken to say that *thumos* was commonly taken to mean brief and non-intense anger.

24. Chadwick 1996, 143–150, discusses *thumos* without throwing any light on the kind of anger the word refers to. Origen attempted to distinguish the terms by saying that *thumos* was *orgē* still on fire while *orgē* was a desire for retaliation (*Exeget. in Psalmos* ii.5 [*PG* xii.1105]), but we may suspect him of desiring to put the *orgē* of the biblical

Seneca comments on the relatively large number of Greek anger nouns, by the standards of Latin.[25] By Hellenistic times an educated Greek certainly seems to have had at his or her disposal a wide choice of words for referring to the angry emotions.[26] This remains true even when we make an allowance for the illusion of synchronicity which can be created by casual glances at Liddell and Scott's lexicon. It is hard to resist the conclusion that this wealth of vocabulary means something.[27] But what? Linguistics scholars have debated throughout the twentieth century whether such richness in a particular semantic field in a particular language has any great significance. The wider question is whether we can ever correlate features of particular cultures with linguistic variables.[28] Much has been written about the "Sapir-Whorf hypothesis," which is sometimes taken to refer to lexical abundance and is sometimes said to state, roughly speaking, that languages influence the thought of those who use them (which might be hard to falsify).[29] None of these matters needs deciding here, but I take it that this lexical abundance is evidence not simply that "the Greeks" were interested in this particular aspect of their lives but that they were really preoccupied with it.[30]

Can we not be more specific? The Greeks' anger vocabulary was already a refined one when Homer wrote, and it continued to evolve in

---

god in a good light. Basil of Caesarea (*Adversus iratos* 6 end [*PG* xxxi.369]) claimed that there was a great difference between the two, which was plainly never true; his opinion is that *thumos* is a kind of kindling or sudden vaporization "of the emotion," while *orgē* is a lasting distress and a continual longing for retaliation against those who have injured us.

25. *De ira* i.4.2.

26. And there are other common terms which happen not to have been mentioned so far, such as *paroxunesthai*, "to be annoyed by."

27. According to Nussbaum 1994, 243 n. 4, "the large number of anger-words seems to be evidence of an intense interest in [it] in both the Greek and Roman worlds," to which I would only object that Latin is not especially rich in this respect. She implies that neither fear nor love had such a rich vocabulary in the classical languages; with respect to fear, this judgement could be questioned.

28. For a linguistics perspective, see Lucy 1992, especially ch. 3.

29. Not that this was precisely what Sapir or Whorf ever thought, apparently (Kay & Kempton 1984).

30. Cf. Ward & Throop 1992, 75. On how to discuss lexical abundance, see H. H. Clark 1996, 341.

important ways at least until the time of Aristotle;[31] during all of that period, one might say, many Greeks were greatly concerned to describe with clarity (*saphēneia*—one of their favourite intellectual virtues) the past, present or potential anger of themselves and others. Now, an anthropologist has reported that Tahitians theorize a lot on the subject of anger, and have a rich vocabulary in this area, but actually feel anger only rarely.[32] What I am suggesting here is not that the lexical abundance of Greek with respect to the angry emotions shows that they were irascible, but simply that they were aware of the varieties of such emotions. This may be taken as a symptom of the fact, which is known independently, that throughout the period just specified they were greatly interested in distinguishing proper from improper anger. We might modestly ask linguistics to take this case into careful consideration when Sapir-Whorf is next under the microscope.

Let us return to the matter of the correspondence between Greek and English terms. We have already discussed *mēnis,* and we shall examine it further in Chapter 7. As for *cholos* and (in its mature usage) *orgē,* it is not in doubt that they had fields of reference very similar to "anger." Like us, the Greeks generally used the same words to describe both short-lived outbursts of anger, accompanied by obvious physical symptoms, and the sort of anger that can continue for years.

What then did *orgē* mean exactly in classical Greek? There is usually thought to be a trouble-free correspondence with "anger."[33] Aristotle offers us two approaches, both analytic rather than in the conventional modern sense definitional. Here is the account in *De anima:* emotions, he says, all belong to the body as well as to the soul, so anger

> must be defined as a movement of a body, in a particular case aroused
> by such a cause, with such an end in view. This at once makes it the
> business of the natural scientist to inquire into the soul . . . But the nat-
> ural scientist and the dialectician will in every case offer different defi-

31. It seems to have been he who coined the word *aorgēsia,* Anon. *In EN Comm.* (*Commentaria in Aristotelem Graeca* XX), 136; the commentator Aspasius was less sure (*Comm. in Aristot.Gr.* XIX, 1, 53.6). But both commentators say that the term *aorgētos* already existed.

32. Levy 1984, 218–223.

33. Thus in the index of Sihvola & Engberg-Pedersen 1998 we read: "orge: see anger."

nitions, for example in answer to the question "What is anger?" The latter will call it a desire for revenge [*antilupēsis*] or something like that, the natural scientist will call it a boiling [*zesis*] of the blood [or heat] which is about the heart.[34]

In the *Rhetoric* he naturally adopts the dialectician's approach, but he gives a more detailed version of it:[35] anger is "the desire, accompanied by pain, for perceived retaliation [*timōria*] for some perceived slight to oneself or one's own, the slight not having been deserved."[36] (This passage is, by the way, frequently mistranslated—there is nothing in the Greek about a "conspicuous" slight or "conspicuous" retaliation).[37] Earlier he had also explained that no one is angry with "those whom vengeance clearly cannot overtake, or those who are far more powerful than he is; against such people they are not angry, or at any rate less so."[38] The implication is clear that while *orgē* is an emotion, it is only *orgē* if it leads to action or comes close to leading to action; the feeling by itself, restrained by, for example, the prudential inadvisability of showing anger against someone "far more powerful," scarcely

34. *De anima* i.1.403a16–32. Renehan 1963 demonstrated that the words translated in square brackets are an interpolation of about the fifth century A.D. For a physical definition of *thumos*-anger: Pl. *Crat.* 419e (cf. Mansfeld 1992, 18); for another early physiological explanation of *orgē*-anger, see Hipp. *Reg.* i.36. For commentary on the *De anima* passage, see Frede 1992, 103–107.

35. Not in contradiction with the *De anima* passage: Nehamas 1992, 295 = 1994, 262. It is interesting that both in the *De anima* and in the *Rhetoric* Aristotle seems to maintain some scholarly distance from the definitions he suggests.

36. Aristot. *Rhet.* ii.2.1378a31: "ὄρεξις μετὰ λύπης τιμωρίας φαινομένης διὰ φαινομένην ὀλιγωρίαν εἰς αὐτὸν ἢ τινὰ τῶν αὐτοῦ, τοῦ ὀλιγωρεῖν μὴ προσήκοντος." R. Kassel's text is slightly different: "ὄρεξις μετὰ λύπης κτλ. ἡ τῶν αὐτοῦ ὀλιγωρεῖν μὴ προσηκόντων." Cf. *Nic.Eth.* v.8.1135b28–29. Only a very lengthy discussion could deal comprehensively with the wealth of material in *Rhet.* ii.2–3.

37. See Cooper 1996, 255 n. 23; W. V. Harris 1997b. Most of the trouble stems from the translation by W. R. Roberts, erroneously followed by, among others, Averill 1982, 80; Solomon 1993, 4; Kemp & Strongman 1995, 400; Stocker 1996, 24; Gill 1996c, 198 n. 78.

38. *Rhet.* i.11.1370b13–15: otherwise getting angry would not be sweet—which he assumes that it is, quoting *Iliad* xviii.109 (it is "much sweeter than dripping honey"); so too *Rhet.* ii.2.1378b1. On the apparent contradiction between the statement that *orgē* is sweet and Aristotle's claim that it is accompanied by pain, see Fillion-Lahille 1970, 51–54.

counts.[39] Another comment clearly indicates the same thing: people do not become angry *(ouk orgizontai)* with those whom they fear or regard with awe, "for it is impossible to fear and be angry <with someone> at the same time"[40]—which would plainly be untrue if *orgē*, like "anger," referred primarily to a feeling rather a propensity for action. This reading of *orgē* is confirmed, I suggest, by the fact that some other Greek emotions—*eleos* (approximately "pity"), for example—are as much dispositions to action as they are interior feelings.[41]

Such a definition of anger as the one in Aristotle's *Rhetoric* may seem inadequate. Adult humans, not to mention children, often feel and express anger even when they are in no position to avenge themselves or retaliate, and they certainly sometimes feel angry—with themselves, for example, or with their own children—without any desire for revenge at all.[42] (Aspasius, the commentator on Aristotle, seems to have been the only ancient writer to make this point).[43] One can be angry with a friend or colleague without actually wishing for revenge or punishment: modern Western emotions are sometimes so mild.[44]

It would be absurd to suppose that Aristotle's definition of *orgē* was seriously mistaken. This was what *orgē* was. But two observations are necessary, one about Aristotle's conception of a definition, the other about a rather different kind of *orgē* which is also visible in the same chapter of the *Rhetoric*. In the first place, Aristotle's notion of meaning derives not, in the normal modern way, from an analysis of a theoretical totality of all uses of a given term, but from paradigm cases. A leading Aristotelian scholar called this kind of meaning the "focal meaning" of a term.[45] And in all ages the quintessential scene of anger, because it is so full of unpredictability and drama, is a display of titanic

---

39. It should be noted that the meaning of *orgē* is not being extrapolated from the texts of authors who preached against it and who could therefore be suspected of exaggerating its intensity.

40. *Rhet.* ii.3.1380a32–34.

41. See Dover 1974, 196.

42. Cf. Vlastos 1991, 190.

43. Aspasius (*Comm. in Aristot.Gr.* XIX, 1, 46.4–5) says that fathers who are angry with their sons do not wish to inflict retaliatory pain *(antilupein)*.

44. According to Nussbaum 1993, 244, modern anger includes the wish to do harm, but that is not invariably the case. For an anthropologist's idiosyncratic definition of anger which unconsciously echoes Aristotle's *Rhetoric*, see Myers 1988, 593.

45. Owen 1960, 169 = 1979, 17 = 1986, 184; and see Leighton 1988, 76.

rage, which no one can continue for long. It would thus be pointless to criticize Aristotle for ignoring anger that is not accompanied by a desire for revenge: the paradigm of *orgē* included a desire for revenge (and the paradigm of modern anger may include it too). That did not in itself discredit *orgē*, since—as we shall see in some detail in Chapters 7 to 9—a desire for revenge or for vengeful punishment was in the eyes of most people (though not of everyone at all periods of either Greek or Roman history) entirely respectable, and not a cause for embarrassment or shame. It is not to be doubted that *orgē*, and *ira* too, very commonly included a frank desire for revenge.

But when Aristotle had uttered this definition, he was evidently not satisfied, and he veered away for a moment to a different kind of anger. People grow angry, he says, when they are in distress *(lupoumenoi)*, for the person who is in distress is aiming for something.

> If then someone else opposes him directly in any way, such as by preventing him from drinking when he is thirsty . . . if people work against him or fail to work with him or otherwise vex him while he is in this state, he becomes angry with all of them. Hence those who are sick or poor or in love or thirsty, or in general desirous of something which they do not obtain, they are irascible.[46]

The sort of anger briefly under discussion here is wish-frustration, not a reaction to "slighting," or at least so it seems.[47]

We might not want to accept without some qualifications the common notion that the fifth- and fourth-century Greeks still lived in a shame culture rather than a guilt culture.[48] But Aristotle's analysis of

---

46. *Rhet.* ii.2.1379a12–19. R. Kassel held that the section beginning "Hence those who are sick" was inauthentic, and one can readily understand why.

47. Cf. Elster 1999, 62 n. 30. Without knowing Greek, Elster astutely observes (62) that Aristotle's *orgē* is not the same as "anger." He wants to call Aristotle's vengeance-anger "wrath," but that word is archaic, and there is unfortunately nothing archaic about revenge. Elster (63–64) was misled by the translation of W. R. Roberts into thinking that the words translated above as "the slight not having been deserved" might mean "at the hands of men who have no call to slight one," which is simply wrong unless one emends the text in a wholly unnecessary way (there *is* a divergence in the MS readings, but it is not relevant). Nonetheless Elster is correct to draw attention to the social character of Aristotelian anger.

48. What I mean by these terms is "a culture in which ethical standards depend on social interactions and interpersonal judgements," and one "in which they depend

orgē undoubtedly supports this idea: "slighting" is an essential part of the arousal of anger (even when he considers wish-frustration, he rapidly veers back to slighting), and revenge is an essential part of its expression. Other comments underline the point, above all his long list of those against whom people are angry, which is matched by a list of those with whom people are not angry but even-tempered.

> People grow angry with those who laugh at, ridicule or jeer at them, for they are insulting them [*hubrizousi*]. [Many other kinds of provocation follow] . . . They are angry with those who slight us before five classes of people, their rivals, those whom they admire, those whom they wish to be admired by, those they are in awe of, and those who are in awe of them.[49]

Honour is much of what is at stake in these two lists: the behaviour which is expected to provoke anger is more or less out in the open, and anger itself is presumed to be out in the open too.[50]

Do ancient writers recognize that one can be angry with oneself? A famous story in Plato's *Republic* has interesting implications in this respect. Leontius is said to have been angry with himself (the word *orgē* is used) for ghoulishly desiring to look closely at the corpses of executed criminals outside the walls of Athens[51]—but in Plato's eyes it was not Leontius *himself* who was the target of the anger, it was the appetitive element in his soul: the story is recounted with the precise purpose of proving that the appetitive element and the passionate element are separate from each other, as if "being angry with oneself" were in fact an impossible concept. And in fact "being angry with oneself," in the sense of experiencing *orgē* against oneself, is rarely attested in antiq-

---

the individual's independent sense of right and wrong" (to borrow the succinct language of Gill 1996c, 66; cf. Dodds 1951, 17–18).

49. *Rhet.* ii.2.1379a31–1379b37, ii.3.1380a9–1380b29.

50. Cf. D. L. Cairns 1993, 383, who writes that "Greek definitions of anger tend . . . to stress the reference of that emotion to one's own honour and status," citing [Pl.] *Def.* 415e11; Aristot. *Top.* iv.5.127b30–31, vi.13.151a15–16, vii.1.156a32–33, in addition to the present passage. Another interesting feature of Aristotelian *orgē* is that it is never altruistic, unlike "hostility," which we are all supposed to feel against thieves and informers as classes (*Rhet.* ii.4.1382a2–7).

51. *Rep.* iv.439e–440a. This passage has sometimes caused scholars to hallucinate, but that need not bother us here. For the context see, e.g., Annas 1981, 140–141.

uity, Menander's comedy *The Self-Punisher (Heautontimoroumenos)* notwithstanding, until the fourth century A.D.[52] This was probably because *orgē* was more vengeful, and in a sense more extrovert, than "anger."[53] And Seneca could even say that *ira,* a somewhat wider term than *orgē,* was not *ira* unless it went beyond mental disturbance and included some kind of attack *(impetus)* (he may admittedly have been engaging in some special pleading).[54]

All or most of the many definitions of *orgē* which later writers offer are more or less simplified versions of the one in Aristotle's *Rhetoric,* not that most of their authors will have known the Aristotelian text. There is one important difference. Chrysippus said that *orgē* was "the desire to retaliate against [*timōrēsasthai*] one who seems to have performed an injustice contrary to one's deserts."[55] "Injustice" has replaced "slight"—which should probably be taken as a symptom of a certain shift from shame culture to guilt culture, since later writers generally followed Chrysippus in this respect and not Aristotle.

Poseidonius *may* have written (the evidence is less clear than is sometimes supposed) that *orgē* was "a desire to punish a person by whom you think you have been hurt unjustly."[56] Similarly Cicero said that *ira* was "a longing to punish a person who seems to have harmed <you> unjustly."[57] Cicero had also written, rather differently, that it

---

52. In Terence's version of the play, a character (not the hero) says, "mihi nunc ego suscenseo" ("It's with myself that I'm angry now") (915), meaning, "What a fool I have been!" According to one of the *sententiae* of Publilius Syrus (at the very end of the Republic), "iratus cum ad se rediit sibi tum irascitur," "as soon as the angry man comes to himself, he is angry at himself" (311 Meyer). Real self-anger: Marcus Aurelius in Fronto, *Epist.* iv.13 (I.216 Haines). For the fourth-century evidence, see M. Oberhaus on Greg.Naz. *De ira* 1. Cic. *De fin.* v.10.28–29 discusses the paradox of self-hatred.

53. To *chalepainein* with oneself was less problematic: see, e.g., Pl. *Soph.* 230b.

54. *De ira* ii.3.4–5.

55. *SVF* III.395 = Stobaeus, *Ecl.* ii.91.10; the relevant section of III.396 = Diog.Laert. vii.113 is almost identical.

56. Lactant. *De ira dei* 17.13 = fr. 155 E–K (but Lactantius will have had this from a lost passage of Seneca). This interpretation depends on the reading "aut ut ait" (see I. G. Kidd's note on Poseid., loc. cit.); if the correct text were "alii ut ait," which is possible, the definition would be one *reported by* Poseidonius (not that this would matter for our immediate purposes).

57. *Tusc.Disp.* iv.21: "libido poeniendi eius qui videatur laesisse iniuria."

was the mark of an angry man "to desire to inflict as much pain [*dolor*] as possible on the person by whom he seems to have been harmed."[58] Seneca's definition in *De ira* is lost in a textual lacuna; according to Lactantius, he said that *ira* was "a desire to avenge an injustice."[59] All this suggests once again that *orgē* was normally aggressive and open. And so indeed Plutarch seems to say: simply add power to *orgē* and it becomes *phonos*, murder.[60]

Was an attack of *orgē* thought of as being essentially brief? Demosthenes, speaking against Meidias, claimed that behaviour that went on "for many days in succession" could not have been angry but must have been deliberate. This, however, was plainly special pleading aimed at invalidating his opponent's use of anger as mitigation.[61] And when Aristotle classifies as *pikria*, bitterness, that anger which people maintain for a long time, he is not denying that it continues to be anger ("bitter people are angry for a long time").[62] In Isaeus I the speaker argues that the *orgē* of the testator Cleonymus, whose will is being contested, had eventually abated, but even he is not denying that it went on for several years.[63]

An interesting fourth-century B.C. usage of *orgē* and *orgizesthai* suggests that action, as well as feeling, was a standard ingredient, for these words came to mean, for a time, not only "anger" and "to be angry" but also sometimes "punishment" and "to punish."[64] The orator Lycurgus speaks of "the extreme *orgē*" when he apparently means the death penalty.[65] Some further implications of this usage will be followed up later (Chapter 10), but is obvious that it came into being in a

---

58. *Tusc.Disp.* iii.19: "proprium est enim irati cupere, a quo laesus videatur, ei quam maxumum dolorem inurere."

59. *De ira dei* 17.13: "cupiditas ulciscendae iniuriae"; and in i.3.3 Seneca says that his definition is not very different from Aristotle's, which he gives as *cupiditas doloris reponendi* (he obviously knew what Aristotle said about this from some other Stoic or Stoics, not directly: cf. Setaioli 1988, 143–145). Cf. *De ira* ii.22.2.

60. *Ad principem ineruditum* 6 (*Mor.* 782c).

61. Demosthenes xxi.41.

62. Aristot. *Nic.Eth.* iv.5.1126a19–20.

63. *orgē:* i.11, 13, 19.

64. Hirzel 1907, 417. But I do not take all the texts he cites in the same way.

65. *Against Leocrates* 138; cf. Dem. xxiv.118, and for *orgizomai*, xxiii.168. The uses in xxi.147 and xxiv.218 seem less determinate.

world in which the ordinary Athenian male citizen found nothing in principle at all wrong with *orgē*. Demosthenes spoke of certain persons' *justly* incurring *orgē* (xvi.19). When this meaning disappeared (after about the time of Menander's play on the subject of *orgē* in 322/321?), the reason was presumably that, while punishment was as necessary as ever, *orgē* had come under a shadow. But this is to rush ahead. What matters here is that what orators envisaged as anger was not the jurors' inner rage but their infliction of concrete penalties.

I suggest that all or most of what was thought of in the period, say, 450 B.C. to 300 A.D. as *orgē*-anger and *thumos*-anger was by modern standards quite furious and intense, though some of it was long-lived.[66] A corollary might be that a good deal of what we regard as anger was either referred to by milder terms, such as *chalepotēs,* or even considered too trivial to be attended to or mentioned.[67]

This hypothesis would help to explain the stance of the "absolutist" ancient critics of anger: an ancient person could easily believe that the wise man should never be angry without giving up the prerogative of being irritated, and—more important—without stinting on the punishment of his or her slaves or the reprimanding of children.[68] Marcus Aurelius claimed, sincerely perhaps, that he was without *orgē,* but he admitted within a few pages that he had often expressed annoyance (he uses the word *chalepainein*) with his philosophical companion Rusticus.[69]

There may be other ways of clarifying the meanings of Greek anger terms. The intensity of *cholos, orgē* and *thumos* is confirmed by their fre-

---

66. I would not disallow some exceptions: but in Pl. *Charm.* 162d, where *orgizesthai* might be thought to mean "to be annoyed," the tone is playful (cf. ἔδοξεν) and lightly erotic (cf. the next note); and Kleinknecht et al. 1968 [1954], 384, were simply in error to translate *orgē* as "irritation" in Soph. *Ant.* 280, 766 and *OT* 337, 405. It may be that in late-antique Greek, however, the meaning of both *orgē* and *thumos* widened to include mere annoyance; so the usage of Libanius somewhat suggests, e.g. *Or.* i.17 *(orgē)*, 25 *(thumos)*. Cf. Longus iii.34.1, Athen. xiv.624a, and some of the curse tablet evidence (third-century A.D. and later) reviewed by Faraone, forthcoming.

67. In Hellenistic times, *orgē* and other "strong" anger words are occasionally used as virtually technical terms for a beloved's disdain: Theocr. xxiii.13–14; cf. Verg. *Ecl.* ii.14, iii.81.

68. The absolutist position had other roots too: see Chapter 15.

69. *To Himself* i.1, i.17.14.

quent association with madness. King Cambyses is mad as well as irascible, Sophocles' Ajax too; indeed Homer's Achilles can sometimes
seem thoroughly unstable.[70] In the more domestic world of Menander,
the similarity between even quite comprehensible *orgē* and madness is
insisted on.[71] "That anger [*thumos*] is nothing short of madness," wrote
Galen, "one can learn from the things that angry people do."[72] Lucian
explains how the unreasoning and repeated *orgē* of old men against
their family members gradually turns into madness, and how women's
orgē may do the same.[73] Roman writers, for instance Horace and Seneca, make the association between madness and *ira*.[74] In Latin, *furor*
and cognate terms seem to combine and confuse the two mental
states. No doubt some of these texts were intended to hurt the repute
of persons who were irate, or even irascible, but not mad in any narrow
sense, and others were intended to detract from the respectability of
anger itself. It remains true that modern anger reaches only infre-
quently the intensity which would justify equating it with madness.

This book would have no subject if the Greeks and Romans had not
very often assumed, from Homer onwards, that people can limit or
suppress or eliminate their own anger. Indeed they are sometimes
rather naive about human beings' capacity for doing this. But very often they perceive *cholos, thumos, orgē* and the rest as impersonal forces
or forces beyond the individual's control. We sometimes of course
make the same assumption, with major consequences in the sphere of
criminal law, but we seem to do so less than the Greeks did; if so, the
reason is partly at least that these Greek anger terms usually referred

70. At *Il.* xxii.346–347, for instance (where cannibalism is envisaged), though it is
not clear how we should read this passage; for further discussion, see Chapter 7. For
the concept of *lussa*, somewhere between rage and madness, see Chapter 14.

71. See Chapter 12. Anger as madness became a commonplace in Hellenistic and
Roman philosophy: Fillion-Lahille 1984, 296 n. 47.

72. *De propriorum animi cuiuslibet affectuum* 5.2: "they strike and kick and tear their
clothes, they shout and glare, they do everything until . . . they grow angry with doors
and stones and keys." Cf. Soranus 2.8 = 19 (p. 31, line 90 Burguière et al.).

73. *Abdicatus* 30, where the speaker remarks that there are many Greek words for
different kinds of madness. For a Greek text identifying the passions (*pathē*) with
madness, see Aristides Quintilianus, *De musica* iii.25.

74. Hor. *Odes* i.16.5–9 (with still further parallels listed by Nisbet & Hubbard),
Epist. i.2.62, Sen. *De ira* i.1.3–4; cf. Cic. *Tusc.Disp.* iv.77.

to almost irresistible forces, to states more intense than most anger. (Impersonal-force language is suitable for use when the speaker needs an excuse or is on the defensive, as Achilles is in *Iliad* IX. Similarly, in the *Agamemnon*, Clytemnestra places the responsibility for the murder she has committed on an avenging demon, *alastōr*).[75] It is a simplification to say that "emotions, for the Greeks, are *pathē*, affections: things that happen to us."[76] But it very often seems true, and Aristotle found it necessary to argue, in his discussion of the difference between voluntary and involuntary actions, that actions performed out of anger *(thumos)* or desire are in fact voluntary (but a little later he says that actions performed through *thumos*—clearly he means *thumos* as anger—are very far from being done out of deliberate choice).[77] Later we shall meet plenty of instances in which *orgē* was thought of as a sickness.

Closely linked with the intensity of the main anger words in Greek is the supposition of some classical writers that anger cannot be hidden. As we shall see, they were well acquainted with anger which keeps out of sight. There was a very famous case, Odysseus' long-concealed anger with the suitors in the second half of the *Odyssey*—but that was part of a scheme concocted by the most devious of the heroes.[78] When on one occasion in Thucydides the Spartans feel *orgē* against Athens *but do not show it,* this is worthy of comment (i.92). Seneca says explicitly that *ira* cannot be hidden.[79] Since the angry man inevitably reveals his condition, a man who seems calm can claim not to be angry, as in the re-

75. *Il.* ix.646–647 (for a somewhat different reading see Gill 1996b, 256); contrast xix.66–67. Earlier in the book, however, when Phoenix describes Meleager's anger in impersonal-force terms (ix.553–554), he is simply emphasizing its strength. Clytemnestra: Aesch. *Ag.* 1497–1504 (on which cf. Irwin 1994, 64–65).

76. Hankinson 1993, 187. He refers to Soph. *Ant.* 781–800, Eur. *Med.* 530–531, *Hipp.* 443, Pl. *Phaedr.* 244a and Gorgias *Enc.Hel,* all of which concern the overwhelming power of eros. In Soph. *OT* 524, being "compelled by *orgē*" is offered as an excuse.

77. *Nic.Eth.* iii.1.1111a22–1111b3; iii.2.1111b18–19 ("deliberate choice" is how I translate *prohairesis*, for the contrast between actions performed out of *orgē* and as a result of *prohairesis*, see also Theophrast. fr. 97 Wimmer = 650 Fortenbaugh et al. [II, p. 494]). No need to reopen here the question of the exact meaning of *hekousios* and *akousios* for Aristotle (cf. Hardie 1980, ch.8).

78. It was for this reason, perhaps, that Odysseus was sometimes thought of as *ou dusorgos,* not irascible, Soph. *Phil.* 377. For the possibility of bottled-up anger, see also *Iliad* i.80–83.

79. *De ira* i.1.5.

pulsive story which Gellius tells us about Plutarch:[80] he ordered one of his slaves, who happened to be educated in philosophy, to be whipped, and while the punishment was being inflicted, the slave objected that the author of a book about eliminating anger should not give in to it. Plutarch replied, so the story goes, that he was *not* acting out of anger, arguing that his face and words showed no such emotion. Normal anger, in other words, was so vigorous or expressive that witnesses could be in no doubt of its existence. Of course many people will have been fully aware, as Cicero was, for instance,[81] that it is entirely possible to be angry even while restraining one's tongue, but the general presumption was that the tongue would not be restrained. This was obviously likely to make eliminating anger seem all the more necessary.

Cases of extreme anger in the anger-control texts should not by themselves determine how we understand *orgē* or other Greek anger terms, for when the critics of anger wanted to give examples of its operation they naturally chose spectacular cases, such as Galen's biter of keys, or the man in Philodemus who bit off someone's nose, or the Phoenician *trōktēs* (approximately, chiseller) who jettisoned his entire cargo in searching for a single tetradrachm.[82] The ostensibly most severe critics of anger are quick to turn to extreme manifestations— Cicero, for instance, to the mythical anger of Atreus and Thyestes,[83] which one might think somewhat irrelevant to the real life of late-republican Rome. But the linguistic evidence we have been examining is remarkably consistent, and more important, perhaps, considerable quantities of it come from moderate critics of anger such as Aristotle and Menander who had no conceivable interest in trying to misrepresent the nature of *orgē*. And as we have seen, Greeks had plenty of words for other anger-like emotions.

Linguists have studied the range of anger metaphors which are used in American English, reaching some fanciful conclusions but at the same time underlining the importance which metaphors may possess

80. Gellius i.26. It was recounted to him by Calvisius (or less probably Calvenus) Taurus, apparently a friend of Plutarch's (i.26.4).

81. *QF* i.1.38.

82. The key-biter: Phld. *De ira* fr. 8 Indelli; the nose-biter: *De ira* 5 (col. xiii.21); the *trōktēs:* ibid. 5 (col. xv.21–30). For a husband kicking his wife in consequence of *orgē*, see Chariton i.4.12.

83. *Tusc.Disp.* iv.77.

in expressing the understanding of anger which prevails in a given culture.[84] It is claimed that the figurative language which American English uses about anger is "based on a cultural theory of the physiology of anger, the major part of which involves heat and internal pressure."[85] This supposed "cultural theory" might be regarded as a typical academic over-intellectualization of linguistic practice, but nonetheless it seems probable that the study of Greek (and Latin) metaphor might lead us to a clearer view of how the classical world understood its various anger concepts.

The obstacles are serious, however. Padel put together a splendid collection of the metaphors which the Athenian tragedians used for emotions,[86] but she drew no conclusion which is of broad significance for this study. And the metaphors imagined by a great or even not so great poet were his own personal prerogative—even in the un-private world of classical Greece (thus, paradoxically, the great poets may be the people to keep away from). Furthermore, in order to be confident that one has discovered from metaphorical language the understanding(s) of *orgē* and all the other terms that the Greeks and Romans used for angry emotions, one would be well advised to engage in a lengthy comparative study.

When *cholos*-anger is compared to honey and to (blinding) smoke,[87] we are made to feel that it is insidious rather than overwhelming, and we seem to be a long way from getting a full view of Homeric *cholos*. Equally vivid, and equally inconclusive, is the comparison of Odysseus' indignant heart to a barking dog.[88] The image of a gale-force wind conveys *orgē*'s externality.[89] In the *Medea* the nurse says that the heroine, who throughout the play is said to be suffering from *orgē*

---

84. Lakoff & Kövecses 1987. But their sole source on English usage was an edition of Roget, and their work was inexact (they take the expressions "He has a ferocious temper" and "He has a fierce temper" to be instances of a "dangerous-animal metaphor," 206).

85. Lakoff & Kövecses 219.

86. Padel 1992.

87. Hom. *Il.* xviii.109, 110.

88. *Od.* xx.13–15; nothing explicit is said about his indignation or anger. Cf. Sappho, fr. 126 Diehl = 158 Voigt.

89. Ar. *Frogs* 997–1003, cf. *Knights* 430–433. See further M. Oberhaus on Greg.Naz. *De ira* 477f., a commentary which is rich in parallels to Gregory's anger metaphors and similes (see esp. p. 198).

and *thumos*, has in consequence become a bull, a metaphor for an angry person which recurs periodically from Aeschylus onwards.[90] Hector as a poisonous angry snake in the *Iliad* implies the deadliness of *cholos* (xxii.93–97); lions, lionesses and wild boars also seem formidable.[91]

But perhaps most often and most importantly *cholos*, *orgē* and *thumos* are compared to fire and to boiling liquids.[92] Greeks blazed with anger from Homer onwards, and the river in Hades where some of the angry are plunged is the Puriphlegethon, "River Fire-Blazing."[93] Metaphor and scientific statement are not always distinct: a person or some element in the person was often said to boil with anger, but Aristotle asserts, as we have seen, that a natural scientist would define anger as the boiling of blood around the heart.[94] Such concepts are perhaps sufficiently widespread to count as a "cultural theory."

Latin was poorer than Greek in its vocabulary for anger-like states. That is presumably one reason why those Romans, Cicero and Seneca for instance, who are in theory "absolutists" can be convicted of occasionally equivocating about *ira*—for it was harder to dispense entirely with *ira* than with *orgē*. After *ira*, *iracundia*, *indignatio* and less common words, for instance the Ciceronian *stomachari*, Latin speakers had to turn to terms such as *dolor* which were on the edge of the semantic field of anger though often associated with it.[95] Cicero offered the previously unattested word *excandescentia* to mean "nascent anger which

90. Eur. *Med.* 92; cf. 188, and Aesch. *Choeph.* 275.

91. For lions and anger, see Tyrtaeus 10 and other passages listed by Nisbet & Hubbard on Hor. *Odes* i.16.15. Lionesses, wild boars: see Eur. *Med.* 188 and Antisthenes, *Odysseus* s.6, respectively. There are also verbal associations which are usually not straightforward metaphors or similes, e.g. with drunkenness (for the evidence, which is mainly of Roman date, see Oberhaus on Greg.Naz. *De ira* 160–165).

92. For example, Agamemnon's eyes blaze with fire in *Il.* i.103, Achilles' in xix.16–17, those of Antinous in *Od.* iv.662. For "extinguishing" anger, see *Il.* ix.678. See also Kingsley 1995, 101–102. For *cholos* associated with monstrous fire, see [Aesch.] *PV* 368–371. For the "bubbling vat of anger," see Achilles Tatius vi.19.

93. Pl. *Phaedo* 113c, 114a. Hot liquids commonly stand for anger in other cultures too: Lakoff & Kövecses 1987; Shaver, Wu & Schwartz 1992, 204–205.

94. Aesch. *Septem* 708, Soph. *OC* 434, Pl. *Crat.* 419e, *Tim.* 70b; Aristot. *De anima* i.1.403a31.

95. For *dolor* meaning something close to "anger" see *TLL* s.v. III.B, a long paragraph. Our side experiences intense *dolor* when insulted: e.g. Cic. *QF* ii.3.2.

has just come into being,"[96] but it did not catch on. Seneca claimed that Latin was rich in anger adjectives: *amarus, acerbus, stomachosus, rabiosus, clamosus, difficilis, asper,* "which are distinctions between angers."[97] And the best poets knew how to vary their vocabulary.[98] But in fact *ira, iracundia* and *indignatio* have to perform many duties, covering tantrums and annoyance as well as towering rages. The term *iracundia* can mean either irascibility and bad temper or prolonged anger, and occasionally it just means anger in general.[99] There are some *irae* (instances of anger) which "do not go beyond a word of complaint and a show of coolness," says Seneca in the same context. When Cicero implies that an angry action is something more intense than an action done *vehementer, acriter* or *animose,*[100] he is merely engaging in some special pleading in order to demonstrate that an absolute rule against anger is in fact reasonable and also that he himself had never acted in anger in his political life.

The term *ira* and its correlates had sometimes to do duty for mild anger, but the range included intense anger, for Cicero said, as we noticed earlier, that it is characteristic of the angry man to wish "to inflict as much pain as possible" on his victim[101]—which is too extreme for much modern anger.[102] *Ira* also included anger expressed in non-modern ways. Here is an incidental observation of Seneca's: "On account of *ira,* we have often thrown away a book because it was written in rather small script, or torn one because it had mistakes in it, we have ripped up garments because they displeased us."[103] The violence of

96. *Tusc.Disp.* iv.21. Thus this term was meant to correspond to the Stoic definition of *thumos.*

97. *De ira* i.4.2.

98. See Rieks 1989, 175–176, for a list of fifty-seven terms (nouns, verbs, adjectives) which are used for *Zorn* and *Raserei* by Vergil, Ovid, Lucan or Statius; but only one of the nouns in question, *ira,* unambiguously means anger or a kind of anger.

99. Instances in Cic. *QF* i.1.37 (also *Tusc.Disp.* iv.27), Suet. *Claud.* 38, Hirtius, *BG* viii.19.8, respectively.

100. *Tusc.Disp.* iv.51.

101. *Tusc.Disp.* iii.19. Cf. Sen. *De ira* i.9.3.

102. Veyne 1993, 105, briefly observes that Senecan anger is often the equivalent of "violence, cruauté, indignation, animosité, ressentiment et même ([*De ira*] i.18.2) malveillance," rather than *colère.*

103. *De ira* ii.26.2.

this tearing and ripping would strike Seneca's modern social equivalents as highly indecorous. (Seneca's first-person plural is not an autobiographical guarantee, and such events may have been very rare). But the suspicion grows that the ancients were somewhat more prone to violent anger against inanimate objects than we are.

In short, the primary Greek words which are always taken to mean "anger" and "to be angry" refer to intense and openly expressed anger emotions; *ira*, however, while probably somewhat influenced by Greek usage, covered a somewhat wider range.

CHAPTER 4

The Minds of Ancient Authors

Poetry then is a sort of address to the people.
Socrates in Pl. *Gorg.* 502d

This book is a study of doctrines and society. The aim is to discover, within the limits of the possible, why a number of ancient authors wrote in the ways they did about the control of angry emotions. Problems of interpretation will be legion and will take up most of the rest of our space. But certain ways of approaching literary texts and the visual evidence (for there is some visual evidence) require a brief apologia before we go any further.

What is at issue here is the interpretation of texts or monuments as bearers or representatives of doctrines or ideologies. This is not in the main a problem about philosophers, professional or amateur. Aristotle and Philodemus, Cicero, Seneca, Galen and Plutarch, and all or almost all the other theoretical writers about anger we shall be considering were indisputably didactic. The main general question we shall have to confront with respect to philosophical texts is the nature of the audiences which philosophers, in various ages, expected and actually reached. There could be considerable variation, as we shall see, but a pattern is also visible: it usually included a high degree of oral teaching or discussion, an extremely limited circulation of full written texts (the whole concept of "publication" is ill adapted to the ancient world), and the more or less accurate transmission of ideas by more or less admiring later philosophers. It also included a biographical tradition,[1] and a somewhat haphazard percolation of often distorted teachings into the general population of the educated. In the Hellenistic world, especially, this population was sometimes surprisingly extensive, but in general it was limited by the well-known failures, quantitative

1. Cameron 1995, 187.

71

and qualitative, of Greek and Roman education (and also, of course, by the indigestibility of philosophy itself).[2]

However, we shall very often be concerned not with philosophers but with poets, historians and others whose didactic quotient is somewhat unclear, or at any rate not clear in advance. At the extreme furthest from philosophy, many passages in which ancient authors refer casually to anger are *not* to be thought of as didactic in any way. Subject matter chosen for other reasons, warfare above all, will mark a narrative with anger or its ugly effects. Very often, however, the discussion is going to revolve around texts that fall between the didactic and the undidactic, or that have been variously classified as one or the other (Athenian tragedy, for example). It is fairly obvious that a political-social-moral ideology of the kind we are investigating can be expressed in any number of ways, and without open preaching. So how are we to read the many literary texts which, without being overtly didactic, seem to imply some lesson about anger or about controlling it? A full answer will emerge as the book progresses.

It is possible to practise high aesthetic disdain. Vladimir Nabokov told how he responded when, in high school in 1917, one of his teachers required him to explain what Gogol intended to teach in *Dead Souls*—what he intended to *show*. The annoyed and annoying adolescent replied that Gogol merely intended to "show" General Betrishchev's crimson dressing gown.[3] But the youthful poet was probably wrong.

Even when the individual is elusive, we can more or less describe the historical context of each text, and the political and social needs which can plausibly be supposed to have helped to bring it into being.

Even when a didactic intention is rather clearly absent, we may hunt for doctrinal clues. I will not revert here to the (as I suspect) rather complex case of Petronius' evident interest in *ira*. But take for instance the romance writer Chariton. *Chaereas and Callirhoe* is a long way from being a moral tract or even a *roman édifiant*. But it refers to a great many outbursts of *orgē*, and it reveals, if rather opaquely, something of how Chariton and his audience (well-educated Greeks of the first cen-

2. On Hellenistic education, see W. V. Harris 1989, 129–139. Cicero, *Tusc.Disp.* ii.8, comments on the fact that while everyone read Plato "reliquosque Socraticos," only loyalists read Epicurus (and he could have said the same about Epicurus' rivals).

3. B. Boyd, *Vladimir Nabokov: The Russian Years* (Princeton, 1990), 128–129.

tury A.D.) thought about anger, such as how a cultured and sensible woman was supposed to deal with her own *orgē* when rejecting unwanted sexual advances.[4] The great mass of surviving Greek and Latin texts allows us to build up a picture of such conventional views and of less conventional opinions.

There is no call to construct a dilemma as to whether one should study authors' intentions or audiences' responses.[5] It is self-evident that every ancient writer had a known or imagined audience, and that each audience or, better, each element in each audience (for in the theatre, especially, audiences will have been very heterogeneous), will have accorded to poets, philosophers, historians, and others what it regarded as the appropriate amount of authority to give political or social or moral instruction.

Some divergent views already existed in antiquity, for example about the claims of Athenian tragedy. The epigraph at the head of this chapter should be restored to its context, which is Socrates' (Plato's) distinction between pleasure and the good, together with his assertion that tragedy, among other kinds of performance, aims exclusively at pleasure, at what he calls flattery of the audience. When he says that poetry is a sort of address to the people *(dēmēgoria)*, he means that it does nothing more than try to gratify them, "without regard for what is better or worse."[6] But this is the same Socrates who a moment later makes much the same charge against Themistocles and Pericles;[7] in other words, relying on such a partisan view is a highly unreliable way of trying to discover the intentions of the tragic dramatists. Plato's continuing war against tragedy resulted in part from the fact that he regarded it as a serious rival to philosophy in the field of moral authority.

Let us go back to the case of Homer. The theory that he had no didactic intent has little to be said for it. Havelock went too far in the other direction in treating the *Iliad* and the *Odyssey* as "tribal encyclopaedias" of previously oral knowledge.[8] But Homer had something

4. Chariton vi.5.8.

5. About this I disagree with Lada 1993, 94.

6. *Gorg.* 500e–502d. Presumably we are meant to include the great dramatists who were working while Socrates was still alive.

7. *Gorg.* 503cd.

8. Against a didactic Homer, see, for instance, Hogan 1981, 21; for the opposite extreme, see Havelock 1982, 122–149, and the same author elsewhere. According to

large he wanted to tell contemporary hearers, and possibly readers, about the workings of *mēnis* and *cholos,* and more specifically about the proper limits which men should impose on them (so at least it will be argued). It is true that the discoverable history of Homer-reception only begins, practically speaking, in the late-ish sixth century with Xenophanes and Heraclitus, so that the poet's likely attitude towards his original audience is largely a matter of conjecture. His own account of the social role of the archaic bard might conceivably be misleading. But his extensive use of what we may call "exemplary tales" is a sure indication of his attitude. For him and for his audience, angering the priest of Apollo leads to plague; Agamemnon believes and acts on a dream, but it is a disastrous deception sent by Zeus; the insubordination of the demagogue Thersites is violently put down by Odysseus; Paris the handsome paramour turns out to be a coward and an ineffectual fighter; and so the pattern continues. These tales in most cases involve both moralistic and pragmatic judgements. This is the earliest known form of what has been referred to as the classical Greek habit of "justifying one's opinions and actions by appealing to mythological examples and precedents."[9]

To most modern readers of the *Oresteia* the anger theme is visible enough, and conspicuous, but that leaves us far from a definite answer to the classically slippery question of Aeschylus' own intentions.[10] The question is all the more difficult because, like all other classical poets, Aeschylus is still often read and interpreted by scholars who are more or less indifferent to the poet's public role. However, we may presume that Aeschylus desired to win the first prize at the great civic festival of the Dionysia (as in this case he did), and we may also presume that he intended to stir some emotions in his initial audience. But we can believe all this without denying that he simultaneously intended to offer a lesson about civic behaviour, at a level above that of everyday poli-

---

Segal 1992, 29, "the Homeric bard does convey moral judgments and ethical insights . . . , but he does not define himself in terms of such tasks"; that is an intuitive judgement.

9. Verdenius 1970, 11 (see the whole passage, 11–15).

10. See Dover 1974, 14–18, for appropriate cautions concerning the use of tragedy to discover the opinions of the poet, with special attention to the demands of characterization.

tics.[11] Such a lesson is unlikely to have been original or very personal—on the contrary, it is likely to have been a vivid expression of an idea which part, at least, of the audience already believed in.[12]

Another and for the moment final example: Polybius' views about *orgē*, if he had any, are immersed in a very long narrative, and may perhaps be incidental to his main themes. His sense of historical relevance is quite strict, and he shows no desire to distract the reader with side issues. Nor is it clear exactly what his thoughts about anger were: sometimes they seem Peripatetic, but sometimes he appears to be categorically against anger. Nevertheless, Polybius was a didactic spirit if ever one lived, and he gives proof of a deep interest in the conflict between emotions and reason in decision-making.[13] In short, he probably intended to offer something of a lesson about anger, but it was only a fragment of his teaching about political and military affairs.

Did the ancient authors who wrote about anger *possess authority to instruct?* A great lesson about civic behaviour depends for the validity that its hearers and readers assign to it on its being uttered by a person with a recognized position of some kind. A recognized occasion adds to the authority of an oral communication. The epic poet singing or reciting at court gains some authority from having been chosen to address the ruler and his circle. The dramatist making his characters perform at a great religious festival, the orator addressing a deliberative or judicial assembly, possessed authority in virtue of both position and occasion. These, in the absence of mass media, were the chief occasions on which Greeks and Romans could be said, more or less literally, to be addressing the community.

So far we have been concentrating on "original" audiences, a fuzzy

11. See Meier 1990 [1980], 87–89, 119–121 (though here, I think, he should have distinguished more and less alert sections of the audience). "The whole design of the *Eumenides* is informed by political thought" (98). I find the attempt of Burnett 1998, 71–72, to show that the Athenian tragic stage was a transgressive place where rules were reversed wholly unconvincing. Which is not to deny that there was a subversive side to Euripides (see Chapter 11).

12. In the view of B. M. W. Knox 1977, 219 = 1979, 311, the great dramatists "are not . . . original thinkers; they reflect and use, dramatize and intensify the thought and feeling of their time." True up to a point, but in Euripidean Athens there was no single set of thoughts and feelings.

13. Pédech 1964, 210–229.

but useful concept. An even more difficult set of questions concerns the *later* authority of our anger-control texts. By the late fifth century, perhaps much earlier, the *Iliad* was the authoritative text on the subject of anger.[14] Philosophers generally shared this view, so that Aristotle, for instance, repeatedly referred to it when he was writing about *orgē*. He believed that Homer meant to criticize Achilles: he sees that the poet in some sense wanted the hero to cease his anger against the corpse of Hector, and elsewhere he seems to hold that Homer recognized the excessive quality in Achilles' irascibility.[15]

For eight hundred years or more the Homeric poems were set before the impressionable mind of every Greek child who received any kind of formal education.[16] Other literary works gradually joined the educational canon in a subordinate capacity. Eventually the *Aeneid* achieved a similar educational dominance in the Latin world, supported by a range of lesser classics. And the canon was read and performed for its own sake, not simply as part of formal education. The political, social and moral influence of these literary canons, which is a matter for a more general cultural history, is hard to estimate. Plato notoriously attributes wide moral influence to the poets, in the first place to Homer.[17] But of necessity we must ask, while we are studying the various doctrines which Greeks and Romans framed with respect to the angry emotions, how much they took for granted what they saw as the lessons taught by the great writers of the past.

Which raises a swarm of questions as to what (if anything) Homer and Euripides, to mention the most important non-philosophical names, were thought to have taught on this subject. Did the ancients in general think that Homer intended to criticize Achilles for being implacable in anger? The intelligent recognized the hermeneutic dif-

14. As is confirmed by the Achillean traits in Aristophanes' depiction of the wrath of Aeschylus: see Tarkow 1982. For some of the ways Homer was read after his own time, see Richardson 1975 and 1992. According to to Plutarch (*De cohibenda ira* 4 [*Mor.* 455a]), Achilles was actually slow to burst out against Agamemnon (not that he doubted Achilles' irascibility: *De virtute morali* 11 [*Mor.* 31ab]).

15. *Rhet.* ii.3.1380b28–31, quoting Apollo's words in *Il.* xxiv.54; *Poet.* 15.1454b11–15 (the point is unaffected by the textual variants here).

16. On the importance of the Homeric poems in Greek education and thought, see in general Buffière 1956, esp. 10–13; Marrou 1965, 39–41, etc.

17. *Rep.* x.606b–d, etc.

ficulties involved in reading such a text: "Some say the poet's meaning is one thing, and some another."[18] But there certainly were "lessons" drawn from the canon: Horace, simply to take one instance for the present, read Homer as a teacher of a simple doctrine of controlling *ira*:[19]

> He who does not restrain [*moderabitur*] his anger will wish to undo what hostile passion suggested as he made haste to retaliate with violent hatred and revenge. Anger is short-term madness.

And many who lived in worlds very remote from Homer's, Epictetus for instance, criticized (or palliated) the anger of Homeric Achilles not only as a reality but as a paradigmatic reality of *orgē*.[20]

There is visual evidence too which can help us to understand ancient attitudes towards the angry emotions. It would be hard to contend that the classical Athenians were unwilling to contemplate scenes of anger, given their evident tolerance for stage quarrels and arguments. Yet a certain reluctance to look upon the disfigured may have led to there being fewer representations of the angry emotions in ancient art than we might have expected. Not that such scenes are difficult to find, whether it is a matter of Achilles about to draw his sword to strike Agamemnon,[21] Achilles being visited by the three-man embassy of *Iliad* IX,[22] or a Euripidean *Medea*.[23] More genre-like scenes of anger seem to be rare, however. It might be possible to recognize one in a mosaic scene from the Villa di Cicerone at Pompeii, one of a pair "signed" by Dioscorides of Samos. It appears to show three angry women railing at

18. Pl. *Prot.* 347e.

19. *Epist.* i.2.59–63; cf. ii.1, a poem in which the *Iliad* is read as a treatise on moral philosophy. And see Max.Tyr. xxvi.5.

20. *Diss.* i.28.24.

21. Kossatz-Deissmann 1981, nos. 428–434; most of this evidence is Pompeian.

22. Ibid. nos. 437–460. The tradition is older here (the earliest evidence is archaic), perhaps because the story allowed Achilles to be veiled and sorrowful-looking rather than being in a transport of rage.

23. M. Schmidt 1992. Most of these representations are naturally of Medea as the murderer of her children. These are all human subjects, be it noted, not divine, even though divine anger was such a commonplace.

a boy, probably a slave; but if, as is usually thought, we are looking at characters wearing theatrical masks, their emotional condition may not be precisely represented.[24]

A change which occurred in the practice of Greek artists in the fourth century B.C. is highly relevant to part of the argument of this book. Sculptors and painters began to represent emotional states for their own sake. The central figures in bringing about this change are thought to have been the sculptor and architect Scopas of Paros and the painter Aristeides of Thebes. Scopas carved famous figures of Eros, Himeros (Desire), and Pothos (Longing), and also Furies and Maenads who must have given him opportunities in this direction.[25] Pliny the Elder remarks that Aristeides was the first painter to depict character and "what the Greeks [he says] call *ēthē*" and in addition the strong emotions, the *perturbationes*.[26] There obviously must be a connection between these developments,[27] datable to the third quarter of the fourth century, and the philosophy of the same period. Scopas and Aristeides could have heard plenty of reflection about the strong emotions, the *pathē*, and they can be imagined to have had among their admirers people who were much interested in such things (which raises an unanswerable question about how far the intellectual interests of Athens at this time extended to other cities).

Some of the most useful information which emerges from the visual sources concerns revenge, and in particular the acceptability of very violent revenge. *The Punishment of Dirce* is a conspicuous example. This was a mythical scene of sadistic revenge which was popular from about

24. In the Museo Nazionale, Naples. It is well illustrated in *EAA* s.v. Dioskourides no. 3 (1960), opposite p. 132. R. Bianchi Bandinelli (ibid.) identified the scene as the consultation of a witch, but the fact that the old woman has a cup in her hand is against this—she is a "typical" old woman (cf. I. C. Cunningham's commentary on Herodas, p. 57). For a lost Roman mosaic depicting angry women, see Simon 1938, 171.

25. See in general A. F. Stewart 1977. Nothing is known about the appearance of Scopas' Furies, except that they were *not* frightening (Paus. i.28.6).

26. *NH* xxxv.98: "is omnium primus animum pinxit et sensus hominis expressit, quae vocant Graeci ἤθη, item perturbationes." None of the eleven subjects of his which Pliny lists has to do with anger, however. The Roman understanding of *ēthē* seems to have been that it meant the milder emotions (Quintil. *Inst.Or.* vi.2.9).

27. There were fifth-century predecessors: Stewart 1977, 73.

400 B.C. onwards, its most famous manifestation being the statuary group from the Baths of Caracalla known as the Farnese Bull.[28] *The Punishment of Dirce* and other scenes of the same kind can be differentiated from the sadistic cruelty which figure so largely in Renaissance and baroque painting, for in that age the sympathies of the imagined viewer were supposed to be aligned with the suffering of the victims. *The Punishment of Dirce* had no such agenda but was judged to be a delightful decoration for the imperial baths, as such works had been for private houses.[29] To all of this visual evidence we shall return.

28. See Heger 1986 (the Farnese Bull: pp. 636–637).

29. *LIMC* records this as the subject of wall paintings at eight sites in Pompeii and Herculaneum.

CHAPTER 5

A Tradition of Self-Control

Prominently displayed on the sixth-century Alcmaeonid temple at Delphi was the maxim "Nothing in excess,"[1] and moderation has often been thought of as an ideal of the classical Greeks. Did the archaic—or classical or later—Greek interest in controlling or eliminating anger grow out of a more general ethic of moderation, or good sense, or observance of limits, or self-control? The ill-defined virtue of *sōphrosunē*, which can have any of these meanings (and others), might in theory be suspected of being the great source from which anger control flowed.

The history of Greek self-control and moderation has still to be written. The early roots of this ideology are diverse. One is precisely the archaic Greek struggle over the angry emotions which will be described in Chapter 7. Another is the heroic virtue of *aidōs*, which is normally translated as "shame" (but is in fact even more difficult to translate than *orgē* or *thumos*). This is the "prospective, inhibitory emotion" that, to put it very briefly, leads a person to respect the honour of others.[2] A third is a certain prudential attachment to moderation which is first made explicit in the *Works and Days*.[3]

---

1. Parke & Wormell 1956, I:387–392.
2. D. L. Cairns 1993, 432; concerning moderation see esp. 130–135.
3. Hes. *WD* 694. West ad loc. cites comparanda from Theognis (614, 694), Solon (4c.3), and Pindar (*Pyth.* ii.34, *Isthm.* vi.71), Eur. *Med.* 125, and so on. *Pyth.* ii.21–89 is the story of Ixion, who offended by both violence and misdirected *erōs*, and was punished by Zeus.

Of more debatable relevance is a vague though discernible Greek tradition of kindness or mildness.[4] And of very doubtful authenticity are the sayings of the Seven Wise Men, at least one of which refers to emotional control.[5]

There was no easy way of conceptualizing "self-control" in Homeric Greek or archaic Greek in general. We should not force the concept on to the Greeks of that period. They had no such categories as "emotions" and "appetites," although every sane person knew that emotions and appetites had, most of the time, to be kept within limits. Homer and Hesiod, the archaic lyric poets and Solon give the impression that the angry emotions were the first ones to become the subject of careful reflection. That impression might be a misleading result of their particular interests, but probably not (Homer, Hesiod, Sappho, Solon and Theognis cover, after all, a wide range of interests). It is apparently not until the fifth century that we encounter any reflection about the possible desirability of controlling such emotions as sexual passion or envy or hatred or grief—or even fear, in spite of the fact that mastering fear was certainly a commonplace part of the war-torn life of Greece in archaic times. But Pindar can imagine an excess of *erōs*, and tells the story of how Ixion offended as a result of his *erōs* for Hera; while Sophocles makes the Chorus in the *Antigone* describe at some length the harm which sexual passion can cause.[6]

It should be said in passing that there is no good evidence that philosophers before the time of Socrates were particularly interested in emotional self-control.[7] Heracleitus seems to have written very cryptically (we have no context) that "it is difficult to fight against *thumos*, for whatever it wants it buys at the price of life," which helps not at all.[8]

---

4. De Romilly 1979 devoted an elaborate study to Greek "douceur," even though this concept lacks a Greek equivalent or set of equivalents. She studied, among other things, *praos* words, which are often treated by the sources as being something like the opposite of anger words. But while *praos* words go back to Homer, the quality of *praotēs* ("even temper," sometimes "kindness") begins to receive heavy attention only in the early fourth century (De Romilly 37).

5. Chilon in D-K I:63 (no. 15): "control <your> *thumos*." Chilon was also supposed to have said, "When you are wronged be reconciled, when you are insulted take revenge" (D-K I:63, no.20).

6. Pind. fr. 127, *Pyth.* l.c.; Soph. *Ant.* 781–800.

7. The evidence about Pythagoras will be discussed in Chapter 13.

8. Heracl. 22 B 85. Even Aristotle seems to take this phrase quite differently in *Pol.*

More relevant is the observation attributed to Democritus, presumably a sort of response to Heracleitus, that "it is difficult to fight against *thumos,* but it is the job of the rational [*eulogistos*] man to conquer it."[9] Unfortunately we have no information as to when during his long career Democritus made this pronouncement (it may not be pre-Socratic at all), but it is likely in any case that by *thumos* he meant mainly "anger."[10]

By the 420s, however, the control of certain emotions and appetites was under vigorous discussion at Athens. Angry emotions, by now a far from novel subject, received the attention of Sophocles *(Oedipus Tyrannus)*, Euripides (*Medea* and *Hippolytus* especially), Herodotus and certainly others. Some crucial words began to take on new colouring, in particular *sōphrosunē*. This ideal had achieved a measure of prominence in the sixth century, and in fifth-century Athens it was regarded as one of the great virtues. However, it had not traditionally been a matter of emotional self-control, but rather was a matter of good sense and sensible behaviour. (It is all right to draw a contrast between *sōphrosunē* and *hubris*[11] as long as one remembers that the latter term, which is also hard to translate,[12] means "insolent violence" as well as "violent insolence"; in other words, it is a propensity to action as much as a psychological condition). Even in the early fourth century *sōphrosunē* was not considered by some to be primarily a matter of emotional control, as is reasonably clear from Plato's *Charmides,* where it is a large part of the subject matter.[13] By the time of the *Hippolytus* (428),

---

v.11.1315a28–31 and in *Nic.Eth.* ii.3.1105a7–8 (he also refers to it in *Eud.Eth.* ii.7.1223b23–24). If *thumos* meant anger or something like it on this occasion, the sense of Heracleitus' statement was probably negative (in spite of Lossau 1992, 60). He may only have meant that anger makes an opponent formidable (cf. *Pol.* l.c.). But one must deplore claims to know the "deeper sense" (Mansfeld 1992, 18) of a fragment which no one can translate with confidence. One commentator glosses it by saying that "yielding to irrational anger [is] seen as a kind of suicide by self-conflagration" (Kahn p. 243), but there is no textual basis whatsoever for supposing that Heracleitus distinguished between rational and irrational anger.

9. 68 B 236. His B 46 says that "it is magnanimity to bear a fault *praeōs,* in an even-tempered fashion."

10. See, for instance, Claus 1981, 148.

11. North 1966, 16–17, 33–50, and so on.

12. Cf. D. L. Cairns 1994, 77–78, on the problem of defining this term.

13. The inadequate definitions which Socrates shoots down are (1) that *sōphrosunē*

however, *sōphrosunē* had acquired a particular association with the control of *erōs,* both female and male, and consequently in that play it is the subject of almost obsessive comment (especially because good sense and refusing *erōs* might lead in different directions).[14] The antisexual connotation continues, and was no doubt one of the reasons why Plato chose, as Socrates' interlocutor on the subject of *sōphrosunē,* the delicious adolescent Charmides.

There are other signs that *sōphrosunē* was extending its range. In Euripides' lost play *Philoctetes,* produced in 431—on the same day, therefore, as the *Medea*—, it had been contrasted with undying *orgē.*[15] A somewhat obscure and quite undated text of Antiphon the Sophist seems to show it moving in the direction of emotional self-control.[16] Thucydides too appears, at least at one point, to be leading in the direction of an "anti-emotional" concept of *sōphrosunē* (though the only emotion Thucydides shows himself to be interested in is in fact *orgē*).[17] A character in Euripides' *Andromache,* in the early 420s, had contrasted the quality of being *sōphrōn* with the behaviour of the angry

---

is "doing everything in an orderly way and quietly" *(hēsuchē);* (2) that it is shame, *aidōs;* (3) that it is doing one's own business; (4) that it is doing good things; and (5) that it is knowing oneself. His own definition is that it is "knowledge of knowledge." In the *Gorgias, sōphrosunē* is primarily contrasted with *akolasia,* roughly "unbridled behaviour." None of this should give the impression that it was necessarily easy to practise *sōphrosunē:* Aristotle, for instance, only allowed that a person was *sōphrōn* if he/ she not only abstained from the bodily pleasures but enjoyed doing so (*Nic.Eth.* ii.3.1104b5–7).

14. *Hipp.* 667, 731, 949, 995, 1007, 1034–1035 (*sōphro-* appears eighteen times in this play, not to mention other *phren-* and *phron-* words); cf. *Andr.* 235, 345–346, 595–596, and *IA* 543–544. Many other such passages are listed by North 1966, 76 n. 105. But she is somewhat off target in saying (33) that Euripides sees *sōphrosunē* "chiefly as the control of the emotions and appetites"; the emotions in general are not explicitly involved.

15. Fr. 799 Nauck (strictly speaking, it is *to sōphronein* which is in question here; for the context see Müller 1992, 121–122). I wonder whether Gill 1996c, 212, is right to translate Soph. *Ajax* 677 (440s), "How shall we fail to learn *to be self-controlled* [*sōphronein*]?" *Sōphronein* in line 1264 may need to be translated in the same way.

16. Antiphon 87 B 58 D-K; there are assorted textual problems here, but "blocking the immediate pleasures of the *thumos*" is contrasted with *sōphrosunē.* The passage perhaps concerns appetites rather than emotions (North 1966, 89, illegitimately introduces the notion of "passion").

17. Thuc. i.84 (King Archidamus speaking): the quality of *sōphrosunē* seems to be

(the *thumoumenoi*).[18] But *sōphrosunē* was still so much a matter of choosing the right course of action that in the *Orestes* (408) Tyndareus is made to say that he would have accounted Orestes as *sōphrōn* if he had exacted revenge from his mother:[19] even now, in other words, *sōphrosunē* was not necessarily a matter of emotional control. In the *Bacchae* Dionysus announces, in expectation of Pentheus' return, that he will deal patiently with the king's raging, remarking with ironic and sinister sententiousness that "it is the mark of a wise man to practise sensible good temper [*sōphron' euorgēsian*]."[20]

Also in the 420s one had begun to hear talk about other excessive emotions besides anger and sexual passion: thus when the nurse in the *Hippolytus* discourses about avoiding excessive *philia* (loving affection), she is expressing a somewhat novel and perhaps not very authoritative opinion.[21] And envy, *phthonos*, came in for criticism in Euripides' *Ino*.[22] But it would still have been very difficult to generalize about the emotions in Greek, because neither *pathos* (suffering) nor its verb *paschō* took on an emotional sphere of reference until at least the 420s and probably later: after two somewhat dubious fifth-century references, we have to wait until Plato's *Phaedrus* in the 380s to encounter *pathos* meaning something close to "emotion."[23] When Aristotle lists

---

associated with, among other things, not being goaded into angry action (section 2 end). But the meaning he normally gives to *sōphrōn* is the usual one, "sensible."

18. *Andr.* 740–742—where P. T. Stevens ad loc. translates *sōphrōn* as "reasonable."

19. *Orestes* 500–503.

20. *Bacchae* 641: πρὸς σοφοῦ γὰρ ἀνδρὸς ἀσκεῖν σώφρον' εὐοργησίαν. That the reference is to *orgē* as anger, not temperament, is confirmed by line 647. E. R. Dodds detects "lightness of tone" in Dionysus' speech (commentary, p. 152).

21. Eur. *Hipp.* 253–266; but the way she refers to the phrase "Nothing in excess" (265) shows that the audience will have found it easy to understand its relevance to *philia*.

22. Fr. 403 Nauck; this was probably a play of the 420s too, for it is apparently referred to in Aristoph. *Ach.* 434 (425 B.C.). Concerning pity, cf. Lada 1993, 113.

23. The dubious references are Democritus 68 B 31 D–K (cf. C sect.2)—but it may be later, and many, including H. Diels himself, have seen the passage as inauthentic; and Thuc. iii.84.1 (genuine Thucydides in my view: p. 179), where the meaning is probably not "emotion" (see further pp. 342, 344). Pl. *Phaedr.* 265b has *erōtikon pathos*. Sorabji 2000, 17, seems to miss this linguistic development.

the *pathē*,[24] there may be a sense of innovation in using the plural form.

A self-restrained life was not unanimously admired in classical Athens or in other Greek environments.[25] The prime exhibit is the might-is-right theorist Callicles in Plato's *Gorgias* (which was probably written in the 380s too). It has been said that he asserts that "the proper use of courage and intelligence is not to repress the passions . . . but to gratify them."[26] This, he says, is bound to be the course of action of any man who has power to follow it. But even now there is no theory about the "passions" in the sense of emotions:

> *Callicles:* What do you mean by "ruling oneself"?
> *Socrates:* Nothing complicated, just what most people mean: being sensible [*sōphrōn*] and in command [*enkratēs*] of oneself, ruling over the pleasures and desires which are inside one.[27]

In other words, neither Socrates nor Callicles is in fact represented as theorizing about what Aristotle called the *pathē* (passions). The new fourth-century word was *enkrateia,* which is normally translated as "self-control" or something similar. That translation is permissible as long as one realizes that *enkrateia* in pre-Aristotelian texts normally refers to pleasures and desires, to eating and drinking, to sex, sleep and warmth.[28] In the *Gorgias* it is entirely clear that the "desires" which Socrates and Callicles are discussing are the more straightforward appetites, such as hunger and thirst—they are certainly not talking about the emotions. It is an exception when, in a text written in the 370s, Isocrates includes among the things which *enkrateia* may be expected to control not only profit, pleasure and pain but also

24. *Nic.Eth.* ii.5.1105b20–23 (desire, anger, fear, boldness, envy, joy, affectionate love, hatred, longing, jealousy, pity—to translate them conventionally).

25. See Cohen & Saller 1994, 42; they take it that Plato expects that "most Athenians [will] be far more sympathetic towards [ridicule of the self-restrained life] than towards Socratic *askēsis.*" There were also those who equated *sōphrosunē* with cowardice: see Aristoph. *Peace* 1297, Thuc. iii.82, Pl. *Rep.* viii.560d.

26. Dodds, summarizing in his *Gorgias* commentary, p. 291.

27. Pl. *Gorg.* 491de.

28. E.g., Xen. *Mem.* i.5.4, ii.1.1–18.

orgē.[29] Even when Aristotle discusses *enkrateia* and its opposites *akolasia* and *akrasia* (lack of restraint, lack of will power) in the *Nicomachean Ethics,* as he does at considerable length, the primary reference is to pleasures and desires, and when *enkrateia* is spoken of in connection with emotions such as *thumos* or *orgē,* they have to be identified; *enkrateia* on its own refers to pleasures and desires.[30]

Did any philosopher prior to Aristotle articulate a general theory about restraining the emotions? That depends on how one takes a pair of passages in Aristotle's own writings. Many of the foundations for a theory had been laid, including the sanctification of *sōphrosunē*—which may have contributed to Aristotle's doctrine of ethical moderation. Plato had had a good deal to say about things which were (later at least) categorized as emotions, for example about *philia* (friendship, loving affection) in the *Lysis.* In the *Phaedrus* he famously compares the soul to a charioteer with two horses—and the bad horse seems especially vulnerable to emotion,[31] but it does not represent emotions.

Aristotle at all events remarks that "they" define the virtues as "certain impassivities" *(apatheias tinas)* or "tranquillities" *(ēremias),*[32] and this has commonly been taken to be a reference to freedom from emotion;[33] in other words, it has been supposed that *apatheiai* means much the same in this context as *apatheia* was later to mean for the Stoics. Perhaps so. But it is hardly clear that he is referring to an explicit theory about the emotions or passions. A true doctrine of emotional impassivity may have had to wait for the Stoics after all. For us, however, this is a side issue.

The temporary failure of the Greeks to form a concept equivalent to "the emotions" would please some recent theorists who have found

---

29. i.21: "practise self-control [*enkrateia*] in all the things by which it is shameful for the soul to be controlled—profit, *orgē,* pleasure and pain."

30. *Nic.Eth.* vii.4.1147b34, 1148a12.

31. Pl. *Phaedr.* 254c *(orgē),* 254e (fear).

32. *Nic.Eth.* ii.3.1104b24–25; see also *Eud.Eth.* ii.4.1222a3–5, where *apatheia* is used in the singular and the MSS attribute the definition to "everyone."

33. E.g., Sorabji 2000, 194. Controversy ensues as to who "they" may have been—perhaps the sympathizers of Democritus or of Pyrrho. But Aristotle presents the definers as people in general.

emotions to be too much of a conceptual *mélange* to have much if any value.[34] As we shall see in the last chapter of this book, there are some serious moral-philosophical disadvantages in lumping all emotions together. Some things can plausibly be said about emotions in general that cannot plausibly be said about rage.

34. Griffiths 1997. See Wierzbicka 1994, 155–156, for a moderate view.

CHAPTER 6

Philosophies of Restraining Rage

For the sake of convenience and clarity, it will be useful to set out in a single chapter the principal ideas about anger—and especially anger control—of those Greeks and Romans whose explicit thinking on the subject can be traced in some detail.[1] Which means starting with Plato. For centuries before his time some Greeks had thought that, sometimes at least, it was possible and desirable to rein in *mēnis* and *cholos,* and in the fifth century the notion had spread that a man of good sense, and certainly a man who claimed to philosophize, ought to be reluctant to express *orgē*-anger and ought to be able to prevent himself from acting out of *orgē*. But now the discussion became much more theoretical.

In their various ways, Empedocles, Antiphon the sophist and Democritus had been moving towards a discussion of the subject. Empedocles' view of the world was founded on a theory about *neikos,* discord, and *philotēs,* love,[2] which suggests that he may have had some explicit opinions about anger. Antiphon and Democritus, as we have already seen, had something to say about the angry emotions, and possibly a great deal. But otherwise the Presocratics are not known to have touched the subject, and all the explicit and detailed theorizing seems to be in the future. As for Socrates, he is an unsolved problem in this as

1. Techniques of anger therapy will be discussed later (Chapter 15).
2. Guthrie 1962–1981, II:152–183. The Strasburg Empedocles tells us nothing new here.

in so many other respects. On balance it seems likely that the historical Socrates did talk about anger,[3] and it will be maintained in Chapter 8 that it is possible to describe his "reformist" teaching with respect to revenge; nevertheless, Plato undoubtedly attributed to him ideas on the subject which were not his own.[4]

Some of the most influential ancient philosophizing about the emotions was done by people like Epicurus and Zeno whose teachings on the subject are only known to us in the barest outline. One cannot operate as if ancient thinking on this (or any other) subject consisted of what is attested in texts which have survived intact until the present day. Furthermore this chapter is intended to convey not only what philosophers and moralists said about anger but *how much* was written on the subject. Therefore, although most of our attention will go to what is at least fairly well attested,[5] there will also be some speculation.[6] At the end of the chapter, an appendix lists all the monographs about the "passions" *(pathē)* in general (including *apatheia,* or absence of passion) or about anger itself which are known to have been written by the early fifth century A.D., even if only the title is known.

The Platonic dossier is quite complex and in some respects quite surprising. It includes not only texts in the famous dialogues such as the *Republic, Phaedrus, Timaeus* and *Laws,* but also, for instance, the strange sub-tragic melodrama which makes up the setting of the early dialogue *Euthyphro.* The main subject of that dialogue is piety—how to define it—but anger also seems to be present as a subsidiary topic. The narrative framework includes, besides Socrates being indicted for im-

---

3. No single argument proves this, but many things make it likely, including his theory that philosophy should undertake the job of caring for the health of the soul (see Chapter 14) and Plato's account of his behaviour in the hour of his death. Cf. Quintil. *Inst.* iii.1.12: the sophists Prodicus, Hippias, Protagoras and Thrasymachus discussed the role of the emotions in speech-making.

4. E.g., at *Phlb.* 47e.

5. *Quellenforschung* has run its course; for a very brief guide to what has been written about the sources of the principal anger monographs, see Indelli 1988, 64.

6. It is not impossible that Plato's younger contemporary Archytas of Tarentum offered teachings about the angry emotions (so Cicero thought, *De rep.* i.38.60: "ergo Archytas iracundiam videlicet dissidentem a ratione seditionem quandam animi esse iure ducebat, atque eam consilio sedari volebat"). This evidence is ignored in the edition of D-K, but it gains some plausibility from Archytas' expertise in music.

piety and for "corrupting the youth," the murder of one of the slaves of the family of Euthyphro by a serf of his, a murder which was committed in drunken *orgē;* the killing of the serf by Euthyphro's father; and the highly unusual prosecution of the father by the son, a proceeding which naturally angered the father and the rest of the family (*aganaktei,* no doubt an understatement).[7]

Shortly afterwards, however, we are told that it is no use defining the holy as "what is dear to the gods," because what causes enmity and outbursts of anger *(orgas)* between the gods is, in effect, disagreements about morality.[8] Yet Socrates has been made to say earlier that he does not believe in stories about the quarrels of the gods,[9] and that, presumably, would also have been Plato's position, that the gods cannot really feel anger against each other.[10] All this may lead us to suspect that the young Plato himself entertained a distaste for vengeance and *orgai,* a distaste which is quite to be expected in a loyal follower of Socrates. And in the *Phaedo,* too, we shall see Plato both aligning himself on the side of emotional restraint and including disdain for anger among Socrates' heroic characteristics.

In other dialogues Plato's attitude towards anger control seems markedly different.[11] We sometimes get the impression that anger has joined the side of the angels, for instance when he writes about that central doctrine, the three-part division of the soul.[12] This ideally takes the form of the governance of the appetitive element in the soul by the rational element, with the cooperation of *to thumoeides,* the spirited or angry or passionate element.[13] The sole or at least primary object of

7. Pl. *Euthphr.* 4a–e. On how to read this dialogue, see Furley 1985.

8. *Euthphr.* 6e–8b.

9. *Euthphr.* 6b. The idea that divine beings do not feel strong emotions can probably be traced back to Xenophanes of Colophon (21 A 35 D-K, with Frohnhofen 1987, 68–69), though he will not have used the term *apathēs.*

10. For the first appearance of the idea that gods should be above even anger towards humans, which is in Euripides (who does not endorse it), see Chapter 8.

11. For this difference, cf. Dillon 1983, 508.

12. In *Republic* II and III, Socrates finds fault with the hostilities attributed to the gods but not specifically with their anger against each other. Homer is *not* criticized for having described Achilles as irate.

13. On Plato's doctrine of the tripartite soul, see among many others Ferrari 1985; Gill 1996c, 245–260.

restraint is held to be the appetitive element, and Plato claims that *to thumoeides* will cooperate:

> *Socrates:* But for the *thumos* to side with the desires, when reason decides that it should not be opposed, is a sort of thing which I believe that you have never observed occurring in yourself, nor, as I think, in anyone else.
> *Glaucon:* Certainly not.[14]

And a little later:

> *Socrates:* We say that in the factional strife [*stasis*] in the soul, *to thumoeides* contributes its fighting power to the side of reason.[15]

In the famous charioteer-and-horses parable in the *Phaedrus,* the good horse, which corresponds to the *thumoeides* element in the soul, is entirely obedient to the charioteer (reason).[16] This is essential for Plato's theory of the ideal state: the warriors have to be loyal to the guardians or the entire utopia collapses, and the analogy between the state and the soul collapses unless *to thumoeides* is obedient to reason.

So far, everything might be explicable by reference to a somewhat artificial distinction between dangerous *orgē* and valiant *thumos.* But the *Republic* also, much later, shows Plato holding that there should be some restraints on angry emotions, including *thumos.* To avoid lawless desires, we must first mollify *to thumoeides* and avoid entering into outbursts of anger *(orgai)* with people.[17] Anger *(thumos)* is among the emotions which, regrettably, "poetry feeds and waters instead of drying them up; she lets them rule, though they ought themselves to be ruled

---

14. *Rep.* iv.440b. Certain difficulties of interpretation can be neglected here. Nor need we ask whether the story of Leontius and the corpses, told in 439e, really confirms this theory. It is interesting that Plato seems in this passage (440ab) to be approaching a doctrine that there can be irresistible desires, but there is no trace of a doctrine of irresistible anger.

15. *Rep.* iv.440e. But the assertion is diluted at 441a (cf. Williams 1973, 205), where we are told that the *thumoeides* is by nature the ally of the rational element *unless* the former "is corrupted by bad upbringing."

16. *Phaedr.* 253d–254e.

17. *Rep.* ix.572a. In 571e the man of sound character is said to be untroubled by the appetitive element in the soul because he has given it neither too much *nor too little,* which is "ventilationist" doctrine in embryonic form; cf. v.465a.

so that we may become better and happier."[18] As we would expect, a man who is especially expert at arousing (and extinguishing) the anger (orgē) of crowds, such as the sophist Thrasymachus of Chalcedon, is regarded with suspicion.[19] And the bad horse in the *Phaedrus* gives way to *orgē* when it is subjected to discipline (253c).

However, the later account of the soul given in the *Timaeus*,[20] which is rather different from the one in the *Republic*, contains the notion that *thumos* can be counted on to support reason against appetites as well as the notion that it is hard to mollify. It is also, incidentally, in the *Timaeus* that we encounter for the first time an explanation in physiological terms of how anger works. Here one may doubt whether the semantic variation—Timaeus speaks not of *orgē* but of *duskolia* and *dusthumia* ("irritation and misguided passion" would, I suggest, be the best translation)—makes any fundamental difference.[21]

In the *Laws*, Plato seems to say that anger is necessary against wrongdoing (v.731b), but this is *thumos*-anger, indeed *thumos gennaios* ("noble anger"), and it is plain that he would not have written *orgē* quite as readily. He evidently means anger in appropriate form and quantity, and the sentiment is hardly surprising in a period in which the word *orgē* could be used to mean "punishment." It is natural for him to imagine his lawgiver as being angry (xi.927d). Curable criminals, however, deserve not anger but pity (v.731c). And the childhood training sketched in the *Laws* aims to produce characters that are not irritable (*duskola*) or quick-tempered (*akrachola*) (vii.791d).

A striking and original feature of the criminal code propounded in Plato's *Laws* is that it deals explicitly with crimes committed in anger (*orgē*), categorizing some crimes as committed in anger, as distinct from those which are voluntary or involuntary (*Laws* v.731cd). As we

18. *Rep.* x.606d.
19. *Phaedr.* 267c.
20. *Tim.* 69c–72d; on anger: 69d.
21. Ibid. 86e–87a: "For whenever the humours [*chumoi*] which arise from acid and saline phlegms, and all humours that are bitter and bilious [*cholōdeis*] wander around the body and find no external vent but are confined inside, and mingle their vapour with the movement of the soul and are blended with it, they implant diseases of the soul of all kinds, varying in intensity and extent; and as these humours penetrate to the three regions of the soul . . . they give rise <in the *thumos*> to all manner of *duskolia* and *dusthumia*." Cf. Hipp. *Humours* 8–9.

shall see, Plato is rather lenient with those who commit such crimes, by the standards of contemporary Athens.[22] Coming on top of the texts just quoted from *Republic* IV, this has the effect of almost removing anger from surveillance, and of making one suspect that Plato would never have been likely to censure his own anger but would rather have passed it off as a rational and justified response to wrong-doing.

Thus by the time Aristotle reached Athens and began to study with Plato in 367/366, *to thumoeides*, the psychological faculty which was supposedly responsible for anger, was one of his teacher's important doctrines, and during the following years *orgē* was sometimes a subject of discussion in the Academy, perhaps with conclusions which were more "permissive" than some fifth-century thinking might have led us to expect.

Aristotle himself addresses the subject of *orgē* rather frequently.[23] It is clear that he considered excessive anger to be a weighty problem (the long list of vices he provides in the *Eudemian Ethics* starts with *orgilotēs*, irascibility), and he gave it his careful attention. In addition to passages in the works just cited, the philosopher is said by Diogenes Laertius to have written a book about the passions *(pathē)*[24] and another which, whatever its exact title, would have concerned *orgē*.[25] But

---

22. Angry murders: *Laws* ix.866d–869e. Angry assaults: 878b–879a. The terms *thumos* and *orgē* seem to be used indifferently here.

23. *De anima* i.1.403a3–b19, i.4.408a35–408b19, *Eud.Eth.* ii.3.1220b37–1221b16, iii.3.1231b5–27, vi (= *Nic.Eth.* vii).6.1149a25–1149b27; *Nic.Eth.* iv.5.1125b26–1126b10, cf. ii.7.1108a7–9; *Pol.* v.10.1311a33–1312b38; *Rhet.* ii.1.1378a21–2.1380a5. See also *Topica* iv.6.127b30–32, viii.1.156a32–33 (an early treatment). On the fragments and pseudo-fragments of Aristotle concerning anger, see Becchi 1990, esp. 72–75. The special bibliography includes Aubenque 1957, Fillion-Lahille 1970, Fortenbaugh 1970, Gastaldi 1987, Leighton 1988, Sherman 1989, Becchi 1990, Cooper 1996, W. V. Harris 1997b.

24. Diog.Laert. v.24. The word *pathē* may be translated "emotions," so long as it is understood that *pathos* is seldom if ever used to refer to quiet emotions such as nostalgia and impatience, and that the *pathē* include "agitated desires and aversions, notably agitated desires for food, drink and sex, and agitated aversions to bodily pain, physical harm, financial loss, and death" (Cooper 1998, 71 = 1999, 449).

25. Diog.Laert. v.23 lists among his works a book with the title περὶ παθῶν ὀργῆς (*On Feelings of Anger*[?]), and some (including Fortenbaugh 1985, 215) have accepted this even though it is dubious Greek. Others have taken the correct text to be περὶ παθῶν ἢ περὶ ὀργῆς (see further Laurenti 1979, 65, and in his joint commentary with

if these books ever existed, it is surprising that they left no definite trace of themselves. If Aristotle really did write a book *peri pathōn,* he may have been the first to do so, or he may have been preceded by Xenocrates, Plato's second successor as head of the Academy. The information that Xenocrates wrote a book about the *pathē* also comes from Diogenes,[26] but it may be more reliable, since Xenocrates, being much less famous, is less likely than Aristotle to have been the subject of careless scholarship in Hellenistic times.

Aristotle's definitions of *orgē* we have already discussed in Chapter 3. He fits it into his moral scheme of excess, moderation and deficiency: between the excess, which is irascibility, and the deficiency, *aorgēsia* ("habitual absence of *orgē*") or *analgēsia* ("indifference"), lies the virtuous mean *praotēs*,[27] the best translation of which is not the conventional "mildness" but "even temper"[28] or sometimes "kindness." What matters, in his opinion, is not that one should avoid anger as such, and not that one's character or temperament should somehow be situated half-way between irascibility and "habitual absence of *orgē*," but that one should be angry with the right people for the right reasons—with people who have truly done one some injury—and also in the right manner and at the right moment and for the right length of time.[29]

G. Indelli on Plutarch, *De cohibenda ira,* pp. 13–14; this was also accepted by O. Gigon in his edition of Aristotle's fragments [Berlin & New York, 1987]; Becchi 1990, 74, was sceptical), which is not in itself a very convincing title. Kenny 1978, 42, argued that that the word *orgē* should be emended to *hormē;* the book would have been called *On the Influence of the Passions.* But Aspasius, in saying that he could find no definition of *pathos* in the works of the early Peripatetics, implies that there was no Aristotelian treatise about the passions (*Commentaria in Aristotelem Graeca* XIX, 1, 44.20–21; cf. O. Bloch 1986, 140), and he may have been right.

26. Diog.Laert. iv.12. The remains of Xenocrates' works were edited by R. Heinze (Leipzig, 1892); fr. 3 seems to say that philosophy was invented "to bring to an end the turbulent element in practical life."

27. *Nic.Eth.* ii.7.1108a4–9 (using the term *aorgēsia*). In *Evd.Eth.* he uses the term *analgēsia* instead of *aorgēsia* (ii.3.1220b38); cf. Becchi 1990, 66–67. Strictly speaking, the mean does not have a name, but "since we call the intermediate person *praos,* let us call the mean *praotēs.*" But the condition of *praotēs,* he thinks, "inclines towards the deficiency [of *orgē*-anger]" (*Nic.Eth.* iv.5.1125b28).

28. Horder 1992, 44 n. 8.

29. *Nic.Eth.* iv.5.1125b27–1126b10, developed somewhat from *Eud.Eth.* ii.3.1221a15–17.

Achieving the mean requires one to meet these criteria; it does *not* mean experiencing a moderate amount of anger, for while moderate anger is sometimes appropriate, in some circumstances—according to Aristotle—the correct reaction to provocation would be vigorous and prolonged anger, in others mild irritation.[30] "In the right manner" will include the question whether to *act* on one's feelings or not.[31] Even temper "inclines towards the deficiency [of anger]," he says, presumably meaning that when in doubt the sensible man usually restrains his anger; "for the even-tempered man is not vengeful, but rather tends to forgive."[32]

The person whose anger fails to meet these criteria is said to be irascible *(orgilos)* if he gets angry quickly and with the wrong people and for the wrong reasons and more than is right but soon ceases to be angry.[33] He is called quick-tempered *(akrocholos)*, says Aristotle, if he is ready to be angry with everything and on every occasion, bitter *(pikros)* if he is hard to appease and retains anger for a long time,[34] obnoxious *(chalepos)* if he is angry at the wrong things, more and longer than is right, and cannot be appeased except by revenge.[35] But these character labels should not give the impression that it is beyond the individual's power to choose: for Aristotle, acts performed in anger are voluntary, though not free.[36] His view is that "irrational emotions seem . . . to

30. See Urmson 1973, 225–226 = 1980, 160–162. Cf. Horder 1992, 45 ("If someone is confronted by the illegal torture of their loved ones, the experience of only a moderate amount of anger would be too mild a response, failing to meet the mean").

31. Ps.-Aristot. *MM* 1202b19–21, Aristot. *Nic.Eth.* 1149a25–26. With some justice, Horder 1992, 62, complains that Aristotle does not clearly distinguish feelings of anger from acting on them.

32. *Nic.Eth.* iv.5.1125b28–1126a3. Cf. Becchi 1990, 79.

33. I write "he" not "he or she" because I am not sure that Aristotle would have used the same criteria for women.

34. "For they hold in their *thumos*. Relief comes when they retaliate; for revenge relieves them of their anger, producing in them pleasure instead of pain. If this does not happen they retain their burden; for owing to its not being obvious, no one even reasons with them, and to digest one's anger within oneself takes time. Such people are troublesome to themselves and to those closest to them." Here, as in Pl. *Rep.* ix.571, there is the basis at least for a ventilationist argument about anger.

35. This sentence paraphrases *Nic.Eth.* iv.5.1126a13–28. See also *Eud.Eth.* ii.3.1221b10–15 on the *oxuthumos*, the *chalepos*, the *thumōdes* and the *pikros*.

36. Fillion-Lahille 1970, 54.

belong to man, so that the actions done from anger and desire are the man's actions; hence it would be absurd to treat them as involuntary."[37]

As for deciding in particular cases what the right manner, the right length of time and so on might be, we are told that the decision rests with "perception."[38] To know how Aristotle's reason or right reason would decide whether any particular instance of anger achieved the mean requires consideration of his wider ethical theory. He observes that particular cases are both complex and subjective.[39] His general principle is that "the wise man has an adequate and true conception of *eudaimonia* [happiness, in the highly specific Aristotelian sense], and makes [his own *eudaimonia*] his end in life"[40]—but it is hardly clear how this is to be translated into action (or restraint). An effect of wisdom is to restrain emotions to some extent,[41] but when and to what extent? Aristotle offers some hints, but hardly more: the irascible man is hard to live with,[42] while the *aorgētos* is slavish and foolish, for "it is considered slavish to put up with an insult or suffer one's friend to be insulted" (so it is plain that repute and shame will play their parts).[43] And Aristotle's approving attitude towards revenge[44] implies that he looked tolerantly on a great deal of *orgē* which some earlier and contemporary Athenians, not to mention most Hellenistic philosophers, would have disapproved of.

On the political plane, however, Aristotle seems to assume that *orgē*-anger is harmful: one of the two reasons why monarchical rule is inferior to other forms of government is that, in his view, one man is much more liable to be carried away by anger *(orgē)* or some other emotion than are the many, who are unlikely all to become angry at the same

37. *Nic.Eth.* iii.1.1111b1–2.

38. Ibid. iv.5.1126b4.

39. Ibid. ii.9.1109b14–26, iv.5.1126b3–4.

40. Hardie 1980, 215. See the whole of his ch. 11. On the meaning of the practical wisdom *(phronēsis)* of the model man (the *phronimos* or *spoudaios*), see Gastaldi 1987, 107.

41. Cf. *MM* i.34.1198b19–20.

42. On the importance of "living together" in Aristotle's ethics, see Hardie 1980, 332.

43. *Nic.Eth.* iv.5.1126a3–8; cf. *Eud.Eth.* iii.3.1231b10–15.

44. See Chapter 8.

time.[45] Which is not of course to deny that there is appropriate anger. And for all the cool analytic tone he employs when he writes about anger in the *Rhetoric*, he is decidedly disdainful about books on rhetoric which deal with personal attacks and pity and anger but not with methods of proof.[46]

Towards *thumos*-anger, Aristotle shows himself more indulgent. In a brilliantly evocative passage he argues that unrestrained *thumos*-anger is less disgraceful than unrestrained "appetites":

Anger [*thumos*] seems to listen to reason to some extent, but to mishear it, as do hasty slaves who run out before they hear the whole of what one says, and then muddle the order, or as dogs bark if there is simply a knock on the door, before looking to see if it is a friend; so anger [*thumos*], by reason of the warmth and hastiness of its nature, though it hears, does not hear an order, and rushes to retaliate. For reason or imagination informs us that we have been insulted or slighted, and anger, reasoning as it were that anything like this must be fought against, heats up [*chalepainei*] of course straightaway [whereas appetites do not obey reason at all, and are therefore more disgraceful] . . . for the person who is unrestrained in respect of anger [*thumos*] is in a sense controlled by reason . . .

Further, we forgive people more easily for following appetites that are natural, since we forgive them more easily for following such desires as are common to all human beings, and insofar as they are common; now, anger [*thumos*] and bad temper [*chalepotēs*] are more natural than the desires for excess . . . Further, those who are most given to plotting against others are most unjust. Now a *thumōdes* [anger-prone?] person is not given to plotting, nor is anger itself—it is open.[47]

Peripatetics, or some of them, were later said by their critics to have maintained that anger was more or less indispensable for courage or indeed for any resolute action.[48] Aristotle himself, however, did not

45. *Pol.* iii.15.1286a28–36.

46. *Rhet.* i.1.1354a16–17.

47. *Eud.Eth.* vi = *Nic.Eth.* vii.6.1149a25–1149b27.

48. Phld. *De ira* 6 (cols. xxxi.24–xxxii.29) (some Peripatetics say removing *orgē* cuts the nerves of the soul, others that it is necessary for boldness, etc.); Cic. *Tusc.Disp.* iv.43 (the Peripatetics consider *iracundia* to be the whetstone of bravery, etc.); Sen. *De*

make any such claim about *orgē*. (He certainly distinguished *orgē* from *thumos*—though quite how remains unclear).[49] What he had said about courage and anger was this:

> People apply the term *thumos* to courage; for those also seem to be courageous [he has been discussing other forms of courage] who rush like wild animals at those who have wounded them, because courageous men <among others> are *thumoeideis* [passionate] . . . Men of courage act for the sake of what is noble, but *thumos* works with them . . . the courage that comes through *thumos* seems to be the most natural, and to *be* courage if choice and purpose are added. Human beings suffer pain when they are angry [*orgizomenoi*], but are pleased when they exact their revenge; those, however, who fight for these reasons are pugnacious [*machimoi*] but not brave; for they do not act for the sake of the noble, nor as reason directs, but from passion [*pathos*]; they have, however, something similar to courage.[50]

For him it is the quasi-courage of the barbarians such as the Celts which stems from *thumos*. In short, Aristotle makes no claim at all that *orgē* is necessary for courage; *thumos,* on the other hand, is a component of some acts of courage, or collaborates with them; but there are other forms of courage that do not involve *thumos.*

The most extraordinary event which has to be registered in this chapter is the tragic disappearance of real Aristotelianism soon after the philosopher's death. If Hellenistic and Roman philosophers had engaged with his views, their own would have been much more interesting. As it was, most of the tradition got lost in a quagmire of technicalities and equivocations.

In this same general period, during the maturity of Aristotle or soon after his death but in any case independently of him, the father of

---

ira i.9.2 (cf. 17.1, iii.3.1) (a supposed quotation from Aristotle which is very unlikely to be trustworthy: see Setaioli 1988, 148–150, against Fillion-Lahille 1970, 62–63).

49. Rightly emphasized by Dirlmeier in his commentary on *Nic.Eth.*, pp. 343–344. Ignoring this distinction not only prevented the Romans from understanding Aristotle but also continues to have deleterious effects (e.g., in Indelli's commentary on Phld. *De ira,* p. 206, and in Burnett 1998, 8).

50. *Nic.Eth.* iii.8.1116b23–1117a9, cf. *Eud.Eth.* iii.1.1229b28–32. I read *pherousin* in 1116b24.

philosophical scepticism, Pyrrho of Elis, preached and practised emotional detachment.[51] This may have been related to his admiration for Democritus.[52] In any case the passions were becoming a standard subject for philosophizing. Aristotle's illustrious student Theophrastus wrote a work about the passions and another about retaliation (timōria).[53] It may have been he who made the first attempt to distinguish orgē explicitly from thumos.[54] The third-century Peripatetic Hieronymus of Rhodes also had at least something and probably a great deal to say about anger.[55] But whatever the degree of Aristotle's general influence on Hellenistic philosophers,[56] it is evident that the latter, to their great detriment, did not, with respect to the passions, take proper account of his arguments.

Some time in the first half of the third century there had appeared the first monograph specifically about anger. It was the soon almost forgotten work of the popular philosopher Bion the Borysthenite.[57] But before he wrote it, some radical new doctrines had appeared.

The condition of the Epicurean Wise Man is psychic tranquillity, ataraxia, and Epicurus thought of achieving this state as the only proper aim of philosophy.[58] One of his well-attested thoughts is simply

51. Diog.Laert. ix.66 and 68, Euseb. Praep.Ev. xiv.18.19. Cf. Cic. Acad. ii.130 = L-S 2F. Biographical embellishment is not to be excluded.

52. The admiration: Diog.Laert. ix.67 (L-S 1C).

53. Diog.Laert. v.45. On his supposed book peri orgēs, see Regenbogen 1940, col. 1485.

54. At any rate, he did distinguish them, according to fr. 72 Wimmer = 438 Fortenbaugh-Huby (he seems to have said that one was more intense than the other). His theory of punishment: 154 Wimmer = 526 Fortenbaugh-Huby.

55. Since he is referred to by both Seneca and Plutarch on the subject of anger, he is commonly supposed to have written a peri orgēs or a peri aorgēsias (cf. Pohlenz 1896, 334–338; Becchi 1990, 71), and in his edition of Hieronymus (Basel & Stuttgart, 1959), F. Wehrli hesitantly printed frr. 21–23 as part of a peri orgēs. On the other hand it does not seem likely that the second-century Peripatetic Sotion of Alexandria was the author of the Stoicizing fragments peri orgēs ascribed to a certain Sotion by Stob. Ecl. iii.14.10, 20.53–55 and iv.44.59 (pace Cupaiuolo 1975, 88; for one of the several other philosophers called Sotion who was probably the author, see below p. 112).

56. He was not much read by the Stoics: Sandbach 1985. Sandbach overlooks the Stoics' debt to Aristotle's definition of orgē.

57. Phld. De ira 2 (col. i.17). The content is entirely conjectural.

58. See Ep.Pyth. 85–86 (L-S 18C); cf. Gnom.Vat. 54 (L-S 25D). On Epicurean views

that we should be busy with our own psychological health.[59] He probably also wrote that a philosopher's discourse *(logos)* is "empty"

> by which no *pathos* [suffering, passion] of a human being is taken care off [*therapeuetai*]. For just as there is no gain from a medical skill which does not cast out the sicknesses of bodies, so there is no gain from philosophy if it does not expel *pathos* from the soul.[60]

Both here and at about the same time in Zeno we can see the ambiguity of the word *pathos* (which, as we saw in the last chapter, had been building up over several generations) exacting its price: if it was a suffering, it was undesirable—yet, to judge from Aristotle's list (desire, anger, fear, boldness, envy, joy, affectionate love, hatred, longing, jealousy, pity),[61] virtually any vigorous emotion was now likely to be considered a *pathos* and hence *automatically* undesirable.[62]

Epicurus' desire to provide *ataraxia* made him suspicious of all strong emotions. He believed, for example, that the gods were not subject to anger, thus bringing into flower an idea which had been germinating since at least the days of Euripides: the first of his *Kuriai Doxai (Master Doctrines)* said that a god "is exempt from outbursts of anger [*orgai*] and partiality, for all such things are weaknesses."[63] As the acceptance of human anger became more limited, so divine anger, although deeply rooted in ordinary people's beliefs, continued to lose credibility with philosophers. The supreme importance of tranquillity

---

about the emotions, see Annas 1989 (cf. Annas 1992, 123–173). On the Epicureans and anger: cf. Asmis 1990, 2395–2399; Procopé 1993.

59. *Gnom.Vat.* 64.

60. Fr. 221 Usener. The fragment was rejected by G. Arrighetti, but accepted by L-S (25C). It appears, with minor variations, in two places, anonymously in Porphyry, *Ad Marcellam* sect. 31, at the end of a passage which shows signs of Epicurean influence (Sodano 1991, 36), and in the anthology of Stobaeus (*Anth.* II p. 22, lines 16–21 Wachsmuth). There it is attributed to Pythagoras, but Stobaeus has been thought to preserve some of Epicurus' opinions under Pythagoras' name (cf. E. Bignone's edition of Epicurus [Bari, 1920], 180 n. 1), and this is likely to be one of them.

61. *Nic.Eth.* ii.5.1105b20–23.

62. Cicero naturally noticed that πάθος sometimes could and sometimes could not be translated by *morbus*, sickness (*De fin.* iii.35).

63. *KD* 1 (*Epicurea* ed. Usener p. 71; L-S 23E, 23G). See also *Ep.Hdt.* 77 (L-S 23C). Cf. Eur. *HF* 1342–1346 (Heracles speaking), Phld. *De ira* ch. 7 (col. xliii.23). Later references to this doctrine are fairly numerous: e.g., Cic. *De natura deorum* i.45.

in the eyes of the Epicureans made them insist on this point: according to Lucretius, the gods are not "won over by virtuous service or touched by wrath."[64]

But concerning what Epicurus himself wrote about anger we know only a little. His special work on the emotions, *Views about Emotions against Timocrates*,[65] is all lost, as is virtually all of another work, *Utterances (Anaphonēseis)*, in which he said something about anger and in particular about the meaning of the term *thumos*.[66] We do not even know for certain whether, like his follower Philodemus 250 years later, he made a distinction between "empty anger" and "natural anger."[67] Students of Epicureanism tend to construct a composite of Epicurean thought about anger, even though we know that the Epicureans sometimes disagreed with each other on this subject. Epicurus himself did not in any case condemn all anger, for he distinguished between being angry *(to thumōthēsesthai)* and being moderately angry,[68] and between the "justified" *(kata to deon)* and the "unjustified" anger of parents towards their children.[69] He *may* also have said that though the wise man will be unusually susceptible to emotion, it will not hinder him from being wise; this was a claim which Philodemus did not accept.[70]

The Epicureans are commonly reputed to have been undeviating followers of the master's doctrines, and even the Stoics are often thought to have done little more than bring out the implications of their founder's teachings. In consequence many modern students of

64. Lucr. i.49 = ii.651. See too vi.71–78. Cf. Nussbaum 1994, 252.

65. Our source is Diog.Laert. x.28. Being in letter form, it was probably quite summary. According to Annas 1989, 146, "the need to analyze and discuss such emotions as anger is implicit in the Epicurean programme from the outset," but it is not known how thoroughly Epicurus addressed this need.

66. Fr. 3 Usener = fr. 8 Arrighetti, from Phld. *De ira* 7 (col. xlv.5–7). For the implications of this title, see Sedley 1973, 59, who suggests that it concerned the natural or original meanings of words. According to Philodemus, the author distinguished between moderate and excessive *thumos*-anger.

67. Otherwise Philodemus might have said so in *De ira* 7, col. xlv.7–8. Cf. Erler 1992, 190. But Epicurus probably did make the distinction, since he distinguished between natural and empty desires, *Ep.Men.* 127 (L-S 21B); cf. Procopé 1993, 371.

68. Phld. loc. cit. In line 8 we are presumably to understand or insert ὀργίζεσθαι.

69. *Gnom.Vat.* 62. But this is not much trusted as genuine Epicurus.

70. Diog.Laert. x.117 (L-S 22Q, with their discussion, II.142). Philodemus' opinion: cf. *De ira* 5 (col. xviii.35–40).

Hellenistic and Roman philosophy have neglected the intellectual history of their subject. And often, of course, we just do not know what individual Hellenistic philosophers said. The whole study of Hellenistic philosophy is the study of a lost library—but that is no excuse for supposing that all the books in it fell into neat categories which did not evolve.

The variety of Epicurean thought about anger is clear from the fact that Philodemus' *De ira* criticizes other philosophers who are reasonably well attested as Epicureans: these were a certain Timasagoras,[71] who may have held that anger resulted from a natural instinct and was therefore inevitable,[72] and one Nicasicrates. The latter saw not only "empty anger" but also "natural anger" as unacceptable; in other words, he came to the same conclusion as the "absolutist" Stoic opponents of anger to whom we shall shortly turn: even "natural anger," in the view of Nicasicrates, obscures the mental faculties (*logismoi*) "with respect to itself," hinders friendship, and brings many other unspecified disadvantages.[73]

We come now to the earliest ancient monograph about anger which in large part survives, Philodemus' *De ira,* which was probably written in the 60s.[74] When the papyrus becomes legible,[75] the author is already cataloguing the evil consequences of *orgē*, including ill health,[76] and he then explains that describing these consequences is a useful method of prevailing on people not to give in to anger. The catalogue continues down to column xxxi; while the angry commit parricide and sacri-

71. For this man as an Epicurean, see Longo Auricchio & Tepedino Guerra 1982, 406–407, basing themselves on a new reading of *P.Herc.* 19/698. See also Phld. *De ira* 4 (col. vii.7). See, further, Indelli's commentary, pp. 150, 154–155; Procopé 1993, 378–381.

72. So Longo Auricchio & Tepedino Guerra 411, arguing from *P.Herc.* 1044 fr. 34.

73. Phld. *De ira* 7 (cols. xxxviii.34–xxxix.7). For the view that he was an Epicurean: Indelli's commentary, pp. 223–224; Procopé 1993, 382.

74. It seems likely that the work had been written before Cicero and apparently Caesar began showing interest in the subject in the years from 63 onwards (cf. Chapter 9).

75. *P.Herc.* 182. For the proportion of Philodemus' book—rather less than half of the original, apparently—that is preserved in readable condition, see Obbink 1991, 79. The title was probably περὶ ὀργῆς. There is no reason (*pace* Rawson 1985, 296) to think that it was part of a more general work.

76. Ch. 4 (cols. ix.27–x.40). This seems to be original.

lege,[77] the underlying theme throughout this section seems to be the multi-faceted absurdity of the angry man's behaviour. Philodemus also conjures up a physical caricature of the angry man, with his flashing eyes, red face, gnashing teeth, glowering expression and raised voice—a hideous figure for Greeks, who were accustomed to associating physical excellence with moral excellence.[78]

Next, in a transitional section, the author attacks the allegedly Peripatetic thesis that anger is indispensable for self-defence and for punishment.[79] It is possible, he says, to fight well without anger, and the angry fighter is actually at a disadvantage—he becomes rash and disobedient.

Then Philodemus turns to the exposition of his own argument to the effect that "natural" anger, by which he means anger arising from sufficient reasons, is a good thing and can be felt even by the Wise Man, who will not experience "empty" or immoderate anger.[80] In Philodemus' view, the Wise Man may experience *orgē*, but he will not desire punishment or revenge (thus he implicitly contradicts Aristotle's definition of *orgē*).[81] Nor will he suffer from the intense form of anger to which Philodemus (contrary to ordinary usage) gives the name of *thumos*,[82] for he will not entertain false, exaggerated opinions about the harm that is done to him.[83]

77. Ch. 5 (col. xiv.8–29).

78. Fr. 6. See also Cic. *Tusc.Disp.* iv.52 (and for the numerous later versions of this topos, see Indelli's edition of Philodemus, p. 135). No doubt there had been earlier Hellenistic precedents. From *Il.* i.104, xix.365–366, onwards, the physical symptoms of anger had often been mentioned. Bad men were ugly from Thersites onwards.

79. Ch. 6 (cols. xxxi.24–xxxiv.7). Some of the opinions attributed to the Peripatetics here were Aristotle's, others not.

80. The distinction between empty and natural: ch. 7 (col. xxxviii.1–6). Sufficient cause: ibid. (cols. xl.26–xli.25). Philodemus' περὶ παρρησίας *(On Frank Speaking)* lends support to the anger of the philosophical teacher (fr. 10.10–11, 87.8, and apparently 2.1–7).

81. Ch. 7 (cols. xlii.21–25, xliv.22–35).

82. Ch. 7 (cols. xliii.14–19 [Indelli's text], xliii.41–xlvi.13). It is rather obvious that although *orgē* and *thumos* were not exactly synonyms (because *thumos* could refer to a person's spirit, in other words the faculty of feeling emotions, as well as to an anger-like emotion), Philodemus' distinction between the two terms is artificial. Chrysippus had also made an artificial distinction between the two, but a different one (see below). Indelli's note on this matter (p. 243) is misleading.

83. Ch. 8 (col. xlvii.36–41). For further details see esp. Procopé 1993, 375–377.

The other surviving exponent of Epicurean *ataraxia,* Lucretius, avoids the difficult problems about anger. He imagines early mankind tiring of primitive revenge and legislating against violence. The human race

> was fainting from its feuds, and hence submitted more readily of its own will to statutes and strict rules of law. For because each man in his anger sought to avenge himself more fiercely than is now permitted by just laws, for this reason men were utterly weary of living in violence. (v.1146–1150)

We are told that the heart must be purified, otherwise great attacks of desire will tear a person in pieces (v.43–46). But as a good Epicurean, Lucretius is not an "absolutist" about anger, he is simply in favour of moderation, and what is to be avoided is "running too headlong to bitter bursts of anger."[84] No doubt he believed in the admissibility of "natural anger," though he does not express such an opinion in so many words. He finds fault with the man of ox-like nature who "will take some things *clementius aequo,* more indulgently than is right."[85] What is most characteristic perhaps is the violence, sometimes macabre violence, of Lucretius' imagination, and that has encouraged a recent critic to see "angry aggression" as a major organizing principle in Lucretius' great work—which seems to me a distorting exaggeration.[86] What is most original perhaps about Lucretius on anger is his radically negative attitude towards warfare, which he contrasts with the anger-free life of the gods.[87]

We can now turn back chronologically to the beginning of Stoicism. The founder Zeno apparently wrote a book about the passions (*pathē*),[88] and he described a *pathos* as "an irrational and unnatural

---

84. "iras . . . ad acris," iii.311. But such a character cannot be completely changed. Reason cannot expel the emotions completely (iii.316–319).

85. Lucr. iii.302–304, 313.

86. Nussbaum 1994, 239–279. This involves a good deal of violence to the evidence: *ira* is not, for instance, said by the poet to have been a component of sexual passion, contrary to the impression given by Nussbaum 259–261. However, no one will deny that *ira* was in some respects an important component of Lucretius' doctrines: for example, one of his principal purposes was to convince people that they had nothing to fear from the supposed anger of the gods (v.1194–1197, etc.).

87. The great prayer to Venus for peace (i.29–49) was a radical departure.

88. Diog.Laert. vii.4, 110.

movement of the soul" and "an impulse which is excessive."[89] Thus he was, or at any rate seemed to be, opposed to all affect. And indeed the Stoics embraced the remarkable idea that absolutely all anger was to be avoided. Zeno's thinking on this point may not have been explicit,[90] but his younger contemporary and follower Dionysius of Heraclea laid it down that the Wise Man never becomes angry (and on this count he criticized Homer's Achilles).[91] This must have been in harmony with Zeno's doctrines.

Zeno, so it seems, made a laudable attempt to distinguish between *mēnis, thumos* and *orgē*,[92] but he did not possess a technique which would have allowed him to do that satisfactorily. And once he had decided to treat as the four primary emotions desire, fear, grief and pleasure, making anger a form of desire, deep philosophical trouble was almost inevitable. For while a prima facie case could be made out for the Wise Man's suppressing these four emotions, it really was not quite so easy to argue against the moral propriety of all anger whatsoever. All the same, one can scarcely be surprised that the critique of anger in Greek culture which we shall be examining in the next chapters now finally led to an overt "ban" on all *orgē*, especially perhaps because the recently dominant Peripatetics had seemed, at least superficially, to be somewhat permissive on the subject. A reaction was due. Zeno's doctrine about the emotions was to exercise great appeal; and no doubt

---

89. *SVF* I.205: κίνησις ψυχῆς ἄλογος παρὰ φύσιν, ὁρμὴ πλεονάζουσα. Cf. 206. On Stoic teaching about the emotions, see Forschner 1981, 114–141; Striker 1991, 61–73; Annas 1992, esp. 37–87. For commentary on the Zenonian definitions, see Graeser 1975, 145–154. Zeno was possibly the first to speak of any anger as unnatural (Aristotle, however, had measured it on a scale of naturalness).

90. The argument from silence carries some weight here. Seneca's assertion (*De ira* i.16.7 = *SVF* I.215) that Zeno said that the soul of the Wise Man may show scars left behind by the passions, even if it is authentic, which is highly doubtful (cf. Setaioli 1988, 259–260), would not justify supposing that Zeno would have agreed with Seneca's gloss to the effect that the Wise Man may feel hints or shadows of the emotions ("suspiciones quasdam et umbras adfectuum").

91. Cicero, *Tusc.Disp.* iii.18–21 (= *SVF* I.434): after quoting *Il.* ix.646–648, where Achilles says that his heart is swollen with anger, Dionysius said that any swollen body part must be in a defective state, and that that applied to the soul too. The soul of the Wise Man is never in such a state, but an angry man's is; therefore the Wise Man is never angry.

92. Diog.Laert. vii.114: he said that *thumos* was *orgē* that was just beginning (Stoics often repeated this: *SVF* III.395–397).

much of the attraction of Stoicism was always for those who, as a result of temperament or experience, desired to deaden their emotions to the greatest possible degree.

Starting from the Aristotelian opinion that the purpose of living is *eudaimonia,* happiness, Zeno asserted that happiness consisted of the *euroia biou,* the good or smooth flow of life.[93] Exactly what this meant to him or to his followers is not clear,[94] but since the above-mentioned Dionysius wrote a book about *apatheia,*[95] absence of passion or impassivity, he at least, if not Zeno himself, presumably recommended it.[96] This ideal later evolved into Ciceronian-Senecan *tranquillitas animi.*[97]

Other Stoics fairly soon wrote about the emotions, but their particular doctrines are often unknown to us. Among Zeno's students, Ariston the Bald of Chios cannot have avoided the subject, since he thought that the only philosophy that counted was ethics.[98] Zeno's successor as leader of the sect, Cleanthes of Assos, wrote a little versified dialogue between Reason *(logismos)* and Anger *(thumos),* the implications of which are uncertain.

> "What, Anger, do you wish? Tell me that."
> "I, Reason? To do everything I want."
> "That is royal indeed; but say it again."
> "That whatever I desire will come to pass."[99]

93. *SVF* I.184 (cf. L-S 63A). There is no room here to discuss in detail how the Stoics thought that anger worked; the most important point (Ioppolo 1995, 26) is that all the Hellenistic Stoics thought that the emotions were voluntary movements of the soul for which the individual was responsible.

94. See Irwin 1986, 225; L-S I.398–400; Long 1989, 88–94 = 1996, 189–195. This was not at all what Aristotle meant by *eudaimonia.*

95. Diog.Laert. vii.166.

96. According to Diog.Laert. vii.117, however, "the Stoics" distinguish between the *apatheia* of the Wise Man and the *apatheia* of the bad man "which means that he is callous and relentless."

97. See Sen. *De ira* ii.12.6, *Ep.* 92.3, as well as *De tranq. animi.*

98. Diog.Laert. vii.160 end. He is not known to have written a book on the passions (as is sometimes said, e.g. by Cupaiuolo 1975, 88; Fillion-Lahille 1984, 17), but almost any of his attested writings (listed in Diog.Laert. vii.163) may have dealt with them. Cf. Fillion-Lahille 19.

99. *SVF* I, pp. 129–130; L-S 65I. But there is no evidence that he wrote anything else about the *pathē,* and the topic is absent from the long list of his book titles in

Herillus the Carthaginian and Sphaerus, both in the third century, are specifically attested as the authors of works entitled *On the Passions*.[100] But much the most successful Hellenistic Stoic work about the passions or about anger was the one written by the mid-third-century leader of the school Chrysippus. It was relatively detailed (it contained four books), and its ancient influence can be judged by the fact that the surviving "fragments" fill no fewer than twenty-three pages in the standard edition.[101]

Chrysippus defined the passions as perverse judgements,[102] which accords with his "absolutist" opposition to anger and all other passions. Cicero complained that Chrysippus and other Stoics spent too much time *defining* the emotions, and too little considering how to cure souls[103]—which seems somewhat captious as far as Chrysippus is concerned, since it was one of the latter's innovations to have written, as part of his work on the emotions, a book which became known as the "therapeutic" book.[104]

In addition to some kind of therapy, the important doctrinal innovations of the post-Zenonian Stoics affecting the emotions were twofold: they introduced some approved emotions, and eventually they conceded that even the Wise Man might feel some sort of preliminary feelings which were not really emotions. Neither of these innovations can be dated with any precision, and indeed some scholars think they were part of the founder's own teaching; much more probably, they

---

Diog.Laert. vii.174–175. A story was told about his refusing to get angry (vii.173), which probably implies that the subject of anger entered into his teaching.

100. Diog.Laert. vii.166 (Herillus also wrote a book called *Medea* which presumably discussed *orgē*), 178.

101. It is nonetheless difficult to reconstruct Chrysippus' thinking about the emotions (see, among others, Glibert-Thirry 1977; Annas 1992, 103–122; Donini 1995), partly no doubt because of the hostility of one of the main sources, Galen (it has been observed that "ancient philosophic polemic did not operate with any rules of fair play," Long 1992, 50 = 1996, 67).

102. *SVF* III.459 (L-S 61B, 65G); cf. 412. As to what exactly he meant by this, and whether Zeno had already expressed this opinion, see recently Ioppolo 1995, 26–28. If passions are judgements, philosophers will obviously claim to be able to correct them.

103. *Tusc.Disp.* iv.9.

104. See Chapter 15.

were later modifications in which Chrysippus took some part. In the first place, the Wise Man was permitted three emotional dispositions, though only three. It was a strange list: joy *(chara)*, wishing *(boulēsis)*, and watchfulness or caution *(eulabeia)*.[105] These were the *eupatheiai*, good emotional states, "rational" ones corresponding respectively to the three "irrational" emotions, which were pleasure, desire, and fear.[106]

The Stoics said from early on that the Wise Man was a very rare creature: Chrysippus and others admitted that there had been very few of them, and Chrysippus made no such claim for himself,[107] but the Stoics persisted in formulating much of their moral instruction as if the Wise Man's perfection were attainable. Eventually they had to concede that mankind was not simply divided into the wise and the foolish, and they came to believe that the individual could achieve moral progress.[108] This doctrine of progression does not mean that the Stoics ever approved of anger, but it did make their position a degree more intelligible. One way or another, a Stoic who gave in to a fit of anger or pity could find excuses for himself. However, most Greeks and Romans who became aware of Stoic ideas, even if they were well read like Cicero or Plutarch, took little or no notice of the refinements of Stoic moral theory and perceived the Stoic commandment about anger as an absolute one.

Antipater of Tarsus, in the mid-second century B.C., was the first important Stoic to follow Borysthenes in writing a work specifically about anger, in at least two books.[109] But we know virtually nothing about it.

---

105. See esp. Cic. *Tusc.Disp.* iv.11–16 (= *SVF* III.438; he translates them as *gaudium, voluntas* and *cautio*), Diog.Laert. vii.116 (= *SVF* III.431, L-S 65F). It is Cicero who indicates that it was only the Wise Man who was held by the Stoics to be capable of these feelings (with respect to *gaudium*, he does not say this explicitly). Some attribute this scheme to Zeno, but its parentage, though unclear, is very probably later. Indeed the way Cicero mentions Zeno in *Tusc.Disp.* iv.11 implies as much.

106. See Forschner 1981, 139–140. On the whole difficult concept of *eupatheiai* (*constantiae* to Cicero, *Tusc.Disp.* iv.14), see Brennan 1998, 54–57. For "preliminary feelings" of anger, which are probably a later development, see below.

107. *SVF* III.545 (L-S 66A, qq.v. for related texts); cf. Sen. *De ira* ii.10.6.

108. This thought was probably already present in Chrysippus: Diog.Laert. vii.91. Cf. Luschnat 1958; Kidd 1978, 247–248, 255–256; L-S I.385–386, 427–428.

109. Athenaeus xiv.643 (quoting from Book I) = Antipater fr. 65 (*SVF* III p. 257). For the identification of this Antipater, see Indelli's commentary on Phld. *De ira,*

Then we pass to the "middle period" of Stoic philosophy, which principally means the Rhodian philosophers Panaetius and Poseidonius. Panaetius' psychology differed from that of the earlier Stoics, and he took a somewhat less rigid line with respect to the emotions. So at least it seems from Cicero, who in a very Greek passage says that virtue has the job of "restraining the *pathē* . . . and making the impulses [*hormai*] obedient to reason."[110] This statement may deviate significantly from old-Stoic views, which had insisted on the *elimination* of *pathē* and disobedient *hormai*.[111] In fact Panaetius' whole system of virtues and emotions differs from what the older Stoics had propounded,[112] and he even seems to have done away with the ideal of *apatheia*,[113] to replace it with a less extreme doctrine of psychological tranquillity.[114]

Poseidonius' opinions about the passions also deviated sharply from early Stoic thinking, but in spite of his wide influence on later writers, his positions are mostly hard to discern.[115] That we can say rather little that is definite about his views on anger is all the more regrettable since he evidently gave the subject detailed thought: he wrote a monograph about *orgē* in at least two books, as well as a work about the *pathē*.[116] We know that he reverted to the tripartite psychology of Plato, and we can probably assume that he followed the earlier Stoics in suggesting that all *orgē*-anger was to be avoided. At the same time, it may

---

p. 211 (Philodemus refers to him in ch.6 [col. xxxiii.34–40]: he is said to have reported the habitual advice of athletic trainers not to grow angry, *mē thumou*). Antipater's views about marriage will appear in Chapter 12.

110. Cic. *De off.* ii.18.

111. I follow Rist 1969, 183, in thinking that this sentence represents Panaetius' thinking more precisely on this point than does *De off.* i.69.

112. Rist 1969, 190–196.

113. Gellius xii.5 = Panaetius fr. 111 Van Straaten.

114. Rist 1969, 196.

115. He continues to be the main battlefield as far as Hellenistic theories of the passions are concerned: see Sihvola & Engberg-Pedersen 1998. Recent contributions include L-S I.422–423; Nussbaum 1993, 109–114; Sorabji 1997, 197–202; Cooper 1998; Sorabji 2000, 93–132. Conflict arises chiefly because of uncertainty about (1) the fairness of Galen's use of Poseidonius in his critique of Chrysippus, and (2) the extent to which Seneca used him in his *De ira*. Neither question is vitally important for this study.

116. Anger in more than one book: *P.Ross.Georg.* I.22 = fr. 36 E-K. The *pathē*: frr. 30–35 E-K. As to how he defined *orgē*, see Chapter 3.

very well have been he who devised the doctrine of the *propatheiai* ("pre-emotions"), the first impulses to emotion which even the Wise Man may feel (but which of course he will know how to control), a doctrine which Seneca took from a Greek source in a passage in which some scholars have diagnosed heavy Poseidonian influence.[117] The effect of this notion will have been to modify Stoic absolutism about the passions still further.

Why then no emotions in Stoic morality? Philosophers answer this question by describing the chain of reasoning which the Stoics used, filling in the gaps to some extent.[118] A historian, by contrast, must ask why the main positions of the ancient philosophers in question appealed to them. Philosophers, across the continents and the ages, have known very many chains of reasoning. Why did this particular one attract certain Greeks and Romans? The Stoics, or at least the earliest ones, believed that it was both possible and morally right to feel no *pathē*. These odd opinions, especially the second, must be treated as matters of cultural history, not simply as the conclusions of arguments.

The next text we are going to examine, the fourth book of Cicero's *Tusculan Disputations,* poses the problem in an acute fashion. The most remarkable feature of Cicero's writing about anger (the same ideas appear briefly in *De officiis*) is that even though he was never a Stoic, he advocated complete abstention from anger and from all the other strong emotions too.[119] Such a position was for him one of the most attractive aspects of Stoicism. He criticizes what he takes to be Peripatetic doctrines about the passions—a kind of vulgar Aristotelianism (he is not likely to have read the *Nicomachean Ethics*). *Perturbationes animi,* his expressions for the *pathē* or passions, are taken to be self-evidently bad, and the opinion that anger is natural or useful, for ex-

117. *De ira* ii.4. Every imaginable opinion has been canvassed about who invented the *propatheiai* (see Ramondetti 1996, 23–26). The term is first attested, not impeccably, in Philo, *Quaest. in Gen.* fr. 1.79 (Philo, Supplement vol. II, p. 190 Marcus). But was the idea already there *avant la lettre?* The supposed citation from Zeno in Sen. *De ira* iii.16.7 is not good evidence. Seneca is our main source on this topic: see ii.4.2 in particular. Poseidonius' influence is fairly obvious in the early chapters of *De ira* II (Fillion-Lahille 1984, 163–169).

118. E.g., Striker 1991, 61–73; Cooper & Procopé 1995, 5–10.

119. What he had written fifteen years earlier in *QF* i.1.38 was a degree less clear-cut.

ample in assisting people to be brave, is denied with counter-examples.[120] Anger is the worst of vices.[121] The orator must put on a show of anger, not feel the emotion itself.[122] "All those things [the emotional *perturbationes*, apparently] spring from the roots of error: they should not be clipped or pruned but torn out and dragged out by the roots."[123] And he proceeds to set out his psychological therapy.

This stance is all the more interesting because Cicero had made his career as an orator, and the practical needs of the orator obviously made it impossible to stay aloof from emotions. In the *Orator* (46) he wrote frankly that he had used every possible means of arousing anger in juries when he had needed to do so, and felt anger himself.[124] In view of this, it might be possible to accuse the author of the *Tusculan Disputations* of superficiality. It is more useful to learn the lesson that Cicero took up emotional "absolutism" even though it seemed to be at odds with the way he constantly conducted himself.

In harmony with Cicero's "absolutism" about anger is the claim he makes in *De officiis* that "god never becomes angry or does harm."[125] He assures us that "all philosophers" agree with this notion. This assertion was probably exaggerated, and in fact the educated public, like everybody else, continued to assume that divine beings could be irate— Vergil will serve as an instance of a highly educated person who made that assumption (though not in his case without some hesitation).[126] Philosophers, however, desirous of logical consistency, found emo-

---

120. *Tusc.Disp.* iv.39–50.

121. Ibid. iv.43, 54.

122. Ibid. iv.55 ("simulare non dedecet"). Cf. Sen. *De ira* ii.14.1, ii.17.1.

123. *Tusc. Disp.* iv.57. For an absolute prohibition of anger see also *De off.* i.89; it is not clear whether he mentioned anger specifically in his exclusion of emotion in i.69.

124. *Orator* 131–133 ("est faciendum etiam ut irascatur iudex"); he celebrates his own *vis animi*, and looks to Demosthenes as his only worthy forerunner in this respect. The contrast with *De Orat.* i.220–222, ii.185–196 (55 B.C.), will be discussed briefly in Chapter 9.

125. *De off.* iii.102. Sext.Emp. *Pyrrh.* i.162 says that it is a "dogma of the philosophers" that the divine is *apathes*, free of passion.

126. For divine anger, see Tac. *Hist.* ii.38. For texts showing the popular belief in the anger of the gods, see Versnel 1985, 258, 260; examples can easily be multiplied. Cf. Juv. i.49–50, xiii.93.

tional disturbances such as *orgē* and *ira* to be incompatible with the psychic tranquillity without which divine happiness could not now be imagined.

Two more lost philosophers may have had influential things to say about anger in the century which elapsed between the *Tusculan Disputations* and Seneca's *De ira:* the Roman Q. Sextius and Seneca's Greek philosophy teacher Sotion. The former offered therapeutic advice about anger,[127] presumably in writing, and since he is referred to favourably by Seneca, his views can be assumed to have been at least broadly similar.[128] The contours of Sotion's philosophy are even harder to make out, since there were as many as four philosophers of that name in the century and a half prior to Seneca. A philosopher named Sotion wrote a work in at least two books about *orgē*,[129] and it is reasonable to assume both that this author was Seneca's teacher and also that Seneca made considerable use of his *orgē* work.[130] (*De ira* does not name Sotion, but that is of little consequence). For present purposes, however, what matters is simply that yet another philosopher wrote a somewhat lengthy work about *orgē*-anger and *may* have been the source of much of the material in Seneca's monograph.

The "absolutist" stance with respect to anger was widely shared by the surviving Roman-imperial writers of works about philosophy—Seneca, on occasion Plutarch, Musonius Rufus, Epictetus, Marcus Aurelius.

Seneca's *De ira*,[131] at about 25,000 words the longest of the surviving ancient treatises on anger, was probably written in 49 or 50,[132] when

127. Sen. *De ira* ii.36.1 ("Quibusdam, ut ait Sextius, iratis profuit"); cf. iii.36.1, *Ep.* 64.2.

128. See further Cupaiuolo 1975, 108 n. 16; Fillion-Lahille 1984, 257.

129. Stob. *Ecl.* iii.20.53.

130. Fillion-Lahille 1984, 261–272, puts the case for his influence on large parts of the work, with excessive confidence. Seneca's references to Sotion: *Ep.* 49.2, 108.17 and 20. The resemblance between the short citation from Sotion in Stobaeus loc. cit. and *De ira* ii.10.5 is held by some to be important.

131. The large bibliography can be traced through such recent works as Malchow's commentary (1987), Cooper & Procopé 1995, Ramondetti 1996, and Rudich 1997, 17–106. Fillion-Lahille 1984 remains useful.

132. After the assassination of Caligula (January 41), because of the blunt comments about him (i.20.8–9, ii.33.3–4, iii.18–19); before 52, because the work was addressed to Seneca's older brother as "Novatus," the name which he is known to have

the author, who was about fifty, was nevertheless near the beginning of his career as a philosophical writer. The work has the same general form as Philodemus' book and no doubt many others: an analysis and a denunciation of anger, followed by therapeutic advice.[133]

After a section on the definition of anger, largely lost, Seneca attempts to refute Peripatetic views, discussing whether anger is natural (no), and whether it is sometimes useful, either for the sake of courage or justice or for producing *magnitudo animi* (no again, on all counts). In Book II the initial subject is whether anger begins "by choice or from without" *(iudicio an impetu)*, the answer being, in cases of true anger (many reservations follow about what is to be counted), "by choice." The Wise Man will not be angry (ii.6–10), not even at what is disgraceful (for otherwise he would never have a quiet moment). Further arguments are produced to demonstrate that anger is not useful, and not inevitable, and not characteristic of freedom or nobility.

The author now passes to remedies (ii.18 to the end of iii), which we shall discuss in detail in Chapter 15. The final section of the book tells us how to cure the anger of others (iii.39–43).

Seneca's position is nominally "absolutist,"[134] but he modified this

---

surrendered by 52 at the latest (because of being legally adopted). It has sometimes been argued that Seneca wrote *De ira* during his exile, or in 41 before exile began (so Giardina 2000). However, 41 is not a plausible date, for whatever the real reason for his exile (according to Cassius Dio [lx.8], the real reason was hostility of the new emperor's young wife, Messalina, towards his mistress Iulia Livilla), exile is unlikely to have been slow in coming. Once he had been sent away, it was Seneca's primary concern to get Claudius to relent. Now the emperor, as we shall see, was most definitely aware of the problem of imperial anger, but whether Seneca would have considered it tactful to publish implied advice on this subject is highly questionable. He avoided any such allusion in the exilic *Consolatio ad Polybium* (43–44), which in spite of its toadying to the emperor failed to bring about his recall—which suggests that Claudius was still at that time irritated by or suspicious of Seneca. Seneca had never been an intimate of the emperor, and the teaching about anger which is offered in *De ira* goes further than Claudius himself would have gone. The standpoint of the *De ira* is that of a high-ranking courtier, not an exile.

133. The analytic and denunciatory part goes down to ii.17. Not that *De ira* always maintains this structure successfully.

134. *De ira* i.7–11 (cf. iii.1.1). The gods are never angry, he implies (ii.27.1), but his indirect way of putting this received philosophical notion ("di inmortales, qui nec volunt obesse nec possunt; natura enim illis mitis et placida est . . ."; he goes on to say

doctrine somewhat in allowing that even the Wise Man may feel "a certain light and tenuous commotion" and the first unavoidable impulse to anger *(animi ictum)*.[135] There is even a risk, he thinks, in bringing up children not to be angry: we may blunt their *indoles*, their innate good qualities, such as a competitive spirit (ii.21.1–5). In another work, he even promised to write about the manner in which one ought to be angry with enemies,[136] and in yet another he distinguishes between sicknesses of the soul *(animi morbos)* and emotions *(adfectus)*, and emphasizes that the man who is very close to perfection can still feel the latter.[137]

Furthermore he works some of the time with a definition of anger so limited that an absolute exclusion of anger loses much of its force:

> A man thinks himself injured and wishes for revenge, but dissuaded by some consideration immediately calms down . . . Therefore that primary disturbance of the mind [*agitatio animi*] which is excited by the impression of injury is no more anger than the impression of injury is itself anger . . . There can never be any doubt that . . . anger involves attack [*impetum*].[138]

Hence the Wise Man has some leeway, all the more so because although he is not allowed to feel *ira*, he is permitted to use *vis*, force.[139] As the Stoics had long said, there were in any case only a few Wise Men in each generation (ii.10.6), so that for any individual it remains a scarcely attainable end. And to cap it all, the whole matter is determined by a man's particular physical combination of the four elements fire, water, air and earth; if he has a lot of fire in him he will be irascible, and apparently there is not much that he can do about it—a quite modern touch.[140]

---

that they are not to blame for the weather) may be an attempt to avoid contradicting Graeco-Roman common sense.

135. Ibid. i.16.7; ii.4.2.

136. *De clem.* i.12.3.

137. *Ep.* 75.11.

138. *De ira* ii.3.4–5.

139. Ibid. ii.17.2. He may also for certain purposes simulate anger: ii.14.1, 17.1.

140. Ibid. ii.19.2. An enigmatic passage of Diog.Laert. (vii.115) attributes to the Stoics the view that the *eukataphoriai* of the soul, its propensities, included quarrels *(erides)*—which also seems to be a limitation of free will.

How to interpret the *De ira* is a complex question which will occupy us later. The quality of Seneca's philosophizing is in this case mediocre—he even finds it difficult to maintain a distinction between anger and hatred,[141] and he has no clear-cut position about what counts as *ira*. He also has the displeasing habit of attributing to great philosophers such as Aristotle and Zeno statements which, in all likelihood, they did not make (it is not probable that Seneca made use of lost books of Aristotle).[142] Quintilian was right, even if his motives were mixed, when he said that Seneca was "lazy at philosophy but a fine chastiser of vice."[143] This is nonetheless an exceedingly important book for the understanding of ancient culture, especially in virtue of the author's and the presumed readers' political eminence. For reasons which remain to be elucidated, Stoic teaching about anger was now thought to be needed in Latin (Seneca was probably the first to write such a treatise in that language). Seneca's views about the passions were also presented less directly in his "theatrical" works—in reality, purely literary productions. On occasion, in his *Medea* for instance,[144] *ira* is a central theme and the author's Stoic views are openly on display.

Seneca's own mentality is not yet our subject, but it must be remarked that it, too, is complex. The chastiser of vice was a scopophiliac: his creative imagination "was filled with luxuriantly erotic scenes of violence,"[145] and this applies to some sections of *De ira*[146] as much as to the theatre scripts.

141. E.g., at i.20.4.

142. For the absurd view that Seneca used lost works by Aristotle, see Laurenti 1979; Fillion-Lahille 1984, 203–210. As to the separate question whether Seneca represented Aristotle's views accurately, see Cooper & Procopé 1995, 27; iii.3.1, for instance, is a rank misrepresentation of what the philosopher had written. The allusion to Zeno at i.16.7 (= *SVF* I.215), to the effect that the soul of the Wise Man shows the scar of anger, is probably anachronistic, as was remarked earlier.

143. "in philosophia parum diligens, egregius tamen vitiorum insectator," *Inst.* x.1.129. Quintilian deplored Seneca's stylistic influence. For Seneca's obtuse attitude towards logic, see Barnes 1997, 12–13.

144. See Nussbaum 1993, 437–483, where, however, there is much to disagree with.

145. Barton 1992, 23.

146. See, for instance, his account of the punishment inflicted on three innocent

Finally, it is worth taking note of the sheer hardness of the multimillionaire moralist: if anger were a good, it would characterize "the most perfect" people. Instead we find that the angriest people are children, the old and the sick, for "the weak," he says tersely, "are by nature complainers" (i.13.5).

The most radical of the Roman Stoics was an Italian knight of Greek culture, Musonius Rufus—he of the "life-long therapy"—a younger contemporary of Seneca's. Musonius diverged somewhat from his Stoic loyalty: instead of arguing, as the Stoics normally had, that the Wise Man would realize that apparent harm done to him was not real harm, he preferred to say that the Wise Man would forgive, just as the Spartan sage Lycurgus had supposedly forgiven the young man who had blinded him in one eye (fr. XXXIX). One should not sue a man from whom one has suffered "outrage" *(hubris)*. Rather, one should bear the injustice *praōs*, in an even-tempered fashion: "We should not be implacable towards those who have wronged us, but rather a source of good hope to them, [which is] characteristic of a civilized and benevolent way of life."[147] As we shall see later, he acted on his disapproval of anger. But his surviving writings give us no other details of his thinking on the subject.

Musonius' most illustrious student was Epictetus, whose views about anger seem at first sight to have been conventional Stoicism: nothing will make the Wise Man angry.[148] The Wise Man regards nothing as his own except his own decisions, and thus he cannot be affected by any insult or any loss.[149] Epictetus repeats at some length (i.28) the view that anger is nothing more than a mistaken judgement, based on sense impressions.

But if we pay proper attention to Epictetus' terminology, we see that he goes a mile further than any previous or indeed subsequent Greek philosopher, Stoic or otherwise. For what is under discussion in the

---

soldiers by Cn. Piso (i.18), or of the mutilation of M. Marius at the orders of Sulla (iii.18)

147. Muson. fr. X (p. 78 Lutz): ἡμέρου τρόπου καὶ φιλανθρώπου ἐστίν.

148. *Diss.* i.28.10, cf. 18.21.

149. Ibid. iv.5. Anger is the target here, with Socrates the good example (for having tolerated his wife and son) and Nero the bad example; but most of the time the things to be avoided are referred to as fighting and insult.

first of the texts just referred to is not simply *orgē* but also *chalepotēs,* annoyance.[150] The chapter is entitled "That we ought not to be *annoyed* [*chalepainein*] with human beings, and what is important and unimportant among humans?" Another chapter (i.18) is entitled "That we ought not to *chalepainein* with those who err." Epictetus has plenty to say about strong forms of anger: the philosophical man "will not be angry with anyone [*oudeni orgisthēsetai*], will not be annoyed with anyone [*oudeni chalepanei*], will not revile anyone, will not blame anyone, will not hate, will not take offence at anyone." He criticizes Achilles for the incorrect judgement which led to his *orgē* (i.28.24). But he most distinctly goes beyond the traditional critique of *orgē,* and even beyond the known thinking of Musonius Rufus, in attempting to exclude the milder emotion *chalepotēs.* He often repeats the term *chalepainein,* and shows no sign of equating it with *orgizesthai,* so that it is clearly an intentional selection. It remains a matter of speculation whether Epictetus' experience as a slave had given him extra understanding of *chalepotēs,* which was no doubt how philosophically minded people tended to classify their own outbursts of ill temper against slaves.

Epictetus' independence from conventional Stoicism is also indicated by some of his ideas about other kinds of emotions. The Stoics did not believe in feeling or showing pity, but that was not Epictetus' view. With respect to Medea, you should not be angry—"why do you not, if anything, rather pity her? As we pity the blind and the lame."[151] As for fear, Epictetus' analysis was tolerant enough to be cited by a Stoic philosopher who on a certain voyage showed himself to be a less than intrepid sailor.[152] But that emphatically does not mean that Epictetus was sympathetic to those who showed symptoms of the angry emotions. A so-called philosopher who was a Roman gave way to

150. This is admittedly an imperfect translation, as i.28.9 suggests (the word is applied to a possible audience for Euripides' *Medea*); it can mean "to take something ill." See further iii.15.10, where it is said that being a philosopher means giving up or at least strictly controlling not only *orgē* but also annoyance, *dusarestein.* Socrates as portrayed by Xenophon also desired to limit *chalepotēs* (*Mem.* ii.2–3), as Epictetus probably knew.

151. i.28.9, cf. 18.9.

152. Gell. xix.1 = fr. 9 Schenkl. The philosopher showed every symptom of terror, but justified himself by referring to a passage in which Epictetus said the Wise Man does not *assent to* terrifying impressions.

chalepotēs in Epictetus' presence, and said that desisting would make him like Epictetus—that is, a Greek slave.[153] In other words, Epictetus held that any persistent display of *chalepotēs* was unacceptable.

Epictetus puts the virtue and psychic well-being of the individual at the centre of his system. What does philosophy claim? Not, he said (and here he is discussing anger in particular), to regulate a person's relations with others, but to teach him to regulate his own interior life (i.15.4). Yet the scale of Epictetus' optimism goes very far beyond this: if on Stoic principles we avoided contentiousness, that would produce "love [*philia*] in the household, concord in the *polis* and peace between nations, <and would make people> thankful towards god and confident at all times."[154] The conclusion of this chapter is also atypical of ancient philosophers:

> We, however, although we are capable of writing and reading these things, and praising them when we read them, are nowhere near capable of being persuaded of them. Therefore the proverb about the Spartans, "Lions at home, but foxes at Ephesus," will fit us too: lions in the lecture room, foxes outside.

Plutarch's principal comments are to be found in his essay *On the Habitual Absence of Anger (peri aorgēsias)*,[155] but he also wrote about anger in *On Moral Virtue* and *On Tranquillity of Mind*. It is possible (the evidence is slight) that he also wrote a specific treatise entitled *On Anger*.[156] He frequently pursues this interest in the biographies.[157] "Let no one," he writes, comparing Theseus and Romulus, "acquit Romulus of unreasoning *thumos* or hasty and senseless *orgē* in dealing with his brother, nor Theseus in dealing with his son; but the cause which

153. iii.8.7, though the point of the story is not absolutely clear.

154. iv.5.35–37. These are the subjects of most of the rest of this book.

155. Recent work includes an edition and commentary by R. Laurenti & G. Indelli (*Sul controllo dell'ira*) (Naples, 1988); Becchi 1990.

156. The single surviving "fragment" (fr. 148 Sandbach, from Stobaeus) does not inspire much confidence, and it is an obvious possibility that the title περὶ ὀργῆς in the "Lamprias Catalogue" of Plutarch's writings is a mistake for περὶ ἀοργησίας (but fr. 148 does not correspond to any section of the surviving essay). For a detailed discussion, in which the authenticity of the fragment is assumed, see Laurenti in his joint commentary, pp. 18–23; Becchi 1990, 84, also accepts it as authentic.

157. On *orgē* in Plutarch's lives, where it is an almost obsessive topic, see Alexiou 1999.

stirred <Theseus'> anger leads us to be more lenient towards the one who was overthrown by a stronger provocation," and so on at some length.[158]

It has been said that Plutarch does not aim at the uprooting of anger,[159] and while this is formally true, the form of *De cohibenda ira* is a dialogue in which one speaker recounts to the other the successful treatment he has undergone for *orgē*. The narrator begins by referring favourably to the "absolutist" Musonius Rufus,[160] goes on to give his views about therapeutic methods, remarks in passing that anger *(thumos)* is the most hated and despised of the emotions,[161] contradicts in detail arguments that are used in favour of anger by Peripatetics,[162] and in spite of Plutarch's admiration for Plato distances himself from Plato's moderate views on the subject.[163] Whereas Aristotle had coined the word *aorgēsia*, "habitual absence of *orgē*," to refer to a vice, an extreme of which he disapproved, for Plutarch this was something to be aimed for. Thus he seems, all in all, to be an "absolutist." We must not, he says, call things by pretty names, claiming that anger is *misoponēria* (righteous indignation).[164]

When, therefore, near the end of the essay,[165] Plutarch writes that "those of whom it is true that righteous indignation causes them frequently to be overwhelmed by anger [*orgē*], should get rid of its excessive and violent form," thereby implying that the righteously indignant may properly feel *moderate* anger, we are compelled to conclude that Plutarch did not work out a consistent position.[166] Or rather that he

---

158. *Comp. Thes. et Rom.* 3; for other reflections about anger, see especially *Coriol.* 21 and *Comp. Alc. et Coriol.* 2 and 4, where Coriolanus' anger is judged to have been worse than that of Alcibiades, *Comp. Phil. et Titi* 1. *Pericles* 5 seems to praise the statesman for his extraordinary control over his anger. These examples can be multiplied.

159. Becchi 1990, 86.

160. *De cohibenda ira* 2 (*Mor.* 453d).

161. Ch. 5 (*Mor.* 455e). For the antecedents of this thought (going back to Eur. *Med.* 1079–1080), and more or less exact parallels, see Oberhaus's n. on Greg.Naz. *De ira* 8.

162. Ch. 8 (456e–457c).

163. Ch. 8 (457c).

164. Ch. 14 (462e).

165. Ch. 16 (463b).

166. In ch. 10 (458c) he had already praised the *metriopatheia*, moderation in passion—which contrasts with *apatheia*—of Camillus, Metellus (presumably Numidicus, consul in 109 B.C.), Aristeides and Socrates.

followed the absolutist line in most of *De cohibenda ira* only because he was repeating a sort of large-scale topos.[167]

The slightly more latitudinarian view is also the one taken in *On Moral Virtue*.[168] In the lives, he sometimes condones anger or comes extremely close to doing so.[169] The younger Cato "was not quickly moved to anger or easily liable to it, but once angered he was inexorable," and Plutarch seems to have approved of the famous angry speech by which Cato, in opposition to Caesar, ensured the death of the subversive Catilinarians.[170] It may also be relevant that Calvisius Taurus, a friend and philosophical admirer of Plutarch's, was an advocate of moderating the passions, and specifically anger, as against excluding them.[171] Like Cicero and Seneca, Plutarch was inconsistent. Now it is possible that in Plutarch's case the reason for this was a real development in his philosophical views; more probably, he made use of a familiar literary form to put forward in his monograph a purer and simpler view than his own.

On one subject Plutarch devised an interesting compromise (it may not really have been original with him): faced with the philosophical tradition that there could be no such thing as divine anger, but also with an ancient tradition and a widespread conviction that gods were sometimes angry, he offered this solution: the Olympians, the real gods, do not show anger; only lesser divine forces do, the Furies *(Erinues)* and *daimones*.[172]

The most fertile ancient writer on the subject of anger whom we have not yet considered is the great physician Galen. He wrote about anger mainly in *De placitis Hippocratis et Platonis (On the Doctrines of Hippocrates and Plato)*, in a little-studied work *De moribus (On Morals)*, which is preserved in Arabic, and above all in *De propriorum animi cuiuslibet*

---

167. So Dillon 1977, 189; Donini 1982, 118.

168. *De virtute morali* 4 (*Mor.* 443c), 12 (451d, 452a–b). Cf. *De lib.ed.* 14 (*Mor.* 10e) for a sensible attitude.

169. E.g., in *Aratus* 45.

170. Plu. *Cat.Min.* 1, 23 (admiration for another display of Catonian *orgē*: ibid. 3).

171. Gell. i.26.10–11. Cf. Laurenti in his joint commentary on *De cohibenda ira*, pp. 26–27. Calvisius wrote some *Commentarii* (Gell. i.26.3) in which anger was discussed.

172. *De cohibenda ira* 9 (*Mor.* 458bc).

affectuum dignotione et curatione (On the Diagnosis and Care of the Passions of the Soul),[173] but also in many of his other productions. The first of these works he wrote in part to vindicate Platonic psychology, and he argued in favour of the tripartite division of the soul and against the monistic psychology of such Stoics as Chrysippus. But he did not derive his whole philosophy of the emotions from Plato, far from it. *Diagnosis,* his most important statement on this subject, begins on an eclectic note, referring to Plato and three other authorities, namely Aristotle, Chrysippus, and a contemporary Epicurean philosopher called Antonius. The latter wrote a book entitled *Concerning the Surveillance of one's own Passions (pathē);*[174] Galen's view of him seems to have been mixed: he accuses him of obscurity, but he nonetheless treats him as a writer worth commenting on.[175]

Galen's opinions about anger were certainly not Epicurean, not at least in any traditional sense. In fact he was an "absolutist," or nearly so; in other words, he was close to the Stoics:

> I thought the first step was to free oneself from one's *pathē* . . . And there are *pathē* of the soul which everybody knows: *thumos, orgē,* fear, grief, envy, and extreme desire. In my opinion, excessive vehemence in loving or hating anything is also a *pathos;* I think that the expression "moderation is best" is correct, since no immoderate action is good. How, then, could a man eradicate *(ekkopseie)* these things if he did not first know that he had them?[176]

Eradication is the aim. Galen denounces anger in now familiar terms: it is madness; the man who surrenders to it is a wild beast. It is a sick-

---

173. That is to put these three works in their chronological order: see *De moribus* p. 26 Kraus, and *De propriorum* 6.1. For *De placitis,* the best edition, with translation, is P. De Lacy's (*CMG* V.4.1.2, Berlin, 1978–1984). *De moribus* survives only in abridged form in Arabic: it was first published by Kraus 1939 and translated by Mattock 1972 and Rosenthal 1975. The best edition of *De propriorum* is that of W. De Boer (in *CMG* V.4.1.1, Leipzig & Berlin, 1937); it was translated by Harkins 1963 (who is not always precise) and by P. N. Singer (1997). For an account of Galen's views about the emotions, see Hankinson 1993.

174. *De propriorum* 1.1–2.

175. Apart from the fact that Galen called him *philomathēs* (xix.629 Kühn), very little else is known about this man (*PIR*[2] A798). Plato, Aristotle, Chrysippus: 1.4.

176. *De propriorum* 3.1–2.

ness of the soul, a vice which he hates.[177] One notes that although Galen is hostile in *De placitis* to Chrysippus, he does not even hint that the latter or any other Stoic went too far in criticizing *orgē*.

Galen has been accused of giving no clear answer to the question of the moral acceptability of anger,[178] and of having believed that there was good anger as well as bad.[179] These, I suspect, are errors, resulting from the fact that Galen believed in moral progression and, since he was of a more patient temperament than some of the great Stoic moralists, was prepared to think well of people who made progress towards overcoming their propensity to anger, even when their progress was not yet complete.[180]

> A man cannot become free from anger [*aorgētos*] as soon as he resolves to do so, but he can keep in check the repulsive side of his anger; and if he does this frequently, he will then discover for himself that he is getting angry less than he formerly did.

By careful training a man can reach the point at which "he will become only a little angry <even> over serious matters, if he will follow a practice of mine."

> When I was very young I imposed upon myself a rule which I have observed throughout my life, never to strike any slave of my household with my own hand.

And later:

> If you will never be a slave to passion [*thumos*], if you will always reason everything out and do everything you think without emotion to be best, you will be a good and noble man.[181]

All this is taken from *On the Diagnosis,* which must be regarded as Galen's definitive statement about anger. *De moribus* seems, however, to have taken up a somewhat different position: in the first place it distin-

---

177. Ibid. 5.2, 5.3–4, 5.5, 4.5.

178. Hankinson 1993, 203–204, suggesting that Galen must have been willing to accept the functioning of the "passionate element" in the Platonic soul.

179. So Manuli maintained (1988, 191).

180. The following quotations are from *De propriorum* 4.5–6.

181. Ibid. 5.4; cf. *De moribus* p. 31 Kraus.

guishes between two different anger-like emotions, a milder Arabic *ḥarad* which we feel towards those we love, and a more extreme Arabic *ghaḍab* which we feel towards others.[182] This distinction is unknown elsewhere with respect to Greek words for the angry emotions, and therefore it is impossible to be sure which Greek terms appeared in the original—perhaps *to chalepainein* and *orgē*, more likely *to aganaktein* and *orgē*.[183] In either case the distinction is artificial, though we may applaud the renewed attempt to differentiate the various terms. Here Galen also seems to have assigned a role to anger in some kinds of courageous behaviour,[184] whereas the more detailed exposition in his later work appears to exclude this.

We are almost at the end of the original ideas formulated in classical antiquity about the control of anger, though we are not yet near to the end of the writing of books on the subject. The emperor Marcus we can hardly count as a theoretician of anger control. He includes such control among the virtues he claims, and we shall consider in Chapter 10 the significance which such a claim had when it was made by an absolute ruler. Marcus was not altogether an orthodox Stoic with respect to the emotions (even if there could still be said to be an orthodoxy), for he says that "the sins of desire are worthy of more reproach than the sins of anger" (because they bring pleasure), a notion which he attributes to Theophrastus.[185] But he was an "absolutist" Stoic too in his opposition to *orgē*-anger.[186]

In an earlier chapter we encountered "ventilationism," the idea that unexpressed or repressed emotions get stronger and consequently need to be allowed a safety valve of some kind. No Greek or Roman seems to voice such thoughts until we come to the Neoplatonists. The ostensible origin is in the passage in Plato's *Timaeus* in which Timaeus gives a hydraulic account of certain angry emotions.[187] Plotinus de-

---

182. *De moribus* p. 31.

183. In *De placitis* iii.5.10, *aganaktein* seems to be milder than *orgizeshthai*.

184. *De moribus* pp. 31–32.

185. *To Himself* ii.10. Cf. Aristot. *Nic.Eth.* vii.6.1149b24.

186. *To Himself* vii.26; cf. 22. In ii.1 he says he cannot be angry *(orgizesthai)* with a relative, having explained that in a sense all humans are his relatives. In iv.3.3–4 he argues against *to duscherainein*, irritation.

187. Cf. Pl. *Tim.* 86e–87a.

vised a physical theory of the origins of attacks of *orgē*, and distinguished between the kind of *orgē* which distorts reason and the kind that proceeds from reason.[188] But the Neoplatonists must have continued to discuss the mechanics and handling of the passions, and when Iamblichus came to refer to the matter, he made a novel assertion which must count as the most important new idea about anger to appear in late antiquity.

The context includes the assumption that it is desirable to achieve *apatheia*.[189] Iamblichus' theory is that when the powers of human passions, the *pathēmata*, are "hemmed in on all sides," they grow stronger; if they are allowed to act briefly and within certain limits, "they rejoice moderately and are fulfilled," after which they are purified and can easily be brought to an end. This effect can be achieved by watching dramatic and "sacred" performances. This set of ideas was echoed and in two respects developed further by the Neoplatonist Proclus: performances of tragedy and comedy do not contribute to the purging of the passions, because they arouse them too much; but the statesman, the *politikos*, should nonetheless contrive the catharsis of the emotions somehow or other.[190]

More traditional ideas about the control of anger were often repeated in the fourth century. The most vocal pagan exponent of these ideas was perhaps Libanius. The cultivated Antiochene professor discoursed about the private and public ills that anger gives rise to, and roughly a millennium after Homer, he thought it worthwhile to write an attack on the character of Achilles.[191] In his autobiography he pointedly claims to have kept out of the *orgē*-inspired violence of the other students at Athens.[192] Since Libanius also wrote an encomium of Achilles,[193] we naturally doubt whether any of this needs to be seen as anything more, or less, than a demonstration that Libanius was a man of good character and an accomplished rhetorician.[194] In fact, as we

---

188. *Enn.* iv.4.28. Cf. Emilsson 1998, 348–351; Sorabji 2000, 203.
189. This and what follows are to be found in *Myst.* i.11; cf. iii.9.
190. *In Platonis Rem Publicam* I.49–50 (cf. p. 42) Kroll.
191. *Vituperatio irae* (VIII.315–324 Foerster). Achilles: VIII.282–290.
192. *Orat.* i.21; for the students' anger, cf. s.25.
193. VIII.235–243 Foerster.
194. Elsewhere Libanius demonstrates his skill by portraying an old *duskolos* (ill-

shall see, there were occasions in Libanius' career when discourse about anger—the anger of the emperor—came to have some severely practical importance.

Christian moralists also had much to say about anger. How ideas from outside the Graeco-Roman tradition affected their thinking, and how they dealt with the problem of divine anger, we shall see in a separate chapter (16). For the present it will be enough to describe the fourth- and fifth-century Christian literature on the subject.

Between the 360s and the 430s no fewer than five church fathers wrote discussions of anger which have survived. As we shall see when we come to investigate the role of anger in late-antique discourse about imperial power, there are plenty of other symptoms of a revival of interest in the subject. It was once again a sin worth denouncing— exactly why, we shall consider later. Brief descriptions will be enough, since these works are all highly derivative even by the standards of anger-control literature. In the 360s or 370s Basil of Caesarea wrote a sermon *Against the Angry,* in which he claims to be opposed to all anger but actually permits some because of Old Testament texts.[195] A few years later another Cappadocian, Gregory of Nazianzus, who studied at Athens together with Basil, wrote a verse attack on *thumos,* at 546 lines the longest of his onslaughts on particular vices.[196] John Chrysostom wrote a sermon called *About Rage and Anger:* it was ostensibly uncompromising, while allowing the faithful to hope that god

---

tempered man), *Decl.* 26–27 (VI.493–563 Foerster); these are comedy turns (cf. D. A. Russell 1983, 90).

195. *Hom.* 10 (κατὰ ὀργιζομένων), *PG* XXXI.353–372. Alluding to Ephesians 4:31 and quoting Matthew 5:4 (the Sermon on the Mount: the *praeis,* the even-tempered, will be rewarded), he concludes (ch. 7 = 371a) by saying that we should rid ourselves of all *orgē* and *thumos* and shouting. The less rigorous view in the previous chapter is ostensibly based on Matthew 5:22 (the more permissive of the two versions of the text) and on instances of justified anger in the Old Testament (368bc). Basil's younger brother, Gregory of Nyssa, also seems to have based his relatively permissive views about *orgē* on Matthew 5:22 (*De beatitudinibus* 6 = VII, 2, pp. 146–147 Jaeger; cf. also *PG* XLVI.61).

196. κατὰ θυμοῦ: *Carmen morale* 25, *PG* XXXVII.813–851. The date of composition was 382 (M. Oberhaus's commentary, pp. 1–4). It was the first disquisition on anger in verse, as far as is known. There is also a great deal about anger in the monastic writings of Evagrius of Pontus, a protégé of the Cappadocians: C. Stewart 2000, 66.

would punish those who provoked them.[197] Nemesius, bishop of Emesa, was a Platonist and therefore, in the short section of *De natura hominis* which he spends on *thumos*, less single-mindedly against it.[198] John Cassian, finally, wrote a long chapter in his *Institutiones* on *ira*.[199] These are all classicizing works, which form part of the amalgamation of Christianity with those elements of classical culture which high-ranking ecclesiastics regarded as acceptable and profitable.

This then is the main philosophical tradition of the Graeco-Roman elite. At the end of antiquity comes a useful reminder that there were other currents of thought (apart from Judaism and Christianity). For a number of years the young Augustine was a follower of the third-century Babylonian sage Mani, who enjoyed widespread influence in the Roman Empire. As a Manichaean, so Augustine tells us,[200] he traced the evil in this world to a dyad consisting of *ira* and *libido*, anger and lust. It would be interesting to know whether the Manichaeans, too, were moral "absolutists" in either of these spheres.

When one considers how fortuitous our knowledge is of many of the works mentioned in this chapter, those of Philodemus and Antonius for instance, or Poseidonius' *On Anger*, it becomes obvious that there must have been many other philosophical books about the passions and about anger. But it is unlikely that anything very influential disappeared without leaving a trace.

What should the history of philosophy be like? Before leaving the philosophers for a while, we must comment on one aspect of this fundamental question. Two divergent views are in conflict, though there seems to be deplorably little concentrated discussion of the matter. On the one hand are ranged those philosophers who study the philosophers of the past (and here, naturally, we shall concentrate on those who study Greek and Roman philosophy). By and large such scholars try to understand and explain the views of ancient philosophers as products of chains of reasoning (and their interest is often in the real strength of the chain—that is to say, in the validity of the argumenta-

---

197. περὶ ὀργῆς καὶ θυμοῦ, *De ira et furore*, *PG* LXIII.689–694.

198. *PG* XL.692 (ch. 21). He says that *thumos*-anger is the *doruphorikos*, bodyguard, of reason.

199. *Inst.* viii ("De spiritu irae") (*CSEL* XVII, pp. 149–165). He was virtually an "absolutist."

200. *Conf.* iv.15 (p. 71, lines 29–30 Skutella).

tion). On the other hand stand those who (like the author of this book) maintain that both the interests and the conclusions of philosophers are very often influenced by social, political, religious and other factors. This conflict has sometimes been seen as a conflict between "internal" and "external" methods of constructing the history of philosophy, but that terminology may give unwarranted precedence to the "internal." It might be better to talk about "technical" and "cultural" explanations.

This divergence has long been familiar, in one form or another, to all intellectual historians. How severe it is at present this book may help to reveal, for while I attempt to treat Greek and Roman philosophers with respect, I also offer "cultural" explanations of certain trends in ancient philosophy. There are, or at least were until recently, experts on Greek philosophy who treated such explanations with disdain. These are the people who think or come close to thinking that "philosophy lives a supra-celestial life, beyond the confines of space and time."[201] This curious view can only be defended by pointing out particular "cultural" explanations that are insufficient to account for particular philosophical trends or conclusions.

Meanwhile there is serious work to do. The history of all philosophy has both technical and cultural aspects. The aim of this book, insofar as it concerns philosophy, is to discover all of the main reasons why ancient philosophers adopted certain specific positions concerning the morality of the angry emotions.

Appendix: Treatises on the Emotions and on Anger

The limitations of such a catalogue should be obvious, for other philosophers certainly wrote about anger: for example, Metrodorus and Hermarchus the Epicurean (see Philodemus), not to mention Cicero and Epictetus. The order here is chronological.

Author	Title	Evidence, in the case of works not extant
Xenocrates	περὶ παθῶν	Diog.Laert. iv.12
Aristotle	περὶ παθῶν	Diog.Laert. v.24
[Aristotle	περὶ παθῶν ὀργῆς	Diog.Laert. v.23]

201. Barnes 1979, ix–x.

Author	Title	Evidence, in the case of works not extant
Theophrastus	περὶ παθῶν	Diog.Laert. v.45
Epicurus	περὶ παθῶν δόξαι πρὸς Τιμοκράτην	Diog.Laert. x.28
Zeno	περὶ παθῶν	Diog.Laert. vii.4, 110
Dionysius of Heraclea	περὶ ἀπαθείας	See n. 94
Herillus of Carthage	περὶ παθῶν	Diog.Laert. vii.166
Hieronymus of Rhodes	(?) περὶ ὀργῆς	See n. 58
Bion the Borysthenite	περὶ ὀργῆς	Phld. De ira 2 (col. i.17)
Chrysippus	περὶ παθῶν, in four books	Diog.Laert, vii.111, etc.
Sphaerus	περὶ παθῶν, in two books	Diog.Laert. vii.178
Hecato	περὶ παθῶν, in two books or more	Diog.Laert. vii.110
Antipater of Tarsus	περὶ ὀργῆς	Athenaeus xiv.643
Poseidonius	περὶ παθῶν	Frr.30–34 E-K (all from Galen)
Poseidonius	περὶ ὀργῆς, in more than one book	P.Ross.Georg. I.22
Philodemus	περὶ ὀργῆς	
Q. Sextius[202]	?	Sen. De ira ii.36.1
Sotion	περὶ ὀργῆς	See n. 58
Seneca	De ira	
Plutarch	περὶ ἀοργησίας	
Galen	περὶ διαγνώσεως καὶ θεραπείας τῶν ἐν τῇ ψυχῇ ἰδίων παθῶν	
Ps.-Andronicus of Rhodes	περὶ παθῶν[203]	
Basil of Caesarea	κατὰ ὀργιζομένων	
Gregory of Nazianzus	κατὰ θυμοῦ	
John Chrysostom	περὶ ὀργῆς καὶ θυμοῦ	

202. There is insufficient reason to believe that the Augustan philosopher Arius Didymus wrote a peri pathōn, pace Cupaiuolo 1975, 88, but it is possible.
203. This Stoic-eclectic work, of quite uncertain date, survives; it was most recently edited by A. Glibert-Thirry (Leiden, 1977).

PART II

Anger in Society
and in the State

CHAPTER 7

The Heroes and the Archaic State

The first Greeks who thought and wrote about the negative consequences of anger were mostly, it seems, concerned with the world outside the household, with the community at large. And it is the history
of the control of angry emotions in society and the body politic which
we shall construct first, without (it is to be hoped) artificially keeping
out of sight what was being said about anger *within* the household.

Anger, or rather *mēnis* together with *cholos*, is the central abstract
theme of the Greeks' master-text, the *Iliad*. The first line of the poem
announces the *mēnis* of Achilles as its subject, and sets its tragic emotional tone:[1]

> Wrath—Goddess, sing the wrath of Peleus' son Achilles, murderous,
> doomed, that cost the Achaeans countless losses, hurling down to the
> House of Death so many sturdy souls (*Iliad* i.1–4),[2]

and the hero's rage, first against his overlord Agamemnon, later
against the Trojan prince Hector, gives the poem its principal structure.[3] Because Agamemnon had refused to allow Apollo's priest
Chryses to ransom his daughter, the god inflicted a plague on the

---

1. On the matter of tone, see J. Griffin 1976, 171–172.

2. Trans. R. Fagles, except that I have replaced "rage" with "wrath."

3. On the wrath of Achilles as the dominant theme of the work see, e.g., Kirk's
commentary, p. 46. But I do not share his view that the *Iliad* underwent a long period
of nearly verbatim transmission before being written down; see rather Morris 1986,

Achaean army, and agreed to relent only when Agamemnon, partly thanks to Achilles, had learned his lesson and resentfully given up his captive. To compensate himself, Agamemnon takes from Achilles the latter's favourite captive, Briseis. In response Achilles, who is only prevented by the divine intervention of Athene from making the conflict with Agamemnon far worse—he goes as far as to reach for his sword[4]—withdraws from the Achaean fight against Troy. The opening book of the poem gives an unforgettable account of the two leaders' steadily rising rage.

Achilles is now so lacking in loyalty that he asks his divine mother, the sea-nymph Thetis, to appeal to Zeus for a Trojan victory (i.408–412). He refuses to relent his anger against Agamemnon, though begged in reasonable terms to do so by a delegation of other authoritative heroes (ix.192–692). His withdrawal from the fighting has by now had severe consequences for the Achaeans, and his refusal to relent contributes to, can indeed be said to cause, the death of, among others, his dear comrade Patroclus.[5]

What does Achilles learn from these happenings? He quickly learns that one should not let anger lead one to disobey a god (i.216–218). Much much more slowly he learns a less obvious lesson. Grieving bitterly for Patroclus, he addresses his mother:

> I wish that strife would disappear from among gods and men, and anger [*cholos*] too, which makes even the wise man get into an evil temper [*chalepēnai*], anger which is much sweeter than trickling honey and spreads like smoke in the breasts of men—as Agamemnon king of men

---

85–88. For an especially stimulating discussion of the *Iliad* poet's treatment of anger, see Alles 1990.

4. "He [Agamemnon] broke off, and anguish gripped Achilles.
   The heart in his rugged chest was pounding, torn . . .
   Should he draw the long sharp sword slung at his hip,
   thrust through the ranks and kill Agamemnon now?—
   or check his rage [*cholon*] and beat his fury down?
   As his racing spirit veered back and forth,
   just as he drew his huge blade from its sheath,
   down from the vaulting heavens swept Athene." (i.188–194, trans. R. Fagles)

5. Patroclus also caused it himself by disobeying Achilles: compare xvi.684–691 ("fool that he was," xvi.686) and xvi.80–96 (see also Redfield 1975/1994, 106). In addition, his death was fated.

made me angry on this occasion. However, what is done is better left alone, though we resent it still, and we must by force curb the dear passion [*thumos*] in our breast.[6]

Achilles now directs his fury towards Hector, the slayer of Patroclus, with deadly effect.[7] In blind rage during the fight with Hector, he says, strangely as well as savagely,

I wish only that my spirit and fury would drive me to hack your flesh away and eat it raw for the things that you have done to me,

thereby seeming to proclaim at the same time the most extreme rage imaginable and the recognition of certain elementary limits.[8]

The last part of the poem turns on the question whether Achilles will relent his anger towards his now dead adversary. Will he yield to the entreaties of Hector's father, Priam (the supplication in Book XXIV is broadly parallel to the embassy in Book IX) for the return of Hector's body? Under divine orders and out of pity for Priam—but without any detectable relenting of his rage against Hector—he finally agrees to hand over Hector's remains, and the poem thus reaches a kind of resolution:

Then Achilles called the serving-women out: "Bathe and anoint the body—bear it aside first, Priam must not see his son."[9]

He feared that, overwhelmed by the sight of Hector, wild with grief, Priam might let his anger *(cholon)* flare and that he himself might once again be aroused, cut the old man down and break the laws of Zeus.

Many of the other individual humans in Homer are said to experience attacks of anger. For the *Iliad*, it is enough to mention the frequent outbursts of Agamemnon himself, or the raging of Diomedes, Priam or Paris. Patroclus was sent into exile as a boy because he killed

6. *Il.* xviii.107–113. The formal end of his anger against Agamemnon occurs at xix.67.

7. On the shift from the first anger to the second, see Lossau 1979, 125. Achilles' *cholos* towards Hector (it is never called *mēnis*): xv.68; xviii.322, 337; xix.16; xxiii.23.

8. *Il.* xxii.346–347. For the eating of raw human flesh as the imagined result of extreme anger, see *Il.* iv.34–36. Hecuba is less restrained in her desire than Achilles: xxiv.212–214. On vestiges of cannibalism in the heroic age, see Glotz 1904, 56.

9. *Il.* xxiv.582–586, trans. R. Fagles but slightly adapted.

another boy in a quarrel, "not wishing to, in a burst of anger [*cholōtheis*] about some dice" (xxiii.85–88). The anger of the heroes is commonly marked by scowling and insulting, and often by rapidly executed physical violence. Then there is the anger against Penelope's suitors and the maids which Odysseus keeps under control, or at least out of sight, for many books in the second half of the *Odyssey*, until the moment comes for revenge and punishment (Book XXII).[10] Sometimes it was difficult for Odysseus to restrain himself, for instance when he was insulted by the swineherd Melanthios (xvii.217–238), but, biding his time, he accepted the suitors' insults—for the moment.[11]

As for revenge in the Homeric world, no one feels embarrassment about exacting it,[12] and since Greek revenge is normally a result of anger, this implies that in principle the archaic Greeks saw nothing wrong with anger. Exacting revenge on an appropriate scale was not only entirely proper but often more or less obligatory; I take that to be what Achilles implies when he says (*Il.* xviii.90–93),

> For I have no wish to live and linger in the world of men, unless before all else Hector is struck by my spear and loses his life, paying the penalty for <killing> Patroclus the son of Menoetius.

Revenge can sometimes be very brutal: Melanthios suffered not only death but mutilation, inflicted by the lord Odysseus' underlings "with wrathful heart";[13] Achilles killed twelve prisoners of war to burn on

10. Odysseus is not said in so many words to be angry with the suitors, at least until xxii.59 (sometimes the poet seems to go out of his way to *avoid* attributing anger to him, e.g. at xviii.348; it is the suitor Eurymachus who feels *cholos*, 387). In the famous scene at the start of *Od.* XX, he is thinking evil thoughts about the suitors (5) when the maids emerge from his palace, provoking an angry reaction which he keeps to himself (which in ancient eyes could mean that he overcame his anger: Galen, *De placitis Hippocratis et Platonis* iii.3.2–5).

11. *Od.* xxiv.163. Concerning Odysseus' ability to control his temper, see Van Wees 1992, 136.

12. What we are talking about here is not revenge in a precise sense, but retaliatory violence (*timōria* in Greek), for although no dictionary and few commentators seem to notice the fact, English "revenge" normally follows a delay (cf. Burnett 1998, 2). Homeric Greek had a special word for "unavenged": *nēpoinos*.

13. *Od.* xxii.477 κεκοτηότι θυμῷ; he had tried to help the suitors at a crucial moment.

Patroclus' funeral pyre (*Il.* xxiii.175–176). Heroic revenge is, however, usually limited in certain ways.[14] What is most striking here is that the punishment for homicide in the Homeric world is normally exile, not more killing (it is an unanswerable question whether this was really the predominant practice in Homer's time). A certain stirring of decency leads Odysseus to insist that when vengeance has been completed, there should be no exulting over the dead ("for it is not holy").[15] But this is the man who, by controlling his own anger, had been able to exact revenge against superhuman odds—to the obvious satisfaction of the original audience.

It is to be noted that vendetta (in the English and French sense of an unending exchange of serious acts of violence) and even feuding (a sporadic long-term exchange of many acts of hostility) are little if at all known in the sources about archaic Greece,[16] let alone later. But, to repeat, retaliatory violence on an appropriate scale was not frowned upon.[17] In the *Odyssey* the hero expects that his revenge against the suitors—the appropriateness of which the poem never of course questions—will lead their relatives to attempt to exact further revenge.[18] The poet thought that this was a reasonable expectation.[19] When Halitherses tries to dissuade the suitors' supporters from such revenge, his advice is rejected by the majority of the Ithacans (xxiv.465–466), and it takes the intervention of a god to bring retaliation to an end. Athene instructs Odysseus: "Hold your hand, and bring this civil strife to a finish, lest you arouse the anger [*cholos*] of ever-watchful Zeus, the son of Cronus" (xxiv.543–544); and she imposes oaths on the contending parties. According to one commentator, we should see this conclu-

14. Cf. Gehrke 1987, 139–140.

15. *Od.* xxii.411–412, lines often deleted by editors. Cf. *Il.* xvii.19. But gloating is fairly common in Homer (Odysseus had gloated over the Cyclops): Saunders 1991, 19. On the end of the *Odyssey*, see Svenbro 1984.

16. Concerning the absence of feuding, see Parker 1983, 125. As to the meaning of the term, cf. Herman 1998, 610.

17. On the matter of scale, cf. Saunders 1991, 17.

18. *Od.* xx.42–43. He has expressed this expectation earlier too: see the commentary of J. Russo et al. on xxiv.413–548.

19. *Od.* xxiv.353–355, 430–434. It is not necessary to debate here the possibility that the last book of the *Odyssey* was a later addition; for the François Vase (ca. 575) as a *terminus ante quem*, cf. Burkert 1987, 47.

sion in general terms: Zeus and his daughter Athene will replace the old system of vendetta.[20] On the contrary—the feud might have continued indefinitely if gods had not intervened, as they needed to in order to give the story satisfactory closure. As to whether the poet is describing how vengeance worked in his own time, or imagining how it had worked in the heroic age, we shall return to the question.

No doubt Hesiod was giving a view of revenge which was widely accepted in his own and Homer's time when he recommended not a *lex talionis* in the strict sense (an eye for an eye), but something still more violent: "Be careful to avoid the anger of the immortal gods . . . If <a man> wrongs you first, offending either in word or deed, remember to repay him double."[21]

To return, however, to Homer and anger: his interest in it is still stronger than the above description suggests, for anger permeates the divine sphere as well as the human one. As soon as a god appears in *Iliad* I, he is angry:

> What god drove them [Agamemnon and Achilles] to fight with such a fury? Apollo, the son of Zeus and Leto. Angry [*cholōtheis*] at the king he swept a fatal plague through the army—men were dying and all because Agamemnon spurned Apollo's priest. Yes, Chryses approached the Achaeans' fast ships to win his daughter back . . . Down <Apollo> strode from Olympus' peaks, storming at heart with his bow and hooded quiver slung across his shoulders. The arrows clanged at his back as the god quaked with rage [*chōomenoio*], . . . and the corpse-fires burned on, night and day, no end in sight. (i.8–52)[22]

Gods are angry with mortals when their power is challenged, and when they think that they are receiving insufficient worship or deference,[23] and for a variety of reasons they are angry with each other.[24] The gods' frequent surrenders to anger in texts of this period proba-

---

20. Russo et al., commenting on this passage. They say "patriarchal" system, but patriarchy has nothing to do with the matter.

21. *Works and Days* 706–711.

22. Trans. R. Fagles, slightly adapted. The direct consequences of Apollo's anger continue down to line 487.

23. On the latter point, see Van Wees 1992, 93–94.

24. See, in general, Irmscher 1950.

bly reflect the way that men expected all very powerful beings to be-have.[25] Divine anger also provided an explanation of disasters that were otherwise inexplicable, such as the plague sent by Apollo. In the *Homeric Hymn to Demeter,* a seventh- or sixth-century text, the goddess's anger over the loss of her daughter, Persephone, which is a principal theme,[26] is said to be what caused a universal famine.[27]

Divine anger can be arrayed on the side of moral rules. Homer would clearly not have gone as far as a character in Aeschylus who claimed that the *kotos* (resentful anger) of Zeus was a beneficent rul-ing force,[28] but Zeus is emphatically said to get angry *(kotessamenos chalepēnē)* at those mortals who make crooked judgements in the agora and drive out justice *(Il.* xvi.386–388). This was not as exceptional as has been supposed.[29] In fact the evidence in Homer for the belief that the gods are concerned about the observance of the norms of human conduct is fairly extensive.[30] The laws of hospitality and the sanctity of oaths are supposed to be especially important to them. And when the gods intervene in cases of human anger, it usually seems to be to re-strain it, as with Athene and Achilles in *Iliad* I, not to inflame it.

Hesiod's gods, slightly later, are scarcely less irascible than Homer's.[31] Their anger is also used for moralizing purposes: both gods

25. Cf. Morris 1986, 125–126; but the view that Homer's gods differ from the heroes "only quantitatively, not qualitatively" is too simple, omitting as it does pre-cisely the human tendency to collaborate.

26. Lines 251–333, and also 83, 91, 338–339, 349–350, 354, 467–468. Cf. N. J. Rich-ardson's note on lines 305–333.

27. Cf. *Works and Days* 240–247. For divine anger as a cause of natural calamities in Near Eastern texts, see Considine 1969, 116–120.

28. That seems to be the implication of "the highest fear among mortals" in *Suppl.* 478–479.

29. By Redfield 1975/1994, 76. The gods are said to be against crime, and Zeus is apparently seen to preside over the rules of hospitality, *Od.* ii.66–68. One can easily see how Gastaldi 1987, 108, reached the conclusion that "in epic poetry these feel-ings [such as anger] are completely divorced from ethical implications," but it is not true.

30. For details, see Saunders 1991, 35–39. Parallels in Hesiod: Saunders 39. The ev-idence is set in its Near Eastern context by Considine, 1969, 102–107. For a cogent theory as to why Poseidon is angry with Odysseus in the *Odyssey,* see Lidov 1977.

31. *Works and Days* 47, 53, 138, 303, etc.; *Theog.* 315, 928, etc.

and men are said to be indignant *(nemesōsi)* with those who do not work.[32]

In epic times, to put it briefly, *mēnis, cholos, thumos* and other forms of anger seem to have been natural phenomena. Both gods and powerful mortals indulged in them as a matter of course, without shame. In the imagined universe of the *Iliad* and *Odyssey,* the gods and heroes need their anger, or at least some of it. It seems entirely natural that in this honour-conscious world (no need for us to decide whether it ever existed in this form) the heroes should be irascible, and that the greatest hero should be the most irascible.[33] But it is not in fact nature that is in question; rather, it is a precise social structure. Honour in this society leads to frequent expressions of anger for a number of more and less obvious reasons.[34] In the first place, the heroes are all warriors, and their prowess is demonstrated in warfare. Classical writers often argued that real courage was not in fact founded on anger, but ferocity linked the two forms of behaviour together, and the aggressiveness of the Homeric hero carries with it a measure of irascibility.[35] And we expect the angry hero to want to fight the enemy—which adds to the tension in the first two-thirds of the *Iliad.* The close association of anger and warfare may even be the reason why the second half of the *Odyssey* actually *says* little about Odysseus' anger, even though it clearly exists. In any case, the aggressiveness of the warrior tends to spill over into life within the community.[36]

32. *Works and Days* 303–306. Zeus protects justice, 225–285, but here his anger is merely implicit.

33. A number of scholars have attempted to describe the social ethos of the world inhabited by the Homeric heroes; I have found the accounts of Redfield 1975/1994 and Van Wees 1992 the most instructive. Neither, however, pays much attention to the anger of the gods. Not only were the gods prone to anger but so, quite often, were the *hērōes,* i.e. semi-divinized deceased humans: see Fontenrose 1968.

34. Few will agree with Vegetti 1995, 40, that in the Homeric world there existed no "shared moral order" which could limit the action of a hero. For the precise structures created by *timē* (honour), see esp. Riedinger 1976.

35. It is perhaps not altogether to the credit of Paris when he disclaims anger (*Il.* vi.335). The riddle of his anger has been much discussed (see Heitsch 1967), but it does not concern us here.

36. Cf. Van Wees 1992, 66–67.

Two other factors are important, I think, in making a measure of irascibility vital to the Homeric hero. The first concerns his relations with his approximate peers, with whom he is to some extent in competition—for honour, for booty (Chryseis and Briseis included), and ultimately for power—while also collaborating with them. This is not only a matter of increasing one's honour but also of retaining the honour one already enjoys, for the supply of honour is limited if not fixed.[37] The gods are similarly in angry competition with each other.

The second factor concerns the hero's social inferiors. Showing anger was a prerogative of the gods and of princes. Calchas the seer explains:

> A prince is the stronger one when he is angry with a commoner; for even if he swallows his anger [*cholos*] on the day itself, afterwards he preserves his ill-will [*kotos*] in his heart until he can put it into action. (*Il.* i.80–83)

That is how things are. One possible implication is that it is not (always) safe for the prince to let his anger show. But in any case, as the episode of Thersites in *Iliad* II shows, an attempt by a person of lower rank to express anger against a member of the princely order was likely to be severely suppressed.[38] Later on, it is true, the Achaean fighters are said to direct *cholos* against Agamemnon,[39] but that is probably a sign of the partial disintegration of his command. This is all reasonably clear, regardless of whether we think that the *Iliad* and *Odyssey* systematically support the interests of the princes.[40]

Since honour by definition has to be recognized, and the Homeric heroes do not go in for tacit assertions of superiority such as titles or special costumes (other than armour), they have to express their superiority as well as feel it. That leads them to let their anger show, both when they witness an attempt at disturbing the social order (which was rare, according to the possibly quite misleading impression given by Homer), and when they feel threatened by their peers. Thus

37. Cf. Van Wees 64–65.
38. Cf. Van Wees 83–85.
39. *Il.* xiii.108–113, xiv.50; cf. xix.85–86.
40. On this topic, see Morris 1986, 123–124.

Telemachus has to learn anger, with the help of Athene, in order to become an adult member of a princely family.[41]

It may also be suspected that Homeric anger often has yet another function, acting as a kind of "justification" for unpleasant or uncooperative behaviour. The *Iliad* requires Achilles to have a reason for his non-cooperation which the poet and his audience can respect. In later times, Achilles was occasionally mocked for having made a great fuss about very little. For the economy of the *Iliad*, his resentment has to take on the grandiose guise of *mēnis*, which is intelligible to the audience as the source of serious trouble-making.[42]

As to how to express one's anger, that is occasionally the subject of an internal debate in the Homeric poems. Odysseus of course has the prudence (again, with some help from Athene) to keep his indignation with the maids to himself (*Od.* xx.1–55). Achilles decides not to pass from words to violence against Agamemnon when Athene orders him not to and tells him that Hera "loves and cares for" both him and Agamemnon equally—which means that his status is assured (*Il.* i.190–222).

Now, the theory has been advanced that anger in general helps to maintain social hierarchy.[43] That is a very dubious proposition as far as contemporary life is concerned, but Homer might well have given his assent to something similar. It is noticeable that when Odysseus is putting a stop to the panicked flight of the Achaeans in *Iliad* II, he shows (feigned?) anger to those of inferior rank while remaining reasonably polite to the more distinguished. Still more to the point: when the mutinous Thersites makes his complaint, Odysseus reacts angrily and Thersites is put brutally in his place; popular discontent instantly disappears (so Homer would like his audience to believe).[44] That is what

41. Van Wees 1992, 126–127. "All of us humans here on earth are *duszēloi* [very touchy]," Odysseus artfully says to King Alcinous (*Od.* vii.307), meaning perhaps that Alcinous might have been annoyed by Odysseus' debatably appropriate behaviour.

42. I do not claim that I have exhausted here the functions of anger in the Homeric world; note for instance that in *Il.* xxiv.248–262 Priam is driven to anger by his grief.

43. So Plutchik 1980, 146–147; but his meaning is not wholly clear.

44. Odysseus and the panic: *Il.* ii.188–206. The Thersites incident: ii.211–278 (popular resentment: *koteonto*, 223). Cf. Finley 1956, 122–124. This is the earliest Greek instance, incidentally, of the anger of a collective.

ought to have happened. In later times, leading men had to choose their moments to be angry, especially if they were political leaders in free republics (this was something which Pericles and Julius Caesar were both well aware of). What the powerful needed in most ancient states, since the citizens were not usually as easily subdued as the followers of Thersites, was not anger, at least not openly displayed anger, but cunning and dignity and a reputation for magnanimity.[45]

While the poet understands that gods and heroes *must* feel anger and may be led ineluctably to act on their anger, he was in my view highly critical of the unrelenting anger of Achilles. Rather than taking a neutral position about all displays of anger, as has been asserted,[46] he was sometimes neutral and sometimes negative (at least in the case of Achilles), without losing sight of the heroic imperative which drove Achilles to behave as he did. The wrath of Achilles is already referred to as harmful *(oulomenēn)* in the very second line. Scarcely has the dispute begun when the wise old Nestor deplores anger, without taking sides:

> Alas, what great sorrow is coming to the land of Achaea! What pleasure for Priam and the sons of Priam, and what joy the other Trojans would feel if they knew.[47]

By the time we reach Book IX, the inaction which is the consequence of Achilles' anger has had dreadful effects.[48] Agamemnon, for his part, has now belatedly relented. It is plain that the senior emissaries he sends to Achilles see the latter's behaviour as excessive. They dwell on the harm the Achaean forces have suffered from his unrelenting wrath. "Come, Achilles," says Phoenix,

> tame your great spirit [*thumos*]. Your heart should not be pitiless, for the gods themselves come round, who have even greater prowess, hon-

---

45. Aristotle explains that aristocratic and oligarchic governments can survive if their leaders treat people decently (*Pol.* v.8.1308a3–13; v.9.1310a2–12 extends the principle to democracies).

46. Adkins 1982, 292–326, esp. 310. Lossau 1992, 60, says that anger was "ennobled" by Homer.

47. *Il.* i.254–284. His wisdom is made explicit, 253 (and for Nestor being sententious again about civil strife, see ix.63–64, a passage quoted in Philodemus, *De ira*).

48. So too has the anger of Agamemnon: Redfield 1975/1994, 95–97.

our and strength <than you> . . . For there exist Supplications, *daughters of mighty Zeus,* lame, wrinkled, sideways-glancing, and they occupy themselves with following Ate [Destruction] about. Ate is strong and swift, which is why she easily gives them the slip and runs ahead of them all over the earth, bringing harm to mankind. Behind her, the Supplications make things better. He who treats the daughters of Zeus with respect when they come near, him they praise highly and to him they listen when he requests something. But he who rejects them and flatly refuses—they go to Zeus the son of Cronus and beg that Ate may follow that man, so that he may be suffer harm and pay the price.[49]

Phoenix emphasizes the message by telling at length the story of Meleager: how Meleager, penetrated by anger "which swells the hearts even of the wisest" (ix.553–554), therefore withdrew from a war, and so came within an inch of ruining his own people (the Aetolians).[50] The story serves to bring home to its hearers that behaviour such as that of Meleager or Achilles has consequences for the community as well as for the individual. Phoenix's purpose was not to suggest that a hero should avoid feeling or expressing anger ("until now," he says, "there was nothing wrong with being angry," ix.523), but that he should be willing to yield to persuasion and relent. Meleager relented when he was told of the military consequences of his behaviour. And by postponing his reconciliation too long, Meleager found that he had to fight without the material compensation which he might have received. Not only Phoenix, but later Apollo and even Patroclus say that Achilles is not behaving like a human being.[51] On the day following

49. *Il.* ix.496–504. The speech is the longest in the *Iliad,* 172 lines, which indicates its importance (not just the loquacity of the elderly speaker). Agamemnon has already commented that Hades alone is truly implacable (ix.158–159), but that might be dismissed as a self-interested view. The divine messenger Iris uses a similar tactic with Poseidon at xv.203: "noble hearts can be won over." On the use of digressions in the *Iliad,* see Austin 1966.

50. *Il.* ix.529–599. As B. Hainsworth remarks (commentary on ix.524–605, p. 130), "the mythological paradigm is part of the Homeric rhetoric of persuasion." On the parallels between the Meleager story and Achilles', see esp. Edwards 1987, 226–227, and for bibliography on this point, Rabel 1997, 129.

51. Phoenix: *Il.* ix.515–526; Apollo: xxiv.39–54; Patroclus: xvi.33–35. See further Redfield 1975/1994, 7–8, who, however, seems to overstate (19–21) the degree to which the actions of Achilles are depicted in the *Iliad* as predetermined by his status.

the embassies described in Book IX, Achilles persists, trapped now by his angry vow even though his anger itself has receded and he admits the fact, and so Patroclus goes to his death.[52] Scholars have written lengthy commentary on what it is in Achilles' character which makes him behave in this way, but in Homeric terms the answer is plain: anger. And his decision not only runs counter to the interests of the community of which he still claims to remain a part[53] but also damages its main enterprise, warfare.[54]

The second of Achilles' two great angers was also seen by the poet of the *Iliad* as (in the end) excessive, apparently, for Zeus eventually disapproves of the way Achilles has treated the corpse of Hector.[55] Apollo had vigorously protested, saying that Achilles "has no decency in his heart," and that "it is unseemly to rage against senseless earth"—that is to say, a dead body (xxiv.40, 54). Achilles' protector Hera angrily protests (without defending Achilles' anger), but Zeus quickly settles the dispute in favour of Apollo.[56] Achilles has gone too far in pursuit of revenge.

Homer, I maintain, was attempting to teach his audience general lessons about anger, the central theme of the epic. But to gain a more secure idea of Homer's purpose, we must describe the context in which he wrote. The attitude of Homer—in my eyes, a single poet writing as well as singing in the late eighth or, perhaps more probably, early seventh century[57]—towards his original audiences is impossible to recover. That the story-singers (*aoidoi*) represented in the archaic epic are themselves respected figures[58] may involve an element of wishful thinking, but down-to-earth considerations show that the successful ones had the attention of some, at least, of the men of power. Without

52. Gill 1996c, 124–125, resists this. See, rather, Alles 1990, 173.

53. On this point, cf. Gill 142–143.

54. He has an answer: he does not *need* the honour of the Achaeans: *Il.* ix.607–608, with Van Wees 1992, 138.

55. *Il.* xxiv.113–115. Van Wees 129–130 seems to ignore this evidence.

56. On this dispute and how it is settled, see Long 1970, 127–128.

57. On the absolute chronology of Homer, see *inter tot alios* West 1995, Van Wees 1997, 216 (both in favour of a seventh-century date). My argument would not be radically affected if there were no single master hand.

58. See Segal 1992. For their activities and audience, see also Thornton 1984, 25–31; Burkert 1987, 47–48.

the assistance if not outright patronage of the well-to-do, the *aoidoi* could not have functioned successfully, unless they were themselves well-to-do, of which there is no sign at all. Only a person of extraordinary resources, such as a local monarch, could afford the social occasions at which the story-singers commonly performed, or the writing material, presumably papyrus, that was necessary for the writing-down of poems of Homeric length. The corollary is that such local grandees sometimes felt intense interest in the bards' productions. The very fact that story-singers—and they alone, apart from seers, priests, physicians and builders—sometimes had the attention of the kings and lords of archaic Greece in virtue of their esoteric skill[59] certainly gave them opportunities and responsibilities for shaping the behaviour of their hearers. The story-singers probably could not rely for their living on the large-scale Panhellenic gatherings of the kind apparently first instituted in the eighth century (the Olympic Games and so on), and it may be doubted whether these were the initial targets.[60] They needed lords.

The expression "civil society" has become one of the vaguest in the language, but we cannot avoid it. State structures—"civil society" in the older pre-Hegelian sense of the expression[61]—were beginning to emerge in some places in Greece well before 700 B.C. The colonization of several new cities in the West during the 750s and succeeding decades showed that communities were learning the advantages of cooperation.[62] This had led to the attractive suggestion that Homer, being aware of "the dangers of the old aristocratic belligerence for the new ventures into cooperation," may well have devised the plot of the *Iliad* with this in mind.[63] But this formulation is unsatisfactory, for the poem

59. See *Od.* xvii.384–385, and commentators.

60. In spite of Wade-Gery 1952, 14–18 (who picturesquely remarked that "for the performance of the *Iliad* we have to suppose something comparable to Wagner's Bayreuth Festival," 14); Morris 1986, 123; and others.

61. Later we shall be concerned with "civil society" in a wider sense—the entire agglomeration of a population's shared institutions and practices. For the older sense, which lasted from Aristotle (*Politics* i.1.1252a7, *hē koinōnia hē politikē*) to Kant, and the Hegelian transition, see Riedel 1969, esp. 141–166; Cohen & Arato 1992, 83–91.

62. Cf. Snodgrass 1986, 14. The fortification of Smyrna, which used to be dated to the ninth century and so played an important part in the history of the polis, is now dated to the seventh century.

63. Thornton 1984, 147.

contains no hint that belligerence, in a precise sense of the term, is bad, or that wide-ranging cooperation is among the poet's concerns. The missing ingredients are two: they concern the military functioning of the early state, a large part of its raison d'être, and its methods of internal dispute settlement.

The problem of individual anger is likely to have been a pressing one in the archaic Greek cities in which the *Iliad* gained and retained its following. These were communities in which the social contract was limited and fragile: in many places about 700 B.C., the Greek city-state was still emerging from the pre-polis community,[64] and it was a place without strong built-in authority, a place where the claim of the city-state on the individual, and the right of the city-state to restrain the behaviour of the individual, must constantly have been in question.[65] Even kings were relatively weak and insecure.[66] Any military operation, indeed any common undertaking, might be weakened or destroyed by the angry quarreling of its leaders.[67] The military cohesion of the city-state was often no doubt the most pressing issue, given the quite belligerent character of the entire culture and the high price of defeat in a world of agrarian economies. The activity which above all put a strain on the cooperativeness of the members of these early city-states was warfare, in which the well-being of the community sometimes suggested that powerful individuals should subordinate their personal preferences to the ruler or rulers.[68] The plethora of "tyrants" who ruled in archaic Greece after coups d'état shows that ruthless individualists often came out on top.

64. For views about the state of the polis in the world described by Homer, see Runciman 1982, Starr 1986, Seaford 1994, 1–29. Seaford also raises the interesting question of Homer's silence about vendetta. The formulation I use in the text is not intended to deny the rethinking of Greek state-formation which is exemplified and required by C. Morgan's paper on the *ethnē* (Morgan 1991). For a theory about the particular relevance of the *Iliad* to colonies, see Alles 1990, 182–185.

65. Was anger felt to be especially characteristic of town life? The occupational rivalries Hesiod refers to—those of potters, builders, beggars and singers—point in that direction.

66. Raaflaub 1989, 28–29. See also Geddes 1984, 28–36, who, however, exaggerated the point.

67. Cf. Thornton 1984, 146.

68. We need not decide here between competing views about the formations that were most used in archaic Greek warfare. For a persuasive account, see Snodgrass 1986, 14–17.

At the same time, the struggle to replace a system of private vengeance with a system of criminal law was still at a very early stage of its development: this was in part a struggle against anger. A large proportion of early criminal law concerned crimes which were likely to have their origin in uncontrolled anger, and likely to be avenged in anger. We may speculate that in Greek society when it was still stateless, displays of anger played a very important part in settling disputes, for the anthropological literature shows that in such societies disputants "try to mobilise public opinion in support of acts of self-help" or turn to arbitration;[69] in either case the archaic Greeks will have given full vent to their indignation. In the worlds of Homer and Hesiod, strife tended to spread from individuals to groups.[70] Both poets probably recognized that, as one scholar has written in a legal context, "the animosity of some injured parties would, if unchecked, be destructive to the community."[71]

In other words, Achilles should be seen not only as an anachronistic relic of a past, partly mythical age, but as an emblem of the lack of cooperativeness and discipline which might easily have made a leading man a danger to his own city-state at the time when Homer was a poet. For present purposes it matters little whether there ever actually existed a world with the social and political characteristics described in the Homeric poems, because the interest of Homer's behavioural instruction is independent of his historical "accuracy."

The specific appropriateness of the *Iliad* for its own time raises the question whether Homer's predecessors had previously told a broadly similar story about the wrath of Achilles. It can be assumed that storytelling bards had been singing about Achilles for generations before Homer, and the poet himself, as it happens, indicates clearly that other poets had often recounted the heroes' wrath.[72] It seems very

---

69. Humphreys 1983a, 230, with references. See also Lintott 1982, 18–22.

70. Latte 1946, 66–67 = 1968, 238 (also in Berneker 1968, 83). *Il.* xviii.502 is the *locus classicus;* cf. Ar. *Clouds* 1322–1323.

71. Saunders 1991, 17. He sees in Homeric society "a strong revulsion against extreme behaviour." For an earlier account, see Latte 1931 = 1968, 252–267 (also in Berneker 1968, 263–314).

72. *Il.* ix.525 (cf. J. Griffin 1986, 43). Some Homer critics used to argue that there must have been an older version of the *Iliad* without the resolution of Achilles' sec-

likely that the story of the wrath of Meleager was in some sense a fore-runner of the *Iliad*.[73] There is, however, no way of settling the issue whether the *Iliad* was the first epic, or the first written epic, to portray the broadly negative effects of a hero's unrelenting rage. It seems un-likely that the idea was wholly original, yet the theme of anger is han-dled so artfully in the *Iliad*[74] that this aspect of the poem, at least, should probably be seen as the work of a single man, or of at most two or three successive poets.

The early history of the Homeric poems invites speculation. What did it mean to put them into written form in a world in which quick-reading literacy was a special skill? Was this decision—which may not have been made by the poet himself but by a patron—inspired in part by a wish to propagate ideas? It is at least a plausible hypothesis that well-to-do patrons saw the poems as reinforcing certain social struc-tures and certain notions of behaviour.[75] Having more or less taken written form in the decades after rather than before 700 B.C., the *Iliad* and *Odyssey* had to compete for a long period with other epics, and did not achieve their Panhellenic dominance until the late sixth century.[76] Of all the epic-singers of archaic Greece, Homer was the one who eventually gained by far the greatest fame. What counted in this pro-cess of far-from-natural selection? In the case of the *Iliad* it would be reasonable to guess that this was in part because the wrath of Achilles continued to arouse intense interest.

---

ond anger provided in Book XXIV: see Burkert 1955, 99–100, 127–128. See *Od.* viii.74–82 for another narrative song about a quarrel (between Odysseus and Achil-les); Finkelberg 1998, 145–147, comments on this passage.

73. Cf. Lesky 1968, cols. 757–759; R. Janko on *Il.* xiii.459–461; Alles 1990, 182.

74. Consider, for instance, how the fearsome quality of Achilles' anger is rein-forced by the parallel anger of Apollo in *Iliad* I, the often commented-on skill with which Odysseus and Phoenix try to mollify Achilles in Book IX, the way in which Patroclus stirs Achilles' pity in Book XVI, etc., etc.

75. Cf. Morris 1986, 123–125. For the suggestion that the leading men of Homer's time claimed legitimacy by associating themselves with Mycenaean heroes, see Morris 128–129.

76. Cf. N. J. Richardson's edition of the Homeric Hymn to Demeter, pp. 5–6. But the story told in the *Iliad* was perhaps not finalized until the fifth century (Lamberton 1997), and the crucial ideas about *mēnis* and *cholos* may not go back as far as 700.

There are signs in Hesiod at close to the same date that a kind of debate was taking place about the advantages and disadvantages of anger. Such is the impression strongly given by the lines at the beginning of the *Works and Days* in which Hesiod distinguishes between good strife and bad strife *(eris)*[77] and goes on to say without a strict logical connection that it is good for there to be competition,[78] for

> potter is angry [*koteei*] with potter, craftsman with craftsman, beggar is jealous [*phthoneei*] of beggar, and singer of singer.

Now *eris* is not anger, though it may give rise to it, but *kotos* is in fact a kind of anger. There may be nothing more here than existing proverbs[79] about the nasty effects of the division of labour, but the question whether *kotos* is a good thing is implicitly raised.

But Zeus, says Hesiod,

> has ordained this law for humans, that fishes and wild animals and birds should devour one another, for justice [*dikē*] is not in them; but to mankind he gave justice, which proves far the best.[80]

This was still a sermon which needed to be preached in the early seventh century B.C. (and it is still needed in the twenty-first century A.D.), when both criminal and civil law were as yet rudimentary even in the most advanced Greek city-states.[81] Homer and Hesiod can be said to have made a case for anger restraint at a time when the Greek city-state was coming into being. It was an important function of archaic Greek discourse about anger to make it easier for citizens to coexist effectively.

The early history of Greek law is too poorly known for us to give any chronology to the process in the eighth or seventh centuries. Homer

77. *Works and Days* 11–26. The word *eris* had been applied by Homer to the conflict between Achilles and Agamemnon, *Il.* i.8.

78. The coherence of this passage is well explained by Gagarin 1990. The immediate reference is presumably to Hesiod's own *Theogony*, lines 225–232.

79. See M. L. West's commentary.

80. *Works and Days* 276–279. See also *Theogony* 75–93 (the Muses help princes, *basilēes*, settle disputes peacefully in the agora [89]).

81. The large literature can be approached through Humphreys 1983a and Gagarin 1986.

and Hesiod themselves are the best evidence. Homer ascribes to the heroic world rudimentary law courts, and it is a reasonable guess that in his time courts, where they existed, functioned in the way he describes. This will have meant without written statutes, and without any official assistance in executing a favourable judgement. But at least there was the beginning of a judicial system.

Neither *dikē*, however, nor written laws would ever in themselves guarantee the cohesion of the city-state, and the discourse about anger had implications which went beyond civil society in the restricted sense of state institutions. The citizens also had to *wish* to keep their disputes within the limits imposed by law. They had to be willing to restrain their own anger. This involved nothing less than, in Norbert Elias's words, a "transformation of the whole structure of our personality,"[82] and the appearance of a new kind of man who desires to meet something like Aristotle's standard of "even temper" *(praotēs)*.

The ideal of social life which for Homer is the opposite of unrestrained rage was conveyed to Achilles by his father, Peleus, when the son was setting out for war—it is *philophrosunē*, friendliness or affability *(Il.* ix.256). Peleus did not explain to his son how to combine *philophrosunē* with the behaviour of a heroic warrior. However, the public project which the Greeks began in the archaic period and continued in classical times was not simply the construction of the polis as a political form or of a set of criminal laws for each city-state. They also constructed a system of social regulations which touched on many spheres of life, and at their most ambitious made *philophrosunē* into a sort of ideal, without of course giving up the agonistic aspects of their culture. The *Iliad* heroes already appear to think, part of the time at least, that it is inappropriate for them to exchange angry words, for—so one of them (Aeneas, addressing Achilles) asserts—that is how women behave (xx.251–255):

> What need is there of strife and quarreling between us? As if we were women who get angry about some bitter conflict, go out into the middle of the street and quarrel with each other, saying many things that are true and many that are not, <for> anger urges them to.

82. Elias 1988, 180.

At the games in *Iliad* XXIII, Achilles—of all people—tells angry Ajax and Idomeneus to stop their petty quarreling, *epei oude eoike*—because it is indecorous or, perhaps, unreasonable (xxiii.473–493).

Help can be obtained here from Elias's book *The Civilizing Process* (1939), which attempted to trace the formation of the state and the growth of civilized society in the early-modern West, with the latter process depicted as above all the rise of emotional self-control.[83] The civilizing of society began, in Elias's view, in the sixteenth century, and he took practically no notice of the first time it occurred, in antiquity.[84] What induces the individual to control his aggressive instincts? Not only self-interest but the internalization of restraining doctrines.[85] Elias himself was acutely conscious of the difficulty of measuring such changes and of relating them to changes in social structure, but the internalization of restraining doctrines also took place, very imperfectly of course, over a long period in the history of archaic Greece. It can be glimpsed through the text of Homer and seen more clearly in later texts we shall shortly be inspecting.

In recent years, Elias's theory has become a classic and has been subjected to a good deal of criticism, merited and unmerited.[86] In my view, he described a real historical process but did so partially and inaccurately, which was scarcely avoidable. What is suggested here is that the process had an important precursor in the classical world.

The possible objections to any such thesis as the one propounded

83. *Über den Prozess der Zivilisation* (Basel, 1939), cited here from the translation by E. Jephcott (Oxford, 1982). Elias paradoxically makes no reference to Freud. For a new view of the mediaeval origins of European civility, see D. Knox 1991, who is concerned, as Elias often was, with manners rather than emotional restraint. Several of the contributors to Rosenwein (ed.) 1998 make guarded use of Elias's framework.

84. He makes his excuses for this (48), and his comments about antiquity are mainly about economic formations (303–306).

85. *The Civilizing Process* 448–492, 499–524. For discussion see, among others, Opp 1983, 165–171; Kuzmics 1988; van Krieken 1989; D. Knox 1991, 108. Elias paid far too little attention to such matters as the imposition of actual state power through law courts and police. And it is most unclear whether the growth of refinement really has anything to do with the self-restraint of violence.

86. The more "patriotic" kind of mediaevalist is naturally offended by his simplistic treatment of the Middle Ages: Rosenwein 1998, 238. Elias's use of the mediaeval sources is now commonly judged unsatisfactory. For a harsh critique, see Robinson 1987. •

in these pages about Homer's views on anger are plain. In the first place, more and less attentive hearers and readers of Homer have been busily and subjectively attributing moral judgements to Homer since antiquity,[87] without in most cases elucidating the real beliefs of the poet. So we must be circumspect. The harm done by Achilles' wrath, or by Meleager's, does not necessarily mean that the poet himself thought that it would have been better if they had "behaved differently." But at least no one should deny that these heroic withdrawals were, in the epic, the causes of the harm described.

Furthermore the use of the word *mēnis* for the anger of Achilles against Agamemnon, even though it is also called *cholos,* may well set it apart from the sort of anger which an archaic Greek human might feel. Achilles is the only mortal whom Homer represents as being angry *(ochthēsas)* with a god (Apollo).[88] Can anything indeed which is said or implied by Homer about the behaviour of that "strange, magical figure" Achilles, as Redfield called him, be applied to ordinary people?[89] "God-like" *(dios)* Achilles may be a degree too divine to be subject to human rules; at the same time, he is emphatically mortal.

In modern times, the "Hamlet syndrome" ensures that every middle-class member of the audience has the opportunity to identify temporarily with the Prince of Denmark, but is that how the mind of an epic poet's audience worked in early Greece? Did the high and the not-so-high members of Homer's original audiences see some of the actions he described as exemplary, and other actions as the opposite? I argued in Chapter 4 that a limited didactic intention was indeed present,[90] and we can assume that the poet was correct in supposing that his audience would be receptive to this. As a practical project, admittedly, conveying any large meanings was a severe challenge for the

---

87. Cf. Buffière 1956, 251–256. The view of Adkins 1982, 318, that the poet of the *Iliad* cannot have been trying to inculcate "cooperative excellences," is based on the fallacious supposition that he would in that case also have to have been teaching "quietism or pacifism," which he obviously does not.

88. *Il.* xxii.14.

89. The phrase is from Redfield 1975/1994, 28.

90. Even Verdenius 1970, 20–25, who argued against attributing too much didacticism to Homer, detected some in the social and moral spheres, and concludes that the moral of the story of Meleager "is meant for Achilles, but also for the audience" (25). For a theoretical range of possible audience responses, see Jauss 1982, 152–188.

poet of works as elaborate as the *Iliad* and *Odyssey:* one may wonder how many in the audience were ever in a position to take in the salient themes of the whole compositions.

Another possible objection to the thesis that, by telling the story of the wrath of Achilles in the way he did, Homer meant to deliver a "political" message might be that the poems seem to know nothing of the polis "in its classical political sense" (to use Finley's words).[91] But in fact the political polis is visible in Homer,[92] and in any case the suggested objection is fallacious, since it is behavioural instruction which we are prospecting for, and *that* might be found even in purely mythical form. Furthermore the poet, though he readily tolerates anachronism, would have made a grave, almost unthinkable mistake to introduce too much of contemporary political or social organization into his work.

A final objection might be that the *Iliad* contains so much *other* anger, both divine and human, besides that of Achilles. Why should Achilles give way if Agamemnon and Apollo, for instance, do not? But eventually Agamemnon *is* forced to relent, and Apollo does so too (quite promptly), for even the gods—with the exception of Hades—can be brought round.[93] In Aristotelian terms, what is wrong with Achilles' two great angers is that they do not continue for the right length of time, and some of the time at least they are not "in the right manner."

Homer can hardly be said to teach Aristotelian even temper. Quite apart from his glorification of military prowess, which could be considered perfectly compatible with even temper, he accepts great quantities of human and divine anger as being quite normal. It was hardly a great restriction to suggest that Achilles' treatment of the corpse of Hector eventually exceeded reasonable limits. What he does teach is a very limited kind of self-restraint, as was appropriate for his time. The effects of Achilles' anger against Agamemenon fall in part on Patroclus and on himself, but what makes the poem weigh so heavily is the fact that the effects fall on the community in arms: it is the

91. Finley 1956, ch. 2. The word is there of course: *Il.* xviii.490.
92. Van Wees 1992; see also Scully 1981; Morris 1986, 104; Seaford 1994, 1.
93. *Il.* ix.158–159, 497.

Achaean warriors who, through no fault of their own, suffer from the individual hero's lack of self-control.[94] The *Iliad* is, among other things, a lesson against uncontrolled and unassuaged wrath, both *mēnis* and *cholos*. To call it that is not to reduce it in any way, any more than it reduces the *Odyssey* to call it an epic of deserved and well-executed revenge.

In Chapter 1 I distinguished between conventional rules about when anger can be shown and non-conventional rules demanding stricter standards of emotional control or behaviour. It is to be doubted whether, in this respect, Homer went beyond reinforcing contemporary ideas which were already widely agreed to.[95] But he reinforced those ideas with such force that in later times commentators and the more simple sort of philosopher took him to have meant Achilles (and sometimes Agamemnon too) as an example of the awfulness of anger.[96] This became part of the Greek educational tradition. Eleven hundred years after Homer, Achilles was still the archetype of the excessively angry man.

Archaic Greek poetry after Hesiod presents, on the one hand, unembarrassed displays of anger, for instance in the poetry of Alcaeus and Semonides and above all in that of Archilochus,[97] and on the other hand, some interestingly critical comments about anger, most but not

94. "Quidquid delirant reges, plectuntur Achivi," as Horace disrespectfully remarks (*Epist.* ii.1.14).

95. Cf. Van Wees 1992, 134.

96. Among commentators see, e.g., *Schol. Graeca in Iliadem* ed. Erbse, I, 3 line 12; [Plu.] *De Homero,* however, which supposes that Homer took a sort of Peripatetic view of *orgē* (ii.135, p. 71 Windstrand), refers favourably to Achilles' rejection of the embassy in *Iliad* IX (ii.169, p. 93 W.).

97. See, e.g., Alcaeus, frr. 129, 348 (and Horace called his verses *minaces*, threatening, *Odes* iv.9.7); Semonides 7 West, the fountain of misogynistic literature, especially lines 17–18, where the angry husband is imagined knocking out his wife's teeth with a stone; Archilochus frr. 114, 172, 188. Some of the lines of Theognis mentioned below should be included here. Someone, an Epicurean apparently, later described Hipponax and Archilochus as the "trainers" of the irascible (Sext.Emp. *Adv.Math.* i.298–299). Archilochus was criticized for his abusiveness by Pindar, *Pyth.* ii.55—a sign of the times?

all of which are so lacking in context as to be hard to interpret securely.

The first general advice against anger in European literature seems to have been written by Sappho, whom I quoted earlier:

> When *orgē* is spreading through your breast, it is best to keep your yapping tongue in check.[98]

This may not of course mean that one is to forget one's anger, any more than the returning Odysseus did. And in its unknown original context it may have had to do with purely private relations. Nor is there any context for the fragment in the corpus of Theognis which pronounces as follows:

> Being angry [*cholōtheis*] with a man, don't reproach him with soul-grinding poverty. Zeus tips the balance this way and that, now to be rich, now to have nothing.[99]

Here the instruction is probably not directed against anger itself, but there is some suggestion of a recipe for cooling social conflict. Another fragment in which the poet announces that "nothing is more unjust than anger [*orgē*]" may, if it is authentic, lead in the same direction.[100] However, yet another Theognidean fragment apparently expresses a straightforwardly traditional attitude towards revenge for loss of possessions: the poet desires to drink the blood of those responsible.[101]

Two writers lead us unequivocally back to anger's nasty political effects, namely Alcaeus and Solon. Alcaeus wrote about the desirability of forgetting *cholos* and "relaxing soul-consuming strife" in the context of violent conflict in seventh-century Mytilene.[102] In a poem written by the early sixth-century Athenian legislator Solon, the control of anger within the city is seen as vitally desirable: the culminating effect of *eunomia* (good order or lawfulness) in the city is that it

98. Fr. 126 Diehl = 158 Voigt.
99. Theognis lines 155–158. MSS read χολωθείς, some editors χαλεφθείς, following Stobaeus.
100. Lines 1223–1224.
101. Lines 349–350. Cf. also lines 188–192.
102. Fragment 43 Diehl. See Page 1955, 235–237.

straightens out distorted judgements, pacifies the violent, brings discord to an end, brings to an end the anger of ill-tempered strife [*eridos cholon*]; it makes all men's affairs correct and sensible.[103]

This is part of Solon's wider advocacy of moderation and restraint inside the polis.[104] One consequence was that 200 years later he, and Cleisthenes too, were associated in the public mind with the virtue of even temper or *praotēs*.[105]

The lines of Sappho, Theognis and Alcaeus cannot be given any precise function, but Solon's poem about good order was evidently meant for as many of the citizens of Athens as possible, and it must have become and remained rather accessible, since it was quoted at length by Demosthenes (xix.255)—without the slightest intention of bringing to an end "the anger of ill-tempered strife." Solonian Athens was not as democratic a state as fifth- and fourth-century Athens usually was, but it is evident that it allowed a good deal of political freedom to many of its citizens, evident too from what happened a generation later, in the time of Peisistratus, that the threat of political violence was real. Solon's lessons were intended to help the Athenians to survive their own freedom.

It seems all the more logical that Solon should have written in favour of *eunomia*, since he presided over reforms which certainly sprang from angry discontent with current conditions and provoked angry discontent from those who stood to lose by those reforms. Of course the political significance of calls for anger restraint will always depend on who—rich or poor, for instance, oligarchs or democrats—is called upon to relent, to end his ill-temper, or whatever the precise formulation may be, and in what circumstances. The call itself, as it survives as a text for us to read, is ambiguous, and not easy, in this case, to fit into the story that is told about Solon in every book about Athenian politics. Normally one reads nowadays of a moderate Solon who brought

103. Solon fr. 4.36–39 (the translation is mostly M. L. West's). Cf. Seaford 1994, 100.

104. See Saunders 1991, 46. For visual evidence of the rise of social solidarity in early sixth-century Athens, see Hölscher 1999, 27–28.

105. Isocr. *Areop.* 20. For the association of democracy and *praotēs*, see Dem. xxii.51, [Aristot.] *Ath.Pol.* 22.4, etc. (and see also M. D. Hall 1996, 74). But *Ath.Pol.* 16.2 also calls the tyrant Peisistratus *praos*.

about some palliating reforms of a limited nature in a socially stratified system which he had no intention of revolutionizing.

Whose anger did Solon wish to calm? Those who were dissatisfied with changes which did not go far enough? Or those who lost something in the process of reform? Perhaps not that of any single social group. If we knew how Solon's text circulated, we might get closer to an answer. A written text strongly suggests that a social elite was the legislator's target.[106] But that does not necessarily mean that the *cholos* he wished to staunch was that of the rich. If it was his policy to secure the privileges of the elite "by granting minimal rights to the poor,"[107] it may well have been the latter who felt anger, before or after this policy was put into effect. And it is possible that the primary conflict in Solonian Athens was not between social classes at all, but between clans.[108]

It may plausibly be supposed that Plutarch was referring to a piece of authentic legislation when he wrote that a Solonian law forbade "speaking ill" of people in temples, in court, in official buildings and at games, for the fines Plutarch mentions are so small as to sound archaic.[109] If so, Solon's interest in civic tranquillity is confirmed.

The other sixth-century writer who would probably be of great interest here if his work were better preserved is Italy's first great poet, Stesichorus. We know, for example, that he wrote at some length about the struggle between Eteocles and Polyneices, the sons of Oedipus,[110] a story which could easily be used as a morality tale directed against rage and was so used by fifth-century poets. It is only with Pindar and Aeschylus that we can pick up the trail once again.

106. Cf. W. V. Harris 1989, 61; Ober 1989, 158.
107. Ober 64.
108. As once was argued by Ellis & Stanton 1968.
109. Plu. *Sol.* 21.1; cf. Wallace 1994, 111.
110. See esp. fr. 222(b) Page-Davies (*PMGF* I, pp. 213–218).

CHAPTER 8

Living Together in the Classical Polis

The political and social dangers from excessive anger ebbed and flowed, for every Greek city-state had its share of violence, both political and non-political. When the sources start to grow slightly more abundant, in the 460s and 450s, anger, angry behaviour and their effects on the city already seem to be under discussion, in Athens at least, and the theme is developed in various ways in fifth- and fourth-century texts. The earlier tradition, say at the time of the Persian Wars, must have been mixed: on the one hand, there was a Solonian doctrine of self-restraint, sketched in the previous chapter. On the other hand, there was the memory of fierce political struggles, including the expulsion of the Peisistratids, a story which must in all its versions have been full of anger[1]—and it was a story which in the eyes of most Athenians had a happy ending.

The classical Greek city could not do without the military virtues, and Athens least of all, after it committed itself in the 470s and 460s to maintaining a widespread hegemony. Every city was more or less constrained to fight at fairly frequent intervals. Meanwhile each city had its own internal strife, usually organized along class lines and in any case concerned with the distribution of power. Neither form of struggle, external or internal, made angry personalities valuable, but they did to some degree privilege aggressive leaders, and aggressive followers too. Athens' imperial power was the product of, among other things, persistent aggressiveness towards the outside world, and *praotēs*

---

1. Cf. Arist. *Pol.* v.10.1311a33–39.

was often lacking, even in the early decades. What was dangerous to Athens itself was the angry violence which made itself felt in internal politics in such vital years of reform and reaction as 462–461, 411 and 404–399.

These Athenians, in common with many other Greeks, had acquired, in and since archaic times, a historically extraordinary degree of political freedom. But it was always an asset which they could lose or squander. Some people, the Pericles of the Funeral Oration for example, articulated the reasonable idea that freedom's survival depended on the citizens' showing courage.[2] Which was a natural thought in time of war. For us, it is an almost equally obvious thought that preserving the freedom of the full citizens, and their privileges with respect to the other members of the community, required them to show self-restraint and mutual respect. In our times, after all, there are plenty of countries in which lack of self-restraint on the part of a few (there seem to be no ochlocracies nowadays) most distinctly limits the freedom of the citizen. Just think of Rupert Murdoch or Silvio Berlusconi.

The Athenians seem to a large extent to have internalized the notion that their freedom would only survive if they were able to limit the action of their own passions, including especially their own anger.[3] For there to be courage, there had to be *thumos,* spirit, passion, but on the other hand if there was too much *thumos*-anger, terrible civil conflict *(stasis)* was a likely consequence. Plato says almost as much in *Republic* VIII, where he claims that democracy leads to a de facto anarchy in which even the slaves and the animals are infected with the spirit of freedom. After that, so he maintains, comes tyranny (viii.563b–e).

Who, then, spoke against the angry emotions in the changing political conditions of fifth- and fourth-century Athens, and on what grounds and for what reasons? To what extent was the train of thought outlined in the previous paragraph articulated and believed in?

The great channel which connected men of ideas with the mass of the citizens in classical Athens was the tragic theatre, which was perhaps not the less important for being restricted to a single annual festival

2. Thuc. ii.43.4; commentators point out the parallels in 36.1 and v.9.1.
3. See Gomperz 1927, 28–29; Vegetti 1995, 59–60.

of nine plays. Thirty-two plays survive, plus a large number of "fragments," from a period of seventy years. As we have already seen, the tragedians probably intended to impart lessons from time to time about matters of moral and political principle. That does not mean that they constantly strove to win their audiences over to intellectual points of view, certainly not to novel ones. Much of their purpose was not argumentative at all. But when an acute critic writes that Sophocles "presupposes a consensus on [moral and intellectual] issues; and his aim was to move and entertain,"[4] that is a mixture of truth and gratuitous assumption. We have no reason at all to suppose that there existed a consensus on all the larger issues which a poet might address, or that a poet would refrain from endorsing or, if he was as original as Euripides, contradicting the dominant opinions.

What the tragedians made their characters say was dictated in the first place by the needs of characterization and plot, of course. A great deal might be required by the conventions of the genre itself.[5] Furthermore, what characters said on the tragic stage was not necessarily taken with great solemnity by all of the audience, and contemporaries must have known, as Aristotle did (*Pol.* viii.7.1342a18–21), that theatrical audiences were partly cultivated and partly banausic.

Nevertheless, the great dramatists were certainly capable of combining characterization and plot with advice to the audience. And the audiences were large in relation to the size of the total citizen body, with probably about 15,000 persons attending; partly in consequence, the occasion was special. Famous or notorious plays were remembered years after they were performed. Furthermore, Athenian theatre was in a sense official, the chorus—that is to say, the right to produce a set of plays at the festival of Dionysus—being granted by the archons. This award offered the poet an unrivalled opportunity to put a point of view before the citizen body. And he could expect his audience to express its reactions.[6]

---

4. Heath 1987, 77.

5. See Parker 1983, 14–15.

6. See Pl. *Rep.* vi.492b. By implication these would be political feelings. For the view that the winning of a first prize at the Great Dionysia reflected, to some extent, popular approval of a play's perceived message, see Martin 1958; but it is hard to define what it was that made Euripides unpopular with the judges (influenced by mass

What then is Athenian tragedy really about?[7] The central difficulty is to decide the relative importance of individual and public concerns. Are we to think of Orestes and Oedipus, Clytemnestra and Hecuba, Jason and Theseus, as individuals struggling with personal trials, or as public figures acting in dramas that were in some sense political? The rage in Aeschylus' *Seven against Thebes* (467 B.C.) is a case in point: the quarrel between the brothers Eteocles and Polyneices is a family affair, but it can also signify the horrors of bloody fratricidal strife metaphorically and much more widely. Here we have to do with civil society in the simplest sense. And we always have to bear in mind that few of the things that happened to an Athenian male were considered to be his exclusively private concern. The family relations of the figures who peopled the tragic stage were also, to varying degrees, matters of public significance.

While anger was frequently alluded to and represented in the tragic theatre of fifth-century Athens, what the tragic poets wished to say about it, if anything, is always hard to state with confidence. No two scholars will read the evidence in exactly the same way.

At first the theme is secondary or in the background. In Aeschylus' *Persae* (472) the anger of Xerxes is not explicit, although it might have been. The shade of King Darius praises the emotional balance of his predecessor Cyrus (a figure whom Herodotus used more emphatically in this connection).[8] In the *Seven against Thebes*, while the whole plot

---

opinion?) and at the same time popular with those who granted choruses. For useful comments about the original audiences' likely reactions to tragedy, see Easterling 1997, 24–25.

7. According to a perceptive fantasy of J.-P. Vernant, "the true subject matter of tragedy is social thought and most especially juridical thought in the very process of elaboration. Tragedy poses the problem of law" (Vernant 1970, 279). But this is of course only one level of meaning. Tragedy represents horrendous events within a few great mythical families (Arist. *Poet.* 13.1378a19–22): hence it "touch[es] many issues, including politics, social conditions, the relations between men and women [and, it may be added, between parents and children] and between humans and gods, and the world of timeless, universal unconscious fantasy and dreams" (Simon 1978, 91). The most important contribution to this debate in recent times is J. Griffin 1998.

8. *Persae* 767 (*phrenes* guided his *thumos;* cf. *euphrōn* 772), with H. D. Broadhead's n. on 769. For the view that the play shows a certain paradoxical ambivalence towards Xerxes, see Griffith 1998, 44–65.

concerns the armed struggle between the two brothers, its emotional content is not perhaps as heavily emphasized as it might have been (or as heavily as it was to be later in Euripides' treatment of the same story in the *Phoenissae*). Not that emotional extremes are lacking: Eteocles, the ruler of besieged Thebes, angrily denounces the Chorus of Theban Women for having panicked (*Septem* 181–202). The bitter hostility of Polyneices is described, and the Chorus admonishes Eteocles not to be carried away by passion (variously described) against his brother.[9]

In Aeschylus' *Supplices* it is the anger of Zeus which receives attention. It was maintained earlier that an old Greek tradition did sometimes array divine anger on the side of moral rules, and that is its role here. This anger is therefore presented in a wholly positive way.[10] The king and the city must give in to it.

Human anger can be just too: it happens to be at the beginning of the *Agamemnon* that we meet the first explicitly just anger in Greek literature—the *thumos*-anger which took the Greeks to Troy.[11] But it is the internal harmony of the city which is conspicuously under discussion in the *Oresteia* (458). In the *Agamemnon* and *Choephori*, anger, though it is in ample supply, is not itself the subject of any other remarkable comment, but in the *Eumenides*, the last play of the trilogy,

9. *Septem* 631–708. Polyneices is seeking revenge (638); he is well-named because Polyneices means "He of Much Strife" (658). The Chorus tells Eteocles not to be of the same emotional state (*orgē*, but the meaning "anger" clearly also impinges) as his brother (677–678). He must not be carried away by "*thumos*-filling, spear-mad Ate [Destruction]" (686–687) (LSJ translates *thumoplēthēs* as "anger-filled," wrongly). Many interesting details of this exchange, and of other tragedies, have to be passed over here.

10. The Danaid suppliants threaten Pelasgus, the king of Argos, with Zeus's *kotos*, angry resentment, if he does not have pity on them (385–386, 427). He sees the force of this: respect for Zeus's angry resentment is "the highest fear in mortal men" (478–479). The Argives bow to this threat (616), and the Danaids dwell on the positive consequences (625–709). The Egyptian pursuers of the Danaids are belligerent, showing their *kotos* (744, cf. 757, 763), but the Argives compel them to withdraw.

11. *Ag.* 48; this was accompanied by a desire for vengeance (41, 58–59), and these feelings result in intense bursts of rage (*orgas ateneis*, 71). It would be interesting to know whether here and in another fifth-century text in which just anger is spoken of, Soph. *El.* 610–611, there was some reluctance to couple fierce *orgē* directly with justice. Cf. also Eur. *HF* 276.

the question has to be resolved whether the anger of the Furies (the Erinues, the implacable spirits of vengeance) should be allowed to punish Orestes for his matricide. After the Athenian jury has in effect acquitted him, Athene has to pacify the Furies' continuing rage.[12] For a time they are unappeased, maintaining their *kotos,* but eventually the goddess's promises of honours in Athens win them over, and their *kotos* passes from them.[13] She has told them that they must not stir up anger between the citizens of Athens, "make them mad with wineless rages [*thumōmata*]";[14] the Athenians are instead to concentrate on foreign wars (which recalls the beginning of the trilogy).

As the end of the trilogy approaches, the Chorus of now transformed Furies prays that

> never may *stasis,* insatiable of evils, roar within the city, may the dust not drink the dark blood of the citizens and, out of passion for revenge [*di'organ poinas,* 981], eagerly embrace the city's ruin through retaliating murders.[15]

Whether taking up a position against the violent expression of vengeful, anger-driven feuding within the city in this fashion has a partisan political meaning is not immediately clear. In any case no attempt is being made to drive angry disputes, as such, out of the city: the poet imagines a way in which the Areopagus obtained (some of) its jurisdiction, and it is a milder jurisdiction than that of the Furies, but Athene is made to say, all the same, that the Areopagus will be *oxuthumos,* harsh-spirited, in judging.[16] Nonetheless it is obvious that the Eumenides' prayer against vengeance is an attempt to display divine support for a basic code of political coexistence. The sentiment was unoriginal, but its prominence in the *Oresteia* probably means that it had immediate relevance in the years just after the reforms (462) and

12. *Eum.* 796–880. Their anger is excessive: ὑπερθύμως ἄγαν, 823.

13. 881–915. But Athene does not envisage that the Furies will give up their potential for anger against those who deserve it: *Eum.* 937, with A. H. Sommerstein's note.

14. 858–863, esp. 860. The presence of lines 858–866 in the original play has often been doubted, but see the mainly convincing defence of them by Carey 1990.

15. *Eum.* 976–983 (for *organ* as "anger" here, see MacLeod 1982, 130 = 1983, 26). We need not decide whether there is a specific contemporary reference; Dodds asserted it ("a reminder of the fairly recent murder of Ephialtes and an appeal to the radicals not to pursue a vindictive policy," 1960, 24 = 1973, 52), MacLeod denied it.

16. *Eum.* 705. Cf. MacLeod 1982, 129 = 1983, 25.

the murder of Ephialtes, and also that bloody political strife was a reality or a lively danger. Since Aeschylus' support for the Argive alliance which was the centrepiece of the reformers' foreign policy is clear,[17] I take it that he thought that they were more likely to be the victims than the perpetrators of "retaliating murders"—indeed they already had been—but the opposite case can be argued. The campaign against vengeful *kotos* within the city is any case reasonably discernible.[18]

Prometheus Bound is perhaps more concerned with the angry emotions than any of the dramas so far discussed, but it is very hard to interpret, all the more so since it has been fairly conclusively shown not to be the work of Aeschylus,[19] and all the more so because we do not know the terms on which Prometheus was *un*bound later in the same trilogy. If the play were by Aeschylus, we might be more confident that Prometheus was putting himself in an equivocal position by not showing fear of the anger of the gods,[20] and that there was nothing at all wrong with Zeus's remaining wrathful until the end. As it is, we learn two important things from this play about (some people's) attitudes towards anger. One is what many Athenians, both at this date and later, would have felt was wrong with controlling one's anger: it would have amounted to unacceptable softness.[21] The other great novelty is that, for the first time in an extant text, anger is very clearly treated as a sickness (*PV* 375–380):

> *Prometheus:* . . . I will bear my present destiny, until the heart of Zeus is surfeited with anger [*cholos*].
> *Ocean:* Do you not understand, Prometheus, that words are the physicians of the illness of anger [*orgē;* or, of a sick disposition]?[22]

17. *Eum.* 287–291, 667–673, 762–774, etc.

18. It may well also be relevant that Aeschylus' lost and undatable play *The Myrmidons* (*TGF* III, frr. 131–142) seems to have presented Achilles in a poor light because of his unrelenting anger (cf. Dangel's edition of Accius, p. 291). But the fragments were read differently by Snell 1953 [1948], 104–105.

19. Griffith 1977; West 1990, 51–72. The *PV,* like Sophocles and Euripides but not Aeschylus, uses *cholos* (among other words) for anger, which is another small argument against Aeschylean authorship.

20. *PV* 29 (Hephaestus' explanation of his behaviour).

21. As it did in the eyes of both Zeus and Prometheus: see M. Griffith on *PV* 79–80, citing 188, 379, 907–908, etc. Cf. Soph. *Ajax* 651, Eur. *Med.* 291, 1052.

22. ὅτι/ ὀργῆς νοσούσης εἰσίν ἰατροὶ λόγοι. Some have taken *orgē* to mean "temperament" here, but it makes little difference, since the reference is clearly to the

Prometheus: Yes, if someone softens the <angry> heart at the right moment, and does not forcibly constrict the swollen spirit [*thumos*].

This exchange has nothing directly to do with anger in the city, but it clearly signals that the kind of anger known as *orgē* had become or was becoming, in the 450s, an object of disapproval. And from this time onwards the tragic theatre often presented spectacles of anger producing appalling effects on individuals, for instance in Sophocles' *Ajax* (440s). Prometheus is a noble figure, but he is also an angry *daimōn*, and he suffers for it.

Another aspect of political life, besides intense strife in a free city, which brings anger into debate in the fifth century is the behaviour of monarchical rulers. The earliest wrathful rulers in fifth-century literature who are meant to be criticized for their anger are Menelaus and Agamemnon in the second part of *Ajax,* when they tyrannically attempt to prevent the dead hero's brother Teucer from burying his remains, only to be persuaded to relent by Odysseus.[23] The anger of monarchical rulers will be explored fully in Chapter 10. But as it is presented in fifth-century texts it sometimes raises other political issues. A prime instance is Sophocles' *Antigone* (about 442).

The King Creon of this play behaves like an evil tyrant, though he is far from being a stock figure.[24] His anger with the dead Polyneices, who had led an attack on the city, and with Polyneices' sister Antigone, who champions his right to burial, is inflexible; and he loses his temper with the guard who reports that Polyneices has indeed been buried (*Ant.* 280–326). Creon's son Haemon asks him with tact to give up his *thumos* (718), but Creon relents too late, so that Antigone, Haemon, and Creon's wife, Eurydice, all die. One can easily understand what has led at least one critic to say that anger is Creon's tragic fault, *hamartia.*[25]

But anger is not the monopoly of the ruler, for Haemon and his

---

cholos of line 376; Thalmann 1986, 496, argued strongly for the translation "anger." Ocean does not know that Prometheus does indeed have some words which will bring about a reconciliation with Zeus (522–525), though they are not words of mollification.

23. *Ajax* 1047–1373. On how to read this part of the play, see Heath 1987, 200–208.
24. Winnington-Ingram 1980, 125–127.
25. Stanford 1983, 33. For this understanding of the term *hamartia* see, e.g., Dover

champion Teiresias both show anger too.[26] And far from seeing Creon as a monster and Antigone as a heroic victim, much of the audience may have seen Antigone as a transgressor. Demosthenes, a century later, was to quote Creon from this play, at length, on the overriding importance of the city's interest in relation to the individual's.[27] For him and his audience, Creon remained an entirely legitimate authority, anger or no anger. And, as Sourvinou-Inwood has shown, Creon was from an Athenian point of view quite justified in denying burial to Polyneices if the latter was a traitor.[28] What this argument misses, however, is that the gods decide that the burial was in fact justified;[29] Creon had been wrong, and he accepts the fact, too late. Thus Demosthenes wrenched the lines that he quoted out of their original context and into his own (quite understandably). Anger, I suggest, is a crucial element in Sophocles' telling of the story, for while some of Creon's opponents surrender to it, Creon is the irascible character in the play, and it is his irate decision which more than any other human action leads to death and misery.[30]

A certain tendency is visible in the 440s and 430s to theorize about past human progress and about the internal bonds within human communities. The evidence is very fragmentary. In or soon after 446

1974, 152. But Creon is not the hero, and the concept of *hamartia* may not be strictly appropriate.

26. Haemon: 766 *(orgē);* Teiresias: 1084–1086 *(thumos).* Perhaps Antigone too, for at 875 the Chorus says that *autognōtos orga* has destroyed her; but the meaning is almost certainly "self-willed temperament."

27. xix.247, quoting *Ant.* 175–190.

28. Sourvinou-Inwood 1989, esp. 137–139; readers should not give up because of the author's claim that she knows "the correct . . . reading of the *Antigone*" (136).

29. *Ant.* 988–1090. Sourvinou-Inwood 146–147 tries to deal with this problem, unsuccessfully in my view.

30. At this point Sophocles falls largely silent, since only one complete play of his *(OT)* survives from a more-than-thirty-year period after the *Antigone* (with the *Electra* probably appearing in 409). Just as Aeschylus seems to have criticized the anger of Achilles in his *Myrmidons,* so did Sophocles in a lost and undated drama called *Sundeipnoi (Banqueters Together),* which therefore became a staple of the anger-control literature: see Philodemus, *De ira* 5 (col. xviii.16–24), with Indelli's commentary. But fr. 565 Pearson/Radt shows that it must have been a satyr play; in other words, it was possible to make fun of Achilles' temper. Fr. 929, from an unknown play and also undated, is interestingly critical of *orgē,* associating it with drunkenness.

the elderly Pindar, at the beginning of *Pythian* VIII, made Tranquillity (Hesuchia) into a living being, describing her as the daughter of Dike, Justice, and as "the one who makes cities great." "You hold the master keys of counsels and of wars."[31] The Chorus in the *Antigone* gives a brief account of human progress, including an enigmatic reference to *orgē*.[32] The account of the emergence of polis life which Plato much later attributed to Protagoras may possibly be authentic and hence traceable to the same period: the gods gave mankind *aidōs* and *dikē* (this was traditional thinking), and that enabled them to live in cities.[33] None of this refers directly to controlling the angry emotions, but the implication is plain that citizens must control their public behaviour within the city for the sake of the city's strength.

It was probably in this same period, before the Peloponnesian War, that the sophist Antiphon wrote a book called *On Concord*.[34] Such a work may have had something to say about political anger, especially since we have some evidence that Antiphon (and other sophists) were interested in what, running the risk of anachronism, we can call the emotions.[35] It is also to this period that scholars have wanted to trace an early form of social-contract theory.[36] Sophists of the generation of Hippias, Socrates and Critias seem to have gone at least part of the dis-

31. *Pyth.* viii.1–4.

32. They include among the things that mankind has learned speaking and thinking and "the dispositions that regulate towns" *(astunomous orgas)*, *Ant.* 354–356. The original theory of Allen (2000, 51) that this phrase means "*anger* that is city-regulated and/or city-regulating," has very little to recommend it.

33. Protagoras speaking in Pl. *Prot.* 322bc: "Their practical skill was sufficient to provide food, but insufficient for the war against wild animals—for they did not yet possess the art of running a city, which includes the art of war . . . Now when they came together, they treated each other unjustly, . . . so they once again scattered and began to be destroyed. Zeus therefore, fearing that our species would be wholly wiped out, sent Hermes to bring *aidōs* and *dikē* to mankind, to be the principles of organization [*kosmoi*] of cities and the bonds of friendship." Opinion has been divided as to whether this story really comes from Protagoras, as seems very likely; see C. C. W. Taylor's commentary; D. L. Cairns 1993, 355.

34. 87 B 44a-71 D-K. On Antiphon, see Gomperz 1927, 61–66. B 58, especially, seems to show that in his opinion "it was mistaken to believe that a man could hurt his neighbour without being hurt himself" (Pohlenz 1966 [1955], 70).

35. On Antiphon and distress, see Chapter 14.

36. Kahn 1981.

tance towards formulating such a theory, without, as far as we know, making reference to the need for some degree of emotional restraint as part of such a compact.[37] Nonetheless these events are highly relevant to the current enquiry, not least because they reinforced a tendency to question the traditional ethic of revenge.

The morality of revenge eventually changed somewhat. Is there any evidence of this before the Peloponnesian War?[38] No doubt most Athenians continued to believe something like what the Chorus says in the *Choephori*, namely that the unavenged dead eventually reveal their *orgai*, bursts of anger.[39] But Aeschylus is not likely to have been isolated in deploring some kinds of revenge. Socrates may be the crucial figure, but since the chronology of his intellectual development is so uncertain, let us look first at a development which has a fairly precise chronology—a linguistic change. The Greek language continued to use the same root-word, *timōr-*, for both punishment and revenge, even though the two practices had been partially distinct for a very long time. Hence it would have been difficult to formulate any general criticism of revenge. But a change occurred about the middle of the fifth century. Not that *timōr-* words began to mean anything different.[40] Rather, new words for "punisher" and "to punish," *kolastēs* and *kolazein*, entered the (literary) language, being first attested in the *Persae* (472 B.C.) and *Ajax* (440s), respectively.[41] That chronology seems to fit rea-

---

37. For Hippias as a possible social-contract theorist, see Guthrie 1962–1981, III.138, and for Socrates, ibid. 140. For Critias, see D-K 88 B 25, with the comment of E. R. Dodds on Pl. *Gorg.* 483b. See, further, *Gorg.* 492c, *Rep.* ii.358e–359a.

38. It can be assumed that the saying attributed to the seventh-century sage Pittacus of Mytilene, "Forgiveness is stronger than revenge" (Diog.Laert. i.4.3), is apocryphal embroidery on the legend that Pittacus had forgiven the murderer of his son.

39. Aesch. *Choeph.* 326. In *Choeph.* 899–903 Orestes' hesitation over killing his mother to avenge his father is stunningly short-lived. On revenge in tragedy, see esp. Said 1984, 48–50, with whom, however, I cannot agree on all points; little illumination results from seeing vengeance as a form of exchange, since this perspective tends to eliminate the anger which is normally a vital part of the revenge sequence.

40. Herman 1998, 614, says that *timōria* slowly came to mean punishment, but a wealth of evidence shows that it continued to be ambiguous.

41. Aesch, *Persae* 827, Soph. *Ajax* 1108, 1160 This was probably in origin a metaphor from the cutting back of plants. When Aristotle comes to distinguish between *timōria* and *kolasis*, he says (*Rhet.* i.10.1369b12–14) that the latter "is for the sake of

sonably well with Plato's representation of Protagoras (such an influential intellectual figure at this time) as one who held advanced,
non-retributive views about punishment.[42] Plato repeatedly makes
Protagoras use the "new" word *kolazein,* the dramatic date being in the
430s.

According to one view, the clearest opponent of revenge in fifth-century Athens was Socrates, and it is plausible to suppose that the historical Socrates came to reject the traditional principle that one should do
harm to one's enemies, and to believe instead that "we should never
return evil for evil to anyone." It is also, however, plausible to suppose
that he expected that "those who believe or will believe this" would be
few.[43]

The great revenge tragedy is of course *Medea* (431). While there was
much to be said on Medea's side[44] (and hence a powerful play), Euripides made her revenge disproportionate. But it would be very hypothetical to suggest that he intended a more general lesson about revenge. And if we look forward to what the tragedians said later about
revenge, we find that the accepted beliefs had changed little if at all
since the time of the *Oresteia.*

It is true that when Euripides presented the dilemma of Orestes
(should a son who has divine sanction for doing so avenge his father,
even though it means killing his own mother?) in his *Electra* (about
416?), he makes Orestes blame the foolishness of Apollo's instructions, but even Aeschylus' Orestes had had his doubts.[45] Sophocles'
Electra is a singularly difficult case. To the modern sensibility, Electra
and Orestes may seem excessive in the manner of their revenge
(Aegisthus is to go unburied), and Electra is so dominated by strong
emotions that it may be hard to think that proper Athenian citizens
will have approved of her conduct.[46] Yet it would be inaccurate to

---

the person who suffers it, the former for the sake of the agent, that he may receive
satisfaction." It is most doubtful whether Hecataeus of Miletus used the word *akolasia*
(*FGrH* 1 F 169).

42. *Protag.* 324ab. He is made to maintain that the retributive attitude is irrational.

43. See Vlastos 1991, 194–199. The former quotation is from *Crito* 49c, with
Vlastos's legitimate addition of the words "to anyone"; the latter is from 49d.

44. The Chorus of women says that Jason suffers justly, *Med.* 1231–1232.

45. And the result is the same as in the *Oresteia.* The matter is discussed from 967
to the end of the play (cf. Vlastos 1991, 183). Foolishness: 971.

46. The non-burial: *El.* 1487–1488. Emotionalism: Burnett 1998, 122–123.

say that the poet was questioning the traditional ethos of revenge.[47] In Euripides' *Orestes* (408) Tyndareos is made to praise the fathers of old for having in effect banned the practice of vendetta.[48] But it was in any case probably a thing of the past, at least as far as Athens was concerned. And to step away from tragedy for a moment, the orator Antiphon shows that it was still persuasive to say in an Athenian court that "an aggressor deserves to be answered not with the same as he gave, but with more and worse."[49]

Medea, on the eve of the Peloponnesian War, problematizes anger as well as revenge;[50] *orgē* is one of its principal themes. Much of what I have to say about this play will appear in Chapter 11, where its significance for the anger of women will be explored. It will be argued that while in the end Euripides suggested no radical conclusions on that subject, he did at least question the conventional Athenian thinking. Anger in any case is at the centre of the drama, Medea's anger that Jason has deserted her for another wife. Jason sententiously tells her that he has often seen what an untreatable evil *(amēchanon kakon)* is harsh anger *(orgē),* and explains that the alternative is "to bear lightly the wishes of the stronger."[51] Pretending to be resigned (to put Jason off his guard), Medea blames her own *orgē* (882–883). Just before the messenger scene which announces the death she has arranged for Jason's bride, she concludes her monologue with words which were quoted over and over again by later writers, from Chrysippus onwards:

I know well what awful harm I am about to inflict, but my passionate rage [*thumos*] overbears my thinking [*bouleumatōn*], rage that brings to humans their greatest harm.[52]

47. However, Electra herself expresses some doubt about blood revenge: *El.* 580–583.

48. *Orestes* 507–525. This is merely a topos, according to C. W. Willink on *Or.* 507–511.

49. iv.β.2. On balance it seems to me that Antiphon the Sophist should be distinguished from this man.

50. In addition to the passages quoted in this paragraph, see 38–39, 91–94, 99, 109, 120–121 (the powerful do not give up their *orgai* easily, says the nurse), 129, 160–167, 172, 176, 271, 319–320, 520, 590, 615, 637–638—and that is simply in the first half of the play.

51. *Med.* 446–450.

52. 1078–1080. How to understand *thumos* and *bouleumatōn* has been endlessly discussed. Diller 1966 argued that *thumos* here means "Leidenschaft," passion; but Eu-

The great innovations in the *Medea* are two, the suggestion that a woman's vengeful rage may have been just (more of that later), and the contrast between the angry emotions and reason.[53] The latter notion makes a relatively brief appearance, and a very peculiar one, for it is within a framework of deception. It was *logoi,* the heroine says (she is lying), in other words the process of thinking things through, which led her to give up her anger. She describes what these thoughts were, refers to them as such *(ennoēsas'),* and refers to her previous state of rage as *aboulia,* unwisdom; but now, she says, "I have come to a better conclusion" *(ameinon bebouleumai).*[54] Jason sees this as the victory of a reasoning process over anger (he is, of course, wholly deluded).[55] Both

ripides probably would not have made Medea say that *thumos* brought humans their greatest harm unless he meant "anger." The *bouleumata* which have been referred to before (769, 772, 1044, and as recently as 1048) were Medea's plans to kill her children. But she cannot be made to say that her anger has mastered her plans to kill her children! Therefore we have to choose: either *kreissōn* (the word paraphrased above as "overbears") means "in control of" (Diller 1966, 274), which is unlikely (Reeve 1972, 59; Lloyd-Jones 1980, 58), or *bouleumatōn* refers not to Medea's murder plan but to her now discarded intention of taking her children from Corinth to Athens (1043–1048, 1056–1058; cf. Lloyd-Jones 1980, 58). The latter option is preferable, but even if it is the wrong one, there is still a contrast in these three lines, as briefly in an earlier scene, between anger and thinking. (The *principal* conflict in this monologue is, however, between vengeful anger and maternal affection). The authenticity of 1078–1080 has often been questioned, but the denunciation of *thumos,* though commonplace later, seems to fit the intellectual context of 431 very well. Some scholars have wanted to dismiss as an interpolation much of Medea's monologue, because of real and supposed incoherences in the speech, which excellently convey the heroine's state of mind. For the conservative view taken here see, among others, Lloyd-Jones 1980; Foley 1989, 66–67. Cf. Marzullo 1999, 191 n.*. It might not matter terribly, from a cultural-historical point of view, whether some or most of this speech was written by a Hellenistic poet rather than by Euripides. It seems to me, however, that the whole speech, including the most disputed lines, 1078–1080, are almost certainly Euripides' own work.

53. Some critics seem to have overreacted to the earlier analyses of this contrast: Lloyd-Jones 1980, 52, for instance, claims that there is no such contrast, because the monologue of 1021–1080 shows her maternal feelings in conflict with her determination to exact revenge. Cf. Foley 1989.

54. 872, 873–881, 882–883, 893.

55. 909–913. According to Foley 1989, 64, Medea "cleverly mimics Jason's own mode of ethical reasoning." I suspect that Euripides is mocking either a sophist or Sophocles, or both.

of them are relying on a notion which is readily understood by the audience: thinking things through (sometimes) leads a person to desist from *orgē*.[56] It is odd that the priority of the *Medea* in this respect has not been acknowledged. Soon, however, the contrast between *orgē* and reason became commonplace.[57]

And it has to be understood what this priority means: not that Euripides necessarily devised this concept by himself, but rather that the idea had been crystallizing in Athenian intellectual circles for several years, perhaps a decade or two. It was only in the 420s, in my view, that Herodotus brought his finished work, in which there is a very marked contrast between rationality and the angry emotions, before the public,[58] but many prefer an earlier date, and in any case the historian must have formulated his views of Cambyses and Xerxes long before he finished his history. Another possibility is that before 431 Democritus may already have expressed something like the opinion I noted earlier on the subject of *thumos*-anger and rationality.

One apparent novelty is unlikely to have been a real one. Medea is a "barbarian," as we are repeatedly reminded. It so happens that this is the first time anyone makes the association of irascibility and being a barbarian, unless once again we want to give Herodotus the priority. In any case, the connection, notwithstanding its absence from Aeschylus' *Persae*, probably went back to the great age of the Persians Wars with the Greeks between 499 and the 470s.

The political theme in the *Medea* has to do with gender politics, not with politics in the conventional sense. Neither is the *Hippolytus* (428), in which once again anger is crucial and destructive, in any obvious way a play about politics. Kings are irascible, but that was hardly a surprise to anyone brought up on Homer, and at Athens, in any case, the message had no practical importance at this time. *Oedipus Tyrannus*

56. Does the fact that this contrast is largely confined to this deception scene imply that Euripides thought that the power of *logoi* to overcome angry passion was not very great?

57. See for instance, besides Herodotus, Soph. *OT* 524, 584; Antiphon v.71–73 (about 415 B.C.).

58. There is no strong positive argument for an earlier date, while the rather numerous scattered allusions to events in the 420s would have been difficult to graft on to the work in ancient conditions of book production.

(early 420s) also has a lot of anger in it. As the play opens, it is the city's afflictions which the priest puts before the audience, and the king's public role is constantly in the foreground.[59] The play seems to be about individual humans, it is true, about fate and *hubris,* and not about kingship; the last utterances of both king and Chorus dwell on the private and familial consequences of what has happened. But before his discovery, Oedipus emerges as a man of uncontrollable temper, both in his classic scenes of anger with the prophet Teiresias and with Creon, and in his account of the murderous encounter at the Three Roads.[60] How was this seen or meant to be seen by the initial audience? Probably in a most unfavourable light, in spite of the foreordained character of the hero's disaster. What produces a tyrant is *hubris,* says the Chorus,[61] and although the link between Oedipus' anger and his *hubris* is not defined, a link was clearly thought to exist. The mechanism which turns Oedipus' tragic fault into disaster is *orgē*-anger, *orgē* when he kills his father at the Three Roads.[62] The reputation of *orgē* displayed in the public sphere is thus low, and it seems to be a matter of great concern at this time to both Sophocles and Euripides.

It almost goes without saying, however, that Euripides should not by any means be seen as a soft-hearted opponent of all conflictuality. In the *Supplices,* after the great King Theseus has been made to say that one should not react to moderate injustice with anger,[63] he nonetheless proceeds to make war against Thebes, and at the end of the play (1213–1226) Athene herself promises revenge to the sons of the Seven.

We can usefully turn aside from tragedy to consider a text produced for quite other purposes within a few years of this play. It constitutes our first look at an Athenian orator, so it is worth remarking that the evidence of the orators is an extremely valuable gauge of the citizens'

---

59. *OT* 22–30, 93–94, 247, 630, 635–636, 878–880, etc.

60. 334–630, 804–813 (Laius paid an unequal price [810] for the blow he struck). Yet at the beginning of his clash with Teiresias, Oedipus' annoyance is easily comprehensible. In *OC* Oedipus is very much a man of wrath (1274, 1328, etc.; Winnington-Ingram 1980, 275–279), but that play cannot be explored here.

61. *OT* 873. Note also their support for rivalry that is healthy for the city, 878–880.

62. παίω δι' ὀργῆς, *OT* 807. He had of course been provoked.

63. Eur. *Supp.* 555–557 (but cf. 476).

prejudices.[64] Cases we know about were commonly serious ones—lives were sometimes at stake—and the speakers had to show accurate respect for the jurors' opinions. It is therefore a minor landmark when the orator Antiphon, in his famous speech *On the Murder of Herodes*, asks the jury to make up its mind without *orgē* or prejudice, which are, he says, the worst of advisers. "It is impossible for a man who is angry to make a good decision, for <anger> destroys the means by which he may make <sensible> decisions, his judgement [*gnōmē*]."[65] The accused on whose behalf Antiphon composed this speech was pleading for his life, probably with success.

Euripides continued to write political plays from time to time, such as the *Troades* in 415. Many of the plays of the war period are concerned with the characters and passions of individuals and with individual fates. However, it remained a function of tragedy to hold up to the audience the public horrors of bitter rivalry between those who should have been restrained by ties of blood. Such rivalry could be presented as a tragedy of anger, and this is what happens in Euripides' *Phoenissae*, in 409, at a time when the subject of civil war could not have been more actual, as much as in the *Seven against Thebes*. Eteocles and Polyneices conduct an angry exchange on stage before leaving to fight to the death. The poet constantly makes it clear that he sees anger as a cause of this conflict, and he emphasizes the consequent sufferings of Thebes.[66] A familiar theme, a commonplace but much-needed message.

Tragedy raises another essential topic, the anger of the gods, or rather human criticism of it. Divine anger is omnipresent, sometimes as the mainspring of the plot, sometimes on the margins. Only one character in any surviving play asserts that a god is angry unjustly, in spite of what were seen as the dreadful consequences of divine anger. In the *Ajax* the destruction of the hero results not in the first place

---

64. Cf. Herman 1996, 13–14; but he goes too far in relegating other kinds of texts to unimportance.

65. v.71–72. No doubt Antiphon had said such things before. See also sect. 91.

66. In favour of a political interpretation of the play, see in general Rawson 1970. The cause of the fraternal strife may have been *eris* (351) or anger (461) or the *mēnimata* of Ares against Cadmus (934). The quarrel on stage: 594–637. The sufferings of the city and its people: 4, 239–246, 881–885, etc.

from his anger but from the anger of Athene with Ajax, caused in turn, we are told, by his own arrogance, in particular with regard to the goddess herself.[67]

The plot of the *Hippolytus* is based on the anger of a god, for the hero's death is a consequence of the anger of Aphrodite,[68] just as the troubles of Heracles and his family in the *Heracles* are a result of the anger of Hera, that perennially wrathful goddess. Scholars have warned us against supposing that any criticism of the gods is intended,[69] and according to the conventional modern view, such a thing is scarcely to be expected in public discourse at Athens in the fifth century.[70] All the same, Hippolytus' old manservant does suggest to Aphrodite that she should as a god be wise enough to overlook Hippolytus' folly.[71] In the *Bacchae*, finally, Cadmus laments Dionysus' judgement (1346–1349):

> *Cadmus:* . . . you go too far.
> *Dionysus:* For although I am a god I was insulted by you.
> *Cadmus:* Gods should not imitate the angers [*orgas*] of humans.
> *Dionysus:* Long ago my father Zeus decided these things.

It is the great historians who show that in the last three decades of the fifth century a more emphatic critique of anger, which was then to develop throughout the history of classical culture, was taking shape.

Herodotus' reflections on anger, some in his own voice but most attributed to his characters, are extensive and of vital importance for this study. "I praise this law <of the Persians>," he says, that forbids the king to punish anyone, or anyone else to do incurable harm to one of his slaves, "until calculation shows that the offender's wrongful acts are more and greater than his services"; then and only then is he allowed to apply his anger *(thumos)* (i.137). After King Cambyses kills the son of his courtier Prexaspes,[72] Croesus, a regular source of wisdom, ad-

---

67. Her anger: *Ajax* 656 *(mēnis)*, 757 *(mēnis)*, 777 *(orgē);* its cause: 761–777. It is not therefore correct to say that anger is Ajax's tragic *hamartia* (Stanford 1983, 33).

68. Her anger is *thumos* (1328) but never *orgē*.

69. E.g., G. Bond in his commentary on the *Heracles*, xxiv–xxvi.

70. But see, e.g., Soph. *Trach.* 1264–1274.

71. *Hipp.* 120. The Chorus expresses a very angry attitude towards the gods at 1146.

72. Hdt. iii.34–35.

monishes him, invoking Cyrus, another Herodotean source of wisdom: "Your majesty, don't entrust everything to your youth and anger [*thumos*], but master yourself, hold yourself in. It is good to think of the future."[73] Periander, tyrant of Corinth, tells his furious son to think "what kind of thing it is to be angry [*tethumōsthai*] with one's parents or one's betters" (iii.52).

Without insisting excessively, the historian makes anger the vice of the tyrant and of the insane or nearly insane Persian king—of Periander and, above all, of Cambyses and Xerxes.[74] Sometimes it infects other powerful Persians, but it is a vice which King Cyrus, whom Herodotus so much admires, knows how to control.[75] When anger takes hold of Cambyses or Xerxes, it is often for a poor reason, and the result is often horrendous. Not indeed always—the Persians *did* conquer Egypt after Cambyses invaded the country in anger. But Cambyses murdered his own sister, in exchange for a bitter reproach; Herodotus has two versions of this story, both obviously apocryphal, which makes it all the more valuable as evidence for his own thinking. And Cambyses murdered his faithful courtier's son with an accurate arrow shot in order to prove that he was not mad. When the loyal Lydian Pythius asked Xerxes that, of his five sons, one might be exempted from the Greek expedition, the king, after a little comment underlining that he has no control over his *thumos*, had Pythius' favourite son cut in half and marched his army between the two halves.[76] And so on.

In fact we can go considerably further. An unpublished paper by H. G. Edinger shows in effect not only that *orgē* and *thumos* are mainly negative emotions in Herodotus but that, in his history, no Greek leader ever makes a decision in anger.[77] Indeed it can be said that Greeks of whom Herodotus approves very seldom feel *orgē*, *thumos*

---

73. iii.36. He then has to flee for his life.

74. There is no intention here of reviving the theory that Herodotus' history was a tract against *turannoi*.

75. Periander: iii.51–52 (not without justification or regret); Cambyses: iii.1, 25, 32, 34, 35; Darius: iv.166.2 (?); Xerxes: vii.11 (after he had received what Herodotus thought was good advice), 39, 210, 238 (mutilating the corpse of Leonidas), ix.111; Cyrus: i.156 (but on the other hand see i.141). Cf. above for Aeschylus on Cyrus' self-control.

76. iii.32, 35; vii.39.

77. An exception is Miltiades' last expedition, to Paros, the real motive for which is

or *cholos*.[78] It is a rare occasion when the Alcmaeonid Megacles feels and acts on *orgē* towards his son-in-law Peisistratus because the latter had "unnatural" sexual relations with Megacles' daughter.[79] The only Greeks who are said to feel *thumos* are the Medizing Thessalians (viii.27, 31), and it has already been noted how rarely Athenian crowds are represented by Herodotus as violent[80]—in part no doubt because it was so, in part because of Herodotus' fondness for his adopted city. Herodotus speaks of divine anger only in exceptional circumstances, and clearly found the concept inappropriate.[81] The term *mēnis*, however, which, when it is used of humans, is interpreted by Edinger to mean collective anger over an offence against a norm of conduct, *is* occasionally attributed to Greeks who are worthy of respect.

This pattern is not to be taken as an accidental feature of Herodotus' narrative, which is in general carefully constructed to sustain certain interpretations of the great patterns of events. We are meant to look down upon Cambyses and Xerxes because of their lack of self-control, and to see their failures as consequences of their moral defects. These two were the threatening foreigners par excellence, who could be both demonized and rendered vulnerable by means of their vices. We may presume that Greeks had already invented an association between barbarians and uncontrolled emotions before Herodotus' time,[82] but this, after the *Medea,* is where we first encounter it. Anger as an attribute of the Other fulfilled such fundamental functions that it was to have a long career, lasting throughout the history of classical culture.

---

alleged by Herodotus to have been an *egkotos,* grudge, on Miltiades' part (vi.133). Not coincidentally, the expedition was a disaster.

78. On occasion he seems to avoid anger terminology carefully: e.g., vi.129 (Cleisthenes and Hippocleides), ix.5 (when a certain Lycidas proposed accepting Persian peace terms, the Athenians, *deinon poiēsamenoi,* "having protested vigorously," stoned him to death).

79. i.61. In vi.85 a speaker implies that the Spartans had acted out of *orgē* when they punished King Leotychidas for taking a bribe, but his clear intention is to suggest that they may one day relent.

80. Above, p. 14.

81. The story about Zeus Laphrystios in vii.197.3 *(mēnin)* is an exception. Does it make a difference that it was only a self-serving local *logos* (s.1)?

82. For the invention of the barbarians in the fifth century, see esp. E. Hall 1989.

But there is more, because the lack of angry passions in the counsels and actions of the approved Greeks is intended as a lesson about how to behave in public affairs (perhaps private as well, but Herodotus is, after all, a political historian). The significance of all this can only be that in the 430s and 420s, the period when the text was being put into writing, Herodotus felt strongly that virtually all manifestations, indeed virtually all sentiments, of anger were better avoided. This must have been a carefully considered view, and it goes beyond anything expressed by the tragedians. Was it a reaction to contemporary events? The effect on Herodotus' initial audience, which must have been small, was to evoke a Greek political past which for all its tensions was a great deal more orderly than the ugly present of the Peloponnesian War, at least as Thucydides describes it. In the golden past, political and social anger were by and large kept under control—so it was claimed.

Herodotus seems to have views about revenge which fit his treatment of anger. At the beginning of his history we are informed of the Persian belief that only fools revenge themselves for the kidnapping of women (they would not have been kidnapped if they had not wanted to be), and later, more clearly, after the terrible revenge which Pheretime of Cyrene—Greek but a woman—inflicted on the city of Barca and her own horrible death, we are told that "excessively severe revenge makes people the subject of the resentment of the gods."[83] The notion that revenge can be excessive is implicit in the description of vengeance in the Persian court in Book IX (78–79). Indeed it seems that in Herodotus it is generally (not always) barbarians and women who are motivated by revenge.

Herodotus does not apparently disapprove of absolutely all revenge: in fact "the greatest act of revenge [*tisis*] of which we know," as he calls it, seems to receive his approval. Hermotimus of Pedasus, so the story runs (viii.105–106), was castrated as a boy by Panionius the Chian, who made a business of selling eunuchs to the Persians. But in due course Hermotimus rose to become the most influential eunuch at the court of Xerxes, and when the Persian was preparing to invade Greece, this Hermotimus found himself in Mysia, where he happened

83. i.4, iv.200–205.

to meet Panionius once again. Pretending friendliness, the eunuch got Panionius and his family into his power, forced him to castrate each of his four sons, and compelled them in turn to castrate their father. It is possible, however, that Herodotus intended to imply that Hermotimus' talionic, or more-than-talionic, revenge was feminine and barbarian—these being characteristics which Panionius himself had bestowed on his future avenger by castrating him and sending him to Persia.[84]

Whatever he thought about revenge, Herodotus was one of the first surviving writers to create an opposition between anger and rational decision making. The notion had roots, going all the way back to Homer, and it must draw to some extent on Herodotus' discussions in Athens in the 440s and 430s. It is in any case deeply written into his narrative, for the central event of his history, Xerxes' invasion of Greece, would not have taken place, Herodotus seems to imply, if Xerxes had reflected carefully instead of giving in to anger. "It is good to think of the future," Croesus had remarked to Cambyses.

The most extensive fifth-century statement of civil ideals is to be found in Pericles' Funeral Speech, which in reality was an essay by Thucydides intended to reflect the great democratic leader's thinking. Pericles is made to specify that the Athenians do *not* show anger, *orgē*, to their fellow citizens "when the latter do something according to pleasure."[85] In other words, they were still in 431 able to avoid *stasis*, civil strife (and Thucydides implies that much of the credit for this belonged to the opponents of the democracy).[86] And Pericles, it is also implied, was well aware of the civic dangers of anger. A little later, *orgē* drives the Athenians to prosecute and fine him (ii.65.3).

This is a subsidiary element in the Funeral Speech, but what Thucydides has to say about *orgē* in his famous analysis of *stasis*—political strife—in Book III is more emphatic: war is a violent teacher which

84. Burckhardt thought that Herodotus fully approved (1898, 323), and he undoubtedly tells the story *against* Panionius.

85. "Something according to pleasure": ii.37.2. Farrar 1988, 156, asserts that *orgē* in Thucydides means "the entire [!] range of impulsive, instinctual, emotional behavior," which is obviously false.

86. For "doing something according to pleasure" as a way of referring to democratic behaviour, see Cohen 1995, 42, 54–55.

makes most men's angry passions *(orgai)* suit their immediate needs; he means, I suppose, that they do not know how to postpone expressing them. In the terrible new world of *stasis,* the angry man was trusted. The Corcyraeans were the first to display such *orgai* towards each other. The political hell which Thucydides describes in this passage is not simply a hell of anger, but anger is one of its main elements.[87] He also seems to have written (iii.84.2) that in these conditions "human nature . . . was pleased to show itself incapable of controlling its *orgē*."[88]

Another strong critique appears in Thucydides' Mytilenaean debate. Because of *orgē*, he says, the Athenians decided to kill all the adult male inhabitants of Mytilene and enslave the rest of the population. When they begin to change their minds, Cleon—the worst man in the entire book, in Thucydides' eyes—argues that an injured man should punish quickly while his *orgē* is still sharp, and that therefore Athens should *not* relent.[89] Diodotus, on the other hand, argues that haste and *orgē*, anger "which comes into being," he says, "with ignorance and narrowmindedness," are opposed to good decision making. Diodotus' point of view—which derives not from generosity but from the calculation that moderation is in Athens' interest—prevails, and most of the Mytilenaeans are spared. Thucydides, being Thucydides, does not tell us openly that this was a good thing, but it is reasonably clear which course of action he preferred.[90] There is a regular insistence on the conflict between *orgē* and rationality.[91]

Thus Thucydides lays considerable stress on the harm which anger

87. The discussion of *stasis:* iii.82–83.

88. Since antiquity most, though not all, commentators have claimed that iii.84 was not written by Thucydides; so too does the most recent of them, S. Hornblower, with some hesitation. It is difficult to go against the negative judgement of J. Classen, A. W. Gomme and K. J. Dover (1994, 84) in this matter. But see the strong argumentation of Christ 1989, supported by Maurer 1995, 114, in favour of authenticity. One of the most suspect phrases is *apaideusia orgēs* ("the ignorance caused by anger"), which is apparently derived from iii.42.1.

89. Huart 1968, 158, pointed out that Thucydides does not explicitly describe Cleon himself as angry or irascible (though he calls him violent, *biaios*).

90. iii.36–49 (the passage quoted: iii.42); Thucydides' view of Cleon: iii.36. For the contrast with Pericles see Connor 1984, 79 n. 1.

91. E.g., ii.11.4, 21.3; iii.42.1; vi.57.3, 59.1; cf. Huart 1968, 161–162.

does within a state and to its external affairs. It should not be assumed that he dogmatically condemned all political anger. The orators who stirred up the anger of the Syracusans in 413, for example, are given inflammatory words without necessarily being blamed.[92] But the historian makes a point of saying that it is contrary to Spartan custom to act out of anger,[93] and attributes to sensible King Archidamus the claim that the Athenians as a people are particularly likely to act irrationally out of anger, the Athenians "who claim to rule others" and are normally the invaders, not the invaded.[94] A few pages later, Thucydides duly shows them being angry with Pericles because of the Spartan invasion of Attica, and their anger with him becomes a constant refrain.[95]

But in parallel with Herodotus, Thucydides rarely attributes *orgē* to Greek political leaders, who from time to time are seen calming the angry *dēmos*.[96] By contrast, he makes the Persian satrap Tissaphernes act out of anger.[97] We may suppose that when Thucydides says that the old tyrant-slaying heroes Harmodius and Aristogeiton acted because they were angry, he intended to detract from their fame.[98] But he did not, I think, intend to detract from that of Pericles when he said that the latter's authority with the Athenians was so great that he could even speak to them angrily *(pros orgēn),* that is to say without suffering for it.[99]

92. vii.68.1: "Let us be convinced that in dealing with an adversary it is most just and lawful to claim the right to slake the fury of the soul in retaliation [*timōria*] on the aggressor, and further that to punish enemies is, as the saying goes, the greatest of all delights."

93. v.63.2. Plu. *Lyc.* 12 purports to describe the traditional Spartan system for teaching young men to keep their tempers.

94. ii.11.7–8, with the notes of J. De Romilly and S. Hornblower.

95. ii.21.3, 59.3, 60.1, 64.1, 65.1, 65.3; see Huart 1968, 160–161.

96. Thuc. ii.22.1, 59.3, 60 (all Pericles), v.63.2 (King Agis), viii.86.5 (Alcibiades).

97. Huart 1968, 158–159. Tissaphernes: viii.43.4.

98. vi.57.3; cf. 56.2. Cf. the commentary of Gomme, Andrewes & Dover, IV, p. 322.

99. ii.65.8. Many say that *pros orgēn* means "so as to provoke their anger"; so Huart 159–160, who points out that Thucydides never elsewhere attributes *orgē* to Pericles. And this was how he was idealized later, Plu. *Per.* 39, in spite of contemporary references to his anger such as Ar. *Ach.* 530 (which may admittedly be pure fantasy). But Pericles' anger can be understood—see Dover 1974, 30, on the role of the "angry, mi-

This way, incidentally, lies the solution of one of the most intractable problems of traditional fifth-century history. The reason why Thucydides underplayed in Book I the role of Athens' Megarian Decree, or rather Decrees, in bringing on the Peloponnesian War is that the climactic decree, the one proposed by Charinus (but during Pericles' ascendancy),[100] was a quintessential example of policy being driven by anger. Thucydides was unwilling to admit that *orgē* played such a crucial role in the policy of the statesman he so much revered, and he therefore greatly underemphasized the decrees' importance as a cause of the war. This solution could and should be written up at length.

During the Peloponnesian War and in its aftermath, a number of Greek cities experienced real crises. These were often situations in which the state's Weberian "monopoly of force," which was never in any case absolute in a Greek city,[101] broke down; in other words the state itself was breaking down. It must have been well before the war that Herodotus formed his views on anger and politics, and the *stasis* described by Thucydides had also been welling up in many cities even before 431.[102] We do not know when Thucydides wrote his response to the crisis—it could well have been as early as the 420s, or it may have been after 404. But it is clear in any event that both historians came to attribute an enormous value to both the leaders' and the citizens' ability to control their rage.

By the last years of the fifth century a ready resort to *orgē* in politics was probably seen by many reflective Athenians in a negative light; Thucydides probably expected much of his audience to agree with him about this. Behind his opinion lay his political experiences in the 420s and also, one may suspect, a conservative feeling on the part of a

---

natory moralizer" in Athenian society—whereas it is hard to see why Pericles, who was not a prosecutor, would have addressed the people "with a view to making them angry."

100. For bibliography and analysis, see P. A. Stadter on Plu. *Per.* 30.2–3.

101. See Hunter 1994 on the circumstances in which it was considered legitimate for an Athenian citizen to resort to violence.

102. See, e.g., Thuc. i.19, 24.2–5, 115.2. According to one view of the Athenian Empire, he ought to have said far more about *stasis* during the Pentekontaetia.

member of the social elite that the right to be angry belonged more to themselves than to "those of no account."[103]

In Aristophanes' *Knights* (424) the *dēmos* is described as an irritable old man, "rustic in temper [*agroikos orgēn*], a lot-chewer, irascible [*akracholos*]."[104] And in the *Wasps* (422) the old man Philocleon, fond admirer of the people's champion Cleon, is as irascible as could be, like all the popular jurors who make up the Chorus—that is why they are wasps. Their wrath seems to imply that the citizens of the democracy, or at least the supporters of Cleon, are unfit to exercise power. But matters are more complicated: some scholars have understandably suspected that much of the audience found old Philocleon, rather than his sensible son Bdelycleon, to be the character in the play with whom they could most identify.[105] Euripides, on the other hand, in his *Supplices* (late 420s) makes King Theseus out to be a sort of democrat, but a democrat without sympathy for the lowest of the three social classes, which he says "lets loose its evil stings [again, they are like wasps] against the men of property" (*Supp.* 242), which obviously implies inappropriate anger.

The *dēmos* of virtually every Greek city showed anger from time to time, and understandably so, as in the case of Athens and Alcibiades (Thuc. viii.56.5). Lying, disappointment and conflicting interests are, after all, standard components of politics in any state in which there is even a minimum of freedom, and they inevitably produce anger. The great years of wrath at Athens came in 404–403, with a stunning military defeat, foreign occupation and bloody civil strife, with more than 1,500 citizens put to death by the oligarchic group which came to be

103. Aristotle's phrase, *Rhet.* ii.2.1379b10–13.

104. *Knights* 41–42, cf. 537. The whole furious argument between the Paphlagonian, Demosthenes and the Sausage-Seller (273–497) is intended as a representation of democratic politics in action.

105. For an interesting if one-sided reading of the *orgē* in this play, see Allen 2000, 128–134. The irascibility of Philocleon and the Chorus: *Wasps* 223–227, 242–244, 278–280, etc. Yet Philocleon has been judged simpatico (Dover 1972, 125–126). In line 1030 the poet claimed for himself the *orgē* of Heracles.

known as the "Thirty Tyrants"[106]—an enormous number for a community of this size. By late 403, the worst was over,[107] except for an event which was to have deep effects on Greek intellectual life—the anger of many Athenians with Socrates, leading to his trial and execution.

The killings carried out by the Thirty Tyrants and the Reconciliation effected in 403 between the democrats and the "moderate oligarchs" illuminate the practical notions about political vengeance, and hence about political anger, which now prevailed. It is true that the Spartan king Pausanias played a certain role in getting the Reconciliation accepted,[108] but the Spartan garrison soon left, and the Athenians had to decide for themselves whether to make it work. The principal results were five: the Thirty Tyrants who had run the anti-democratic state were exempted from the amnesty (and subsequently they were demonized by public opinion); all other vengeance, even vengeance by litigation, was passed up; but somewhat later the anti-democratic hard core was attacked at Eleusis and its commanders killed; four years after the Reconciliation, the aging philosopher who was held to have been the intellectual mentor of Critias, head of the junta of 404, was put to death; and lastly, the Athenians were proud of the Reconciliation, and it served as part of the ideological basis of the restored democracy until it was supplanted by outside force in 322.

Something a little strange had happened to revenge at Athens. Indeed, it has recently been argued that the early fourth-century Athenians adopted a morality which was explicitly hostile to revenge. And not only to violent retaliation but even to seeking revenge through litigation.[109] That conclusion goes too far:[110] it can only be sustained by very selective use of the available evidence. It is true, however, that the

106. [Arist.] *Ath.Pol.* 35.4, etc.

107. On the great Reconciliation which restored the democracy see, among many others, P. J. Rhodes's commentary on the *Ath.Pol.,* esp. pp. 462–473. *Ath.Pol.* 40.3 warmly praises the achievement; cf. Lysias ii.64. There had been plenty of anger in recent Athenian politics: *Ath.Pol.* 34.1, 36.1, 38.2.

108. Xen. *Mem.* ii.4.29–33. My understanding of these events owes a good deal to an unpublished paper by David Cohen.

109. Herman 1994, 1995, 1996.

110. W. V. Harris 1997a.

fourth-century Athenians admired some human qualities that ran directly counter to vengefulness, such as forgivingness and magnanimity.[111] Restraining oneself in the face of provocation could be claimed as a virtue. In Demosthenes LIV, for example, *Against Conon* (a speech of the 350s or 340s), the speaker Ariston makes a point of asserting that, in spite of his anger and hatred against Conon and his sons, he did not try for revenge, even legal revenge ("I simply resolved . . . to take care to have nothing to do with people of that sort").[112] The truth or untruth of his claim is not, as it would be vogueish to maintain, immaterial, but it cannot be discovered. Yet in any case it is clear that while the right to exact revenge, of certain kinds in certain circumstances, was still thoroughly accepted, restraining one's claim to avenge oneself on a fellow citizen was also much approved. In all likelihood the Athenians put this ideal into practice from time to time (it is hard to be sure, since the forensic orators were such ruthless liars). Ideology, at all events, to some extent favoured the omission of vengeance.

But no one should be surprised that the same social class at Athens could, at the same time, still openly *support* the ethic of revenge, assisted by the ambiguity of *timōr-* words which was mentioned earlier (they covered both punishment and revenge). Individual views must

111. On the former, see Dover 1991, 179–180. On the latter, Dover 1974, 190–195.

112. Dem. liv.6; Harris 1997a, 366. But neither Demosthenes' speech against Meidias nor Isaeus IX *(On the Estate of Astyphilus)* supports Herman's thesis. Further: with regard to Lysias I—Euphiletus' defence against the charge of having murdered Eratosthenes, whom he had allegedly caught in bed with his wife, a sequence of events which is normally taken to be a typical case of Greek revenge—it is not correct to say that Euphiletus tries to avoid saying that he had exercised revenge (see Harris 1997a, 365). It is interesting, however, that he employed the superficially plausible argument that he had taken vengeance *not* on his own behalf but legally and indeed on behalf of his (male) fellow citizens (all of them potentially outraged husbands). Nor does Lysias III *(Defence against Simon)* do anything to suggest that revenge had lost legitimacy. The speaker, who had allegedly suffered property damage and other wrongs at the hands of Simon, says that "he preferred to go without satisfaction for these offences." However, the reason for this restraint was not that exacting revenge would have been deplored by the Athenians who heard this speech, but that, as the very next phrase shows, the speaker was embarrassed by one particular aspect of his original dispute with Simon (Harris 364–365). There is no claim here that going without retaliation is especially virtuous.

have differed (it is enough to remember the existence of exponents of "might is right" opinions, such as Callicles), and the less one's anger was involved, the easier it was to be magnanimous. A mid-fourth-century litigant said: "It is to exact vengeance [from the defendant] that I shall pursue this case, for he started the hostility." Everyone, this speaker claimed, encouraged him to take revenge and told him that he would be "the most cowardly of men" if he did not. One is not "begrudged retaliation [*timōreisthai*]" against the person who wronged one.[113] What is most interesting here may be the speaker's slightly defensive tone. But one cannot dismiss Aristotle's views on the specious grounds that he was not an Athenian; it is possible that Athens differed slightly from some other places, but Aristotle spent most of his adult life there, and it is not plausible to suppose that he diverged much from local opinion when he classified exacting revenge and refusing to be reconciled as noble, *kalon*, whereas "to put up with insults to oneself, and to overlook those done to one's friends, is regarded as [note the reference to public opinion] servile."[114]

When we turn back to anger, we encounter a similar ambivalence in public attitudes. In the fourth century the repute of *orgē* at Athens was so mixed that litigants could invoke it or deplore it according to their convenience, just as a modern pleader invokes or deplores severity according to the needs of the moment. In other words, *orgē* in the abstract was unattractive, at least to most people, but it was often regarded as justified in particular circumstances.

The well-informed author of a study of Greek penology reached the conclusion that the fourth-century Athenian legal system was "an uneasy amalgam of two sets of assumptions," namely an "older, unreflect-

---

113. [Dem.] lix [*Against Neaira*].1, 12, 15. For the strong probability that Apollodorus, the son of Pasion, was the author, see Trevett 1992, esp. 50–76.

114. *Rhet.* i.9.1367a20–22, *Nic.Eth.* iv.5.1126a7–8. Herman dismisses this evidence for what contemporary Athenians were thinking on the grounds that Aristotle "was writing for posterity" (1994, 109) or that he was "a single theoretician brought up at Pella" (1998, 615)—not, in the circumstances, relevant considerations. Aristotle also quotes the saying, which is referred to by Thucydides (vii.68.1), that revenge is the sweetest of all things (ibid. and *Rhet.* i.9.1370b30). It was after 400 that *The Punishment of Dirce* became a popular artistic subject, in the wake of Euripides' representation of the story, and Heger misses the violence of the revenge in emphasizing that Dirce was the "real offender" (1986, 642).

ing acceptance of anger as normal and legitimate; and . . . the new assumption, at least implicit in the formal legal machinery, that the facts are paramount."[115] And it is true that fourth-century advocates deplored anger, as Antiphon had done earlier, when it suited them to do so. This was made easier by the cultural history we have just been examining, or rather by those Athenians and others who at least since the 420s had from time to time put the strong angry emotions in a unflattering light. "An honourable citizen," Demosthenes virtuously claims,

> should not ask a jury impanelled in the public service to take care of an anger or a hatred or anything like that for his own benefit, and he should not go to court for such purposes. As much as possible, he should not have such things in his nature, but if it is necessary, he should manage them in an even-tempered and moderate fashion.[116]

There is no doubt a heavy dose of hypocrisy here, as there was when Aeschines in turn used this argument.[117] But such statements make no sense unless they reflect part of the accepted ideology. It was also recognized that *orgē* was a common source of crime,[118] and that a testator under the influence of *orgē* may have acted against his real wishes (and hence that his will should be set aside).[119]

We can turn for a moment to another kind of writing, namely the sage platitudes of a teacher who educated men for public affairs. Isocrates' *To Demonicus* (370s) included advice against *orgē*:

> Practise self-control [*enkrateia*] in all the things by which it is shameful for the soul to be controlled—gain, *orgē*, pleasure, and pain. You will attain such self-control if you [among other things] . . . manage your *orgē*

115. Saunders 1991, 99–100.

116. xviii.278 (cf. Dover 1974, 192). Cf. xlii.12: the moderate man who minds his own business does not rush to court.

117. Aeschin. ii.3 (where inflaming anger is contrasted with using "just arguments," and it is taken to be self-evidently bad that Demosthenes wanted "to call forth [the jurors'] *orgē*"); iii.4 (he speaks of his opponents as "obtaining judgements not on the basis of the laws, but with anger on the basis of ad hoc decrees").

118. E.g., Dem. liv.25.

119. Isaeus i.13—*orgē*, through which we all make mistakes (cf. 10, 18).

towards those who offend against you as you would expect others to do if you offended against them.[120]

In the social elite there was now, evidently, a degree of disgrace attached to extreme displays of *orgē*.

As for the "new assumption" that the facts were paramount, it is itself a fiction. Fourth-century litigants do attempt to convince juries of their versions of "the facts," but they also, for instance, love character assassination and misrepresenting the law.[121] And Antiphon's speeches show that, as we would in any case assume, these habits went well back into the fifth century. In fact they probably went back to the very earliest Athenian litigation. The orators in the *Iliad* know very well that they have to stir up emotions, notably anger. From the beginning the sophists had dealt with the importance of the emotions to public speaking.[122] And in his sketch of the art of rhetoric in the *Phaedrus*, Plato alludes to the technique of *deinōsis*, or "horrification,"[123] in effect a technique for working on the audience's anger.

Plato himself naturally took a more Olympian view of this sort of oratorical technique. In the *Phaedrus*, a man who is especially expert at arousing (and extinguishing) the anger of crowds, such as the sophist Thrasymachus of Chalcedon, is regarded with some suspicion. "The mighty Chalcedonian," Socrates says,

is the winner for tearful speeches aimed at arousing pity for old age and poverty, and he is also clever, as he said, at arousing the masses to anger, and at soothing them again by his charms when they are angry,

120. i.21. 1.30–31 spells this out: "Be affable in your relations with those you deal with . . . You will be affable if you are not quarrelsome or hard to please and if you are not competitive with everyone, and if you do not harshly oppose the *orgai* of those you deal with even when their *orgē* is unjust; you should instead give way to them when they are in a passion, and rebuke them when they have stopped." His defence of platitudes: ii.40–41.

121. On the role of "the facts" in Athenian court oratory, see Cohen 1995, e.g. 76.

122. Quintil. *Inst.* iii.1.12. Every successful speaker of classical times knew this: for Cleon, for instance, see Thuc. iii.38.1.

123. Pl. *Phaedr.* 272a. Quintil. *Inst.* vi.2.24 defines this as "rebus indignis, asperis, invidiosis addens vim oratio": "in which skill above all others Demosthenes was extremely formidable."

and he is first-rate at both devising and eliminating calumnies on any grounds whatsoever.[124]

This is not a neutral account.

Demosthenes, the leading practitioner, and Aristotle, the theorist and instructor, are both candid about the need to stimulate *orgē*-anger. Demosthenes often explicitly attempts to excite the *orgē* of his audiences in both political and judicial contexts,[125] and he owed much of his success to his ability to stir his hearers' emotions.[126] He takes it for granted that it was right and proper for the jury in, for instance, his prosecution of Meidias to feel *orgē*,[127] and this no doubt reflected general opinion:

> But this habit my opponent has, men of Athens, this device of entangling in yet more trouble those who take just proceedings in their own defence, is not something which should cause me alone to be indignant and resentful while you overlook it. Far from it. All of us should be equally angry [*orgisteon*], for people should reason and observe that the likeliest of you to suffer easy maltreatment are the poorest and weakest, whereas the likeliest to act insolently [*hubrisai*], and then to avoid punishment for it and hire men to get up legal actions in retaliation, are the loathsome rich. So such conduct must not be overlooked.

Other contemporary orators commonly present judicial anger as proper and indeed desirable.[128]

Aristotle's most detailed anatomy of anger arises from his desire to meet the orator's needs. "Clearly," he says,

> one must, by means of the speech, bring the judges into the state of those who are irascible, and show one's opponents to be responsible

---

124. *Phaedr.* 267cd (cf. D-K 85 B 6).

125. Political contexts: *Third Philippic* 31 and 61; *On the Crown* 18 and 138; *On the False Embassy* 7, 265, 302, etc. Judicial contexts: xxi.57, 123 and *passim;* liv.42, etc.; [Dem]. xlv.7, 53, 67.

126. Cf. Dion.Hal. *Dem.* 22, and cf. Quintil. vi.2.24 again.

127. xxi.34, 46, 147, 226. It is probable that Demosthenes really did prosecute Meidias, in spite of Aeschin. iii.51–52; see the assessment of the problem in D. M. MacDowell's edition of Demosthenes XXI, pp. 23–28. The propriety of judicial *orgē* taken for granted: e.g., Lys. vi.17, xxxi.11; Dem. xxiv.118 (it will be calibrated to the seriousness of the offence). The passage quoted in the text is xxi.123–124.

128. E.g., Isocr. xviii.4, 36; xx.6, 9, 22; Dinarchus, *Against Demosthenes* 2.

for those things that are the causes of anger [*eph'hois orgizontai*], and that they are the sort of people against whom anger is directed.[129]

To this end he gives a highly detailed description of the kinds of people who would commonly provoke the hearers to anger and of the reasons for their anger.[130] The detail brings before us an Athenian citizen's world marked by an intense competition for respect and standing.[131] But the important point here is that *orgē* is treated as a respectable instrument of persuasion.

Demosthenes boasts that he did not physically strike back when Meidias struck him, "although," he says, "I fully sympathize with Euaion and anyone else who has defended himself when dishonoured" (Euaion had actually killed his assailant in anger, but was convicted by only one vote in the ensuing prosecution; xxi.72–76). One should not, he says, fight off insolent bullies at the moment of anger, but refer them to the courts, which have the function of protecting victims (xxi.76). In other words, there is no embarrassment about admitting to *orgē*, even though it can if mishandled lead to deplorable results; it should be expressed through the proper institutional mechanisms. One could even put forward one's *orgē* as an excuse for the sort of thing that Meidias was supposed to have done, striking another adult male citizen of similar status on a public occasion; whether the plea had much effect is unclear.[132]

Anger for proper motives and in proper quantities was so far from

129. *Rhet.* ii.2.1380a2–5.

130. *Rhet.* ii.2.1379a30–1380a5. Concerning instruction on the arousing of emotions, see Solmsen 1938, 391–394. According to Fortenbaugh 1970, 64 (= 1979, 149), Aristotle made the use of emotional appeals a more respectable part of oratorical practice than it had been before; it is more likely that he simply gave a better analysis of the psychological basis of existing practice, while ignoring the moral objections which Plato had raised in the *Phaedrus*.

131. Cohen 1995, 62–63.

132. xxi.41. Few classical Athenian men are likely to have thought that one should avoid anger in responding to an act of *hubris;* cf. Lys. iii.39 (if a man who is in love and "is deprived of the object of his desire" does not show anger and an immediate desire to retaliate, his story is not credible), Dem. xxi.72. What was not so easy to excuse was the prolonged anger known as *pikria*, bitterness (e.g., Dem. liv.14). Acting out of fresh anger was more excusable, apparently: Lys. xviii.19. For anger as an excuse, cf. Lys. x.30, where, however, the speaker says that "the lawgiver [i.e., the law] gives no pardon" to it (a matter we shall return to shortly). Cf. Saunders 1991, 110.

being disapproved of at Athens in the mid-fourth century that punishing crime could be spoken of naturally as involving the public's *orgē*.[133] In the *Crito* Plato imagined the laws of the city being judicially angry and requiring to be humoured, but one notes that the anger concept used here is the relatively mild *chalepainein;* later on, however, an older and less Socratic Plato did not mind attributing *orgē* to his ideal lawgiver.[134]

To some extent, then, there seems to have been a division of opinion about the acceptability of *orgē*-anger. But several extra comments are needed. First of all, it will not be sufficient to say that Demosthenes neglected to learn from Herodotus, though that is likely enough. No educated Athenian can have been ignorant by the 380s/370s of the fact that *orgē*, as a style of interaction, had been subjected to some criticism. But there was no need to agree wholeheartedly with the criticisms—all the less so because one could simultaneously think that a statesman should avoid acting out of anger and that certain private offences or, to put it in an Aristotelian way, forms of slighting required one to be angry. Or one could think that *orgē* was normally excessive but that *to chalepainein* was perfectly all right. One's milieu obviously mattered too: philosophers and teachers could preach ideals, while men who were pleading in court understandably used arguments which were more practical than utopian.[135]

Plato made a close connection between temperament and the merits of political systems. In *Republic* II he asks how in the ideal state the

---

133. Aeschin. iii.197. Especially if the guilty were rich: [Dem]. xlv.67. Cf. Pl. *Protag.* 323e–324a, where Protagoras is shown taking it for granted that it is annoyance that leads the punisher to punish; nonetheless he has (on the basis of 324ab) earned credit for the theory that people do not punish retributively. Allen 2000, 50, gives a misleading impression about the acceptability of *orgē* in the Athens of the orators by using an eccentrically wide definition of punishment and by lumping together (348 n. 2) a miscellany of texts relevant and irrelevant (such as Isocr. xiii.1, Lys. xv.12); her attempt to diminish the number of texts in which speakers deprecate anger seems disingenuous.

134. Pl. *Crito* 51b, 54c; *Laws* xi.927d.

135. And utopian arguments could be used for all sorts of purposes: the speaker of [Dem]. xxv.89–92 passes easily from a eulogy of Athenian harmony *(homonoia)* to a demand (which was unsuccessful) that his opponent should be executed for a techni-

"guardians" can be both spirited *(thumoeideis)* and ill-tempered to enemies, and at the same time even-tempered with each other; the answer
is, as a result of education in philosophy.[136] This education will notoriously *not* include reading Homeric accounts of the gods' quarrelling
with each other. Too much music, he claims, would also make the potential guardians not harmonious but "ill-tempered [*akracholoi*] and
irascible [*orgiloi*] instead of spirited [*thumoeidous*], and full of sour-
ness."[137]

So rulers who are not irascible with each other are clearly an essential part of the just Platonic polity, and Plato does not think it necessary to explain or spell out all the effects of anger in unjust political systems. It seems largely inconsequential in Books VIII and IX
when he associates anger not with democracy or even tyranny, but
"timocracy," whatever that means exactly (rule by the men of honour?).[138] It is in the soul of the "timocratic man" that the passionate element *(to thumoeides)* is said to dominate.[139]

The elderly Plato seems to have grown more indulgent towards anger, at least in the penal sphere. It is worth considering the penal doctrines which he put forward in the *Laws* in the context of actual Athe-

---

cal offence. In *Laws* xii.934–935 Plato argues for the banning of rhetorical abuse, on
the grounds that giving in to *thumos*-anger is uncivilized, subhuman and irresponsible
(see Koster 1980, 10–11). The angry orator "fills his *orgē* with evil banquetings"
(935a).

136. *Rep.* ii.375b-376c. The elimination of family life will prevent there being
much quarreling or litigation among the guardians. Then comes the startling addition: "And there will be no justification for lawsuits between them for acts of violence
or assaults, *for we shall say that it is fine and just for men to defend themselves against others
in the same age group,* thereby compelling them to stay physically fit . . . If anyone of
them should get into a passion [*thumoito*] against another, he would <therefore>
vent his *thumos* on such a person and be less likely to proceed to greater quarrels"
(v.464d–465a). I suppose that it was distaste for the democratic law courts, combined
with an artificial distinction between *thumos* and *orgē*, which caused Plato to imagine
turning back the clock like this.

137. *Rep.* iii.411c. He is here making Socrates contradict an already long established opinion about the psychotherapeutic power of music (for which see Chapter
14).

138. Plato speaks of timocracy as a Spartan form of government, or Cretan, *Rep.*
viii.544c, 545a.

139. *Rep.* viii.548c, 550b. This is because his angry mother has taught him to seek
retaliation, *timōria* (549e).

nian penal practice. We can recognize that classical Greek cities did not in a strict sense possess penal systems[140] but still ask what Athenian criminal law and legal practice had to say about crimes committed in anger. The great ambivalence which seems to reign in American criminal law concerning the value of emotion, of anger in particular, as an excuse or exculpation[141] may warn us not to expect complete consistency on this subject in other legal systems.

Some homicides likely to be the result of anger were legally condoned by Athenian law, such as, unsurprisingly, the killing of a man caught in illicit intercourse with a member of the assailant's immediate family.[142] Wounding, at least, was held to be more serious if the act was done with malice aforethought (ek pronoias)[143]—and thus less recognizably under the impact of anger. (Aristotle makes it reasonably clear that acts performed in anger were not considered to have been performed ek pronoias).[144] In the case of homicide, it appears that unpremeditated killings were classified as unintentional.[145] The punishment was life-long exile, without loss of property; and the murderer could be pardoned by the victim's relatives if they felt like it. Since the angry murder was no doubt in most cases unpremeditated,[146] it was therefore, by modern standards, subject to rather lenient treatment.[147] And as we have already seen, anger could be used as an acceptable mitigation.

In the *Laws* Plato theorizes about the circumstances in which the city should show judicial anger or should keep its anger under control.[148] The important distinction is between curable criminals and in-

140. M. D. Hall 1996, 73.

141. Kahan & Nussbaum 1996.

142. With his wife, mother, sister, daughter or established concubine: MacDowell 1978, 114; Cohen 1991, 99–109.

143. MacDowell 123–124.

144. *Nic.Eth.* v.8.1135b26–27.

145. Demonstrated by Loomis 1972. Cf. Gagarin 1981, 31–37.

146. But the intention to *harm* was taken to be sufficient evidence of premeditation, even if there was no evidence of intention to *kill;* see Loomis 93.

147. The punishment for intentional homicide in classical Athens was capital. The leniency of the Athenians towards passionate crimes may have been a consequence of wide support for the opinion that the angry emotions often act as irresistible external forces.

148. *Laws* v.731cd. Every citizen, he has just remarked (731b), should be *thumoeidēs* (strong-willed, spirited) but also as *praos* (even-tempered) as possible.

curable ones. Against the latter we have to fight, and we cannot do that without *thumos gennaios,* "noble anger" (at the same time, he avoids commending *orgē*).[149]

He also most remarkably makes a special subject out of the penology of specifically angry murders and assaults, and his recommendations are strikingly lenient. The utopian legislator distinguishes the involuntary cases from the voluntary, but also creates a borderline category between involuntary and voluntary for cases in which the action proceeds from *thumos* or *orgē*.[150] Within the category of killing in anger, he further distinguishes two sub-categories, killings committed on the impulse of the moment and immediately repented, and those committed by persons who, stung by insults, exact revenge later and do not repent. In the first case the punishment in the ideal city of Magnesia is to be two years' exile, in the second, surprisingly, nothing more than three years' exile. Thus Plato was more systematically lenient than the Athenian state was with the homicide defendant who had acted in anger.[151] One reason may have been his positive opinion about *to thumoeides,* the passionate element in the soul. Another reason was that Plato did not want his code of criminal law simply to protect the community: he wanted it to cure the souls of the criminals as well.[152] Curable criminals deserved pity, not anger. Unfortunately he does not explain how the unrepentant avenger is to be cured.

Insofar as anger is associated with a particular social class in fifth- and fourth-century texts, it is with the poorer section of the *dēmos.* The connection is already there in Aristophanes and Thucydides. In a democracy, Plato alleges, the *dēmos* gets angry *(aganaktein)* "if people are subjected to anything which hints at slavery" (by which he probably means any legal or official limitation of their actions as individu-

---

149. *Laws* v.731b (perhaps this even means "magnanimous anger"; cf. Dover 1991, 181).

150. Angry murders: *Laws* ix.866d–869e. Angry assaults: 878b–879a. The terms *thumos* and *orgē* are used indifferently here.

151. ix.866d–867e. It is not clear to me whether the penalties prescribed in the *Laws* for angry assaults were more or less harsh than those inflicted in contemporary Athens.

152. *Laws* ix.862b; cf. Saunders 1991, 144–147.

als).[153] Nor is this view entirely confined to the enemies of the *dēmos:* the poor *(penomenoi)*, as Aristotle says, are among the groups of people who are irascible and easily excited.[154] Demosthenes attempted for his own purposes to inflame the popular jurors' anger against men who were rich,[155] clearly presupposing that there was plenty of fuel for him to ignite.

Anger could naturally be attributed to other political actors, not only the *dēmos.* Aristotle takes it for granted that on the political plane *orgē* is harmful: the primary reason why monarchical rule is a bad thing is that, in his view, one man is much more liable to be carried away by anger or some other emotion than are the many, "and then his judgement is necessarily perverted," whereas, he claims, a great number of people are unlikely all to be carried away by emotion at the same time.[156] In all this there is no formal contradiction of what he wrote in the *Nicomachean Ethics* about the admissibility of appropriate anger, but the assumption seems to be that in political life anger is generally to be avoided. And it is not necessary for courage in battle either. Associating anger with the barbarians in the now traditional way, he claims that when barbarians show courage under the impulse of anger—the Celts are named—it is only a kind of quasi-courage; real courage is based, so he maintains, on reason.[157] The ideal Greek citizen-soldier is implicitly constructed as a man with a high degree of control over his own anger.

But when in *Politics* V Aristotle comes to analyse the failure of constitutions, or as we might say, of regimes, anger seems less conspicuous

153. Pl. *Rep.* viii.563d. Cf. vi.493cd.

154. *Rhet.* ii.2.1379a17. What causes the *aganaktein* of the masses in an oligarchy: *Pol.* v.8.1308b33–38.

155. xxi.123, [Dem.] xlv.67.

156. *Pol.* iii.15.1286a31–35: "The many are less likely to go astray. Just as a large volume of water is harder to pollute, so the mass of the citizens is less likely to go astray than the few; and the individual's judgement is bound to go astray when he is overcome by *orgē* or some other such emotion, whereas it is a very difficult thing for all the <citizens> to be angry and fall into error at the same time." [Aristot.] *Ath.Pol.* 22.4 refers to the habitual *praotēs* of the *dēmos* (which was something of a commonplace with Athenian speakers: M. D. Hall 1996, 74). There is some ambiguity about Aristotle's attitude to monarchy: Walbank 1984, 76; D. Miller 1995, 234–239.

157. *Nic.Eth.* iii.8.1117a4–9, cf. *Eud.Eth.* iii.1.1229b28–32.

than a reader of, say, Thucydides might have expected. We are told the conditions which prevent the masses from becoming very annoyed with an oligarchic regime,[158] but emotions are not much a feature of this book until Aristotle comes to speak about the fall of monarchies. However, anger is often nearby, for the philosopher has a good deal to say about the phenomenon of *stasis*,[159] in which anger is an inevitable element; he takes it for granted that *stasis* is evil.

When he reaches monarchies, we are naturally told about some of the anger-driven violence and conspiracy that had brought down tyrants, "for a tyrant's cruelty may take many forms, and each becomes a cause of *orgē*" (*Pol.* v.10.1311a33–34). In the background is the anger of the monarch himself, which inevitably gained importance for the Greeks when first Philip II of Macedon and then Alexander became the dominant figures at Athens and elsewhere. Examples: the Peisistratids at Athens, and so on. "Many attacks on them have occurred because of <people's anger at> the rulers' sexual offences against their subjects." More examples. Many assassination attempts against monarchical regimes have also been motivated by anger at physical violence, he says, with yet more examples (v.10.1311b6–36). It may be that Aristotle did not particularly regret any of these actions; on the other hand, they are explicitly treated as the intervention of irrationality.[160]

In the last phase, therefore, of classical Athenian democracy, *orgē*-anger in the political sphere had a somewhat complicated reputation. Having been the subject of criticism in the age of the Athenian Empire, it had continued to appear quite regularly as a vice or a form of excess. It was regularly contrasted with reasoning and reasoned behaviour. The opposite style of comportment, which was epitomized in the word *praotēs*, was frequently alluded to as an ideal. But practitioners and theorists both recognized that even *orgē*, not to mention less extreme forms of angry emotion, might have positive civic and political

158. *Pol.* v.8.1308b33–40.
159. *Pol.* v.1.1302a8–13, v.7.1308a31–33.
160. v.10.1312b27–34: "Often anger is more effective than hatred [in attacks on tyrants], since men who are angered attack more eagerly because the emotion does not make use of reasoning."

effects. It was difficult to separate it from *thumos* and indeed from courage.

The Athenian democracy of the fifth and fourth centuries has been praised for its success in limiting the scale of violence between citizens, and it deserves credit for having kept political violence to a minimum, except in the great defeat-year of 404 and its immediate aftermath. And this was not a police state, quite the reverse.[161] Athens the city achieved a remarkably high level of freedom of speech, and tolerated quite intense personal abuse, as Aristophanes abundantly demonstrates. There were some legal limitations to slander,[162] but an attempt to penalize "verbal abuse" *(kakēgoria)* as a criminal offence[163] seems to have had little if any practical success. Freedom of speech was highly prized. Thus the Athenians could, if we concentrated on their internal political affairs, be said to have kept anger within reasonable bounds.

They spurred each other on to this achievement by means of an arbitration system[164] and a criminal law system, and also by means of a shared social and moral code. Part of this code was a complex discourse about *orgē* whose general tendency was towards restraint.[165] Not that this should lead us to regard the Athenians as saints. And a psychological account of fifth/fourth-century Athenian men must also take into account their sometimes exceptionally violent behaviour towards foreign populations, at least in the days of the great empire—the extreme examples of horror being their massacres at Scione and Melos.[166] As to whether the Athenians diverted on to their slaves and their own family members the *orgē* which they attempted to restrain in dealing with each other, that is a question we shall consider in Chapters 12 and 13.

161. There was policing (mainly public slaves at the disposal of the magistrates), but it clearly did not aim at intervening in all violence between citizens, or even violence committed in public space (cf. Hunter 1994, 3).

162. Wallace 1994, 109.

163. Isocr. xx.3, Dem. xxi.32. Such a law was desired by the elderly Plato: *Laws* xii.934e.

164. On which see Gernet 1939.

165. Another element was the discourse of *homonoia,* concord, for which see Thériault 1996.

166. Which are not said by Thucydides to have been motivated by anger. But it is a reasonable deduction from Isocrates iv.101–102 (380 B.C.) that what non-Athenians saw on the latter occasion was an act of ill-tempered revenge.

Never again after the deaths of Demosthenes and Aristotle do we have enough evidence to be able to construct contemporary views about political or civic anger in any Greek city. Not that city life came to an end with Alexander, as some scholars used to imply; not that Hellenistic philosophers can have been uninterested in this subject, for the early fathers of Stoicism, to go no further, Zeno, Cleanthes and Chrysippus, are all known to have written about both political philosophy and the emotions. But the opinions of two Hellenistic figures only can be established in any detail, Polybius and Philodemus, both of whom, as it happens, expected and must have found readers in both the Greek and the Roman social elites.

Some further words about Stoicism, however: its hostility to the passions does not seem at first glance to be rooted in the political realm (even Epictetus, who made the political advantages of the elimination of the passions explicit, claimed to put the *individual* at the centre), but the political implications were there from the beginning. In other words, we can hardly doubt that the early Stoics—and their supporters—already saw that the elimination of *orgē* had political advantages as well as others. This will have applied all the more to such politically conscious Stoics and Stoicizers as Poseidonius and Cicero. But it was left to Seneca and Epictetus, as far as we know, to bring out the political benefits of this particular Stoic doctrine.

Polybius was both a strong believer in reason and a student of non-rational behaviour. Angry emotions appear in the historian's narrative and in his asides at many vital junctures. What makes the Roman army superior to that of the Carthaginians is that Roman soldiers (so Polybius says, simplifying unduly) are citizens, fighting for their own country and children; they are not technically superior to the Carthaginians, but they win because "they can never relax their anger *(orgē)*— they persist with obstinate resolution until they have overcome their enemies" (vi.52).

But the most important strength of the Roman state, Polybius thinks, lies in the Romans' extreme respect for the gods, which he notoriously attributes to manipulation by the upper class, manipulation which is aimed at controlling the common people—for the mass of any population, he says, is "full of lawless desires, unreasoning *orgē* and violent *thumos*" (vi.56.11). Speaking in general terms, but making a prediction about the future of Roman politics which it is reasonable to see as his disguised description of contemporary affairs, he says that when the *dēmos* becomes convinced that it is being cheated by its leaders, it will, "in passionate resentment and acting under the dictates of anger," refuse to obey (vi.57.8). Thus popular *orgē* is useful in war and deleterious in peacetime. But it is also clear that Polybius makes much of the anger of populations which he dislikes: a case of frightful popular anger occurred at Alexandria in the year 200, in reaction against the government of Agathocles.[167] And the Aetolians, whom Polybius loathed, are naturally represented as giving way to *orgē*.[168]

Just as in Herodotus the enemy rulers tend to be overcome by anger, so in Polybius some of the principal opponents of Rome are irascible characters: this applies to Hamilcar Barca, and to the Carthaginians as a nation in the period prior to the Second Punic War (it is no accident that they are "barbarians"), and it applies to King Philip V, and to his son Perseus the last king of Macedon.[169] What Polybius says about the Roman general who was held responsible for losing the Battle of Trasimene, C. Flaminius, confirms the general pattern: he went down to defeat because he was full of *thumos* and "started to utter indignant complaints" *(eschetliaze)*.[170]

The Roman Senate, on the other hand, is rarely and only in rather special circumstances said to have expressed anger: the one clear case seems to have concerned the Rhodian ambassadors of 169.[171] This in

---

167. xv.25–33. Cf. Eckstein 1995, 132, with some further examples.

168. iii.3.3, 7.1 (with Eckstein 212–213).

169. Hamilcar Barca: iii.9.7; the Carthaginians in general: iii.10.5, 13.1; Philip V: many references, making up an entire portrait (cf. Pédech 1964, 223–224)—see in particular v.11.4, vii.13.3, viii.8.1, xi.7.3, xvi.1.2, xvi.10.3, xvi.28.8, xxii.13.7, cf. vii.13.1; Perseus: xxiii.7.5.

170. iii.82; cf. iii.81.9 (unreasoning *thumos*).

171. Liv. xliv.35.4 ("ingentem iram patrum"; cf. 14.13) paraphrases a lost section of Polybius; this anger was directed at Rhodian ambassadors who, showing a poor knowledge of the peculiar psychology of the Romans, dared to advocate peace between Rome and Macedon. According to Eckstein 1995, 96 n. 38, the Senate was also angry with the Rhodians in Polyb. xxix.19, but he does not say so explicitly. In xxvii.6.3 Polybius says that King Perseus' ambassadors came to Rome in order to "mollify" the Senate. All this intriguingly hints that Polybius saw that the Senate was in fact largely responsible for beginning and prolonging the war against Perseus (cf.

spite of the fact that it is constantly at loggerheads with the rulers and representatives of foreign states.

Polybius felt a marked distaste for so-called "tragic" historiography, in other words historical writing in which intense emotions are described.[172] That presumably made him self-aware when he depicted his own characters in the grip of powerful emotions. His narrative use of anger is even less likely to be accidental than the patterns we observed in Herodotus and Thucydides (less likely also because of all the writing about the passions there had been in the interim). But he was not as strict or consistent an opponent. In a programmatic passage, he assumes that he and his readers seek for those "who will share our anger" (sunorgioumenon) (iii.31.9). And while he very seldom seems to mention the orgē of the Senate, he allows that it has been necessary to soften "the orgē of the conquerors,"[173] the Roman conquerors that is, whose interests he had striven to promote. It could of course be said that Polybius did not shrink from harsh practical reality, and some Greeks at least may have derived advantage from his unpatriotic behaviour: his fellow Megalopolitans honoured him with a public inscription in part precisely because he had "ended the Romans' orgē against the Greeks."[174]

Thus Polybius uses charges of surrendering to anger to blacken the names of those whom he disapproves of, which leads to the conclusion that his contemporary readers, or at least the Greeks among them, while not rigidly against all manifestations of anger,[175] believed that it should be dominated or excluded.

In an earlier chapter, we saw that while Philodemus of Gadara admitted the existence of a morally permissible "natural" anger, he spent much of his energy in his De ira on a wholesale denunciation of all orgē and thumos. This lack of clarity and finesse includes what he has to say

---

Harris 1979, 228). In xxx.31.12 a Rhodian ambassador speaking to the Senate is made to refer to the Romans' orgē against his city.

172. On which see Walbank 1972, 34–40.

173. xxxviii.4.7. This phrase is a probably a symptom of his having felt some real doubts about Roman imperialism in the years after 146.

174. The Megalopolitans: Paus. viii.30.8.

175. And Polybius recognizes (v.93.4), in a less partisan way, that shortage of public funds commonly leads to anger.

about anger in political and civic life. For he seems to be a determined critic:

> Neither a judge nor a senator nor an assemblyman nor a magistrate nor in short anyone can be just when he is in the grip of angry passions [*pathesin orgilois*]. The angry become despotic, suspicious, liars, treacherous, dishonest, deceitful, ungrateful, and egotistical.[176]

But he shows no interest in defining what this means. Is all anger whatsoever included in his condemnation? Elsewhere we are told that the angry man is asocial, and loves war and revenge.[177] In reality it is likely that this theorist made some room for justified political and civic anger, perhaps in one of the many lost sections of *De ira;* but in the main he was intent on denunciation.

In *Civilization and Its Discontents* (1930) Freud observed, fitting his own work together with a traditional belief, that "in consequence of [the] primary mutual hostility of human beings, civilized society is perpetually threatened with disintegration."[178] We need not endorse either Freud's view of human nature or his fear of the age of iron to see that the threat is indeed perpetual. That is especially true if civil society in a wider sense is in question, and not simply the state—if, in other words, we are concerned about civil cooperation and decency. These things were all the harder to achieve in antiquity because of the relative lack of participatory institutions, and all the more difficult for the Greeks because of the agonistic nature of their culture, and also perhaps because of the tradition, which weakened greatly in the fourth century, of heavy citizen participation in warfare. But some Greeks identified strong expressions of anger as one of the enemies of political processes and inter-citizen relationships as they ought to be; and because of this they came to favour, in varying degrees, the control of *orgē.*

---

176. *De ira* 5 (col. xxviii.22–33; cf. xxix.20–25).

177. *De ira* 7 (col. xliv.22–26). Fr. 12 Indelli tantalizingly seems to distinguish the anger of the poor and the rich. For his oddly apolitical way of approaching the anger of kings, see Chapter 10.

178. Freud 1961 [1930], 69. "The law is not able to lay hold of the more cautious and refined manifestations of human aggressiveness" (71).

CHAPTER 9

The Roman Version

On the day of Rome's foundation, the founder killed his brother in a fit of anger.[1] This element in the foundation story is likely to have been archaic, but it was still acceptable in Livy's time (and it could be given a positive cast: Romulus was willing to kill *even* his brother, such was his determination to defend the new city wall). Vergil, however, saw that in the new, officially harmonious Augustan age, Romulus and Remus would have to be reconciled.[2] Then there is the endlessly discussed end of the *Aeneid:* in the last lines of the national epic, the hero puts the enemy Turnus to the sword in a transport of rage, without presumably undermining the political program of the poet's patron and friend Augustus (but many disagree). It is clearly not going to be easy to discover how far, when, and why, the Romans came to believe in a measure of anger control, or what this had to do with their views about the internal order of their state and society.

The aristocracy of the mid-republican period, the earliest Romans we can study in any detail via texts, was a highly contentious group. Its members competed with each other fiercely, though most of the time non-violently, for public office and honours. Senators also showed themselves periodically to be short-tempered as well as arrogant in

1. Liv. i.7.2: "inde cum altercatione congressi certamine irarum ad caedem vertuntur."
2. *Aen.* i.292, with the comment of Wiseman 1995, 145. Horace did not approve of the fratricidal squabble, *Epod.* 7.18–20.

dealing with foreign states. But political and religious and social institutions, sustained by a highly adaptive ideology, succeeded in maintaining the internal cohesion of the state, while permitting competition to proceed. As for angry behaviour towards other states and their inhabitants, some Roman leaders, from the time of Flamininus (consul in 198) onwards, learned a modicum of tact in dealing with the Greeks,[3] but until the very late Republic there is no indication that any Roman political figure set much store by restraining his temper with respect to other states or their populations.

Is there anything to discuss in this chapter, one may wonder, other than the Hellenization of the Romans? Was the Cicero of *Tusculan Disputations* IV, or the Seneca of *De ira,* attempting anything other than a demonstration of his own cleverness in adapting Greek philosophy and literature to a Roman public? Did they have anything to say in those works which was important for Roman politics or Roman society? Seneca and many other Romans did indeed offer doctrines about how emperors should behave, and how their subjects, especially their courtiers, should behave too. But first let us consider more broadly how the Romans adapted and developed Greek thinking about the restraint of the angry emotions between citizens in the political and civic spheres—staying alert to the fact that the central Latin concept, *ira,* is a wider one than Greek *orgē.*

Through the thick mist that envelops most Latin literature before Cicero, we catch glimpses of works which put classic scenes of Greek mythological rage before Roman audiences.[4] When Cicero wished to describe the quarrels of Agamemnon with Menelaus and of Atreus with Thyestes, he quoted the versions adapted for the Roman stage some two generations earlier by Accius.[5] What this adaptation had done to the moral framework of the original Greek stories can sometimes be detected: Accius, for instance, wrote a play called *The Myrmi-*

---

3. In the account of Greek opinions about Roman imperialism in Polyb. xxxvi.9, not even the critics of Rome refer to Roman irascibility, possibly because it was not much noticed, more probably, in view of xxxviii.4.7, because Polybius' respect for Roman power persisted.

4. This was probably the kind of context in which Ennius had called anger "the beginning of madness" (Cic. *Tusc.Disp.* iv.52).

5. *Tusc.Disp.* iv.77.

dons in which Achilles seems to be much more on the defensive over his anger against Agamemnon than he ever is in the *Iliad*.[6] Indeed he seems to be on the point of being tried for treason. Perhaps a Roman audience at this date (somewhere within the period between 140 and 100), with its tradition of military discipline still largely intact, would not have tolerated easily a hero who set his rage, however justified, above the orders of his commanding officer.[7] Yet we do not normally think that Roman playwrights were delivering messages to receptive audiences "about matters of moral or political principle" (as was said about the Athenian tragic poets). No one should doubt the political importance of the theatre in the middle and late Republic,[8] but in spite of the fame some playwrights achieved, they never acquired the authority of the great tragic poets of Athens.

Mid-republican Roman society was too structured and in some ways too disciplined for anger in public life to be an issue. There were of course occasional times of intense civic strife, and the possibility of further angry conflict was visible to Polybius and presumably to others.[9] Perhaps the angriest man to become conspicuous in Roman politics for a long time rose to prominence at the very end of Polybius' life, and embodied the popular aspirations Polybius detested—namely, Gaius Gracchus.[10] But there are no reliable details.[11]

It would never, I think, have occurred to any mid-republican Roman to suggest that anger, rather than the ambition and corruption of his

6. See especially lines 108–113, 118 Dangel = 452–457, 462 Warmington; the last of these lines is "ego me non peccasse plane ostendam aut poenas sufferam." For Aeschylus' *Myrmidons* as a principal source, see J. Dangel's edition, pp. 290–295.

7. But Accius was generally quite hard on the Homeric heroes (Dangel 38–39).

8. Cf. Wiseman 1995, 133–138.

9. Val.Max. ix.3.1–8 lists some angry incidents.

10. Plutarch alleges that he was harsh and passionate *(thumoeidēs)* *(TG* 2); cf. Dio Cassius fr. 85.

11. An anecdote suggests that Gaius was self-conscious about his own irascibility. Realizing that he was often carried away by anger as he was speaking in public, he arranged to be attended by a slave with a musical instrument who on such occasions sounded a soft note, "on hearing which Gaius would at once remit the vehemence of his passion and speech, and become milder." But this story is Plutarch's *(TG* 2), and it is quite likely to have been distorted by his interest in anger therapy. Cicero's earlier and more credible version simply has it that Gaius used a flautist to regulate the pitch of his voice *(De orat.* iii.225–227).

opponents, was responsible for the often intense tensions in public life. But there was certainly plenty of public anger expressed in the last century of the Republic, in the shape of slave rebellions as well as Italian discontent and strife among the Romans of older citizen stock. The responses of the Roman elite were practical: they answered serious opposition with more or less firm measures of repression, while from time to time *popularis* politicians attempted to inflame the anger of the city *plebs*. On the theoretical level, the response was not very profound, as far as we can tell: Cicero's efforts, unless the loss of most of Books IV and V of his *Republic* is obscuring something important, were substantially limited to nostalgia for the past, combined with a somewhat desperate desire for a benevolent *rector* or Leader who would keep the lower orders in their place.

But the growth of Roman interest in philosophy had roots going back well before 150 B.C.; by the last decade of the second century this interest affects a certain number of senators and a few others, and it spreads out among other educated persons after the Social War.[12] In the late Republic some notion of the primary ethical views of the famous Greek philosophical schools could be assumed among the upper social elite, municipal as well as metropolitan. No doubt this knowledge was often superficial, but many people were now well enough informed to know that anger could be of questionable moral standing.

Of great importance here is the letter Cicero wrote to his younger brother Quintus in late 60 or early 59 B.C. to give him advice about the governance of the province Asia, which the younger Cicero had been ruling for some two years. It deserves to be quoted at length (*QF* i.1.37–40):

> There is one point about which I shall not cease to instruct you, and insofar as it is within my capacity I shall not tolerate any exceptions in your reputation [i.e., I shall attempt to cure you of your only vice]. Everyone who comes from there ["Asia"] speaks of your good character, integrity and kindliness [*humanitas*], but there is one reservation in their encomia of you, and that concerns irascibility [*iracundia*]. This vice is considered, even in this private, normal life I lead, to be a sign of irresponsibility and weakness, but nothing is so unbecoming as show-

12. Ferrary 1988, 602–615.

ing harshness [*acerbitatem animi*] while one holds the highest office. I will not undertake to describe to you now what is always said by learned men about irascibility, since I don't want to be prolix and secondly because you can easily find out from many authors' writings . . .

[38] This is what practically everybody reports, that as long as you keep your temper, they find you the pleasantest person in the world; but when you are upset by some fellow's rascality or wrongheadedness, you become so exasperated that everyone longs for the return of your kindliness . . . And I am not now urging you to do what is perhaps difficult in human nature at any time, but especially at our time of life, and that is to change one's disposition and suddenly to pluck out some evil deeply ingrained in the character; but this much advice I do give you, that if you cannot possibly avoid it, because anger [*iracundia*] takes possession of the mind before reason has been able to prevent its being so possessed, in that case you should prepare yourself beforehand, and reflect daily that what you have to fight against is anger, and that when the mind is most under its influence is just the time when you should be most careful to bridle your tongue; and indeed I sometimes think that this is as great a virtue as not feeling anger at all. For the latter is not exclusively a sign of strength of character, but also occasionally of slowness [*lentitudo*]; while to govern one's mind and speech when angry, or even to hold one's tongue and retain one's sway over mental perturbation and resentment, that though not a proof of perfect wisdom, is a mark of great natural ability . . .

[39] Passion, curses and insults are not only inconsistent with literary culture and *humanitas*, they are inimical to the dignity of imperial office, for if one's outbursts of anger are implacable, that is a sign of extreme harshness, but if they are capable of being mollified, that is a sign of frivolity—which is, however, to be preferred to harshness.

The long letter from which this passage is taken was a somewhat formal literary performance,[13] in which Cicero modestly put himself in the role of a former philosopher-ruler giving counsel to another philosopher-ruler.[14] The writer takes it for granted that Quintus, who was an educated man but not an intellectual, would understand a discus-

13. Cf. D. R. Shackleton Bailey's commentary, p. 147.
14. Cf. Rawson 1989, 239–240.

sion of anger control, and could easily find out, if he did not already know, what the extensive philosophical literature had to say about anger. Meanwhile, an important political issue was at stake, namely the acceptability of a provincial governor to those he ruled over and to those whose interests he could affect. Locally, this power was very personal and in consequence subject to the governor's passions. In the following letter, Marcus spells out in considerable though allusive detail how his brother had offended both Greeks and Romans by his sharpness and irascibility.[15]

There is evidence that talk about anger control was in these years familiar to people well outside senatorial circles.[16] When Cicero defended the consul-elect L. Murena in 63, he was addressing a jury made up of property-owning Romans, most of whom can have had no special education in philosophy. Prosecutor in the case was the younger Cato, tribune-elect and inflexible Stoic. This was the way to attack him (*Mur.* 61–63): "There was a certain man of genius, Zeno . . . his rules are of such a kind as this: the wise man . . . never forgives anyone's crime . . . a man worthy of the name cannot be mollified or placated, only the wise man is handsome or rich . . . it is as bad a crime to kill poultry unnecessarily as to suffocate one's father . . . You said something in anger. 'The Wise Man [Cato is imagined as saying] is never angry.'" Whereas, according to the Platonists and Aristotelians, so Cicero goes on, the wise man sometimes does get angry. We may draw the conclusion that it was by now possible to discuss anger control, if only in very general terms, before an audience such as made up the judicial panel trying Murena. Elsewhere Cicero confirms that he really did make such comments in the speech he delivered.[17] And

15. i.2.4–7. But *QF* ii.16.3 end suggests that in later years Quintus himself looked back on Marcus' advice as something of a joke. *Att.* i.17.1–4 shows at some length how one made excuses for such a person ("irritabilis animos esse optimorum saepe hominum et eosdem placabilis").

16. In attacking another provincial governor, Verres, Cicero had earlier made some use of the accused's supposedly furious outbursts: *II Verr.* v.106, etc. Part of the point was that the provincials reacted with their own indignation to unjust treatment (sect. 115), just as the slaves we shall be considering in Chapter 13 did.

17. The published speeches are not of course transcripts of what was really said, but *De fin.* iv.74 seems to show that the substance of the *Pro Murena* passage was actually delivered to the *iudices* (jurymen) ("omnia peccata paria dicitis. non ego tecum ita iam iocabor, ut isdem his de rebus, cum L. Murenam te accusante defenderem.

among the *periti homines*—that is to say, those who were interested in philosophy—it was by now possible to assume a notably higher level of knowledge.

It is a pity that we cannot know whether Caesar really gave a speech at the great Catilinarian debate in 63 anything like the one which Sallust later attributed to him. He is made to comment emphatically on the trouble that can come to prominent people who show *iracundia* (*Cat.* 51.12–14), and he or Sallust must have been thinking of real damage to a man's reputation. "A public man is expected not to be angry: what in others is called *iracundia* is called in a public official arrogance and cruelty."

By now a reputation for irascibility seems to have been genuinely harmful. Whatever the origin of these words of Sallust's, Caesar's self-presentation, even before he became dictator, shows a distinct interest in anger. The great political innovator already seems to have applied his mind to the matter by the time of his first consulship in 59, if not earlier. Dio's account is striking: Caesar as consul tended to ignore Cicero's insults, he says, but

> he did not disregard him entirely. For although Caesar possessed in reality a rather mild nature [*epieikesteran* (= *clementiorem*)], and was not at all easily moved to anger [*ethumouto*], he nevertheless punished many, since his interests were so numerous, yet in such a way that it was not done in anger [*di'orgēs*] nor always immediately. He did not indulge in *thumos* at all, but watched for the right moment, and he caught up with most of his enemies without their knowing about it . . . he visited his retribution secretly and in places where one would least have expected it, both for the sake of his reputation, in order to avoid seeming to have a wrathful character, and also so that no one should learn of it beforehand.[18]

---

apud imperitos tum illa dicta sunt, aliquid etiam coronae datum"). In their presence he was naturally more polite: "non est nobis haec oratio habenda in imperita multitudine aut in aliquo conventu agrestium" (*Mur.* 61). The obvious comparison is with the passages in *In Pisonem* (59–60, 68–72) in which he made mock of his opponent's alleged philosophical views; but casual allusions before juries (e.g., *Pis.* 20, 37) are clear indications that such men were expected to know something about the great philosophical schools.

18. xxxviii.11.3–5. More reflection about anger attributed to Caesar: xxxvii.55.2.

A cold and treacherous enemy, in other words.[19] It is hardly to be doubted that this sort of analysis of Caesar's conduct had already started in the 50s,[20] and I take it that it started with Caesar himself. It looks as if he knew the prescriptions of the philosophers, and how to make use of them.[21] The year 59 or 57 is the most likely date for Philodemus' tract *On the Good King according to Homer*,[22] which Caesar may well have read (it was addressed to his father-in-law and ally, L. Calpurnius Piso[23]). There seems at all events to have been political credit to be gained as early as the 50s by avoiding the appearance of an irascible character, or by gaining the positive reputation of being able to control one's anger. The dictator's *clementia* ideology was practically predetermined.

Yet another reason for thinking that a reputation for irascibility or the reverse may really have carried weight is that anger control is reasonably prominent in the description which Cicero gives of the ideal Leader in his *Republic* (54–51 B.C.). Authoritative historical figures, Scipio Aemilianus and Laelius, are exploited there in the interests of the argument that the state should be ruled by one man, just as the *animus* should be ruled by reason, with the passions, anger in particular, eliminated.[24]

19. "What strikes a modern observer most in Caesar's conduct [in 59] . . . is the masterly way in which he put his opponents morally in the wrong," wrote Gelzer, with no apparent irony (1968, 78).

20. But Dio Cassius' speeches are notoriously unreliable, and there is no really firm evidence that Caesar was interested in anger until as late as 49. Furthermore, Dio used Caesar as a model for the behaviour of emperors in his own time (cf. Millar 1964, 80–81).

21. Such as the warning of Philodemus against the enjoyment of punishing, *De ira* 7 (col. xlii.21–25). Rawson's judgement (1989, 242) that Caesar was not interested in philosophy was in part mistaken; of course such statements are always relative, but his behaviour and language with respect to anger suggest *informed* calculation.

22. For 59: Murray 1965, esp. 178–181, and T. Dorandi's edition, pp. 39–46. For 57: Paolucci 1955. Momigliano argued (1941, 152–153 = 1960, 380–381), as have others, that it was written when Caesar was dictator, and that cannot be excluded.

23. See ch. 9 (col. xliii.16).

24. *De rep.* i.38.59–60. He represents Laelius as claiming, to Scipio's applause, that though he was sometimes angry he did not allow *iracundia* to dominate his soul, and as referring to the authority of Archytas of Tarentum. There must be no place in the ruler's soul, Laelius says, for *libidines* or *irae/iracundiae*. No expectation here, there-

There is only one Roman who in the entirety of Caesar's writings is said to have been affected by *iracundia*—his enemy and one-time fellow consul Calpurnius Bibulus.[25] It was probably a serious matter when Caesar was in effect called upon, at the beginning of the civil war which led to his dictatorship, to respond to charges of *iracundia* and excessive anger. An emissary came from Pompey to try to make peace: he invited Caesar "to give up his party spirit [*studium*] and anger [*iracundia*] for the sake of the state" (this is all recounted by Caesar himself), and "not to be so seriously angry [*adeo graviter irasci*] with his personal enemies" as to harm the state too. Caesar answers with a whole chapter of self-justifying argumentation.[26] The appearance of excessive anger was now a political liability,[27] and in March 49 Caesar had time to explain to correspondents that his "new method of winning" the civil conflict consisted of mercy *(misericordia)* and generosity *(liberalitas)*,[28] a most striking statement for a hard-headed warlord in the middle of a campaign. Another watchword was *lenitas*, kindness (*BC* iii.98.2).

And he succeeded in spreading the message. In the speeches which Cicero wrote to cajole Caesar when the civil war was practically over, he portrayed him as a man of mercy, claiming on one occasion that Caesar's self-restraint, including his control over his temper, was even more remarkable than his conquests and made him comparable to a god.[29] This was all the more admirable because civil war is preeminently a time of *iracundia*.[30] Caesar's own interest in anger is confirmed in an unexpected way: one of the prominent adornments of the most important of his monuments, the temple of Venus Genetrix, was a pair of paintings, for which he paid a huge sum, by the contem-

fore, that *to thumoeides* will ally itself with reason. Hellenistic denunciations of strong anger had done their work.

25. *BC* iii.16.3 (the word is repeated). See Syme 1978, 224.

26. *BC* i.8.3, i.9 (where he avoids referring directly to his anger, except with "aequo animo tulisse," sect. 3).

27. It would be interesting to know when the story was invented that the tyrannical Sulla died in a fit of rage (Val.Max. ix.3.8).

28. Transmitted as Cic. *Att.* ix.7C.1.

29. Cic. *Marc.* 8–9: "animum vincere, iracundiam cohibere"; cf. *Deiot.* 40, *Lig.* 29.

30. *Marc.* 9. Some people thought that Caesar followed up his forgiveness of M. Marcellus (consul in 51) by having him murdered (Cic. *Att.* x.1.3).

porary artist Timomachus of Byzantium. The subjects, rather incongruously, were Medea and Ajax[31]—a pair linked to each other by their rage.

Since Caesar saw displays of anger in such a negative light, it is not surprising that he continued the practice of Herodotus and other Greeks who had associated irascibility with barbarian enemies, thus denigrating both: Caesar makes the German prince Ariovistus a man of *iracundia*,[32] and later this was a tedious topos. Tacitus, for instance, did the same for the German Arminius and for the Batavian rebel Civilis and his followers.[33]

It would be rather poor method to gauge the opinions of the Roman upper class by means of the gnomic lines of Caesar's protégé Publilius Syrus, but there is nonetheless some interest in the fact that his sentiments about *ira* and *iracundia* are negative (he praises revenge, however).[34]

At all events, the notion that anger should be *completely* avoided had emphatically not, in the late Republic, won the assent of all Romans. It is in Cicero's philosophical works that one finds the "absolutist" doctrine on this subject; elsewhere he is more moderate. That does not mean that his expression of "absolutism" was casual or "insincere," but it imposes a certain caution. Cato will have been unusual in being a root-and-branch preacher against the passions. There is no reason to think that Caesar went beyond the view that public figures should maintain appearances in respect of anger. And the traditional atti-

31. Plin. *NH* vii.126, xxxv.26 ("praecipuam auctoritatem publice tabulis fecit"), 136. This picture of Medea was often written about by epigrammatists (see A. S. F. Gow & D. L. Page on Antipater of Thessalonica xxix [*Garland of Philip* II, pp. 43–44]); they emphasize how well Timomachus represented her emotions, including anger. A Herculaneum painting of Medea (Naples, Archaeological Museum, inv. MN 111436, often illustrated) is probably a copy of Timomachus' work.

32. *BG* i.31.13, and for Gauls, see vi.5.2, vii.42.2. For the *ira* of the Gauls ("which that race cannot control") see also Liv. v.37.4.

33. *Ann.* i.59, *Hist.* iv.13, 21, 29. See also Sen. *De ira* ii.15, Tac. *Germ.* 25.

34. Esp. 87 Meyer, 88, 290 ("iracundiam qui vincit hostem superat maximum"), 301, 311, 319, 344, 345, 514, 638, 679. But see 230, 455. Revenge: 270, 323, 334, 580. Line 127 may be recommending "ventilation": "cui nolis saepe irasci irascaris semel"; cf. 550. Line 695 may possibly sum up his point of view: "tarde sed graviter <vir> sapiens irascitur."

tudes subsisted. When *viri fortissimi,* vigorous public men, are injured they resent it, when they are angered they are carried away *(efferuntur),* when they are provoked they fight (Cic. *Cael.* 21). In the *First Philippic* Cicero asked Antony not to be angry if he, Cicero, spoke his mind, but realizing that in the circumstances this was too much to ask, "I ask him to be angry with me as with a fellow citizen," which meant stopping short of violence *(Phil.* i.27).

It was recognized that an effective orator needed to display anger as well as stimulate it. It may be that in *De oratore* (of 55 B.C.) Cicero tried to avoid directly endorsing this view when he attributed it to the unrefined though highly successful orator of the previous generation, M. Antonius (consul in 99).[35] The latter is imagined as mocking the philosophical opinions of those who had theorized about anger.[36] Nine years later, however, in his *Orator,* Cicero stated with greater frankness that he had used every possible means of arousing anger in juries when he had needed to do so, and that he had felt anger himself.[37] And while Cicero's philosophical works are "absolutist" about anger, his private attitude admitted bursts of appropriate anger, both in his friends[38] and in himself: "Insane wretch," "I am bursting with indignation."[39] These lines were written under the extreme provocation of Caesar's invasion of Italy in 49, which seemed likely to overthrow most of what Cicero had struggled for in public affairs (this anger he no doubt felt to be altruistic). Nonetheless his letters may leave the impression that he also made some serious effort to avoid anger when he could.[40]

Roman revenge also seems to have undergone some real but limited

35. Antonius' practice: ii.189–204. The pretending option: ii.189.

36. *De orat.* i.220–222. But he is interestingly represented as assuming that "omnia haec" (apparently expressions of anger) "are thought to be bad, troublesome and to be avoided in our daily life together" (221).

37. *Orator* 131 ("est faciendum etiam ut irascatur iudex")–133; Cicero celebrates his own *vis animi,* and looks to Demosthenes as his only worthy forerunner in this respect.

38. E.g., *Att.* i.17.4 ("irritabilis animos esse optimorum saepe hominum et eosdem placabilis").

39. *Att.* vii.11.1 ("O hominem amentem et miserum"), vii.12.3 ("dirumpor dolore")—this at the beginning of the civil war.

40. See, e.g., *Att.* vi.3.8, vii.18.2 ("stomachari desinamus").

criticism.[41] We must be careful not to invent an unhistorical story here, and it may well be that traditional beliefs already held that revenge should be strictly in proportion to the offence committed, and that one should always seek legal redress, not violent retaliation. Vendetta in the Anglo-Saxon sense was probably never approved in the historical period. But it must be emphasized that even in such a relatively civilized location as Cicero's writings on rhetoric, the existence of a general right of revenge (*ius ulciscendi*) is taken for granted.[42]

Orators of the first century B.C. argued, when it suited them, that "punishment" exacted outside the legal system was to be deplored.[43] Nothing surprising about that. But a passage of Lucretius suggests that, within the elite at least, opinion had moved somewhat further. He contrasts the present day with the time before a social contract came into being: in those days "each man in his anger sought to avenge himself more fiercely than is now permitted by just laws" (*De rerum natura* v.1148–1150). But that is very vague. So was Cicero when he spoke about revenge after he returned to Rome from exile in 57. His speech of thanks to the *populus Romanus* comes, at its close, to the question of retaliation. Marius, Cicero reminds the audience, had avenged himself in blood "with an angry heart" when he came back from exile in 87; but he, Cicero, will instead employ oratory—as if he had any alternative. "I will avenge individual crimes," he asserts—but by good political leadership and other peaceful means. At the end of this section, Cicero said something else—a textual problem prevents us from knowing exactly what—about the good repute which attaches to the man who is *neglectful* about revenging himself.[44] And he wrote piously in a philosophical work that "there is a limit to vengeance and punishment," hardly in itself a radical thought.[45] An anonymous late-

41. There seems to be no general account of this matter, but see Y. Thomas 1984, who, however, sometimes fails to distinguish revenge from general expressions of hostility.

42. *Topica* 90, *Part. Or.* 42 (and see *Sulla* 46); cf. *De inv.* ii.65–66, 161.

43. *Rhet. ad Her.* ii.15.22, Cic. *De inv.* ii.27.81 (specifically against revenge). Cf. Y. Thomas 1984, 74.

44. *Post red. ad pop.* 19–23 ("qui in ulciscendo remissior fuit, in eo consilium aperte laudatur," Peterson; the MSS have "in eo aperte utitur," or something similar). Marius was supposed to have been a man of anger: *Phil.* xi.1.

45. *De off.* i.34: "Sunt autem quaedam officia etiam adversus eos servanda a quibus

republican writer rejects the notion of violent revenge as barbaric.[46] Philodemus as well as other philosophers opposed it, as we saw earlier. And the cause of *clementia* received further advertisement when it became part of Caesar's propaganda arsenal.

Whatever the nature of the political struggle in the late Republic—whether it was mainly a struggle within the upper class, as implied by the still dominant *Roman Revolution* of Ronald Syme, or whether popular discontent and reactions to it were also vitally important (as it is tempting to think)—it was undoubtedly a time of strong political passions. As far as the urban *plebs* is concerned, these passions defy analysis.[47] To start with, the sheer numbers were such as no city on earth, not even Alexandria or Beijing, had ever seen; and inevitably the sources incorporate the biases of the elite. The trend towards political violence began in the middle of the second century and accelerated in the 80s. It had its roots in the heightened unscrupulousness of the senators, few if any of whom disdained violent methods by the 50s, as well as in the restlessness of the poor—and also of the slaves.[48]

If the political rage of the late Republic gave rise to any Thucydides-like reflections about the role of strong emotion in political *stasis,* they are lost to us. There is, however, some reflection of late-republican *stasis* in the great philosophical poem of Lucretius. In the passage just referred to, he tells a traditional story: experience of violence and feuds *(inimicitiae)* made the human race become more willing to submit to the rule of law: "because each man in his anger sought to avenge himself more fiercely than is now permitted by just laws, for this reason men were utterly weary of living in violence" ("est homines pertaesum vi colere aevum") (v.1150). He explains that violence recoils on the man who is guilty of it. Law thus exists in part to limit the operation of anger. More difficult to comprehend fully is what he has to say about

---

iniuriam acceperis. est enim ulciscendi et puniendi modus"). Cicero often represents *inimicitias deponere* and *redire in gratiam* as positive acts.

46. Ps.-Sall. *Epist. ad Caes.* i.3.4.

47. For a good short account of the ways in which the city *plebs* expressed its discontents in the late Republic, see Purcell 1994, 676–680.

48. Quite apart from the great slave rebellions, it would be worth studying all the signs of slave owners' nervousness in the late Republic, including the vivid warning uttered in Philodemus' *De ira* 5 (col.xxiv.17–36), and such passages as Cic. *Cat.* iv.12, *Mil.* 87, 89.

warfare when he addresses Venus at the start of the poem. Having made the request, revolutionary for a Roman of this time, that Rome be freed from warfare (he even seems to include foreign wars), he contrasts the existence of humans with that of the gods. The placid existence of the latter is "untouched by anger," and we may be left with the implication that it is anger which leads humans to fight so many wars.[49]

It is likely that the critical Epicurean and Stoic views about *orgē*-anger and *thumos*-anger, having been translated into criticism of *ira*, began to have a certain effect on people's opinions even outside the circles of those who had an intense interest in philosophy. One recalls the evidence that Epicureanism had acquired a numerous following in Italy during the last generation of the Republic (Cic. *Tusc.Disp.* iv.7), a following which must admittedly have been partly dilettantish in character.

The political and civic consequences of these philosophically based criticisms of anger at Rome were in a sense nil.[50] But *ira*, like *clementia*, became a weapon in the propaganda wars which accompanied the long painful transition from republic to monarchy, and as such probably had some effect. Under the new system, from Caesar's dictatorship onwards, since the anger of the ruler was of intense practical importance at the center of power, anger discourse took on a new life—as we shall see in the next chapter.

Although the civil wars of the years 49 to 30 were a time of anger, anger which touched the lives of every Roman, the great contemporary writers who make civil strife their subject do not for the most part make anger the culprit. Both Vergil (*Eclogues* I and IX) and Horace (*Epodes* VII and XVI) avoid the theme in the political poems they wrote in the 30s. In the end, however, in the culminating work of his lyric poetry, Horace alluded to the wars which were now twenty years in the past in these terms (*Odes* iv.15.17–20): "With Caesar as guardian of our affairs, no rage [*furor*] or violence between the citizens will drive out peace, and no anger which sharpens swords and makes wretched cities

49. i.29–49. It is fairly plain that it is war in general, not simply civil war, which Lucretius wishes to be rid of ("per maria ac terras," 30, suggests that without fully proving it).

50. Their effects on the private individual may of course have been profound.

their own enemies." The poet simultaneously identifies part of the real psychology of the civil wars, and awards the new dictator the prize for having put a stop to the workings of an appalling vice.

The official version was that the civil wars had been fought for the sake of revenge.[51] But this very claim allows us to catch a glimpse not only of evolving imperial ideology but also perhaps of evolving Roman attitudes towards revenge. Fighting the Battle of Philippi in 42 against the assassins of his "father," Caesar, Octavian (with or without Antony) promised a temple to Mars the Avenger (Mars Ultor).[52] Appian's narrative of these times, which emphasizes Octavian's determination to avenge the famous assassination, presumably reflects the official line; Octavian is shown praising Achilles' vengeful reaction to the death of Patroclus.[53] The old ethos of revenge was clearly alive and well—never better, one might say, since Mars Ultor was a new conception.[54]

After Actium there is some retrospective Roman discourse about political anger such as the passage in Horace quoted above: we used to fight with each other because of excessive *ira*. But now the main contemporary questions about anger control in the public sphere concern emperors (and those petty emperors, the provincial governors). Can the emperor be prevailed upon to restrain himself? How should his subordinates react to his rage? Such matters will be dealt with in Chapter 10. But there is also the separate issue, anger between citizens.

The history of such anger could in theory follow many paths—the anger of and against gladiators,[55] the anger of hungry town populations in times of shortage, the anger of communities against each other (neighbouring towns; Greeks and Jews in Alexandria and elsewhere), anger against religious dissidents. But the track we are follow-

51. In the official version, the war against M. Antonius was of course a foreign war.

52. The sources include Ov. *Fast.* v.573–377, Suet. *Aug.* 29; cf. Cassius Dio xlvii.42, xlviii.3.

53. App. *BC* iii.13.

54. As to the manner in which Augustus dealt with this later, when it turned out to be inopportune to emphasize revenge against citizens (the temple of Mars Ultor was not dedicated for a full forty years, and by then the supposed victims of the *ultio* were not Romans but the Parthians), see the following chapter.

55. Gladiators were volunteers (Veyne 1999), and unconscious rage may have been an important part of their psychology.

ing, though it will bring us in sight of each of these themes, is a different one: the repute of the angry emotions, and the origins of attempts to restrain them.[56]

Before completing the transition to the new period of monarchy and, soon, absolute monarchy, let us consider a political historian, Livy, and a political poet, Vergil, who can perhaps help to indicate to us what point Roman thinking about *ira* had reached by Augustan times.[57]

It was mentioned before that Livy makes heavy use of anger words. While such terms are scattered throughout his history, they are used with particular frequency in Book II,[58] which describes the murderous strife and virtual civil war among the Romans after the expulsion of the last of the Tarquins. Livy's first ten books in general, the era of the "Struggle of the Orders" and Rome's rise to power in Italy, are only slightly less irate. The contentiousness of the age when the republican state was under construction stands out from his narrative, and it is probable that he gave at least some thought to *ira/iracundia*. The historian had written philosophical dialogues[59] which presumably concerned moral philosophy, and in his history there are occasional (banal) asides on the subject.[60] *Ira* and related words are immensely commoner in his usage than, say, *avaritia* words or *odium* words.

Not that Livy was an uncompromising critic of anger, far from it. He is supposed by some scholars to have been deeply influenced by Stoicism,[61] but he sometimes attributes *ira* to people whom he evidently approves of, including the Roman Senate and victorious Roman armies,[62] as well as to others. That in itself makes any theory that he was

56. In the Greek world, the spectre of popular *orgē* reappears from time to time: *IGRR* i.864 (line 20), Dio Chrys. iii.49.

57. It is not of course suggested that their opinions were necessarily typical, but we can take it that in their principal works they were addressing the Roman elite at large.

58. There is also plenty of *indignatio*. In Book II we find forty-three instances of *ira*, *iracundia* and *irascor* (of course other terms are relevant too); twenty-nine in Book VIII is the next largest concentration.

59. Sen. *Ep.* 100.9.

60. E.g., xxxiii.37.8: "then it was clear how much strength *ira* has for stirring the spirit [*ad stimulandos animos*]"—and the Romans slaughtered their enemies almost to a man.

61. Walsh 1963, 59, 64, 94.

62. The Senate: e.g., ii.5.1, xxiii.25.6, xliv.35.4 *(ingentem iram)*. Armies: e.g., ix.14.9,

in any serious sense a Stoic quite untenable. Admittedly a patriotic historian of Rome faced a difficult task if he held Stoic views—but he could at least have followed Polybius in suggesting that the Senate was almost always guided by reason not passion.

As for contemporary lessons, the fact that he often makes kings irascible[63] confirms his contemporary reputation for republicanism or something like it. The monarch of his own time noticed,[64] but was much too sensible to do anything about it; after all, it was the last of Augustus' intentions to institute overt *regnum*.

The closing lines of the *Aeneid*, in which the poet describes Aeneas' furiously angry killing of Turnus (xii.945–952), have become a notorious scholarly problem. Investigating the history of anger criticism shows without too much difficulty what the solution should be. But before we come to that issue, we must consider Vergil's general attitude towards anger.

Let it be said at once that neither issue is to be approached by *labelling* the poet, whether as "Stoic," "Epicurean," "Aristotelian," or anything else.[65] Next, we should admit that *ira* was an important topic in the *Aeneid*. Not only was the climax of the poem a scene of anger, the whole framework of the epic is provided by the anger of the goddess Juno against the hero.[66] If the legitimacy or seriousness of her anger were to be denied, the poem would be in severe danger of collapsing. Admittedly the *Aeneid* is not "about" *ira* in the same way as the *Iliad* is "about" angry emotions. And we might conclude that this anger of Juno's is merely part of an ambitious but not altogether successful attempt on the part of a regime poet to breathe life into the traditional gods. But at least the anger of Juno and other Vergilian gods proves

---

x.5.2, xxxviii.25.16. Hardly any Roman is likely to have been in the least troubled by the fact that Roman armies sometimes showed *ira* towards foreigners: cf. Vell. ii.119.2.

63. Kings are irascible (so is the *plebs*): i.36.4; ii.6.1, 7, 12.12, 13.7, 19.10; xlii.25.8. In ii.3.3 royalist traitors say there is a place for royal anger.

64. Tac. *Ann.* iv.34.3.

65. Cf. Gill forthcoming.

66. *Aen.* i.3–4. This anger is not surrendered until a few pages from the poem's end, xii.841: "adnuit his Iuno et mentem laetata retorsit." For the pervasiveness of anger in the *Aeneid*, see Wright 1997.

that the author of the *Aeneid* cannot possibly be considered an Epicurean,[67] even though as a young man he had had a connection with
Philodemus.[68]

It is plain that some kinds of anger are acceptable to Vergil. Even
if, as some think, he intends to undermine Aeneas at the end of
the poem by showing him in the grips of rage, it is not to be believed
that this (explicable) anger was supposed to delegitimize Aeneas altogether. Elsewhere he writes of "just anger."[69] And in Book VIII no less a
personage than the beneficent hero Hercules gives way to furious anger in exacting vengeance—clearly vengeance which Vergil thought
was thoroughly deserved—from the monster Cacus.[70] Yet anger in the
Aeneid is associated above all with the arch-enemy Turnus.[71] And there
is something angular, at the very least, about Aeneas' rage at the end
of XII: the economy of the poem does not require it; the dramatic circumstances do not require it; the whole tendency of the high culture is
against showing a great hero being overwhelmed by an ugly passion.[72]
The solution to this dilemma concerns the person of the *princeps*, and
will therefore be presented in the next chapter when we are examining the anger control of rulers.

Educated Romans of Augustus' time were well aware that philosophers had often found fault with angry emotions. Some of them held
more or less strict Stoic views on the subject. Most, however, probably
assumed an attitude which was a simplified form of Aristotle's—in
other words, they approved of *ira/iracundia* when it was directed in appropriate quantity against an appropriate target (and *ira* was such a
wide term—it was difficult to be altogether against it). While they may

67. *Pace* Erler 1992. The private Vergil is obviously unknowable.

68. For the papyrus linking Philodemus with Vergil (who was some forty years his
junior), see Gigante & Capasso 1989.

69. *Iusta ira:* x.714; cf. viii.500–501. Vergil quite often justifies anger elsewhere
(Laurenti 1987, 21).

70. viii.219–261 constantly emphasizes Hercules' passion ("ter totum fervidus ira /
lustrat Aventini montem," 230–231, etc.).

71. F. Cairns 1989, 71, 74.

72. For a solution to this problem, see the next chapter. Gill (forthcoming) argues
effectively that for most of the *Aeneid* the poet purposefully associates Aeneas with
unangry responses, which makes it all the more desirable to find a specific explanation for the ending.

not have been quite as enthusiastic about revenge as Aristotle seems to have been, they had no difficulty at all in approving it if the provocation was sufficient. The ideal woman of the time, "Turia," when she is eulogized in an inscription, is praised for, among other things, having avenged her parents.[73] Horrendous crimes—those of Cacus in the *Aeneid,* or later the supposed poisoning of Germanicus—were naturally thought of as being suitable occasions for revenge; Vergil describes Hercules as "the great avenger."[74]

How, it may be asked, did Roman law regard crimes of anger and acts of revenge?[75] One kind of violent revenge was legally sanctified: the Julian law on adultery, the definitive statute on that subject for several centuries, permitted the betrayed husband or his wife's father to kill the intrusive male, subject to certain conditions, and the guilty woman's father was permitted to kill her too.[76] But we should not take it for granted that these were the actual social practices in Augustan times: Augustus was busy for his own reasons making a demonstration against adultery, and the government seems to have recognized that, even when cuckolded, few real-world husbands will have wanted to go as far as murdering the paramour if he was a respectable citizen.[77] A

73. *Laudatio Turiae* I, lines 5 and 8 (to be read in the edition of Durry & Lancel).

74. *maximus ultor, Aen.* viii.201. For the case of Germanicus, see Suet. *Cal.* 3.

75. The subject here is the pre-Severan law of the Roman Empire; some later developments will be mentioned further on. In the late Republic, when Milo was charged under the Lex Pompeia *de vi,* Cicero seems to have thought of pleading, among other things, that his client had acted out of anger (*Mil.* 35), but he did not do so directly, and such a plea would have been a rhetorical obfuscation—perhaps not without some possible effect, however, for otherwise he would not have mentioned the matter.

76. *Dig.* xlviii.5.24–25. The father-in-law could do this lawfully only if he killed both wife and lover (he had to kill them "prope uno ictu et uno impetu . . . , aequali ira adversus utrumque sumpta," 24.4, cf. 33 pr. [this was the jurists' interpretation]); see further Mommsen 1899, 624. It was thought to show exceptional *robor,* toughness, to kill an unmarried daughter for a sexual liaison, even when the lover was a slave: Val.Max. vi.1.3. The husband's right to kill was also limited to those whose social status was impaired in certain ways (at least so the third-century jurist Macer said, xlviii.5.25 pr.; was this part of Augustus' law?).

77. The husband who stayed married and let the paramour go was liable to punishment for *lenocinium, Dig.* xlviii.5.30 pr., "for he ought to have been angry with his wife."

husband who killed his adulterous wife was deemed guilty of murder, though second-century emperors said that his punishment should be reduced because of the resentment *(dolor)* he felt.[78]

Generally, of course, revenge was supposed to be judicial not personal. This sort of revenge was taken for granted: one of the Cyrene Edicts shows that *not* avenging (by means of prosecution) the death of a relative would have been remarkable.[79] We have seen that Athenian law courts and some Greek legal theory made a certain amount of room for uncontrolled anger as a mitigating plea. The criminal law of classical Rome, however, did not regard loss of self-control as a mitigation of any offence, with the exception noted above, unless this was a result of madness. Nevertheless, in several matters of civil law, jurists sensibly ruled that statements made in anger could be declared invalid or inoperative.[80]

Let us turn once more to Seneca. His purposes in writing *De ira* seem to have been multiple: in part they were literary, in part they were therapeutic. Insofar as they were political, they concerned the behaviour of the emperor and the reactions of his courtiers (see below).[81] In addition, we can learn from this text Seneca's opinions about how other Romans (those of his own social class, naturally) ought to behave when anger is in question. He claims to make it possible to enjoy *tranquillitas animi*. But that, for a man in Seneca's position or indeed for any Roman of rank, involved intricate social interactions: not for him the relatively simple life of a philosopher.

The judgement that it is risky to be angry with an equal, insane to be angry with a superior, and squalid *(sordidum)* to be angry with a social inferior is merely a prudential social and political maxim (*De ira*

---

78. *Dig.* xlviii.5.39.8; cf. xlviii.8.1.5. Cohen 1991, 118, maintains that at Rome "the natural impulse of the husband is to avenge adultery in blood," but he relies too much on the artificial and macabre world of Seneca senior's *Controversiae*, and the law was as stated in the text. It was supposed that in the elder Cato's time a husband was permitted to kill his adulterous wife if he caught her in the act (Gell. x.23.5), but this must have been at most a dead letter by the first century B.C.

79. *Cyrene Edict* (*FIRA* I no. 68 Riccobono) I, line 34.

80. *Dig.* xxii.3.29.1, xxiv.2.3 (see, too, l.17.48) (in both situations it is female anger which is held to render an intention inoperative, but in the second instance this was probably to women's advantage).

81. But iii.2 also contains the sketch of an interesting reflection to the effect that anger is the only emotion which can affect a whole nation.

ii.34.1). So much for philosophical principles. But Seneca recommends, with detailed examples of his own practice, a nightly examination of conscience with respect to anger. What follows is one of the few sections of *De ira* which appears to consist of the author's own sustained reflections and not simply the more or less skilful cutting, pasting and recasting of earlier material.[82] And here it is the author's social relations, and by implication the reader's, that are the focus of attention as much as his psychic well-being. Addressing himself, he imagines himself having spoken too pugnaciously in a debate (moral: keep away from the ignorant), having admonished someone too candidly (moral: in future, consider whether the person can bear the truth), having been upset at a party by jokes and comments at his expense (moral: keep away from parties with the common people). It is noticeable that all this advice gives excuses for Seneca as well as indicating how one can avoid anger. Other situations in which he imagines himself being misguidedly angry are these: on a friend's behalf when the latter is mistreated by a rich man's concierge, or again at a dinner if he (Seneca) is assigned an insufficiently honorific place, or yet again when someone speaks badly of his talents *(ingenium)*. A sensible public man does not, he implies, grow angry when someone insults him (unlike Cornelius Fidus, who burst into tears when a fellow senator called him a "plucked ostrich").[83] Seneca undertakes the difficult task of showing that these offences against one's dignity (for that is what most of them are) do not merit anger. All this was practical advice for the smooth conduct of the social life of the upper-class male.

Seneca's advice about anger concerns other areas of public life too, including both penology and foreign affairs. He does not bother with the masses: the multitude in the forum is a crowd of wild beasts, except that wild beasts are less aggressive (ii.8.3). Scholars who have supposed that Seneca was addressing a mass public which cut across social classes are grossly anachronistic.[84] His penological theory, at all events, is cor-

---

82. iii.36–38. A little earlier, in iii.33.1, the thought that "most of the fuss is about money," whether it is anger in the family or in the state, seems as formulated to be original with Seneca.

83. Seneca expresses his disapproval of this reaction in *De const.* 17. Presumably most senators would have grown angry and replied in kind.

84. I have in mind the usually well-informed Cupaiuolo 1975, 167, who does not realize the limitations of Roman education and book circulation. According to

rective or curative. Since man's nature, at its best, aims at kindness, it is not *poenae adpetens,* eager to punish.[85] Revenge is an inhuman word.[86] He contrasts punishment as a remedy with punishment inflicted in anger, and naturally prefers the former.[87] We are a little surprised to hear a Stoic saying that the anger-free judge will often let a guilty party go free if he seems likely to reform (i.19.5)—not that such notions are likely to have had much impact on real-life judicial behaviour.[88]

And even Seneca's condemnation of revenge has something equivocal about it, since he allows exceptions. In saying that "it is often better to dissimulate than to revenge oneself" (ii.33.1), he allows room, on undefined terms, for any claim that in a particular case revenge would be better—provided, of course, that it is not angry but cold-blooded.

Seneca, like many other imperial writers, repeats the topos about the anger of the barbarians. He contends that "those who live towards the frigid north have harsh temperaments that are, as the poet says, 'very like their native skies,'" whereas empires generally occur in milder—that is, Mediterranean—climates.[89] In part, this simply continues the long tradition of attributing irascibility to the Other, with the corollary that we Romans are good at limiting our anger. The irascibility of the barbarians—sometimes idealized now as *free* people— continues as long as there is any Roman literature.[90]

The at-first-glance strange contrast between empires and the world of anger makes sense in the new period of Roman imperialism now beginning, in which educated Romans thought of Rome as having brought not only justice and law, *iura et leges,* to the conquered peo-

---

Donini 1982, 40–41, Stoic doctrines enjoyed some diffusion in "the lowest classes of Roman society," which at the very least gives the wrong impression. They were not in any case the object of Seneca's interest.

85. *De ira* i.5 and 6.4. But the most important text is *De clem.* i.20–24. Protagoras and Plato and others (cf. Cupaiuolo 1975, 116 n. 82) had already opposed retributive punishment.

86. *De ira* ii.32.1. The MSS read "ultio et talio," but editors have seen that one noun or the other has to go; since Seneca seems to use *talio* to mean "retribution" in general (*Ep.* 81.7), it is not important which.

87. Punishment as remedy: i.16.2–4, 19.5 and 7.

88. For some subsequent controversy about the principles of penology, see Gell. xx.1.

89. ii.15.5; the poet is unknown.

90. See, e.g., Lucian, *Toxaris* 8 (Scythians); Xen.Eph. ii.3.5–6, etc.; Heliod. ii.12.4; *Pan.Lat.* vi.10.2 (Franks); Themistius, *Or.* x.131bc. For Tacitus, see above, n. 33.

ples, but also *humanitas* and harmony.[91] This thought did not logically entail giving up military expansion on the frontiers, but it is true that Seneca asserted that it was *ira* that led rulers into misguided foreign wars.[92] Now that imperial expansion had decelerated for severely practical reasons, there could be some real discussion at Rome about the justification for expansionist wars, and this discussion can be traced from Seneca's time until that of Cassius Dio, and indeed beyond.

In short, Seneca appears to have a wide range of concerns about anger's political and social effects. We should not dismiss any of them as entirely rhetorical or frivolous; on the other hand, the most serious probably involve the figures we have not yet examined in detail, the emperor and the courtier.

Musonius Rufus, Seneca's younger contemporary, went a good deal further, as we might have expected. By Roman standards, he was an apostle of mildness. As we saw in Chapter 6, he argued that the Wise Man should forgo retaliation, and should not even go to court when he has suffered "outrage" *(hubris)*: "We should not be implacable towards those who have wronged us, but rather a source of good hope to them, [which is] characteristic of a civilized and benevolent way of life.[93] Musonius was quite widely admired in "all social orders," according to Pliny, meaning both inside and outside the Senate. In this age, the 60s and 70s of the first century, this could happen to a prominent Roman who was held to be a man of philosophical principle. It would be mistaken to deny him any practical influence among those who frequented the same social and intellectual circles.[94]

The social limits of this influence were vividly illustrated in 69. With

---

91. A vital text here is Plin. *NH* iii.39, written under Vespasian: Italy was chosen by the gods to "unite scattered empires, to make manners gentle, to draw together in converse by community of language the jarring and uncouth tongues of so many nations, to give mankind civilization [*humanitatem homini dare*], and in a word to become throughout the world the single fatherland of all peoples." The idea that a Roman administrator should show *humanitas* was old, but most of the passage quoted is, as far as surviving texts go, original.

92. *De ben.* vi.30.5. But for Pliny and Trajan, a barbarian king could deserve the emperor's *ira* and *indignatio: Pan.* 16.5.

93. Musonius fr. X = p. 78 Lutz.

94. Plin. *Ep.* iii.11.7 mentions that he had *omnium ordinum adsectatores*. For his influence among contemporaries and near contemporaries, see Lutz 18–20. He was sent into exile both by Nero and by Vespasian (Lutz 14, 16).

the Flavian army of Antonius Primus on the outskirts of Rome, the new usurper Vitellius sent a senatorial delegation to make terms. Musonius, though only a knight, joined in, but his attempts to expound to the angry soldiers the blessings of peace and similar themes were found ludicrous or boring, and in spite of his rank he narrowly escaped violence. "Poorly timed philosophy" (intempestiva sapientia), Tacitus comments.[95] A poorly chosen audience too. Musonius saw where there was anger, and rashly went to confront it. On a later occasion his choice of audience, while superficially more reasonable, turned out to be almost equally over-optimistic: we are told that a Roman philosopher, and there can be little doubt that it was Musonius, reproved the Athenians for staging gladiatorial combat—that great expression of unconscious rage—in no less a place than the Theatre of Dionysus. The Athenians were so annoyed with the philosopher over this matter, says Dio Chrysostom, that he decided to give up Athens and go to live somewhere else.[96]

It was the accepted wisdom of the imperial age that anger characterized barbarians, and that anger inside the body politic was a principal cause of civil wars. These were both ancient ideas to which first- and second-century Rome contributed nothing more than elegant reformulations. Encapsulating 200 years of Rome's violent internal struggles in a single chapter of his Histories, Tacitus remarked that the armies of 48 B.C. and 42, and those of Otho and Vitellius, were all driven into battle by the same forces—the anger of the gods and the furious passion (rabies) of mankind (ii.38). The most interesting Tacitean remark about anger may be the most famous one—his claim that he is able to write the history of emperors from Augustus onwards "sine ira et studio," "without anger or affection" (Ann. i.1). The accumulated ill repute of the angry emotions is likely to have required that a declaration of impartiality should be in these terms.

Besides Seneca and Musonius, the other great apostle of emotional restraint as a vital element in political Stoicism was of course Epictetus: he supposed that avoiding "contentiousness" would produce, among other benefits, "concord in the polis and peace between nations"

---

95. *Hist.* iii.31; Cassius Dio, who does not mention Musonius, says that Primus' soldiers were in an angry mood (lxv.19.2).

96. Dio Chrysostom xxxi.122, who does not name Musonius; for this old identification see Lutz 17 n. 60.

(iv.5.35–37). The first of these consequences, which fitted Epictetus' generally fatalistic politics, was by now banal; the second was still a distinctive point of view. The Roman Stoics—some of them anyway—had also taken up a distinctively humanitarian view of slavery (as we shall see in Chapter 13). All in all, therefore, it is not enough to see Stoic morals as merely an expression of the hegemony of the dominant social elite. Anger control was in the interest of that elite as a whole, but suggested to them certain ways of behaving which they did not unanimously want to accept.

Not that political anger was always seen in a negative light—we must not let our account be unduly influenced by morally superior intellectuals. It was Aelius Aristides, of all people—scarcely a man to slander the imperial power—who pronounced with satisfaction that under Roman rule political trouble-makers are punished: they are overtaken by the *orgē* and revenge of Rome (*To Rome* 65, 143 A.D.). No hint here that *orgē* might be disapproved.

Juvenal's satires, however, suggest how the traditional ethos had changed. In the first part of his collected works, his *persona*, like that of his predecessor Persius, is the satirist in his pure form—that is to say, bursting with fury. "How can I express the amount of anger that burns in my fevered liver?" (i.45). "Facit indignatio versum" ("outrage compels me to write")—the famous phrase well expresses the essence of the first six satires, which culminate in a misogynistic attack on marriage sustained at outlandish length. These satires gain some of their force from the very fact that anger has been attacked from so many directions: the angry poet knows that he may be thought to be behaving badly—the works of anger are among his targets, after all (i.85)—but such is the provocation that he cannot restrain himself. He justifies his *indignatio* at the supposed degeneracy of contemporary Rome in ample detail.[97]

We might possibly expect this atrabilious *persona*, which draws on a very long literary tradition including the prototypical Roman satirist Lucilius,[98] to be maintained (though the subtle variations within Horace's *Satires* and so-called *Epistles* might have warned us). Instead, it is

---

97. For a succinct account of this justification, see Anderson 1962, 146–149 = 1982, 278–281. For the interchangeability of *indignatio* and *ira* in some imperial writers, see Anderson 158 n. 6 = 290 n. 6.

98. Angry, or pretend-angry, poetic invective flourished greatly at Rome; cf. the

not only abandoned but negated. In Juvenal's later satires, at least from Satire Ten onwards, the poet takes on a *persona* which sometimes expresses scorn, but turns against all passion. He urges the reader to ask for a soul which "knows not how to be angry" *(nesciat irasci)* and has no desires.[99] What, if anything, in the way of personal experience may have given rise to the new personality of the poet we cannot know. Part of the purpose is obviously to instil a philosophy of acceptance. This is how we should probably take Satire Thirteen, which treats at length the indignation felt by Calvinus (because of a bad debt), indignation which finds the satirist thoroughly unsympathetic.[100] Satire Fifteen describes an incident of bestial cannibalism in Egypt, for which the poet says that *ira* was to blame (or *furor* or *rabies* or hatred)[101]—yet another horror story attributing extremes of angry behaviour to the Other.

Satire Thirteen is in fact a prolonged attack on *vindicta,*[102] revenge. Punishment will not make good a financial loss, and revenge is (usually? always?) contrary to philosophy *(sapientia).*[103] In any case it is not as effective a punishment as the torture inflicted by a criminal's own conscience and his fear of divine wrath. The culminating argument is that revenge is especially enjoyed by women.[104] All this is likely to represent an important strand in contemporary Roman thought. Satire Thirteen shows that the dubious moral status of revenge and of inappropriate anger was familiar to, and accepted by, a large proportion of moderately educated Romans.[105] But Juvenal's position was not extreme: the addressee is chided because his reaction seems to Juvenal to

---

pseudo-Vergilian *Catalepton* 13, as well as the well-known works of Catullus and Horace.

99. x.357–362. On the programmatic nature of this change, see Courtney's commentary, p. 446. Braund 1988, esp. 189, argues that the transition was gradual.

100. On Satire Eleven, cf. Anderson 1962, 157–158 = 1982, 289–290.

101. xv.131, 169.

102. See esp., but not only, lines 174–249. For a recent treatment, see Braund 1997, who, however, somewhat mistakes the target.

103. xiii.189–191 (". . . quippe minuti / semper et infirmi est animi exiguique voluptas / ultio"). Note that he explicitly rejects Stoicism, xiii.121, but invokes Chrysippus (184).

104. xiii.191–192.

105. Moderately indeed if they thought that Thales had been a critic of revenge (xiii.184).

be *disproportionate* to his loss;[106] and the very end of the poem seems to promise that the wrongdoer will suffer in the end, to the addressee's delight.

It can be hypothesized that from Seneca's time onwards a certain number of highly educated Romans felt increased concern about the propriety of revenge.[107] It would be simpleminded to assume that such speculations had no effect at all on contemporary behaviour, and we shall see later that during the succeeding century there was a certain tendency within the Roman upper class to regard slaves in a more humane light, a tendency which was to have some surprising legislative effects in the reign of Antoninus Pius. The Roman Empire was still full of curse tablets, casual violence, litigation and religious contention; the extreme ferocity of magical spells, in particular, must strike any reader.[108] Nonetheless it should be assumed that the widespread and often intense disapproval of *orgē* and *ira* on the part of articulate second-century opinion had some effect on the *public* expression of the angry emotions.

Not that the personal price was necessarily very heavy:

> Philagrus of Cilicia was . . . the most hot-tempered [*thermotatos*] and splenetic [*epicholōtatos*] of the sophists, for it is said that once when someone in the audience was dozing off he went so far as to strike him on the cheek . . . But though he lived among many peoples and won a great reputation among them for his skill in handling rhetorical themes, at Athens he showed no skill in handling his own bilious temper [*cholē*] but started a feud with Herodes just as if he had come there with that purpose . . . [Once while he was displaying (artificial) anger in a rhetorical display,] his voice was extinguished by his *cholē*—this happens with splenetic people. Later on, however, he won the chair <of rhetoric> at Rome, though at Athens he was deprived of his proper fame for the reasons I have explained.[109]

---

106. xiii.11–17, 124–144, 247–249.

107. The idealism of the emperor Marcus went further: he wrote that it is the mark of a human being to love even those who make blunders, and one should forgive the wrongs of others against oneself and not get angry (*To Himself* vii.22, 26).

108. For the material, see Gager 1992, and see more specifically Versnel 1998, 247–267. A wide-ranging study of Roman imperial sadism is overdue.

109. Philostratus, *VS* ii.8 (578–580); *PIR*² P 348. On the quarrelsome propensities of the second-century sophists, see Bowersock 1969, 89–100.

Philagrus' enemy and fellow sophist Herodes Atticus (consul in 143) was something of a contrarian voice on the subject of anger, and his career, too, suggests what one could get away with. But it cannot have been pleasant for him in old age to have to respond to Athenian charges of "tyranny" before his former pupil the emperor Marcus; it seems probable that his quarrelsome and ill-tempered nature had been at least partly responsible.[110]

As to how much disapproval of revenge was still left in Severan times, one may be sceptical. The Severan evidence includes the "indictment for unavenged death," *crimen mortis inultae,* a charge which was supposed to follow failure to avenge a murder.[111] Even though the imperial government's motive was to disqualify heirs in order to justify seizing property, something is revealed about the acceptability of revenge.[112]

Anger and the need to control it are not absent from the literature of the Roman Empire of the second to fourth centuries, far from it. But the reasons why anger is an issue mostly seem to concern either the relationship between the emperor and his subjects, or family peace, or the psychic well-being of the individual—and the pretensions of philosophers who claimed to be able to ensure it. All these themes will need treatment in their own contexts.

110. The contrarian voice: Gellius xix.12 describes a speech he gave "against the *apatheia* of the Stoics," in which he argued that it was both impossible and undesirable to eradicate the passions, undesirable because they were intimately linked to man's good and useful qualities (here he was following his teacher Calvisius Taurus). In so saying, he seems to have been justifying some of his own personality traits: see Philostr. *VS* ii.1; *PIR*² C 802. The charge of tyranny (notwithstanding his extensive philanthropy): *VS* 559. He was probably responsible for the violent death of his wife, cf. *VS* 555–556. See in general Tobin 1997.

111. *C.Iust.* vi.35.1 pr.; cf. *Dig.* xxix.5.9, xxxvii.14.23 pr.

112. On the representation of *The Punishment of Dirce* in the Baths of Caracalla, good evidence of the Roman enjoyment of sadistic punishment, see Chapter 4.

CHAPTER 10

Restraining the Angry Ruler

The anger of rulers as rulers is not overtly criticized in the texts that survive from archaic Greece,[1] but the figure of the angry ruler was an insistent part of the critique of the angry emotions from the fifth century onwards. In the 470s Pindar makes it a monarch's virtue that he is *praus*, good-natured, with his subjects.[2] The earliest instances of implied criticism appear to concern Menelaus and Agamemnon in Sophocles' *Ajax*, and Creon in *Antigone*, both in the 440s. Menelaus claims that his and his brother's behaviour is justified by the latter's royal power, and Agamemnon is driven to admit that "it is not easy for a *turannos* to obey the rules of religion" *(eusebein)*.[3] In neither play is it easy to think that the association of royal power and anger is accidental,[4] or likely to have gone unnoticed by the original audience. Should we say the same about other, later, tragedies in which royal rage was dramatized in great detail, and in a partly political fashion—such as, most notably, *Oedipus Tyrannus* and the *Bacchae* (King Pentheus)?[5]

---

1. In *Od.* iv.687–695 Penelope is represented as claiming that a moral debt is owed to Odysseus because as king he did not maltreat his subjects, as was his right (691); but anger is not explicitly in question.

2. *Pyth.* iii.71; cf. iv.136. In Hes. *Th.* 90, the princes use "gentle words" to correct the people.

3. See, respectively, *Ajax* 1050, 1067–1076; 1350. There had been at least one attack on tyranny in an earlier play, Eur. *Peliades* fr. 605 (455 B.C.).

4. It appears next in Eur. *Med.* 119–121 (the *orgai* of tyrants).

5. This question could be debated at length. Oedipus: see Chapter 8. Pentheus:

There was so much else for the audience of these plays to feel and to think about. Yet the association is insistent in the later works of Euripides.[6] The most probable solution is that the Athenian audience of these years was accustomed to the thought that a monarchical ruler was likely to be irascible: the messenger who comes to tell Pentheus about the Bacchants fears to speak because he associates royalty and excessive anger (*Bacch.* 671). But a good king such as Erechtheus could be shown advising his successor to rule mildly.[7]

Unprovoked and unrelenting anger were for Herodotus prime characteristics of the evil ruler. Cambyses and Xerxes are the leading examples, the Medes Cyaxares and Astyages were others, and Periander of Corinth goes a fair distance in the same direction.[8] Cambyses attacked both Egypt and Ethiopia out of anger. He did insane things to members of his own family; then came the turn of his courtier Prexaspes (Hdt. iii.34–35):

> He is said to have asked Prexaspes, whom he especially honoured . . . and whose son was his wine-server, the following question: "What sort of man do the Persians think I am, and what do they say about me?" "Master," Prexaspes replied, "you are highly praised by them—except that they say you are too fond of wine" . . . This enraged [*thumōthenta*] Cambyses: "So now," he said, "the Persians say that devotion to wine has driven me out of my mind and made me insane. They said something quite different before [for he recalled being flattered by them on an earlier occasion]" . . . It was the memory of this incident which made him, on the present occasion, say in a rage [*orgēi*] to Prexaspes: "I'll soon show you whether the Persians speak the truth or are insane themselves when they say this. Here is your son standing in the entrance: if I shoot him through the middle of the heart, I shall have proved the Persians' words empty and meaningless.

Bacch. esp. 343–357, 509–514, 640, 671, 981 (λυσσώδη), 997; cf. 50–51 (the *orgē* of Thebes under the command of Pentheus).

6. Besides the *Bacchae*, see *IT* 1474, *Helen* 1642–1679 (in both cases gods order non-Greek kings to cease their anger). Wilamowitz restored a similar sentiment in a line of the *Cretans* (fr. 82 [*Nova Fragmenta Euripidea* ed. Austin], line 43).

7. Eur. *Erechth.* fr. 362 (= 14 Carrara), line 6 (about 422?).

8. See Chapter 8. Cyaxares: Hdt. i.73. Cf. Nauhardt 1940, 60.

He drew his bow and duly shot the boy through the heart.

To suggest, in the case of Xerxes, that Herodotus was merely report-ing "the facts" reveals a tone-deaf reader,[9] for Xerxes' rages are part of a highly elaborate literary narrative. The anger theme (irascibility or its converse) is frequently used for the rest of antiquity to create a neg-ative or positive view of a historical or contemporary ruler. The key ele-ments, cruelty, injustice and folly, are already present in Herodotus.

A king's willingness to control his anger had apparently become a prominent part of his image in Persia before it is known to have done so in Greece.[10] One of the great inscriptions of Darius I (522–486) from Naqsh-i-Rustam near Persepolis proclaims among other things the following:

> What is right, that is my desire. I am not a friend to the man who is a
> Lie-follower. I am not hot-tempered. What things develop in my anger,
> I hold firmly under my control by my thinking-power. I am firmly rul-
> ing over my own <impulses>. The man who cooperates, him accord-
> ing to his cooperative action, him thus do I reward . . . What a man says
> against a man, that does not convince me, until he satisfies the Ordi-
> nance of Good Regulations. (trans. Kent).[11]

The implication is that there had already been important discussions about royal anger in Persian court circles, and that the Persians had a system of psychological concepts which was adequate for such pur-poses. However we may wish to characterize the cultural relations be-tween Persia and Greece in this period, the Naqsh-i-Rustam text makes it a degree more likely that royal anger was also a subject of discussion in any number of Greek cities on the fringes of the Persian Empire.

It seems clear that by Herodotus' time the effects of a king's anger

9. Waters 1971, 75–76.

10. The question of priority need not detain us. Darius' language may have been traditional; Cambyses' wrath may have been notorious among his Greek contempo-raries.

11. Kent 1953, 140 (lines 16–24, out of sixty lines); physical location and bibliogra-phy: 109 (on the Persian king's reluctance to punish, see Hdt. i.137). The suspicious may like to know that this translation corresponds in most (not all) relevant respects to the one offered by Herzfeld 1938.

had become part of a conscious critique of a form of government. In the historian's famous constitutional debate,[12] the Persian nobleman Otanes recalls the *hubris*—which is not "pride" but something more like "aggression"—of Cambyses, and asserts, in his critique of monarchical government, that the two vices of a monarch are *hubris* and envy. In consequence of *hubris*, a king cannot be satisfied: he is annoyed *(achthetai)* if you abase yourself too little, but also if you abase yourself too much.[13] Herodotus did not think that well-ordered monarchy was impossible,[14] but he evidently held that such a political system could exist only if the monarch controlled his whims and avoided arbitrary violence against his subjects.[15]

In the same general period in which Herodotus reached these conclusions (long before he put the finishing touches to his history in the 420s), Pericles had come to exercise something close to one-man rule at Athens. His position of power was attacked by some as tyrannical or god-like,[16] and evidently gave rise to an intensified debate about the merits of such a form of government. A democratic leader, so Thucydides implies (ii.65), would normally avoid any demonstration of anger (except of course against ideological or foreign enemies), and Pericles' different behaviour corresponded to his anomalous position.[17] A decade and a half after his death, in Alcibiades' time, the issue of one-man rule once again became one of practical significance in the internal politics of the city.[18] Gradually, we may suppose, the no-

12. Identifying the sources of this text is a well-worn problem (see D. Asheri's commentary; cf. also Stroheker 1953–54, 383 n. 4). I assume that much of it arose from a treasury of ideas shared by a number of intellectuals in Athens by about the 430s, and also that a number of points, unidentifiable, were Herodotus' own.

13. iii.80.2–5. We are warned not to presume that this was Herodotus' own view of monarchy (Asheri, *ad loc.*), which is sound method but probably over-cautious.

14. With this statement cf. Flory 1987, ch. 4, who, however, exaggerates somewhat.

15. Note not only the anger control of Cyrus (Hdt. i.156) but also the strict behaviour of the Median ruler Deioces (i.100.1); and see iii.80.

16. The earliest known criticisms of Pericles as a quasi-tyrant are attributable to the partly pre-Aristophanic playwrights Teleclides and Cratinus (see P. A. Stadter's commentary on Plu. *Per.*, pp. lxvi–lxvii).

17. For the restraint advised by Theseus in Euripides' *Supplices* (422), see lines 555–557.

18. Cf. Thuc. vi.15.4.

tion formed of the monarchical ruler who would, unlike Alcibiades, be morally equal to his role. That would involve the control of certain passions, and among them anger.

The Athenians were not ready for one-man rule. In some actual monarchies, the ruler's temper, good or bad, became a significant part of what we can scarcely avoid calling his image. When Euripides, in Macedon in 408–407, wrote a tragedy called *Archelaos* for the contemporary king of that name, he sermonized against anger,[19] with the obvious intention of suggesting that his patron was above such an emotion. (Dionysius, the ruthless empire-building first tyrant of Syracuse, knew what he was doing when in the 390s, as a crude form of self-advertisement, he named his three unfortunate daughters Virtue, Self-Restraint (Sophrosune) and Justice.[20] The last two names, taken together, will probably have contained the implication that he had his temper well in hand).

The earliest Greek treatise about monarchy was written by Socrates' follower Antisthenes, probably in the 390s, and was called *Archelaos* (with reference to the king of Macedon) *or On Kingship*.[21] The earliest which survives, however, is the piece which Isocrates sent to the Cypriot tyrant Nicocles in or soon after 374. This therefore is the first definite example of Greece's "Mirror of Princes" literature, a series of didactic portrayals of the ideal ruler.[22] Monarchical government had

19. *Archel.* frr. 257–259. Not that one would want to understate the difficulties of interpretation.

20. Plu. *De Alex. Magn. fortuna* 5 = *Mor.* 338c, etc. This, a hundred years after Darius, is the first known reaction by an actual Greek ruler to theorizing about monarchy (Stroheker 1953–54, 409). Dionysius nonetheless became famous for his anger: Plu. *De tranq.* 12 = *Mor.* 471e. On Dionysius and revenge, see De Sensi Sestito 1997.

21. Diog.Laert. vi.18.

22. For the whole subject, see Hadot 1972. There has been a certain amount of confusion about the purposes of the works by Isocrates and Xenophon which have the best claims to be of such a general type. A recent theorist, noting the apparent irrelevance of such writings to the practical Athenian politics of the restored democracy, has suggested that in reality they aimed at a restoration of the now marginalized Athenian aristocracy (Eder 1995), which scarcely makes sense. The Athenian context is in any case not the only one: while Isocrates' and Xenophon's anti-democratic yearnings were largely futile in the 370s and 360s as far as Athens was concerned, the big intellectuals of the time operated (as indeed the sophists had done) in a larger

made a notable comeback at the end of the fifth century.[23] Isocrates professes from the beginning to be speaking to monarchical rulers in general. He expects, so he claims (ii.8), to benefit both them and their subjects (by making governments more *praos,* or even-tempered). There is no knowing precisely what he intended the "Cyprian Orations" to achieve, but the easiest supposition is that he wished to combine self-advertisement with some assistance to a ruler, Nicocles, who may well have been in some sense his student and certainly gave him money.[24] This will not exclude the possibility that Isocrates also wanted to suggest that monarchy was in general an acceptable form of government.

Among Isocrates' instructions to Nicocles is this: "Do nothing in anger, but simulate anger when the occasion demands it. Show yourself stern by overlooking nothing which men do, but even-tempered by making the punishment less than the offence. Be unwilling to show your authority by ill temper [*chalepotēs*] or by undue severity in punishment."[25] In a similar vein, Isocrates wrote in his eulogy of Nicocles' father Euagoras that the latter had "inspired fear not by showing ill temper [*to chalepainein*] to many, but because he far surpassed all others in character."[26] When he wrote a speech for Nicocles to direct to his Cypriot subjects, Isocrates again touched the theme of anger, from the ruler's point of view: "Don't think that it is their natural dispositions alone which make tyrants ill-tempered [*chalepoi*] or even-tempered [*praoi*], but the character of the citizens as well; for many before now have been compelled by the depravity of their subjects to rule more harshly than they wished."[27] If tyrants have a reputation for irascibility, in other words, it is not entirely their fault. This is the first time that a classical text seeks to excuse royal anger.

Thus by the time of the great rise to power of the Macedonian kings

---

Greek world. For ancient encomia more generally, see the edition of Menander Rhetor by D. A. Russell & N. G. Wilson, pp. xiii–xviii.

23. Eder 1995, 162.

24. On the latter point: xv[*Antidosis*].40. For an unflattering glimpse of Nicocles, see Aristot. *Pol.* v.10.1311b4–6.

25. ii[*To Nicocles*].23–24.

26. ix[*Euagoras*].45.

27. iii[*Nicocles or the Cyprians*].55.

from the 350s onwards, the Greeks had long been used to evaluating monarchical rulers partly by reference to their anger or their ability to control it.[28] After the Battle of Chaeronea (338), the cities of old Greece became subject to monarchical power, and the manner of its operation became a matter of larger importance.

Alexander of Macedon's explosive rages were already famous in his own lifetime.[29] One may suspect that most of his harshness was carefully calculated policy, but his evil temper, perhaps exacerbated by heavy drinking, seems well enough authenticated. What matters here in any case is what was *believed* about him. His significance in the present context is that although he was widely seen as a man of wrath, he was also regarded by many Greeks as a great hero. Like Achilles, whom he greatly admired,[30] the figure of Alexander thus tended to undermine the cultural opposition to the expression of passionate anger.

The charge sheet was fairly long, though most of it is in fact trivial by comparison with his decade-long career of bloodthirsty conquest. The most famous incident was and is the murder of his friend Cleitus the Black in 328, which Arrian describes as follows:

> [Cleitus objected to the flattery which was heaped on Alexander of Macedon at a hard-drinking symposium]. When he [Cleitus] uttered these thoughts, Alexander was hurt. I do not commend Cleitus' words either; I rather think it enough, amid such drunkenness, for a man to keep his feelings to himself, while avoiding the ill-conceived flattery of the others. However, when some even mentioned the achievements of King Philip, most unjustly suggesting that Philip had done no great or

28. In 346 Isocrates was already asking Philip II to show *praotēs* and *philanthrōpia* towards the Greeks (v.116–118). Aristotle cannot have left the subject untouched in his lost monograph *On Kingship* (one recalls his comment about kingly anger in *Pol.* iii.15), for which see Diog.Laert. v.21 and frr. 646–647 Rose. Cicero may imply that this work was written for Alexander when he was still *adulescens* (*Att.* xiii.28.2–3).

29. It did not occur to Arrian, the historian who used the contemporary sources Ptolemy and Aristobulus, to deny, when he came to sum up Alexander's character (vii.29), that *oxutēs* (harshness) and *orgē* were two of Alexander's three weaknesses (Arrian proceeded to palliate them).

30. See most recently Mossman 1988, 83–85 (repr. 1995, 209–212).

wonderful deeds . . . , Cleitus could no longer control himself and spoke honorifically of Philip's achievements, belittling Alexander and what he had achieved. Being now quite drunk, he heaped abuse on Alexander, saying in particular that after all Alexander owed his life to him . . . and holding out his right hand with a superb air he said, "This, Alexander, is this very hand that saved you then." [Alexander leapt up in anger *(orgē)*, and Cleitus went on insulting him] . . . and, as some say, Alexander snatched a spear from one of his bodyguards, and with this struck and killed Cleitus; but according to others, he took a long pike from one of the guards, and killed him with this . . . I myself strongly blame Cleitus for his insulting behaviour towards his own king; Alexander I pity for what happened, since he thereby showed himself to have been defeated by two vices by neither of which should any man of self-discipline [*andra sōphronounta*] be overcome, namely anger and drunkenness.[31]

Alexander's destruction of rebellious Thebes in 335 and the enslavement of the survivors were seen by the Greeks as acts of rage.[32] Then there was his anger against his companion Hermolaus, which led to the Conspiracy of the Pages in 327,[33] and his anger the following year at the unwillingness of his army to proceed beyond the River Hyphasis to conquer the rest of India.[34] The catalogue could continue.[35] These stories tended to proliferate in succeeding centuries,[36] but they were also sometimes accompanied by claims that Alexander had repented certain of his most notorious rages, or blamed them on the god Dionysus.[37]

31. Arrian iv.8–9. Plu. *Alex.* 51.6 makes Alexander speak in Macedonian on this occasion—because he was behaving like a barbarian?

32. Arrian says nothing of his anger, but see Polyb. v.10.6; Diod.Sic. xvii.8.2 and especially 6; Plu. *Alex.* 13.2. However, Alexander did nothing in this campaign which was not readily understandable from a policy point of view.

33. Arrian iv.13.2, etc.

34. Arrian v.28, etc.

35. Plu. *Alex.* 9–10, 22, etc.

36. Thus, e.g., the crucifixion of 2,000 of the survivors of the siege of Tyre because of Alexander's anger, Curtius iv.4.16, may be an "embellishment."

37. Supposed repentance over Cleitus: Arrian iv.9.1–4; over Thebes: Plu. *Alex.* 13. Blaming Dionysus: Arrian iv.8.2, 9.5; Plu. ibid.

The Greeks were divided about Alexander. In his own time, obviously, many detested him. Theophrastus—author apparently of two books about kingship—was critical.[38] The early Stoics must have found it impossible to overlook his rages, and Chrysippus seems not to have been an enthusiast.[39] But the glamour of vast conquests, human nature being what it is, overshadowed the king's moral failings. Ptolemy and Aristobulus were his effective apologists. After Chrysippus the next definite judgement we hear from a philosophical writer is from Panaetius, who was an admirer.[40] Polybius too was dazzled by the glory of Alexander, and attempted to convince his readers that Alexander had in fact behaved decently after the sack of rebellious Thebes in 335: he was extremely angry, he enslaved the surviving inhabitants and levelled the city to the ground—but he respected the temples of the gods (v.10.6–7). Eventually the figure of Alexander came under renewed attack—from Romans who were Stoics or under Stoic influence, and were thinking as both Stoics and Romans.[41]

From Alexander's time onwards, most Greeks were ruled by kings or were more or less liable to come under royal power, and a more ample literature arose about kingship. But we know little about its contents. The historian Theopompus of Chios gave formal written advice to Alexander, and the latter's pet philosopher, Anaxarchus of Abdera, wrote a monograph *On Kingship*.[42] Zeno's *Republic* cannot have avoided the subject; then the Stoics Cleanthes, Persaeus, and Sphaerus all felt compelled to write still further works entitled *On Kingship*.[43]

---

38. But perhaps for merely personal reasons: the evidence is Cic. *Tusc.Disp.* iii.21. He wrote a book about kingship and another about the education of a king (Diog.Laert. v.42).

39. Fears 1974, 130. Eratosthenes' enthusiasm may be less important.

40. He classed him among men who had performed "magnas res et salutares" (Cic. *De off.* ii.16)—which may not have excluded his disapproving of Alexander's anger.

41. For Alexander's Roman reputation, see esp. Fears 1974. For his irascibility, see among others, Liv. ix.18 (his great vice was *trux et perfervida ira*), Sen. *Ep.* 113.29; *De ira* iii.17, 23.1; Dio Chrys. i.6. All this served to make the position of the actual emperor more difficult.

42. *FGrH* 115 T 48 (according to which another Theopompus also wrote about kingship); D-K 72 B 1–2.

43. Cleanthes: Diog.Laert. vii.175; Persaeus: vii.36; Sphaerus: vii.178.

Euphantus of Olynthus, the teacher of King Antigonus Gonatas, did so too, for the benefit of his former pupil.[44] All of these works are likely to have had something negative to say about irascibility. It is suggestive that in Cleanthes' dialogue between Reason and Thumos, he drew a parallel between the imperiousness of anger and of kings.[45] What survives, however, is first the atypical *Letter to Philocrates* of Pseudo-Aristeas (a Jewish text probably written in the second century—after 145 B.C.?), the main subject of which is the translation of the Septuagint,[46] and second, Philodemus' treatise *On the Good King according to Homer,* which evidently (parts of it are known from a papyrus) gave a certain amount of space to the consideration of anger.[47] Because of their anger, kings and such are treated as dangerous creatures in his *De ira.*[48]

Demetrius of Phaleron, the Athenian politician, is said to have recommended the buying and reading of "the books about kingship and *hēgemonia*" to King Ptolemy I,[49] and it is possible that the advice was taken. One would not easily believe, however, that philosophers' advice made much difference to Hellenistic kings. None of the kings, not even Antigonus Gonatas, is known to have engaged in negotiation about the use of royal power, which is not surprising, since none of the kings had to contend with a powerful internal aristocracy such as existed in Augustan Rome, the only imaginable interlocutor in such negotiations. But it would be simplistic to assert that the philosophers never exercised any influence at all. Persaeus and Euphantus are, after all, attested within Antigonus Gonatas' court circle.[50] Greece, furthermore, always had public opinion, and intellectuals could to some ex-

44. Diog.Laert. ii.110.

45. *SVF* I, p. 130 line 1; L-S 65I (quoted, p. 106).

46. The fragments about kingship belonging to the neo-Pythagoreans Diotogenes and Ecphantus are, I think, to be dated to the Roman Empire (cf. Delatte 1942; Burkert 1971, 48–49). The texts are in Thesleff 1965, 71–75, 79–84.

47. Note the reference to *thumos* in connection with Achilles in col. xii.6–8 (ed. T. Dorandi). In cols. xxiv.6–xxv.19, the subject was the desirability of *praotēs, epieikeia* and similar virtues in the behaviour of the king, with Cambyses cited (xxiv.18–19) as a counter-example (it is not clear whether anger was referred to explicitly).

48. Kings and tyrants: ch. 4 (col. xi.13–23), cf. 5 (col. xix.2–8).

49. Plu. *Apophth. Regum = Mor.* 189d.

50. Persaeus: *Index Stoic.Herc.* col. xiii (= *SVF* I.441, p. 97); Euphantus: see above. Hieronymus of Rhodes was on good terms with Antigonus Gonatas, Diog.Laert. iv.41.

tent affect it. A sizeable number of stories circulated later about the anger of kings in the early third century.[51] The striking thing is how many of them were intended to reflect favourably on the kings:[52] Magas of Cyrene, for example, had been made fun of in a play by Philemon, but when a shipwreck put the dramatist in Magas' power, the king limited himself to sending a soldier to touch Philemon's neck with a sword and to giving him, as an insult, some children's presents. So says Plutarch, meaning to put Magas in a good light.[53] Ptolemy I and Antigonus Gonatas, among others, are also portrayed positively.[54] What had happened was that a proportion of Greek intellectuals now depended on kings or hoped to depend on them; hence the irascible monarchs of Herodotus and Euripides tend to disappear from view.

Part of the *Letter* of Pseudo-Aristeas consists of a holy man's extended fantasy in which the seventy-two learned translators are entertained at a series of sumptuous dinners given by King Ptolemy II Philadelphus. They are asked their advice about how he should rule. Each one replies with a pious banality and is complimented by the king, who concludes by giving them all generous presents (sect. 294). The guests have a certain amount to say about clemency and about anger. In particular, when the king asked one of them how he could avoid anger *(thumos)*, he was told (sects. 253–254) that he should "take thought for the fact that he exercised absolute power, and so caused death if he became angry, and that it would be useless and grievous if he took life away from many just because he was the master. Since everyone was his subject and nobody opposed him, why would he get angry? He should realize that god rules the whole world benevolently and without any anger [*orgē*]. 'Your majesty, you must follow his example.'"[55]

51. They found their way in particular into Plutarch's monograph; also into Seneca's. The latest of them seems to concern Magas of Cyrene, Plu. *De coh.ira* 9 (*Mor.* 458a). Hieronymus of Rhodes might possibly be Plutarch's source (cf. R. Laurenti, in his joint commentary with G. Indelli, p. 70).

52. There were exceptions, concerning, e.g., the tyrant Apollodorus of Cassandreia (*RE* no. 43, Sen. *De ira* ii.5), and Lysimachus (iii.17). On the harmony which generally prevailed between Hellenistic philosophers and kings, see Habicht 1994, 243–244 (there were exceptions here too: 237).

53. See above, n. 51.

54. Plu. 9 (*Mor.* 458a and 457e, respectively).

55. Elsewhere, too, the letter pays attention to clemency (sects. 188—this is the

Other Hellenistic thinkers probably elaborated the contrast between monarchies which administered the laws and those that allowed the king's anger to rage.[56]

At about the same time as the composition of the *Letter to Philocrates*, Polybius was also expressing his opinion about kings and anger. Like Herodotus, he makes the enemy rulers men of wrath—in his case, Hamilcar Barca, King Philip V of Macedon, and Philip's son Perseus. This was not because Polybius was systematically against monarchy as a form of government;[57] he judged kings according to what he saw as their merits,[58] including their capacity for controlling their anger. Philip II of Macedon, for example, is said to have behaved mildly towards Athens after the Battle of Chaeronea, avoiding *thumos* towards them.[59] The historian was simultaneously giving vent to his own rancour and offering instruction in the art of rational government, an art which needed to be understood by Hellenistic statesmen (before it was too late) and by Roman senators.

---

first piece of advice the king receives—192, 207, 208) and controlling the passions (222, 256). The ruler must rule himself: 211. He is also told to avoid *eris* with his wife (250). For a discussion of the letter's sources and credibility, see Fraser 1972, ii.696–704.

56. Thus Diodorus Siculus (i.71.1), in his idealizing account of the archaic monarchy of the Egyptians, says that "the kings were not allowed to render any legal decision or transact any business which happened to come up, or to punish anyone gratuitously or in anger or for any other unjust cause but only in accordance with the established laws relative to each offence." For the claim that law, not *bia* (violent force) was the foundation of the Macedonian monarchy, see Arrian iv.11.6 (ironically, Callisthenes the historian, whom Alexander unjustly executed, is speaking), with Mooren 1983, 219–232. As for the inscriptions and papyrological texts which allow us to see how Hellenistic kings desired to present themselves to their subjects, they do not lower themselves to speak of anger, but they do from time to time proclaim the respect of the kings for established law (Schubart 1937, 7–8 = 1979, 98).

57. See Welwei 1963, esp. 185–186. On the character of the laudable ruler according to Polybius, see Welwei 140–156.

58. Eckstein 1995, 273–275.

59. v.10.3: "he did not add *thumos* to his exploits," and stopped fighting "as soon as he could take the opportunity to show his *praotēs* [even temper] and *kalokagathia* [gentlemanliness]." There was some truth in this (cf. Walbank's commentary), but Polybius prettified his picture of Philip by ignoring the latter's behaviour towards Thebes (Pédech on v.10.5). The immediate point of all this was to blacken still further the reputation of a more recent Macedonian king, Philip V.

The first Romans who in republican times found themselves in positions of near-monarchical power were the governors of provinces. From an early date some of them had succumbed to the temptation to behave like tyrants, but by the middle of the second century B.C. there was discussion at Rome about how governors of provinces should comport themselves. Most were no doubt guided mainly by what they could get away with, but repute and resentment could matter too, and by the 60s B.C., at the latest, it was worth making a serious effort to avoid a reputation for irascibility. For the first time, in fact, the anger of the sole ruler acquired a degree of political importance.[60] The anger of the governor was to be feared, but it might be possible to use the bad reputation of the angry emotions to prevail upon him to take a different view. At Tarsus, in triumviral times, Boethus, a poet who had been put in charge of the city, was charged with a swindle concerning olive oil. In court before M. Antonius, he deprecated the latter's anger. He referred to a poem he had written in the general's honour and compared himself to Homer, "who had sung the praises of Achilles, Agamemnon and Odysseus." To which, however, the prosecutor replied that Homer had not stolen Agamemnon's oil (Strabo xiv.674).

Some of the worst stories of anger continued to be generated under the principate by Roman officials in the provinces, such as Messalla Volesus in Asia under Augustus, who is said by Seneca to have gloried in having had 300 people decapitated in a single day.[61] For Seneca, a typical man in a rage is a proconsul, "leaping down from his official platform" (*De ira* i.19.3), thus losing his much-needed dignity. When Philo wanted to traduce Pontius Pilate, he labelled him rancorous and evil-tempered.[62] The issue continued as long as there were men of education among the rulers: Juvenal advises the man who has been ap-

60. The theory was that no official could act justly in a state of rage: Phld. *De ira* 5 (col. xxviii.22–26). The practical situation was that provincial governors could not forget for long (cf. Cic. *QF* i.1.23) that they would soon leave office and become vulnerable.

61. *De ira* ii.5. "O rem regiam!" he allegedly exclaimed. Consul in 5 A.D., he was later convicted of maladministration in his province.

62. *Legatio ad Gaium* 303. How you *defended* a governor who evidently did not have very good control over his *iracundia* can be seen in Tac. *Agr.* 22 end: at least he was not secretive about it.

pointed to govern a province to control two vices—anger *(pone irae frena modumque)* and greed. And he warns that too much violent punishment in a province will cause trouble back at Rome for the man responsible.[63] Although governors enjoyed wide penal discretion,[64] there was some truth in this. Lucian attributed similar advice to the philosopher Demonax: when a newly appointed governor asked his opinion about how to rule, he said, "Without rage [*aorgētōs*], talking little and listening much."[65] The context was not only the governor's wide discretionary power but also, commonly, a real rivalry between the governor and the local authorities.[66]

The Christians duly inherited both the difficulty of dealing with high officials who were sometimes inclined to let their vexations rip, and the propaganda possibilities which such anger created. In consequence, martyrdom narratives quite frequently make mention of the rage of provincial governors and city prefects, to the virtual exclusion of other reactions they may have felt.[67] Not that anti-Christian anger is shown as exclusively the anger of rulers: crowds and minor officials sometimes feel it too. Nor is the rage of the enemy an explicit target of the Christians' attack: it is simply an element in their denigratory narrative technique.

Innumerable speeches were made to arriving Roman governors, praising them for a host of virtues which it was hoped that they would display. A rhetorical manual of Diocletianic date explains how to do it:

> Subdivide the praise of actions into the four virtues: wisdom, justice, temperance, courage . . . Under justice, you should include humanity [*philanthrōpia*] to subjects, gentleness of character, and approachability

63. viii.88, 135–139.

64. MacMullen 1986a, 150 = 1990, 206.

65. *Demonax* 51. The previous section tells how Demonax prevailed on an angry governor to relent. For the story of Nicetes of Smyrna and his successful mollification of yet another irate and vengeful governor, see Philostr. *Vit.Soph.* i.19 (pp. 511–512).

66. For evidence that irascibility continued to affect governors' local reputations, see Lib. *Or.* xx.28.

67. E.g., *Acta Carpi* 9 (Musurillo 1972, 22), *Acta Iustini* C.4 (Musurillo 54), *Acta Cononis* 5.4 (Musurillo 190), *Acta Irenaei* 5.1 (Musurillo 298), Eus. *HE* v.1.58 (Musurillo 80), *Mart.Pal.* 8.6.

... Do not simply state virtues ... but treat the topic also by considering the opposite: he is not unjust, not irascible, not inaccessible.[68]

The relationship between governor and provincials was a microcosm of the emperor's relationship with his subjects, with the obvious difference that the emperor's subjects had no legal form of recourse.

Caesar, as we have seen, was alert to the possibilities of both positive and negative publicity concerning anger, and his assassination was the most dramatic Roman consequence of thinking about anger and revenge, for if he had not practised *clementia*, mercifulness, he would probably have lived much longer. Nonetheless *clementia*, together with the less formalized attempt to claim that the ruler could control his anger, was part of his legacy to Caesar Octavianus. This *clementia* was the virtue which the dictator most insistently claimed, at least from 46 onwards.[69] Unlike a number of other abstract qualities, it had never previously received a temple; but in 45 the Senate voted a temple for the Clementia of Caesar. The word *clementia* did not mean precisely freedom from anger—it referred to behaviour, not to an emotional condition—but there was obviously a connection. One's degree of control over one's anger necessarily affected one's ability to apply clemency.

Octavian duly made use of the *clementia* inheritance, apparently as early as 42.[70] It was certainly not a novelty when it was included among the four carefully chosen cardinal virtues listed on the golden shield he received in 27.[71] A regime poet, Horace, claimed that Augustus had superseded the era of anger, and after Actium we can see Augustus apparently distancing himself somewhat—though by no means entirely—from the notion that it had been his mission to exact vengeance from those fellow Romans who had assassinated Caesar.

---

68. Menander Rhetor, II [part 10].415, lines 24–26, and 416, lines 5–7, 12–15 (p. 166 Russell & Wilson). This kind of speech had the technical label *prosphōnētikos*.
   69. Cf. Weinstock 1971, 233–243.
   70. Cassius Dio xlviii.3.6.
   71. *Res Gestae* 34.2: the other virtues were *virtus, iustitia* and *pietas*.

There was some imperial boasting about revenge in 19 and 18 B.C., when coin types associated the recovery of Roman standards from the Parthians in 20 with the words "Mars Ultor."[72] But the great temple in the Forum of Augustus was not dedicated until 2 B.C., a decidedly strange forty-year delay since Philippi.[73] It is tempting to suppose that while revenge exacted from the Parthians never lost its glitter, revenge against fellow citizens—so much a mark of the triumviral regime—did not altogether suit Augustus and his doctrine of *clementia*. When the Forum Augustum temple was finally completed, it was associated with the supposed revenge inflicted on the Parthians.[74] The transition can, as it happens, be observed—in a poem (*Odes* i.2) which Horace wrote some time in the years 30 to 27.[75] And the account in the *Res Gestae* of what Augustus had done to the assassins seems to be carefully measured: "Those who slaughtered my father I drove into exile [moderation], avenging their crime by means of legal judgements [more moderation]; afterwards when they made war on the state I twice defeated them in pitched battles."[76]

But the evidence about Augustus and anger is much more extensive. Not long after he obtained supreme power, he shed some tears over the suicide of one of his subordinates, Cornelius Gallus the poet, complaining that he alone was not allowed to be as angry with his friends as he wished.[77] Apocryphal? We cannot know. As with Alexander of Macedon, the anger of Augustus generated many stories, and it is hard

72. *RIC* I (revised ed., 1984) nos. 28, 39, 68–74, 103–106, 114–120, 507. Augustus may have had a small temple of Mars Ultor built on the Capitol to house these standards (Cassius Dio liv.8.2–3, but see C. Reusser in *LTUR* III, 230–231).

73. On the whole matter, cf. Bonnefond 1987, 270–277.

74. The "Parthian" standards were displayed there, *RG* 29.2.

75. The poem is politically as well as in other ways a remarkable performance, for while it adulates Octavian as "Caesaris ultor" (44), it suggests that the recently concluded war really was a deplorable civil war (21), not a war against Cleopatra, and that the energy would have better spent on conquering Parthia (22), *vengeance* against whom is presented as Octavian's next task (51–52). For the date, see R. G. M. Nisbet & M. Hubbard's commentary, pp. 17–19.

76. *RG* 2 ("Qui parentem meum trucidaverunt, eos in exilium expuli iudiciis legitimis ultus eorum facinus [i.e., by the Lex Pedia], et postea bellum inferentis rei publicae vici bis acie"); cf. Y. Thomas 1984, 75.

77. Suet. *Aug.* 66.2. The date was 26.

to know what is authentic. The story about Gallus comes from a relatively reliable source (Suetonius' early lives are not to be underestimated).

Plutarch is the great source of tales about this matter. It is he who tells us about Octavian's exchange with a former teacher, the Stoic philosopher Athenodorus of Tarsus:

> Athenodorus . . . asked to be allowed to go home because of his old age, and Augustus consented. But when Athenodorus was taking leave of him, he said "Whenever you get angry [*orgistheis*], Caesar, don't say or do anything before repeating to yourself the twenty-four letters of the alphabet." Augustus seized his hand, and said, "I still have need of your presence here," and detained him for a whole year, quoting the line "No risk attends the benefit that silence brings."[78]

The philosopher suffered for his self-righteous advice, but the more interesting point is that Octavian was assumed to have been receptive to advice about his *orgē:* such a story could not have been told about, say, Alexander.[79]

The same collection of Augustus' sayings also shows him forgiving the Alexandrians for their opposition, but by contrast physically attacking a young man who was said to be the lover of his daughter Iulia—an action which Augustus then repented—and finally it shows him nailing a trusted slave to a ship's mast for the crime of eating a prize quail.[80] These and other reactions on the part of Augustus described in this collection come from a single matrix: they display a set of rules for an acceptable emperor. Thus Augustus showed magnanimity to the Alexandrians, who for practical reasons were best conciliated; in the second case, he dealt vigorously but briefly with his daughter's sup-

78. *Mor.* 207c (*Sayings of the Romans,* Caesar Augustus no. 7). The subject was Athenodorus, son of Sandon, *PIR²* A 1288.

79. According to Grimal 1945, 271, Plutarch was naive to suppose that Octavian would have been interested in Athenodorus' teachings about anger. Rawson 1985, 245, was sceptical about the story on the grounds that it is inconsistent with Athenodorus' mission to put the affairs of Tarsus in order.

80. *Sayings* 3, 9 and 4, respectively (the last is quoted below in Chapter 13). Anger is only mentioned in the second case, in which the victim supposedly calmed the *princeps* by reminding him that he had made a law—i.e., he could seek legal redress. *Sayings* 14 and 15 also show him relenting anger.

posed paramour; and in the case of the prize quail he inflicted a typically brutal Roman punishment on a slave for a trivial offence. The important thing was a carefully calibrated response, and a willingness to relent when dealing with citizens. The emperor's subjects, however, have no power to resist unless they are collectivities (like the Alexandrians), and not much even then.

We are now, I think, in a position to solve the problem of the anger of Aeneas. Both sides in the recent war of words about the ending of the *Aeneid* seem to be somewhat in error (though both of them have reasonable things to say). When in furious anger Aeneas kills Turnus—"Inflamed by Furies and terrible in his anger . . . he sank his weapon in his enemy's breast, blazing"—he is *neither* acting as a perfect Augustan hero exacting legitimate revenge, *nor* subverting the poem's political meaning by falling into emotional excess.[81]

We are not necessarily invited by the poet to decide whether the father of the race did the right thing in angrily killing Turnus.[82] We are told, at the climax of a very long preparatory narrative, that this happened. With much justification scholars have pointed out that Turnus had offered ample provocation, and that the Roman tradition still believed in exacting revenge from foreign enemies.[83] No less a figure than the god-man Hercules had acted out of rage and been driven by Furies in *Aeneid* VIII, which seems to legitimate the rage of Aeneas (but Hercules was eliminating a monster, not concluding a war).[84]

---

81. There is no need to give the full bibliography of this dispute: Braund & Gill 1997 will lead one back into it. Incidentally, the modernizing anti-Augustan interpretation was already formulated during the Renaissance: Kallendorf 1999.

82. It is as well to remember that there is a vast amount of anger in the *Aeneid,* as was inevitable in a work which emulated the *Iliad.*

83. Stahl 1990, Galinsky 1994 (though there is a good deal to argue with in both accounts). Quint 1993, 78, does not convince me that the statues of the Danaids in the temple of Apollo Palatinus gave an "imperial sanction" to Aeneas' act; the murders they carried out appeared on the baldric of Pallas (*Aen.* x.497–498), true enough, but there it is a *nefas.* It is more than slightly wrong to say that the *Aeneid* "preached" revenge (Quint 81).

84. "hic vero Alcidae furiis exarserat atro / felle dolor" (219–220), "furens animis" (228). Hercules in Book VIII as a model for Aeneas at the end of XII: see, e.g., Gransden 1984, 211; Wright 1997, 183. Most of the *furor* in the *Aeneid* is viewed negatively (Farron 1985, 622), but *furere* is used of Aeneas several times, and in viii.494 Etruria is moved by *furiae iustae.*

Matters could perhaps have turned out otherwise: Aeneas nearly decided to spare Turnus.[85] Vergil thus with consummate skill turns our minds for a moment to *clementia*. But Aeneas, though represented throughout the poem as a kind of proto-Augustus, is not simply a mechanical copy of what Augustus claimed to be. He belonged to heroic times; he had fought with Achilles. To act *furiis accensus* in those times and circumstances was inevitable. Aeneas was, precisely, terrible. He probably needed to be. But he also fails a moral test which Vergil had intentionally devised, namely Turnus' submission.[86] Nowadays, of course—it is implicit—we have in Caesar Augustus a still greater leader. With admirable finesse, in short, Vergil makes Aeneas heroic—*merely* heroic, modern readers are tempted to think—while a still greater role is left for Augustus. It was after all *his,* Augustus', *Aeneid*.[87]

We should get away from the notion that if Aeneas fails a moral test, the politics of the *Aeneid* cease to make sense. On the contrary: Aeneas' wrathful action leaves room for the moral success of Augustus, prince of *clementia,* the man who advertised his willingness to forgive. This was a primary element in Augustus' politics in the years in which the *Aeneid* was taking shape.[88] Aeneas, unable to control his anger (though not of course so reprehensible as to feel anger without good reason) is imperfect; Augustus on the other hand replaces anger with *clementia*.

Augustus was greatly annoyed when Ovid first brought out *The Art of Love* (about 1 B.C.), but it would have been clumsy to take any severe measures against a famous poet who furthermore had once been thought an acceptable candidate for the Senate. This emperor could

---

85. *Aen.* xii.939–941.

86. It would have been easy for Vergil to make Aeneas kill Turnus in combat, as Achilles had killed Hector; instead of this, Aeneas incapicitated Turnus but left him in a state to submit and ask for mercy; the victor refused. See, above all, Perret 1967, 352. In *Aeneid* VI he had been told to "parcere subiectis."

87. Ov. *Trist.* ii.533.

88. Syme 1939, 299 (he practised clemency "when murder could serve no useful purpose"). See also M. Barden Dowling's forthcoming book about *clementia*.

do nothing but nurse his fury[89] (many later ones would not have hesitated), until in 8 A.D. the poet somehow compounded the offence and found himself banished to the wastes of Moesia. Ovid repeatedly attempted to persuade the *princeps* to recall him from exile by suggesting that his anger was misguided and that he ought to relent.[90] But he was left in Moesia, having perhaps inflamed the ruler's anger all the more by harping on *Caesaris ira* in public.

By the time of Seneca, Augustus had become a model emperor. It could be admitted that he had been prone to anger in youth and had done many things which he looked back on with regret[91]—which was a hefty admission in his case, since he was only eighteen years of age when he first wielded political power. Seneca tells an elaborate tale, situated in 16–13 B.C., in which Livia teaches Augustus to make use of *clementia* towards a potential assassin.[92] The tradition was unanimous that Augustus exercised a certain degree of self-control. "He did and said many memorable things from which it is clear that anger did not rule him"[93]—a nicely phrased judgement, since it left room for angry outbursts. Plutarch's stories we have already analysed. Cassius Dio's report of what people said about Augustus on his death emphasizes that his anger was not ungovernable (lvi.43.3). In senatorial circles, this was a matter of concern.

From Augustus' time onwards, the positive or negative character of a Roman ruler—and of a potential ruler—could be signalled by his control over his anger, or the lack of it. The recently published senatorial decree of 20 A.D. about Germanicus and Piso beatifies the late prince by reference to his *moderatio* and *patientia*,[94] and the Tacitean

89. Nisbet 1982, 56 = 1995, 159.

90. *Caesaris ira: Epist. ex Ponto* i.4.29, 9.28, 10.20, and seven other times, ten in the *Tristia; principis ira* is also common. In the view of Syme 1978, 224, "the error of Caesar Augustus [in not recalling him] played into Ovid's hands." But it was only a moral victory, or rather a literary one.

91. Sen. *De clem.* i.11.1; cf. i.9.1

92. i.9.2–12. The same story was re-written, and apparently re-dated, by Cassius Dio lv.14–22.

93. *De ira* iii.23.4. Seneca goes on to describe his patience in dealing with the tiresome historian Timagenes of Alexandria.

94. Line 26 (Eck, Caballos & Fernández 1996, p. 40, with their commentary, 153–154); cf. line 167. Perhaps Germanicus needed defending against charges of display-

description of Sejanus as a man of anger and vengefulness,[95] though written under Trajan, probably reflects what was said about him after his fall in 31. Philo's denunciation of Caligula's frequent extreme rage is a clear example; conversely, he includes in his praise of Tiberius the latter's alleged freedom from anger.[96]

It was a matter of substance as well as image, for the stable government of the Roman Empire depended on the effective cooperation of the ruler and the elites, as all but the most foolish emperors realized. The control of inappropriate anger had become part of the ideological basis of that peculiarly ideological kind of rule which was that of the Roman emperors. At the same time, an emperor needed to be thought capable of anger against contumelious or corrupt subordinates: the Roman Empire was no kindergarten.

The monarchy was already by the middle years of Tiberius' reign nearly absolute,[97] which meant that it depended entirely on the emperor's character and perception of his own self-interest whether he attempted to control his anger, a matter of literally vital importance for his family, his courtiers, for the senatorial and equestrian orders, and occasionally for others. The age of Tiberius was frightening enough for the senatorial elite; that of Caligula was a terrifying nightmare which allowed of no complaint until it was over. Caligula is credibly said to have stated in the Senate on one occasion that there were only "very few" members with whom he was still angry. "This state-

---

ing inappropriate anger (cf. Tac. *Ann.* ii.57.3). Line 27, by contrast, attributes to Piso *feritas morum* (hence some suspicion that the story about him in Sen. *De ira* i.18.3–6 is based on disinformation). It is an interesting question whether a prior reputation for irascibility would have hindered one's rise to high office: Piso was allegedly *ingenio violentus* (Tac. *Ann.* ii.43), but even if it was true, was it appreciated before he reached the heights?

95. *Ann.* iv.3.2 (but Drusus, the son of Tiberius, was partly to blame); cf. Cassius Dio lviii.3–4. *Ann.* iv.6–7 emphasizes that it was the death of Drusus that marked a shift towards absolute monarchy. The Tacitean context repeatedly alludes to the evil tempers of members of the Julio-Claudian dynasty: Livia (iv.12.4), Tiberius (17.2, 21.1), Agrippina, widow of Germanicus (52.2, 53.1).

96. *Legatio ad Gaium* 254, 260, 261, 268, 366–367, etc.; Tiberius: 303.

97. So it was suitable that the year 28 saw the decision to erect an altar in Rome to *clementia* (Tac. *Ann.* iv.74). The judgement of Yavetz that it was Tiberius, not Augustus, "who broke the backbone of the Roman aristocracy" (1996, 121) is surely correct.

ment," says Dio, "doubled the anxiety of every one of them, for each was thinking of himself."[98]

In the beginning, Claudius clearly intended to do better:

Being conscious of his own *ira* [liability to outbursts of anger] and *iracundia* [which here seems to mean "proclivity to persisting anger"], he excused both characteristics in an edict, and he promised that his outbursts of anger would be short and harmless, and that his *iracundia* would not be unjust.[99]

The date of this promise will obviously have been soon after Claudius' accession in 41.[100] But the actual effect was apparently slight: Claudius had no compunction about avenging himself on enemies (Suet. 42.1), and left numerous casualties.[101]

Claudius' edict was not his only public allusion to his own anger. In a much-discussed letter of 41 to the Alexandrians, he employs two phrases which imply some reflection about imperial anger: he declines to investigate who started the fighting between Jews and Greeks in Alexandria in 38, but threatens punishment against anyone who renews the violence, "guarding within myself unrelenting anger [*orgē ametamelētos*] against those who renew the struggle." And a few lines later, he tells them that if they do not cease "this damnable and obstinate *orgē* against each other," "I shall be forced to show what a benevolent *hēgemon* is like if he is changed into just *orgē*."[102] Both phrases, and

98. Cassius Dio lix.25.9; cf. 26.4. Caligula may very well not have been angry at all on this occasion; the pretence would have been enough to spread terror. By the time Seneca wrote *De ira* (49 or 50), Caligula's reputation was deeply tainted by absurd rages: it was said, for instance, that he had grown angry with the heavens and Jupiter because thunder interrupted a dramatic performance (Sen. i.20.8–9). More Caligulan rage: ii.33.3–4, iii.18–19. In reality it was not so much Caligula's anger which the court and the elite had to fear as his cold-blooded cruelty.

99. Suet. *Claud.* 38.1.

100. Cf. Fillion-Lahille 1984, 273. This text is not in itself overpowering evidence that Julio-Claudian emperors saw imperial anger as a major issue, since Claudius sometimes put forth edicts on ludicrously trivial subjects (Suet. 16.4).

101. According to the *Apocolocyntosis* (14), Claudius killed 35 senators, 221 knights, and others as "countless as grains of sand." For his irascibility, see also *Apocol.* 6, Tac. *Ann.* xi.26.2.

102. *P.Lond.* vi.1912 (= E. M. Smallwood, *Documents* [I] no. 370), lines 77–78, 79–82.

in particular perhaps the expression "guarding within myself unrelenting anger," seem to strike a personal note.[103] There are even hints of an
obsession. Claudius did not need the essay by Seneca to lead him in
this direction, and indeed Seneca would have thoroughly disapproved.
As a Roman of good education, Claudius will often have read about
orgē and *ira,* and he may also have learned something at the court of
Augustus. His angry threats show, however, that the ruler's anger was a
danger outside the court as well as within it.

Seneca wrote *De ira* with various purposes in mind, but much of it is
concerned with absolute rulers and their courtiers. The book could
scarcely avoid politics, and yet the ice was fragile: it is in fact a proof
that Claudius had genuinely changed his attitude towards Seneca and
not simply accommodated Messalina's wishes, that Seneca had strong
enough nerves to suggest in public—very guardedly, however—how
an emperor should behave, all the more so because his views and those
of Claudius appeared to differ sharply.[104]

Seneca's essay hints almost from the beginning that the ruler must
control his temper.[105] It recounts the fates of political leaders who have
been struck down by anger (*De ira* i.2.2)—they had been *victims* of anger, but as all readers will have known, what had happened to them
was often the consequence of their own anger or their otherwise tyrannical behaviour.[106] He argues for scepticism in listening to *criminantes,*
traducers (ii.22.3–4). The Athenian tyrant Hippias is the negative example cited; Alexander of Macedon, on the other hand, was so sceptical of an informer that (unlike some cautious members of the Julio-
Claudian house) he risked being poisoned.[107] "The rarer that modera-

---

103. The phrase *orgē ametamelētos* seems not to be attested in any earlier writer.
"Just *orgē*" was part of official parlance: see for instance the Augustan document *SIG*³
780 (= *FIRA* ed. Riccobono, III no. 185 = R. K. Sherk, *Roman Documents from the Greek
East* [Baltimore, 1969], no. 67), line 22. For Roman *orgē* as a proper part of provincial
government, see the previous chapter.

104. It is doubly erroneous to say (Nussbaum 1994, 405) that *De ira* contains "references to Claudius' own semi-philosophical writing on anger."

105. But the Wise Man is permitted to use *vis,* as we saw earlier (ii.3.4–5, 4.2, 17.2).
In *De clem.* i.5.6 we are told that a king should not show inexorable anger.

106. See Cassius Dio lix.25.8 for Caligula's fear of the vexation he had caused
among his courtiers.

107. Seneca commonly taught lessons by means of Persian or Greek examples; cf.

tion is in kings, the more it deserves praise": Julius Caesar burned some incriminating letters without reading them. Although Caesar was in the habit of being angry in moderation, Seneca says, he preferred to avoid knowing what might have made him angry (ii.23).

It was quite unnecessary for Seneca to point out how different the behaviour of subsequent Caesars had been. But the virtue of *moderatio* is not difficult, he says, for even tyrants with their swollen personalities have sometimes repressed their cruelty. Seneca recites at length stories of Persian and Macedonian kings famous for their anger, underlining the high price of giving a king good advice (iii.14.6). "Though it is expedient for subjects to control their passions, especially this mad and unbridled one, it is even more expedient for kings" (iii.16.2). Then he turns to Roman examples, all of them either republican or concerning Caligula. Then back once more to Persian and Macedonian rulers (iii.20–21). Then finally Seneca tells at relative length the tale of Augustus' relations with Timagenes of Alexandria, showing that the latter was treated by the emperor with what passed for indulgent restraint. Augustus often warned Timagenes to speak more moderately, and later excluded him from the imperial house. Timagenes continued to give *recitationes* of his histories and was received everywhere; he carried on his *inimicitiae* with Augustus, but no one feared his *amicitia*—an extreme contrast with what happened at court from Tiberius' time onwards (iii.23.4–8). Then almost at the end of the monograph we come to the famous story of Augustus and Vedius Pollio[108]—which finds a useful role for the anger of an emperor. In short, Seneca presents an account of imperial anger which seems to emphasize the desirability of moderation rather than overtly advocating it; which was quite understandable, given the author's circumstances as a courtier.

The actual politics of the Claudian court are suggested even more clearly by the somewhat tortured advice which Seneca offers to members of the emperor's entourage. When he tells the story of Cambyses and Prexaspes,[109] he at first blames the grovelling courtier. Then comes hesitation; then the case of Harpagus, victim of the wrath of

---

the clever example in *De ben.* vi.30.5–31.12 (the *ira* that led Xerxes into an undesirable war).

108. iii.39. More on irrational royal anger: *Ep.Mor.* 47.20.

109. Quoted at the beginning of this chapter.

Astyages the Mede, which seems to change his mind and lead him to state what was obviously his calculated conclusion. "This sort of restraint [pretending to have enjoyed eating one's own children, like Harpagus] is necessary, particularly for those whose lot is court life and who are invited to the table of a king."[110] The philosopher advises those who involve themselves in politics to show submissiveness to the emperor.[111] As he had written earlier, if you are wronged by "a king" and you are guilty, accept his justice; if you are innocent, accept your fate (ii.30.1). Reason calls for endurance, since "failure to bear with equanimity a single insulting word has led to exile . . . indignation at the slightest infringement of liberty has brought on the yoke of servitude."[112] How do you survive to old age in the service of a king? Seneca quotes a man who had achieved this feat: you do it "iniurias accipiendo et gratias agendo," "by accepting wrongs and giving thanks."[113] Prexaspes, in short, did right to toady to Cambyses and not show anger.[114]

What distinguished tolerable from intolerable emperors, from a court and senatorial point of view, was not primarily whether they observed legal forms: Tiberius and Claudius did that, and as Syme observed, "governments are never at a loss for lawyers."[115] What was crucial was the emperor's character and intellect—did he believe every informer, was he malevolent, could he (above all) resist the temptation to grow angry? And over these matters courtiers and senators had little or no influence. There remained only retrospective denigration. Flavian and later writers had a splendid time pointing out the tyrannical irascibility of the Julio-Claudian monarchs.[116] A prime exhibit is the

110. All this is in iii.14–15.

111. Cf. Rudich 1997, 83–87.

112. ii.14.4. "Wrongs done by the powerful should be borne with a cheerful look, not just patiently," ii.33.1.

113. Ibid. Most senators presumably agreed with Tacitus' view that polite *obsequium* was essential (*Agr.* 42, etc.).

114. iii.14.5. Everyone understood that showing anger in addressing an emperor was normally suicidal: cf. Philostr. *VS* ii.1 p. 561.

115. Syme 1958, 408. Cf. Dio Chrys. iii.43 for a formula which allowed emperors to have it both ways.

116. Jerphagnon 1984, in cataloguing the stereotypical qualities of a negatively viewed Roman emperor, includes cruelty but misses irascibility.

Octavia, a drama of Flavian date and unknown authorship which recounts the end of Nero's first wife, with heavy emphasis on the irascibility of the emperor and his unwillingness to rein in his passions
as Seneca advises.[117] Epictetus later joined in the chorus of those
who recalled Nero's supposedly short temper.[118] Tacitus' depiction of
psychological states is more complex than most, but he lets us know,
for instance, that Tiberius was thought to have spent his Rhodian
exile "concentrating on his anger, his deceptiveness and his secret
lusts."[119]

Pliny's panegyrical address to the emperor Trajan (September 1,
100) might in theory let us know whether there was still room for some
informal negotiation between ruler and Senate. After two years in
power, much was still unclear about what sort of emperor Trajan
would be. It is commonly assumed that the much-revised speech which
we possess represented, at the least, a widely held senatorial view of
emperor-senator relations.[120] Not that Pliny as a new suffect consul was
the Senate's most authoritative spokesman. Many other consuls had
carried out the same duty before,[121] and the survival of this particular
speech results mainly from the vanity of the author and from his energy in getting the pamphlet into circulation.[122] Furthermore his caution and ambition will have combined to produce a text which would
not cause the emperor any offence.

117. Nero's *ira: Oct.* 255, 438–438bis, 543, 821, 830, 858–859, 876 (*tumor,* if that is
the right text); Seneca's advice against it, 472–491 (esp. 474) (invoking Augustus;
Nero easily turns this around, 505–527). But Octavia, too, suffers from *ira* (176; *dolor*
as well), as does Agrippina (635), as had Claudius (265), and as will the *populus* (572–
573; cf. 784, 802). The gods are angry with the family of Octavia (258), and the god
Cupido, Desire, can be angry too (813). All this confirms that Latin was ill-provided
with terms for emotions.

118. Epictet. iv.5.18.

119. *Ann.* i.4.4. Cf. *Agr.* 4 (Caligula), *Ann.* xi.26.2 (Claudius). Domitian too:
Agr. 42.

120. For the expansion of the speech, see *Ep.* iii.18. When Pliny says (*Ep.* iii.13.2)
that in this genre "nota vulgata dicta sunt omnia," he seems to confirm the value of
his own panegyric as representative text.

121. See Durry's edition, pp. 3–4. The nominal function of such a speech, which
was delivered under a senatorial decree, was to give thanks to the emperor for the
consulship (*Pan.* 4.1, *Ep.* iii.18).

122. As to how one did that: Valette-Cagnac 1997, 140–158. The speech's survival
was also a consequence of its use by later panegyrists (Wallace-Hadrill 1981, 312).

The speaker puts his energy into blackening the regime of Domitian, and the implications for Trajan are of the vaguest.[123] The previous regime had induced profound pessimism, so it was claimed (*Pan.* 27.1), whereas now, "above all, your nature is such that under your power it is both a pleasure and an advantage to rear children. No father now need fear more for his son than the hazards of human frailty; the list of incurable illnesses does not include the emperor's anger [*principis ira*]." The hope of *libertas* and *securitas*—that is, security of rights and property—are the most important encouragement. If Trajan had been able to, he would have restored life and fortune to the many whom Domitian had slaughtered and despoiled, but in default of that he did not collect debts to the *fiscus* which had been incurred before his accession; a different emperor would have been angry with the non-payers (*Pan.* 40.5). And what a contrast between the relaxed *salutationes* (levees) of Trajan and the terrifying ones in the palace of Domitian, where the emperor was characterized by "arrogance on his brow, *ira* in his eye, a womanish pallor spread over his body, and a deep flush on his face to match his shameless expression."[124] Being a model of *benignitas* and *indulgentia*, the new emperor requires the senators to speak freely, and of course they will.[125] Trajan even dispels or thwarts the anger of others.[126] It is hard to see why anyone would deny that this is imperial propaganda.[127] The implicit recommendations are entirely anodyne.

It has been suggested that in 100 Pliny entertained "political illusions" about Trajan, and put a "neo-Stoic" programme before him in the *Panegyricus*.[128] Neither claim convinces: Pliny never shows any par-

---

123. Indeed *Pan.* 8.5 suggests that pro-Trajanic anger would have been quite understandable at the time of Trajan's adoption: it would have been an "inritamentum . . . irarum et fax tumultus" if anyone else had been chosen. As to what it was really like in Domitian's court, in the early years, it is hard to say: Martial, seeking the emperor's patronage, says that his previous request had been turned down by a Domitian who had shown no annoyance, "nulla nubilus ira" (vi.10.5).

124. *Pan.* 48 (where the "we" who attend the levees are senators).

125. *Pan.* 21.4, 66 (66.3: the favour of an unpredictable emperor may be even more dangerous than his anger).

126. *Pan.* 28.3 (the *plebs*), 43.1. In 70 Vespasian had attempted to allay *dolor* and *ira* between senators, according to Tac. *Hist.* iv.44.1.

127. The view of Durry 1956, 231; K. Latte and R. Syme demurred, ibid. 237–238.

128. Molin 1989 ("illusions," 794).

ticular affection for Stoicism,[129] and his text is a combination of calculated flattery and insinuated requests, the former inevitably taking up most of the space.[130] The situation of Pliny and his colleagues could have been worse: casualties were after all very light in the Trajanic Senate, and it was still possible to give the emperor implied advice; nonetheless ambitious senators were of necessity his servants.

Anger, or at any rate intense anger, naturally continues to be a mark of a deplorable emperor, good temper of an acceptable one. There is no need to rehearse every occurrence of these motifs throughout the era of Hadrian,[131] the Antonines,[132] and the Severans.[133] Cassius Dio's comment on Trajan sums up in simple terms the main things senators desired from the ideal emperor: "he put no trust in slanders, and was no slave of anger [*orgē*]. He refrained equally from the money of others and from unjust murders" (lxviii.6.4).

Not that there were no changes. Hadrian's self-control in this department seems to have been most uncertain. A dreadful tale was told about his blinding of a slave (see Chapter 13); anger played a part in his killing of the leading architect Apollodorus, and may well have

129. It was not only emperors who showed a marked lack of affection for philosophers in this period (two expulsions by the Flavians): proper senators kept their distance (cf. Syme 1958, 533–555, etc.), and there are no philosophers among all of Pliny's correspondents.

130. Which is not to deny that there is a somewhat admonitory tone about Pliny's generally critical remarks about previous emperors (cf. Molin 786–787, *Pan.* 45.1). In Dio Chrysostom's four essays on kingship, also written while Trajan ruled, anger is not much emphasized; in *Or.* ii.75–76, however, the good king is defined in part by reference to his control over his anger and his willingness to remit it. Plutarch, in his brief incomplete essay *To an Uneducated Ruler,* pronounces that the ruler should avoid *duskolia* (bad temper) and cultivate *praotēs* (even temper), chs. 2–3 (*Mor.* 780a–781a; a ruler's *orgē* may turn into murder, ch. 6 = 782c).

131. The most interesting evidence is provided by the coin types that are referred to in the next paragraph.

132. Was the story of Pius' *praotēs* towards a sophist, Philostr. *VS* i.25 p. 534, contemporary? Marcus advertised his control over his *orgē*: *To Himself* i.1, i.9.9 (he never showed even the appearance of *orgē*), xi.18.20–23. On his famous *praotēs* with respect to Herodes Atticus, see *VS* ii.1 p. 561.

133. See for instance Cassius Dio's portrait of Domitian: "he was not only bold and quick to anger [*orgilos*], but also treacherous and secretive," etc., etc. (lxvii.1.1). Cf. also lviii.5.3–4, and esp. lxxv/lxxvi.7.4 on Septimius Severus. In Philostratus, see *VS* i.8 p. 489 end.

been the real cause of the mysterious death of the emperor's love-object, Antinous.[134] But what is relevant for present purposes is that he showed himself the most creative of all emperors in advertising his supposed virtues on his coin types, including—to mention simply those which involve anger control—*indulgentia, patientia* and *tranquillitas*, as well as the traditional *clementia*.[135] The disappearance of *patientia* from the coin types after Hadrian, and the disappearance of *indulgentia* and *tranquillitas* after the reign of Antoninus Pius,[136] obviously suggest a loss of interest in such aspects of the emperor's image. Caracalla may even have turned the old ideology on its head by having himself represented in official portraits as the man of the angry scowl;[137] but *vis* rather than *iracundia* will have been the desired impression.

How did Roman thinking on this subject develop under the changed conditions of the later empire, from Diocletian down to the early decades of the fifth century? A large body of evidence survives concerning the emperor's virtues: not only the canonical Latin panegyrics (eleven, dating from the years 289 to 389) but also the relevant work of Menander Rhetor (who sets out the now well-established conventions),[138] and the panegyrical texts of Eusebius, Julian, Themistius (with a response by Constantius II), Libanius, Symmachus, Ambrose, Synesius and Claudian.[139] In much of this literature, anger control tends to disappear into a generalized gentleness and *philanthrōpia*,[140]

---

134. Apollodorus: Dio lxix.4.5. Antinous: the story that he was drowned in the Nile is thoroughly implausible.

135. *RIC* II Hadrian nos. 212, 213, 361, 417, 708–709 *(indulgentia)*, 365 *(patientia)*, 222–223, 367, 730 *(tranquillitas)*. "In offering a gallery of imperial virtues, the mint responds to the mood of the times," in the view of Wallace-Hadrill 1981, 313.

136. The last two qualities make brief reappearances in the third century.

137. Wood 1986, 29, writes of "the effect of brute strength and intimidating anger which these portraits seek to convey." The best known example is the bust in Berlin, Wood fig. 1. For an occasion when Caracalla may have pretended to be angry, or to be more angry than he felt, see Philostr. *VS* 607 end.

138. Esp. Treatise II, parts 1–2 (of Diocletianic date).

139. For a summary account of this literature, see Hadot 1972, cols. 601–619.

140. See, e.g., Liban. *Or.* lix.160–162 (348 or 349), Themistius, *Or.* i and xix; cf. Liebeschuetz 1972, 106; Wiemer 1995, 233. In the Latin panegyrics, the emperor

and the emperor's control over his anger is rather conspicuously absent from the Latin prose panegyrics.[141]

On most occasions when we hear imperial anger being discussed in this era, we seem to be witnessing demonstrations of professional skill without even the vestigial political significance which such discussions had possessed in the second century. Three authors in particular are in question, Libanius, Claudian and Synesius.[142]

In 362–363 the emperor Julian and the people of Antioch had a famously disagreeable encounter before the ruler left to fight his campaign in Mesopotamia. Hoping to rescue the situation, the leading local rhetorician, Libanius, composed two documents in the form of speeches, a placatory one addressed to Julian himself, and another on the subject of the emperor's anger addressed to the Antiochenes—in reality to the social elite of Antioch—in order to warn them of the seriousness of their situation.[143] But when Libanius attempted to cool the emperor's anger against the Antiochenes,[144] he was speaking from a position of exceptional privilege, and to an emperor of even more exceptional character. Julian knew all about the problem of imperial anger, as he shows in a surviving letter, which also, however, makes it obvious that the senator who received it is likely to have found the emperor's written rebuke unnerving.[145]

Much later, in 387, when an anti-imperial tax riot at Antioch put the entire population, including the *curiales,* in danger of retribution, and the now septuagenarian Libanius tried to help his native city ward off

---

must be "noble, wise, brave, dignified, kind, merciful, just, devoted to his people, chaste in his private life, moderate, generous, truthful, prudent, self-restrained, modest" (Born 1934, 23). Goodwill even towards barbarians could be recommended on occasion: Liban. *Or.* xix.16.

141. ii.36 and 45 are thus unusual.

142. There are other sources too, for instance Eusebius: *Triakontaeterikos* 5 (p. 203, lines 30–31; p. 204, lines 5–9 Heikel) refers briefly to Constantine's supposed control over his anger.

143. Liban. *Or.* xv and xvi. On the intended audience of xvi *(To the Antiochenes on the Emperor's Anger)*, see Wiemer 1995, 198–199.

144. For explicit mentions of the emperor's *orgē: Or.* xv.4, 22, 34–35 (the barbarians are dominated by anger, but we Greeks forgive; even Achilles relented), 71, 82. The speech could not be delivered to Julian *(Or.* xvii.37), but no doubt Libanius had intended that it should be.

145. Julian, *Letters* 82 (50 ed. Wright) (444a).

the displeasure of Theodosius, something quite different was going on. He wrote, among other things, two speeches (XIX and XX) addressed to the emperor. Many considerations lead to the conclusion, spelled out at length, that Theodosius must cease his *orgē*.[146] However these were not really speeches at all, but written texts which were not intended to influence Theodosius' immediate policy—for he had already decided it. Besides flattery,[147] the purpose was very clearly a demonstration of Libanius' professional skill and standing as a rhetorician.[148] Libanius and his friends perhaps hoped that Theodosius might actually learn a lesson,[149] but anger was too sensitive an issue to be mentioned to the all-powerful ruler while there was any chance that he might still be suffering from it, especially as he lacked the education which would have enabled him to understand such comments.

Both of the relevant texts of Claudian belong to the second half of the 390s. After the fall of the praetorian prefect Rufinus in 395, the young Alexandrian poet attempted to win credit for himself at court by joining in a campaign of vilification, which included harsh anger among the charges.[150] In January 396 Claudian celebrated the third consulship of the eleven-year-old emperor Honorius with a flattering poem, and two years after that he devoted a 656-line poem to the adolescent's next consulship. Both works allude to anger, as a way of blackening the name of the defeated and dead enemy Arbogast[151] or laundering the reputation of the emperor's recently deceased father, Theodosius—now endowed with a gentle and forgiving nature.[152]

---

146. Liban. *Or.* xix.45–47.

147. Antioch experienced Theodosius' anger for only half a day: Liban. *Or.* xx.12–end, esp. 14, including comparisons with Diocletian, Alexander of Macedon, Philip II, Constantine, Valens, Constantius and Vespasian—none as lenient as Theodosius. Cf. *Or.* xxiii.13. In reality, Theodosius "maintained military discipline by burning men alive or more often cutting off their hands" (MacMullen 1986a, 158 = 1990, 212).

148. Cf. A. F. Norman's comment in his Loeb edition of Libanius, vol. II (1977), p. 240. See Chapter 6 for Libanius' essays about Achilles.

149. For evidence that Theodosius was well disposed towards the orator, see Liebeschuetz 1972, 28–29. The intended audience of these "speeches": Liebeschuetz 26–28.

150. *In Rufinum* i.224–239.

151. *De III Cons. Honor.* 104–105 ("ultrices in se converterat iras tandem iusta manus").

152. *De IV Cons. Honor.* 111–116 (" . . . mitis precibus . . . paci non intulit iram"). This work puts in the mouth of Theodosius a speech of advice to his son, including a

The ambitious poet thus advanced his career by the skilled and more or less elegant adaptation of traditional formulae. It is hardly to be believed that either Honorius or the real ruler of the western empire in 398, Stilicho, was ready to pay any attention to advice about emotional control.[153]

In his so-called speech *To the Emperor on Kingship* Synesius of Cyrene, at this time an ambassador from Cyrene to the court at Constantinople, gives some emphasis to the control of the passions: "The first essential quality of a king," he says, "is to rule himself."[154] He quotes *Medea* 1078–1079 on the subject of anger. Arcadius is asked not be annoyed when his court is criticized.[155] Other themes, in particular the desirability of a simple imperial lifestyle and the undesirability of Goths in imperial service, not to mention imperial greed, take up considerably more space. Synesius had come to ask for a reduction in Cyrene's taxes, and the extreme frankness of part of the text makes it impossible to suppose that Arcadius or his courtiers were confronted with it in this form.[156] "He says what he would have liked to say in his real *presbeutikos*."[157] The real audience may not have been in Constantinople at all but in Cyrene.

---

philosophical-mythological pastiche about Prometheus, which leads (without much logic) to the conclusion that rulers ought to govern their emotions and in particular their anger (*De IV Cons. Honor.* 214-352, esp. 225–268 on the emotions and esp. 241–266 on anger).

153. According to Cameron 1970, 380, the eulogist's purpose in lines 214–352 was "to entertain, not instruct." There are naturally political nuances which we are not called upon to explore here. Did the imperial regime itself desire to advertise its benevolence to the small elite which encountered texts of this kind? Did Claudian's powerful patrons, who can in part be identified, wish to send a hint from Rome to Milan of what they expected of Stilicho's regime? *De VI Cons. Honor.* of 404 (660 lines) avoids emotional control, commenting favourably (111) on the anger which Theodosius had brought to bear on his enemies.

154. Ch. 10 = pp. 22–23 Terzaghi.

155. Ch. 14 = p. 29 Terzaghi. The date is 399 or, according to others, slightly earlier.

156. It is true that in 404 Synesius claimed that he had addressed the court more boldly than any earlier Greek (*On Dreams* 148d = p. 176 Terzaghi). Yet Synesius remained on good terms with high-ranking officials. Lacombrade 1951, 79–87, offered a conspicuously weak defence of the speech's authenticity, by which he apparently meant its precisely fidelity to the speech actually delivered. Are we to believe that Synesius called the emperor a jellyfish to his face (ch. 14 = p. 30 Terzaghi)?

157. Cameron & Long 1993, 134. Some scholars think that this extreme candour is

It remained a commonplace of political discourse that the ruler ought to restrain his rage. This can be seen once again in the great historical work of the age, that of Ammianus Marcellinus.[158] Constantius II and Gallus cut bad figures in Ammianus' narrative, and his comments about the brothers Valentinian and Valens make his views clear: he remarks that at the beginning of his reign Valentinian (364–375), to counteract his reputation for harshness, "sometimes strove to keep his savage impulses under control," but gradually this quality, made worse by bitter anger, took command. There follows a little analysis of anger.[159] If only Valens had known how "to restrain his power, to resist unbounded desire and implacable *iracundiae,* and to know—as the dictator Caesar used to say—that the recollection of cruelty is a wretched support for old age."[160]

The Roman emperors of the late fourth century wielded almost absolute power.[161] They ruled by edict, they put their enemies to death, they appointed officials at will. Like all absolute rulers, they depended on a minimum of consensus, the important body of opinion being the army. There were also, however, aristocracies, and maintaining a degree of their support meant paying a certain respect to the

---

intelligible if we suppose that Synesius' work is a manifesto for one party of courtiers, temporarily out of power, against another, but that is unconvincing, since the text will have at the very least made Synesius vulnerable to the emperor's deep displeasure. It was probably not circulated (when it was actually written is another matter) until after Arcadius' death in 408. We can believe in Synesius' courage, but not in suicidal tendencies.

158. His reputation for reliability gains somewhat from the fact that in spite of his high opinion of Julian he neither credits him with uniform good temper nor omits particular instances of his anger; he limits himself to saying that Julian treated very gently some who plotted against him and punished them with inborn mildness. Julian being angry: e.g., xxii.13.2, xxiv.5.10; reaction to plotters: xxv.4.9.

159. Constantius: e.g., xiv.11.23, xx.2.5, xxi.16.9; Gallus: xiv.1.10. Valentinian: xxvii.7.4. "Hanc [iram] enim ulcus esse animi diuturnum, interdumque perpetuum, prudentes definiunt [to whom is he referring?], nasci ex mentis mollitia consuetum, id asserentes argumento probabili, quod iracundiores sunt incolumibus languidi, et feminae maribus, et iuvenibus senes, et felicibus aerumnosi," ibid.; cf. 7.7.

160. xxix.2.18. Valentinian apparently died of a heart attack brought on by a fit of rage: xxx.6.3.

161. Liebeschuetz 1972, 106, writes of the "unlimited power of the imperial office"; but he was well aware that for a variety of reasons the emperor could not always get his way.

way an Augustan or at least a Trajanic ruler was supposed to have behaved.

Sermonizing after the death of Theodosius in 395, Ambrose asserts that compassion called the emperor back from taking vengeance, and that he "was readier to forgive, the greater the emotion of *iracundia* had been."[162] "What foretold his forgiveness was that he had been irate [*indignatum*]; and what was feared in others, anger, was desired in him . . . He preferred to reprimand as a father than punish as a judge." Ambrose quotes a psalm which says "Be angry and do not sin."[163] Ambrose was the first to eulogize an emperor almost exclusively on the basis of Jewish and Christian texts,[164] and the Christianness of what Ambrose prescribes is obvious—not restraint, but repentance, real or (in this case) imaginary, after unrestrained behaviour.

Classical allusions to royal anger are usually critical in some way, or offer defence against criticism of an individual. The mediaeval tradition seems to have been neutral or positive to a much greater extent, to judge from a recent study.[165] What then were the functions of this critical discourse?

We can isolate six distinct functions. In the first place, irascibility or its opposite, an even temper, is used to create a negative or positive view of a historical or contemporary ruler. The negative portrait is often that of a *foreign* king, and there is an obvious link to the discourse of patriotism and xenophobia.[166] Second, anger takes a certain part, though not a central one, in debates about rival forms of government, not only grand theoretical debates about the merits of kingship and democracy but also, occasionally, more practical discussions about the acceptability of individual power. Third, starting with Isocrates such texts could actually help rulers (Nicocles of Cyprus, or a Roman provincial governor) to manage their subjects. Fourth, they could help to

162. *De obitu Theodosii* 12–13 (*CSEL* lxxiii.377).
163. Ibid. 14 (Psalms 4:5).
164. Cf. Hadot 1972, col. 618.
165. Althoff 1998. It is a distortion to say that when, from the eighth century, the gentler emotions once more began to figure largely in the "Mirror of Princes" literature, this was a *Christian* rulership ethic (Althoff 74). It was, but it had also been a classical rulership ethic—or, better, representation.
166. Another illustration: the supposed rage of Lysander, Plu. 19, 22, 27, 28.

establish the skill and prestige of the author (Isocrates, Pliny, Libanius and the like). Kings and their successful or more often unsuccessful attempts to control their angry emotions served as examples in the specialized anger-control texts. Fifth, from the time of Augustus in particular, tales about imperial anger and *clementia* were used to set up a general standard to which emperors ought to aspire; under the less despotic kind of emperor, there might even be an element of negotiation between the emperor and the upper elite (Trajan and Pliny?). And finally, descriptions of the angry conduct of rulers might also serve as instruction in rational political behaviour for their subjects, especially their courtiers (Seneca).

CHAPTER 11

A Thesis about Women and Anger

Shall they not cease, the empty reproaches of men?
Euripides, *Melanippe in Chains* (Page, *Greek Literary Papyri* no. 12, lines 19–20)

Women have so far been mainly absent from this account of ancient politics and society. Livia and Messalina appeared in the last chapter in the unusual role of conciliators, but almost nothing has been said so far about the ways in which women's anger is discussed in Greek and Latin texts.

The angry emotions were feminine. A persistent topos, or rather stereotype, on record from Homer to the Council of Elvira, represented women as the irascible sex. The Erinues (in Latin, Furiae), the spirits of retribution, were conceived to be feminine. Just as women were unduly liable to give in to other passions and appetites,[1] so they easily surrendered to the angry emotions, and their anger was seldom if ever justified. In this chapter I shall attempt to explain the socio-political function of this stereotype, and shall also point out those few texts which may be read as attempts to subvert it.

Women's anger, at the start of the twenty-first century, is a highly politicized subject, which means that its historical manifestations—in any period—are difficult to keep in clear focus. Whereas psychiatric opinion now regards much anger with suspicion and believes that excessive anger requires treatment, feminist thinkers are divided about anger's usefulness to women. Here, for example, is a characteristic passage from a recent book:

Women are continually in situations of subordination that produce anger (e.g., often not having control over their bodies, making less money than men with the same education, responsibilities, and experience; being the recipients of [physical] abuse ten times more fre-

1. Cf. Kurke 1997, 142.

quently than are men), but the culture still largely denies them direct expression of that emotion.[2]

Other feminists, however, have argued that for women's real careers and in real politics, anger is largely counter-productive, and that the same applies to their private lives. The philosopher Elizabeth Spelman has observed that "those who unjustly wield power and authority over others will be pleased if those they oppress find some way to censor their anger," but also that "encouraging persons in subordinate positions to recognize why they have the right to or why they ought to be angry must be done with concern for the consequences of their acting on that anger."[3] To what extent, one wonders, did Greek and Roman women think that they had the right to be angry or to show anger?

The ancient stereotype is not confined to intensely misogynistic or misogamic texts such as the famous diatribe of Semonides of Amorgos or the sixth satire of Juvenal. It is almost pandemic, so to speak, and appears in many genres; writers who conspicuously avoid it (Philodemus, for example) will require special consideration for that reason. It is not simply a cliché, it is (of course) a hostile stereotype, as is evident from the beginning. In the *Iliad*, Aeneas asked Achilles:

> What need is there of strife and quarreling between us? As if we were women who get angry about some bitter conflict, go out into the middle of the street and quarrel with each other, saying many things that are true and many that are not, <for> anger urges them to.[4]

Deplorable behaviour, according to the code of Homeric man. It is to be noted that the imaginary female anger which incurs hostile male comment is not simply anger directed against free men; anger between women, and anger towards slaves, could also be spoken of negatively. Whether it is only the physical, extrovert, anger of *orgē* which is denigrated or delegitimized, or milder anger too, is a vital question which we shall only be able to answer after a close look at a variety of texts.

2. McBride 1993, xiv.
3. Spelman 1989, 272 and 271. See also Burack 1994.
4. *Il.* xx.252–255.

The most vengeful character in Homer, on the verbal level, is probably Hecuba, who, faced with Priam's diplomatic project in *Iliad* XXIV, expresses her desire to eat Achilles' raw flesh. The nurse Eurycleia in the *Odyssey* also seems particularly vindictive.[5]

Certain angry mythical women seem to have been constantly on the educated male mind, above all Clytemnestra and Medea. Both of course have powerful reasons for their anger. Clytemnestra is nonetheless always a monster, and once she emerges as a specifically angry figure, in the *Oresteia*, that is what she remains. As we have already seen, philosophers and orators returned obsessively to Medea, from Chrysippus to Synesius. Numerous other tragedies contemplated women's rage (we shall be paying special attention later to *Medea*, *Hecuba*, and the two surviving *Electras*), and some contemplated the anger of goddesses (the *Hippolytus* includes a hint of criticism directed at Aphrodite).

Mingled in with the negative stereotype are positive admonitions: Deianeira, faced with her husband Heracles' unfaithfulness, resolves to win him back, but she professes not to be angered, for, she says, she does not know how to be angry *(thumousthai)* with him. For it is not proper, she continues a moment later, for any sensible woman to grow angry *(orgainein)*.[6] Now, it is necessary for the sake of Sophocles' plot that Deianeira should not be carried away by rage, but should rather employ Nessus' (as it turns out) fatal magic. All the same, we may perhaps assume that her sententious comment about *orgē* was conventional male opinion.

This raises the old question whether women were present during the performance of Athenian tragedies. Scholars continue to disagree, but the balance of the evidence seems to show that *some* women were

---

5. *Il.* xxiv.212–214, *Od.* xxii.407–412. I reluctantly leave aside the plentiful archaic evidence about angry goddesses, since they seem no angrier than the male gods.

6. Soph. *Trach.* 543, 552–553. (The rare word *orgainein* seems simply to have been a metrical convenience the tragedians used instead of *orgizesthai*). Somewhat similarly, an unidentified character in Euripides' *Phrixus* (fr. 819 Nauck) appears to take the restraining of *orgē* and *dusthumia* as one of a wife's principal merits. In Eur. *IT* 993, Iphigeneia virtuously tells Orestes that she is not *thumos*-angry with her late father.

present. Some female members of metic families were probably present, and a small number of citizen women.[7] It does not follow that the dramatists ever had a female audience in mind, but women's presence does help us to make more sense out of some didactic texts we are about to examine.

Readers who recall Herodotus' artful treatment of the angry emotions, as it was outlined in Chapter 8, will recognize that the language which he uses about angry women is unlikely to be arbitrary. Pheretime, ruler of Cyrene, was responsible for impalements, mutilations and enslavement, which the historian calls "excessively severe revenge" such as "makes people the subject of the resentment of the gods."[8] Is gender a mere incidental here? Probably not, because when Pheretime is first introduced she behaves in a conspicuously "unfeminine" manner.[9] But since there is plenty of impaling, mutilating and enslaving carried out by men in Herodotus' narrative, the questions remains a delicate one, and in general he does not hastily attribute angry emotions to women.[10]

Female rage as a joke was sitting there waiting for Aristophanes to make use of it in the *Lysistrata*. Lysistrata and her friends are eventually assailed by the Athenian police, the Scythian Archers, whom they promptly defeat. "What did you expect?" Lysistrata asks, "Did you think that you had come out against *slave* women, or didn't you realize that [free] women have *cholē* [bile, fighting spirit] in them?"[11]

The younger contemporary of Aristophanes who opened his mind to a drastically different social role for women was Plato. The latter's proposal that in the just state women should be eligible to become "guardians" leads in *Republic* V to a famous discussion of women's abili-

---

7. In favour of the thesis that women were allowed to attend, see most recently Henderson 1991; on the other side, Goldhill 1994.

8. *epiphthonoi ginontai*, iv.205.

9. iv.162.5.

10. When the women of Athens stoned to death the widow and children of the councillor Lycidas, who had been receptive to Mardonius' peace proposal (ix.5), no emotion is mentioned. Herodotus seems to take their reaction to be a natural one.

11. 463–465. That the women are angry is confirmed by 435–448 and 550, and by the *orgē* they provoke in their opponents (505).

ties. It is asserted that while women "will be the weaker partners," they are sometimes qualified to be rulers:

> May a woman then not be either philosophic or anti-philosophical, either spirited [*thumoeidēs*] or spiritless [*athumos*]?
> Yes again.
> Then there will be some women capable of being guardians, and others incapable. For these qualities were those for which we chose our male guardians.
> Yes indeed.[12]

This exchange may be thought to imply that Socrates regarded women as no more likely to surrender to *thumos*-anger than men are—but he does not explicitly state this conclusion. Later, in the *Laws*, Plato reverts to the old stereotype of women's irascibility: one should pity those criminals who could be cured and not punish them in anger and bitterness *like a woman*.[13]

The only people an ordinary Greek woman might punish angrily were the family's slaves, and free women's irascibility towards slaves may already have been criticized in the fourth century B.C., as it certainly was later. A woman's influence in the public sphere being necessarily indirect,[14] women might be suspected of goading their sons to give vent to political anger, and that too was probably disapproved.[15]

Are there any Greek texts of classical (i.e. pre-323) date in which a woman's anger is represented as right or just or is fully approved of? We shall explore shortly the possibility that Euripides' *Hecuba* should

---

12. *Rep.* v.455e–456a. In iii.396d he speaks of wrangling, quarreling women but then also holds up for disapproval men who behave similarly.

13. *Laws* v.731d (*mē akracholounta gunaikeiōs pikrainomenon diatelein*). And see xii.934e.

14. They could not sue or testify. Allen 2000, 112, is misleading when she says that they could "initiate . . . arbitrations," for their official role in arbitrations generally seems to have been limited to testifying about paternity.

15. Pl. *Rep.* viii.549d. Thus Athens seems to have resembled another patriarchal society, that of the Icelandic sagas, where, according to W. I. Miller (1993, 104), "women are expected to goad their menfolk to vengeful action, and men use this goading as an opportunity to discourse disapprovingly about female vengefulness and irrationality."

be read in some such way.[16] A clearer instance, and a most unusual one, appears in the speech which Apollodorus, son of Pasion, gave against Neaera (Pseudo-Demosthenes LIX). Having tried to blacken Neaera's reputation by calling her a prostitute and a bordello keeper, the speaker challenges the jurors with evident passion: if you acquit her of her alleged offence (usurpation of citizen rights), what will you say to your wife, daughter or mother when you go home? Will not the most virtuous women *(hai sōphronestatai)* immediately be angry with you *(orgisthēsontai)* for deciding that Neaera should share in their privileges as citizen women?[17] Since this comment is a piece of public advocacy, it is all the more useful as an indication of general opinion (in Athens in the 340s). But the speaker is also, I suggest, implying a contrast: *even* well-behaved women will be angry, so outrageous would an acquittal be, whereas such *sōphronestatai* do not normally feel *orgē.*

The fifth mime of Herodas confirms that the stereotype was alive and popular in Alexandria in the mid-third century. In this brief sketch (85 lines) entitled *Zelotupos,* "The Jealous One," the "heroine" is a woman named Bitinna, who has been conducting a sexual relationship with her slave Gastron ("Mr. Stomach") and now accuses him in crude terms of being unfaithful to her. She rejects his pleas of innocence and his appeals for mercy, and orders him to be whipped and to be tattooed on the face. In the last five lines, however, on the intercession of a slave woman, Bitinna agrees to postpone the punishments for a few days. She is a disgraceful character, according to the morals of free Greek men: first for having a slave lover; second, I think, for the fury, cruelty and implacability of her anger against the slave when she thinks that he has been unfaithful. So, a double degradation, only a little bit softened at the end, and another irate woman held up to contempt. In the succeeding mime we encounter some more female anger, disreputable again[18]—and we also encounter the line which represents a sort of official doctrine against a woman's anger: "a

---

16. The anger of Phaedra with her nurse in Eur. *Hipp.* 682–712 is at least very easily comprehensible.

17. [Dem]. lix.110–111.

18. vi.1–11, 27–36.

good woman is ready to bear anything" *(gunaikos esti krēguēs pherein panta)*.[19] There were other surviving texts similar in theme to these two sketches, such as an anonymous mime (Page, *Greek Literary Papyri* no.77) in which once again the protagonist is a raging woman slave-holder who has a sexual connection with at least one of her slaves.[20] The anger of the principal character is so sadistic that there should be no doubt that it is being held up for derision.

Herodas III also seems to hold a woman's anger up for derision, though the case is less explicit and straightforward. Metrotime, the principal character, desires to have her schoolboy son thrashed by his teacher, who readily collaborates. Eventually he desists, but Metrotime is unrelenting.[21]

And to turn to a vastly more sophisticated text, when Horace wrote a poem elegantly urging someone to cease being angry with him, the addressee was female (*Odes* i.16).[22] One can believe, if one wishes, that a real person, unnamed, was concerned, but it is much more likely that the occasion was imaginary and that Horace was acknowledging the force of the ancient stereotype. No doubt there had already been plenty of angry women in Roman literature—Ariadne in Catullus 64 stands out.[23] There had been angry males too, of course, but it is clear that when women (fictional or otherwise) appear in literary works they have a much better chance than men do of being labelled as irascible. Another part of this story is the woman who cannot control her anger towards her slaves.[24]

19. vi.39. It is not sufficient to say that these characters "are designed simply to provoke our laughter" (Zanker 1987, 158). Another glimpse of the classic stereotype: Polyb. xv.30.1.

20. Her anger: lines 13, 25, 28, 35, etc. This is a fragmentary text of early imperial date, originally published as *P.Oxy.* III.413 verso, cols. 1–3 (cf. some discussion by I. Cunningham in his commentary on Herodas, pp. 8–9). When Trimalchio tells his guest Scintilla not to be *zelotypa* towards a slave (*Sat.* 69.2), Petronius has in mind texts such as Herodas V.

21. See esp. lines 87–88, 94–97, though there are textual problems.

22. I follow the general line of interpretation suggested by R. G. M. Nisbet & M. Hubbard; the poem is not a palinode.

23. She curses Theseus, 64.132–201, her anger being especially plain at lines 192–201.

24. P. Clark 1998, 123–124, collects texts that propagate this image, including Ov.

A certain Theano was either the wife or the pupil of the philosopher Pythagoras. Many centuries after her death (how many we do not know), someone wrote some spurious Theano letters. She is imagined as an unusually self-controlled woman in virtue of her relationship to Pythagoras, and in one of her spurious letters she is represented as advising a woman acquaintance not to punish her slaves to excess out of *thumos*.[25] But she is not capable of maintaining this level of control: the next letter but one in the collection, also attributed to Theano, is simply a short angry message[26]—such as women typically write to each other, we are led to think. The stereotype in action once more.

To Greek intellectuals of the Roman period, female irascibility was generally a commonplace: it was made use of by Lucian,[27] and by Plutarch,[28] even though the latter, as I shall show in the next chapter, was able to see that much marital anger came from the male side. Galen is a prime exhibit:

> I cannot say what kind of nature I had <as a boy>—to know oneself is a difficult thing even for full-grown men, much more for boys—but I did enjoy the good fortune of having the least irascible [*aorgētotaton*], the most just, the most devoted and the kindest of fathers. My mother, however, was so very prone to anger [*orgilotatēn*] that she sometimes bit her slave-women; she constantly shrieked at my father and fought with him, more than Xanthippe did with Socrates.[29]

And he goes on to speak about his mother's "disgraceful passions." Now, perhaps she really did bite her slave women, but Galen repro-

---

Amores i.14.12–18, *AA* ii.235–244; Petr. *Sat.* 69; Juv. vi.219–224, 475–495; Apul. *Met.* 3.16.

25. *Epistolographi Graeci,* Pythagorae et Pythagoreorum Ep. 6 ed. Hercher (pp. 605–606) = 4 Thesleff (Thesleff 1965, 198), lines 18–23.

26. 8 Hercher (pp. 606–607) = 8 Thesleff (p. 200).

27. *Abdicatus* 28: women have a great deal of irascibility *(orgilon)* in them and frivolity and excitability (?) *(oxukinēton);* they are more liable to various emotions including *orgē* than men are (ibid. 30).

28. It appears from *Marius* 38 (the story of Fannia of Minturnae) that Plutarch regarded a woman who passed up an opportunity for revenge as unusual.

29. *De propriorum animi cuiuslibet affectuum dignotione et curatione* 8.1 De Boer. Cf. Plu. *Ant.* 1.3, *Ant.* 49.2. Writing to his wife, Marcella, Porphyry limited himself to instructing her not to punish slaves in anger *(Ad Marcellam* 35).

duces topoi as items of autobiography, and he may be doing so here; in any case he chose to proclaim his mother's supposed inability to control her rage.

The ideal woman wrote a Theano letter, or she was the heroine of a romance. In the romance written by Chariton, the heroine Callirhoe is propositioned by a eunuch on behalf of the king of Babylon: her first reaction is that she would like to tear his eyes out, but "being a woman of education and good sense [*phrenērēs*], she reasoned quickly . . . , replaced her *orgē*, and responded to the barbarian artfully."[30]

It is possible, however, that most philosophers and people with strong philosophical interests generally avoided this cliché or at any rate treated it with some reserve.[31] Since Aristotle insisted on the subordination of women, we expect him to accuse them of excessive emotionalism. And sure enough, he does say that the rational part of women's souls "is not in command" *(akuron),*[32] which implies that they are more emotional than men. Elsewhere he declares that people are more angry with their *philoi,* their dear ones, than with other people, the reason being (he says) that people think that the former have obligations to them.[33] He *might* perhaps have added that that is why wives are irascible, but he did not do so.

Virtually the only reference to women in the admittedly incomplete *De ira* of Philodemus is a complaint about men who show undue anger to their wives.[34] The Epicureans in general may have tended to reject the traditional sexism on this subject.[35] It so happens that the familiar

---

30. Chariton vi.5.8. The old stereotype is visible in the romances from time to time, e.g. at Achilles Tatius v.5.6–7 and perhaps at Xen.Eph. ii.3.

31. It may also be relevant that amid all his angry characters Menander seems to have included no women.

32. *Pol.* i.5.1260a13. The context is the assertion that there is a woman's form of virtue and of self-restraint, courage and justice; he quotes Soph. *Ajax* 293, "Silence makes a woman beautiful" (words which Tecmessa says are trite, *humnoumena,* 292).

33. *Rhet.* ii.2.1379b2–4.

34. *De ira* 5 (cols. xxii.32–xxiii.2): "If they marry, they accuse their wives of corrupt behaviour and form hasty judgements <about them>" (that seems to be the meaning, but there is a gap in the text immediately after the last word translated here. Indelli takes the meaning to be: "se sono sposati, agiscono sconsideratamente, accusando la moglie di oltraggio)."

35. Cf. Nussbaum 1994, 194 n. 2. Some Stoics were not above passing on hostile

topos is absent from the philosophical works of Cicero.[36] Even Seneca, although he surrenders to the standard stereotype, may be less fond of it than might have been expected. A recent writer has maintained that Seneca believed in the moral equality of the sexes.[37] That may be exaggerated: once in *De ira* he refers to anger as a woman's vice—"it is womanly to rage [*furere*] in anger"—and the same sentiment appears elsewhere.[38] Yet given the length of *De ira,* we might have expected more; not one of his numerous *exempla* of evil temper is female.

With Plutarch we seem at first sight to be back to normal: "Just as with the body a bruise results from a great blow, so with the most delicate souls the inclination to inflict pain produces a greater outburst of anger [*thumos*] in proportion to their greater weakness. *That is why women are more irascible than men.*"[39] And while Plutarch, like Cicero and Philodemus, is capable of seeing women as the victims of male anger,[40] the old stereotype persists: a wife "should have no emotion [*pathos*] of her own, but should share her husband's seriousness or playfulness, soberness or laughter." If the husband commits "some little error" with a *hetaira* or slave-woman, the wife should not *aganaktein* or *chalepainein*—that is, make a fuss or get cross (it follows that she should not even think of giving way to *orgē*).[41] On the other hand, as we shall see in the next chapter, Plutarch's somewhat novel view of marriage as a partnership includes both an unprecedented degree of concern about familial anger as well as an awareness that husbands are responsible for a good proportion of it.

A properly organized community, from the point of view of Greek and Roman men, was one in which women knew their place, and knowing

stories about Xanthippe, the wife of Socrates: Antipater of Tarsus fr. 65 (*SVF* III p. 257).

36. For a supposedly criminal woman furiously applying torture to slaves, see Cic. *Cluent.* 177.

37. Mauch 1997.

38. Sen. *De ira* i.20.3; *De clem.* i.5.5.

39. *De cohibenda ira* 8 (*Mor.* 457ab). See also 9 (457c).

40. Cf. *Coniugalia praecepta* 2, 3, 39 (*Mor.* 139e, 143e).

41. *Coniugalia praecepta* 14, 16 (*Mor.* 140a, 140b); cf. 28 (141f–142a). It is assumed in 27 = 141f that *orgē* in a marriage comes from the wife's side.

their place involved, among other things, avoiding anger. The stereotype we have been examining implies that there was almost no legitimate place for women's anger in the classical city. The point of the stereotyped angry woman is that she represents an attempt at the thorough denigration, indeed delegitimization, of female anger.[42] The moralistic anti-anger tradition we have been examining was only in part "absolutist": a great deal of anger was actually approved of even by philosophers, particularly by Platonists and Peripatetics. The ordinary educated Greek male of Hellenistic and Roman times (not to mention earlier Greeks, not to mention Romans) was by no means opposed to all male anger whatsoever; but about women's anger he knew what to think. The message of the texts we have been examining is, to borrow words from Spelman, that while "members of subordinate groups are expected to be emotional, indeed to have their emotions run their lives, their anger will not be tolerated."[43]

It might be objected that there are other kinds of people who are stereotypically angry in ancient texts—the elderly, for instance. Was their anger meant to be delegitimized too? To some extent perhaps it was, but as we shall see in Chapter 14, attitudes towards paternal anger were in fact quite complex, and an angry old father might be thought to have a degree of justice on his side.

Thus the argument is that the *orgē* of women was held up for disapproval or derision so often in Greek literature that we should detect a dominant tradition of delegitimization. But not of all anger whatsoever, for the texts we have been examining have for the most part been concerned with *orgē* and *thumos*. So the campaign was not as severe as it might at first seem. The rules established by the Greek male did not go as far as to say, for instance, that a wife could not express some annoyance, *chalepotēs*, towards her husband now and again.

But why exactly should Greek and perhaps Roman men have wished to reserve anger for their own use? An ingenious theory has proposed that the cognitive component in anger, emphasized both by Aristotle and by contemporary psychology, and indeed taken for granted by most ancient thinking on the subject, means that anger is *judge-*

42. Cf. Allen 2000, 115, who registers the passages in tragedy in which angry or punishing women are referred to as masculine.
43. Spelman 1989, 264.

mental.[44] To be angry, it has been argued, is to put oneself in the position of judge, which for a woman in a patriarchal society means to be insubordinate. Greek men were unwilling to have women pass judgement on them.

This is a not implausible if somewhat metaphysical interpretation. Anger often no doubt seems judgemental to its targets, in all ages. But we may hesitate to equate the cognitive event, which is invariably or almost invariably involved in being angry, with an act of judging. Appropriating anger for themselves was, rather, a matter of strengthening men's social and sexual control. Greek men simply wanted their wives (and also their concubines and *hetairai,* and daughters too) to do their duty without excessive complaint. An argument in favour of this view is that they wished to censor not only the anger of women against the dominant male but also their anger against slaves and against each other. It is hard to think that the free male found anything inappropriate in a free woman's *judgement* about a slave's behaviour—for it was part of a housewife's job to superintend the slaves. It was not that men needed to establish their control over the household.[45] Rather, a double purpose is served. A lesson is offered against a woman's extreme anger towards slaves, for such anger was an impediment to the smooth running of the slave system (we shall see exactly why in Chapter 13). And female anger against slaves could also be used, as in the mimes of Herodas, to reassert women's weakness of character.

This male instrumentalization of anger fits, as it is easy to see, into a wider set of beliefs about the excessive emotionality of women, a belief which goes back at least to epic times and the unfaithful wife Helen. The tragic theatre provides ample evidence, and Aristotle was doubtless merely one among innumerable Greek men who believed that women were more emotional than men. Anger, however, is—together with sexual desire—the emotion which most clearly requires, in the view of the Greeks, different rules for women and men.

Women were expected to fulfil their socially assigned roles, and without too much complaining. In my view, Athenian women had unusually strong grounds for complaint, since they lived in a system which was not only patriarchal but also, even by the standards of patri-

44. Spelman 265–270.
45. As P. Clark maintains in an important discussion, 1998, 124.

archal societies, quite inconsiderate of their feelings. However, it is an extremely speculative business to reconstruct the emotional atmosphere of, say, classical Athenian marriages, and I postpone consideration of the question to the next chapter in order not to complicate the argument unnecessarily. It is evident in any case that the morality of anger between wife and husband was not usually symmetrical: in other words, it was a long time before philosophers suggested that husbands should exercise restraint over their anger towards their wives. Philodemus and Cicero are the earliest surviving authors to suggest such as thing (though they are not likely to have been the very first).

The Epicureans may have rejected the traditional stereotype of the woman who surrenders to anger. It seems, however, that it had been subjected to critical scrutiny long before, in Athenian tragedy.

First it should be said that although we are attempting to interpret the inert texts of Sophocles and Euripides, we must allow for the probability that in the actual staging the actors did their utmost to exploit the theatrical possibilities of raging fury. That is to say, anger may have stood out in performance even more than it does in silent reading.

To begin with, the role of prominent female characters in the extant plays of Sophocles is more often to placate angry passions of one kind or another than to express them. Tecmessa plays that role among others in the *Ajax*,[46] as does Jocasta in *Oedipus Tyrannus*.[47] Finally, much later, in the *Oedipus at Colonus*, Antigone calms her father's rage and then attempts to mollify her brother Polyneices.[48] These are all quite brief scenes, and they should be taken not as a message of any kind but as evidence of one way in which Sophocles and some of his contemporaries imagined women as behaving.

Three Euripidean plays in particular show the poet exploring the subject of women's anger: *Medea, Hecuba* and *Electra* (to put them in chronological order). These plays seem to show a certain progression, from an appalling demon of female anger, who, however, has an excellent reason to be angry *(Medea),* to a violent collective act of angry fe-

---

46. *Ajax* 368, 588, 594; her husband is of course the target.
47. *OT* 634–702. She intervenes between her husband and Creon.
48. *OC* 1181–1203, 1420–1443.

male vengeance which is paradoxically given a measure of approval *(Hecuba),* to an act of female vengeance which is horrible but fully accepted *(Electra).*

Medea, as we have already seen, is permeated with *orgē.*[49] Medea has also gone to great lengths in the service of another passion, *erōs.*[50] The consequences of her anger are recounted to us unsparingly, and while there is room for argument about the precise ways in which Euripides adapted the plot, there can be no doubt that he made Medea a more violent and ruthless character than was necessary: the tradition did not require him to make her the killer of her children.[51] Not only is she murderously angry, she is fully conscious of being so. Medea's revenge, especially the murder of her two small children, seems to be the maximum of horror that a woman (lacking armed force) could inflict. Furthermore her anger, though perhaps it is natural, is unrelenting: what is most wrong is that she does not desist.[52] And in spite of her "masculine" resolution, Medea is depicted as a representative woman: "We were born women," she says, "incapable of performing noble actions, but such skilled architects of every kind of harm."[53]

When Jason finally appears on stage, he begins by sententiously telling his wife that he has often seen what an untreatable evil harsh anger is, and he explains that the alternative is "to bear lightly the wishes of the stronger."[54] All very simple and true, but the play also contains a violently contrasting theme, namely that Medea has a case. This is not a subjective reaction to Medea's dramatic situation: Chorus and cult both take us in the same direction. Medea is rescued by Aigeus, king of Athens, in the last scene of the play, and Attica becomes for her as for so many other tragic personages a final haven. The Chorus of Corinthian women says that Jason suffers justly *(endikōs).*[55] Revenge was not

---

49. P. 169.

50. On the linkage between Medea's *erōs* and her anger, see Friedrich 1993, 225.

51. B. M. W. Knox 1977, 194 = 1979, 295–296.

52. She is δυσκατάπαυστος (109); cf. 878–879.

53. *Med.* 407–409. Cf. 569–575, 908–913 (it is unsurprising [*eikos*], Jason says, for a woman to be angry in Medea's situation; then, in his delusion, he praises her for having changed her mind).

54. 446–447, 449.

55. 1231–1232; this is before Medea has killed her children.

yet in 431 much questioned at Athens, and the quasi-masculine Medea almost inevitably exacted it.

We should conclude that Euripides intended to startle his audience out of its wits (and his trilogy was duly ranked third and last) by setting before them the disastrous anger of a barbarian woman who had good reason to be angry. No one would want to reduce this extraordinary work to a simple formula. The uniqueness and strangeness of the plot almost defies one to draw general conclusions. But what I think we see is Euripides' representation of a woman who—although she has all the determination and astuteness of Odysseus, so much so that she can see the value of carefully dissembling her emotions—is in the end ruled by unrelenting anger. At the same time, her anger was justifiable, at least while she was encompassing the death of the new bride Glauce.

In *Hecuba* (of about 424) a woman's anger also has terrible effects. The second half of the play reveals how Hecuba's son Polydorus, the last Trojan prince, who had been sent to the court of King Polymestor of Thrace, was after the fall of Troy murdered by Polymestor for his gold. Hecuba, though now an enslaved prisoner, manages to requite Polymestor: in combination with other enslaved Trojan women, she blinds him and kills his sons. The cooperation of a group of violent women[56] must have made the act seem all the more unpalatable to the male audience. Polymestor prophesies strikingly that Hecuba will be changed into a dog with fiery-red eyes (1265).

Agamemnon, however, the play's presiding figure, adjudicates in Hecuba's favour. In fact he is complicit in her actions (898–904), and we may therefore suspect that Hecuba's case is meant to receive sympathy—even though it is represented as a female mastery *(kratos)* over men (883). Polymestor's crime made Hecuba into an angry and vengeful woman, and an even more resolute one than Medea, but her anger is not delegitimized—far from it. A modern critic speaks typically of the "degradation" which Hecuba brings upon herself,[57] but the common classical Greek reaction is also likely to have included the view that she delivered a justified act of revenge. It is interesting that although the play contains a lot of anger, *orgē* words, so common

56. *Hec.* 1052, 1061–1075, 1095–1096, 1120, 1151–1172, foreshadowed by 886.

57. Kerrigan 1996, 194 ("she sinks to the level of her enemy"). Cf. Allen 2000, 115–116.

in the *Medea,* are never heard. When Agamemnon catches sight of Polymestor after he has been blinded, he says, "It was indeed a great *cholos* that the doer of this deed had for you and your children."[58] This linguistic oddity is presumably to be taken as a sign that Hecuba's anger is not to be demonized. A recent reading of the play makes much of the moral ambiguity of the heroine's revenge,[59] which one might be inclined to dismiss as the 1990s fashion—but in this instance a reading of this kind seems just right. The play is terrifying, but it is at the same time one of the most understanding depictions of female retaliation to have survived from Greek antiquity.

Euripides' *Electra* (about 416?) also shows us female vengeance in action. The heroine impels her sometimes hesitant brother to avenge Agamemnon's death by murdering Clytemnestra (967–987). Her hand as well as Orestes' is on the sword as it does its work (1225). When the killing has been done, the Dioscuri appear and conveniently place the blame on Apollo; they also explain how the cycle of killing will come to an end. To that extent, Electra is justified,[60] and a violent woman can be said to have been presented with some understanding. It is to be noted, however, that Electra's anger against Clytemnestra is mentioned only indirectly; it may be that Electra's virile revenge is acceptable to poet and audience partly because it is *not* the product of violent and unreasoning passion.

Finally, Sophocles' play on the same subject, which was produced somewhat later.[61] The heroine's anger is an explicit theme, and she seems to gain credit from attempting to resist it and, ultimately, blame for surrendering to it. Sophocles saw that Electra's revenge had to be built on her anger, and he allowed no palliation of that anger. The Chorus tells her early in the play to turn her *cholos* over to Zeus, and she is aware of her *orgē* and what can be said against it.[62] When Clytemnestra in her turn is angry, Electra regains a degree of calm (lines 516–629), but at the climactic moment she urges Orestes on to

---

58. *Hec.* 1118–1119.

59. Mossman 1995, esp. 163–209, a first-rate account.

60. See esp. 1296–1297.

61. In 413, according to Dale 1969, 227–229; shortly before 409, according to Bremer 1991, 328–329.

62. *El.* 176–177; 222; 331 and 369.

still greater violence in his murder of Clytemnestra.[63] This time there is no resolution: we are left with the terrible consequences of Electra's rage. What the poet and his audience imagined as happening when the play was over is a vexed scholarly question, but the poet conspicuously does not bring the Dioscuri or anyone else to Electra's moral rescue.

It is to be concluded that few male Greeks considered in any period that there was much room for legitimate female *orgē*. The limitations included in this statement must be attended to: the discussion is about intense anger, not about every minor form of irritation, and there are exceptional situations such as the one envisaged in *Against Neaera*. And there were those, such as Euripides and presumably some members of the Great Dionsyia audience, who perceived the strangeness of the imbalance which arises when rage is permitted to one sex but not the other.

This has for the most part been a Greek chapter, and so it will remain. The stereotyped angry woman appears from time to time in Latin sources (Dido in the *Aeneid* is an unforgettable example), but her real life is with the Greeks and the most Hellenized Romans—so at least it may be hypothesized.

To a certain extent, it is true, the stereotype carries over into Latin literature, but that is often for specific reasons. One of these was the logic of slavery: Roman writers such as Ovid, Petronius, Juvenal and Apuleius make play from time to time with the more or less inappropriate anger or cruelty of women towards slaves.[64] In Juvenal VI, of course, a wife's anger is one of the main motifs.[65] It is also noticeable that in some Roman authors, the anger of Juno, the female anger that is most deeply rooted in the literary tradition and for various reasons least vulnerable to criticism, is represented as eventually calming down[66]—for it would have been indecorous if it had continued for ever.

63. 1414–1415; cf. 1483–1484.

64. Ovid, *Amores* i.14.16–18; Petr. *Sat.* 69.2; Juv. vi.219–224, 475–495; Apul. *Met.* iii.16.

65. Cf. lines 268–270.

66. Catull. 68.139 (whatever the correct text should be), in addition, of course, to *Aen.* xii.841.

Which leads to the complex case of the angry goddesses in Ovid's *Metamorphoses.*[67] The dominant passion of the male deities in the *Metamorphoses* is sexual.[68] What drives the frequently present female deities, however, is rage. They are angry because male gods have betrayed them (Juno's anger with Io, for example), or because their own sexual advances have been rejected (Circe and Glaucus), or because humans have outraged their dignity (Diana and Actaeon) or failed to honour them (Venus and Atalanta and Hippomenes).[69] As in the *Aeneid,* Juno is the deity most often said to have given way to anger. How to interpret all this? Divine anger was needed to explain the macabre transformations that are the poem's subject. But there are other factors at work. One is probably a literary game being played with just the Greek stereotype we have been examining. And Venus, punishing Atalanta and Hippomenes, sounds like a sexualized Ovidian version of a Roman matron who has had some slaves whipped, or put to death: "I was changed into sudden anger, I resented being treated with disrespect, and to see to it that I would not be scorned in future, I made an example of them and roused myself against them both."[70]

We have come a long way from building a civil society in the turbulent world of archaic Greece. We have seen how the discourse of anger control served to assist that achievement, and how a more ambitious discourse about the angry emotions attempted to counteract some of the natural tendencies towards political and social conflict in the classical period of the Greek polis. This was apparently the source of the original impulse to make the control of the strong angry emotions a matter of importance. By the late Roman Republic there was something of a Roman counterpart to the Greek doctrines that favoured the limita-

67. While literary and religious traditions determined to some extent what he could say about divine beings, the poet's opinions were worldly ("expedit esse deos," *Ars Am.* i.637) and his manipulation of the narrative all the more revealing.

68. At the beginning of the poem, however, Jupiter is led by anger to destroy almost the entire human race, i.177–312.

69. For all this, see Nagle 1984. There cannot be much doubt that anger and especially vindictiveness are associated by the poet with *female* divinities: Nagle 241.

70. *Met.* x.683–685. The poet sometimes says that a goddess's revenge went beyond what was just: iii.253 (Diana), 333 (Juno), cf. iv.547–550.

tion or even elimination of such emotions, and it too had a largely political reference. The critique of anger had always provided ammunition for negative or positive propaganda about monarchical rulers, and this was even, spasmodically, a matter of practical importance, not least with respect to those little kings, the governors of Roman provinces. But this critique was not wholly benevolent in its effects: in particular, it helped not only to exclude women from political affairs but also to take away from them, as far as possible, one of the foundations of an independent personality, the right to rage.

PART III

Intimate Rage

CHAPTER 12

Family and Friends

We have seen how, from the beginning of Greek history, life outside the household began to suggest that restraining the angry emotions had positive effects, and began to create a discourse about anger control. We have traced the Greek and Roman development of talk about limiting the anger of citizens and of rulers. Is there a similar history to construct with respect to private life?[1]

From a twentieth- or twenty-first-century Western standpoint, the family ought perhaps to be the place from which to *begin* a historical study of anger. The majority of us probably have an ingrained post-Freudian suspicion that most deeply felt anger derives in some way from the hostility between parents and children or from hostilities between spouses or spouse-equivalents. Aristotle asserted that the family was "an earlier and more essential institution than the state,"[2] and it may be that the nature of angry Greek emotions, and also the earliest ideas about the desirability of reining them in, were influenced by this

---

1. The predominant Greek and Roman concepts of family, namely *oikos* and *familia*, both normally include the slaves. But we can look first at *philoi*, that is to say close kin and friends (on the meaning of *philos*, see esp. Goldhill 1986, 79–83). As for the structure of the Greek and Roman household, nuclear, extended, or something else, it may have some bearing on the subject of this chapter, but it is not yet clear how.

2. *Nic.Eth.* viii.12.1162a16–18. But he appears to take the opposite view in *Pol.* i.2.1253a19–20.

fact. Furthermore some Greeks and Romans evidently considered that family anger—the anger of the unfilial son, of the overbearing father or husband, of the disloyal brother—was the worst sort of anger, if not the fundamental kind of anger. The classical Athenians were not as fond of eternal damnation as Christianity was to be, but they did consign to Hades those who had ill-treated their parents.[3] In the *Phaedo,* the people who are immersed in the fire-blazing river Puriphlegethon in Hades are the people who "out of anger [*orgē*] have done some act of violence against father or mother."[4] After Achilles, Agamemnon and Odysseus, the mythological characters most often mentioned in this book are probably the enraged wife Medea and the warring Theban brothers Eteocles and Polyneices.

We are going to encounter plenty of texts which suggest that the classical Athenians were well aware of the special potential for provoking anger which is inherent in family relations and in friendship. Aristotle had an explanation for this: we are more angry with our *philoi* (family and friends) than with non-*philoi* because we think the former have obligations towards us.[5] In the *Politics* he makes the same point rather differently:[6] "This [being fierce, *agrios*] is a feeling which men show most strongly towards their friends [*sunētheis*], if they think they have received a wrong at their hands,

3. Aesch. *Eum.* 269–273, Ar. *Frogs* 149–150; cf. *Clouds* 1447–1451.

4. Pl. *Phaed.* 113e–114b. The full route of such people after death is spelled out in some detail: "Those who are curable, but are found to have committed great sins, who, for instance, out of anger [*orgē*] have done some act of violence against father or mother and have lived in repentance the rest of their lives, or have slain some other person under similar circumstances," all of these go to Tartarus for a year, then those who have assaulted their parents emerge by way of Puriphlegethon and beg those they have wronged to admit them to the Acherusian lake; those who do not now obtain mercy are sent back to Puriphlegethon. One implication of all this is that those who assault their parents but do *not* feel prolonged remorse are destined for an even worse fate in the afterlife. For the texts which reflect the obvious fact that classical Greeks thought that the gods required mortals to respect their parents, see Golden 1990, 213 nn. 94, 95. Plato so much disliked the type of democratic leader who became a "tyrant" that he compared him to an Arcadian werewolf (*Rep.* viii.565d)—and the tyrannical man even abuses his parents (ix.574a–c).

5. *Rhet.* ii.2.1379b2–4.

6. *Pol.* vii.6.1328a11–17.

as indeed is reasonable, for, besides the actual injury, they seem to be deprived of a benefit by those who owe them one. Hence the saying, 'Cruel is the strife of brothers,' and again, 'Those who love in excess also hate in excess.'

We might also suggest that, since by Aristotle's time the expression of anger outside the household was very much inhibited, it was likely to be diverted against those who were *inside* it. But of course different kinds of anger against *philoi* require different explanations, a topic we shall explore further. In any event, Aristotle could take it for granted that "we are more angry with *philoi*."

In archaic and classical Greece, however, at least down to the time of Aristotle, criticism of anger mostly seems to concern not intimate rage within the family but anger in the city. Anger in the city seems to have been regarded as a more pressing matter. Not that family anger is rare in the archaic texts. About the early life of Phoenix, who tried so hard to persuade Achilles to relent, we are told one big thing in *Iliad* IX— that he had a furious dispute with his father, Amyntor, which might even have ended in parricide, though after all it ended with Phoenix's flight.[7] It is an angry and semi-Oedipal tale (Phoenix slept with his father's mistress and nearly killed his father). Yet nothing momentous comes of it—it was a private matter, not the kind of thing which made an epic by itself. Again, Odysseus' father, Laertes, did *not* take the admirable Eurycleia (who later became Odysseus' nurse) to bed, "but avoided the anger [*cholos*] of his wife."[8]

As for the divine family on Olympus, in Homer it practically lives for anger.[9] The whole *Iliad* is an angry struggle between wife and husband, Hera and Zeus, with the latter's daughter Athene constantly at the front and many other family members joining in. When we first meet this family group in the *Iliad*, husband and wife are seething with dislike, and so the relationship goes on. This struggle is mostly light relief from the awful events unfolding among mortals, but it gives a vivid

7. ix.448–480; I take it for granted that lines 458–461 are authentic. Anger: 454–463.

8. *Od.* i.429–433.

9. See Edwards 1987, 132–134.

view of how a Greek poet of about 700 B.C. imagined a dysfunctional family. Homer and his audience had a certain taste for scenes of marital and father-son discord. In short, the poet was not uninterested in family anger. At the same time, there is no sign that he wishes to teach lessons on the subject.

The Greeks naturally possessed some traditional norms of family behaviour. Anger might reinforce these norms, as in the case of Laertes, but it could also give rise to undesirable conflicts and to misery. The archaic poets not surprisingly lent some support to the notion of family harmony. In its own way, the *Odyssey* celebrates marital loyalty and happiness, and not only through the central tale of Penelope and Odysseus.[10] The harmony of brothers in the Homeric poems is also remarkably consistent—the great fraternal conflicts of mythology such as the one between Eteocles and Polyneices seem to belong to a later age.[11] This indubitably reflected a behavioural ideal of Homer's time.

When Hesiod imagines a range of evils which will mark the end of the current age of iron, his jeremiad gives the family a prominent place:

> Fathers will not agree with their sons, sons will not agree with their fathers, nor will guest and host or comrade and comrade; nor will brother be dear to brother as before. Men will dishonour their aging parents . . . , they will blame them, chiding them with harsh words, hard-hearted, not knowing of the vengeance of the gods. They will not repay their aged parents the cost of their nurture . . . , and one man will sack another's city.[12]

This is not quite a critique of anger, and nothing is said about husband and wife, but peaceful relations between parents and children and between brothers were already, presumably, traditional ideals. Similarly, later in the poem: "[with anyone] who abuses his aged father at the cheerless threshold of old age and attacks him with harsh words, Zeus

---

10. Odysseus delivers an encomium of marriage to Nausicaa, vi.180–185. Cf. Simon 1988, 18–19.

11. See Said 1993.

12. *Works and Days* 182–189. For the ancient Near Eastern parallels, see M. L. West's note on 182–186.

himself will be angry [*agaietai*]."[13] In Semonides of Amorgos, an angry husband is astonishingly imagined knocking out his wife's teeth with a stone,[14] but even Semonides, woman-hater though he seems to have been, has a vision of harmonious marriage, for the single laudable kind of woman "grows old with a husband whom she loves and who loves her, the mother of a handsome and well-reputed family."[15]

But we can tell a much more specific and cogent story if we consider the prevalence of certain kinds of anger between relatives in classical antiquity, and the springs of the desire to control that anger.[16]

The forms of anger within the classical family can sometimes be quite unmodern, and they suggest further questions. We expect fathers and sons to rage or at least seethe at each other from time to time, but some of the Greek texts are strange to us. In the *Nicomachean Ethics* Aristotle illustrates his contention that temper *(thumos)* and testiness or harshness *(chalepotēs)* are more pardonable than (certain) desires, by sympathetically imagining a man defending himself for beating his father: "Well, he said, he beat *his* father, and grandfather beat the father before him; and this fellow, he said, pointing to his little boy, will beat me when he gets to be a man. It runs in our family!"[17] He goes on: "And the man who was being dragged out of the house by his son used to say 'Stop!' when they got to the front door. 'That's as far as *I* dragged *my* father.'" The philosopher's humorous intention does not obscure the fact that these imagined acts come from a world remote from us. If the classical Greek family was like this, we may be inclined to think, it was perilously close to being dysfunctional, and dysfunctional in a world in which the economic and social functions of the family were more essential than they are often considered to be in the

13. See the whole passage, *Works and Days* 327–334. ἀγαίεται and its cognates are rare words of somewhat unclear meaning, but Zeus' reaction is obviously negative. See West on 331–332 for later parallels. Cf. Theognis 821–822, Pind. *Pyth.* vi.26–27.

14. vii.17–18.

15. vii.86–87, trans. Lloyd-Jones (slightly adapted).

16. Notwithstanding the insurmountable difficulties that affect even the documentary evidence (cf. Arnaoutoglou 1995 on marital disputes).

17. *Nic.Eth.* vii.6.1149b4–13.

modern West. What is most striking is the author's near acceptance of the normality of the angry violence of son towards father. And this is not imagined as adolescent anger but as that of a young man who is already a father himself. Was this the principal kind of filial anger to be encountered in classical Athens?

It does not take much effort of understanding to see that the patriarchal family, characterized by arranged marriages, little or no courtship, and a sexual double standard, as well as strong paternal authority,[18] is likely to have been the site of great amounts of rage. It is also plain that controlling rage in the family is almost as much in the interests of the dominant male himself as of women, children and the elderly. But while patriarchal family systems of the kind just described are widespread, the Greek family seems to have been especially combustible. It is possible to suggest why—but first we should consider more closely the nature of family relations in classical Athens. It will hardly be necessary to insist, either here or later in this chapter, on the utter inadequacy of the sources for judging such complex and intimate matters: we are at the outer limits of historical speculation.

As far as Athenian husbands and wives are concerned, the general view seems to be that their relationships must usually have been lacking in affection and emotional satisfaction.[19] Much of the time Athenian husbands openly directed their affections and sexual attention elsewhere. The ample Athenian evidence for concubines and "courtesans" (*pallakai* and *hetairai*)[20] and for the male pursuit of adolescent

18. For the first two of these aspects of the Greek family, see Lacey 1968, 106–108 (very misleading, however, on the subject of a woman's access to divorce, which was in practice almost nil), 113–114; Vérilhac & Vial 1998, 210–227; on paternal authority cf. Golden 1990, 80–114. It has been argued that divorce was relatively infrequent (Cohn-Haft 1995), but the significance of that is not clear.

19. See D. Cohen 1991, 167, for references to the literature. It is to be noted that celibacy was rare, and rarely recommended (Theophrastus wrote that the wise man would not marry: fr. 486 Fortenbaugh-Huby = Jerome, *Adversus Iovinianum* i.47; see further Barigazzi 1965, 35).

20. Davidson 1997, esp. 73–77, a refreshing improvement over some recent writing on the subject. See also Kurke 1997. Athenian reality is distorted if one translates *hetaira* simply as "prostitute" (Pomeroy 1997, 151): relations with *hetairai* had some duration, involved socialization as well as sex, and sometimes at least engaged the emotions; see Theoph. *Char.* 17.3, 27.9, among many other passages (and cf. Dover

boys[21] makes it readily apparent that by most standards an Athenian marriage was likely to be unloving. Concubinage made some men practically bigamous, and there is no reason to think that their wives, or the concubines and *hetairai,* were reconciled to this practice.

It can be assumed and admitted that some men deeply loved their wives,[22] but a knowledgeable author who set out to show that loving husbands were common found himself citing on the one hand texts which reveal the enthusiasm of husbands for having sex with their wives, and on the other hand the hopes of male authors that wives will be passionately attached to their husbands[23]—both entirely predictable phenomena which do very little to invalidate the notion that real-life Athenian marriages were, emotionally speaking, less satisfying than most. The same scholar even cites lines from the *Medea* which follow Jason's famous expression of his wish that there were a way of having children without the nuisance of women's existence—for the Chorus responds, as a Chorus would, by reproaching Jason for his betrayal.[24] No one will deny that it was common and respectable at Athens for husband and wife to feel mutual *erōs* for each other,[25] and the ideal of marital devotion received a certain amount of expression in epitaphs and in the iconography of tombstones.[26] The conventional morality included solidarity between parents and children as well as between spouses.[27]

The felicity or otherwise of married couples is admittedly hard to

---

1989, 20–21). Starting a relationship with a *hetaira* just after getting married might be thought excessive: Men. *Epitrepontes* fr. 1 Körte-Thierfelder. The overall effects of casual sex with "flute-girls" or ordinary slaves are hard to judge: it could certainly give rise to quarrels (for evidence concerning household slaves, see, e.g., Men. *Dusk.* 461–463).

21. See, above all, Dover 1989, 60–68, 81–91. According to conventional opinion, this too could be overdone: cf. Ar. *Wasps* 1025, Xen. *Oec.* 2.7.

22. Cf. Lefkowitz 1986, 68, who, however, neglects the crucial factors that hindered this. Cf. also Patterson 1998, 234 n. 28, even though she professes (228) to scorn such questions.

23. D. Cohen 1991, 167.

24. Eur. *Med.* 570–575. Hippolytus is made to echo, or rather to elaborate, Jason's thought in Eur. *Hipp.* 618–624.

25. Cf. Xen. *Symp.* 8.3. See also Sutton 1981, esp. v,232.

26. On both matters: Humphreys 1983b, 105, etc.

27. This is too obvious to need references, but cf. Lysias ii.65.

judge—hard enough in the here and now, and perhaps impossible across the divide that separates us from classical Greece. Most of the evidence about the degree of emotional satisfaction which Athenian marriages provided is so refractory. This is obviously true about tragedy,[28] comedy and forensic speeches, and it also applies to the works of Xenophon. The sensible husband Ischomachus in Xenophon's *Oeconomicus* professes an ideal of marital love and partnership,[29] but this is ideology, not sociology. Xenophon's dialogue contrasts Ischomachus with Socrates' initial interlocutor, Critoboulus, whose emotional life, insofar as it is revealed, consists of pursuing boys.[30]

The mutual hostility of husband and wife is a central subject of Athens' great tragic theatre. Even when a wife has heroically sacrificed herself for her husband, the Chorus is liable to imply that such a wife is atypical.[31] But what—if anything—does it signify about actual Athenian marriage that whereas Andromache and Penelope are the most memorable wives in Homer, the most famous wives of fifth-century tragedy are the horrendous figures of Clytemnestra and Medea?[32] Why indeed did family relationships become the predominant subject matter of tragedy?[33] These things could not have happened if the citizens had not been worried about the problems of family life, and deeply disturbed in their relationships with their wives or with the prospect of marriage. That does not mean of course that their own family lives were much like those of Agamemnon or Hippolytus, for the events of tragedy were of necessity more horrific than most of ordinary life. But when the obsession is added on to the structural facts already mentioned (mistresses and boys), it suggests that among the men of prop-

28. See Humphreys 1983b, 70–71.

29. He wishes to be a property-partner and a body-partner who is "worthy of love," *axiophilētos,* and imagines her loving him "from her soul," *Oec.* 10.3–5. He does *not* speak of his love for his wife.

30. *Oec.* 2.7 (cf. *Symp.* 8.2).

31. Eur. *Alc.* 474–476.

32. Admittedly, Clytemnestra is already a frightful murderess in the *Odyssey;* but see Simon 1988, 18–20, on the differences between her Homeric and her Aeschylean representation.

33. Historical themes disappeared. A shift occurred from "any story at all" to stories about "a few families" (Aristot. *Poet.* 13.1453a17–22).

erty at least (not everyone could afford mistresses or boys) contented marriages were rare.

Two facts are particularly striking about the sexual-affective relations of the free adult Athenian male. In neither case is he unique or even uncommon, but nonetheless these are specific characteristics: he quite often had more or less open ties with women other than his wife, and a relatively high proportion of his affective relations were with other males. This applied to ordinary sociability as well as to amorous relationships,[34] and the great traditional settings for male socialization, the symposium and the gymnasium, invariably excluded wives. The continuity of these sexual and social practices at Athens and elsewhere in Hellenistic and Roman times is not to be taken for granted in every detail, but it scarcely needs demonstrating that a passionate male interest in adolescent boys was remarkably constant, as visible in the *Anthology* and in Lucian as in the fifth- and fourth-century B.C. sources.[35] Nor is it correct to suppose that such ties ceased with marriage.[36]

From an emotional point of view, therefore, we may expect many angry Athenian wives, all the more so because, as was argued in Chapter 1, there was no full Greek equivalent of modern depression. And angry husbands, too, since the pederastic relationships which were often their most intense attachments were inherently short-lived.[37] The standard target, the *erōmenos*, was an adolescent, and in practice he was seldom much older.[38] Even the *erastēs*, the lover, was not meant to be

34. For *philia* outside the household as a prerogative of men, see Eur. *Med.* 244–247. The fact is assumed in such texts about friendship as Pl. *Lysis* and Aristot. *Nic.Eth.* VIII and IX. There may, however, have been an element of wishful male thinking about this, as can perhaps be seen in *Nic.Eth.* ix.11.1171b10–11.

35. A famous Hellenistic marriage contract is sometimes referred to in this context, in which the wife's side tried to take precautions: "Philiscus shall not be permitted to bring in another wife besides Apollonia, or to keep a concubine or boy" (*P.Tebt.* i.104 = *Select Papyri* i.2, 92 B.C.). See more generally Cantarella 1992 [1988], 70–77; Sutton 1992, 26.

36. See Cantarella 89. For the normality of a married Athenian male's pursuit of an *erōmenos*, see, e.g., the story in Arist. *Pol.* v.3.1303b22–26.

37. Cf. the comments of Calame 1996, 123, about the "anxiety and depression" created by the brevity of homoerotic ties in archaic Greece.

38. Dover 1989, 84–87; Cohen 1991, 195; drawing on Pl. *Protag.* 309ab, *Symp.* 191e–192a and Aeschin. i.41.

elderly.[39] It has sometimes been an aspiration of contemporary gay scholars to find emotionally satisfying adult-to-adult gay relationships in the historical Greek world, and the search is not altogether futile. There was, moreover, a restless and energetic minority of the male population which evidently took great pleasure in the sometimes painful ephebe-hunt. But the *erōmenos* seldom seems to have been fully adult, and for the ageing male even the role of *erastēs* was usually no more than a memory.

No kind of historical statement—except those which concern the mental processes of individuals—is more uncertain than such claims about the emotional states of sizeable categories of people. We have learned to distrust, for instance, those who used to tell us that until the blessed twentieth century parental love was weak, shallow, imperfect.[40] It is extremely perilous to extrapolate emotions on the basis of modern reactions; all the same, it is absurd to ignore the fact that Athenian marriages were subjected to terrible pressures, even by the standards of patriarchal societies. We cannot suppose that in a society which professed an ideal of an ultimately monogamous and harmonious marriage (Odysseus back in Ithaca), wives were somehow resigned. One cannot write honestly about the Greek family's emotional life without taking into consideration the plain facts of Greek social and sexual history.

Not much experience of history, anthropology or indeed life is needed to prevent us from being surprised that the Athenians simultaneously cherished an ideal of marital affection and ignored it; something similar can be found at Rome in some periods and in many a capital city ever since the Enlightenment. David Cohen has accurately identified the contradictions within the Athenian system of laws and norms with respect to homoeroticism,[41] but contradictions spread

39. W. V. Harris 1997b, 364–365.

40. See L. A. Pollock, *Forgotten Children: Parent-Child Relations from 1500 to 1900* (1983).

41. Cohen 1991, 171–202, with useful anthropological background (173–174). His strategy is to argue that conjugal relations at Athens were less problematic than is usually supposed, and homoerotic relations more so. But in my view Dover 1989 conveyed the unalloyed enthusiasm of Athenian men for attractive striplings in a more convincing way.

even more widely. And whereas in many cultures homoeroticism has flourished as a distinctly minority pursuit even within the social elite, it was much more firmly established at Athens, and the ideal of marital affection was thereby weakened. Indeed the latter ideal was not much insisted on, and its psychological depth is in any case suspect, since it served the purposes of producing legitimate heirs and guarding the household.[42]

Some writers have maintained that frustration, frustrated desires and frustrated aims, are the origin of all or most feelings of anger.[43] Thus an anthropologist maintains that, according to the "most common" view, "we become angry when we are frustrated by our inability to pursue our goals, generally because someone or something stands in the way." She sees this as specifically American, claiming that to a certain extent Americans believe that they have a *right* to get what they want.[44] At first glance such a theory looks simply like what it is, the result of reflecting on American consumer society, and it therefore seems unlikely to have much relevance to antiquity and to the agonistic, communal, less materialistic world of classical Athens. We shall certainly want to leave rights out of the matter in constructing an analogous theory about the ancients.

It may be hypothesized, however, that the social and family structures of the classical Athenian world did in fact frustrate even free people, both men and women, in their desire to maintain satisfactory emotional relationships. Relatively hostile relations between the sexes, combined with pederastic ties which were normally short-lived, can be imagined to have left most adult Greeks emotionally isolated, and irascible. Depression in modern societies is primarily the result of failed

42. As is said in the well-known text [Dem]. lix [*Against Neaera*].122 (commentary is not necessary in this context). See also Xen. *Mem.* ii.2.4–5.

43. Izard 1977, 329–330, maintained that anger occurs when one is "either physically or psychologically restrained from doing what one intensely desires to do," not claiming, however, that all anger is of this kind. For a later, less clear, account by the same author, see Izard 1991, 230–238.

44. Lutz 1988, 177–178. She makes this observation in the course of a careful comparison between anger and an anger-like emotion she encountered among her study population.

relationships.[45] In antiquity, there being no depression, or not much, the consequence was rage.

Is it possible to generalize about the tone of father-son relationships among the classical Athenians? The truly relevant evidence is slight in quantity, and it could hardly be more slippery to handle. A historian who attempts to extract social history from Aristophanes is in danger of despair; even extracting social rules is difficult. But of course there is no doubt that conventional society thought sons owed respect to their fathers, and no doubt either that fathers and sons sometimes quarrelled.[46] The splendidly wrought, and fraught, father-son relationships in the *Clouds* and the *Wasps* stay in our minds. But diagnosing a generalized "conflict of generations" at Athens during the first decade and a half of the Peloponnesian War can be no more than guesswork, since sources of the same kind are largely lacking for almost all other periods of Greek history.[47] While strain between young men and old makes itself audible with intriguing frequency during the 420s,[48] and the all-out war between Athens and the Peloponnesians is likely to have intensified it, the causes were for the most part perennial.

We may reasonably suspect that Theseus in Euripides' *Hippolytus,* who angrily and unjustly banishes his son, is in part an elaboration of an irascible and overbearing father well known to many members of the audience, and that the quarrels between Creon and Haemon in the *Antigone,* and between Admetus and his father, Pheres, in Euripi-

---

45. Mathes, Adams & Davies 1985; Oatley 1997, 323.

46. Nothing much can be built on single quarrels, such as that of Pericles with his eldest son, Xanthippus (Plu. *Per.* 36).

47. The prime recent exponent of such a view has been Strauss 1993, who, however, admits (136) that intergenerational conflict was an "age-old motif." For a reductio ad absurdum, see Laín Entralgo 1970 [1958], 39: "The souls of young Greeks during the seventh and sixth centuries . . . must have experienced with deep inner vexation the ambivalence between the strong moral and affective bondage to patriarchal custom and a growing desire for independent existence, a desire which . . . remained almost always unsatisfied until the second half of the fifth century."

48. Note especially Eur. *Supp.* 232 (King Theseus), 250 (the Chorus), in addition to the *Clouds* and *Wasps.*

des' *Alcestis* (both prewar plays, be it noted), are in part stylized versions of quarrels which really took place in Athenian families.

As for extracting real family relations from comedies such as the *Clouds* or the *Wasps,* it can only be done with careful reservations. Strepsiades may seem to be the first *iratus senex* in Greek literature, but in fact the irascibility of the elderly was already a topos: in the *Eumenides,* of all places, Athene seems to a make a joke at the Furies' expense, saying that she will put up with their *orgai* because they are older than she is.[49] Both the *Clouds* (423) and the *Wasps* (422), however, hinge on reversals of paternal authority, and this must mean that, in those years at least, the behaviour of fathers and sons towards each other was under close scrutiny. The *Birds,* too, touches the topic (414): it seems to make room for father beaters or even father killers in utopian Cloudcuckootown—though eventually the attitude of the character who is called "Father-beater" *(Patraloias)* is rejected.[50]

What is most remarkable about father-son conflict in the classical Athenian texts is that the son is already an adult (he is himself a father in the passage of the *Nicomachean Ethics* quoted earlier), and that sons use not just angry words but violence towards their fathers. (Adolescent sons would probably not have been acceptable stage characters— and they would have been unable to beat their fathers.) The climax of the *Clouds,* which began with Strepsiades in despair over his son's extravagance, is the son's culminating outrage: Pheidippides beats his father, in part on stage, and having now been schooled by Socrates, at his father's insistence, provides a rhetorical justification for doing so.[51] We have been well warned not to forget that this scene is clowning and farce,[52] but that truth obviously does not hinder the conclusion that for much of the audience, part of the joy of the last part of the play was to see the tables neatly turned on a tiresome and irate father.

Strain between father and son characterized a whole epoch. A considerable element in Cyrus the Younger's army, according to Xeno-

---

49. Aesch. *Eum.* 848.

50. *Birds* 757–759, 1337–1371, with N. Dunbar's note on the latter passage. See also *Frogs* 274, 773; *Eccl.* 639–640 (with R. G. Ussher's note).

51. *Clouds* 1321–1446.

52. Reckford 1976, esp. 108–110.

phon, was made up of Athenians who were "running away from" their fathers and, strangely enough, their mothers.[53] Again, one of Lysias' speakers claims it as a mark of exceptional virtue that he had never "spoken against" his father in all his thirty years (xix.55). The suspicion grows that the offence for which Plato consigned men to the River Puriphlegethon was not so very rare. He assumes himself that when a boy grows older he will, at least, be in conflict with his parents.[54]

But to return to violence: there are very many references in Athenian literature to father-beating besides those in Aristophanes and Aristotle which have already been mentioned, for it was a cliché of oratorical attack.[55] In the fourth century it was supposed that there was a Solonian law which forbade anyone who assaulted his father or mother from being a public speaker.[56] All this presupposes that fathers suffered a certain amount of physical assault, though perhaps not in the social circles of the famous orators.

It is hardly possible to speak about the tensions of Athenian father-son relationships without speculating about their psychological basis. This cannot be deduced from any general theory. The most we can properly do in the present state of knowledge is to discriminate between more and less salient factors. In the latter category we may wish to put the likelihood that, because of short life expectancy, more than 70 percent of Athenian men had lost their fathers before they themselves got married, and that the majority of twenty-year-olds were already fatherless.[57] Adoption, however, was common, and so was the remarriage of widows.[58] Thus, most young men had a substitute father alive, if not their biological father.

The custom of passing on control of family property while the father

---

53. *Anab.* vi.4.8. The word *apodedrakotes* seems to exclude the possibility the young men were simply fortune hunters. Conflict with father as a motive for mercenary service: Men. *Samia* 623–631.

54. *Laws* vi.754b.

55. See, for instance, Lysias xiii.91.

56. Aeschin. i.28.

57. I spare the reader the calculations which give rise to these numbers. Golden 1990, 111–112, suggests that the likely demographic facts limited father-son conflict over property.

58. Adoption: Lacey 1968, 145–146; remarriage: 108–109.

was still living[59] may possibly have had a negative effect on the harmony of many families. And the strong expectation, not unreasonable in the economic conditions of classical Greece, that sons would recompense their parents for their upbringing[60] was fated to sporadic disappointment, since—as Aristotle explains—parents love their children more than they are loved by them.[61] Disharmony is all the more likely because neither the time nor the extent of such "surrenders" of property was predetermined. Disinheritance was also possible. Unconscious sexual rivalry between father and son may also have had an important effect, given the normal disparity between the ages of husband and wife, and the extreme youth of the latter.[62] Another source of resentment will have been child exposure, undoubtedly quite common at Athens by the late fifth century;[63] most of those who were exposed did not live to tell the tale, but the survivors, both those who had been exposed and, probably in a different way, those who had not been, are likely to have felt some consequent hostility towards their fathers.

There is also a history of relations between brothers. In Homer the extraordinary thing is how harmonious such relations seem to have been.[64] Perses in the *Works and Days* gives us a radically different kind of relationship, but there must still have been some shock when, in the fifth century, from the time of Aeschylus' *Seven against Thebes* onwards, poets began to describe bitter fraternal conflicts in the mythological world. Now, in real-life classical Athens there were possible sources of fraternal conflict, as in any society. The system of partible inheritance may have led to numerous disputes, but then so does virtually any system of inheritance.[65] There may have been, as we shall see, a different

59. Lacey 128–131; Golden 1990, 107–111.

60. See, e.g., Eur. *Supp.* 361–365.

61. *Nic.Eth.* viii.12.1161b18–27. We may admit that this was a good account of Greek attitudes, even if it is not universally applicable.

62. *Contra* Golden 1990, 105–106. Aristotle recommends that women should marry at eighteen, men at thirty-seven (*Pol.* vii.16.1335a29–30), but it is hardly disputed that the actual median ages were lower: for girls about fifteen, for men about thirty.

63. Viljoen 1959; Golden 1981; W. V. Harris 1994, 4 (where the reference to Pl. *Theaetet.* should have been to 161c).

64. Said 1993, 301–307.

65. On the harmony of brothers, see Golden 1990, 115–121.

kind of reason why the anger texts eventually paid attention to disputes between brothers.

Those who transgressed against the traditional norms of sexual or family behaviour—the unfaithful wife, the disloyal brother or son—were always liable to execration. As to when anger began to be isolated as an element in family relations, and when the angry husband and father began to be criticized, we always have to fear that we are being misled by the accidents of source survival. No fifth-century text contains explicit admonitions about any variety of anger within the family, but sometimes it is made very clear that anger is to blame for terrible harm. Tyrannical rulers in Herodotus harm members of their own families, as we saw earlier. As for the tragic theatre, that universe of blood and psychic anguish, it probably reflects and makes use of contemporary attitudes about family relations rather than taking any controversial stance about them. This applies, for example, to such tragedies of family anger as the *Seven against Thebes* and *Oedipus Tyrannus*. The Chorus in the *Alcestis* is simply behaving according to accepted standards when it tries to make peace between Admetus and Pheres (lines 706–707). Other plays, *Medea* and perhaps *Hippolytus* (another play in which the angry emotions are almost overwhelmingly present),[66] may have been more original in their approach to certain kinds of anger within the family. In all these plays, the horror of the story arises because events lead ineluctably to the angry breaking of one or more laws of family conduct. Medea's duty to her children is plain, and in male Athenian eyes her duty to Jason was also strong. Part of the force of the *Hippolytus* comes from the fact that there was supposed to be some limit to the extent of a father's *orgē* with a son: Theseus underlines this in saying, too late, that respect for the gods has changed his attitude (*Hipp.* 1257–1260).

Oedipus Tyrannus, as we saw in Chapter 8, presents us with an intractable problem of interpretation. Is this version of the Oedipus myth, the West's most disturbing metaphor of filial relations, about filial an-

---

66. Theseus' anger: see 1313–1324; cf. *orgē* 900, *menos* 983, *orgas* 1124, *ōrgismenos* 1413, *orgai* 1418. That of Hippolytus with Phaedra: 581–668 (cf. 689); that of Phaedra with the nurse, 682–709.

ger at all? It is not about a typical struggle between father and son; in fact the story is so strange that it seems intended to be unique. But this is a play of anger all right, and the consequences fall on members of the hero's family. In my view, the original audience was intended to feel *both* that Oedipus was culpable for fatally mistreating his father at the Three Roads *and* that Oedipus had suffered terrible harm from the father who had abandoned him as an infant—*and also* that Laius had had no choice, since a reliable oracle had foretold that Oedipus would kill him.

Another complicating factor is metaphor. Euripides presumably wrote the *Phoenissae* because the strife between Eteocles and Polyneices was a traditional and powerful theme, but also because civil war was a present danger to the Athenians of 409 B.C. The force of this myth, widely felt in the Greek world and indeed beyond it, was not merely perhaps that brothers should agree—that was hardly a problematic contention—but also those who were *metaphorically* brothers, that is to say, fellow citizens, should agree.[67]

Classical Athenian morality does not seem to have been much interested in reining in the angry emotions of fathers or husbands, but the mature Plato took it for granted (*Soph.* 229e–230a) that the kind of anger that a good father applied to an erring son was *to chalepainein*, which was milder than *orgē*. Socrates himself was apparently thought by some to have gone further. Xenophon attributes to the philosopher two sermons about anger, neither of which seems at first glance to go beyond a recasting of conventional morality. In the first he appears as a champion of filial loyalty, telling his eldest son, Lamprocles, to give up his bad temper towards the boy's mother, Xanthippe (*Mem.* ii.2.1). The son complains of his mother's temper, but Socrates recommends gratitude and a prudent unwillingness to offend the gods and earn a reputation for ungratefulness. Similarly in the following chapter, Socrates is shown trying to persuade the younger of two feuding brothers to initiate a reconciliation, mainly on general prudential grounds. Being grateful to one's mother and keeping on good terms with one's brother: unoriginal advice. Yet there is a hint here of something new,

---

67. Similar in form but in my opinion less cogent is the theory of Strauss (1993, 144–148), that conflicts over paternal authority during the Peloponnesian War were in fact conflicts over authority and change more generally.

for these little lessons are not in fact about *orgē*, they are about instances of *chalepotēs* (annoyance)—though it is evidently persistent and
intense annoyance. Is that an accident? More probably Xenophon is
claiming that Socrates taught that *even* the milder of the two emotions
is to be restrained in these familial circumstances.

The prudential aspect of these two sermons is noteworthy, though it
cannot be assumed to be new. It evidently corresponded to a widespread kind of thinking. Half a century later we encounter something
similar when Demosthenes claims to describe the concord *(homonoia)*
which (normally) exists within the family, a *homonoia* which was to be
achieved by mutual tolerance between young and old in spite of their
conflicting desires.[68]

Plato was at the time when he wrote the *Republic* simultaneously a
radical and a conservative as far as the family was concerned. Democracy, he asserted conservatively, leads through excessive liberty to sons'
losing proper awe for their fathers,[69] and he complained about women
who nag their husbands for not being ambitious enough.[70] In the *Laws*
he predictably complained that the mythological tradition under-
mined respect for parents (x.886c). None of this, however, is specifically given as criticism of anger.

It was implicit, however, in Aristotle's advice about appropriate and
inappropriate *orgē* that there should be limits on all kinds of family anger and that marital anger in both directions should be restricted.
Theophrastus' essay *On the Passions* is unlikely to have avoided talking
about family relations. Unfortunately we can at first glance have no
clear notion where either of them drew the lines, and it *appears* to have
been only the founders of the Hellenistic philosophical schools who
established family anger in general as an explicit object of criticism.

This hypothetical trend towards a philosophical critique of family
anger coincided approximately with an increasing propensity of ordinary citizens, those anyway with some education, to take thought
about family relationships. The primary evidence for this in the late
fourth century is in the theatre of Menander. New Comedy notori-

68. Dem. xxv.88. Whether Demosthenes himself is the author is immaterial here.
69. *Rep.* viii.562e; cf. v.465a. In *Crito* 51b the personified customs of Athens are represented as implying that even an angry father ought to be revered.
70. *Rep.* viii.549d.

ously put the emotions on display more insistently than earlier comedy, and by doing so manipulated the emotions of the audience, thus creating a genre of theatre whose descendants are very much with us;[71] but in Menander's case, at least, there was also an element of didacticism about the emotions.

His first play, produced in 322/321 B.C. when Menander was only about twenty, was actually entitled *Orge*, and presumably dwelt at length on *orgē*'s harmful effects. (The few remaining fragments show little sign of this, however.)[72] Orge was probably a character in the play,[73] and it is obvious from Menander's other plays—*Samia, Duskolos* and *Perikeiromenē*, in particular[74]—as well as from the Menandrian plays of Terence, that it was rage between members of families, not political rage, which was the subject.

In the *Samia (The Samian Woman),* so it has been persuasively argued, anger is the principal theme:[75] both of the main male characters of the older generation (Demeas and his neighbour Niceratus) fly into spectacular rages around the central events of the play, and in the final act the young hero, Demeas' adoptive son, Moschion, also shows his anger. It would be easy to dismiss the significance of all this. For one thing, the play being a comedy and a New Comedy, everyone recovers (except perhaps the rape victim Plangon, but that is another story). And anger might be not much more than a technical device aimed at intensifying dramatic interest. Besides, Demeas, Niceratus and even Moschion all have reasons for their anger which are, to say the least, substantial: Demeas, for instance, believes that his *hetaira,* Chrysis, has had a child by his own son Moschion. Niceratus rages because his virgin daughter has been raped. Some of the manifestations of anger are indeed extreme: in fury over Moschion's having made his daughter

---

71. It is unfortunate that his immediate predecessors are so poorly known.

72. The date: Körte 1931, col. 710; Schröder 1996, 36–37. Whether he won the competition is unclear. The fragments are 303–311 in the Körte-Thierfelder edition.

73. Cf. Dover 1974, 142–144. Lussa ("Raging Madness") had been given a role by Euripides in the *Hercules Furens.*

74. Interesting lines about anger in the *Duskolos* include 17, 102, 108–123, 129–131 (almost all poor farmers are irascible, *huperpikroi*), 467–468; in the *Perikeiromenē (A Girl with Short Hair,* referred to by Sandbach line-numbers), 151, 366–368, 379–380 (as supplemented by Wilamowitz), 986–988.

75. Groton 1987; the date was probably 314 (Arnott 1998, 35–36).

pregnant, Niceratus tells the young man's father to get angry and blind him; later he threatens to burn the baby and murder his own wife.[76] But in Athenian eyes Niceratus had been subjected to appalling provocation; and it is to be noted that, in any case, he fully relents without having performed any frightful action.[77]

The frequent occasions on which this play compares anger to madness, or identifies it with madness,[78] suggest a critical attitude on Menander's part. Nor is there any difficulty in casting him as a conscious thinker about an abstract theme such as anger. Not only had he written a play on this very subject but he had also been a pupil of Theophrastus,[79] the leading intellectual figure in Athens after the withdrawal of Aristotle in 323. Theophrastus' interest in the subject (more or less predictable in a follower of Aristotle) we noted earlier. Furthermore the theme reappears in some of Menander's other plays, including the lost *Adelphoi* from which Terence took most of his play of that name.[80]

Menander should not be imagined as an extreme opponent of *orgē*, still less of anger more generally; in fact he may more or less have followed Aristotle.[81] The influence on him of the Peripatetics, which was recognized in antiquity, has been established with a wealth of convincing detail.[82] As for his views about anger, short fragments dragged from

76. Lines 499–500, 553, 560–561. In Sandbach's view, line 554 indicates the scene is farcical. He also supposed that the reference was to *Demeas'* wife, not Niceratus'.

77. Lines 588–612.

78. Lines 216–217, 279, 361, 363, 411–412, 415, 419, 563, 620, 703. The assertion that the angry are mad can also be found in a contextless fragment of Menander's contemporary Philemon (fr. 156 Kassel-Austin): "We are all mad whenever we are angry" (this thought appears in a slightly different form in Men. *Monost.* 503. For its earlier history see Chapter 14).

79. Diog.Laert. v.36. This does not of course prevent Menandrian characters from speaking disrespectfully about philosophy (*Samia* 725—a line which in fact shows that Menander and his audience thought of philosophy as being concerned with such things as father-son relationships).

80. Ter. *Adelph.* didasc.5. On the anger theme: Lord 1977. See also Ter. *Heaut.* 915–923.

81. According to Indelli (commentary on Phld. *De ira* p. 228), Menander disapproved of anger, but thought that a man should be angry when he had really been insulted.

82. Barigazzi 1965, Gaiser 1967.

their contexts must of course be treated with constant caution. For what it is worth, a fragment of one of his plays is against unreasoning anger *(orgēs alogistou)*, while another treats *orgē* as a natural consequence of an insult, and yet another seems to excuse the anger of someone because he is greatly in love.[83] Philodemus, in order to cap an argument, quotes the dramatist's lines, "Whoever does not get angry, gives ample evidence of his baseness."[84] Another Menandrian vignette: in the *Samia*, when the plot seems to have been resolved, the *jeune premier* Moschion touchily starts another crisis by suddenly announcing he is furiously angry that his father had suspected him. In a few lines he seems to calm down, but he then *pretends* to be angry in order to have the pleasure of hearing his father beg him not to leave home,[85] manipulating emotions like a skilled orator. And the response of his father includes this surprising statement: "I love you because you are angry"[86]—presumably because he thinks (rather generously in the circumstances) that his son's anger is a mark of fine character.

But what matters for present purposes are not the precise views of Menander about anger, which are irrecoverable, but the evidence he provides for contemporary Athenian and particularly Peripatetic interest in anger between *philoi*. The attention he gave to family rage also raises the intriguing possibility that the ordinary intelligent Athenian was more interested in this matter than philosophers were. We should assume that this interest took the form of an increasing receptiveness to doctrines of emotional control, so that when the doctrines of Epicurus, Zeno and their immediate disciples emerged, some people found them easy to sympathize with or accept. But Menander's interest in the emotions and especially his interest in family anger suggest

83. Fr. 519; fr. 620, lines 9–10; fr. 599 ("he who loves most is angered by the smallest cause").

84. Phld. *De ira* 7 (col. xxxviii.24–27) = Menander fr. 725. Philodemus quotes the passage in support of his assertion that "natural" anger is a good. An alternative reading yields the meaning "gives evidence of ample baseness"; see Indelli's commentary on Philodemus, which also reviews (pp. 226–227) the sentiments about anger attributable to Menander. Fr. 599 (= 659 Kock), quoted above, was seen by Lord 1977, 198, as a "remarkable parallel" to Aristotle, but the parallel is only approximate, and we do not know who spoke the fragmentary lines or in what circumstances.

85. *Samia* 616–724.

86. 695: ὅτι μὲν ὀργίζει, φιλῶ σε.

that it was not, as might otherwise have been imagined, Epicurus or Zeno but the Peripatetics who made family anger into an important theme in moral philosophy.

Not that one would want to discount the originality of Menander's own ideas. The most credible Menander is one who was well aware of the problem of controlling anger and of some of the bad effects that might follow it, and indeed had given thought to these matters, but who entirely approved of "reasonable" anger.

To a considerable extent, the opinions of Epicurus and Zeno about anger can be deduced from their known opinions about the passions in general. A serious follower of Zeno will have had no difficulty from the first in learning that ideally he should eliminate all anger whatsoever from his family relations. The earliest Epicureans were faced with a more complicated ethical system. As far as family anger was concerned, they probably received some guidance from Epicurus himself. He is not likely to have distinguished between the justified (*kata to deon*) and the unjustified outbursts of anger (*orgai*) of parents towards their children, as we know in fact that he did,[87] without providing a measure of explanation.

Both Epicureans and Stoics will presumably have used examples of family anger as material for attacking anger in general. Neither school, however, argued against anger on the basis of its social or familial affects, and at first they do not seem to be interested in the functioning of the traditional family. The Stoic Antipater of Tarsus wrote a work about marriage in which he endorsed the opinion that a good wife restrains her *orgē*.[88] But it is not in fact until Philodemus and Cicero that we have explicit evidence for philosophers' criticizing expressions of anger within the family. We may end this section with Philodemus, for although he may have had Roman as well as Greek readers in mind, his teachings are entirely Greek. He mentions rage within the circle of *philoi* (family and friends) fairly frequently.[89] The changes from classical times are marked. Unlike earlier moralists, he complains about the behaviour of irate men towards their wives: "If they marry, they accuse their wives of corrupt behaviour and form hasty judgements <about

87. *Gnom.Vat.* 62 (Epicurus fr. 6 Arrighetti [pp. 152–153]).
88. *SVF* III Antipater fr. 63 (p. 255).
89. *De ira* 5 (col. xiv.9–16; col. xvii.8–10; cols. xxii.32–xxiii.2; col. xxiv.1–4; col. xxvii.26–30; col. xxviii.3; col. xxix.19–20; col. xxx.5–6: companions as well as *philoi*).

them>."[90] And at last a Greek finds fault with anger against children: anger is not *like* madness, it *is* madness "when it kicks children and tears off their tunics."[91] Yet there is something strangely listless about his comments on these matters, and it is plain that he is retailing topoi, presumably of Epicurean origin. This in fact is the main importance of the Philodemus evidence—to suggest how Hellenistic writers, Epicurean but also Stoic and perhaps even Peripatetic, had extended the critique of anger to protect the more vulnerable family members.

All in all, one may say that the Greek discourse of anger control did receive a certain amount of impetus from the desire to prevent hostilities inside families—hostilities which are likely to have been unusually severe. The playwrights of the fifth and fourth centuries explored the matter. But family anger was no more than a spasmodic concern of the fourth-century and Hellenistic moralists, and one can see why: while the self-control of the subordinate members of the family was taken to be a self-evident good, virtually no one was greatly interested in questioning the system of subordination by making a major issue out of, say, the rage of husbands. The Epicureans, with their unusual concern for the quality of human relationships, certainly took some thought for family anger. But for the most part the discontents of the Greek family persisted, unremedied by philosophers.

When Cicero desired to criticize the Peripatetics, who held that anger assisted courage, he tried to show the supposed absurdity of their position by shifting attention to family life. From the point of view of a senator of late-republican times, the most insidious thing which the Peripatetics had said about anger was that it assisted soldierly courage.[92] But "this warrior irascibility of yours [*ista bellatrix iracundia*]," he says to

90. *De ira* 5 (cols. xxii.32–xxiii.2). Two generations later, when Dionysius of Halicarnassus was idealizing the Romans, he claimed (xx.13) that they believed that husbands should not be unjust to their wives: in other words, a husband's behaviour was now of some significance to a Greek intellectual. To put the matter in terms of anger might have implied an improbable amount of philosophical awareness in the old Roman worthies.

91. *De ira* 5 (col. xvii.8–10). "Kicking" is a restoration in the text but seems reasonably secure. In Dion.Hal. loc. cit., another of the notions he attributes to the Romans is that fathers should not be too "bitter" or too lenient with their children.

92. Cf. *Tusc.Disp.* iv.48–54.

them, "when it has come back home, what is it like with your wife, children and slaves? Do you think that it's useful there too?"[93] The inspiration for this thought was Greek. The implied rule of conduct—restraining one's temper at home—might, as far as spousal and parental relations are concerned, be said to fit the needs of any society whatsoever. As we have seen, the classical Greek world seemed to have particular need of such a code.

The Romans may have needed one rather less, since married Roman women were less disadvantaged than most Greek wives had been and still were.[94] On the other hand, father-son relations seem to have had their own specifically Roman strains.[95]

How large a role does family anger play in Roman discourse about anger in general? It is present, but it is not central. In Cicero's *Tusculans,* for instance, the detailed discussion of anger starts with the brothers Agamemnon and Menelaus quarrelling, yet the focus of his brief discussion is not on keeping the peace between brothers but on the awful actions to which *even* brothers can be reduced by anger.[96]

The Roman ideal of marital harmony is famously expressed in the funerary inscription known as the *Laudatio Turiae*—the acting out of an elderly widower's grief[97]—and in numerous epitaphs and literary texts.[98] The Latin epitaphs in which a marriage is commemorated as having been "sine ulla querela" ("without a disagreement"), or some equivalent, are extremely numerous.[99] Roman marriages may not have

93. *Tusc.Disp.* iv.54.

94. See in general Gardner 1986.

95. The great difficulty of keeping any such entity as "the Romans" reasonably precise with respect to time and social class is obvious. I am generalizing here about the educated upper elite in the period 100 B.C. to 250 A.D.—until the end of the chapter, where I descend to a later date.

96. *Tusc.Disp.* iv.77.

97. In truth, most upper-class Romans, the males at least, would probably have regarded this text as excessive in length.

98. Treggiari 1991, 229–261; for a brief but balanced account of the affective lives of Roman wives and husbands in high classical times, see Dixon 1992, 83–90.

99. Lattimore 1942, 279, collected some 140 instances of *sine ulla querela,* almost without going outside *CIL;* he notes that the formula is mostly Italian, not provincial. For the other formulae, see ibid. n. 108: *sine lite, controversia, reprehensione, offensa, offensione, discordia, stomacho, bile, iurgio,* are all relevant to the present study. These, too, are mainly Italian phrases. Lattimore has only one instance of *sine ulla iracundia*

been as strained as those in classical Athens. For one thing, homo-erotic interests, though commonplace in (at least) the upper class from (at least) the second century B.C. until the mid-second century A.D., took a different and probably less preoccupying social form than they had among the Athenians.[100] Divorce was easier. Nevertheless it was still hard in practice for a woman to initiate a divorce,[101] and the usual features of patriarchal society, such as arranged marriage, may have been aggravated in some ways by the presence in well-to-do households of large numbers of slaves, with all their potential for complicating the intimate lives of the owner's family. The literary tradition of male hostility to marriage corresponded to what was at least a substantial strand in Roman thinking,[102] but it has to be balanced against a considerable body of literary evidence for married couples in various states of ardour and contentment.

A classically difficult person in Roman literature and upper-class life was the *dotata uxor,* the wife with a large dowry.[103] In virtue of her privileged position, she had more freedom of speech than was given to the ordinary wife. She was angry and, for mercenary reasons if no others, needed placating. It never seems to be explained why she is angry in the first place; was this simply the anger which resulted from most wives' experience of Roman marriage?

That experience included, according to some, a certain male acceptance of male violence.[104] But several distinctions are necessary. There is no reason to suppose that *extreme* angry violence against a wife was

(*CIL* vi.10812 = *ILS* 8387), a fact which is presumably to be explained by a desire for euphemism: an epitaph cannot congratulate the deceased on not having come to blows with the surviving partner.

100. Not a matter which lends itself to quantification. C. A. Williams 1999 reviews both recent studies and the evidence, and shows that male slave owners exploited their young male slaves sexually as a matter of course. The pursuit of the free *adulescens,* however, was a matter of serious reproach, and probably not very common, if one considers the Roman citizen community as a whole.

101. Treggiari 1991, 481, etc.

102. See E. Courtney's commentary on Juvenal VI.

103. See especially Papinian in *Dig.* xxix.6.3, with Treggiari 210; Saller 1994, 129. The problem was not of course entirely new: cf. Aristot. *Nic.Eth.* viii.10.1161a1–2.

104. P. Clark 1998, 120–122 ("assaults on women [by their husbands or lovers] are not expressly condoned . . . but they are made to appear explicable and venial," 120).

ever approved in any way: it was the subject of horror stories concerning tyrants such as Cambyses and Nero and the irascible multimillionaire consul Herodes Atticus.[105] In relationships with other women, however, a degree of violence could be a matter for male preening—"grata est vis ista puellis" ("girls like that sort of violence").[106] As for the sort of angry violence that caused a bruise rather than a wound or a miscarriage, many Roman husbands probably found it unproblematic (much will have depended on individual temperament); eventually, however, a contrary ideal gained some acceptance, as we shall shortly see.[107]

As for father-son relationships at Rome, they have traditionally been supposed to be dominated by the severe, not to say brutal, rules of *patria potestas*. These rules nominally gave fathers the right to put their sons to death in certain circumstances, and more than nominally limited the financial independence of sons with living fathers.[108] Paternal power was to some extent a myth, but it was also a myth in the sense that it had a serious meaning: it used patriotism and fatherly authority to reinforce each other.[109] Roman fathers, unlike Athenian ones, did not pass on family property while they were still alive, and it is quite likely that many sons found the relationship onerous. Yet there was a tradition of family solidarity, and it would be naive to think that the duty of sons to respect their fathers normally produced severe hostilities. The significance of the fact that many fathers died before their sons grew up is debatable, as at Athens, but by the late Republic some people at least felt that traditional *patria potestas* was in its full form uncivilized.[110] Fathers and sons must often have quarrelled, but, *patria po-*

---

105. Hdt. iii.32.4, Tac. *Ann.* xvi.6, Philostr. *VS* 555; see Clark 120–121. The horrendous blinding of the elder Agrippina by a centurion acting on Tiberius' orders (Suet. 53) was, I suppose, an imperial prerogative.

106. Ov. *AA* i.673.

107. P. Clark 1998, 119–120, rightly points to Petr. *Sat.* 74–75 (Trimalchio and Fortunata) as evidence that the upper class thought of a husband's public violence, abuse and physical threats towards his wife as extremely vulgar.

108. Cf. Saller 1994, ch. 5. For the view that the son's legal inability to control his property was typically no more than nominal, see 123–127; the contrary view probably deserves to be restated.

109. W. V. Harris 1986, 90–91.

110. Cf. Liv. viii.12.1.

testas notwithstanding, there is less reason than at Athens to suppose that such quarrels became serious enough to cause public anxiety.[111] And if we turn to the relations of fathers with their very young sons, and ask whether, for example, Roman fathers gave way to violence when they were enraged by their sons or daughters, Roman writers do not seem to be very interested.[112] That may be because a measure of corporal punishment or child abuse was taken for granted, with respect to sons, or because there was in fact quite little of it,[113] but in any case it is not a large element in discussions about *ira*.

Thus the discourse of the Romans about anger concerned political relations and, as we shall see in the next chapter, slavery, but had quite little to say about anger between relatives. Convinced Stoics, from the younger Cato onwards, will have been opposed to all *orgē*-anger within the family, as they were to all such anger in other relationships as well. But Seneca's anger monograph is about anger between man and man outside the domestic context, it is about politics and about therapy, and it has relatively little to say about family anger. Wives receive only a very glancing allusion.[114] It is foolish to be angry with children, he says, or with people who are not much more sensible than children (ii.26.6). A brief litany of family conflicts is quoted from Ovid.[115] And that is all. Even the radical Musonius, while he held unusual opinions about the way men should treat women and maintained that women could be educated in philosophy, simply advises women to restrain their *orgē* if they want to be good wives,[116] and he has nothing to say about the *orgē* of husbands.

A generation later a certain change occurred. Consider, first of all,

---

111. Cf. Evans 1991, 166–194; Saller 1994, 119–132.

112. See above for Cic. *Tusc.Disp.* iv.54.

113. Saller 1994, ch. 6, demonstrated that whipping was generally reserved for slaves but did not fully resolve the matter of physical punishment. Seneca apparently thought that the corporal punishment of children was sometimes necessary (*De const.* 12.3; cf. Saller 142) but also implies (11.2) that in his world it was normal to be fairly indulgent.

114. *De ira* iii.35.1: the irascible man is imagined as being annoyed that his wife has answered him. Seneca lists her between the freedman and the *cliens;* the essay is much more interested in slaves than in wives.

115. ii.9.2, quoting *Met.* i.144–148.

116. Fr. III (p. 40, line 21 Lutz).

Plutarch's views about marriage—which are easy to misunderstand since, as we have already seen, he instructed women to accept a subordinate role. In spite of that, there is a new emphasis on partnership in marriage which goes beyond the ideals put forward in earlier works from the *Odyssey* onwards.[117] A number of scholars have recognized Plutarch's apparent originality in this respect.[118] He strikingly maintains that husbands should avoid sleeping with women other than their wives.[119] And the upper class more generally seems to have turned in this period towards monogamous fidelity and uxoriousness, and to some extent away from the marauding sexual habits of earlier times. Pliny's letters indicate what was aspired to, in his circle at least.[120] It would, I think, be hyper-sceptical to suppose that this alteration in ideals had no effect whatsoever on actual behaviour.

And Plutarch's essay about anger control shows more interest in anger towards *philoi* than Seneca's *De ira* does. That might simply be a consequence of their different political roles and the presumable differences in the readers they had in mind—imperial and senatorial circles on the one side, a more diverse group of the highly educated on the other (though we shall not forget that Plutarch's principal speaker

117. *Con.praec.* 11, 34, etc., with Goessler 1999 [1962], 110–111. One treats such prescriptive writing sceptically, of course. And when Epictetus says that one of the aims of philosophy is *philia* in the family (iv.5.35), we should not forget that he has just represented the philosopher as the indifferent victim of his irate wife and son (s.33).

118. Foucault 1986 [1984], 148 and 162 (rightly referring to Antipater of Tarsus as a forerunner: see *SVF* III Antipater fr. 63 [pp. 253–257]); Moxnes 1997, 282. It is frustrating that we cannot give a date to the treatise on marriage known as Ps.-Aristotle, *Oeconomica* III (preserved only in a thirteenth-century Latin translation): in my view, some of it is definitely not ancient, and so I do not propose to use it here. Given the highly fragmentary state of the earlier advice literature about marriage, opinions will continue to differ about the extent of Plutarch's originality. But it would be most unwise to follow Saller 1994, 6, in supposing that a single saying attributed by Plutarch to the elder Cato (*Cat.Mai.* 20) shows that Plutarch's own teaching was traditional; apart from other factors, that biography is thoroughly contaminated by philosophy. A new degree of sensitivity is suggested by Plutarch's (speaker's) emphatic assertion that he would not wish his wife or daughters to see or hear him in the repulsive state of *orgē* (*De coh. ira* 6 = *Mor.* 455f).

119. 44 = *Mor.* 144cd; cf. 16 = 140b

120. *Ep.* iv.19, vi.4 and 7, vii.5 (all admittedly performances both rhetorical and egotistical). For further discussion of the change in values in this period see Cantarella 1992 [1988], 187–188; Evans Grubbs 1995, 56–60.

in this work is a Roman senator). We may, however, assume that within limits (this was not after all a culture which set a high value on "sincerity") each of them reveals which victims of anger he thinks are most in need of sympathy. In Plutarch's view, it is our *philoi* who mainly suffer from our rage.[121] We may be angry with anyone or anything, and he tells plenty of stories about kings; but it is friends, wives and children who are constantly evoked.[122] "We see that . . . in the company of anger [*orgē*], husbands generally cannot endure even their wives' chastity [*sōphrosunē*], nor wives their husbands' love, nor friends each others' company. Thus neither marriage nor friendship is tolerable if anger is present; but without anger even drunkenness is a light burden . . . Madness by itself is treated by Anticyra [i.e., hellebore], but if it is mingled with anger it produces tragedies and awful stories."[123]

For the first time, I think, in the ancient discourse about anger control, this essay gives the reader the impression that family anger is really a central part of the problem, an impression heightened by the allusions to anger against slaves. What is most noteworthy, however, is Plutarch's attention to wives.

There also seems to have been a change with respect to notions of child rearing, once more a change that limited the scope for legitimate anger. A good case can be made for supposing that severity towards children gradually went out of favour in the last decade or two of the first century and the first decades of the second.[124] It is admittedly a case that depends on a handful of texts, in particular on Quintilian's stated opposition to corporal punishment in education and on some observations made in his later *persona* by Juvenal.[125]

---

121. *De coh. ira* 5 = *Mor.* 455c. Here *philoi* probably means "dear ones" in general, even though it means "friends" a few lines later.

122. Friends: 455f (it is not necessary to write out all the chapter numbers), 460f, 461b, 462ab, 462e, 463c, 464a. Wives: 455f, 457a (presumably), 460f, 461b, 461c, 462ab, 464a. Children: 455f (the speaker's daughters), 462e, 464a (but not 457a, where *paidaria* means slaves, not *bambini* as in the edition of R. Laurenti and G. Indelli). Also brothers, 462c, and animals (dogs, horses and mules), 457a.

123. Ch. 13 = *Mor.* 462a. Against *orgē* in marriage: *Con.praec.* 27 = *Mor.* 141ef.

124. Dating such changes is admittedly difficult; others have offered much earlier dates, e.g. Manson 1983, Evans 1991, 171. Wiedemann 1989, 93–100, sees something of a change in the correspondence of Fronto.

125. Quintil. *Inst.* i.3.14–17, without precedent as far as I know. See Juvenal xiv.47 for the striking phrase "maxima debetur puero reverentia" ("your son is entitled to

This new attitude applied to youth as well as childhood. A letter of Pliny's puts on display, as so often, the conventional senator under the influence of *humanitas:*

A man was chastising his son because he was buying horses and dogs rather too extravagantly. After the young man had left, I said to the father: "Well now, did you never do anything that could be criticized by your father? Dare I say you have <so acted>? Don't you sometimes do something which, if he were suddenly the father and you were the son, he would criticize with equal seriousness? Are not all men led astray by some error? Does he not indulge himself in this while someone else indulges in that?"[126]

The correct attitude, from the point of view of Pliny and his friends, was, we may assume, at least a measure of indulgence, this being, however, an attitude which was not at all universal and needed to be asserted.[127] He advertises a similar doctrine of patience or indulgence towards slaves—which should make us wonder whether we are in the presence of anything more than pious aspirations. But we can take it to have been widely agreed among the Greek and Roman elites of this era that a father's anger towards his son might easily be excessive and illegitimate.[128]

A quite different ideology is on display by the time we come to the world of the fourth- and fifth-century Christian fathers. There are, it

---

very great respect"; the point is that we should set our children a moral example). The child-welfare scheme put into effect by Nerva and Trajan was meant to alleviate the hardships of the children of poor Italian families, though it had other functions too.

126. Plin. *Ep.* ix.12. There had always been differences of opinion about the amount of strictness or indulgence to be meted out to the youth: see Eyben 1993 [1987], esp. 16–17.

127. Saller 1994, 125, rightly draws attention to the similarity between this tale and comedy, e.g., Plaut. *Epid.* 382–391. But it is very unlikely that a Roman senator of Plautus' time, or of Cicero's, would have advertised (though he might have given) advice such as is contained in this letter. Cf. the next chapter for Pliny's views about anger directed against slaves. Elsewhere Pliny treats the anger of testators towards potential heirs as a sign of social malaise (so it seems: *Pan.* 43.1).

128. The sentiment in *Dig.* xlviii.9.5, that paternal power ought to consist of *pietas* (respect), not *atrocitas,* probably goes back to Hadrian. For the deplorableness of an old man's anger against his son, see Lucian's *Abdicatus.*

is true, church fathers, Basil of Caesarea for instance, who occasionally see family anger as something worthy of their concern.[129] But Lactantius, to prove that there is such a thing as just *ira*, turns not to the judge, who he says should punish without emotion, but to the anger we may feel towards those who are in our power—our slaves, children, wives and students.[130] When we see them doing wrong, he says, "incitamur ad coercendum," we are provoked to punish them, and in so doing we rightly, so it is implied, show *ira*. Even two centuries earlier, many Romans would probably have assented to this. But a genuine change had occurred, or was occurring.

The lack of a comprehensive study of the late-antique family makes itself felt here. Did Roman family relations become even more brutally authoritarian? It seems impossible to say. One cannot perhaps build very much on the violence of Augustine's father towards his mother, even if it was rather common in their particular milieu.[131] Augustine's assumptions and admonitions are more germane. He takes it for granted that a man must "tame" his sons and compel the obedience of his wife.[132] In his view, a man's wife was his slave *(famula)*—he says as much.[133] She, needless to say, is permitted no anger at all: Augustine's mother, Monnica, is praised for having avoided quarrels with her husband, and for having convinced her friends to put up with their married servitude.[134] All this implies that, with respect to family anger, the Christians had discarded the highest aspirations, first known to us in the pages of Philodemus and Cicero.

---

129. *PG* xxxi.356a.

130. *De ira dei* 17.16.

131. *Conf.* ix.9.19 ("sicut benevolentia praecipuus, ita ira fervidus," a paradox which pagan writers would have found it hard to sustain). Patricius was of curial rank. Augustine implies that other fathers at Thagaste were the same (cf. Shaw 1987, 31 n. 119).

132. See *De utilitate ieiunii* 4.5 (*CC-SL* xlvi.235). His support for the authority of the *paterfamilias: CD* xix.16.

133. *Enarr. in Psalmos* 143.6 (*CC-SL* xl.2077). Similarly *Sermo* 332.4.4 (*PL* xxxviii.1463), all the more significant for being addressed to a Christian public, not a handful of adepts. Rist 1994, 213, somewhat incoherently attempts to soften Augustine's teachings. Musonius Rufus had written rather differently that a good wife was willing to do work which some people would consider servile (ch. 3, p. 42 line 8 Lutz).

134. *Conf.* ix.9.19.

This is not altogether surprising, since part of their programme for dominating the intimate lives of the faithful was the demotion of family relations.[135] The rhetorical trick was to allow more space for family anger but also to depreciate family life as the site of inevitable quarrelsomeness. Jesus was believed to have given instructions to his followers that they should hate their parents, wives, children and siblings,[136] and when Augustine preached about the conflict between this and the biblical duty to respect one's parents, he said that the family must give way before the imperative to martyrdom—metaphorical martyrdom, presumably, since Christianity was now the established religion. He recognized that family members might be angry when they were let down by an extreme Christian, and there were no real-world consolations to offer for this.[137] Gregory of Nyssa, in his tract in favour of virginity, included among the thousand and one things that are wrong with married life jealousies and fights, and the sufferings they lead to.[138]

The family was often present at, but was seldom at the centre of, the classical debate about anger. To some extent the texts are fairly predictable. The need for texts in favour of restraining anger towards parents and brothers may be seen as the natural product of societies in which family solidarity was of vital importance. Some elements in the discussion are less predictable. Texts in favour of restraining anger towards wives and children may be seen as parallel to the need for texts that tended to restrain all-powerful rulers. In both cases law and custom left the victims defenceless, or nearly so, against the rage of the stronger. But whereas it was a rather elementary rule of self-preservation that a ruler should show anger with discretion (like Augustus), it was only a relatively sophisticated society that produced the rule that the patriarchal head of a household should struggle not to show anger towards his wife or children.

---

135. Not that one should ignore the church's support for the sexual fidelity of husbands: Augustin. *Sermo* 224.3 (*PL* xxxviii.1095).

136. Luke 14:26–27.

137. See the new sermon published by Dolbeau 1992, 292–297.

138. *De virginitate* 3 (VIII, 1, p. 265 Jaeger), a profoundly silly chapter.

CHAPTER 13

Slavery

It is a disgrace to rule over slaves but to be enslaved by pleasures.
Isocrates i.21

A constant source of anger throughout classical antiquity was the relationship between slave-owner and slave. It gave rise to both the anger of the maltreated or humiliated slave and the anger of the slave-owner, for the owner was destined to be repeatedly frustrated by slaves who ran away or shirked or disobeyed or, if they obeyed, did so in the wrong spirit.[1] Virtually all slave-owners must at the very least have come close to anger from time to time, and very few external restraints existed; for the Roman master during many centuries, virtually none. Eventually, under the Roman Empire, the government offered some legal protection to slaves, but it can never have had more than a marginal effect.

The institution of slavery depended on vicious punishments and the threat of them, but also on winning the slaves over to more or less willing submission. What was at stake was not only the slave's work and in a broad sense productivity, but also the safety of the owner and his or her family and possessions.

Why should punishment calmly inflicted cause less trouble with slaves than angry punishment? There were at least two salient factors: one was the owner's ability to judge rationally when his or her own behaviour was going too far, from a prudential point of view; the other factor, possibly more important still, was dignity, a vital attribute in any system of personalized authority.

1. It is not my intention in this chapter to extrapolate loosely from other systems of slavery, but at this point it is hard not to recall the words of a scholar with an unsurpassed knowledge of the primary sources for U.S. slavery: "Typically, they [the owners] always wanted something; typically, the servants failed to measure up," etc. (Genovese 1976 [1972], 333).

Masters should restrain their anger towards their slaves, it was commonly said. The first surviving manifestation of this thought, or of something very like it, is Herodotus' comment on punishment among the Persians. He praises the Persian law that forbids anyone to do incurable harm to one of his slaves, "until calculation shows that the offender's wrongful acts are more and greater than his services"; only then is the master allowed to vent his anger *(thumos)* (i.137). The historian does not explain exactly what he thinks is gained by this display of fairness within a system of harsh and arbitrary punishments. Another comment of the same years is also enigmatic: the "Old Oligarch," in his diatribe against Athenian democracy, complains that there is so much "indiscipline" at Athens among slaves and non-citizens that you cannot hit them, and "a slave will not stand aside for you"; the Athenians let slaves and non-citizens dress so well, he says, that you cannot tell them apart from citizens.[2] Now Athenians could certainly strike their own slaves.[3] Is it implied here that in some other Greek cities free men were permitted to go about doing violence at will to other people's slaves (as the Spartiates perhaps did to the Helots)? And that the Athenians had learned not to do so? In the fourth century, at any rate, they held it to be illegal *hubris* to assault a slave belonging to someone else.[4]

The logic of slave relations which we find spelled out in fourth-century authors was in all likelihood entirely clear to the Athenians of the 420s, and indeed probably had been at least since, starting in the 480s, Athens had become much richer and had acquired far more slaves. Advice on the subject might even go back to some lost unsuccessful rival of the *Works and Days*. In any case there are occasional hints in the sources, besides those just mentioned, that the late-fifth-century Athenians talked about how to treat their slaves: the audience of the *Clouds* readily understood why the war against Sparta supposedly meant that Strepsiades could not punish his slaves.[5] You could not afford to provoke them at an unstable time when they might run away.

2. Ps.-Xen. *Ath.Pol.* i.10.

3. It was apparently illegal to kill a slave one owned without an official decision to back one up (cf. MacDowell 1978, 80), but that protection probably failed from time to time (see esp. Antiphon v.47–48).

4. Dem. xxi.47–50; this can hardly have applied to the owners themselves.

5. *Clouds* 6–7.

In Xenophon's *Hiero,* the tyrant is made to explain that a tyrant's lot is not a happy one. Among his woes is this (i.28): unless he marries a foreigner, he necessarily has to marry a social inferior; metaphorically she will be a slave, but "the services of slaves are quite unappreciated when shown, and any little shortcomings produce grievous outbursts of anger *(orgas)* and annoyance." Owning slaves, like being a tyrant, inevitably produces *orgē.* And it is Xenophon, as it happens, who is the earliest surviving author to make explicit the notion that when slave-owners give in to anger they often do more harm to themselves than to their slaves. This is in the context of a defeat which the Spartan army suffered at Olynthus because of its commander's failure to control his *orgē.*[6] "One should not even punish a slave in anger," says Xenophon, still less initiate a military attack: "*orgē* is lacking in foresight," whereas intelligence *(gnōmē)* weighs the consequences. Self-defeating *orgē,* in other words, makes him think of the punishment of slaves.

Plato elaborates on the matter, explaining that slave-owners face a dilemma (and it is clear that he had thought through the logic of master-slave relations). There is a difference of opinion, he says in the *Laws,* between those who, not trusting slaves, "treat them like animals, [and] with goads and whips make the slaves' souls not merely thrice-enslaved, but many times enslaved," and those who do "the opposite."[7] A little later, talking about punishment, he explains what happens if punishments are too degrading: you cause *orgē* in the persons punished;[8] the dangers are not explained, since they are fairly obvious. Plato recommends a middle way, neither degrading the slaves nor "pampering" them. At the beginning of the *Republic* he had already used a metaphor which shows one specific reason why slave-owners thought it was in their best interests to restrain their anger to some degree: a slave who had to deal with a master who was raging (*luttōnta*—a strong word) and harsh might well run away.[9] Plato's use of this situa-

---

6. *Hell.* v.3.3–7.

7. *Laws* vi.777a; cf. *Philebus* 58b. In the former passage he quotes lines from the *Odyssey* (xvii.322–323) which suggest rather well, though indirectly, the fear which Greeks felt of their slaves: "When the day of slavery catches up with a man, far-seeing Zeus takes away half of his worth [*aretē*]" (except that Plato wrote "mind" instead of "worth"). The lines may not, however, be authentic Homer.

8. *Laws* vii.793e.

9. *Rep.* i.329c.

tion as a metaphor makes it obvious that every prosperous Athenian slave-owner was familiar with the line of thinking involved. Nor was it merely a matter of the *individual* slave-owner's interests how he behaved. The free, says Plato, have to show solidarity with each other against the slaves; otherwise their lives would be in danger. Xenophon takes it for granted that the free protect each other against the slaves.[10] The legal prohibition of acts of violence against other people's slaves will have been part of this carefully gauged system.

There must have been wide recognition of the dilemma about slave treatment among Athenian men of property, and it reappears in Aristotle's *Politics*.[11] Plato himself puts the matter in a predictably snobbish fashion: in his opinion it was the insufficiently educated man who was likely to be harsh with slaves—instead of despising them.[12] The advice became more explicit still with Theophrastus, who told slave-owners that they should never punish slaves or others while they were angry, but wait until their anger had departed and punish coldly (without forgiving).[13] Theophrastus explains his opinion simply by invoking reason. Reason would have pointed out what Xenophon and Plato had said and implied about the dangers of provoking a reaction.

In the fourth century and later the notion that it was sometimes better not to beat or whip was put into anecdotal form. The first subject of such a story may have been the philosopher Archytas of Tarentum: "How I would have dealt with you," he said to his farm manager in controlled anger, "if I had not been angry."[14] Later it was supposed that Socrates had said to an erring slave, "I would beat you if I were not angry," and similar stories were told about Plato.[15] Hence a

---

10. *Rep*. ix.578e–579b, Xen. *Hiero* iv.3. As to how slaves might express their defiance, see Garlan 1988, 192–196.

11. ii.9.1269b8–11; cf. i.13.1260b5–6.

12. *Rep*. viii.548e–549a.

13. Fr. 154 Wimmer = 526 Fortenbaugh et al. The government of Trinidad was operating on the same principle when in 1823 it ruled that slaves could not be whipped until twenty-four hours had passed after the supposed offence (for the fact, see Higman 1984, 200–201).

14. Aristoxenus fr. 30 Wehrli; Cic. *Rep*. i.38.59, *Tusc.Disp*. iv.78 (quoted here); Val.Max. iv.1 ext.1.

15. Socrates: Sen. *De ira* i.15.3. Plato: Sen. *De ira* iii.12.5–6; see further Riginos 1976, 155–156.

nice paradox such as was desired from a philosopher, together with some advice for living which disguised practical common sense as part of the higher wisdom. The central figure in such tales is inevitably the wise philosopher, not the suffering slave.[16]

Did the prudential reasons for avoiding excessive or excessively overt anger against slaves then predispose the great anti-rage philosophers to think as they did? Each of them presented an elaborate train of thought in favour of emotional restraint. Epicurus is said to have advocated a policy of restraint in the treatment of slaves,[17] but on what grounds we do not know. What the other great Hellenistic philosophers said is also unattested.[18]

Philodemus, however, is unusually vivid on the subject of the *orgē* of the slave-owners. Their experience in the extreme slave economy of Roman Italy,[19] especially after the Sicilian slave insurrection of the 130s, had made this an even more practical question. The Romans of this era, unlike the classical Athenians, permitted owners to execute slaves at will, and generally by the second century B.C. operated a slave system harsher than that of Athens. Poseidonius had attributed the rebellion in part to the owners' violent treatment of their slaves,[20] and this must have been an influential opinion. In a fragmentary passage,

16. As is made clear by the next story in Seneca, according to which Plato caught himself being angry with a slave and asked Speusippus to do the whipping for him. Plato was supposed to have restrained himself with the following thought: "plus faciam quam oportet, libentius faciam" ("[being angry] I shall do more than I ought, and with more pleasure than I ought to feel") (iii.12.7).

17. Diog.Laert. x.118: the wise man will not punish his slaves, but will forgive the good ones. Phld. *De ira* 7 (col. xxxvi.3–4) accuses someone, apparently Epicurus himself, of "calamities" (?) with slaves who were at fault (the meaning of *periptōsis* in this context is obscure; G. Indelli translates the phrase "*l'imbattersi* in servi che sbagliano," which is clearer than the original but not exact).

18. On the early Stoics' lack of interest in actual as distinct from metaphorical slavery, see Garnsey 1996, 133–138. The witticism attributed to Zeno in Diog.Laert. vii.23 suggests that no markedly humane attitude was associated with him (when he was whipping a slave for thievery, the slave said, "It was my fate to steal," to which the philosopher replied, "And to be thrashed"). For the hard attitude of Chrysippus and the Stoics of the second century B.C., see M. Griffin 1976, 258.

19. Extreme at least in the sense that slaves were more numerous than they usually were in Graeco-Roman milieux.

20. *FGrH* 87 F 108.

Philodemus speaks of the threatening reaction of a slave to his master's anger,[21] and in another passage he refers to running away as well as to brutal punishments.[22] But his main surviving comments, which have been neglected by historians of Roman slavery, are as clear as could be. Showing anger towards slaves makes the whole business of controlling and managing them more difficult:

> The natural results <of the master's anger> are not only poor service but difficulties and every kind of misfortune; and when <slaves> are provoked to the limit by roaring rages [brimōseis], by abuse, by threats, by undeserved, frequent and excessive punishments, if they get the opportunity, they kill their masters and they do it with pleasure; if that is impossible, they kill their children and wives; if even that is impossible, they burn their houses and destroy their other property.[23]

That Philodemus was not inventing the risks that slave-owners ran, at least in his own time, is clear enough. Such things certainly happened during the rebellion of Spartacus (73–71). And we happen to know that the super-luxurious "villa," that is to say, country palace, of the senator M. Aemilius Scaurus at Tusculum was burnt down by angry slaves some time in the very late Republic.[24]

Whips, the hook, the cross: these were the basis of the Roman slave system,[25] as everyone knew.[26] The hope of manumission was also indispensable. But the harsh truths were so well known that they did not have to be stated any longer. Varro's *Res Rusticae*, for instance, does not

21. Fr. 12, lines 13–14. Anger towards slaves is also discussed in fr. 13, lines 23–36, but the full meaning cannot be recovered.

22. *De ira* 5 (col. xxiii.36–40).

23. Ibid. (col. xxiv.17–36). See also Plu. *De cohibenda ira* 11 (*Mor.* 459cd). βρίμωσις is first attested in Philodemus and is a favourite with him.

24. Plin. *NH* xxxvi.116.

25. Cic. *Rab.Perd.* 16. In fact the repertoire of "punishments" was much larger: see, e.g., Saller 1994, 147–148.

26. Well, not quite everyone: Dion.Hal. *Ant.Rom.* xx.13 claims that "the Romans believe[d] that a master should not be cruel in the punishments inflicted on slaves," and that the censors imposed this rule. But this is merely part of Dionysius' sometimes desperate attempt to prove to his Greek readers that the Romans were civilized, and in any case leaves it in the air what should be counted as cruel. (Watson 1987, 116–120, laboriously proves that the censors cannot have had anything to do with the matter.)

have as much to say about the actual treatment of slaves as one might possibly expect, and he permits himself a measure of hypocrisy: the *praefecti,* squad leaders, of the slaves on a large estate should use words to maintain order, not floggings.[27] In reality, slaves—often driven to desperation—resorted to suicide even more frequently than one might have predicted.[28]

That the problem of slave obedience was a very serious one in late-republican and early imperial Italy can easily be believed. That was what gave rise to a senatorial decree, the *senatus consultum Silanianum,* which reasserted (10 A.D.) that the domestic slaves of a murdered slave-owner should be put to death regardless of their individual culpability. Ulpian begins his discussion of the decree by saying that "no home can be safe" unless such a rule exists;[29] no doubt the thought was traditional. The chapter of the *Digest* in question is long enough to suggest that the matter was of fairly frequent concern as well as being legally complex.

In high imperial times, it was understood that the proper slave-owner should avoid displays of anger. Augustus himself had a some-what mixed reputation as far as anger control was concerned. Suetonius' account of how he treated slaves is also mixed: "towards his slaves and freed slaves he was as strict [*severus*] as he was easy-going and merciful."[30] He tells five little anecdotes, two to show Augustus being easy-going (he *merely* put in chains a slave who made an insulting comment), three to show him being strict. But no anger is mentioned: the slave-owner stays calm, by Roman standards, as he hands out awful punishments.

From the time of Seneca's *De ira* (49 or 50), for a little over a century, we can see two parallel stories unfold: a discussion about the treatment of slaves, and a series of legislative acts aimed at ameliorating the con-

---

27. *RR* i.17.5. Cicero in effect adopts the restrained attitude which he attributes to Archytas (see above), by attributing an endorsement of it to the younger C. Laelius (*De rep.* i.38.59).

28. Cf. Bradley 1994, 111–112.

29. *Dig.* xxix.5.1 pr.

30. *DA* 67. He could also have mentioned Eros and Vedius Pollio (though in the latter case he was not the owner, which made a difference).

ditions of slave life—for the most part, but not always, in a marginal fashion. The question here is not only how much the problem of slave management affected the general discussion about anger control but also how much the philosophers went beyond dressing up prudential advice as high morality.

The writings of Seneca raise both these problems. In *De ira* the great property-owner positioned himself far above the fray. The primary concerns which he expresses are not to do with the dynamics of slave management, and loyalty to Stoic ideas prevented him from concentrating on what was going on all around him. It is not to be supposed that a man of such extreme wealth worried excessively about the behaviour of his slaves; the age of slave rebellions was past, and with proper care, incidents such as the murder of the city prefect Pedanius Secundus by a resentful slave (61 A.D.) could be avoided.[31] And to show such anxiety while writing moral philosophy would itself have been undignified.

It is fairly apparent in fact that the slave-owners were affected by an underlying fear, as indeed the legal slaughter of Pedanius' city slaves indicates. From time to time resentment overcame single slaves or groups of them and led to a violent attack.[32] But generally speaking, of course, terror, with an admixture of hope, worked: slaves knew that they could not lose their tempers with their masters without quickly suffering frightful consequences.[33] And so the system thrived, in spite of overwork, sexual abuse and every kind of deprivation.

We can very easily believe that Seneca's fellow slave-owners sometimes allowed themselves to lose their tempers over defects in domestic service *(parum agilis est puer)*—insufficiently cooled drinks and so on[34]—also that the philosophically minded tried to rise above such

31. Tac. *Ann.* xiv.42–45. M. Griffin, however, considered that "the number of references to masters' being murdered by their slaves [in Seneca] is remarkable" (1976, 267).

32. For the possibility of rural *seditiones,* see Colum. i.8.17–18. About the murder of the cruel slave-owner Larcius Macedo (Plin. *Ep.* iii.14.1–5; his cruelty, s.1), A. N. Sherwin-White says that "cases were sufficiently rare to merit attention," but even if that is the right way to read the letter, Pliny's anxiety is probably real ("quot periculis quot contumeliis quot ludibriis [sumus] obnoxii," s.5); see also viii.14.12.

33. Cf. Petr. *Sat.* 53 (a slave was crucified for having cursed his owner; fiction of course).

34. *De ira* ii.25, iii.35.

things. Anger with slaves caused financial loss: "How many slaves have irate masters not driven to run away, or to their death?"[35] But it is not a point which much concerns Seneca. He remarks in *De clementia* that fear of being crucified had not always been enough to prevent slaves from avenging themselves for cruelty; but in that passage, at least, he is far more interested in the rage of tyrants.[36]

Rational management is the thing. Why have a slave's legs broken or have him put to death while you are angry if a calm consideration of what had happened would lead to a lesser punishment?[37] The manager of a large estate should exercise firm authority, writes Columella, but he should do so without cruelty.[38] Nevertheless, the prevailing tone of Seneca's comments about slave management is not prudential but moralistic:

> Restraint in ordering slaves about is praiseworthy. Even if someone is your chattel, the question is not how far you can get away with making him suffer, but how much you are permitted to inflict by the principles of equity and right, which require that mercy should be shown even to captives and purchased slaves.[39]

Letter Forty-seven to Lucilius is a relatively long discussion of the relations between master and slave. While the reader is warned that fate may have slavery in store for anyone,[40] the tone is again moralistic. A natural modern reaction is to see this text as mere rhetorical hypocrisy. The wealthy slave-owner asserts the claim of slaves to decent treatment while concentrating on side issues, such as whether certain slaves should be allowed to dine with their masters. He is outraged, or claims to be, not because Vedius Pollio intended (until Augustus intervened) to put a slave to death for an accidental domestic mistake but because he intended to feed him to his man-eating eels.[41] The case of

35. Ibid. iii.5.4.

36. i.26.1; cf. i.24.1.

37. *De ira* iii.32.2.

38. i.8.10. Ill-treatment makes slaves more to be feared: sect. 17.

39. *De clem.* i.18.1.

40. *Ep.Mor.* 47.10 (where the correct reading is *Variana*, not *Mariana*)–12; and the slave you maltreated may eventually obtain his freedom, and become a right-hand man of the emperor, 47.9.

41. *De ira* iii.39.2–5: Augustus, unlike an ordinary person, could use his anger to repress the anger of another. While Vedius had Augustus as a dinner guest, a slave

Pedanius Secundus' slaves, among others, confirms how outrageous treatment of slaves had to be before it was counted as *saevitia*.[42]

But it might be a mistake to dismiss all Seneca's moralizing as empty sentiment; it has recently been read as a "passionate plea."[43] At least he wanted to be thought well of by others of similar bent; he desired a reputation for self-restraint. In the overall context of Roman slavery, Seneca's assertion that slaves are *humiles amici*, friends of humble status, and *conservi*, fellow slaves (of Fate, that is),[44] is well worthy of attention. And the choice between whips and words as instruments of control[45] was to some extent real. A certain horror of enslavement may have affected a large proportion of the less lumpish Greeks and Romans. Athenaeus thought that god showed his anger against the people of Chios because they invented chattel slavery.[46] Such thoughts reflected some reservations about the traditional ruthless Roman exploitation of the enslaved.

---

broke a crystal vessel, and in his anger Vedius ordered him to be thrown to the anthropophagous *murenae* he kept in a fishpond. You would have supposed that this order was a matter of ostentatiousness *(luxuria)*, Seneca very revealingly says, but it was really *saevitia*. The slave begged Augustus to let him die in some other way (it was taken for granted that breaking a *crustallinum* was worth a life). Augustus was upset by the originality of Vedius' cruelty, pardoned the slave, had all the rest of Vedius' *crustallina* broken and the fishpond filled in. But, says Seneca (sect. 5), even a powerful man should interfere with the anger of others only when it is "fierce, inhuman, bloodthirsty." We do not, after all, want to hear from our friends which slaves we may and may not put to death.

42. Nero distinguished between the execution of Pedanius' (very, very approximately) four hundred town slaves, which he enforced, and the *saevitia* which would have been involved in also exiling Pedanius' freedmen (Tac. *Ann.* xiv.45). Cf. the story about ostentatiously cruel punishment under the Republic which Macrob. *Sat.* i.11.3 had from Varro. One could easily, if quizzically, admit that one had been angry with a slave for no good reason, Sen. *Ep.* 12.2 (where it is relevant that the author is admitting signs of old age). Augustus did not have a bad reputation in this department, but Plutarch recounts that when he heard that "Eros [a highly trusted slave] . . . had bought a quail which had defeated all others in fighting and was the undisputed champion, and that Eros had roasted this quail and eaten it, he sent for him and examined him; when he admitted the facts, Augustus ordered him to be nailed to a ship's mast" (*Sayings of the Romans* Caesar Augustus no.4 = *Mor.* 207b).

43. Garnsey 1996, 93; cf. M. Griffin 1976, 256.

44. *Ep.Mor.* 47.1.

45. Ibid. 47.19.

46. vi.265c; cf. Garnsey 1996, 62.

"Newly-purchased slaves," so Plutarch says, "do not inquire whether their master is superstitious, or jealous, but whether he is *thumōdēs* [irascible]."[47] Scarcely a reliable source, it may be thought, but even if there is only a modicum of truth in the assertion, it implies that slaves thought of anger when they might have been thinking of such matters as whether they would get enough to eat. And Plutarch sets out the familiar logic of master-slave relations. Threats cause slaves to run away, and so escape punishment (it seems not to be the financial loss which most upsets him).[48] The problem is that slave-owners have absolute power, so that everything depends on self-control.[49] And the masters hardly even aim to keep their tempers, so it seems: Plutarch, describing a dinner party for which the slaves had neglected to buy bread, asks, "Which of us would not have made the walls fall down with shouts?"[50] If you treat slaves patiently, you often receive better service.[51] Excessive punishment simply makes the slaves keep out of their master's sight, whereas delayed punishment ensures that slaves are not punished mistakenly, or for trivialities like burning the food; and one should not enjoy punishing them.[52] Decorum, apparently, is what requires one not to terrorize the servants while guests are present.[53] It was clearly embarrassing if a visitor to the house encountered a slave who was being whipped[54]—decorum again. All this from one who was a professed "absolutist" about anger. Not being a perfectly convinced absolutist, however, he lets his readers know the prudential arguments against showing anger towards slaves. These arguments will not have prevented Plutarch himself from imposing harsh punishments. And there is in this essay none of the Stoicizing humanitarianism of Seneca. Somewhat similar is the advice given by the undated forger who foisted on Theano (wife of Pythagoras) the advice that a woman should not punish her slaves to ex-

---

47. *De coh. ira* 13 = *Mor.* 462a. Similarly fr. 153 Sandbach, but the passage is probably a mirage—in other words, merely a confused reminiscence of the other.

48. *De coh. ira* 10 = *Mor.* 459a.

49. Ibid. 11 = 459b. The speaker blames his wife and friends for inciting him to severity.

50. Ibid. 13 = 461d.

51. Ibid. 11 = 459c (*siōpēi kai prothumoteron*).

52. Ibid. 11 = 459d–460c.

53. Ibid. 13 = 461e.

54. *De curiositate* 3 = *Mor.* 516e.

cess out of anger, because the victims may run away or commit suicide.[55]

A letter of Pliny's suggests the limits of a wealthy Roman's willingness to let his anger be placated: the senator advertises his intercession
with a friend on behalf of a freedman who had made the friend angry.
He is truly sorry, please forgive him. A whole letter is devoted to this
theme, and a short follow-up thanks Sabinianus for being so *tractabilis*,
ending with the admonition that he should be *placabilis* towards "his
own" *(tui)* when they make mistakes. We note without surprise that it
was only on behalf of a freedman and not an ordinary slave that Pliny
intervened, and no ordinary freedman, either, but one who must have
been an intellectual or a high-level man of affairs, since he was on
friendly terms with the ex-consul.[56]

To take too literally what Martial and Juvenal have to say about the
harsh treatment of slaves would be to fall into an obvious trap. The excesses of slave-owners had been a standard topic of satire since before
Aristophanes,[57] and of criticism too, and the excesses of women's anger had been a commonplace for many centuries. So when Martial
(ii.66) elegantly reproves "Lalage" for having a slave-woman *coiffeuse*
put to death for a single mistake, we know how this fits into gender
politics, and we know that we are not reading a police report. All the
less so, because Martial alleges that the killing was done with a mirror.
Juvenal contrasts wife and husband, representing the former as eager
to crucify a slave even if he is innocent.[58] With the vulgarity which char-
acterizes Satire Six, the poet claims that when a Roman wife is refused
sex by her husband, she shows spite towards her slaves (vi.475–485). In
both passages, it would be reasonable to diagnose projection.

In high-imperial Italy, slave-owners really did have their slaves put to
death at will; it was still in this period entirely a matter for private decision. You were not meant to do it with *ira*,[59] but traditionally no one as-

---

55. See above, p. 271.

56. Plin. *Ep.* ix.21 and 24. The utter lack of specific detail (the freedman is not
even named) may make one wonder whether the case was real.

57. In fact Aristophanes claimed (*Peace* 743–748) to have eliminated the hack-
neyed figure of the supposedly comic whipped slave.

58. vi.219–224. Plutarch takes it for granted that women are the harsh unjust pun-
ishers of slaves, while men oppose them (*Cons. ad uxorem* 4 = *Mor.* 609c).

59. So Tacitus seems to imply in *Germ.* 25, when he says that the Germans, though

sailed your right to do it at all. Nonetheless, the controversy about brutality and severity continued, and by Hadrian's time, it had spread well
outside the world of those with philosophical interests. Juvenal mocks
the hypocrisy of the father who preaches to his son mildness towards
the slaves but practises brutality and torture; the interesting element
here is the doctrine of mildness, even if its effects were minor.[60] The
most famous story about Hadrian's behaviour towards slaves told how
the emperor lost his temper and blinded a slave in one eye with a pen.
He repented, and asked the victim what compensation he would like.
A new eye, the slave replied, unanswerably.[61]

Galen, like Plutarch, gives so much emphasis to anger directed
against slaves[62] that we must suspect that his opinions about anger control in general were stimulated by his experience of slave-owners and
slave-owning. But although he was self-righteous about anger, even he
was not really very demanding when it came to anger against slaves.
He prided himself on the fact that he and his father, by contrast with
his mother, were unusually restrained, which meant that they arranged
for other people to inflict violent punishments on their slaves. About
his admired father, he wrote the following: "Many were the friends he
reproved when they had bruised a tendon while striking their slaves in
the teeth . . . They could have waited a while and used a cane or whip
to inflict as many blows as they wished and to accomplish the act with
reflection."[63] It is all right as long as you don't inflict "incurable injury":[64] anything else is acceptable—and this is the view of a moralist,
not of *l'homme moyen*.

What was probably the first attempt of the imperial government
to restrain slave-owners is known to us from a stark reference in Seneca's *De beneficiis* (iii.22.3): "someone has been appointed to hear cases
involving the mistreatment of slaves by their owners, to control

---

they are restrained in using other forms of coercion towards their slaves, kill them
"non disciplina et severitate, sed impetu et ira."

60. Juvenal xiv.15–24 ("mitem animum et mores modicis erroribus aequos /
praecipit").

61. Galen, *De propriorum animi cuiuslibet affectuum dignotione et curatione* 4.7–8 De
Boer. Galen tells the story as an instance of something which people do: it was not
specifically imperial behaviour.

62. See, for instance, *De propriorum animi cuiuslibet* 4.6, 5.1.

63. Ibid. 4.5.

64. Ibid. 5.3.

[*compescat*] both their *saevitia* and their lust and their meanness in supplying food." The "someone" was the *praefectus urbi*. It is a great pity we do not know the date of this innovation, which seems no longer to have been new when Seneca wrote (probably at the end of the fifties).[65] The first roughly datable measures of a humane kind were the work of Claudius, and these were followed by the Lex Petronia, probably of 61.[66] All these provisions were modest in scope, as were the subsequent enactments of Domitian and Hadrian.[67] Hadrian exiled for five years a woman "who inflicted the most cruel punishment on her domestic slave women for the most trivial of causes,"[68] but that is reported in an isolated fashion, and it may simply have been a whim of Hadrian's, encouraged by the notion that female treatment of slaves was especially cruel.[69] It is probably not true that he ordained that masters could kill their own slaves only after obtaining judgement from a magistrate[70]—that came in the next reign.

A series of more ambitious changes is attributable to Antoninus Pius; they show that the imperial court now had an active policy about

65. The *praefectus urbi: Dig.* i.12.1.8. One of his main jobs was *servitia coercere*, to keep the slave population under control (Tac. *Ann.* vi.11). The job of listening to slaves' complaints has often been thought of as an innovation of Neronian date, for no overwhelming reason.

66. Claudius: Suet. *Claud.* 25, *Dig.* xl.8.2. The Lex Petronia: *Dig.* xlviii.8.11.2 (but what it said exactly is unclear, and while 61 is the most likely date, 19 is also possible; for some discussion of the date, see M. Griffin 1976, 278–280). The real import of the senate decree of 20 about subjecting slaves to proper criminal trials (*Dig.* xlviii.2.12.3) is also uncertain (Westermann 1955, 114, saw it as part of a change in "social consciousness towards slaves"; similarly Griffin 268).

67. For the imperial legislation which sought to restrict the absolute power of owners over their slaves, see further Buckland 1908, 37; Watson 1987, 121–123; Manning 1989, 1532. The latter says (1539) that these reforms were probably intended to serve the interests of the slave-owning class, and did not arise out of humanitarian theory.

68. *Mosaicarum et Romanarum Legum Collatio* iii.3.4 (*FIRA* II, p. 551); *Dig.* i.6.2 end.

69. Watson 1987, 123, recounts this case as if Hadrian *made a practice* of punishing such behaviour.

70. As Buckland asserted (1908, 37), on the basis of SHA, *Hadr.* 18.7 ("servos a dominis occidi vetuit eosque iussit damnari per iudices, si digni essent"), which may of course have been a first attempt to legislate a provision which then had to be reasserted by Pius; but it seems more likely that Hadrian is being confused with his successor, or that his innovation was more limited.

the treatment of slaves. The matter was intimately related to the control of anger, even though the imperial edicts, when they identify the abstract quality to which they are opposed, call it *saevitia,* which is perhaps best translated as "brutality." The most important change was to make it more difficult to put a slave to death: Pius "laid down that one who without cause kills his own slave is as much amenable to justice as one who kills another's."[71] As to how any authority should interpret "without cause," the emperor is not known to have given any guidance.[72] In addition, Pius decreed that masters whose treatment of their slaves was found to reach the level of "intolerable" *saevitia* were to be forced to sell their slaves.[73] The emperor furthermore asserted that slaves should be protected from sexual assault[74] and—more radically still—receive fair work assignments.[75] All these rules still seem to have been in effect in Ulpian's time, sixty years after Pius' death, but it is now generally supposed that the resulting amelioration of the lives of slaves was very limited. The problem for a slave of obtaining access to the provincial governor, let alone winning him over, was normally insurmountable.

Pius wrote that it was in the interest of the slave-owners themselves that slaves should have some recourse against the *saevitia* of their masters.[76] The aim was the obedience of the slaves and "obtaining what you [the owners] need from them without difficulty."[77] Pius invokes as a reason for his opposition to excessive severity the possibility of a "somewhat disturbed state of affairs," which must mean counter-violence by the slaves.[78]

At about the time of Pius' death, the leading jurist Gaius could write (probably in an eastern province) that "at the present day, neither Roman citizens nor any other persons subject to the rule of the Roman people are allowed to use brutal methods against their slaves beyond

71. Gaius, *Inst.* i.53, also quoted in *Dig.* i.6.1.
72. Cf. Mommsen 1899, 616–617.
73. Gaius, *Inst.* i.53; *Dig.* i.6.2 ("durius . . . quam aequum est").
74. Ulpian in *Dig.* i.6.2.
75. *Collatio* iii.3.5.
76. Ibid. iii.3.5, iii.3.6.
77. Ulpian in *Dig.* i.6.2 ("si . . . ad impudicitiam turpemque violationem compellat"), and in *Collatio* iii.3.1.
78. Ibid. ("ne quid tumultuosius contra accidat"); cf. Garnsey 1996, 97.

measure or without cause."[79] He seems to be conscious of having witnessed a degree of reform. Its effectiveness can only have been limited, however. Quite apart from the problem of the slaves' access to the authorities, the best treatment is likely to have been reserved for a relatively small number of privileged slaves.[80]

Our judgement about the effectiveness of governmental intervention in these matters will also depend in part on how much we think slave-owners throughout the Roman Empire shared the emperors' underlying purposes. Had slave-owners absorbed the prudential or the moral arguments which had long been in circulation in favour of moderating angry behaviour towards slaves? There were both legal principles and human weaknesses working in the opposite direction. Pius prescribed that "the power of masters over their slaves should be unimpaired," before setting out to impair them. No doubt owners appealed to this principle, and the temptation to apply coercion and to exploit slaves both as workers and as sex objects was always strong. Executions probably diminished in a marked fashion, since they were after all unnecessary to an effective penal system and, more important, because they might be difficult to keep hidden from the authorities. Everyday *saevitia*, however, may not have diminished much, and the emperor Pius represents the high point of the reforming impulse: not even his moralistic successor is known to have taken any new steps to protect slaves.

Here we may consider an extremely intriguing story which Galen tells in his monograph about the passions. It confirms the suggestion that Galen's standards of *orgē* control were not in fact especially demanding, but it may also suggest that Pius' legislation had had a certain effect as far as killing slaves was concerned. On one occasion the great physician was travelling eastwards with a Cretan friend of irascible character.[81] The two of them were on their way from Corinth to

79. *Inst.* i.53

80. For distinctions between slaves, see Ulpian in *Dig.* xlvii.10.15.44 (by his time, and no doubt earlier, these distinctions affected a slave's de facto rights).

81. *De propriorum animi cuiuslibet* 4.9–13. In other ways he was worthy of respect (Galen gives details), "but he was so irascible [*orgilos*] that he used his own hands against his slaves, and sometimes his feet, but more often a whip or any available piece of wood."

Athens by land, with two slaves only, having sent the rest of the party by sea, when the Cretan lost his temper *(thumōtheis)* with the slaves over some unfindable luggage. He assaulted them with the sharp edge of his scabbard (a long-distance traveller would normally be armed), "inflicting two very serious wounds on the head of each of them." The Cretan fled to nearby Athens, leaving Galen to look after the slaves. At Athens he repented; Galen recounts that when he rejoined his friend, he

> heaped charges on his own head. He took me by the hand and led me to a house; he handed over his whip, stripped off his clothes, and bade me to flog him for what he had done while in the violent grip of his cursed anger [*thumos*]—for that is what he called it.

Galen kept laughing (an odd-seeming reaction, explicable by the absolute unimaginability of a applying a whip to one's friend), and gave him a good talking-to.

How to interpret all this? In the first place, Galen would presumably not have complained if the Cretan had, with appropriate deliberation, subjected the two slaves to a ferocious whipping. Second—as a historian has recently suggested—the Cretan may well have feared the new legal consequences of his act,[82] for why else would he have been eager to be absent if one of the slaves were to die?

At first sight, Antoninus Pius' motives in legislating look as if they were entirely prudential, and this favours a functionalist interpretation of the whole trend towards advocating greater decency and restraint towards slaves. Safe and effective slave management was apparently the uppermost consideration in the emperor's mind. We may think that most of what stimulated the discourse of restraint was a desire to make the slave system run smoothly.

Even the philosophically minded, now as in Philodemus' time, were fully aware of the possible counter-anger of the slaves themselves.[83]

---

82. Hopkins 1993, 10.

83. Cf. Galen, *De placitis Hippocratis et Platonis* v.7.66: slaves are angry when they think they have been punished unjustly (whereas those who have a guilty conscience supposedly accept punishment).

And when Galen's ferocious Cretan repented, there is no sign that it was out of compassion for the injured slaves,[84] and we may suspect that (if the story is true) he was moved by nothing more humanitarian than a concern for his own dignity—an important enough possession. To lose control of one's temper in front of a slave was to hint at one's own weakness.

But prudential motives, while they were very important, probably do not fully account for the reform legislation or the intellectual currents that supported it. To start with, the big slave-owners had long been aware of the practical reasons for avoiding *saevitia:* they did not have to wait for Claudius, let alone Antoninus Pius, to teach them. Pius, furthermore, may well have thought that if he wanted his slave-owning subjects to cooperate, he needed to invoke the practical advantages of his new slave policy.[85] In other words, we do not necessarily have to take an improvement in slave obedience as the sole purpose of his actions.

But it is the culture of the Roman upper class that is in question, not the motives of a single ruler. Slave-owning Romans had learned over a long period that the sensible management of slaves required a measure of restraint. For a long time, probably until the generation of Seneca, that meant no more to them than avoiding gratuitous physical cruelty. Even before that time, individual owners could behave decently towards individual slaves, but for the most part the corrupting, dehumanizing effects of slavery made themselves felt. No Roman worried about showing a normal everyday kind of anger towards slaves. However, as a more humanistic kind of Stoicism gained ground in Seneca's time, additionally affecting some of those who did not count themselves as Stoics, anger directed against slaves came under moralistic as well as prudential attack.

Strong anger itself was widely disapproved by Stoicizing as well as Stoic members of the Roman Empire's elite. The practical reasons persisted, and the desire to maintain one's dignity contributed. To be vigorously angry was now in itself, for some people, a sign of poor moral condition and psychic health—an attitude which we shall be exam-

---

84. There is no further mention of the wounded slaves once Galen has transported them to Athens.

85. Cf. M. Griffin 1976, 274.

ining in Part IV. The slave-owner who restrained his (or her) anger towards a slave in the Senecan-Antonine era was quite likely to be thinking not of the possibly dangerous reaction or of the victim's humanity, but of himself (or herself). There was a kind of self-regarding virtue, neatly and horribly revealed by a comment of Galen's: "those who strike their slaves with their own hands are not such great sinners [*elatton hamartanousi*] as those who bite and kick stones, doors and keys."[86] A ludicrous side effect is the philosopher who is caught in an eternal dilemma between restraining his anger (philosophers harped on this) and reacting to the provocations of his highly imperfect slave. The dilemma is illustrated in detail in the lives of the slave Aesop and their account of his relationship with his philosopher master, Xanthus.[87]

The Stoics and the Christians had theoretical grounds for a serious amelioration in slave treatment, but the influence of the former, such as it was, seems to have diminished after the time of Marcus Aurelius, and the Christians accepted the institution much as they found it. The institution was in any case too deeply embedded in Graeco-Roman society and in the economy to be altered much by any ideology.

Even a very detailed study might fail to tell us conclusively whether the late-antique Romans treated their slaves differently. We do not in any case hear much more, in the voluminous literature of the fourth century, about restraining one's anger towards one's slaves,[88] whether for prudential reasons or theoretical ones. Constantine legislated on the punishing of slaves, but what he said—though it was more "progressive" than pre-Antonine law—was a considerable step backwards from the legislation of Antoninus Pius. In summary, he allowed slave-owners who killed their own slaves without the intention of killing to go unpunished, but classified intentional killings as homicide (*C.Th.*

---

86. Galen, *De propriorum animi cuiuslibet* 5.3.

87. See *Aesopica*, ed. B. E. Perry (Urbana, 1952), trans. L. W. Daly, *Aesop without Morals* (London & New York, 1961). It is hard to say when this element entered the lives of Aesop, some if not all of which continued to be adapted until Roman times. As to whether the reader is expected to side with the slave figure against the owner, see Hopkins 1993, 19 (yes); Hägg 1997, 197 (no).

88. There is a final high-imperial mention in a rescript of Alexander Severus, *C.Iust.* iii.36.5.

ix.12); if a slave died from beating, there was to be no investigation (ix.13). And this was confirmed in the next century by Theodosius. No doubt anything more liberal would now have been altogether unrealistic.

The Council of Elvira (which is variously dated between about 300 and 314) belongs to a time when most of the reform efforts of Antoninus Pius had undoubtedly been forgotten. The canons of the council dealt with pressing issues of morality. Canon Five laid down that "if a woman who is overcome with rage [*furore zeli accensa*] whips her slave woman so badly that she dies within three days, and it is doubtful whether she killed her on purpose or by accident: provided that the required penance has been done," she shall be readmitted to the church after seven or five years, depending on whether the killing was intentional or unintentional.[89] Thus, Christian whippings so brutal that they caused death were common enough to need regulating; and it was decided that if the slave lasted more than seventy-two hours nothing awful had happened. The correct attitude of the slaves, according to the Christian hierarchy, was of course obedience.[90]

89. Canon 5: see *Acta et Symbola Conciliorum quae saeculo quarto habita sunt,* ed. E. J. Jonkers (Leiden, 1954), p. 6.

90. In obeying his master a slave was obeying Christ: Augustin. *Enarr. in Psalmos* 124.7 (*CC-SL* xl.1841).

PART IV

Anger and the Invention of Psychic Health

CHAPTER 14

Anger as a Sickness of the Soul in Classical Greece

Anger could cause great harm in the city and in the household. But ancient perceptions of its harmfulness did not stop there, for many thought that the angry emotions were, or could amount to, a form of psychic ill health. It would be futile to try to make a strict distinction between ancient texts which concern the external effects of anger (city and household) and those which concern the internal ones. What we can establish, however, is that the individual's psychic well-being, and the harm which anger or irascibility might do to it, eventually became important elements in the discourse of anger control.

But how did angry emotions come to be thought of as a suitable object of treatment or therapy? And where did therapy start—in other words, what did such treatments or therapies amount to in pre-Hellenistic times? More generally, what led to that new focus on inner experience which from the late fifth century B.C. onwards[1] led many to see anger as a failing of the individual as much as, or more than, a menace to society or to other people?

The first of these questions is only answerable in the most speculative fashion. In the 450s the poet of the *Prometheus Bound* wrote the lines in which, for the first time, we hear anger being explicitly spoken of in such terms.[2] We must quote the crucial lines again:

1. Cf. Redfield 1994 [1975], 25.
2. [Aesch.] *PV* 375–380.

Prometheus: . . . I will bear my present destiny, until the heart of Zeus is surfeited with anger [*cholos*].

Ocean: Do you not understand, Prometheus, that words are the physicians of the illness of anger [*orgē*] [or, of a sick disposition]?[3]

Prometheus: Yes, if someone softens the <angry> heart at the right moment, and does not forcibly constrict the swollen spirit [*thumos*].

The speakers are referring to the anger of Zeus but presumably also see ordinary human anger as an illness. Some scholars have claimed that part at least of what the god Ocean is made to say here was proverbial or traditional,[4] and it was scarcely original to suggest that words were the best way to overcome someone else's anger (Phoenix and Odysseus knew that). But this is the clearest representation, to date, of anger (or for that matter, of any emotion) as a metaphorical sickness. The notion was to become a commonplace,[5] and indeed it had already become one by the time we reach the *Medea*, some twenty-five years later: by then it was Chorus language to say, between speeches of Medea and Jason, that "a terrible and *hard-to-cure* anger approaches."[6] A little while later, it was sententiously said in *Oedipus Tyrannus* that angry natures are painful for the very people who possess them.[7] All of these sentiments are of course easier to understand when we recall that *orgē* in particular was a more intense and active concept than "anger" is, and more likely therefore to produce vivid physiological symptoms.

Several elements in Greek culture made it natural to think of anger as a sickness—and not only in a metaphorical sense—quite apart from the harmful public effects which had been attributed to it since at least the time of Solon. In the first place, it appears that the archaic and classical Greeks did not construct any definite barrier between physical suffering and intense emotional suffering. One can see this in *Iliad* IX, where Achilles, responding to Ajax, explains that his spirit is (still)

3. For this reading, see above, p. 163.

4. Cf. Laín Entralgo 1970 [1958], 1–31, 42–107; Nussbaum 1994, 49 (but it is Ocean, not the Chorus, who pronounces the second of these comments).

5. See P. Groeneboom on *PV* 377–378. Cicero's translation of 377–380: *Tusc.Disp.* iii.76.

6. Eur. *Med.* 520.

7. Soph. *OT* 674–675 (Creon speaking).

swollen with anger *(cholos)* as a result of the way he has been treated by Agamemnon.[8] The exact implications of the verb *oidanetai* are not clear to us, but it is obvious that Achilles is speaking of a disagreeable physical or near-physical condition.[9]

The ordinary Homeric word for anger, *cholos*, apparently meant "bile" at one time, and the related word *cholē* always did—so that the notion that medical remedies might be applied to anger was almost automatic as soon as anyone identified *cholos* as a noxious influence, which, as we have seen, was already happening in Homeric times. The belief that *cholos* was a kind of sickness must have been well established by the time the term *orgē* took over as the principal strong-anger word. Aristophanes (and occasionally others) used *cholē* as well as *cholos* to mean something close to "anger"[10]—"fighting spirit" perhaps—so it is evident that ordinary Athenians did not distinguish the two terms, or did not do so at all sharply. This presumably means that it was generally believed that anger was a physiological condition. But by this time, a specific part of the human structure had been identified which felt emotions and could be subjected to cures, non-medical cures, and that was the *psuchē*.

To understand the thinking that lies behind the exchange in the *Prometheus Vinctus,* we shall have to descend to a slightly later date. Hip-

---

8. *Il.* ix.646. For Stoic use of this passage, see Cic. *Tusc.Disp.* iii.19. For the verb, see also line 554. Nussbaum 1994, 49, is misleading when she says that "from Homer on, we encounter, frequently and prominently, the idea that *logos* is to illnesses of the soul as medical treatment is to illnesses of the body"; in fact we *never* encounter it in archaic Greek literature. The nearest is perhaps *Il.* ix.507, the passage about the Supplications, in which they are said to "cure" the harm which Ate does to men. The harmful inaccuracy of Nussbaum's discussion is also exemplified by her statement that Empedocles [31 B 111, 112 D-K] "speaks of his poems as providing *pharmaka* (drugs) for human ills," implying that psychic ills are included. But in the text itself the reference is unmistakably to physical ills (111.1, 112.10–12).

9. Various other emotions produced physical symptoms in the epic and melic poets, as love famously does in Sappho 2 Lobel-Page = 31 Voigt, lines 5–16 (cf., among others, Page 1955, 28–30). But it must be remembered that there was as yet no word corresponding to "emotions."

10. *Wasps* 403, *Lys.* 465, *Thesm.* 468, cf. *Frogs* 4, Aesch. *Ch.* 184, Pherecrates 75.5 Kassel-Austin, Ps.[?]-Dem. xxv.27 (if this is the correct reading) and Herodas v.39. In Ar. *Peace* 66, however, *cholē* seems to mean "mania." In the Second Sophistic, *cholē* became a common word for "bitter anger" (Pearcy 1984, 451–452).

pocratic medicine concerned itself mostly with physical illness more or less as we understand that concept, but the experts did not differentiate neatly between physical and psychological ill health, and in this respect they were probably maintaining a traditional attitude.[11] The Hippocratic essay *Airs, Waters, Places* theorizes about the effects of environment on health, but also from time to time claims to know how such factors affect people's temperament.[12] Some of the case reports in Hippocrates' *Epidemics* show that while doctors did not treat anger as such, some of them recognized anger and other psychological states as symptoms. For instance, "in Thasos, a woman . . . was seized with an acute fever [after childbirth]. [Many details follow, ending in the patient's death on the eighteenth day]. The urine of this patient was throughout black[,] . . . coma was present, aversion to food, despondency, sleeplessness, outbursts of anger [*orgai*], restlessness, the mind being affected by *melancholia.*"[13] In *Humours* Hippocrates theorizes that the physical humours produce *dusorgēsiai*, outbursts of rage, as well as *lupai* ("distresses"—this term will reappear shortly) and desires.[14]

The very fact that the principal verb for suffering, *paschō*, eventually came to include the specialized meaning "experience emotionally," while in the same period the noun *pathos* came to mean "passion" or "emotion," suggests that the Greeks often thought of emotions as hostile disease-like forces outside the person. But these lexical developments probably did not take place until well into the fourth century.[15]

11. Cf. Lloyd 1987, 28–29. We have often been warned not to see Graeco-Roman doctors as the exact counterparts of modern physicians: see for instance Nutton 1999.

12. *Airs, Waters, Places* 5, 12 (the people of "Asia" are milder and better tempered, *euorgētotera*, than Europeans, because of the climate), 16, 23–24.

13. *Epid.* iii.17.2 (p. 262 Jones).

14. *Humours* 9.

15. The pre-Aristotelian texts in which *pathos* means passion are at most three: Democritus 68 B 31 D-K, which is not always accepted as authentic (see above, p. 84, and cf. Pigeaud 1981, 17 n. 22), Thuc. iii.84.1 (where, however, *dia pathous* probably means "on account of their suffering": Maurer 1995, 114 n. 18) and Pl. *Phaedr.* 265b. The verb *paschein* means "experience" (passions or emotions) in Isocr. xv.31, Dem. xix.195 (Lysias viii.17 may be seen as a transitional passage: Dover 1974, 126). There is a parallel history of *pathēma(ta)*: Calame 1999, 135, was wrong, I think, to translate the word as "passions" in Ar. *Thesm.* 201, but it commonly has this meaning in Plato (and see Xen. *Cyr.* iii.1.17).

The meaning of *lup-* words is from a modern point of view ambiguous: they can refer to physical pain or to psychological distress. Medicine existed to deal with the former—and the latter too. The first steps in that direction may have been taken by those who tried to deal with major cases of mental instability by non-religious means, though unfortunately we have very little idea when this happened: an allusion to the use of the drug hellebore in Aristophanes' *Wasps* (422) is a *terminus ante quem*.[16]

New ways of dealing with psychological distress *(lupē)* seem to have appeared by the 430s. A Roman imperial writer tells the story that the orator Antiphon—but it is much more likely to have been Antiphon the sophist—opened a sort of clinic at Corinth:

> He is said to have composed tragedies . . . But while he was still busy with poetry, he invented a method of curing distress [*alupias*], just as doctors have treatment [*therapeia*] for those who are sick. At Corinth he put up a sign outside a room near the marketplace saying that he could treat by words those who were in distress; and by finding out from them the causes of their condition he tried to cure with words [*paremutheito*] those who were suffering. But thinking this skill was unworthy of him, he turned to oratory.[17]

The story is sufficiently odd and circumstantial that we should take it seriously.[18] It is intriguing in this connection to recall that the nurse in the *Medea* finds fault with the poets for not having devised the music which will cure *lupai*, which suggests that in 431 someone had recently been claiming to have done so.[19] This may also be the right historical context for Democritus' declaration that "medicine heals the sick-

16. Ar. *Wasps* 1489. But most of the madness cures satirized in this play are religious. I am assuming that [Hipp.] *Regimen* i.35.79–80 was written a little later.

17. 87 A 6 D-K (q.v.) = Ps.-Plu. *Vitae X Orat.* 1 (= *Mor.* 833c). This Antiphon is likely to have been the author of the work *On Concord* mentioned earlier. As for the date, an Athenian could hardly have done such a thing at Corinth after 431. See further Laín Entralgo 1970 [1958], 101–103 (an imaginative but not altogether convincing reconstruction of Antiphon's procedure); Furley 1992, 211.

18. For *paremutheito*, see below.

19. *Med.* 195–198. There might conceivably be an allusion here to Damon, on whose theories about the moral effects of music see West 1992b, 246–247; not that Damon is known to have concerned himself with *lupai*.

nesses of the body, wisdom removes the *pathē* from the soul" (though as we have seen, Democritus may not have used the word *pathē* in this sense).[20] Socrates, however, actually gloried in having caused the Athenians *lupē* by means of philosophizing[21]—there were higher aims than freedom from distress.

It is also possible that people began to think of extreme anger as a sickness because they sometimes saw it as a kind of madness (see Chapter 3). There is something counter-intuitive about this: it can scarcely be supposed that the fifth-century Greeks commonly took *orgē* to be in a literal sense a form of madness. But the evidence is compelling that archaic and fifth-century Greeks did indeed see some outbursts of anger as instances of madness, as many later thinkers did. Homer imagines Achilles saying about Agamemnon, while the king is in the grip of *eris*, angry strife, that he "is raging in his destructive heart, and cannot reason."[22] As Achilles tears into the Trojan heroes in *Iliad* XX and XXI, he seems to us quite insane with rage—though we should recognize that Homer does not say anything explicit to that effect. And there is in the thought-world of Homer an intermediate state between anger and madness, namely *lussa*, a sort of temporary rabid frenzy.[23] The concept was also familiar to the tragedians. In a number of fifth-century texts the distance between powerful anger and madness is certainly not very great. In the *Eumenides*, Athene tells the Furies that they must not stir up anger between the citizens of Athens, and specifically that they must not "make them mad with wineless rages."[24] Sophocles' *Ajax* is another important instance. In Herodotus, writing in the 430s

---

20. 68 B 31 D-K, cf. C 6. The fragment B 290 ("Expel ungovernable *lupē* of the numbed soul by means of reason") is something of an argument in its favour (cf. Laín Entralgo 1970 [1958], 105). It should not be inferred from Pl. *Prot.* 312b–313a that Protagoras conceptualized his own teaching as *therapeia* of the soul, but Socrates may possibly have claimed that Protagoras' teaching had that character (and was bad therapy).

21. Pl. *Apol.* 41e.

22. *Il.* i.342–343: ἦ γὰρ ὅ γ᾽ ὀλοιῇσι φρεσὶ θύει, / οὐδέ τι οἶδε νοῆσαι. For *eris*, see 319.

23. The *Iliad* particularly attributes *lussa* to Hector when he is fighting, *Il.* ix.239, 305, xiii.53 (the *lussa* of Achilles: xxi.542). Personified Lussa is quite common in classical iconography: see Kossatz-Deissmann 1992. See further West 1997, 213–214.

24. ἀοίνοις ἐμμανεῖς θυμώμασιν, 860. See also, for instance, Eur. *Bacch.* 359.

and 420s, the identification of anger and madness is frequent.[25] By the time of Isaeus, being angry can easily be contrasted with being in one's right mind (i.43). Meanwhile the first evidence for a treatment of mental illness by means that a modern medical practitioner might recognize had appeared in the *Wasps:* one of the methods by which Bdelycleon had tried to cure his father is described simply as a verbal soothing (*paramuthoumenos*—just the word that was used about Antiphon).[26]

By the last quarter of the fifth century, in any case, it was not only established but commonplace that *orgē*-anger and *thumos*-anger were somehow or other susceptible to therapy. Not, of course, that there was any agreement as to how. All sorts of notions seem have been explored. For instance, the pseudo-Hippocratic treatise known as *Regimen I* discusses what a regimen can and cannot do to bring about an improvement in the soul—concluding that irascibility (the quality of being *oxuthumos*) was *not* in fact treatable by regimen.[27] The sophist Gorgias light-heartedly set out to prove in his *Encomium of Helen* that the woman who caused the Trojan War was innocent (a good sophistical exercise).[28] Part of his argument was that if love was a disease, it was not something for which a person could be blamed.[29] Nonetheless Gorgias also supposes that words are like drugs *(pharmaka):* they have the power to alter emotional states.[30]

In the same general period Socrates was developing the theory that philosophy should undertake the job of caring for the health of the

25. I would suppose that Philocleon's irascibility in the *Wasps* encouraged Aristophanes to identify his obsession with jury duty as a form of madness.

26. *Wasps* 115. This sounds more like therapy than dissuasion, *pace* Gill 1985, 309.

27. Ch. 36. The same applied to other emotional conditions. The passage is highly theoretical, and others may have disagreed. According to Claus 1981, 152, *Regimen I* shows that "physicians designed actual therapeutic programs for the health of the *psuchē*," but this is far from clear.

28. 82 B 11 D-K. Light-heartedly: sect. 21. Hankinson represents the general opinion when he writes (1993, 187 n. 15) that this work "embodies elements of a serious contemporary debate."

29. Sect. 19. Cf. Saunders 1991, 124–125. On the psychological theory employed in this text, cf. Claus 1981, 148–150.

30. Sects. 8–9, 14. On the latter passage, cf. Nussbaum 1994, 51, who, however, mistranslates it (there is no mention of "increasing fellow feeling").

psuchē, as we shall shortly see in more detail. The best evidence is in Plato's early dialogue *Charmides,* where Socrates speaks of the treatment of the soul as an essential part of medicine, and explains that the aim of such treatment is *sōphrosunē* (self-control), which can be imparted by means of philosophical words. He proceeds to apply his treatment to the self-controlled but confused young Charmides, not by means of anything which we can recognize as psychotherapy, but by his usual cross-questioning *elenchos.*[31]

Finally: another of the conditions which enabled the Greeks to think of anger as an illness was that they developed a clearer or at least more unitary idea of the human personality. The abruptness of this change should not be overstated. The archaic Greeks were not wholly unreflecting about their own emotions, and Homer finds no awkwardness in representing his greatest warrior speaking in the abstract about anger. Odysseus is made to address his own heart, telling it to be patient when he is tempted to kill the disloyal maids prematurely.[32] And from Homer onwards Greeks were accustomed to internal debate; archaic texts often show us people addressing their own heart or spirit.[33] As we have seen, the poet of the *Prometheus Vinctus* found it perfectly possible to talk about anger while supposing that its location was in the heart (an idea which lived on, even when it came to be supposed that the site of the emotions was the *psuchē*). The differences between the archaic period and Plato's, in this respect, are multiple, but not because the Greeks of the earlier period were unable to think in their own fashion about their own emotional states. Rather, they were not *preoccupied* with them, as some people seem to have been in the fourth century B.C.—and others have been almost ever since—nor did they reflect at length either about their psychological well-being or about their own moral condition.[34]

---

31. See esp. *Charm.* 156d–159a (this was probably written about 390), with Gill 1985, 321. Socrates recognizes of course that Greek doctors do not take care of the *psuchē* (156e, 157b). For another account of the emergence of a philosophy of psychotherapy, see Sorabji 2000, 17–19.

32. *Od.* xx.18–21; De Romilly 1984, 11–12. Cf. Achilles in *Il.* i.188–192.

33. Schadewaldt 1926, 201.

34. Heelas 1986, 260, constructs a stark contrast between a tribal world in which discourse about emotions is "sociocentric" and a modern Western world in which it is individualistic. The fourth century B.C. thus becomes a watershed.

The term *psuchē* itself is important, and it has sometimes been held that it was only in the period of Plato's early dialogues, in the 390s, that it was first thought of as the principal site of a person's moral choices and emotional activities, or as the essential element of personality.[35] This view is mistaken, as the following texts show, in spite of their enigmatic brevity (I put them in chronological sequence):[36]

476: Pindar, *Olympian* ii.70: "those who have kept their *psuchē* altogether away from unjust deeds";[37]

440s: Sophocles, *Antigone* 175–177: "no man can be known in *psuchē* and sense and judgement" until he has held office.

440s or 430s: Antiphon, *Tetralogy* iii.*a*.7: "it is your duty . . . to deprive him of the *psuchē* which planned [this crime]."

before 422: Euripides, *Theseus* fr. 388 Nauck: "a *psuchē* just, self-controlled and virtuous."[38]

Thus by the 440s the idea was in circulation that anger was a sort of disease, and also that it could, in some way which no source defines clearly, be treated with words. But it is one thing to talk someone else out of anger (an age-old skill), another to be willing to have one's own anger treated (which presupposes that the angry or irascible person has at least a slight desire to be cured). There is as yet no sign of anything which closely resembles psychotherapy directed towards this or any other emotional condition. The usual suspects are the Pythagoreans and the "Orphics," but no good testimony makes any of them psychotherapists in any proper sense. It is not impossible that, as Iamblichus' biography claims, the historical Pythagoras used music to produce psychological effects (this would have been well before the 440s) and knew songs that would counteract mental suffering, and

35. Claus 1981, esp. 182–183 (but this is a nuanced account). Cf. T. M. Robinson 1970, 8: "Nowhere had it been affirmed [before Plato] that the soul is both the principle of cognition and the 'total' self"; strictly speaking true, but quite misleading.

36. It is unlikely that Philolaus fr. 13 (44 B 13 D-K), which uses *psuchē* in an older sense (cf. Huffman 1993, 318–319), was written before 440.

37. The context may be Orphic: Guthrie 1962–1981, III:468 n. 3. Claus's comments on this passage (1981, 117) are special pleading.

38. Claus 84 too readily dismisses this passage from consideration. For the date, see Schol.Ar. *Wasps* 313. For the development of Socrates' thinking about the *psuchē*, see Claus 156–180.

others that would counteract outbursts of *orgē* and *thumos;* but this is probably a later accretion to the Pythagoras legend.[39] Still less relevant is that original figure Empedocles: he was reputed on one occasion to have saved his host from being murdered by using music to dissipate anger. A young man "in a state of confusion and anger" drew his sword and charged at the host, who had earlier condemned the assailant's father to death, but Empedocles started to play soothing music, thus preserving his host and also saving the young man from becoming a murderer. He became instead the sage's most devoted follower.[40] But this story is now normally rejected as an edifying fiction,[41] and it is hardly to be rescued. It may, however, be classical rather than Hellenistic, for the host's name seems to have been authentic.[42]

What then about possible treatments for this sickness? Some thought that music could be helpful. Scattered references show that this idea began circulating at quite an early date. In the Homeric Hymn to Hermes, the sixth-century poet describes how the god dispelled the anger of Apollo by playing the lyre to him.[43] Such stories must have been the inspiration for the ones about Pythagoras and Empedocles. It seems to have been the Athenian musicologist Damon (who flourished from the 440s to 420s) who first achieved wide publicity for the belief that musical modes and rhythms had profound moral effects on the listeners.[44] By the fourth century the Pythagoreans were claiming that they

39. *De vita Pythagorica* 111; even for Iamblichus this was only an anonymous tradition. Cf. Marrou 1965, 214–215; West 1992b, 31, for stories about Pythagoras, the seventh-century Terpander and other archaic poets who were supposed to have restored calm.

40. 31 A 15 D-K = Iamblichus, *VP* 113. Apparently he was supposed to have sung *Od.* iv.221.

41. E.g., in the editions of Empedocles by Bollack and Wright (pp. 7–13).

42. For the name Anchitus, see Diog.Laert. viii.20.

43. *Hom.Hymn.Herm.* 416–421. Ancient writers (e.g., Aelian, *VH* xiv.23) sometimes said that in Homer, Achilles had calmed his anger by means of his music, but that is not what the poet himself says, *Il.* ix.186–188. The soothing power of music must always have been recognized: cf. Hes. *Th.* 98–103, Pind. *Pyth.* i.1–12.

44. The evidence about Damon (see D-K 37) is slight, but none of it indicates that he was specifically concerned about anger (Marrou 1965, 215, is misleading). The idea that music could have moral effects was already attacked in writing ca. 390 (ap-

could effectively dispel anger by means of music. But it was their own anger, apparently. There is at any rate reasonably good evidence that the Pythagorean Cleinias of Tarentum followed this practice: when he felt he was growing angry, he would play the lyre. "I am calming my temper," he would say *(praunomai)*.[45]

Galen claimed that his hero Plato "correctly wrote the therapies of the *pathē*,"[46] but it was hardly true. Socrates and Plato were very much interested in psychic health,[47] a well-known fact which I shall later try to explain, insofar as it is possible to do so. They were both interested in the formation of the young person's character. And Socrates certainly had a technique.[48] But we cannot call a technique a therapy for passion unless the passions are clearly the target. If Socrates talked every day about virtue and maintained, in the famous phrase, that "the unexamined life is not worth living,"[49] that may be taken as one root of the therapy of the passions, but it is not itself such therapy. "I shall question and examine and cross-examine him, and if he seems to me not to possess virtue, but claims to do so, I shall rebuke him." But the aim is unspecific: that the soul should be very good.[50] The nearest thing in Plato to therapy directed towards the passions are his educational precepts in *Republic* III and *Laws* VII. In the *Republic* he explains which musical "modes" will be used in his utopian scheme of educa-

---

parently), as we know from an anonymous papyrus text (*P.Hibeh* 13: see West 1992a; 1992b, 247). It was later to be attacked again by Philodemus in his *De musica*.

45. Chamaileon fr. 4 Wehrli (in *Die Schule des Aristoteles* VIII) = Athen. xiv.624a; Aelian, *VH* xiv.23. Marrou 1965, 214–215, summarily dismissed this evidence in a passage marked by great impatience with ancient thinking on the subject of the moral influence of music. Aristoxenos fr. 26 Wehrli (*Die Schule des Aristoteles* II) also helps to show that music as therapy was a Pythagorean practice by the fourth century. Cf. Dodds 1951, 79–80.

46. *De placitis Hippocratis et Platonis* v.4.15 (p. 316 De Lacy) (cf. Poseid. fr. 167 E-K).

47. But it is hardly accurate to say that Plato was "convinced that all philosophizing must aim at an improvement in the condition of the soul" (Thome 1995, 241; not a book to rely on).

48. Gill 1985, 321.

49. Pl. *Apol.* 38a.

50. *Apol.* 29e–30a. Much later, in the *Sophist,* Plato wrote of the "purification" *(katharmos)* of the soul, an important stage between traditional ideas of purification (how far such ideas had developed by the late fifth century: Parker 1983, 323) and Aristotle, but he nowhere speaks of purifying the soul of emotions.

tion: the Dorian mode will be used to promote courage, the Phrygian mode will be used to promote moderate and reasonable behaviour in peace-time.[51] In the *Laws* he describes the middle way between luxurious and severe training which will allow children to grow up not to be quick-tempered.[52]

Platonic morality, as we saw in Chapter 6, aimed at a certain level of anger control, and Plato's desire to substitute reeducation for punishment in certain circumstances would logically imply that he thought there were ways of curing some people of criminal habits. But at no point does he descend to detail.[53]

Nor does Aristotle anywhere maintain that psychotherapy of any kind might help people to achieve the mean with respect to *orgē*-anger. But in *Politics* VIII he in turn discusses the educational effects of music, making far-reaching claims:

> It is obvious from many different considerations that we acquire particular dispositions [as a result of music] . . . when listening to theatrical performances everyone is emotionally affected in accord with the performance . . . Now in rhythms and melodies there are resemblances to reality—the realities of anger [*orgē*] and of even temper, also of courage and moderation, and of the opposites of these, indeed of all moral qualities . . . an equable feeling is produced, I think, only by the Dorian mode . . . This is what is correctly said by those who have philosophized about musical education; for they take the proofs of their theories from the actual facts. The same is true of rhythm . . . It follows from all this that music has indeed the power to induce certain habits of mind [*poion ti to tēs psuchēs ēthos*], and if it can do that, clearly it must be applied to education, and the young must be educated in it.[54]

But this is a theoretical educational programme, or rather the sketch of one, not therapy. And Aristotle stops short of promising his readers that if the young are brought up on a strong diet of Dorian-mode mu-

---

51. *Rep.* iii.398e–399c. For the meaning of "mode" (*harmonia*) see West 1992b, 177–189. For parallel characterizations of the Dorian and Phrygian modes in Plato and elsewhere, see West 179–181 and cf. 248–249.

52. *Laws* vii.791c–793a.

53. *Rep.* v.465a should not, I think, be taken as advocating a ventilationist therapy.

54. *Pol.* viii.5.1340a8–21, b3–13. The subject is picked up again in viii.7.

sic, they will manage their anger according to the mean. It should impress us that an intellect such as Aristotle's was convinced that music could change not only moods but also patterns of behaviour.[55] But though stories illustrating this theory were repeated throughout antiquity, listening to music was not to be the main direction of Hellenistic or Roman anger therapy.

The other quasi-therapeutic concept we associate with Aristotle is of course catharsis: tragedy is "a representation [*mimēsis*] . . . accomplishing, through pity and fear, the purging of such passions."[56] But this, though it contains the germ of an idea for psychotherapy, is not actually a scheme for any such thing, and certainly not for the reining in of anger. What later classical writers made of therapeutic catharsis we shall see in the next chapter. As for Aristotle, when at the end of the *Nicomachean Ethics* he comes to consider how people can be induced to behave well, he concentrates on education and legislation. He just takes note in passing of the possibility that individuals may assume the task of "producing the right moral disposition" *(diatheinai kalōs)* in other individuals; the task will require "one who knows," that is to say, has knowledge of moral principles—that is all we are told.[57]

The notion that a person who desires to control the passions needs an individual helper of some kind seems to be part of the general culture by the last decades of the fourth century. An unidentified character in Menander, echoing but going beyond what Gorgias had said a century earlier, proclaimed that the only cure *(pharmakon)* for anger was "the weighty word of a person dear to one."[58] But we may guess that what needed to be cured here was a single attack of *orgē* rather than a habitual disposition.

The roots of the "new focus on inner experience" can be traced back at least as far as the 450s or 440s. Indeed they go back to the Delphic maxim "Know yourself." The change has always proved difficult to de-

---

55. Such an idea is nowadays dismissed as absurd.

56. *Poet.* vi.1449b24–28.

57. *Nic.Eth.* x.9.1180b25–27.

58. λόγος σπουδαῖος ἀνθρώπου φίλου, fr. 518 Koerte-Thierfelder (from Stobaeus).

scribe, not least because our evidence about pre-Socratic philosophy is so pathetically inadequate. But the quarry, as far as this study is concerned, is not the first formulation of an idea in a period whose texts are mostly lost, and which was in any case characterized by a semi-oral culture, but rather a shift in interests.[59]

Sophocles' *Ajax*, produced in the 440s, is necessarily an important exhibit. Jebb called one of the sections of his introduction to the play "The successive moods of Ajax," and Ajax is the first hero of a surviving play who is allowed moods. It was Sophocles who created the soliloquy, and not only in a technical sense but as a means of self-addressed self-analysis on stage.[60] *Ajax*, like the *Oresteia* and many other tragedies, is much concerned with relations between gods and mortals, but it is also concerned with the hero's psychic state.[61] This is sometimes rage—initially because Ajax was not awarded the armour and weapons of Achilles—sometimes madness, sometimes still other things; the culmination is the hero's unique on-stage suicide.

Athenian tragedy is about many things, but it is often about the interior state of its leading characters, and it can be supposed to have contributed to the new obsession with such states. This inner experience was sometimes dominated by anger. *Medea, Hippolytus* and *Philoctetes* put on display the inner workings of angry personages, so does the *Heracleidae* (Alcmene) and the *Bacchae* (Agaue and Pentheus), and so, to a lesser extent, do other plays.

Not everyone took the new introspection with frightful solemnity. As early as 425, in the *Acharnians*, Aristophanes mocked Euripides for something similar, his supposed habit of making his characters address their *thumos* or *kardia* (heart).[62]

Among philosophers, it was Socrates and perhaps Democritus who did the most to hasten the transition to concentrating on inner experi-

59. This phenomenon is quite distinct from the individualism which Dihle 1956, in particular, detected at Athens in the decades before and after 400. Foucault 1986 [1984], 41–43, analysed the ambiguity of this term.

60. See, among others, De Romilly 1984, 78–81.

61. Cf. Simon 1978, 124–130; Winnington-Ingram 1980, 20 (the "theme of madness and sanity, of sense and sickness of mind, pervades the first half of the play"). The second half of the play is also, as we have seen, much concerned with anger and retaliation in different forms.

62. 480–489, with De Romilly 1984, 98 n. 54. Cf. also *Ach.* 356, 450.

ence.[63] Democritus wrote a work about the well-being of the spirit *(peri euthumiēs)*,[64] which suggests a degree of concentrated reflection on the subject not attested for earlier times.[65] Anger was presumably discussed, though we have no evidence of that. As is to be expected, our knowledge of what Democritus had to say about anger is very limited, for we have no more than his statement, quoted earlier, that wisdom removes the "passions" from the soul, and a decontextualized fragment saying that "it is difficult to fight against *thumos* [anger?], but it is the job of the rational [*eulogistos*] man to conquer it."[66]

It was probably Socrates, however, who was most important in bringing about the new attentiveness to self-knowledge and care of the "soul."[67] While we cannot rely on Plato or Xenophon to give us an accurate account of his detailed teachings, it is unlikely that Plato radically misrepresented the actual subjects of the older man's concern. Beyond any reasonable doubt, Socrates made the proper care of the soul, which implied a degree of control over the emotions, into a central concern of his philosophy, perhaps the central concern. It was in Socrates' time, according to Aristotle, that philosophers turned their attention mainly to "useful and civic virtue"[68]—away, that is, from both cosmology and logic. Unless we want to take a position of extreme scepticism about the possibility of knowing the opinions of the historical Socrates, we have to agree with Xenophon and with Plato that he was intent on discussing the psychic condition of the virtuous man.

It seems likely that the tragedians and the philosophers, some of them, learned from each other in the intellectual exchanges of the 440s and 430s. When Nietzsche, in *The Birth of Tragedy*, argued for a connection between Euripides and Socrates,[69] he was grasping at an important point. And when in the *Gorgias* Plato depicts Socrates as tak-

---

63. See De Romilly 176–178, who, however, employs arguments of varying strength.

64. Diog.Laert. ix.46; see 68 B 2c D-K. Cf. most recently Furley 1992, 211.

65. But Guthrie 1962–1981, II:492, was dismissive towards this work, translating *euthumiē* as "cheerfulness" or "contentment."

66. See Chapter 5.

67. See, among others, Gigon 1947, 38–40; Guthrie 1962–1981, III: 467–473; Foucault 1986 [1984], 44.

68. *Part.anim.* i.1.642a28–31; cf. *Metaph.* i.6.987b1–2.

69. Section XIII.

ing a harsh view of the seriousness of the tragedians (tragedy amounts to mere flattery of the audience, he says),[70] he may very well be imposing a view of his own.

It looks as if the period just before the outbreak of the Peloponnesian War in 431 was important. The dramatic dates of Plato's dialogues are normally dismissed as being of no real significance, but it is striking that in the dialogues which he assigns, certainly not by accident, to the years shortly before the war, such as *Protagoras, Charmides* and the first *Alcibiades,* Socrates is represented as being chiefly interested in moral *aretē* (virtue) and in the care of the *psuchē.*[71] In the *Protagoras* the discussion begins from Socrates' anxiety about a young interlocutor's desire "to hand over his own soul [to Protagoras] for care [or treatment; *therapeusai*]."[72] *Gorgias,* set in or about 427, discourses at length about sickness and health of the soul.[73]

The later Socrates was little changed. This is how he is made to describe his occupation in the simple language of the *Apology:*

> My sole activity is to go about urging you [the Athenians in general], both young and old, not to care for your bodies or your property either before or as much as you care for your soul, and I tell you that virtue does not come from money, but . . .[74]

All the dialogues just referred to, except *Gorgias,* are believed to have been written early in Plato's career. Hence they were written while there was still a solid nucleus of Socrates' personal followers still living, and therefore we can hardly think that Plato gravely misrepresented his views. The same is not so obviously true of the most famous "Socratic" text on this subject, since it occurs in the middle-period *Phaedo,* which there is reason to regard as a less faithful account of Socrates' opinions. Having "proved" the immortality of the soul, the philosopher is made to say that "if the soul is immortal, it requires care . . . It cannot escape from evil or be saved except by becoming as good and wise [*phronimos*] as possible." There follows his description of Hades,

---

70. Pl. *Gorg.* 502bc. Cf. the low moral ranking given to poets in *Phaedr.* 248e.

71. *Prot.* esp. 329b–333b, 360e–361c, *Charm. passim, I Alc.* 132bc.

72. *Prot.* 312c.

73. *Gorg.* 477, 503a (for the date, see esp. 503c).

74. *Apol.* 30a. Cf. 29de.

including the fate of those who have "in anger done some act of violence against father or mother."[75] Since this passage is consonant with the others just cited, Socrates' views were probably still unchanged in 399; in other words, he was still preoccupied with the well-being of the soul[76]—all the more so because this also seems to be a characteristic of the Socrates described by Xenophon, a Socrates for whom the highest virtue is *enkrateia,* mastery of oneself.[77]

The matchless last pages of the *Phaedo* show Socrates putting this doctrine into effect. The reader may expect Socrates to control his grief, but he also controls his anger, or rather shuns anger altogether. The public slave comes from the Eleven, and says to the condemned philosopher,

> Socrates, I shall not have to reproach you, as I do others, for being angry [*chalepainousi*] with me and cursing me when, on the instructions of the archons, I tell you to drink the poison. I have found you during this period the noblest and most even-tempered and best man who has ever come here; and now, I am sure, you are not angry with *me*, but with those who you know are responsible.[78]

He weeps and departs, to be pursued by Socrates' praise; but Socrates shows no sign whatsoever of being angry with his persecutors, maintaining his calm till the very end. Plato thus enrolls Socrates in the ranks of those who are above experiencing *orgē*-anger or indeed any other kind.

When Plato writes in the *Republic* about *to thumoeides,* the passionate or spirited element in the soul, its political workings are foremost, but the health of the soul itself is also at issue. There are already hints of this in *Republic* IV,[79] but it appears more clearly in Book IX: "the first

75. *Phaed.* 107cd.

76. Even Bostock 1986, 7–11, while generally sceptical, and with reason, about the historicity of the arguments attributed to Socrates in the *Phaedo,* takes this to be a historical element.

77. Xen. *Mem.* i.1, ii.1, iv.5.

78. *Phaed.* 116cd.

79. See above all iv.443de: justice means making sure that each part of the soul does its own job; it requires establishing self-control (*arxanta auton hautou*) and inner harmony.

object [of the man of understanding] will not be strength or health or good looks, . . . but he will always subordinate physical well-being to the harmony of the soul . . . He will look at the city [*politeia*] which is within him, and take heed that no disorder occurs in it."[80] No one will need convincing that in his mature works Plato is greatly concerned about the state of this "city within."[81] Even the more worldly Isocrates seems concerned, when he is putting forth moral precepts, with harmonious character development as well as with social relations.[82]

But *why*, to revert to our earlier question, did interest in psychic health become so strong among Athenian intellectuals from the second half of the fifth century? We cannot necessarily account for Socrates' or Plato's or Aristotle's every belief. But a historian, while taking care not to treat these or other philosophers as non-distorting mirrors of the times they lived in, must pursue the context. The correct answer is likely to be complicated, and we would wish it to be anchored in social structures and relations; no satisfying account of this matter can restrict itself to the pure history of ideas. What is involved after all is not simply the growth of an intellectual interest but the invention, as far as the West is concerned, of moral philosophy.

Some of the Ionian philosophers had taken an interest in the soul, but this debt can be considered minimal. Socrates *changed* the philosopher's agenda. Nor is it any answer to say that Socrates or Plato thought of the age they lived in as one of moral "decadence";[83] even if they did (and in Socrates' case, the proposition is a dubious one), the belief would have been a banality with no necessary effect.

The new Athens which had come into being after the Persian Wars, growing steadily wealthier and more powerful as the Delian League turned into an empire, gave greater leisure to the elite, and eventually attracted sophists from other cities. In Athens they found citizens who believed (as, admittedly, did those of many other cities) in their right

---

80. *Rep.* ix.591c–e.

81. See for instance *Phaedr.* 248c–249d (part of the charioteer and horses parable briefly analysed in Chapter 6), *Soph.* 227d–231a, *Tim.* 87a.

82. i.21 was quoted above, p. 186. In the present context see esp. sects. 5–7. For the *logoi* which may cure evil desires in the *psuchē*, see viii.39–40.

83. Thome 1995, 9–10, claims that one reason why Plato tried to devise a method of psychotherapy was because he saw himself surrounded by "decadence." That is not quite as absurd as it sounds, since decadence is usually in the eye of the beholder.

to make their own decisions about private as well as public affairs. From the 450s, at least, the tragic poets and (part of) their public encouraged each other to confront moral questions with psychological dimensions to them—one thinks, for instance, of the obstinacy of Zeus and Prometheus in *Prometheus Bound*. It should not be surprising that property-owning Athenians made emotional self-control one of their primary concerns, for emotional control in a slave society could come to the dominant males only from within themselves. We could say that the slave-owning Greeks and Romans had so much moral liberty that they had to create some rules with which to limit it. One of the mechanisms at work here is remorse, a frequent consequence of anger, attested from Homer onwards, and not much studied by psychologists. How ought free men to comport themselves—that was, for the intelligent, an unavoidable question.

The sophists contributed a great deal to the development we are discussing. How exactly? They were interested, after all, in skills, and not much, the *Encomium of Helen* notwithstanding, in psychological well-being. However they—or some of them—claimed to teach *aretē*, virtue,[84] and that road necessarily led to concern about the *psuchē*. They also made it more commonplace to argue in a secular way about emotional behaviour, since they taught rhetoric and politics.[85]

A great shift was going on, in the second half of the fifth century, in what Athens' leading intellects found satisfying in the way of explanations of psychological states. Sophocles' *Ajax*, for all its brilliance, seems almost childish as well as terrifying in its proposal that the horrible mania of the hero was inflicted on him by a goddess. And the last great madnesses on the tragic stage, those shown in the *Bacchae* forty years later, are still imposed by gods. But late-fifth-century intellectuals did not imagine that their emotions, or even their strong emotions, were all caused by divine intervention, and some of them were ready for secular discussion of how *thumos* and the *psuchē* functioned. There was naturally no neat divide between religious and rationalistic theories about human psychology: Socrates was clearly a leading proponent of rational thinking on the subject, but he also notoriously claimed that he had his *daimonion* ("supernatural spirit"?) to

84. Pl. *Meno* 95bc.
85. De Romilly 1984, 17–18, q.v., makes the needs of rhetoric an important force.

guide him. We can say that his *daimonion* was often something like a superego, and it was part of his attempt to understand himself, part of a kind of psychological project. (One would be tempted to say a *failed* psychological project but for the strength of character which is brought out in the *Phaedo*.)[86]

There was an element of ambition, too, intellectual ambition. Few cultures without an actual science of psychology can ever have demonstrated such an awareness of psychological complexity as the Greeks already had by the 430s. It required a high degree of optimism about the capacity of human understanding to think that the interior workings of the human spirit could be rationally analysed, but this was an era (the 450s to 430s) in which rational analysis flourished as never before in diverse fields, including medicine, rhetoric and history writing.[87] The desire for intellectual exploration was voracious, and it extended to self-analysis, with very various results, including the political pamphlet of the "Old Oligarch" and Pericles', or rather Thucydides', Funeral Oration, as well as the more obvious intellectual achievements. In fact the two great historians are themselves proof of this powerful trend towards psychological analysis (as we have seen, they both thought carefully about *orgē*). But the element of ambition linked a number of Athenian projects: it is worth setting side by side the imperial ambition of Athens, culminating in the extraordinary folly of the Sicilian expedition, and the evident belief of such diverse minds as Euripides, Antiphon and some other sophists, Democritus, Socrates and Thucydides that the human spirit may be comprehensible.

So much for the initial impulses. After the execution of Socrates, men with philosophical interests experienced understandable disillusionment with their fellow citizens, and especially with the Athenian democracy,[88] and it is tempting to see concentration on the *psuchē* as part of that reaction. Decades after the event, Plato still had a sense

86. Socrates' religious views are an old problem: one may suspect that in the *Apology* he is made to protest his religious orthodoxy too much, and Aristophanes had made him out to be an atheist (*Clouds* 247–248).

87. For an older discussion of the struggle between reason and religion in the fifth century, see Guthrie 1962–1981, III:226–249. See further Buxton 1999.

88. Note esp. Pl. *Rep.* vi.492bc.

that the self-restrained man could not function in civic life,[89] and his own political experiences at Syracuse did nothing to reverse this view.

But of course Plato and Aristotle also taught and wrote politics. Their audiences were to a large extent made up of members of the social elite,[90] for whom politics was always a possibility and good reputation always a profound need. And their teachings combined psychological and political investigations. The control of anger did not lose its political or social importance in the fourth century: Aristotle's *Politics* and *Rhetoric* were indeed mainly of interest to men with practical ambitions in public life. As Bodéüs has shown, the ethical works too were primarily addressed to those who were concerned with the body politic. Ethics, for the author of the *Nicomachean Ethics,* is a political subject, for it presents essential knowledge with which legislators must fortify themselves.[91] Neither Plato nor Aristotle retreated from the polis to the soul.

It is true that Aristotle seems to go a certain distance further in putting the individual's soul at the centre of an ethical system. The foundation of this system is the belief that "the wise man has an adequate and true conception of *eudaimonia* [happiness?] and makes [his own *eudaimonia*] his end in life."[92] We need not address all the complexities involved in Aristotle's conception of *eudaimonia* (which was remote from any subjective feeling of contentment), for it clear that, in his view, it is "an activity of soul in accordance with perfect virtue."[93] This is the centre of his moral system. But he was always aware that the wise man necessarily lived in a city or *ethnos*. Indeed he insists that the "end" (we might say "fulfilment") of the state is greater and more com-

---

89. Cf. Cohen & Saller 1994, 43.

90. For the impossibility of making the masses *(hoi polloi)* virtuous by means of *logoi*, see *Nic.Eth.* x.9.1179b4–20. They can only be motivated by fear.

91. Bodéüs 1993 [1982], 123.

92. Hardie 1980, 215. See his whole ch. 11. On the meaning of the practical wisdom *(phronēsis)* of the model man (the *phronimos* or *spoudaios*), see Gastaldi 1987, 107.

93. *Nic.Eth.* i.13.1102a5–6. Aristotle's *eudaimonia* does not of course consist of any of the things which ordinary people say are happiness, nor of Plato's absolute good. Rather, "the good for man turns out to be activity of soul in accordance with virtue, and if there is more than one virtue, in accordance with the best and most complete" (i.7.1098a16–18). See further Hardie 22–27.

plete, finer and more god-like, than that of the individual.[94] "Perhaps one's own good cannot exist . . . without a form of government," he writes.[95]

It would be interesting to know whether the audience for philosophy was changing in the time of Aristotle's teaching at Athens, or shortly afterwards. Some have imagined that he himself addressed fairly large audiences,[96] which does not seem plausible. Nevertheless, the reading public had expanded in the fourth century, and the eudaemonist content of Aristotle's ethics, where the central question is how the individual can be happy, had an obvious appeal to the ordinary man. As I noted earlier, Menander shows signs of having truly learned from Aristotle's successor Theophrastus,[97] and it seems likely that the audience for philosophy was widening somewhat, a trend which was to have far-reaching effects in Hellenistic times.

To sum up, the new focus on inner experience was not exclusive. It arose gradually, in a specifically Athenian environment of prosperity, slave-owning and intellectual self-confidence. It was further encouraged by the practical needs of civic life and in particular oratory. And it also resulted from a continuously evolving intellectual tradition, within which Socrates reacted to the sophists, Plato to Socrates, and so on.[98]

The angry emotions had been subjected to a fairly intense critique by some fifth-century Athenians. The criticism had let up somewhat in the fourth century (this is probably not just an accident of source survival). The role of *orgē* in punishment was widely believed in, and the question about anger was refined, by Aristotle, above all, to take the

94. *Nic.Eth.* i.2.1094b8–10.
95. *Nic.Eth.* vi.8.1142a9–10. The word "perhaps" *(isōs)* is presumably ironical.
96. Nussbaum 1994, 56, suggests that students attended Aristotle's lectures "in relatively large groups." Even what Gellius calls his "exotericas auditiones" (xx.5.4) were given as he walked about; but admittedly there was some attempt to reach a larger public, and there must have been some interest on the part of that public.
97. P. 304.
98. Brown 1992, 50, suggests that philosophy turned towards moral issues and the control of the passions in the first two centuries of this era because of "a lurking fear of arbitrary violence, untrammeled by legal and political constraints." While there is something to this, the difficulty remains that such fears were not new in Augustan times, or for that matter in Socratic times.

form of asking whether it was appropriate in a particular situation. But its compatibility with virtue was to receive an enormous amount of further discussion.

Belief in the importance of caring for the soul was, however, transmitted to all the principal philosophical sects of Hellenistic times, and they all therefore had to think about anger as a suspect activity of the *psuchē*.

CHAPTER 15

Can You Cure Emotions?
Hellenistic and Roman Anger Therapy

Hellenistic philosophers are well known to have concentrated much attention on the virtue and the happiness of the individual. Their Roman followers did likewise. That did not mean that they were uninterested in political philosophy:[1] Zeno, Cleanthes, Chrysippus and of course Cicero wrote *Republic*s or similar works,[2] and there was also a substantial sub-philosophical literature about kingship. As we have seen, Seneca's works on moral philosophy had plenty of political content. Hence Hellenistic philosophy as a whole cannot be said to have retreated from politics. This observation should make it impossible to maintain the old clichés about the supposed effects on philosophy of the supposed death of the polis in or about 336–323 B.C. No one would now say, with Tarn, that "man as a political animal, a fraction of the *polis* . . . , had ended with Aristotle; with Alexander begins man as an individual."[3] But until recently at least, one could read that people turned to philosophy in Hellenistic times because of the anxieties they

---

1. As Marrou 1965, 313, correctly observed.

2. Demetrius of Phaleron wrote two books of *Politica,* Diog.Laert. v.80. No one would accuse Panaetius or Poseidonius of being uninterested in such matters. Since Shaw 1985, 28, denied that Cleanthes wrote about the polis, the evidence had better be mentioned: he wrote among other things a *politikos* (Diog.Laert. vii.174, and cf. *SVF* I, frr. 587–588).

3. Tarn 1952, 79.

felt as a consequence of having lost control over their political fate—as if anxieties of this kind were few before Alexander of Macedon.[4]

Epicurus and his followers did of course recommend keeping out of public life.[5] But their view of this matter, though it had a reasoned basis, was not in fact new. Even in high classical Athens, there had been those who desired to keep out of the melee of public life. They were the *apragmones,* the "inactive men," whose presence can be traced back to 431 if not further.[6] They were often men of property and good education. Socrates can be accounted one of their number, though a very eccentric one—and hence the philosophical tradition was closely linked with this outlook. Epicurus is known to have admired Pyrrho the Sceptic's style of life, and it is extremely likely that he consciously followed the latter's belief in *apragmosunē,* keeping out of public affairs.[7] The ideals of *apragmosunē* and *ataraxia* (psychic tranquillity) were not identical, but they were closely linked. Aristotle set out the dichotomy between the political and the philosophical life.[8]

There is nonetheless some obvious truth in the view that Hellenistic and Roman philosophers were especially interested in individual happiness and virtue. The reader will recall what is perhaps the extreme statement on the subject, that of Epicurus: a philosopher's discourse *(logos)* is empty, he said, "by which no *pathos* [passion] of a human being is taken care of [*therapeuetai*]. For just as there is no gain from a

---

4. Glibert-Thirry 1977, 399–400; Bryant 1996, 454 (with a whole story about the lack of social mobility, etc.). Contrast Foucault 1986 [1984], 41–42; Annas 1992, 2 n. 3. For a terse critique of a recent recurrence of the cliché, see Striker 1999, 102; she proposes instead—unconvincingly, to my mind—that the presentation of philosophy as a help in life is to be connected with increased competition between philosophy and other forms of education. My view does not involve denying that Stoicism reacted in some ways to the changed political circumstances of Hellenistic and Roman times (cf. the provocative discussion by Shaw 1985).

5. Epicur. *Sent.Vat.* 58 (= L-S 22 D 1), Diog.Laert. x.119 (= 22 Q 10). This instruction was implicit in the famous and widely ignored advice, "Live your life unnoticed" *(lathe biōsas)* (fr. 551 Usener).

6. On the whole phenomenon, see esp. Carter 1986, Demont 1990; on Socrates, Carter 183–186.

7. See the cogent arguments of Sedley 1976, 136–137. Note esp. Diog.Laert. ix.64, who remarks that there were many who emulated Pyrrho's *apragmosunē.*

8. *Pol.* vii.2.

medical skill which does not cast out the sicknesses of bodies, so there is no gain from philosophy if it does not expel *pathos* from the soul."[9] This attitude was in part a consequence of the internal development of philosophy itself: Aristotle's eudaemonist ethics had shown the way. But a Stoic would not have said such things, and Ariston of Chios went so far as to denigrate the hortatory aspect of moral philosophy, saying that that was work for a *paidagōgos* (a boy's slave attendant).[10] However, Ariston was in this respect a rarity, and in spite of their interest in logic and physics, the Stoics regarded moral philosophy as one of their central activities. Virtually all other Hellenistic and Roman philosophers did so too.

Philosophers of various persuasions claimed incessantly that they could play a role analogous to that of doctors. Chrysippus, for instance, asserted that the art of curing the unhealthy soul "is not inferior, in its specific theory or therapy [*therapeia*]" to the art of medicine.[11] Philo of Larissa, Philodemus, Cicero, Seneca and Dio Chrysostom, among others, echoed this ambitious claim.[12] Unfortunately the philosophers were taking on an enemy which was more difficult to identify than physical ill health, and sometimes hard or impos-

---

9. Fr. 221 Usener. On its authenticity, see above, p. 100. For the medical analogy in Epicurus see *Sent.Vat.* 54 (= L-S 25 D 2). Nussbaum 1994, 13, prejudices an issue by translating θεραπεύεται in fr. 221 as "is therapeutically treated." For a similar sentiment attributed to Xenocrates slightly earlier, see above, p. 94.

10. Sen. *Ep.Mor.* 89.13 (*SVF* I.357): "eum locum [moralis philosophiae] qui monitiones continet sustulit." Cf. Cic. *De fin.* iv.68, Sen. *Ep.Mor.* 94.2 and 48, Sextus Emp. *Adv.Math.* vii.12 ("nurses and *paidagōgoi*").

11. Galen, *De placitis* v.2 (= *SVF* III.471).

12. Philo ap. Stob. *Ecl.* ii.7.2 (Philo was head of the Academy from ca. 110 until the 80s); Phld. *De ira* 3 (col. iv.3–11) (cf. Gigante 1975, Indelli ad loc.); Ps.-Hipp. *Epist.* 23.2 (IX p. 394 Littré); Cic. *Tusc.Disp.* iv.23–33 (complaining about excessive Stoic use of the analogy, which does not prevent him from reverting to it again), iv.58; Sen. *De ira* ii.18.1, 20.4; Dio Chrys. xxvii.7–10 (people only listen to philosophers and physicians when they suffer misfortunes), lxxvii/lxxviii.43–45. For some speculation about the exact advantages which philosophers hoped to gain from this claim, see Edelstein 1967 [1952], 363–364. The notion that the emotionally disturbed were sick had been a commonplace in the general culture since at least the time of Aristophanes; at Men. *Dusk.* 150, for instance, the ill-tempered hero is said to be in ill health.

sible to treat. The deficiencies of philosophy as soul medicine did not, of course, go unnoticed.[13]

What sort of *pathē* or passions of the soul did Hellenistic philosophers have in mind when they spoke of psychic therapy? We should not give anger too much importance here: the three emotions which the Epicureans considered to be the cause of harm were hatred, envy and contempt *(kataphronēsis)*;[14] and of course they were much concerned to eliminate the fear of death. The three basic emotions, according to Stoic doctrine, were pleasure, desire and fear (anger was categorized as a sub-species of desire).[15]

Before we examine the ways in which Hellenistic philosophers proposed to treat undesired emotions, we should look more closely at the social context in which they worked. It has been asserted that in attending to emotions and psychic health, they were "far more concerned [than Aristotle] to show that their strategies can offer something to each and every human being, regardless of class or status or gender."[16] This goes in the right direction, but too far. As far as gender is concerned, Epicurus' attitude was a radical change (though he owed something to both Plato and Aristotle): women were permitted to study philosophy and allowed more autonomy than had been traditional at Athens. A few Stoics eventually adopted a partially enlightened attitude towards women, as we saw earlier, but the average non-Epicurean philosopher remained narrow-minded on the subject, not surprisingly. With respect to social class, there were indeed a few Hellenistic philosophers, mainly Stoics, of markedly egalitarian spirit. And even though many philosophers wrote in a more or less hermetic Greek which only an expert could understand, there was also a measure of popularization. The form of this popularization was probably

---

13. Cf. *Tusc.Disp.* iii.1: "The need for medicine for the soul was not felt as deeply [as medicine for the body] before its discovery, nor has it been cultivated as closely since it became known, nor has it been welcomed and approved by as many people but rather it has been suspected and hated by a greater number."

14. Diog.Laert. x.117.

15. Above, p. 108.

16. Nussbaum 1994, 10. This does an ahistorical injustice to Aristotle, who excluded only those who had not made the first steps in philosophy (it was hardly his fault that those who had were for the most part comfortably-off males).

in the main oral, not so much because the masses were illiterate as because that was the best available way of communicating with ordinary Greek townsmen.[17]

It is by paying attention to education that we can resolve the first issue raised in this chapter. If one is looking for a development in the cultural life of the Greek world between 400 and 250 B.C. which changed the audience for philosophy, it is not to be found in the supposed disappearance of the polis but in the spread of education. Hellenistic literacy remained at premodern levels—of course—but in many cities (and there was much geographical variation) levels of literacy probably reached a peak not surpassed in the Greek world until the early twentieth century.[18] A number of cities aimed at universal education for boys and even for girls.[19] The origins of this trend constitute a delicate historical problem which would lead us too far away from the control of anger, but the fact can hardly be doubted.

Elementary education is one thing, taking an interest in philosophy is admittedly another. But a certain small proportion of those who now acquired a basic education was able to make further progress. Another way of describing the change would be to say that the casual, very much part-time, audience for philosophy increased. Thus two trends mutually reinforced each other: many philosophers paid more attention to the problems of the individual psyche (which made their discourse more interesting to the ordinary man), and the ordinary man was more likely to pay attention to philosophy.[20]

There never was in antiquity any psychotherapy in the Freudian and post-Freudian sense, a series of one-on-one dialogues in which the patient is supposed to do most of the talking and to explore his or her own feelings and fantasies in order to discover the origins of his or her psychic condition and to improve it, while the therapist, ostensibly at

17. It is all right to say that Hellenistic philosophers were interested in "ordinary human lives" (Nussbaum 4, cf. 12) if one means that the philosophers' public was "ordinary" in the sense of being commonplace, but not if one means "ordinary" in the sense of being socially typical.

18. Cf. Harris 1989, 146 (a little pessimistic).

19. Harris 130–133, 136.

20. Epicurus encouraged people to believe that philosophy was accessible to a person of moderate education: fr. 117 Usener (= L-S 25 F), *Sent. Vat.* 27 (25 I 1).

least, gives little or no advice.[21] Nonetheless the reader who supposes that ancient anger therapy can have been no more than a metaphor or a conceit is in for something of a surprise, for there were indeed seriously meant therapeutic techniques and even therapeutic relationships (there was also a certain amount of posturing). Before we describe them, however, it would be useful to set out for comparative purposes what kinds of anger therapy are available *now*, especially as most such treatments no longer conform to the traditional model of psychotherapy.

A practice-oriented American psychologist lists the following types of anger therapy:[22]

1. *Cognitive therapies,* in which the therapist teaches the patient new and more sensible ways of thinking about provocations to anger and about how he or she should react to such provocations.
2. *Relaxation-based therapies,* in which the patient is taught methods of physical relaxation which he or she will be able to summon when provoked to anger, to avoid angry arousal.
3. *Skill-training therapies,* which help the patient to interact with other people calmly in circumstances which are liable to provoke anger.
4. *Exposure-based treatments,* which present the patient with stimuli which would normally cause him or her to be angry, but in an artificial setting which enables the patient to practise self-control.
5. *Cathartic treatments,* in which the patient lets out or drains off his or her pent-up rage in a harmless fashion.

21. Cf. Gill 1985, 307–308.
22. Tafrate 1995, 110, who gives the bibliography in each case. For another very similar list of methods of treatment, see Deffenbacher 1994, 253–266. The latter also includes a category called "response disruption and interference" (254–256), which had its ancient equivalents. Most of these treatments can be combined, and can be applied either to groups or individually. The great advantage enjoyed by modern therapists is that they are likely to realize more clearly than any ancient expert did that anger often arises out of existing emotional tension (see Deffenbacher 1994, 248–249).

The psychologist who drew up this list reviewed the empirical evidence for the effectiveness of such treatments and concluded that all of them *except the cathartic ones* are effective.[23]

Now, the concept of therapy for anger is paradoxical: when one is angry, one desires satisfaction (revenge, according to a common ancient view), not treatment. There are nowadays some "self-referred" anger patients, but most of those who undergo treatment for their irascibility are more or less coerced to do so (hence a delicate problem of establishing a "therapeutic alliance" with the irascible client/patient/prisoner).[24] Plutarch made the point that those who are suffering from psychic passions are unaware of the fact.[25] An angry person may submit to the voice of authority or even to persuasion, but getting a person to relent on a particular occasion is not a therapeutic process. There can be anger therapy only for those who are not at the moment angry, or who at any rate have their anger under control, but who are aware of their own irascibility or some kindred quality and wish to counteract it. There is also the problem of denial, likely to be common in a culture such as that of the Hellenistic Greeks which commonly questioned the propriety of anger: the angry person can always claim that what he or she is showing is some respectable quality such as, for instance, *misoponēria*, hatred of evil.[26]

Did Hellenistic Greeks, or Romans, really submit themselves to anger therapy? The question requires us to decide whether reading a philosophical text about anger is a way of submitting to therapy. Since philosophers, many of them, thought that they were offering psychic

23. For similar conclusions, see S. P. Thomas 1990, 206–207; DiGiuseppe 1995, 145 ("catharsis leads to temporary relief [but] increases the chances that one will become angry in the future"). Tafrate recognizes the provisional nature of his conclusions. The subjects were far too often—more than 60 percent of the time (Tafrate 127)—undergraduate volunteers. However, the most obvious failing of contemporary research design in this area is that it has not led to an assessment of the importance of habit or character formation. And I suspect that the current rejection of cathartic therapy rests on an equivocation: it may not dispel anger, but it may be an effective means of decreasing violence.

24. For a discussion of this problem, see DiGiuseppe 1995, 131–149.

25. *Animine an corporis* 3 (*Mor.* 501a).

26. Plu. *De cohibenda ira* 14 (*Mor.* 462ef). This became a popular stratagem with the Christians.

health, I propose to treat their advice as a kind of therapy; at the same time we have to recognize that, even if the medium is not the message, the skill of the living therapist is what counts most of all. In some well-informed pages of *Le souci de soi* Foucault conjured up a world of interpersonal help over the care of the psychic state,[27] but insofar as such help existed in antiquity, it seems too unsystematic to be accurately described as therapy—at least until the time of Soranus and Galen.

Epicurus evidently thought that he knew how to relieve emotional disturbances, and he included inappropriate anger among those disturbances.[28] But how he proposed to produce this result is not wholly clear. An attempt was made earlier to dispel the notion that Epicurean philosophers merely elaborated what the master himself had said about the emotions. It is not sound method to attribute everything we can find in Philodemus' writings to Epicurus.[29] Nor can we be confident that Cicero's critical account of Epicurus' teaching about treating the sicknesses of the soul, including anger, is a full and fair one. But Epicurus, he says, taught that emotional *aegritudo* could be relieved in two ways, by calling oneself away from thinking about troublesome subjects, and by calling oneself back to thinking about "pleasures" (thus by *avocatio* and *revocatio*).[30] Since he immediately states that Epicurus was of the opinion that "the soul is able to obey reason and to follow where it leads," Epicurus apparently gave the active role to the actual sufferer (what some of his followers came to know as his *tetrapharmakos*, his four-fold medicine, consisted of a summary of his first four "Main Opinions").[31] This was not quite cognitive therapy; we might call it a "distraction therapy."

It was said about Zeno that he particularly favoured the taking of advice—that is, intellectual and probably moral advice;[32] this may have

27. Foucault 1986 [1984], esp. 50–54.

28. Anger among the *aegritudines:* Cic. *Tusc.Disp.* iii.7, 19.

29. Nussbaum 1994, 116–117, treats Philodemus as a faithful follower of Epicurean practice, even though she knows (117 n. 29) that on the subject of anger he was quite eclectic.

30. *Tusc.Disp.* iii.33 (part of fr. 444 Usener).

31. *P.Herc.* 1005 (cf. *Epicurea* p. 69 Usener; Nussbaum 1994, 116).

32. Diog.Laert. vii. 25 end; he improved Hesiod, *WD* 293–294, in this sense. For the friend who helps one to cure *orgē* see the passage of Menander quoted above, p. 351.

encouraged later Stoics to favour inter-personal therapy. The figure of the "consoler," who seems to have appeared in the philosophy of Cleanthes,[33] is also relevant. But the first Stoic who helps us greatly in this enquiry is Chrysippus. One book of his treatise on the passions was known as the "therapeutic" or "ethical" book.[34] Unfortunately most of our knowledge of its contents depends once again on a few remarks made by a hostile witness, in this case Galen. Cicero did not think very much of it either, nor naturally did Philodemus. Cicero complained that though Chrysippus and other Stoics spent much time subdividing and defining the emotions, the part of their discourse devoted to healing the passions was extremely thin ("perexigua"). Philodemus says something different, however, for he classifies Bion and Chrysippus with those "who only denounce < orgē> . . . or do little else."[35]

Part of what Chrysippus had to say on the subject was fairly trite. While the sufferer is actually in the heat of emotion, it is no use interfering: "Anger [orgē] is blind; it often prevents our seeing things that are obvious and it often gets in the way of things which are <already> being comprehended . . . For the passions, once they have started, drive out reasoning and contrary evidence, and push forward violently towards actions contrary to reason."[36] And it was inevitable that, having defined the emotions as perverse judgements, Chrysippus offered an intellectual method of eliminating them: his advice was that someone should make the sufferer aware that the judgement constituting the emotion was false—*cognitive therapy* in other words.[37] Thus, Stoic

33. Cic. *Tusc.Disp.* iii.76 = *SVF* I.576. The Greek for the condition which the "consoler" was attempting to remedy was presumably *lupē* (Donini 1995, 305), a term which could be applied to the passions in general.

34. For this label, see *SVF* III.457, 461, 474 (people sometimes called it the "ethical" book, fr. 461). Cf. Gould 1970, 186–188, Fillion-Lahille 1984, 98–118; Nussbaum 1994, 368; Donini 1995. For a general account of ancient ideas about the psychotherapy of the emotions, see Sorabji 2000, 211–225, 228–272.

35. Cic. *Tusc.Disp.* iv.9; cf. Phld. *De ira* 2 (col. i.13–18, reading βαιόν in line 16).

36. Plu. *De virtute morali* 10 (*Mor.* 450c) = Chrysippus, *On the Failure to Lead a Consistent Life*, *SVF* III.390. Cf. III.475, 484.

37. Cic. *Tusc.Disp.* iii.76–77. "It is necessary to show that every passion is a discordant state," *SVF* III.474 end. More abstractly, it is *logos* which will show the person who calmed down the absurdity of his passion (see *SVF* III.467, which compares this

psychology and Stoic therapeutic claims went closely together,[38] and this was no doubt why later non-Stoics found Chrysippus' therapeutic book so unhelpful. Nevertheless, many agreed with a logical consequence of the Stoic-Chrysippan position: the people who were qualified to correct the "errors" of the passionate were obviously the philosophers.

What is most interesting is that Chrysippus wrote as if he really expected to be an active therapist of people in the throes of anger. "Therefore," he says, "we treat these people who are in the grip of passion [*empathōn*] as if they were out of their minds, and we speak to them as if they had changed character and were not in control of themselves."[39] But if this reference to what "we" do is anything more than a *façon de parler*, we get no other hint of it from the sources. When we hear of the anger-controlling feats of the Stoic sages, it is *their own* anger they are said to have controlled,[40] not that of disciples or patients.

It may be that most of the Hellenistic philosophers before Poseidonius were in fact reluctant or unable to specify therapies for the avoidance of the passions. Perhaps Philodemus was actually being fair when he represented Bion the Borysthenite as having denounced anger but gone no further,[41] and when he criticized an unidentified philosopher (this is likely to have been the Epicurean Timasagoras)[42] who apparently considered that it was useless to describe the negative consequences of anger because angry people have become "unable to reason about the passions."[43]

---

role with the one played by Achilles with respect to the grief of Priam [cf. Voelke 1993, 79]).

38. Cf. Dodds 1951, 239.

39. *SVF* III.475.

40. Diogenes of Babylon, for example, was supposed to have remained calm when a young man spat on him as he was lecturing about anger (Sen. *De ira* iii.38.1 = *SVF* III.50). His reported comment was "Non quidem irascor, sed dubito tamen an oporteat irasci." The younger Cato was also said to have kept calm under the same provocation, Sen. iii.38.2. Cf. Nussbaum 1994, 339–340, on the role of *exempla* in Stoic moral teaching.

41. *De ira* 2 (col. i.11–27).

42. See Indelli's commentary on this passage, pp. 142–143.

43. Phld. *De ira* 4 (col. vii.6–9): ἀνεπιλογίστους αὐτοὺς γεγονέναι τῶν παθῶν. Indelli translates slightly differently: "che gli iracondi non sono capaci di considerare

The main idea for treating anger which the Hellenistic age had inherited from Plato and Aristotle was to use music. But no such doctrine seems to have had much success. The Stoic Diogenes of Babylon had a high opinion of music's moral effects,[44] but others were sceptical, at least as far as anger and strife were concerned, and even Plutarch, who suggests that it can be used against attacks of *orgē,* neither insists much nor explains how this should be done.[45]

We are inevitably stumbling in near darkness on the subject of anger therapy at least until we come to Philodemus. However, there is one other earlier figure whose views on this matter are partly known and may have been very influential, namely Poseidonius. Emotions, he held, involve reason's assenting, under the influence of affective movements (which are not the same as emotions), to erroneous views about externals. But to prevent an emotion which one is liable to experience from occurring, one should imagine in advance, and prepare oneself for, events that would set off the emotion, thus getting used to them[46]—an *exposure-based treatment,* in other words. Poseidonius also seems to have said that if a person's character is going to improve, his or her reason must "acquire knowledge of the truth, and the emotional movements *must be blunted by habituation to good practices.*"[47] That was unoriginal, but Poseidonius may indeed have given special empha-

---

bene le affezioni." It looks as if Timasagoras had pointed out, and Philodemus wanted to ignore, the fact that those who are actually in the throes of *orgē* are typically quite uninterested in being sermonized on the subject.

44. See his frr. 54, 56 in *SVF* III; cf. Nussbaum 1993, 117–118; 1994, 367. Another Stoic echo of such doctrine: Poseid. fr. 168 E-K (applied to the "more passionate," the *thumikōteroi*).

45. Sceptical: Phld. *De musica* iv.11 Neubecker (speaking of civil strife, *emphulios stasis,* col. xix.7), Sextus Emp. *Adv.Math.* vi.19–37, esp. 21–22 (he invokes Epicurus, sect. 27). Plutarch's view: *Coniug.Praec.* 38 (*Mor.* 143c), *Inst.Lac.* (*Mor.* 238b), *De coh. ira* 10 (*Mor.* 458e). The musicologist Aristides Quintilianus held (ii.5 and 9) that some mode or modes could help a person recover from *orgē.*

46. Galen, *De placitis Hippocratis et Platonis* iv.7.7–8 De Lacy = Poseid. fr. 165 (pp. 150–151) E-K. The notion that one can defend oneself against harm by imagining it ahead of time can be traced back at least to Euripides: Newman 1989, 1477.

47. *De placitis* v.5.29 De Lacy = Poseid. fr. 169 E-K end. For Poseidonius' treatment, cf. Cooper 1998, 92–93 = 1999, 476–477.

sis to good moral habits in the control of anger, and it may have been
he who invented the discipline of daily self-examination.

This last observation leads to another: what we can certainly not do
in this chapter is trace each "therapeutic" idea to its source, for the
crucial authors do not survive. But we can discover something about
the variety of the techniques that were suggested, and conversely take
note of some that were not.

With Philodemus we are on firmer ground, but his anger therapy
seems essentially to consist of a more extreme version of the argumentation against anger which he found fault with when it was practised by
other philosophers, for it consists of discoursing about anger's harmful effects. This procedure, he claims, "arouses great horror [*phrikē*],
so that the [potentially?] angry man easily escapes [the harmful ef-
fects]."[48] The result, he claims, is to make the subject "attentive to
therapeia."[49] He or she will then consider "the magnitude and the number" of the evils that result from anger.[50] Thus: a kind of *cognitive therapy* based on shock.

With the aid of Philodemus' essay *On Free Speech (peri parrhēsias)* we
can find out something more.[51] The treatment presupposes a diagnosis of the individual patient by the philosophical teacher, and it consists of the use of arguments directed towards the patient—arguments
mild or harsh, as the case may be, with respect to the patient's moral
condition. The person on the verge of anger is then supposed to consider rationally what the ill effects of his or her anger would be.

We do not know whether Philodemus or any contemporary philosopher ever got the opportunity to put the theory of anger control
into practice. The imagined and the actual audience of *De ira* must
have been very small: that is guaranteed by Philodemus' abstruse and
rebarbative Greek. But he acquired a notable intellectual influence in
first-century B.C. Italy, and may have had real "patients" or at least dev-
otees. And it was apparently in the age of Philodemus and Cicero that
the figure of the live-in philosopher, exemplified by the Stoic Diodotus

48. *De ira* 3 (col. iii.14–18).
49. *Ibid.* (col. iv.17–19; cf. V.9).
50. *Ibid.* (col.vi.19–21).
51. Cf. Nussbaum 1994, 122–126.

in Cicero's own household, became a familiar one in the houses of wealthy Romans.[52] Later on such arrangements were easily satirized,[53] and one will look sceptically on any claim that they led to any serious attempt to control the passions. If one-on-one therapy occurred, as distinct from lectures and conversations with groups, it is surprising that we never hear of it from Cicero or Lucretius. There was, however, an audience for teachings about anger control—a small audience, but an interesting one, including Cicero, Caesar (so it was suggested in Chapter 9), Augustus, Seneca and Claudius.

Cicero's own anger therapy is not in essence very different from that of Philodemus, in spite of the fact the Roman writer had criticized the doctrine of the Epicureans on this matter. More *cognitive* therapy, in other words. Relief from disturbance of the soul can be achieved "when you teach" the falseness of the twin judgements which make up an emotion. In the first place, you should teach that what gives rise to delight or *libido* is not really a good, and that what gives rise to psychic *aegritudo* is not a genuine evil.[54] But, he continues, "the sure and proper cure is if you show that the disturbances [such as anger] are of themselves essentially wrong [*per se esse vitiosas*], and contain nothing either natural or necessary." The first of these two modes of arguing is, he says, *utilior*, more useful (presumably because it eliminates the second mistaken judgement as well as the first),[55] but is rarely helpful and is not to be applied to the *vulgus*—by which he means those who are incapable of philosophical discernment.[56] Both forms of treatment are referred to as forms of *oratio*, oral admonition. What concerns us most here is precisely the most elusive part of this account, namely the identity of the "you" and the listener, and their relationship with each

52. He lived in Cicero's household for many years until his death in about 60 B.C.; see esp. *Acad.* ii.115. Cf. Rawson 1985, 79–83.

53. For Lucian, see below, p. 388.

54. *Tusc.Disp.* iv.60. It is unfortunately not clear what sort of *conturbatio mentis* he has in mind in iv.30, where he speaks of its being removed "curatione et purgatione [this word is conjectural] medicorum."

55. On this point, see Voelke 1993, 75, who, in the wake of Pohlenz 1906, traces the whole argument back to Chrysippus.

56. Therefore all philosophers, he asserts, use the second method and discuss not what causes "disturbances" but the disturbances themselves (iv.62). What this means with respect to anger is talking about the evilness of its effects (iv.77–79).

other. "You" of course are a philosopher, but the listener and the philosopher's relationship to him or her remain unspecified. At the end, being "cured" by philosophy seems an impersonal business.[57]

This continual advocacy of cognitive therapy should not be surprising, given the established Greek ambiguity about error and sin: *hamart-* words cover both the one and the other, from which it seems to follow that if a person does not make a mistake he or she will not sin, except perhaps in cases of severe moral depravity.[58] And advice about anger often came from philosophers, who were perhaps congenitally prone to supposing that correct reasoning would lead to virtuous behaviour. This after all was the Platonic tradition, relatively all the stronger in Hellenistic times because of the neglect of Aristotle. Nowadays, with a more complex understanding of human motives, we tend to dismiss this notion.[59] Yet in contemporary practice cognitive therapy once again has a place.

The Greeks and Romans themselves eventually grew restive with the mainly cognitive way of treating anger. The most important of the new techniques was *daily self-examination*—one of those obvious ideas which nonetheless had to be invented. Who invented it we do not know, for it is already taken for granted in the letter Cicero wrote to his brother about anger in 60 or 59.[60] The Pythagoreans are said to have practised a kind of daily self-examination much earlier, but in order (apparently) to exercise their memory, not to improve their morals.[61] The idea of a daily moral self-examination was favoured by the Stoic philosopher of Augustan times Q. Sextius, who seems like Cicero to have thought of it as a way of limiting anger, and the notion of self-examination was also familiar to a philosophical amateur such as Hor-

---

57. *Tusc.Disp.* iv.82–84.

58. See Dover 1974, 152–153.

59. B. Williams's negative reaction (1997, 212–213) to the argument that Stoic philosophy can function as psychotherapy for the emotions therefore seems characteristic.

60. *QF* i.1.37, quoted above, p. 205.

61. Cicero (*De sen.* 38) makes Cato say that every day he reviewed what he had said, heard and done *Pythagoreorum modo*, to exercise his aging memory; but Cicero is not clear as to what the motives of the Pythagoreans had been. Diog.Laert. viii.22 claims that Pythagoras taught his disciples to practice regular *moral* self-examination.

ace.[62] Sextius, according to Seneca, asked his "soul" as he went to bed, "What ill have you cured today? What vice have you resisted? What part of you is better?"[63] "Anger will cease," Seneca continues, "and become less intense [*moderatior*] if it knows that every day it will have to appear before a judge" (but Seneca then spoils the effect, as we shall see).[64] It is not impossible that the originator of this idea, or at least the person who put it into philosophical circulation, was Poseidonius.

This was another form of self-treatment, and a kind of stratagem for reducing anger. There are other stratagems, varying in their practicality, which first appear in Augustan times. Q. Sextius advised that the angry man should look at himself in a mirror—a fairly useless notion, since it presumably requires the cooperation of the person who is currently raging (Seneca indeed detects this difficulty).[65] Another little stratagem for avoiding anger was offered to Augustus, according to a story of Plutarch's, by the unfortunate philosopher Athenodorus of Tarsus: when provoked, repeat to yourself the letters of the alphabet[66]—a relaxation or distraction which had some potential for helping Augustus, and Plutarch's readers, with their minor irritations.

The appearance of Horace in this account enables us to speculate further about the manner in which an introspective concern about anger had by now affected members of Rome's intellectual elite. Not only was the poet broadly conversant with what the critics of anger had said (that we could have predicted), he also shows signs of being concerned about his own irascibility: he gives it as one of his principal characteristics that he is "irasci celerem, tamen ut placabilis essem" ("swift to anger, but able to relent").[67] But he remains urbane: no Stoic excesses.

62. Hor. *Sat.* i.4.133–138, who admittedly does not speak explicitly of *daily* self-examination.

63. *De ira* iii.36.1; cf. *Ep.* 28.9–10, 83.2 (where he complains that "no one" engages in such introspection).

64. This notion had a considerable future: see Epictet. iii.10.2, iv.4.46; Ps.-Pyth. *Golden Words* 40–43 (see D. Young's ed. of Theognis, p. 90); G. Viansino's note on the *De ira* passage.

65. Sen. *De ira* ii.36.1; cf. Plu. *De cohibenda ira* 6 (*Mor.* 456a), Greg.Naz. *Adv.iram* 87–90. See Sen. ii.36.3.

66. Plu. *Mor.* 207c (*Sayings of the Romans*, Caesar Augustus no. 7), quoted in Chapter 10.

67. *Epist.* i.20.25. For some joking awareness of his own quick temper, see *Sat.*

Our first real opportunity to describe an ancient writer's detailed views about the psychotherapy of anger is presented by Seneca. *De tranquillitate animi* is particularly relevant, as well as *De ira*.[68] While Seneca's thinking about anger was partly directed towards politics, he was also eager to bring about psychic calm.[69] The aim of *De ira* is nominally the absolute elimination of anger, though the practical aim is a little less clear-cut. And he makes "absolutism" itself into a sort of instrument: "It is easier to exclude harmful influences than to govern them," "The enemy must be stopped at the frontier."[70] And before he comes to the therapeutic section itself, he explains (ii.12–13) that the complete elimination of anger is not impossible.

Once again, free use is made of the medical parallel, but when Seneca offers direct instruction about remedies, as he does in the second half of *De ira,* he does so without any mention of courses of individualized therapy, and no therapist is imagined. Seneca professes two aims here: to show the reader how to avoid anger, and to show how, if one is angry, one can avoid "doing wrong." Assorted pieces of sensible and not-so-sensible advice about the first of these matters fill the rest of Book II.[71] Habits are important ("plurimum potest consuetudo"). Avoid excessive drinking or eating; work, but not too much; exercise and relax, but again, not too much (ii.20).

The training of children is the next subject.[72] The problem is to bring them up not to be angry, without "blunting their natural spirit [*indoles*]." Seneca responds to this difficulty at some length, undoubtedly drawing on earlier discussions while giving them the form that suited his own social ambience.

> In conflicts with boys of his own age, we should not let [a boy] be defeated, or get angry . . . Nothing does more to make people ill-tem-

---

ii.3.323. For his familiarity with the literature, see *Odes* i.16. The surviving work of Augustan literature which is ostensibly most concerned to provide therapy for a passion is Ovid's *Remedia amoris* (see lines 795–796 for the medical metaphor).

68. For the suggestion that some of his tragedies were intended as a kind of therapy, see Vegetti 1995, 65.

69. *De ira* ii.12.6.

70. i.7.2, 8.2: the theme fills both chapters.

71. The organization is not strict (*contra* Fillion-Lahille 1984, 288): in Book II he sometimes tells what is to be done if anger takes hold (29.1), while in Book III he sometimes comes back to methods of avoiding anger in the first place (5.2).

72. ii.21; cf. also 20.2.

pered than a soft, comfortable upbringing . . . He will never be able to stand up to negative experiences if he has never been denied anything . . . He . . . should even feel fear sometimes . . . He should never get his way through anger . . . it will help for them to have even-tempered teachers and *paedagogi.*

Above all, he should lead an unluxurious life.[73]

Next comes "cognitive" advice for adults, which can be summarized as follows: they should be sceptical about things which seem to deserve an angry response, they should not be annoyed by trifles or by things or people that have no capacity to harm them, or any wish to do so (ii.22–27). Since none of us is innocent, we should not find fault with others. We should delay angry reactions in order to make them disappear, and the person who is the target of our potential anger may deserve to be excused (ii.28–30). If we think we have been treated unfairly, it may be only because the experience was unexpected, and in any case the power to injure (in return) is "vile and detestable and completely foreign to human nature"—hence punishment must not be angry but precautionary. Revenge is not truly pleasurable (he admits, however, that only a large spirit overlooks injustices, *iniuriae*), and it is often inexpedient to be angry (an anecdote follows about one of the victims of Caligula, and we are temporarily visiting the world of practical advice for courtiers) (ii.31–33). Forgiveness is better, and anger is hard to retract.

Anger, he continues, makes people ugly, and we should imagine anger itself as ugly. And "if the <angry> mind [*animus*] could be shown, if it were enclosed in some transparent substance, its appearance—dark and mottled, inflamed, distorted and swollen—would confound the observer" (ii.36.2).

Anger is also dangerous to the health, and can lead to madness, as witness the case of Ajax (for the amateur soul-doctor, the casebook is partly mythological) (ii.36.4–5). To conclude this section and Book II, Seneca offers the image of anger as a passion so powerful that it overcomes all others. The whole of this section we might sum up as a kind of cognitive therapy based on repulsion or fear.

Book III purportedly attempts to explain what we should do if we

73. Much of this is derived from Pl. *Laws* vii.791c–793a, and most of it is probably taken from Poseidonius.

nonetheless do experience anger. But the author has great difficulty in concentrating on this theme, and turns in the very first chapter to ways of limiting the anger of others. "Each man's character should determine the plan of action." Then it is quickly back to a general denunciation of anger. A sort of new preface in Chapter 5 promises three topics: how not to grow angry, how to stop being angry, and finally how to pacify others.[74] All three sections can be regarded as broadly therapeutic in intent, or broadly literary—not that these categories necessarily exclude each other.

The principal therapeutic sections are (a) a "cognitive" lecture about the evil effects of anger, (b) the advice that we should suppress the symptoms as soon as they appear, (c) "avoid provocations," (d) postpone your reaction, and (e) try to keep it hidden and secret.[75] There follows a list of examples to avoid and another of examples to follow. The next section of the work is, as recent critics have remarked a "disorganized miscellany of advice and reflections,"[76] mostly recurring to themes Seneca has already mentioned. The most important remaining subject is daily self-examination (ii.36–38). In Seneca's case, however, self-examination seems to consist largely of blaming other people for unpleasant encounters, and this moment of self-revelation detracts from the sense of *De ira*'s moral seriousness. Nearing the end, Seneca turns briefly to curing the anger of other people—which might lead us to expect some therapeutic advice in a modern sense. But his advice is vague and hasty: you must approach the angry person "in various ways and *blande* [tactfully]" (ii.40.2).

It is entirely wrong to see Seneca's *De ira* as itself an act of personalized therapy directed towards the author's brother Novatus.[77] Novatus comes into the work only in the most formal fashion.[78] The intent was therapeutic in a more general sense, and not simply analytic. A modern reader may be put off by a certain pornography of violence, but

74. iii.5.2. These are discussed in chs. 5–9 (reading history is supposed to be a good precautionary measure, iii.9.2), chs. 10–38 and chs. 39–40.

75. (a) iii.5.3–6.2, (b) 10, 13.1–6, (c) 11, (d) 12.3–7, (e) 13.1–6. For musical therapy, see 9.2.

76. ii.24–35. Cooper & Procopé 1995, 100 n.52.

77. This misconception is propagated by Nussbaum 1994, 405–426.

78. At the beginning of each book and near the end, at iii.39.1. The imaginary objector who is periodically introduced with *inquis* or *inquit* ("you say," "he says") is simply part of the customary rhetorical furniture (see M. Griffin 1976, 414, 419) and not

Seneca provides a wide range of fairly sensible advice. Its effect no doubt was limited to a very small circle, consisting of the most reflective members of the social elite (fewer still when Senecan prose went out of fashion); but on some of these it can be presumed to have made a strong impression.

Seneca was an "absolutist," in the sense that he disapproved, ostensibly, of all *ira* whatsoever. We noticed earlier the surprising ancient popularity of this somewhat unrealistic doctrine, and some of the factors that encouraged it, including the specific meaning of some of the Greek and Latin words—it was not quite as unrealistic to denounce *orgē* as to denounce anger. But absolutism in this department has had few advocates in modern times: there was no anger in More's Utopia (1516), but that was precisely a utopian vision, and Spinoza too can be said to have been an "absolutist" with respect to anger,[79] but there have been few others.

The intellectual foundations of absolutism were laid in the fifth century B.C.: Socrates himself, as delineated by Plato, was in a sense something of an absolutist.[80] But a passion for absolutes was a distinctively Stoic trait; they also maintained that nothing except virtue was good, and that virtue, and virtue alone, was sufficient for happiness.[81] "Whoever has one [virtue] has all <of them>" was another Stoic pronouncement.[82]

The Stoics formulated an appropriate chain of reasoning in favor of eliminating the passions (we inspected it briefly in Chapter 6). It was in fact a circular chain, essentially of this form: the passions are always excessive (or are vices), what is excessive (or morally unhealthy) is to be eliminated (because it hinders *tranquillitas animi*), therefore the passions are to be eliminated. The argument can be seen in its full simplicity in, for instance, Seneca's *Moral Epistle* 116. But if we do

---

"deep in Novatus' soul" (Nussbaum 407). Novatus' "demand" that Seneca should write (i.1, made much of by Nussbaum) is a well-known topos (see A. Gudeman's commentary on Tac. *Dial.,* p. 41), though it appears here in an interestingly intense form (cf. Sen. *Contr.* i.1.1, "exigitis").

79. Fillion-Lahille 1984, 11. For Spinoza's views, see esp. *Eth.* iii, prop. 45 cor. 1 and prop. 46. But it is not crystal clear, in view of prop. 65, that he was a complete absolutist.

80. *Crito* 49a–b; *Gorg.* 469b, 508e; Gerson 1997.

81. See L-S sections 60 and 58, respectively.

82. L-S 61D 1, 61F 1.

not admit that every *affectus* (emotion) is always necessarily a *morbus* (sickness), or that *tranquillitas animi* is the only good end? The chain breaks.[83] Seneca adroitly claims that the main objection to Stoic absolutism about the emotions is just that it is unrealizable.[84] He naturally denies this. That was an objection which the Stoics had always been used to meeting. They did so in part by putting their morality in the form of a description of what the perfectly wise man will do—who, it was said, was as rare as or rarer than the phoenix.[85] However, it was also a standard Stoic view that virtue was a *consistent disposition (diathesis)*,[86] and while there is some uncertainty as to what they meant by "consistent,"[87] that is a plausible statement, at least—and it may be thought to lead to the conclusion that to be virtuous one must consistently eliminate the passions.

Cicero, too, when he is discussing anger absolutism, hides behind the *sapiens*,[88] the superman who can be said without absurdity to be superior to the passions. He admits that Stoic reasoning on the subject is "rather convoluted" *(contortius)*, but he nonetheless tells us that we must stay with the Stoics because "they use extremely robust and, so to speak, virile reasoning and thinking."[89] It could hardly be plainer that his opinion is not really based on a chain of reasoning at all, even in his own eyes.

The desire for a therapeutic rule was clearly vital. Seneca is the earliest writer who is known to have pointed out this practical advantage of "absolutism." We must now quote the passage more fully:

> It is easier to exclude harmful influences than to govern them [he argued], and easier to deny them admittance than, after they have been admitted, to control them; for when they have established themselves

83. Even Annas 1992, who is extremely indulgent towards the Stoics, admits that their theory of the emotions "to some extent redefines the original phenomena" (103).

84. *Ep.Mor.* 116.7–8.

85. Chrysippus, *SVF* III.545 (L-S 66A), Panaetius fr. 114 (L-S 66C) etc. The phoenix: Sen. *Ep.Mor.* 42.1; Alexander of Aphrodisias, *De fato* 199 (*SVF* III.658 = L-S 61N 2).

86. Diog.Laert. vii.89 (L-S 61A), Plu. *De virtute morali* 3 (*Mor.* 441b–c) (L-S 61B 8).

87. Cf. L-S I, p. 383.

88. *Tusc.Disp.* iii.19–22.

89. iii.22. Later (iv.43) he rejects the Peripatetic argument that one is virile only if one knows how to be angry.

in possession, they are stronger than their ruler, and do not tolerate being cut back or diminished.[90]

This thought is unlikely to have been original with Seneca, and it may go back to almost any earlier Stoic. The logic is commonsensical, and seems parallel to the total-abstention logic of Alcoholics Anonymous (not a single drink, ever). Indeed Plutarch's spokesman about anger uses sobriety and abstention from wine as a metaphor for anger restraint.[91]

In psychological terms the appeal of such statements is not particularly difficult to understand. They are strong and uncompromising statements, and give the illusion of purity. Strenuous moralists can often upstage the rest of the human race, especially those who think in more subtle categories, and the Stoics benefited from this. Even for a Cicero or a Plutarch or a Galen, all of them highly knowledgeable about the faults that could be found with Stoic moral philosophy, it was virtually impossible to resist the allure of the extreme position. It was difficult to argue in favour of *orgē*-anger or even in favour of *ira*.

As for lesser minds, at certain periods they flocked in. Lucian satirized the type. How did you decide that Stoicism was the best philosophy?[92]

> *Hermotimus:* I saw that most people were taking up this one, so I guessed that it was the best . . .
> *Lycinus:* . . . You are hiding the truth from me.
> *Hermotimus:* . . . A lot of people said about the Stoics that they are manly [*andrōdeis*] and understand everything, and that the person who follows this path is the only king, the only rich man, the only wise man, and altogether everything.

Lifelong therapy was needed, the Stoic Musonius Rufus asserted. The power of reason, so he apparently said, resembles not medicine

---

90. *De ira* i.7.2. He develops the thought elsewhere, especially in *Ep. Mor.* 116.
91. *De cohibenda ira* 16 end (*Mor.* 464c).
92. *Herm.* 16; cf. 18 beginning. For a view of Stoicism as the dominant philosophy of the Roman Empire, see Shaw 1985.

(*pharmaka*) but healthy foods, "since it implants a good disposition [*hexis*], along with health, in whoever is accustomed to it" (fr. XXXVI). Admonitions, however, that are offered when the emotions are at their height succeed slowly (*scholēi*) and with difficulty. But what Musonius knew of in the realm of therapeutic practice the surviving excerpts from his writings do not reveal. Epictetus was more demanding (as we saw earlier),[93] but has nothing categorically new to offer in the way of treatment. Some of his therapy is banal: Medea would not have been carried away by fury if someone had shown her that she was deceived in thinking that exacting revenge from her husband was more profitable than saving her children (i.28.8). He strongly emphasizes habits: "If you wish not to be irascible [*orgilos*], do not feed your habit, put before it nothing which will make it grow. As the first step, keep quiet and count the <consecutive> days on which you have not been angry." One must build up the intervals to four days; when you have gone thirty days without *orgē*, sacrifice to god. "For the habit is first weakened, then completely destroyed" (ii.18.12–13). In an earlier chapter I quoted his self-deprecating comments on his own capacity for controlling his emotions (he seems to be thinking mainly of anger), but what is relevant here is that the roles he refers to are still simply those of the writer and the reader (iv.5.36).

The Stoic emphasis on habit appears at about the same time in Plutarch's anger essay. And at last we have clearer references to what sounds like a course of treatment. The first and subsidiary speaker advocates mutual moral inspections of friends or dear ones, and then proceeds to say to his interlocutor,[94] who has overcome his irascibility: "describe to us *as if it were a medical treatment of yourself* the means by which you made your spirit so obedient, docile, accepting of reason, and controlled." It is rational judgement (*krisis*) which represses fits of *orgē*, comes the reply. "To me at least it happened that when I had twice or three times resisted anger I experienced what the Thebans did, who when they had for the first time defeated the Spartans . . . were never defeated by them again."[95]

---

93. See above, p. 117. One who desires to be a philosopher must, among other things, give up his nearest ones, his *oikeioi* (iii.15.11).
94. Plu. *De cohibenda ira* 1 (*Mor.* 453a, 453c).
95. Ch. 3 (454c).

Some familiar advice follows: catch outbursts of anger quickly.[96] Catharsis is rejected, which is intriguing, for although the idea had Aristotelian roots, it had not been in evidence in recent times as a remedy for anger: it may cure other passions, the speaker says, but "anger [thumos] is, rather, inflamed by the things people who are suffering from it do and say."[97] The speaker says that he started his medical cure (iatreia) by studying the rage of others, its effects first of all on the face (he advocates mirror therapy) and voice. He continues this artifice by claiming that he has observed this and that kind of angry conduct.[98] We are told yet again about habits and training.[99] Even delay can contribute to the medical treatment (iatreia) of anger. It is because people feel despised or neglected that they grow angry: "therefore it is necessary to help those who are trying to reject anger" (tois paraitoumenois orgēn), and you do this by convincing them that they have not really been despised or neglected.[100] The speaker preaches a simple life, and concludes by referring to the sacred vow he had made: "first to pass a few days without orgē . . . then one month and two [cf. Seneca]; and so, testing myself, I gradually progressed in time into the front ranks of patient endurance." It was all self-therapy, with a certain amount of help, he says, from god.[101] Thus the iatreia remains not fictitious but metaphorical.

Second-century physicians, some of them at least, believed that philosophy could have a serious effect on irascibility. So Soranus of Ephesus thought, perhaps the leading medical writer of Hadrianic times. We know this from the late-antique writer Caelius Aurelianus, who appears to transmit a large quantity of Soranus. If a patient who is suffering from insanity is willing to hear discussions of philosophers, he says, he should be afforded the opportunity: "for by their words philosophers eliminate [amputant] fear, sorrow and anger [iracundia], and in so doing make no small contribution to the health of the body."[102]

---

96. Chs. 3–4 (454d–455b).
97. Ch. 5 (455c).
98. Chs. 6–10 (455e–458e) passim, 12 (460d).
99. Ch. 11 (459b): ethismos and askēsis.
100. Ch. 12 (460d).
101. Ch. 16 (464b–d), reading καὶ before πειρώμενος in 464c.
102. On Chronic Diseases (Tardae Passiones) i.5.166–7. Cf. Pigeaud 1981, 109–110.

It is, however, in Galen's essay *On the Diagnosis and Care of the Passions of the Soul* that we gain the clearest idea of what ancient anger therapy could be like.[103] Much of what the man of Pergamum has to say on the subject of controlling one's anger is by now entirely familiar, but the role of the helper is emphasized as never before.[104] The author explains that he wants the reader to look for his own faults first.[105] But in case one cannot do that, one needs a helper (a notion which we have seen developing gradually since at least the time of Chrysippus)—and Galen explains what sort of person that should be: someone who does not flatter the well-to-do, someone who leads a disciplined life.

> If you find such a man, talk to him in private and ask him to reveal immediately whatever of the above-mentioned passions [*pathē*] he may see in you. Tell him you will be most grateful for this and that you will look upon him as your deliverer [*sōtēra*] more than if he had saved you from a physical illness. And if he promises to tell you whenever he sees you affected by any of these passions, and then after several days, although he has been spending time with you, he tells you nothing, reproach him and again ask him, still more earnestly than before, to reveal immediately whatever he sees you doing in accordance with passion.[106]

If he tells you that he has seen you commit no such act, do not believe him (various speculations follow as to why he may be unwilling to tell you).

> But if you remain silent . . . when you are [corrected and] freed from your acts of passion, you will soon afterwards find many people who will give you true correction; especially if you show gratitude to your corrector [*tōi mempsamenōi*] after you have, thanks to him, removed the harm from yourself. You will benefit greatly in considering whether he is right or wrong to censure you. If you do this continuously because

---

103. Cf. Hankinson 1993, 198–204 (but Galen does not, *pace* Hankinson 200, emphasize a distinction between controlling manifestations of an emotion and the emotion itself). Galen's work is inexplicably neglected in Nussbaum 1994.

104. Or perhaps we should say, not since the time of Menander.

105. *De propriorum animi cuiuslibet affectuum* 2.5–6 De Boer.

106. 3.4–5. The "above-mentioned passions" are *thumos, orgē,* fear, grief, envy and extreme desire. Anger is the passion Galen is first interested in in this treatise, but later (10.4) he makes *pleonexia* (greed) the fundamental vice.

you have really chosen to become an honourable and good man, you will be one. (*On the Diagnosis* 3.9)

I have quoted from these passages at relative length because their length itself—and Galen continues, explaining how you should behave if your critic appears to have criticized you unjustly, and remarking that it is impossible for the rich or powerful to obtain the candid criticism they need—suggests strongly that such therapy was now taken seriously. Later, Galen returns repeatedly to the notion that one needs a moral critic to point out one's failings.[107] He refers to this method as "the usual one for recognizing and curing all [diseases of the soul]" (7.1).

This "other" does not have to be a physician or a philosopher, in fact he needs no occupational label at all—for few if any occupational labels carried much weight with the social elite of the high Roman Empire. Galen refers to him as a sort of initiate *(epoptēs)* or boy-minder *(paidagōgos)*.[108] Did such people and such relationships exist? Galen does not joke nor does he fantasize.

Galen himself put his case against the passions to many, he says (10.1), but in spite of immediate success, they received little long-term benefit, for in most people the passions are incurable. Now if it is true that Galen did this (and as we have seen, his autobiographical statements are sometimes false), it would be interesting to know whether he was allowed or encouraged to do so in virtue of being a physician, a philosopher or simply a wise acquaintance. Nothing in Galen's text suggests that either physicians or philosophers had succeeded in "professionalizing" such treatment. However, *On the Diagnosis and Care* presents itself as a work of philosophy, and we have sufficient evidence from elsewhere that wealthy Romans of this era sometimes maintained household philosophers.[109]

Another favourite idea of Galen's for overcoming anger involved a crisis of revulsion, rather like the "horror" of anger which Philodemus had hoped to induce in the readers of his *De ira*. That was the point of

107. Ibid. 5.6–8; see also 6.10, 6.12, 6.13.

108. Ibid. 10.2; Harkins 1963, 66, translates "overseer or instructor," incorrectly.

109. The classic text is Lucian, *On Salaried Posts in Great Houses*, where the addressee is a philosopher (sects. 4, 24) who is supposed to take thought for his employer's soul (19; cf. 41).

the story he tells (see Chapter 1) about seeing a man biting a key: this was supposedly the moment when Galen began his "hatred" of anger (*On the Diagnosis* 4.5). The story about the Cretan who wounded his slaves (Chapter 13) has a similar form: crisis, followed by admonition, followed by gradual improvement. "That man took thought for himself and in a year he became a much better man. Even if you do not become much better, be satisfied if in the first year you advance and show a measure of improvement. If you continue to resist your passion and to soften your anger, you will show more noteworthy improvement during the second year" (4.14). Not that Galen innocently believed in full human autonomy: far from it—he held that a large part of character, especially in the young, is determined by "nature" (7.9–10). But it is very noticeable that in *On the Diagnosis and Care of the Passions of the Soul* none of his anger therapy is physical, and he makes no allusion to the claim, which the physician Rufus of Ephesus had made, that sex "causes the greatest angers [*orgai*] to relax."[110] Galen aimed higher than short-term relaxation.

That experts in philosophy such as Galen really did offer therapy for anger is confirmed, I think, by a series of hostile comments made by a famous slightly older contemporary, Lucian of Samosata. In one dialogue, for instance, Lucian makes a physician (who is the son of an irascible father) express the wish "that medical science had a medicine [*pharmakon*] of such a kind that it could check not only the insane but also the unjustly angry [*orgizomenous*]."[111] Lucian knew well that there were philosophers who claimed to have a sort of medicine for unjust anger, and more or less gently mocked them. In a panoramic satire of philosophical sects, he represents Diogenes the Cynic identifying himself as a "doctor of the passions,"[112] not because the historical Diogenes had done so, I think, but because this was among what Lucian considered to be the more absurd claims that philosophers made. And what is the principal character weakness of philosophers? Why, of course, the one they are always harping on, anger: in *The Dead Come to Life, or the Fisherman* he imagines that the philosophers are furiously angry

110. Rufus p. 320 Daremberg-Ruelle (from Aetius), and in Oribasius, *Coll.Med.* vi.38 (I p. 541 ed. Bussemaker-Daremberg), and again in Oribas. *Syn.* i.6.1.
111. *Abdicatus (Disowned)* 1.
112. *Vit.auct. (Philosophies for Sale)* 8.

with him, no less a figure than Socrates taking the lead.[113] Lucian claims that it is not philosophy that he had intended to criticize but contemporary philosophers. They are hypocrites. Their textbooks tell one, among other things, not to be angry, but they are more *orgilos* than little dogs, more quarrelsome than cocks.[114] In at least three other dialogues, philosophers are represented as quarrelsome or irascible: these are his *Symposium, or the Lapiths,* where a Stoic called Zenothemis fizzes with rage; *Tragic Zeus,* where a Stoic ("Timocles") is almost as bad; and *Hermotimus* (a Stoic yet again).[115] Lucian himself doubtless shared the ordinary views of a Greek with some philosophical education and disapproved more or less comprehensively of *orgē*-anger. And there were probably many others like him who combined this attitude with disdain for the pretentions of contemporary philosophers. Insofar as the therapeutic role of the latter is visible in Lucian's writings, it takes the form of greedy toadying to the rich (to be distinguished from fund-raising).[116]

The desirability of anger control was generally admitted by educated Greeks of this era, and they assumed that *paideia,* literary culture, taught one the capacity to restrain one's emotions (hence a certain rivalry between two kinds of education). Nor was this unrealistic, for *paideia* included the art of persuasive speaking, which in turn entailed managing one's outward anger, one's *cholē* and *orgē.*[117]

There is one mild surprise left in the ancient therapy of anger, namely the Neoplatonic theory of catharsis. As was mentioned before, Iamblichus' theory was that when the powers of human passions, the *pathēmata,* are "hemmed in on all sides," they grow stronger. The coun-

---

113. The philosophers' *orgē: Piscator* 4, 8, etc.

114. Sects. 15, 34. See similarly *Fugitivi (The Runaways)* 19.

115. *Symposium* 1, 9, 32, 43–45; *Iuppiter Tragoedus* 35–53 (36 draws attention to the Stoic's ill temper); *Herm.* 9 and 12. For the view that Lucian preferred the Epicureans, see Jones 1986, 26–28. Hostility to the Stoics: ibid. 28–29. For other raging Stoics see, e.g., Plu. *De communibus notitiis* 1 (*Mor.* 1059a).

116. *Piscator* 40, *Symposium* 36, etc.

117. Hence when Herodes Atticus lost his temper with Marcus Aurelius, it was his rhetorical training that ought to have prevented it: "One would have thought that a man trained in this type of speaking would have managed his *cholē,*" Philostratus remarks (*VS* ii.1 p. 561; cf. Brown 1992, 48–49). For the association of *paideia* and anger control, cf. Chariton vi.5.8.

tervailing therapy therefore is to allow them to act briefly and within certain limits, so that "they rejoice moderately and are fulfilled," after which they are purified and can easily be brought to an end. This effect can be achieved by watching dramatic and "sacred" performances.[118] The reader was apparently supposed to think that if the irascible subject grew moderately angry often enough while attending the theatre (but angry against whom? Medea? the wicked personages in classical tragedy arouse pity more often than anger), he or she would be purified of the undesired emotion. Not surprisingly this failed to satisfy even other Neoplatonists, such as Proclus.

No simple narrative can encompass all the therapeutic advice we have encountered in this chapter. Until the first century B.C., it seems very thin; after that it grows somewhat in complexity and sophistication. Actual therapeutic advisers or companions were probably few, and subject to a good deal of scepticism. As to techniques which could be applied, by the sufferer or another person, many of the those which are known to modern psychiatrists occurred to the ancients: cognitive therapies, relaxation therapy (on a very modest scale), exposure-based therapy, cathartic therapy. We have not isolated anything as a "skill-training therapy," but that is probably because this category is hard to distinguish from the cognitive. We have also met a kind of distraction therapy (Epicurus), and cognitive therapy based on delayed response (Seneca, Galen) or on shock, repulsion and fear (Philodemus, Seneca, Galen). But what is most strikingly present in some ancient advice—and most strikingly absent from modern advice—is a heavy emphasis on habit and the importance of establishing habitual control over one's angry emotions (Poseidonius, Seneca, Epictetus, Plutarch, Galen).

Two thousand years later, there is a quite natural tendency to dismiss all this ancient advice. Lord Macaulay was heavily sceptical: "We doubt whether Seneca ever kept anybody from being angry . . . the business of a philosopher was [in Seneca's eyes] to declaim in praise of poverty with two millions sterling out at usury," and so on.[119] Among our contemporaries, Veyne has written that Graeco-Roman thinkers

118. *Myst.* i.11; cf. iii.9.
119. In his essay on Bacon, *Miscellaneous Works* (New York, 1880), II:411.

were "naive in their overestimation of the possibilities of self-censorship and facile in their underestimation of the potency of the censored material"[120] (though that now smacks a little too much of the era of psychoanalysis). Bernard Williams has asked how people like Cicero and Seneca could take Stoic philosophy seriously as therapy.[121] As for Veyne's observation, there is no question that some ancient philosophers overestimated the autonomy of the individual. At the same time, Greeks and Romans often recognized the irresistible force sometimes exercised by the passions, and they did what they could to strengthen one another's resistance to the ones which they saw as harmful. It is not clear that traditional psychoanalysis has ever been more effective in combatting the angry emotions than Galen's advice is likely to have been.

This is not to deny that ancient writing on the subject of anger therapy is generously tinged with naïveté, muddled thinking, posturing and hypocrisy. Preaching against anger became something of a philosophical custom. But none of this meant that the anti-anger tradition was useless. If it sometimes helped to restrain slave-owners, husbands and other family members—and perhaps occasionally a provincial governor or even an emperor—there will have been some gain.

120. Veyne 1987 [1985], 229.
121. B. Williams 1997, 213.

CHAPTER 16

From Sickness to Sin:
Early Christianity and Anger

When Christianity became important in the general history of the Graeco-Roman world, in the fourth century A.D., its moral philosophy included, as we saw briefly in Chapter 6, fervent admonitions about the control of angry emotions. What were the origins of these beliefs? In part they derived from Graeco-Roman traditions, and in part from a separate Christian moral tradition, which, although it had long emphasized the ground it shared with the moral philosophy of the pagans,[1] was in fundamental ways distinct from that philosophy. What then did this Christian moral tradition teach about the control of anger?

What Jesus himself said about the angry emotions, if indeed he said anything, is of little consequence for this study, but we want to determine what his followers *believed* he had said. As it happens, however, the vital evidence, a passage in the Sermon on the Mount recounted in Matthew 5:22a, already existed in two crucially different forms in the second century, and perhaps earlier.[2] One version of this text claims that, after repeating the Old Testament injunction against killing, Jesus added this: "But I say to you that everyone who is angry [*orgizomenos*] with his brother will be subject to judgement." In the other version, it is "everyone who is angry with his brother *without rea-*

---

1. Whittaker 1979 = 1993.
2. Cf. Black 1988. There are no synoptic parallels.

son" who will be punished.[3] It follows that some Christians held that Jesus was against *orgē* (or whatever its nearest equivalent was in Aramaic),[4] but in a moderate or latitudinarian fashion (the "without reason" school).[5] Others held that he had been more strict—although the words "with his brother" left a certain amount of room for moral casuistry.

The New Testament says only once in so many words that Jesus experienced *orgē*-anger, against the "hypocritical" Pharisees.[6] That might or might not suggest at first glance that the ability to avoid showing *orgē*-anger in almost all circumstances was part of the canonical version of Jesus' character. He is also of course represented as recommending forgiveness ("seventy-times-seven times"), while the Sermon on the Mount deprecates revenge and violent reactions ("turn the other cheek").[7] But none of these imperatives was specifically about emotions. And Jesus is in fact represented as having been angry on other occasions in the gospel narratives, even though no word from the root of *orgē* is used: he berated the money changers in the Temple,[8] and other hearers at least once later.[9] Even Christian investigators have

3. The key word is εἰκῇ. This is translated "without good cause" in the New English Bible. But the meaning of the word is closer to "at random" than to "without good cause", so this version of the text may condemn less anger than some readers have thought.

4. The nuances of the Aramaic "equivalent" are not clear. The verb used is likely to have the root *rgz*-like the Greek (I thank Professors S. J. D. Cohen and Seth Schwartz for help with this matter).

5. Pagels 1993, 240, seems to sense that the meaning of the *orgē* referred to in Matthew 5:22 is not simply "anger," for she says that Jesus tells his followers not to express "or, it may be, even experience" anger. The emotion in question was normally expressed as well as experienced.

6. Mark 3:5 (he is said to have reacted with *orgē* to the "obstinate stupidity" of his opponents). When Matthew and Luke tell this story (the healing of the man with the withered hand), they make no mention of anger. Mark 1:41 is another possible case, where the correct text may be either *orgistheis* or *splangchtheis* ("emotionally moved").

7. Matthew 18:22; Matthew 5:39 and Luke 6:29.

8. Matthew 21:12–13, Mark 11:15–17, Luke 19:45–46. But nothing explicit is said about his emotional condition.

9. Matthew 23:33–35, at the climax of a long oration: "You snakes, you vipers' brood, how can you escape being condemned to hell? I send you therefore prophets, sages, and teachers; some of them you will kill and crucify, others you will flog in your synagogues and hound from city to city. And so, on you will fall the guilt of all the in-

concluded that "wrath [undefined] is an integral characteristic of the Jesus of the Gospels."[10]

It would be a mistake to approach the New Testament as if its authors possessed a carefully worked out moral philosophy on this subject.[11] In keeping with the Sermon on the Mount, Paul sometimes spoke against orgē-anger and behaviour that resulted from it. "Do not seek revenge," he wrote, and elsewhere, "Have done with all bitterness and thumos and orgē and shouting and cursing."[12] The latter admonition comes from a letter to the Christians of Ephesus which is quite concerned about their internal harmony. A few lines earlier, however, he had written "Be angry (orgizesthe), but do not sin; let the sun not sink on your anger (parorgismos),"[13] where the message is that anger is permissible but should be acted on with restraint and not over a long period. The Letter of James rather similarly instructs the Christian to be "slow to orgē, for orgē does not work the justice of God."[14] On two occasions the New Testament represents instances of human anger in a positive fashion,[15] but in one case it is merely a matter of aganaktēsis, annoyance,[16] and in the other one Paul is quoting from the Old Testament.[17]

The scholar who has perhaps examined the matter most carefully

---

nocent blood spilt on the ground," etc. (New English Bible). The verb ἐμβριμᾶσθαι, when it is applied to Jesus in Matthew 9:30, Mark 1:43 and John 11:33 and 38, presumably means "to be indignant."

10. G. Stählin in Kleinknecht et al. 1968 [1954], 427. He points to some thirteen other passages.

11. As is often implied, e.g., by Vögtle 1993, 1404.

12. Romans 12:17, Ephesians 4:31; and see Colossians 3:8. Ephesians 2:3 deplores orgē ("we were the children of anger"). In Acts 17:16 Paul is described as having been angry himself (parōxuneto, milder than feeling orgē-anger); so too in Acts 15:39. Various angry emotions are deprecated in 1 Corinthians 13:5 (paroxunetai), 2 Corinthians 12:20 (thumoi), Galatians 5:19 (thumoi).

13. Ephesians 4:26, a quotation from Psalms 4:4. Translators often slant such texts (e.g., "If you are angry . . .," G. Stählin in Kleinknecht et al. 1968 [1954], 421, followed by the New English Bible). παροργισμός, which might theoretically mean "aberrant anger," seems to be a Jewish-Christian synonym of orgē.

14. James 1:19–20.

15. G. Stählin in Kleinknecht et al. 1968 [1954], 419.

16. It had been felt by the Corinthian Christians, according to 2 Corinthians 7:11.

17. Romans 10:19: he quotes Moses' intention to arouse anger.

concludes that "the NT assessment of human anger is mainly recusant."[18] But that already seems to be slightly wrong, for *orgē* is not exactly "anger," and even with respect to *orgē* the New Testament contains a measure of obscurity.

And its teaching about anger is further complicated by the fact that the follower of Jesus is not meant to eliminate anger from his or her universe but to turn it over to God, who will do the punishing for him or her. "Give space to the *orgē* [of God]," says Paul, who imagines God promising to do the avenging.[19] The Christian authorities, while telling the faithful to avoid anger, encouraged them to think that God would annihilate their enemies.[20]

Believing Jews who had been educated in Hellenistic philosophy must quite often have had to think about divine anger.[21] Yahweh was as short-tempered as any other ancient Near Eastern god, or as the Homeric gods.[22] Some Jews nevertheless adopted the Greek philosophical opinion about the divine nature: thus Philo of Alexandria wrote an essay entitled *On the Unchangeableness of God*, in which he denied that god was susceptible to any *pathos*, passion, whatsoever, in spite of the fact that Genesis quoted Yahweh as saying, "I will wipe mankind off the face of the earth . . . because I have grown angry [*ethumōthen*] that I made <them>."[23] That left Philo with the baffling problem why a canonical text had so misrepresented the matter, the only intelligible an-

---

18. Black 1988, 5. See also G. Stählin in Kleinknecht et al. 1968 [1954], 420–421.

19. Romans 12:19; cf. James 1:20.

20. Pagels 1988, 241. This of course has been an extremely robust tradition; see, among others, Kerrigan 1996, 136.

21. Cf. Ps.-Aristeas 254 (but according to E. Sjöberg & G. Stählin in Kleinknecht et al. 1968 [1954], 413, this text is isolated until we come to Philo). The Jewish religious tradition was also against human anger, at least in some forms: see, among others, Wibbing 1959, 54, 93.

22. His anger is sometimes represented as malevolent (e.g., Job 16:9–13) and not only as "righteous" (cf. Pagels 1993). On divine anger in the OT, see J. Fichtner in Kleinknecht et al. 1968 [1954], 392–409.

23. *Quod deus sit immutabilis* 51–52, quoting Genesis 6:7. On the tendency of humans to attribute human passions such as *orgai* to God, see also *De sacrificiis Abelis et Caini* 95–96.

swer being that its author was aiming at the terrorization and moral improvement of the foolish.[24]

The Christians inherited the problem. Does this matter to us? They could, after all, have combined a belief in the anger of their god with the belief that humans never ought to be angry[25]—not a particularly illogical position. But in practice, people who deeply disapprove of the angry emotions are often reluctant to attribute them to their god or gods.

The god of the New Testament continues to be irascible, if less insistently so than the god of the Old.[26] Two gospels make John the Baptist refer to the coming *orgē* (i.e., of God), and Paul speaks of it too.[27] The theme is a beloved favourite in the Revelation of John of Patmos.[28]

Some of the early Greek-language apologists of Christianity dealt with this dilemma of divine anger by siding with the intellectual-pagan view of the divine nature.[29] Clement of Rome stated without equivocating that God was angerless *(aorgētos)* towards his whole creation.[30] Others, including Clement of Alexandria, Tertullian and Lactantius, attempted to explain how it made sense that their God sometimes felt anger even though it seemed to detract from his perfection.[31] In gen-

24. *Quod deus* 62, 68. For a still more desperate explanation, see 70–73.

25. In spite of G. Stählin in Kleinknecht et al. 1968 [1954], 419.

26. See C. Ingremeau's edition of Lactantius, *De ira dei*, p. 15; Vögtle 1993, 1404. According to G. Stählin in Kleinknecht et al. 1968 [1954], 423, "Nowhere in the NT is God's wrath portrayed with the colours of psychical or natural passion, as often in the OT," but while it is true that God's anger in the OT is sometimes more sweeping and is less compensated by love or pity, *orgē* in Hellenistic Greek was inevitably a psychic passion.

27. Matthew 3:7; Luke 3:7, 21:23; Romans 1:18, 2:5 and 8, 4:15, 9:22, etc.

28. Revelation 14:19, 15:7, 19:15 are characteristic. The day of judgement was expected to be the *dies irae*.

29. The texts are catalogued by Ingremeau, p. 18 (a more detailed account was given by Pohlenz 1909). Arnobius, too, was a good pagan in this respect: *Adversus nationes* i.18, vii.5. MacMullen 1984, 18–19, greatly oversimplified when he contrasted the supposedly anger-free traditional gods with the irascible god of the Christians.

30. I Clem. 19.3.

31. Clement, *Stromateis* ii.18; Tertullian, *Adversus Marcionem* ii.27.6; Lactantius, *De ira dei* (but he is clear that God is indeed angry). See further Theophilus, *Ad Autolycum* i.3 end; Greg.Naz. *PG* XXXVII.838–840 (lines 371–398); Tert. *De Anima* 16; Ingremeau pp. 17–22.

eral, Christians who read or heard the canonical texts had to suppose
that God could be angry. Augustine, however, tended to follow his classical training (but of course he had some Christian predecessors in
this respect, not to mention his own past as a Manichaean) and to pro-
nounce in favour of God's "impassibility."[32]

Thus the early Christian tradition about the suppression of human anger was somewhat ambiguous. Paul was generally against the angry
emotions but was not an "absolutist," while the message which one received from the Gospels would depend on the branch of the tradition
one happened to hear, and on what one wanted to hear. Jesus himself
was not represented in the Gospels as being consistently without angry
emotions. Yet some Christian moralists were Stoically inclined as far as
the passions were concerned: Clement of Alexandria, for instance, was
an advocate of *apatheia*,[33] and the author of *The Teachings of Silvanus*
(a Nag Hammadi text probably composed in the third century) was
strongly against *orgē*.[34]

A gospel of forgiveness and pity was bound to be tendentially against
extreme forms of anger. And once Paul had in effect categorized *orgē*-
anger as a sin, the Christian tradition automatically included it in its
"vice-catalogues." Not that classifying anger as a "sin" was original with

32. Hallman 1984, esp. 8–10. The case is not, however, as clear as he thinks, for
while Augustine says that *ira* is attributed to God "by an abuse [of the word], or a pe-
culiarity of language" (*Contra Faustum* xxii.18 = *CSEL* xxv.1.607: one ought to speak
of the "vindicta" of God, he says) and that god is angry only metaphorically (*Enarr.
in Psalmos* 105.32 = *CC-SL* xl.1565; see further *Enarr. in Psalmos* 82.12 = *CC-SL*
xxxix.1144: "meminerimus sane iram dei sine ulla affectione turbulenta intellegere:
ira quippe eius dicitur, ratio iusta vindictae; tamquam si lex dicatur irasci, cum
ministri eius secundum eam commoti vindicant," *De doctrina Christiana* iii.17), he occasionally writes as if God were angry (though with an anger different from human
anger): *De civ. dei* ix.5, and other passages quoted by Hallman; see also *Serm.* 302.20.
The extreme of sophistry concerning this matter is reached in *De civ. dei* xxii.2.

33. *Stromateis* ii.13 end, 18, 20; vi.9; vii.11. Compare the emphasis on controlling
ill-temper *(oxucholia)* in Hermas, *Shepherd,* mand. 5 and 6.

34. *Nag Hammadi Codex VII* p. 84, lines 19–25 (p. 278 Pearson). On the date, cf. M.
Peel's discussion in the Pearson edition, p. 274. This is not a Gnostic text (Peel 267–
270) but shows Stoic influence (260–262). The Coptic text uses the Greek loan word
orgē.

the Christians, for the Greeks had often seen anger as a *hamartia,* and the Romans had no difficulty in applying the word *peccare*.[35] But the basis of anger control was now different: a more or less complex philosopher's conclusion began to give way very slowly to a divinely sanctioned commandment—which one could be forgiven for breaking.

This was a great change, but in a sense it was hardly a change at all. For the Christians, the condition of the individual's soul had paramount importance, but as far as emotional control was concerned, that was no innovation, at least not for people of some education—for, as we have seen, some Greeks and Romans had been concerned about their own psychic health, and consequently with the appropriateness of their own emotions, long before Christianity.

Between the 360s and the 430s, no fewer than five ecclesiastics gave the world their critiques of anger.[36] Other Christians, notably Prudentius,[37] wrote about anger too, and some non-Christians did as well, not to mention the essays about imperial anger which we examined in Chapter 10. This appearance of a revived interest in the morality of anger is not, I think, simply a result of the relatively very large quantity of literature that survives from those decades. One must suspect at least that there really was an increase in production. The reason, rather evidently, is that Christian intellectuals, now much more numerous, still needed to lay down the rules of a Christian morality in terms that would be satisfying to persons of education (no matter if in reality the rules were largely pagan ones).

These texts were not in full agreement with each other. Most though not all of their authors assumed the "absolutist" posture, but some of those who did so, specifically Basil of Caesarea and John Chrysostom, also made some space for Christian anger.[38] Neither Nemesius nor Augustine is fully against it. In fact Augustine opens the flood-gates:

35. For the former term and its meanings, see the index; for the latter see, e.g., Hor. *Epist.* i.2.15–16.

36. Chapter 6.

37. *Psychomachia* 109–177, one of seven scenes of conflict between virtues and vices. For some of the mediaeval reception of this passage, see Little 1998, 14–25, with illustrations.

38. Even Gregory of Nazianzus occasionally permits anger: see lines 1 and 362 of his diatribe.

Scripture subjects the mind to God for control and help, and subjects the passions to the mind for their restraint and control [*moderandas atque frenandas*] so that they may be turned to the purposes of justice . . . in our discipline, the question is not *whether* the pious soul is angry [*utrum pius animus irascatur*], but *why . . . To be angry with the sinner with a view to his correction* [*ut corrigatur*], to feel sorrow for the afflicted so that he may be released from suffering, to be afraid for one in danger to prevent his death—<such feelings> I doubt that anyone could sensibly disapprove.[39]

The controversialist then distracts attention from his general statement by attacking the Stoic view of pity, proceeding to claim sophistically that, in any case, the Stoics "admit passions of this kind into the soul of the wise man."[40] But can the angels feel anger? That for Augustine is the serious question. No wonder anger regained such respectability that in *Paradiso* XXVII, where one might have expected a certain celestial calm, Saint Peter rages fierily against the pope.

We can end this chapter with a set of three complementary judgements about these historical developments. First, the notion that anger of various kinds should be reined in or eliminated was reinforced by entirely new religious sanctions. While it was never clear, even when the sect was new, what the penalty would be for various kinds of angry behaviour, the moral rule was now a matter of religious discipline, in the form of exclusion from one's Christian community[41] and fear of eternal damnation.

Second, the ethic of anger control now spread outside the intellectual elite in a novel fashion. It had not always been their exclusive prerogative in past ages: one thinks of the Attic theatre and of the popularity, at certain times, of simplified Epicurean and Stoic philosophy. Stoicism had a message for the slaves as well as for the free. In imperial times Homer continued to be the best known of all Greek authors, being instilled into schoolchildren in every town if not every village. But Christianity, more than any other ideology in antiquity, aimed for the

39. *De civ. dei* ix.5. For Augustine's partial acceptance of the emotions, see Sorabji 2000, 397–399.
40. Ibid. (*CC-SL* xlvii.254, lines 25–26)
41. For a specific rule prescribing this penalty, see above, p. 336.

uneducated, and its agents came with appropriately simple messages, including authoritative divine words (the Sermon on the Mount) and catalogues of vices.[42]

Third, what Christianity delivered as far as anger was concerned was an ambivalent message. Not that it necessarily appears so at first glance: after all, Prudentius made *ira* an unmitigated evil, and some of the fourth-century ecclesiastics were "absolutists." But we have seen that a degree of ambivalence was already present in the New Testament, and by the time Augustine had finished explaining that it was quite acceptable to be indignant with sinners (an easy way of classifying those who have annoyed you)—whom God will eventually punish in any case—very little anti-anger doctrine may seem to have been left.[43] However, it will readily be conceded that in failing to resolve the problem of distinguishing between sinful and acceptable anger, the Christians were reproducing in another form the more sophisticated failures of the philosophers (and anticipating those of modern anger experts).

42. Galatians 5:19–21, etc. See Wibbing 1959.

43. The first Sahidic *Life of Pachomius* emphasizes (fr. 3) how the saint struggled to overcome his anger. When he had done so, "he did not get angry again as men of the flesh do, but if he became angry on occasion, he was angry after the manner of the saints" (trans. Goehring 2000, 26).

CHAPTER 17

Retrospect and Prospect

The first part of this chapter rehearses the conclusions reached in the body of this work; the second draws out some of the moral, legal and scientific implications—for there are indeed implications in all of those dimensions.

We set out with the purpose of discovering why the Greeks and Romans advocated the reining in or the elimination of angry emotions, taking this to be a problem in cultural history and not a mere matter of analysing the texts. The angry emotions are perhaps never the same from one culture to another (and there are differences across time as well as across space). Virtually all populations know such emotions, but they may categorize them in markedly different ways, and presumably feel them in different ways. In this respect the anthropology of recent decades (the names of Michele Rosaldo and Anna Wierzbicka stand out) must condition everything that is written about classical antiquity.

We examined the main Greek and Roman concepts, trying to avoid being misled by the requirements of particular texts (such as the desire to dramatize instances of *orgē*). We considered the world of metaphor as well as the Graeco-Roman habit of comparing or assimilating the angry emotions to fits of madness. We concluded that the principal Greek terms, most notably *orgē* and its cognates, refer—for most, at least, of their classical history—to intense and active anger: Aristotle makes this abundantly clear, and the other evidence concurs. Since much of the classical critique of anger concerns either *orgē* or *thumos* (which, when it refers to anger, is also intense), it is evident that such a critique means something quite different from what it may seem to mean in translation. It is essentially a more moderate critique than scholars have hitherto supposed.

Latin *ira* had to perform more duties than any single Greek word. It was difficult to reason about *ira,* precisely because, while authors and speakers used the term readily for less intense forms of anger (so that it is safer to translate it simply as "anger" than is the case with *orgē* or *thumos*), philosophically inclined Romans not surprisingly took it to be a true synonym of *orgē.* Hence a built-in confusion about its acceptability.

Having defined the subject matter, we turned to some methodological questions about the use of non-philosophical texts and of images in the investigation of ancient attitudes towards the angry emotions. This led to the hypothesis that we may find didactic purposes scattered fairly widely in certain genres of literature.

Our path then led us to put classical Greek anger control in the context of other early Greek attempts to control the emotions, and of the sanctification of the virtues of good sense *(sōphrosunē)* and self-restraint *(enkrateia).*[1] The interest of the archaic and classical Greeks in controlling anger did not arise out of a generalized admiration for emotional control; rather, it had its own particular foundations. It was only in the fourth century B.C. that the Greeks began to employ the concept of the passions or emotions *(pathē);* there had not previously been any way of referring to emotions as a class. In order, therefore, to discover the basis of the archaic and classical critique of the angry emotions, we must indeed look beyond "nothing in excess" to specific reasons.

To conclude our preliminaries, we reviewed the known opinions about anger control expressed in antiquity by philosophers and the philosophically informed. They produced an extensive literature concerning the passions and the strong-anger emotions, beginning with Plato. Plato glorified the figure of a Socrates who was above anger, and he never apparently admits that there are cases of just *orgē.* But his doctrine about *thumos* is different: it has to be "ruled," but it can be no-

---

1. The reader will scarcely need reminding that these are approximate translations.

ble. Unfortunately he did not define the difference between *thumos* and *orgē*. And with respect to the latter, he is perhaps more accepting than the literature of the immediately preceding generations might have led us to expect. Aristotle's views were very different, and it was of course the Peripatetic tradition that presented the most vigorous philosophical defence of some *orgē*-anger, based on the notion of the mean, or rather on the notion of appropriateness: for the mean, with respect to *orgē*, is to be angry with the right people for the right reasons and in the right manner, at the right moment and for the right length of time. The overall effect of Aristotle's account is to subject particular cases of *orgē* to severe tests, but certainly to give it more latitude than had been the case in the writings of Plato or was to be the case in Hellenistic philosophy of other schools. However, Aristotle does not, any more than Plato did, resolve the obscurity about the difference between *orgē* and *thumos;* it was easier to speak well of *thumos*-anger than of *orgē*-anger, but how to distinguish the two?

Hellenistic philosophers sometimes attempted to answer this question, but whatever the validity of their answers, they did not succeed in imposing clarity. Nonetheless they devised some important new approaches to *orgē*- and *thumos*-anger. The Epicureans formulated a distinction between "natural" anger and "empty" or immoderate anger: the wise man will feel one but not the other. But how, once again, to tell the difference? The Stoics decreed initially that all the *pathē* were unnatural and excessive, and propagated (though they did not invent) the doctrine which I have called "absolutism." This apparent rigour of the early Stoics about the passions was gradually eroded or mitigated: we attempted to chart these changes through the works of Chrysippus, Panaetius, Poseidonius, Seneca and Epictetus as well as lesser figures.

Both Epicureans and Stoics continued for long periods—at least four hundred years—to refine their teachings on this subject. Their influence, especially that of the Stoics, spread far beyond those who considered themselves to be adherents of a particular school, the most conspicuous non-Stoic absolutists or near absolutists being Cicero, Plutarch and Galen. A well-educated member of the Graeco-Roman elite, for a long period from Hellenistic to Antonine times, was inevitably acquainted with the principal philosophical theories about anger control. A sort of high point of moral ambition was reached by

Epictetus when he suggested forgoing not only *orgē* but also *chalepotēs,*
a considerably milder angry emotion which can often be translated as
"annoyance."

Why then did the Greeks and Romans find fault with anger? We first
considered the archaic texts, which take us immediately into political
and civic life. In recounting the heroes' wrath, Homer was following
his predecessors, but he told of the wrath of Achilles in such a way as to
imply disapproval of unrelenting anger—which was a message well
adapted to the times, this being the age of Greek state formation.
Norbert Elias, in spite of his errors, taught us the importance in state
formation of the growth of emotional control. The *Iliad* teaches that a
great man's intense and unrelenting anger can do untold harm, a lesson appropriate to the political world in which Homer lived. Solon
translates such a lesson into the language of direct advice, and adapts
it to the conditions of citizen government in early sixth-century
Athens.

Very many non-philosophical texts of the age from Pindar to
Polybius express negative views about the operation of *orgē,* and sometimes other forms of anger, in public affairs—which is not to say that
all such *orgē* was disapproved. They do so, of course, according to
the practices of their various genres as well as according to the vaga-
ries of individual temperament and opinion. But reflective Athenians
without any doubt engaged in some conscious thought about strong
political anger from at least the time of the *Oresteia* (458). It could
be said that citizen thinking about *orgē* (as it appears in drama and
speeches) became more and more critical down to the late years of the
Peloponnesian War. There seem to have been two principal thoughts
underlying this hostility towards anger: it was irrational, and it brought
on *stasis* (it also typified tyrants and foreign potentates). In the same
period a smaller number of intellectuals (represented for us by
Herodotus and perhaps Thucydides) became virtual absolutists, while
another school of thought, led by Socrates, came to reject the traditional approval of revenge.

The fourth-century Athenian citizen was sometimes inclined to see
anger as a dangerous force opposed to reason; but he was by no means
convinced that all *orgē* was a bad thing, and indeed he regarded the
orgē of the *dēmos* against the wrongdoer as being altogether proper.
The Athenians admired magnanimity while also believing that re-

venge, if it was exacted by appropriate means (which would usually be non-violent) and in appropriate amounts, was legitimate: "To put up with insults . . . is regarded," Aristotle said, "as servile." There was no single attitude towards *orgē*-anger, but *orgē* on behalf of one's own individual interests was thought to be discreditable, certainly in a public figure,[2] and it needed to be turned into the correct channels. At the same time, people sometimes saw *orgē* as a virtually external force whose action excused a person's violent behaviour.

Plato indicated the importance of *orgē* in Athenian thinking about violent crime when he discussed, in the *Laws,* his proposed penology of specifically angry murders and assaults. His views on this topic are remarkably lenient. Nonetheless both Plato and Aristotle were in different ways opposed to the operation of strong anger in the political sphere, and there can be little doubt that in this respect their views broadly corresponded to those of their social peers. The two Hellenistic Greeks whose views about political anger we can trace in any detail, Polybius and Philodemus, were even more markedly hostile to it. The threat of political anger, thought to bring with it both irrationality and *stasis,* was thus more or less constantly present throughout the history of classical and Hellenistic Greece.

Controlling anger in the state assumed some importance at Rome too. Never quite such wide importance, since the Romans had less political *stasis* (and more vertical control) than there ever was in classical Athens—though there was a short exceptional period at the end of the Republic. The Roman elite learned to philosophize about anger from the Greeks, of course, and some of the effects may have been quite superficial. Revenge, for example, is periodically subjected to criticism in Roman texts from Lucretius to Juvenal, but the significance of this is very hard to evaluate. Powerful Romans encountered, however, two sets of political problems that gave the question of anger practical importance. One was the matter of provincial governance: the Roman governor could behave like a tyrant if he wanted to—but in so doing he created risks for himself. Then there was personal power at Rome itself: Caesar saw the value of gaining a reputation for being even-tempered and for exercising *clementia,* and he passed this knowledge on to his adoptive son, after which anger became a standard part of imperial

2. Isocr. i.21; cf. Pl. *Rep.* ii.375b–376c.

image making. Seneca too, though he points out in *De ira* many of *ira*'s political and social ill effects, is most concerned with the anger of the emperor and the counter-anger of the courtier—both of which are to be deplored.

Royal anger had been under discussion since Homeric times. A king's or emperor's or governor's irascibility was an obvious source of danger, particularly in an absolute or a near absolute monarchy, and irascibility or even temper was often part of the perceived character of a historical or contemporary ruler. Cruelty, injustice and irrationality are all involved, but especially the first. The countervailing official virtue was above all *clementia*.

Another thing wrong with anger was that it was feminine. Such was the stereotype throughout classical antiquity. Anger was prominent among the passions that women and goddesses could not resist— though occasionally a fictional heroine succeeded in doing so. The critique of anger thus came to be, among other things, an instrument of male domination, and virtually no one is known to have stood up in any way for the possible justice of a woman's rage.

Turning more specifically to anger within the family, we observed how Greek writers gradually came to deplore angry emotions when these were let loose on one's *philoi*, that is, family or close friends. Not all the stages of this development can be traced, but there is some reason to see the last quarter of the fourth century B.C. as a crucial period (Menander's play *Samia* being an important piece of evidence). Considerably later, to judge from what Philodemus and Cicero wrote, the concern about family anger spread so far that it even questioned the anger of fathers towards their children and of husbands towards their wives. All of this concern about anger between relatives can be presumed to have a strong prudential component, but at the same time it reflected a maturing sensibility.

Prudential considerations were also the original basis for the advice that one should avoid showing anger towards one's slaves, advice which we first encounter in the writings of Xenophon and Plato. At the best such anger will make slaves less inclined to work; at the worst it will provoke them to murder. It is a delicate question whether loftier theorizations of restraint towards slaves, such as Seneca for example formulated, are simply prudence in disguise: scholars are likely to judge this matter according to their individual temperament. In my opinion, we should allow some space for moral aspirations: Seneca was probably too wealthy and also too courageous to worry unduly about the prudential aspects of the matter (at least until the case of Pedanius). And when emperors turned their hand to reforming the treatment of slaves, as some of them did in a modest way in the first century, they were thinking of practicalities; but there may also have been a philosophical influence, and this is even more likely to have been true of Antoninus Pius.

Should we conclude that the language of anger control always served those who were in power? Such a judgement would be too simple. It is easy to see that the restraint of anger is often in the long-term interests of those who rule, whether they are kings or slave owners. A whole class might benefit, quite apart from the slave owners, if the *plebs* restrained its ire against the men of property (but the classical discourse of anger control did not very often reach the *plebs*). Anger control, however, was for the most part in the interest of all who benefited from the smooth functioning of the state or the family—and even of those, such as the slaves and some of the subjects of absolute rulers, who were liable to suffer vicious punishments.

The full functioning of the ideology of anger control benefited those who wielded power by helping to keep the social and political machinery in smooth working order, but also by reinforcing the upper order's belief in its own rationality and decency. The men in power are always strengthened by a belief in their own superior rectitude.

So much, in outline, for the political reasons why Greeks and Romans found fault with anger, and for those that grew directly out of the social structures (family, slavery). It is a more speculative matter to explain how and why anger control became an objective as part of the individual's psychic health. We saw how anger came to be diagnosed as a sickness. We saw how the Greeks became much more interested in their own psychic health and began to believe that philosophy could assist such health. Inappropriate anger, or even any anger whatsoever, came to be regarded as a failing. It was classified with the inability to control various other passions *(pathē)*, and hence became part of a much wider argument. The aim was moral improvement and sometimes tranquillity, either partial (the Epicureans) or total (the Stoics). These programmes were commonly represented as aiming at the victory of reason.

This Graeco-Roman concern for the individual's psychic health produced a lengthy discussion of the appropriate therapies, a discussion which turned up a number of methods similar in principle to those of contemporary psychotherapeutic care. The principal difference from the advice that is given now is that the Greeks and Romans put more emphasis on habit and the importance of establishing habitual control over one's angry emotions. They also aimed more often for the total elimination of anger, or rather of *orgē*-anger. The chief reason for this was that an absolute prohibition was thought to be therapeutically more effective.

Christianity, too, generally assumed a negative view of *orgē*-anger. One eventual effect was probably to take an anti-anger message to more people outside the social elite than had previously heard it. But the message was for several reasons more ambivalent than the anger teaching of the most severe classical moralists. One reason was the ambivalence of a crucial verse in the gospel of Matthew; another was the biblical account of divine anger. And seeing the angry emotions as in need of control was after all a tradition fostered and passed on by the *paideia* of the "pagans."

According to Descartes, there was little to learn from what the Greeks and Romans said about the passions: "The defects of the sciences we have from the ancients are nowhere more apparent than in their writings on the passions. This topic . . . does not seem to be one of the more difficult to investigate . . . yet the teachings of the ancients about the passions are so meagre and for the most part so implausible [that he will mostly ignore them]."[3] In recent generations, however, both Aristotle and the Stoics seem to have been thought better guides to the passions than Descartes. With what justification, one might ask?

One thing we can learn from reading ancient authors—and we could admittedly learn it without them, from wide reading or simply from attending to our experience—is how various the angry emotions are. This at once threatens to invalidate a high proportion of the recent psychological literature on the subject. It is not simply that anger may be of long duration. Much of it is a social and interpersonal phe-

3. *The Passions of the Soul* (1649), part I, sect. 1, trans. R. Stoothoff.

nomenon, hence one which is not to be understood without an understanding of how social pressures help to bring it into being and help to limit its action. One therefore hopes to read no more universal pontifications about anger founded on questionnaires administered to well-fed middle-class American or British twenty-year-olds.

It is also high time that scholars ceased to generalize about the angry emotions as if English were the language of all humanity past and present. If this book has advanced the study of Greek and Roman anger in any way, it is due in good part to the realization that classical Greek anger words, especially *orgē*, meant something distinct from "anger." Anthropologists and even historians have now begun to study the emotions in a genuinely cross-cultural way, and this practice ought to be absorbed by everyone else who claims to tell us about the emotions.

Another lesson to learn is simply that anger is a very dangerous substance. In theory most of us know this, but we scarcely ever draw the conclusion that there should be a grave practical or moral imperative against acting on one's anger—a presumption of guilt, so to speak, against any manifestation of anger.[4] That may well be a mistake.

Should we then follow the Stoics and strongly favour anger control (a telegraphic way of referring to the shared view of Stoic philosophers who did not in fact fully agree with each other)?[5] The harm that anger does is all around us in the form of violence, cruelty, folly and petty spite. That is true even in normal countries; as for the United States, 1.8 million of its inhabitants are in prison at the time of writing, reflecting among other things a vast mass of anger, frustration and vindictiveness. No fewer than 3,652 persons are said to be awaiting execution. Domestic violence, meantime, is a plague throughout the world. Since these phenomena do not impinge greatly on the lives of scholars

---

4. Indeed the author of what was at one time the standard American book about anger observed that he had "emphasized" "the positive aspects of anger" (Averill 1982, 335).

5. What follows is not an argument in favour of Stoicism in general, old or new, but merely an argument about rage. "What is disconcerting about the portrait of the Stoic sage is [not that it would be extremely difficult to achieve such a state of detachment but] rather that it is presented to us as a portrait of perfect virtue" (Striker 1991, 67, a point which she develops in the succeeding pages, ultimately rejecting *apatheia*).

or scientists or literary persons, they are easily forgotten in discussions of anger, or relegated to minor roles. Political anger, too, causes endless horror and hardship. Nowadays it often takes the form of rage against members of some other ethnic group: at any given moment there are likely to be half a dozen or more such violent conflicts under way on assorted parts of the earth. And considerable amounts of harm are done in the name of revenge, collective or individual.[6] Would we not then be better off without anger, or at least without *orgē*-anger?

These reasons for being against anger are moral or prudential-moral (strictly speaking, we have not given reasons but simply referred to some possible bases for arguing against anger). There are also purely prudential reasons why we might be against anger, or certain kinds of anger: we might suppose it to be bad for our health or our career, or our condition after death. Even a moderate degree of irascibility—in the sense of being liable to be carried way by anger—appears to raise our risk of suffering a heart attack.

Before trying to answer the question whether we would on balance benefit from doing without anger, we should revert to and make use of a distinction made in Chapter 1, the distinction between angry actions and speech on the one hand, and angry feelings on the other. A little more elaborately, we can distinguish between feeling anger, expressing it within socially accepted limits, and being carried away by it (rough-and-ready categories). It is one thing to be angry with your employer, another to let him know of your anger, and still another to insult, sue or assault him.

Four kinds of reasons are advanced for opposing the Stoic position and allowing the desirability or the moral legitimacy of at least some anger. (They are not, be it noted, mutually exclusive). First, it is commonly said that without the emotions life would lose its savour, its zest, its humanity. If we gave up anger, would we not lose exuberance too? What would life be without love or pity? Too cold and too boring to bear perhaps, for most people. But that fact does not make it wise or right or desirable to feel or display all emotions whatsoever, including

6. In the United States, views about revenge seem to have sunk to a level appropriate to a neolithic village, but one wonders how much violent revenge there is to match the Hollywood fantasies. After antiquity, revenge began to come under attack again in the eighteenth century.

Schadenfreude, vindictiveness, anger. The category "emotions" is analyti-
cally indispensable, but those who have recently found fault with it[7]
have some good arguments on their side. Emotions are a little like
plants—some emotions are essential to the good life, some plants supply essential nutrients, and in both cases some members of the class
are deleterious.

We have come across a matter of very great importance for the
proper evaluation of anger. A good life does not by any means require
us to feel emotions of all kinds. We are not faced with a pure dilemma
about the emotions, we do *not* have to choose between "those who cry
up emotion and those who cry it down."[8] Do we not admire a person
who is free of envy or of spitefulness? It is desirable that we think about
the angry emotions on their merits and demerits, not simply as part of
the category "emotions" (or *pathē* or *perturbationes*). The current study
of the emotions, above all of anger, suffers in very many cases from a
fatal flaw: the reasoning is all about whether *emotions as a class* are, for
instance, "functional," and anger is simply treated as part of the class.[9]
Some may be functional, others not (or only on certain conditions).

Perhaps the ancients themselves eventually came to the conclusion
that there was some risk in grouping all emotions together. From the
time of Xenocrates and Aristotle, philosophers wrote about the passions, but they mostly ceased to do so with Poseidonius and Cicero,
whereas there continued to be specific works about anger. Did they begin to appreciate that it was hard to generalize about desire, anger,
fear, boldness, envy, joy, affectionate love, hatred, longing, jealousy
and pity? (I repeat Aristotle's list of the principal *pathē.*) Galen's *On the
Diagnosis and Care of the Passions of the Soul* is the apparent exception,
but even though he says his essay is about "*thumos, orgē,* fear, grief, envy
and excessive desire,"[10] *orgē* predominates over all the other passions
discussed, and the title is misleading.

It is at all events not crystal clear—or not yet—that to lead a happy

7. Such as Griffiths 1997.

8. As claimed by S. Blackburn, *TLS,* 29 October 1999, p. 4. On this point he is representative. Sorabji 2000 falls into the same trap.

9. Gross & Levenson 1997 and Keltner & Gross 1999 can stand for many others
here.

10. *De propriorum animi cuiuslibet affectuum* 3.1.

human life, in an Aristotelian sense or an everyday sense, one needs to express anger from time to time. For Achilles, the vigorous anger of *cholos* was sweeter than honey, and most people, most males anyway, have some immediate understanding of what he meant. But on the whole we should not attempt to live like Mycenaean princes.

A modern topos holds that the man of genius is also a man of spleen (I encountered this notion most recently in Shirley Hazzard's memoir of Graham Greene). Is there not something grand about anger? Plutarch knew of the argument that *thumos*-anger was a mark of *megalourgia*,[11] greatness in action—in other words, a mark of a superior person. Only mere mortals need keep their temper. Here too there is something to learn from antiquity, for while two great men were famous for their rage, Achilles and Alexander, the tradition criticized both of them—ambivalently, it is true—and genius was not normally held to be irascible. It was Romanticism, presumably, that created this particular excuse for rage.

A second kind of argument for allowing anger moral legitimacy is that there is really no such thing as anger control, that anger is not in our power, and consequently that it is futile to try to eliminate it or even reduce it.[12] Anger is "not in general voluntary," so a philosopher has written.[13] That seems obviously true, at first glance. We sometimes pretend to be angry, but "real," spontaneous anger, it may be said, is anger that wells up within us whether we like it or not.

This line of argument cannot be sustained. It is rather like arguing that since historians, even the best of them, inevitably make mistakes, they should not strive to avoid making them or be held to account when they do fall into error. More precisely: though it is often difficult for us to understand the aetiology of our own anger, and it is sometimes a real struggle to restrain its expression, everyone knows that, with proper preparation, some self-control is possible. And although society makes allowances for anger, it does not generally forgive violent acts committed in anger unless very grave provocation is present; in other words, it assumes that the subject has *some* capacity for controlling his anger.[14]

11. *De cohibenda ira* 8 (*Mor.* 456f).
12. Cf. Averill 1982, 339.
13. Adams 1985, 3.
14. Of course it could be argued that this is only a pretence: angry murderers

As many ancient writers realized very well, we choose to some extent whether to be *habitually* angry or not: we get into the habit of becoming angry or avoiding anger, and the choice has an element of freedom about it. And even if we cannot prevent ourselves from feeling angry, we can at least learn—as indeed most people do learn—to avoid being carried away by anger and acting on it in harmful ways. Greeks often supposed—naively, according to some—that one could even control, on certain conditions (see Chapter 15), the intense ready-for-action anger that was *orgē*.

A third type of argument against encouraging anger control is that anger is often an indifferent, not in itself a matter for moral censure of any kind. What business was it of Chrysippus' or Galen's if someone bit a key in anger? Is there anything wrong with getting uselessly annoyed when, for example, you try to telephone someone and encounter a tedious maze of recorded messages?

"People here [in Dili, East Timor] have gotten used to the scene: a mob of unemployed young men shoving, shouting and weeping in anger outside the headquarters of the United Nations."[15] And why not? Their anger may not do any good, but it is not clear that we could possibly be right to criticize them. And suppose that the young men of Dili maintained their composure while feeling intensely angry: it would be even more difficult to criticize them for being angry (in that case we might criticize them for not voicing their complaints).

Clearly some anger is harmless. If it is of moderate strength, or if it is expressed in reasonable terms or not at all, if its target is an inanimate object or a person with sufficient understanding to absorb the attack, there need be no deleterious result. It is universally agreed, however, that anger is habit forming, so that even "victimless" anger, even biting a key, may eventually affect your relations with other humans.

A final kind of argument—the most formidable kind—for not following the Stoics is that some or even most anger serves vital purposes, social or personal or both. In antiquity, as we have seen, some maintained that rage could have positive effects. Aristotle and others thought that the individual needed *orgē*-anger in order to avoid the

---

would have to be punished for other reasons even if we held that their anger was entirely involuntary. For a recent philosophical discussion of the question whether we are responsible for our emotions, see Oakley 1992, 122–159.

15. *New York Times,* 22 April 2000, p. A1.

shame of being slighted; the fourth-century B.C. Athenians thought they needed it in order to punish wrongdoers; others apparently thought that it helped one to be courageous. These are not negligible arguments, but none of this is likely to be advanced in so many words by a modern author.

The vital purposes of anger as they are propounded in our times may be categorized as follows:

(1) It can be argued that displaying anger is cathartic. However, the evidence now seems to say that cathartic displays of anger do not cure irascibility, and as for the practical utility of discharging in the direction of underlings the anger which one may secretly desire to vent on those in power, that deserves the adjective which Seneca applied to all anger aimed at inferiors, namely *sordidum*, squalid.[16]

(2) A contemporary favourite is to suppose that anger, or some anger at least, is adaptive.[17] There exists a whole field known as "evolutionary psychology." It can be maintained not only that primitive man needed anger to survive in the wild, but that modern persons need it in order to survive in the jungle of human competition and relationships. In its most sophisticated form (and it often appears in unsophisticated forms), this is not an absurd argument: one of its proponents, calling anger "an agitated, irrational, unpredictable state of aggressive arousal,"[18] suggests that anger is effective because it convinces its target that the costs of "defecting" from his or her relationship with the angry person may be high, and potentially high just because the latter is in an unpredictably aggressive state. But it could equally well be argued that what is adaptive, at least as far as anger is concerned, is self-control. For anger, or at any rate vigorous *orgē*-anger, if it is frequently displayed, eventually puts any relationship at risk. Cooperating with evolution is in any case a ridiculous basis for behavioural decisions: evolution—to be distinguished from social change—does not distribute rewards, still less does it provide a foundation for deciding what is right or just.

(3) Similar but not identical is the type of argument which maintains that anger is functional. Once again we need to be wary of the

16. *De ira* ii.34.1.
17. See above, p. 46, and Oatley & Jenkins 1996.
18. Nesse 1990, 277.

category of emotion: "man cannot perform efficiently in the absence of a fairly high degree of reasonably persistent emotional activation," so it has been declared.[19] Does that mean that we need, more specifically, the angry emotions?

Anger may be needed in order to renegotiate or reshape personal relationships,[20] between woman and man or more generally between family members. It may be needed for similar purposes in the workplace or in almost any institutional framework.[21] Anger may be necessary for self-respect.[22] We saw that there is a debate under way as to whether anger generally helps women to obtain their rights. In theory we might calculate the rewards and risks of feeling different levels of anger or of displaying them. Some healthy verbal confrontations help to consolidate relationships, but most people in complex societies seem to sense without calculation that overtly displayed anger soon starts to backfire. You can profitably rage at your spouse or your parent or your subordinates, but the point of negative return is soon reached, and if you are accustomed to speak in anger you may not recognize that point.

Perhaps simulated anger may help us. Even Seneca allows that there is some need of simulated *iracundia* in both oratory and life.[23] The real trouble here is that simulated anger has to remain a well-kept secret: if the Roman orator's hearers had all been brought up to think that a lot of anger was simulated, no amount of rhetorical rage would have impressed them.

(4) Then there is "righteous indignation," and morally justified anger more generally. It has been well said that

the desire to show up wrongdoers for what they are (as well as having the courage to do so) and the characteristic events associated with the expression of that desire . . . can be attractive features of anger experi-

19. Geertz 1973, 80.

20. See above, p. 45.

21. To put it in psychospeak, functional explanations of emotions argue that they "prioritis[e] and organis[e] ongoing behaviors in ways that optimise the individual's adjustment to the demands of the physical and social environment" (Keltner & Gross 1999, 468).

22. Cf. Burnyeat 1996, 14.

23. *De ira* ii.14.1, 17.1.

enced and expressed in accordance with the [Aristotelian] mean. This attractiveness is part of the aesthetics of character. Unfortunately, because anger as outrage and anger as a loss of self-control share so many features with righteous indignation, . . . they have sucked out a share of the ethical goodness of righteous indignation for themselves.[24]

Very little would ever have been reformed in any sphere of life if there had not been some intervention of anger. Anger, it has been boldly said, "is an important part of liberation from oppression—whether psychological, economic, or political."[25] That hardly needs demonstration. And then there is the matter of extreme personal maltreatment and humiliation: some provocations are outrageous enough to make many of us think that not feeling anger, or restraining it, would be more culpable than showing it.

One trouble is that the anger of the oppressed usually wins them no liberation at all, or wins a small advantage at a high cost. And morally speaking, righteous indignation may not be righteous at all: one person's righteous indignation is notoriously another person's entirely misguided rage. Thousands of humans believe that they feel righteous indignation against abortion rights, but to me they seem at best deluded. I am righteously indignant, so it seems to me, with those who defend the possession of firearms by private individuals; in the United States, such indignation is widely regarded as bizarre. Then there is the matter of degree: no doubt the emperor Constantine was quite right to be angry with the venal officials in his government, but whether the horrifying violence of his response was either decent or effective is another matter.[26]

So how can we tell whether or when we should be angry? One clue may come from the Greeks and their ways of distinguishing the angry emotions (this does not mean forgetting the imperfections of Greek terminology). David Hume saw that there was anger and anger, and "where these angry passions rise up to cruelty, they form the most de-

---

24. Horder 1992, 196–197.

25. Stocker 1996, 286. Cf. Jenkins, Oatley & Stein 1998, 240: "In the West anger is seen as sometimes necessary to protect one's rights, and to maintain a respect for self" (but controlling one's anger can also enhance self-respect).

26. Cf. MacMullen 1986a, 157 = 1990, 212.

tested of all vices."[27] Two scholars in our age who have reflected at length about anger remark that there are plenty of "causes for legitimate annoyance" in the contemporary world.[28] *Annoyance:* that is their well-chosen term. We ought—in my view—to distinguish more between angry emotions, such as annoyance, that do little harm and may be allowed in reasonable quantities on appropriate occasions (subject, in other words, to the Aristotelian rules), and more intense anger, rage in fact. And why not declare rage a general enemy, and make it in Plutarchean language the most hated and despised of the passions?

First, because it has to be admitted that there are some personal outrages—just a very few, things that never happen to most of us—which it would indeed be servile to react to in any other way than with rage.[29] Second, we need rage as members of the community, not for the punishment of wrongdoers—for rage is the enemy of rational penology—but for political change. Now it may be that what we need is *hatred* of injustice and reaction, rather than rage against them. But interests wider than those of the individual may justify anger, since anger can sustain a cause. Human nature being what it is, some political anger will always do harm: the art of civilized government, and civilized international government, consists in creating and maintaining the institutions which will limit the harmful actions of anger (terrorists, ethnic cleansing) without taking away people's opportunities of expressing anger over communal causes.

What modern psychotherapy aims for is usually, as was remarked earlier, not the elimination of anger but its reduction or "management." But that is a largely impractical objective for a number of obvious reasons: most of the people who need psychotherapy never receive

27. Earlier in the same passage (*A Treatise of Human Nature,* part III, book III, sect. iii) he wrote: "We are not . . . to imagine that *all the angry passions* [my italics] are vicious, though they are disagreeable. There is a certain indulgence due to human nature in this respect. Anger and hatred are passions inherent in our very frame and constitution. The want of them, on some occasions, may even be a proof of weakness and imbecility."

28. Stearns & Stearns 1986, 235.

29. Which is not of course an exculpation of violence; indeed Horder 1992 is convincing when he argues that in homicide cases the excuse of provocation should be abolished.

it, and anger is widely perceived as a positive force or, at the least, something which it is dangerous to bottle up. How pleasant it would be if we could eliminate these latter notions. If we tried to follow the Stoics in this respect, we would not eliminate all anger, but we might conceivably, in the end, diminish the amount of harmful rage.

BIBLIOGRAPHY

INDEX

Bibliography

Commentaries are listed separately.

Adam, T. 1970. *Clementia principis: Der Einfluss hellenistischer Fürstenspiegel auf den Versuch einer rechtlichen Fundierung des Prinzipats durch Seneca.* Stuttgart.

Adams, R. M. 1985. "Involuntary Sins." *Philosophical Review* xciv, 3–31.

Adkins, A. W. H. 1969. "Threatening, Abusing and Feeling Angry in the Homeric Poems." *Journal of Hellenic Studies* lxxxix, 7–21.

———. 1982. "Values, Goals and Emotions in the Iliad." *Classical Philology* lxxvii, 292–326.

Alexiou, E. 1999. "Die Darstellung der ὀργή in Plutarchs Bioi." *Philologus* cxliii, 101–113.

Allen, D. S. 2000. *The World of Prometheus: The Politics of Punishing in Democratic Athens.* Princeton.

Alles, G. D. 1990. "Wrath and Persuasion: The *Iliad* and Its Contexts." *Journal of Religion* lxx, 167–188.

Althoff, G. 1998. "*Ira regis:* Prolegomena to a History of Royal Anger." In Rosenwein (ed.) 1998, 59–74.

Anderson, W. S. 1962. "The Programs of Juvenal's Later Books." *Classical Philology* lvii, 145–160. Repr. in *Essays on Roman Satire* (Princeton, 1982).

———. 1964. *Anger in Juvenal and Seneca.* University of California Publications in Classical Philology XIX, no. 3. Berkeley & Los Angeles.

Annas, J. 1981. *An Introduction to the* Republic *of Plato.* Oxford.

———. 1989. "Epicurean Emotions." *Greek, Roman, and Byzantine Studies* xxx, 145–164.

———. 1992. *Hellenistic Philosophy of Mind.* Berkeley & Los Angeles.

———. 1993. *The Morality of Happiness*. Oxford.

Appel, M. A., K. A. Holroyd & L. Gorkin. 1983. "Anger and the Etiology and Progression of Physical Illness." In Temoshok et al. (eds.) 1983, 73–87.

Armon-Jones, C. 1986. "The Thesis of Constructionism." In Harré 1986, 32–56.

Armstrong, D. 1998. Rev. of Braund & Gill (eds.) 1997. *Bryn Mawr Classical Review;* see http://ccat.sas.upenn.edu/bmcr/1998/98.5.10.html.

Arnaoutoglou, I. 1995. "Marital Disputes in Greco-Roman Egypt." *Journal of Juristic Papyrology* xxv, 11–28.

Arnott, W. G. 1998. "First Notes on Menander's Samia." *Zeitschrift für Papyrologie und Epigraphik* cxxi, 35–44.

Arrighetti, G. 1955. "Ieronimo di Rodi." *Studi classici e orientali* iii, 111–128.

Asmis, E. 1990. "Philodemus' Epicureanism." *ANRW* II, 36, 4, 2369–2406.

Aubenque, P. 1957. "Sur la définition aristotélicienne de la colère." *Revue philosophique de France et de l'étranger* cxlvii, 300–317.

Audollent, A. 1904. *Defixionum Tabellae*. Paris.

Austin, N. 1966. "The Function of Digressions in the Iliad." *Greek, Roman, and Byzantine Studies* vii, 295–312.

Averill, J. R. 1982. *Anger and Aggression: An Essay on Emotion*. New York.

———. 1990. "Emotions in Relation to Systems of Behavior." In N. L. Stein, B. Leventhal & T. Trabasso (eds.), *Psychological and Biological Approaches to Emotion*. Hillsdale, N.J., 385–404.

———. 1994. Rev. of K. Oatley, *Best Laid Schemes* (1992). *Cognition and Emotion* viii, 73–91.

Bäumer, Ä. 1982. *Die Bestie Mensch*. Frankfurt am Main.

Barbu, Z. 1960. *Problems of Historical Psychology*. New York.

Barden Dowling, M. Forthcoming. *Begging Pardon: Clemency and Cruelty in the Roman World*. Ann Arbor.

Barigazzi, A. 1965. *La formazione spirituale di Menandro*. Turin.

Barlow, C. T. 1937. "A Sixth-Century Epitome of Seneca, *De ira*." *Transactions of the American Philological Association* lxviii, 26–42.

Barnes, J. 1979. *The Presocratic Philosophers*, 2 vols. London.

———. 1997. *Logic and the Imperial Stoa*. Leiden.

Barnes, J., M. Schofield & R. Sorabji (eds.). 1979. *Articles on Aristotle*, 4 vols. London.

Barraclough, J. 1994. *Cancer and Emotion*. New York.

Barton, C. 1992. *The Sorrows of the Ancient Romans: The Gladiator and the Monster*. Princeton.

Becchi, F. 1990. "La nozione di *orge* e di *aorgesia* in Aristotele e Plutarco." *Prometheus* xvi, 65–87.

Becker, L. C. 1998. *A New Stoicism*. Princeton.

Berneker, E. (ed.). 1968. *Zur griechischen Rechtsgeschichte.* Darmstadt.

Berry, J. W., et al. 1992. *Cross-Cultural Psychology: Research and Applications.* Cambridge.

Bickel, E. 1915. *Diatribe in Senecae philosophi fragmentis.* Leipzig.

Bieber, M. 1930. "Maske." In *RE* XIV, cols. 2070–2120.

Bilde, P., et al. 1997. *Conventional Values of the Hellenistic Greeks.* Aarhus.

Black, D. A. 1988. "Jesus on Anger: The Text of Matthew 5:22a Revisited." *Novum Testamentum* xxx, 1–8.

Black-Michaud, J. 1975. *Cohesive Force: Feud in the Mediterranean and the Middle East.* Oxford.

Blank, D. 1993. "The Arousal of Emotion in Plato's Dialogues." *Classical Quarterly* xliii, 428–439.

Bloch, M. 1961. *Feudal Society,* 2 vols., trans. L. A. Manyon. Chicago. (Original ed.: *La société féodale: La formation des liens de dépendance,* Paris, 1939.)

Bloch, O. 1986. "Un imbroglio philologique: Les fragments d'Aristote sur la colère" In *Energeia: Études aristotéliciennes . . . A. Jannone.* Paris. 135–144.

Blundell, M. 1989. *Helping Friends and Harming Enemies: A Study in Sophocles and Greek Ethics.* Cambridge.

Bodei, R. 1991. *Geometria delle passioni: paura, speranza, felicità. Filosofia e uso politico.* Milan.

Bodéüs, R. 1993. *The Political Dimensions of Aristotle's* Ethics, trans. J. E. Garrett. Albany, N.Y. (Original ed.: *La philosophie et la cité,* Liège, 1982.)

Bonhöffer, A. 1894. *Die Ethik des Stoikers Epiktet.* Stuttgart.

Bonime, W. 1976. "Anger as a Basis for a Sense of Self." *Journal of the American Academy of Psychoanalysis* iv, 7–12.

Bonnefond, M. 1987. "Transferts de fonctions et mutation idéologique: Le Capitole et le Forum d'Auguste." In *L'Urbs: Espace urbain et histoire.* Rome. 251–278.

Born, L. K. 1934. "The Perfect Prince according to the Latin Panegyrists." *American Journal of Philology* lv, 20–35.

Bornkamm, G. 1935. "Die Offenbarung des Zornes Gottes (Röm 1–3)." *Zeitschrift für neutestamentlichen Wissenschaft* xxxiv, 239–262. Repr. in *Das Ende des Gesetzes: Paulusstudien* (Munich, 1952), 9–33.

Borucki, J. 1926. *Seneca philosophus quam habet auctoritatem in aliorum scriptorum locis afferendis.* Münster.

Bostock, D. 1986. *Plato's* Phaedo. Oxford.

Boucher, J. D. 1979. "Culture and Emotion." In A. J. Marsella, R. Tharp & T. Ciborowski (eds.), *Perspectives on Cross-Cultural Psychology.* New York. 159–178.

Bowersock, G. W. 1965. *Augustus and the Greek World.* Oxford.

————. 1969. *Greek Sophists in the Roman Empire*. Oxford.

Boyancé, P. 1972. *Le culte des Muses chez les philosophes grecs*, 2nd ed. Paris.

Bradley, K. R. 1986. "Seneca and Slavery." *Classica et Mediaevalia* xxxvii, 161–172.

————. 1994. *Slavery and Society at Rome*. Cambridge.

Braund, S. H. 1988. *Beyond Anger: A Study of Juvenal's Third Book of Satires*. Cambridge.

Braund, S. M. 1997. "A Passion Unconsoled? Grief and Anger in Juvenal 'Satire' 13." In Braund & Gill 1997, 68–88.

Braund, S. M., & C. Gill (eds.). 1997. *The Passions in Roman Thought and Practice*. Cambridge.

Braund, S. M., & G. W. Most (eds.). Forthcoming. *Aspects of Anger.*

Bremer, J. 1991. "Exit Electra." *Gymnasium* xcviii, 325–342.

Brennan, T. 1998. "The Old Stoic Theory of Emotions." In Sihvola & Engberg-Pederson 1998, 21–70.

Breuer, J., & S. Freud. 1895. *Studien über Hysterie*. Leipzig & Vienna. See Freud 1955 [1895].

Briggs, J. L. 1970. *Never in Anger: Portrait of an Eskimo Family*. Cambridge, Mass.

Brown, P. 1992. *Power and Persuasion in Late Antiquity: Towards a Christian Empire*. Madison, Wis.

Bruneau, P. 1970. *Recherches sur les cultes de Délos à l'époque hellénistique et à l'époque impériale*. Paris.

Brunschwig, J., & M. Nussbaum (eds.). 1993. *Passions and Perceptions*. Cambridge.

Brunt, P. A. 1974. "Marcus Aurelius in His *Meditations*." *Journal of Roman Studies* lxiv, 1–20.

Bryant, J. M. 1996. *Moral Codes and Social Structure in Ancient Greece*. Albany, N.Y.

Buck, R. 1988. *Human Motivation and Emotion*, 2nd ed. New York.

Buckland, W. W. 1908. *The Roman Law of Slavery*. Cambridge.

Buffière, F. 1956. *Les mythes d'Homère et la pensée grecque*. Paris.

Burack, C. 1994. *The Problem of the Passions: Feminism, Psychoanalysis, and Social Theory*. New York.

Burckhardt, J. 1898. *Griechische Kulturgeschichte* II. Basel & Stuttgart.

Burger, R. 1991. "Ethical Reflections and Righteous Indignation: *Nemesis* in the *Nicomachean Ethics*." In J. P. Anton & A. Preus (eds.), *Essays in Ancient Greek Philosophy* IV: *Aristotle's Ethics*. Albany, N.Y. 127–139.

Burkert, W. 1955. *Zum altgriechischen Mitleidsbegriff*. Erlangen.

————. 1971. "Zur geistesgeschichtlichen Einordnung einiger Pseudo-pythagorica." *Entretiens de la Fondation Hardt* xviii, 23–55.

————. 1987. "The Making of Homer in the Sixth Century B.C.: Rhapsodes versus Stesichorus." In *Papers on the Amasis Painter and His World*. Malibu. 43–62.

Burnett, A. P. 1998. *Revenge in Attic and Later Tragedy.* Berkeley & Los Angeles.

Burnyeat, M. 1996. "Gnev i mest" [Russ.], *Hyperboreus* ii, 2, 3–20.

Burton, R. 1652. *The Anatomy of Melancholy,* 6th ed. London; repr. New York, 1864.

Buxton, R. (ed.). 1999. *From Myth to Reason: Studies in the Development of Greek Thought.* Oxford.

Bynum, C. W. 1997. "Wonder." *American Historical Review* cii, 1–26.

Cacioppo, J. T., et al. 1993. "The Psychophysiology of Emotion." In Lewis & Haviland 1993, 119–142.

Cairns, D. L. 1993. Aidōs: *The Psychology and Ethics of Honour and Shame in Ancient Greek Literature.* Oxford.

————. 1994. Rev. of N. R. E. Fisher, Hybris: *A Study in the Values of Honour and Shame in Ancient Greece* (1992). *Classical Review* xliv, 76–79.

————. Forthcoming. "Anger and Honour in Homer's *Iliad.*" In Braund & Most, forthcoming.

Cairns, F. 1989. *Virgil's Augustan Epic.* Cambridge.

Calame, C. 1996. "Sappho's Group: An Initiation into Womanhood." In E. Greene (ed.), *Reading Sappho: Contemporary Approaches.* Berkeley & Los Angeles. 113–124.

————. 1999. *The Poetics of Eros in Ancient Greece,* trans. J. Lloyd. Princeton. (Original ed.: *I greci e l'eros,* Rome & Bari, 1992.)

Camerer, R. 1936. *Zorn und Groll in der sophokleischen Tragödie.* Leipzig.

Cameron, A. 1970. *Claudian: Poetry and Propaganda at the Court of Honorius.* Oxford.

————. 1995. *Callimachus and His Critics.* Princeton.

Cameron, A., & J. Long. 1993. *Barbarians and Politics at the Court of Arcadius.* Berkeley & Los Angeles.

Cantarella, E. 1992. *Bisexuality in the Ancient World,* trans. C. Ó Cuilleanáin. New Haven & London. (Original ed.: *Secondo natura: La bisessualità nel mondo antico,* Rome, 1988.)

Carey, C. 1990. "Aischylos, *Eumenides* 858–866." *Illinois Classical Studies* xv, 239–250.

Carter, L. B. 1986. *The Quiet Athenian.* Oxford.

Casagrande, C., & S. Vecchio. 2000. *I sette vizi capitali: Storia dei peccati nel Medioevo.* Turin.

Cavallini, E. 1984–85. "Sapph. fr. 158V." *Museum Criticum* xix–xx, 7–9.

Chadwick, J. 1996. *Lexicographica Graeca.* Oxford.

Christ, M. R. 1989. "The Authenticity of Thucydides 3.84." *Transactions of the American Philological Association* cxix, 137–148.

Claessen, H. J. M., & J. G. Oosten (eds.). 1996. *Ideology and the Formation of Early States.* Leiden.

Clark, H. H. 1996. "Communities, Commonalities and Communication." In J. J. Gumperz & S. C. Levinson (eds.), *Rethinking Linguistic Relativity.* Cambridge. 324–355.

Clark, M. S. (ed.). 1992. *Emotion.* Newbury Park, Calif. (*Review of Personality and Social Psychology* 13).

Clark, P. 1998. "Women, Slaves, and the Hierarchies of Domestic Violence: The Family of St. Augustine." In S. R. Joshel & S. Murnaghan (eds.), *Women and Slaves in Greco-Roman Culture: Differential Equations.* London & New York. 109–129.

Claus, D. B. 1981. *Toward the Soul.* New Haven & London.

Cohen, D. 1991. *Law, Sexuality and Society.* Cambridge.

———. 1995. *Law, Violence and Community in Classical Athens.* Cambridge.

Cohen, D., & R. Saller. 1994. "Foucault on Sexuality in Greco-Roman Antiquity." In J. Goldstein (ed.), *Foucault and the Writing of History.* Oxford. 31–59.

Cohen, J. L., & A. Arato. 1992. *Civil Society and Political Theory.* Cambridge, Mass.

Cohn-Haft, L. 1995. "Divorce in Classical Athens." *Journal of Hellenic Studies* cxv, 1–14.

Collingwood, R. G. 1946. *The Idea of History.* Oxford.

Connor, W. R. 1984. *Thucydides.* Princeton.

Considine, P. 1966. "Some Homeric Terms for Anger." *Acta Classica* ix, 15–25.

———. 1969. "The Theme of Divine Wrath in Ancient East Mediterranean Literature." *Studi micenei ed egeo-anatolici* viii, 85–159.

———. 1985. "The Indo-European Origin of μῆνις—Wrath." *Transactions of the Philological Society,* 144–170.

———. 1986. "The Etymology of μῆνις." In *Studies in Honour of T. B. L. Webster* I. Bristol. 53–64.

Cooper, J.M. 1993. "Rhetoric, Dialectic, and the Passions." In C. C. W. Taylor (ed.), *Oxford Studies in Ancient Philosophy* xi, 175–198.

———. 1996. "An Aristotelian Theory of the Emotions." In A. O. Rorty (ed.), *Essays on Aristotle's Rhetoric.* Berkeley & Los Angeles. 238–257. Repr. in Cooper 1999, 406–423.

———. 1998. "Posidonius on Emotions." In Sihvola & Engberg-Pedersen 1998, 71–111. Repr. in Cooper 1999, 449–484.

———. 1999. *Reason and Emotion: Essays on Ancient Moral Psychology and Ethical Theory*. Princeton.

Cooper, J. M., & J. F. Procopé (eds.). 1995. *Seneca: Moral and Political Essays*. Cambridge.

Corsini, E. (ed.). 1986–88. *Il polis e il suo teatro*, 2 vols. Turin.

Cupaiuolo, G. 1975. *Introduzione al* De ira *di Seneca*. Naples.

Curry, R. R., & T. L. Allison. 1996. *States of Rage: Emotional Eruption, Violence and Social Change*. New York.

Dale, A. M. 1969. *Collected Papers*. Cambridge.

Darwin, C. 1872. *Expression of the Emotions in Man and Animals*. London.

Dauge, Y. A. 1981. *Le barbare: Recherches sur la conception romaine de la barbarie*. Brussels.

Davidson, J. 1997. *Courtesans and Fish Cakes: The Consuming Passions of Classical Athens*. London.

Deffenbacher, J. L. 1994. "Anger Reduction: Issues, Assessment, and Intervention Strategies." In Siegman & Smith 1994, 239–269.

Deffenbacher, J. L., P. M. Demm & A. D. Brandon. 1986. "High General Anger: Correlates and Treatment." *Behavior Research and Therapy* xxiv, 481–489.

Delatte, L. 1942. *Les traités de la royauté d'Ecphante, Diotogène et Sthénidas*. Liège & Paris.

Demont, P. 1990. *La cité grecque archaïque et classique et l'idéal de tranquillité*. Paris.

De Romilly, J. 1971. "La vengeance comme explication historique dans l'oeuvre d'Hérodote." *Revue des Études Anciennes* lxxxiv, 314–337.

———. 1979. *La douceur dans la pensée grecque*. Paris.

———. 1984. *"Patience, mon coeur": L'essor de la psychologie dans la littérature grecque classique*. Paris.

De Sensi Sestito, G. 1997. "La τιμωρία del 'tyrannos' e del 'basileus': Il caso di Dioniso I e di Alessandro Magno." In M. Sordi (ed.), *Amnistia, perdono e vendetta nel mondo antico*. Milan. 167–185.

Diamond, S. A. 1996. *Anger, Madness, and the Daimonic: The Psychological Genesis of Violence, Evil, and Creativity*. Albany, N.Y.

DiGiuseppe, R. 1995. "Developing the Therapeutic Alliance with Angry Clients." In Kassinove (ed.) 1995, 131–149.

Dihle, A. 1956. *Studien zur griechischen Biographie*. Göttingen.

Diller, H. 1966. "θυμὸς δὲ κρείσσων τῶν ἐμῶν βουλευμάτων." *Hermes* xciv, 267–275. Repr. in his *Kleine Schriften* (Munich, 1971), 359–369.

Dillon, J. 1977. *The Middle Platonists, 80 B.C. to A.D. 220*. Ithaca, N.Y.

———. 1983. "*Metriopatheia* and *apatheia*: Some Reflections on a Controversy in Late Greek Ethics." In J. P. Anton & A. Preus (eds.), *Essays in Ancient Greek Philosophy* II. Albany, N.Y. 508–517.

Dion, J. 1993. *Les passions dans l'oeuvre de Virgile: Poétique et philosophie.* Nancy.

Dixon, S. 1992. *The Roman Family.* Baltimore.

Dodds, E. R. 1951. *The Greeks and the Irrational.* Berkeley & Los Angeles.

——. 1960. "Morals and Politics in the 'Oresteia.'" *Proceedings of the Cambridge Philological Society* clxxxvi, 20–31. Repr. in *The Ancient Concept of Progress* (Oxford, 1973), 45–63.

Dolbeau, F. 1992. "Sermons inédits de Saint Augustin prêchés en 397 (3ème série)." *Revue Bénédictine* cii, 267–297.

Donini, P. 1982. *Le scuole, l'anima, l'impero: La filosofia antica da Antioco a Plotino.* Turin.

——. 1995. "Struttura delle passioni e del vizio e la loro cura in Crisippo." *Elenchos* xvi, 305–329.

Dorandi, T. 1990. "Filodemo: Gli orientamenti della ricerca attuale." In *ANRW* II, 36, 4, 2328–2368.

Dover, K. J. 1972. *Aristophanic Comedy.* Berkeley & Los Angeles.

——. 1974. *Greek Popular Morality in the Time of Plato and Aristotle.* Oxford.

——. 1989. *Greek Homosexuality,* 2nd ed. London.

——. 1991. "Fathers, Sons and Forgiveness." *Illinois Classical Studies* xvi, 173–182.

——. 1994. "Style, Genre and Author." *Illinois Classical Studies* xix, 83–87.

Drake, H. A. 1996. "Lambs into Lions: Explaining Early Christian Intolerance." *Past and Present* cliii, 3–36.

Durry, M. 1956. "Les empereurs comme historiens d'Auguste à Hadrien." *Entretiens de la Fondation Hardt* iv, 213–235.

Dvornik, F. 1966. *Early Christian and Byzantine Political Philosophy: Origins and Background.* Washington, D.C.

Easterling, P. E. 1997. "Constructing the Heroic." In C. Pelling (ed.), *Greek Tragedy and the Historian.* Oxford. 21–37.

Eck, W., A. Caballos & F. Fernández. 1996. *Das senatus consultum de Cn. Pisone patre.* Munich.

Eckstein, A. M. 1995. *Moral Vision in the Histories of Polybius.* Berkeley & Los Angeles.

Edelstein, L. 1952. "The Relationship of Ancient Philosophy to Medicine." *Bulletin of the History of Medicine* xxvi, 299–316. Cited from his *Ancient Medicine: Selected Papers* (Baltimore, 1967), 349–366.

Eder, W. 1995. "Monarchie und Demokratie im 4. Jahrhundert v.Chr.: Die Rolle des Fürstenspiegels in der athenischen Demokratie." In Eder (ed.) 1995, 153–173.

—— (ed.). 1995. *Die athenische Demokratie im 4. Jahrhundert v.Chr.* Stuttgart.

Edinger, H. G. "Anger in Herodotus." Unpublished paper.

Edwards, M. W. 1987. *Homer, Poet of the* Iliad. Baltimore & London.

Ekman, P. 1992. "An Argument for Basic Emotions." *Cognition and Emotion* vi, 169–200.

———. 1998. Edition of Darwin, *Expression of the Emotions in Man and Animals.* New York & Oxford.

Elias, N. 1982. *The Civilizing Process,* trans. E. Jephcott. Oxford. (Original ed.: *Über den Prozess der Zivilisation,* Basel, 1939.)

———. 1988. "Violence and Civilization: The State Monopoly of Physical Violence and Its Infringement." In J. Keane (ed.), *Civil Society and the State.* London & New York. 177–198.

Ellis, J. R., & G. R. Stanton. 1968. "Factional Conflicts and Solon's Reforms." *Phoenix* xxii, 95–110.

Elster, J. 1985. "Sadder but Wiser? Rationality and the Emotions." *Social Science Information* xxiv, 375–406.

———. 1989–90. "Norms of Revenge." *Ethics* c, 862–885.

———. 1999. *Alchemies of the Mind: Rationality and the Emotions.* Cambridge.

Emilsson, E. J. 1998. "Plotinus on the Emotions." In Sihvola & Engberg-Pederson 1998, 339–363.

Erler, M. 1992. "Der Zorn des Helden: Philodems 'De ira' und Vergils Konzept des Zorns in der 'Aeneis.'" *Grazer Beiträge* xviii, 103–126.

Evans, J. K. 1991. *War, Women and Children in Ancient Rome.* London.

Evans Grubbs, J. 1995. *Law and Family in Late Antiquity: The Emperor Constantine's Marriage Legislation.* Oxford.

Eyben, E. 1993. *Restless Youth in Ancient Rome,* trans. P. Daly. London (Original ed.: *De onstuimigen: Jeugd en (on)deugd en het Oude Rome,* Kapellen, 1987.)

Faraone, C. Forthcoming. "*Thumos* as Masculine Ideal and Social Pathology in Ancient Greek Magical Spells." In Braund & Most, forthcoming.

Farrar, C. 1988. *The Origins of Democratic Thinking: The Invention of Politics in Classical Athens.* Cambridge.

Farron, S. 1985. "Furie/furore." In *Enciclopedia Virgiliana* II. Rome. 620–622.

Fears, J. R. 1974. "The Stoic View of the Career and Character of Alexander the Great." *Philologus* cxviii, 113–130.

Febvre, L. 1973. "Sensibility and History: How to Reconstitute the Emotional Life of the Past." In *A New Kind of History and Other Essays,* trans. K. Folca. London. 12–26. (Original ed.: "La Sensibilité et l'histoire: Comment reconstituer la vie affective d'autrefois." *Annales d'histoire sociale* iii [1941], 5–20; repr. in *Combats pour l'histoire* [Paris, 1953], 221–238.)

Fehr, B., & M. Baldwin. 1996. "Prototype and Script Analyses of Laypeople's Knowledge of Anger." In G. J. O. Fletcher & J. Fitness (eds.), *Knowledge*

Structures in Close Relationships: A Social Psychological Approach. Mahwah, N.J. 219–245.

Ferrari, G. R. F. 1985. "The Struggle in the Soul: Plato, *Phaedrus* 253c7–255a1." *Ancient Philosophy* v, 1–10.

Ferrary, J.-L. 1988. *Philhellénisme et impérialisme.* Rome.

Fillion-Lahille, J. 1970. "La colère chez Aristote." *Revue des Études Anciennes* lxxii, 46–79.

———. 1984. *Le* De ira *de Sénèque et la philosophie stoïcienne des passions.* Paris.

Finkelberg, M. 1998. *The Birth of Literary Fiction in Ancient Greece.* Oxford.

Finley, M. I. 1956. *The World of Odysseus.* London.

Fischer, A. H., A. S. R. Manstead & P. M. Rodriguez Mosquera. 1999. "The Role of Honour-related vs. Individualistic Values in Conceptualising Pride, Shame, and Anger: Spanish and Dutch Cultural Prototypes." *Cognition and Emotion* xiii, 149–179.

Flandrin, J.-L. 1976. *Familles: Parenté, maison, sexualité dans l'ancienne société.* Paris.

Flashar, H. 1966. *Melancholie und Melancholiker in den medizinischen Theorie der Antike.* Berlin.

Flory, S. 1987. *The Archaic Smile of Herodotus.* Detroit.

Foley, H. 1989. "Medea's Divided Self." *Classical Antiquity* viii, 61–85.

Fontenrose, J. 1968. "The Hero as Athlete." *California Studies in Classical Antiquity* i, 73–104.

Forschner, M. 1981. *Die Stoische Ethik.* Stuttgart.

Fortenbaugh, W. W. 1970. "Aristotle's *Rhetoric* on Emotions." *Archiv für Geschichte der Philosophie* lii, 40–70. Repr. in Barnes, Schofield & Sorabji 1979, IV:133–153.

———. 1985. "Theophrastus on Emotion." In W. W. Fortenbaugh (ed.), *Theophrastus of Eresus: On His Life and Work.* New Brunswick & Oxford. 209–229.

Foucault, M. 1986. *The History of Sexuality* III: *The Care of the Self,* trans. R. Hurley. New York. (Original ed.: *Histoire de la sexualité* III: *Le souci de soi,* Paris, 1984.)

Fowler, D. 1997. "Epicurean Anger." In Braund & Gill 1997, 16–35.

Fraser, P. M. 1972. *Ptolemaic Alexandria.* Oxford.

Frede, M. 1986. "The Stoic Doctrine of the Affections of the Soul." In Schofield & Striker 1986, 93–110.

———. 1992. "On Aristotle's Conception of the Soul." In M. C. Nussbaum & A. O. Rorty (eds.), *Essays on Aristotle's* De Anima. Oxford. 93–107.

Freeman, D. 1983. *Margaret Mead and Samoa: The Making and Unmaking of an Anthropological Myth.* Cambridge, Mass.

Freud, S. 1955. *Standard Edition* II: *Studies on Hysteria,* trans. J. Strachey et al. London. (Original ed.: J. Breuer & S. Freud, *Studien über Hysterie,* Leipzig & Vienna, 1895.)

———. 1957. "The Unconscious." In *Standard Edition* XIV, trans. J. Strachey et al. London. 159–215. (Original ed.: "Das Unbewusste." *Internationale Zeitschrift für ärtzliche Psychoanalyse* iii [1915]: 189–203, 257–269; often reprinted.)

———. 1961. *Civilization and Its Discontents,* trans. J. Strachey. New York. (Original ed.: *Das Unbehagen in der Kultur,* Vienna, 1930.)

Friedrich, R. 1993. "Medea *apolis:* On Euripides' Dramatization of the Crisis of the Polis." In A. H. Sommerstein et al. (eds.), *Tragedy, Comedy and the Polis.* Bari. 219–239.

Frijda, N. H., et al. 1992. "The Complexity of Intensity: Issues concerning the Structure of Emotion Intensity." in M. S. Clark 1992, 60–89.

Frisk, H. 1952. "μῆνις: Zur Geschichte eines Begriffes." *Eranos* 1, 28–40. Repr. in his *Kleine Schriften* Göteborg, 1966, 389–402.

Frohnhofen, H. 1987. *Apatheia tou theou: Über die Affektslosigkeit Gottes in der griechischen Antike.* Frankfurt am Main.

Fürst, A. 1996. *Streit unter Freunden: Ideal und Realität in der Freundschaftslehre der Antike.* Stuttgart.

Furley, W. D. 1985. "The Figure of Euthyphro in Plato's Dialogue." *Phronesis* xxx, 201–208.

———. 1992. "Antiphon der Athener: Ein Sophist als Psychotherapeut." *Rheinisches Museum für Philologie* cxxxv, 198–216.

Fusillo, M. 1990. "Le conflit des émotions: Un topos du roman érotique grec." *Museum Helveticum* xlvii, 201–221.

Gagarin, M. 1981. *Drakon and Early Athenian Homicide Law.* New Haven & London.

———. 1986. *Early Greek Law.* Berkeley & Los Angeles.

———. 1990. "The Ambiguity of *eris* in the *Works and Days.*" In *Cabinet of the Muses: Essays on Classical and Comparative Literature in Honor of Thomas G. Rosenmeyer.* Atlanta. 173–183.

Gager, J. G. (ed.). 1992. *Curse Tablets and Binding Spells from the Ancient World.* New York.

Gaiser, K. 1967. "Menander und der Peripatos." *Antike und Abendland* xiii, 8–40.

Galinsky, K. 1988. "The Anger of Aeneas." *American Journal of Philology* cix, 321–348.

———. 1994. "How to Be Philosophical about the End of the *Aeneid.*" *Illinois Classical Studies* xix, 191–201.

Gardner, J. F. 1986. *Woman in Roman Law and Society.* Bloomington, Ind.

Garlan, Y. 1988. *Slavery in Ancient Greece,* trans. J. Lloyd. Ithaca, N.Y., & London. (Original ed.: *Les esclaves en Grèce ancienne,* Paris, 1982.)

Garnsey, P. 1996. *Ideas of Slavery from Aristotle to Augustine.* Cambridge.

Gastaldi, S. 1987. "*Pathe* and *polis:* Aristotle's Theory of Passion in the Rhetorics and the Ethics." *Topoi* vi, 105–110.

Gaub, H. D. 1763. *Sermo academicus alter de regimine mentis.* Leiden.

Gaylin, W. 1989. *The Rage Within: Anger in Modern Life.* New York.

Geddes, A. G. 1984. "Who's Who in 'Homeric Society'?" *Classical Quarterly* xxxiv, 17–36.

Geertz, C. 1973. *The Interpretation of Cultures: Selected Essays.* New York.

Gehrke, H.-J. 1985. *Stasis: Untersuchungen zu den inneren Kriegen.* Munich.

———. 1987. "Die Griechen und die Rache: Ein Versuch in historischer Psychologie." *Saeculum* xxxviii, 121–149.

Gelzer, M. 1968. *Caesar: Politician and Statesman,* trans. P. Needham. Oxford. (Original ed.: *Caesar der Politiker und Staatsmann,* 6th ed., Wiesbaden, 1960.)

Genovese, E. 1976. *Roll, Jordan, Roll: The World the Slaves Made.* New York. (Original ed.: 1972.)

Gerber, E. R. 1985. "Rage and Obligation: Samoan Emotion in Conflict." In White & Kirkpatrick 1985, 121–167.

Gernet, L. 1939. "L'Institution des arbitres publics à Athènes." *Revue des Études Grecques* lii, 389–414. Repr. in *Droit et société dans la Grèce ancienne* Paris, 1955, 103–119.

Gerson, L. P. 1997. "Socrates' Absolutist Prohibition of Wrongdoing." *Apeiron* xxx, 4 1–11.

Giardina, A. 2000. "Storie riflesse: Claudio e Seneca." In *Seneca e il suo tempo.* Rome. 59–90.

Gigante, M. 1975. "'Philosophia medicans' in Filodemo." *Cronache ercolanesi* v, 53–61.

Gigante, M., & M. Capasso. 1989. "Il ritorno di Virgilio a Ercolano." *Studi italiani di filologia classica* ser. 3, vii, 3–6.

Gigon, O. 1947. *Sokrates: Sein Bild in Dichtung und Geschichte.* Bern.

Gill, C. 1985. "Ancient Psychotherapy." *Journal of the History of Ideas* xlvi, 307–325.

———. 1995. *Greek Thought,* Oxford.

———. 1996a. "Ancient Passions: Theories and Cultural Styles." In K. Cameron (ed.), *The Literary Portrayal of Passion through the Ages.* Lewiston, Me. 1–10.

———. 1996b. "Mind and Madness in Greek Tragedy." *Apeiron* xxix, 249–267.

———. 1996c. *Personality in Greek Epic, Tragedy, and Philosophy: The Self in Dialogue.* Oxford.

———. Forthcoming. "Alternatives to Anger: Virgil's *Aeneid* and Hellenistic Philosophy." In Braund & Most, forthcoming.

Glibert-Thirry, A. 1977. "La théorie stoïcienne de la passion chez Chrysippe et son évolution chez Posidonius." *Revue philosophique de Louvain* lxxv, 393–435.

Glick, R. A., & S. P. Roose. (eds.). 1993. *Rage, Power, and Aggression.* New Haven & London.

Glotz, G. 1904. *La solidarité de la famille dans le droit criminel en Grèce.* Paris.

Goddard, C. 1991. "Anger in the Western Desert: A Case Study in the Cross-Cultural Semantics of Emotion." *Man* xxvi, 265–279.

Goddard, C., & A. Wierzbicka. (eds.). 1994. *Semantic and Lexical Universals.* Amsterdam & Philadelphia.

Goehring, J. E. 2000. "The First Sahidic *Life of Pachomius.*" In Valantasis 2000, 19–33.

Goessler, L. 1999. "Advice to the Bride and Groom." In S. B. Pomeroy (ed.), *Plutarch's* Advice to the Bride and Groom *and* A Consolation to His Wife. Oxford. 97–115. (Trans. H. M. and D. Harvey from Goessler, *Plutarchs Gedanken über die Ehe* [Zurich, 1962], 44–69.)

Golden, M. 1981. "Demography and the Exposure of Girls at Athens." *Phoenix* xxxv, 316–331.

———. 1990. *Children and Childhood in Classical Athens.* Baltimore & London.

Goldhill, S. 1986. *Reading Greek Tragedy.* Cambridge.

———. 1994. "Representing Democracy: Women at the Great Dionysia." In *Ritual, Finance and Politics: Athenian Democratic Accounts Presented to David Lewis.* Oxford. 347–369.

Gomperz, H. 1927. *Die Lebensauffassung der griechischen Philosophen,* 3rd ed. Jena.

Gould, J. B. 1970. *The Philosophy of Chrysippus.* Albany, N.Y.

Graeser, A. 1975. *Zenon von Kition: Positionen und Probleme.* Berlin & New York.

Gransden, K. W. 1984. *Virgil's Iliad: An Essay on Epic Narrative.* Cambridge.

Gray, J. 1947–1953. "The Wrath of God in Canaanite and Hebrew Literature." *Journal of the Manchester University Egyptological and Oriental Society* xxv, 9–19.

Griffin, J. 1976. "Homeric Pathos and Objectivity." *Classical Quarterly* xxvi, 161–187.

———. 1986. "Homeric Words and Speakers." *Journal of Hellenic Studies* cvi, 36–57.

———. 1998. "The Social Function of Attic Tragedy." *Classical Quarterly* xlviii, 39–61.

Griffin, M. 1976. *Seneca: A Philosopher in Politics.* Oxford.

Griffith, M. 1977. *The Authenticity of 'Prometheus Bound.'* Cambridge.

———. 1998. "The King and Eye: The Rule of the Father in Greek Tragedy." *Proceedings of the Cambridge Philological Society* xliv, 20–84.

Griffiths, P. E. 1997. *What Emotions Really Are: The Problem of Psychological Categories.* Chicago & London.

Grimal, P. 1945. "Auguste et Athénodore." *Revue des Études Anciennes* xlvii, 261–273; xlviii 1946, 62–79.

Gross, J. J., and R. W. Levenson. 1997. "Hiding Feelings: The Acute Effects of Inhibiting Negative and Positive Emotion." *Journal of Abnormal Psychology* cvi, 95–103.

Groton, A. H. 1987. "Anger in Menander's *Samia.*" *American Journal of Philology* cviii, 437–443.

Guthrie, W. K. C. 1962–1981. *A History of Greek Philosophy,* 6 vols. Cambridge.

Habicht, C. 1994. *Athen in hellenistischer Zeit: Gesammelte Aufsätze.* Munich.

Hacking, I. 1999. *The Social Construction of What?* Cambridge, Mass.

Hadot, P. 1972. "Fürstenspiegel." *Reallexikon für Antike und Christentum* VIII, cols. 555–632.

Hägg, T. 1997. "A Professor and His Slave: Conventions and Values in the *Life of Aesop.*" In Bilde et al. 1997, 177–203.

Hall, E. 1989. *Inventing the Barbarian.* Oxford.

———. 1993. "Political and Cosmic Turbulence in Euripides' *Orestes.*" In A. H. Sommerstein et al. (eds.), *Tragedy, Comedy and the Polis.* Bari. 263–285.

Hall, M. D. 1996. "Even Dogs Have Erinyes: Sanctions in Athenian Practice and Thinking." In L. Foxhall & A. D. E. Lewis (eds.), *Greek Law in Its Political Setting.* Oxford. 73–89.

Hallman, J. 1984. "The Emotions of God in the Theology of St. Augustine." *Recherches de théologie* li, 5–19.

Hamma, K. 1983. "The Representations of Helen and Menelaos." *Getty Museum Journal* xi, 123–128.

Hankinson, J. 1993. "Actions and Passions: Affection, Emotion, and Moral Self-Management in Galen's Philosophical Psychology." In J. Brunschwig & M. Nussbaum, *Passions and Perceptions.* Cambridge. 184–222.

Hardie, W. R. F. 1980. *Aristotle's Ethical Theory,* 2nd ed. Oxford.

Harkins, P. W. 1963. *Galen on the Passions and Errors of the Soul.* Columbus, Ohio.

Harré, R. (ed.). 1986. *The Social Construction of Emotions.* Oxford.

Harris, G. G. 1978. *Casting Out Anger: Religion among the Taita of Kenya.* Cambridge.

Harris, P. L. 1989. *Children and Emotion: The Development of Psychological Understanding.* Oxford.

Harris, W. V. 1979. *War and Imperialism in Republican Rome, 327–70 B.C.* Oxford.

———. 1986. "The Roman Father's Power of Life and Death." In *Studies in Roman Law in Memory of A. Arthur Sciller.* Leiden. 81–95.

———. 1989. *Ancient Literacy.* Cambridge, Mass.

———. 1994. "Child-Exposure in the Roman Empire." *Journal of Roman Studies* lxxxiv, 1–22.

———. 1997a. "Lysias III and Athenian Beliefs about Revenge." *Classical Quarterly* xlvii, 363–366.

———. 1997b. "Saving the φαινόμενα: A Note on Aristotle's Definition of Anger." *Classical Quarterly* xlvii, 452–454.

Havelock, E. A. 1982. *The Literate Revolution in Greece and Its Cultural Consequences.* Princeton.

Heald, S. 1989. *Controlling Anger: The Sociology of Gisu Violence.* Manchester, England.

Heath, M. 1987. *The Poetics of Greek Tragedy.* London.

Heelas, P. 1984. "Emotions across Cultures: Objectivity and Cultural Divergence." In S. C. Brown (ed.), *Objectivity and Cultural Divergence.* Cambridge. 21–42.

———. 1986. "Emotion Talk across Cultures." In R. Harré (ed.), *The Social Construction of Emotions.* Oxford. 234–266.

Heger, F. 1986. "Dirke." In *LIMC* III. Zurich & Munich. 635–644.

Heiberg, J. L. 1927. "Geisteskrankheiten im klassischen Altertum." *Allgemeine Zeitschrift für Psychiatrie* lxxxvi, 1–44.

Heim, F. 1992. "Clémence ou extermination: Le pouvoir impérial et les barbares au IVe siècle." *Ktema* xvii, 281–295.

Heitsch, E. 1967. "Der Zorn des Paris: Zur Deutungsgeschichte eines homerischen Zetemas." In *Festschrift für Joseph Klein zum 70. Geburtstag.* Göttingen. 216–247.

Henderson, J. 1991. "Women and the Athenian Dramatic Festivals." *Transactions of the American Philological Association* cxxi, 133–147.

Herlihy, D. 1972. "Some Psychological and Social Roots of Violence in the Tuscan Cities." In L. Martines (ed.), *Violence and Disorder in Italian Cities, 1200–1500.* Berkeley & Los Angeles. 129–154.

Herman, G. 1994. "How Violent Was Athenian Society?" In *Ritual, Finance, Politics: Athenian Democratic Accounts Presented to David Lewis.* Oxford. 99–117.

———. 1995. "Honour, Revenge and the State in Fourth-Century Athens." In Eder 1995, 43–60.

———. 1996. "Ancient Athens and the Values of Mediterranean Society." *Mediterranean Historical Review* xi, 5–36.

———. 1998. Rev. of D. Cohen 1995. *Gnomon* lxx, 605–615.

Herzfeld, E. 1938. *Altpersische Inschriften*. Berlin.

Higman, B. W. 1984. *Slave Populations of the British Caribbean 1807–1834*. Baltimore & London.

Hirzel, R. 1907. *Themis, Dike und Verwandtes: Ein Beitrag zur Geschichte der Rechtsidee bei den Griechen*. Leipzig.

Hölscher, T. 1999. "Immagini mitologiche e valori sociali nella Grecia arcaica." In *Im Spiegel des Mythos: Bilderwelt und Lebenswelt*. Wiesbaden. 11–30.

Hogan, J. C. 1981. "Eris in Homer." *Grazer Beiträge* x, 21–58.

Hopkins, K. 1993. "Novel Evidence for Roman Slavery." *Past and Present* cxxxviii, 3–27.

Horder, J. 1992. *Provocation and Responsibility*. Oxford.

Howell, S. 1984. *Society and Cosmos: Chewong of Peninsula Malaysia*. Oxford.

Howie, J. G. 1995. "The *Iliad* as Exemplum." In Ø. Andersen & M. Dickie (eds.), *Homer's World: Fiction, Tradition, and Reality*. Bergen. 141–173.

Huart, P. 1968. *Le vocabulaire de l'analyse psychologique dans l'oeuvre de Thucydide*. Paris.

Huffman, C. 1993. *Philolaus of Croton: Pythagorean and Presocratic*. Cambridge.

Humphreys, S. C. 1983a. "The Evolution of Legal Process in Ancient Attica." In *Tria Corda: Scritti in onore di Arnaldo Momigliano*. Como. 229–256.

———. 1983b. *The Family, Women and Death: Comparative Studies*. London.

Hunter, V. J. 1994. *Policing Athens: Social Control in the Attic Lawsuits, 420–320 B.C.* Princeton.

Hupka, R. B., et al. 1996. "Anger, Envy, Fear, and Jealousy as Felt in the Body." *Cross-Cultural Research* xxx, 243–264.

Indelli, G. 1988. "Considerazioni sugli opuscoli *De ira* di Filodemo e. Plutarco." In I. Gallo (ed.), *Aspetti dello stoicismo e dell'epicureismo in Plutarco*. Quaderni del Giornale Filologico Ferrarese 9. Ferrara. 57–64.

Inwood, B. 1993. "Seneca and Psychological Dualism." In Brunschwig & Nussbaum 1993, 150–183.

Ioppolo, A. M. 1995. "L'ὁρμὴ πλεονάζουσα nella dottrina stoica." *Elenchos* xvi, 23–55.

Irmscher, J. 1950. *Götterzorn bei Homerus*. Leipzig.

Irwin, T. H. 1986. "Stoic and Aristotelian Conceptions of Happiness." In Schofield & Striker 1986, 205–244.

———. 1994. "Critical Notice" of B. Williams, *Shame and Necessity* (Berkeley & Los Angeles, 1993). *Apeiron* xxvii, 45–76.

Isaacson, R. L. 1982. *The Limbic System,* 2nd ed. New York.

Izard, C. E. 1977. *Human Emotions.* New York & London.

———. 1983. "Emotions in Personality and Culture." *Ethos* xi, 305–312.

———. 1991. *The Psychology of Emotions.* London & New York.

Jackson, S. W. 1986. *Melancholia and Depression: From Hippocratic Times to Modern Times.* New Haven & London.

Jacoby, S. 1983. *Wild Justice: The Evolution of Revenge.* New York.

James, W. 1884. "What Is an Emotion?" *Mind* ix, 188–205. Repr. in K. Dunlap (ed.), *The Emotions* (New York, 1967).

———. 1890. *The Principles of Psychology.* New York.

Jauss, H. R. 1982. *Aesthetic Experience and Literary Hermeneutics,* trans. M. Shaw. Minneapolis. (Original ed.: *Ästhetische Erfahrung und literarische Hermeneutik,* Munich, 1977.)

Jenkins, J. M., K. Oatley & N. L. Stein. 1998. *Human Emotions: A Reader.* Oxford.

Jerphagnon, L. 1984. "Que le tyran est contre-nature: Sur quelques clichés de l'historiographie romaine." *Cahiers de philosophie politique et juridique* vi, 41–50.

Johnson-Laird, P. N., & K. Oatley. 1989. "The Language of Emotions: An Analysis of a Semantic Field." *Cognition and Emotion* iii, 81–123.

Jones, C. P. 1986. *Culture and Society in Lucian.* Cambridge, Mass.

Jordan, D. R. 1985. "A Survey of Greek *defixiones* not Included in the Special Corpora." *Greek, Roman, and Byzantine Studies* xxvi, 151–197.

Kahan, D. M., & M. C. Nussbaum. 1996. "Two Conceptions of Emotion in Criminal Law." *Columbia Law Review* xcvi, 269–374.

Kahn, C. H. 1981. "The Origins of Social Contract Theory." In G. B. Kerferd (ed.), *The Sophists and Their Legacy* (*Hermes* Einzelschrift 44). Wiesbaden. 92–108.

Kallendorf, C. 1999. "Historicizing the 'Harvard School': Pessimistic Readings of the *Aeneid* in Italian Renaissance Scholarship." *Harvard Studies in Classical Philology* xcix, 391–403.

Kassinove, H. (ed.). 1995. *Anger Disorders: Definition, Diagnosis, and Treatment.* Washington, D.C.

Kassinove, H., & D. G. Sukhodolsky. 1995. "Anger Disorders: Basic Science and Practice Issues." In Kassinove 1995, 1–26.

Kawachi, I., et al. 1996. "A Prospective Study of Anger and Coronary Heart Disease." *Circulation* xciv, 2090–2095.

Kay, P., & W. Kempton. 1984. "What Is the Sapir-Whorf Hypothesis?" *American Anthropologist* lxxxvi, 65–79.

Keltner, D., & J. J. Gross. 1999. "Functional Accounts of Emotions." *Cognition and Emotion* xiii, 467–480.

Kemp, S., & K. T. Strongman. 1995. "Anger Theory and Management: A Historical Analysis." *American Journal of Psychology* cviii, 397–417.

Kemper, T. D. 1993. "Sociological Models in the Explanation of Emotions." In Lewis & Haviland 1993, 41–51.

Kenny, A. 1978. *The Aristotelian Ethics.* Oxford.

Kent, R. G. 1953. *Old Persian: Grammar, Texts, Lexicon,* 2nd ed. New Haven.

Kerrigan, J. 1996. *Revenge Tragedy.* Oxford.

Kidd, I. G. 1978. "Moral Actions and Rules in Stoic Ethics." In J. M. Rist (ed.), *The Stoics.* Berkeley & Los Angeles. 247–258.

Kingsley, P. 1995. *Ancient Philosophy, Mystery, and Magic: Empedocles and Pythagorean Tradition.* Oxford.

Kleinknecht, H., et al. 1968. ὀργή, etc. In *Theological Dictionary of the New Testament* V, trans. G. W. Bromley. Grand Rapids, Mich. 382–447 (Original ed.: *Theologisches Wörterbuch zum Neuen Testament* V [Stuttgart, 1954], 383–448.

Kneppe, A. 1994. *Metus Temporum: Zur Bedeutung von Angst in Politik und Gesellschaft der römischen Kaiserzeit des 1. und 2. Jhs.n.Chr.* Stuttgart.

Knox, B. M. W. 1977. "The *Medea* of Euripides." *Yale Classical Studies* xxv, 193–225. Repr. in *Word and Action: Essays on the Ancient Theater* (Baltimore & London, 1979), 295–322.

Knox, D. 1991. "*Disciplina:* The Monastic and Clerical Origins of European Civility." In *Renaissance Society and Culture: Essays in Honor of Eugene F. Rice, Jr.* New York. 107–135.

Körte, A. 1931. "Menandros" (9). In *RE,* cols. 707–761.

Kövecses, Z. 1986. *Metaphors of Anger, Pride and Love: A Lexical Approach to the Structure of Concepts.* Amsterdam.

———. 2000. *Metaphor and Emotion: Language, Culture, and Body in Human Feeling.* Cambridge.

Kossatz-Deissmann, A. 1981. "Achilleus." In *LIMC* I. Zurich & Munich. 37–200.

———. 1992. "Lyssa." In *LIMC* VI. Zurich & Munich. 322–329.

Koster, S. 1980. *Die Invektive in der griechischen und römischen Literatur.* Meisenheim am Glan.

Kraus, P. 1939. "Kitāb al-ahlāq li-Gālīnus." *Bulletin of the Faculty of Arts of the University of Egypt* v.1, 1–51.

Kring, A. M. 2000. "Gender and Anger." In A. H. Fischer (ed.), *Gender and Emotion: Social Psychological Perspectives.* Cambridge & Paris. 211–231.

Kristeva, J. 1989. *Black Sun: Depression and Melancholia,* trans. L. S. Roudiez. New York. (Original ed.: *Soleil noir: Dépression et mélancolie,* Paris, 1987).

Kudlien, F. 1967. *Der Beginn des medizinischen Denkens bei den Griechen.* Zurich.

Kurke, L. 1997. "Sex, Politics, and Discursive Conflict in Archaic Greece." *Classical Antiquity* xvi, 106–150.

Kuzmics, H. 1988. "The Civilizing Process." In J. Keane (ed.), *Civil Society and the State.* London & New York. 147–176.

Lacey, W. K. 1968. *The Family in Classical Greece.* London.

Lacombrade, C. 1951. *Le discours sur la royauté de Synésios de Cyrène à l'empereur Arcadios.* Paris.

Lada, I. 1993. "'Empathic Understanding': Emotion and Cognition in Classical Dramatic Audience-Response." *Proceedings of the Cambridge Philological Society* xxxix, 94–140.

Laín Entralgo, P. 1970. *The Therapy of the Word in Classical Antiquity,* ed. and trans. L. J. Rather & J. M. Sharp. New Haven & London. (Original ed.: *La curación por la palabra en la antigüedad clásica,* Madrid, 1958.)

Lakoff, G., & Z. Kövecses. 1987. "The Cognitive Model of Anger Inherent in American English." In D. Holland & N. Quinn (eds.), *Cultural Models in Language and Thought.* Cambridge. 195–221.

Lamberton, R. W. 1997. "Homer in Antiquity." In I. Morris & B. Powell (eds.), *A New Companion to Homer.* Leiden. 33–54.

Lamberton, R. W., & J. J. Keaney (eds.). 1992. *Homer's Ancient Readers: The Hermeneutics of Greek Epic's Earliest Exegetes* Princeton.

Latte, K. 1931. "Beiträge zum griechischen Strafrecht." *Hermes* lxvi, 30–48. Repr. in Latte 1968, 252–267, and in Berneker 1968, 263–314.

———. 1946. "Der Rechtsgedanke im archaischen Griechentum." *Antike und Abendland* ii, 63–76. Repr. in Latte 1968, 233–251, and in Berneker 1968, 77–98.

———. 1968. *Kleine Schriften.* Munich.

Lattimore, R. B. 1942. *Themes in Greek and Latin Epitaphs.* Urbana, Ill.

Laurenti, R. 1979. "Aristotele e il 'De ira' di Seneca." *Studi filosofici* ii, 61–91.

———. 1987. "Ira." In *Enciclopedia Virgiliana* III. Rome. 20–21.

Lazarus, R. S. 1991. *Emotion and Adaptation.* New York & Oxford.

LeDoux, J. E. 1987. "Emotion." In F. Plum (ed.), *Handbook of Physiology.* Washington, D.C. V:419–459.

———. 1992. "Emotion and the Limbic System Concept." *Concepts in Neuroscience* ii, 2, 169–199.

———. 1996. *The Emotional Brain: The Mysterious Underpinnings of Emotional Life.* New York.

Lefkowitz, M. R. 1986. *Women in Greek Myth.* Baltimore.

Legras, B. 1996. "Morale et société dans la fable scolaire grecque et latine d'Égypte." *Cahiers du Centre Gustave-Glotz* vii, 51–80.

Leighton, S. R. 1988. "Aristotle's Courageous Passions." *Phronesis* xxxiii, 76–99.

Lesky, A. 1968. "Homeros." In *RE* Supplementband XI, cols. 687–846.

Leventhal, H., & L. Patrick-Miller. 1993. "Emotion and Illness: The Mind Is in the Body." In Lewis & Haviland 1993, 365–379.

Levy, R. I. 1984. "Emotion, Knowing and Culture." In R. A. Shweder & R. A. LeVine (eds.), *Culture Theory: Essays on Mind, Self, and Emotion*. Cambridge. 214–237.

Lewis, M. 1993. "The Development of Anger and Rage." In Glick & Roose 1993, 148–168.

Lewis, M., & J. M. Haviland (eds.). 1993. *Handbook of Emotions*. New York & London. (2nd ed., 2000.)

Lidov, J. 1977. "The Anger of Poseidon." *Arethusa* x, 227–236.

Liebeschuetz, J. H. W. G. 1972. *Antioch: City and Imperial Administration in the Later Roman Empire*. Oxford.

Lintott, A. W. 1982. *Violence, Civil Strife and Revolution in the Classical City, 750–330 B.C.* Baltimore.

Little, L. K. 1998. "Anger in Monastic Curses." In Rosenwein (ed.) 1998, 9–35.

Lloyd, G. E. R. 1987. *The Revolutions of Wisdom: Studies in the Claims and Practice of Ancient Greek Science*. Berkeley & Los Angeles.

Lloyd-Jones, H. 1980. "Euripides, Medea 1056–80." *Würzburger Jahrbücher für die Altertumswissenschaft* n.F. vi, 51–59.

Long, A. A. 1970. "Morals and Values in Homer." *Journal of Hellenic Studies* xc, 121–139.

———. 1989. "Stoic Eudaimonism." *Proceedings of the Boston Area Colloquium in Ancient Philosophy* iv, 77–101. Repr. in Long 1996, 179–201.

———. 1992. "Stoic Readings of Homer." In Lamberton & Keaney 1992, 41–66. Repr. in Long 1996, 58–84.

———. 1996. *Stoic Studies*. Cambridge.

Long, A. A., & D. Sedley. 1987. *The Hellenistic Philosophers*, 2 vols. Cambridge.

Longo Auricchio, F., & A. Tepedino Guerra. 1982. "Chi è Timasagora?" In *La regione sotterrata dal Vesuvio: Studi e prospettive*. Naples. 405–413.

Loomis, W. T. 1972. "The Nature of Premeditation in Athenian Homicide Law." *Journal of Hellenic Studies* xcii, 86–95.

Lord, C. 1977. "Aristotle, Menander, and the *Adelphoe* of Terence." *Transactions of the American Philological Association* cvii, 183–202.

Lossau, M. 1979. "Achills Rache und aristotelische Ethik." *Antike und Abendland* xxv, 120–129.

———. 1992. "Aristotelesverfälschung: ὀργή in der 'orthodoxen' Stoa." *Philologus* cxxxvi, 60–70.

Lucy, J. A. 1992. *Language Diversity and Thought: A Reformulation of the Linguistic Relativity Hypothesis.* Cambridge.

Luhmann, N. 1982. *The Differentiation of Society,* trans. S. Holmes & C. Larmore. New York. (Original ed.: *Soziologische Aufklärung: Aufsätze zur Theorie sozialer Systeme,* Cologne, 1970.)

Luschnat, O. 1958. "Das Problem des ethischen Fortschritts in der alten Stoa." *Philologus* cii, 178–214.

Lutz, C. A. 1988. *Unnatural Emotions: Everyday Sentiments on a Micronesian Atoll and Their Challenge to Western Theory.* Chicago & London.

Lutz, C., & G. M. White. 1986. "The Anthropology of Emotions." *Annual Review of Anthropology* xv, 405–436.

Lynch, O. M. 1990. "The Social Construction of Emotion in India." In O. M. Lynch (ed.), *Divine Passions: The Social Construction of Emotion in India.* Berkeley & Los Angeles. 3–34.

Lyons, W. 1980. *Emotion.* Cambridge.

MacDowell, D. M. 1978. *The Law in Classical Athens.* London.

MacLeod, C. 1982. "Politics and the Oresteia." *Journal of Hellenic Studies* cii, 124–144. Repr. in *Collected Essays* (Oxford, 1983), 20–40.

MacMullen, R. 1984. *Christianizing the Roman Empire, A.D. 100–400.* New Haven.

———. 1986a. "Judicial Savagery in the Roman Empire." *Chiron* xvi, 147–166. Repr. in MacMullen 1990, 204–217.

———. 1986b. "Personal Power in the Roman Empire." *American Journal of Philology* cvii, 512–524. Repr. in MacMullen 1990, 190–197.

———. 1990. *Changes in the Roman Empire: Essays in the Ordinary.* Princeton.

Manning, C. E. 1973. "Seneca and the Stoics on the Equality of the Sexes." *Mnemosyne* xxvi, 170–177.

———. 1989. "Stoicism and Slavery in the Roman Empire." In *ANRW* II, 36, 3, 1518–1543.

Mansfeld, J. 1992. "Heraclitus fr. B85 DK." *Mnemosyne* xlv, 9–18.

Manson, M. 1983. "The Emergence of the Small Child in Rome (Third Century B.C.–First Century A.D.)." *History of Education* xii, 149–159.

Manstead, A. S. R., & P. E. Tetlock. 1989. "Cognitive Appraisals and Emotional Experience." *Cognition and Emotion* iii, 225–240.

Manuli, P. 1988. "La passione nel *De placitis Hippocratis et Platonis.*" In P. Manuli & M. Vegetti (eds.), *Le opere psicologiche di Galeno: Atti del III Colloquio Galenico Internazionale.* Naples. 185–214.

Marrou, H.-I. 1965. *Histoire de l'éducation dans l'antiquité,* 6th ed. Paris.

Marsella, A. J. 1980. "Depressive Experience and Disorder across Cultures." In H. C. Triandis & J. G. Draguns (eds.), *Handbook of Cross-Cultural Psychology* VI: *Psychopathology.* Boston. 237–289.

Martin, V. 1958. "Euripide et Ménandre face à leur public." *Entretiens de la Fondation Hardt* vi, 245–283.

Marzullo, B. 1999. "La 'coscienza' di Medea (Eur. *Med.* 1078–80)." *Philologus* cxliii, 191–210.

Mathes, E. W., H. E. Adams & R. M. Davies. 1985. "Jealousy: Loss of Relationship Rewards, Loss of Self-esteem, Depression, Anxiety, and Anger." *Journal of Personality and Social Psychology* xlvii, 1552–1561.

Matsumoto, D. 1990. "Cultural Similarities and Differences in Display Rules." *Motivation and Emotion* xiv, 195–214.

Mattock, J. N. 1972. "A Translation of the Arabic Epitome of Galen's Book περὶ ἠθῶν." In *Islamic Philosophy and the Classical Tradition: Essays Presented by His Friends and Pupils to Richard Walzer on His Seventieth Birthday.* Oxford. 235–260.

Mauch, M. 1997. *Senecas Frauenbild in den philosophischen Schriften.* Frankfurt am Main.

Maurer, K. 1995. *Interpolations in Thucydides.* Leiden.

McBride, A. B. 1993. "Foreword." In S. P. Thomas (ed.), *Women and Anger.* New York. xiii–xv.

Mead, M. 1928. *Coming of Age in Samoa.* New York.

Meeks, W. A. 1993. *The Origins of Christian Morality: The First Two Centuries.* New Haven.

Meier, C. 1986. "Die Angst und der Staat: Fragen und Thesen zur Geschichte menschlicher Affekte." In H. Rössner (ed.), *Der ganze Mensch.* Munich. 228–246.

———. 1990. *The Greek Discovery of Politics,* trans. D. McLintock. Cambridge, Mass. (Original ed.: *Die Entstehung des Politischen bei den Griechen,* Frankfurt, 1980.)

Mesquita, B., & N. H. Frijda. 1992. "Cultural Variations in Emotion: A Review." *Psychological Bulletin* cxii, 179–204.

Mikulincer, M. 1998. "Adult Attachment Style and Individual Differences in Functional versus Dysfunctional Experiences of Anger." *Journal of Personality and Social Psychology* lxxiv, 513–524.

Millar, F. 1964. *A Study of Cassius Dio.* Oxford.

Miller, D. 1995. *Nature, Justice, and Rights in Aristotle's* Politics. Oxford.

Miller, M. C. 1997. *Athens and Persia in the Fifth Century: A Study in Cultural Receptivity.* Cambridge.

Miller, W. I. 1993. *Humiliation, and Other Essays on Honor, Social Discomfort and Violence.* Ithaca, N.Y., & London.

Mittleman, M. A., et al. 1995. "Triggering of Acute Myocardial Infarction Onset by Episodes of Anger." *Circulation* xcii, 1720–1725.

Molin, M. 1989. "Le *Panégyrique de Trajan:* Éloquence d'apparat ou programme politique néo-stoïcien?" *Latomus* xlviii, 785–797.

Momigliano, A. 1941. Rev. of B. Farrington, *Science and Politics in the Ancient World. Journal of Roman Studies* xxxi, 149–157. Repr. in his *Secondo Contributo alla storia degli studi classici* (Rome, 1960), 375–388.

Mommsen, T. 1899. *Römisches Strafrecht.* Leipzig.

Mooren, L. 1983. "The Nature of the Hellenistic Monarchy." In E. van't Dack et al. (eds.), *Egypt and the Hellenistic World.* Louvain. 205–240.

Morgan, C. 1991. "Ethnicity and the Early Greek States: Historical and Material Perspectives." *Proceedings of the Cambridge Philological Society* xxxvii, 131–163.

Morris, I. 1986. "Use and Abuse of Homer." *Classical Antiquity* v, 81–138.

Mossman, J. M. 1988. "Tragedy and Epic in Plutarch's *Alexander.*" *Journal of Hellenic Studies* cviii, 83–93. Repr. in B. Scardigli (ed.), *Essays on Plutarch's Lives* (Oxford, 1995), 209–228.

———. 1995. *Wild Justice: A Study of Euripides'* Hecuba. Oxford.

Moxnes, H. 1997. "Conventional Values in the Hellenistic World: Masculinity." In Bilde et al. 1997, 263–284.

Müller, C. W. 1992. "Patriotismus und Verweigerung: Eine Interpretation des euripideischen *Philoktet.*" *Rheinisches Museum für Philologie* cxxxv, 104–134.

Muellner, L. C. 1996. *The Anger of Achilles:* mēnis *in Greek Epic.* Ithaca, N.Y., & London, 1996).

Muir, E. 1993. *Mad Blood Stirring: Vendetta and Factions in Friuli during the Renaissance.* Baltimore & London.

Murray, O. 1965. "Philodemus on the Good King according to Homer." *Journal of Roman Studies* lv, 161–182.

———. 1967. "Aristeas and Ptolemaic Kingship." *Journal of Theological Studies* xviii, 337–371.

Musurillo, H. 1972. *The Acts of the Christian Martyrs.* Oxford.

Myers, F. R. 1988. "The Logic and Meaning of Anger among Pintupi Aborigines." *Man* n.s. xxiii, 589–610.

Nagle, B. R. 1984. "*Amor, ira,* and Sexual Identity in Ovid's *Metamorphoses.*" *Classical Antiquity* iii, 236–255.

Nauhardt, W. 1940. *Das Bild des Herrschers in der griechischen Dichtung.* Berlin.

Nehamas, A. 1992. "Pity and Fear in the *Rhetoric* and the *Poetics.*" In A. O. Rorty (ed.), *Essays on Aristotle's Poetics.* Princeton. 291–314. Repr. in D. J. Furley & A. Nehamas (eds.), *Aristotle's* Rhetoric: *Philosophical Essays* (Princeton, 1994), 257–282.

Nesse, R. 1990. "Evolutionary Explanations of Emotions." *Human Nature* i, 261–289.

Newman, R. J. 1989. "*Cotidie meditare:* Theory and Practice of the *Meditatio* in Imperial Stoicism." In *ANRW* II, 36, 3, 1473–1517.

Nichols, M. P., & M. Zax. 1977. *Catharsis in Psychotherapy.* New York.

Nippel, W. 1995. *Public Order in Ancient Rome.* Cambridge.

Nisbet, R. G. M. 1982. "'Great and Lesser Bear' (Ovid, *Tristia* 4, 3)." *Journal of Roman Studies* lxxii, 49–56. Repr. in *Collected Papers in Latin Literature* (Oxford, 1995), 147–160.

Nock, A. D. 1933. *Conversion: The Old and the New in Religion from Alexander the Great to Augustine of Hippo.* Oxford.

North, H. F. 1966. *Sophrosyne.* Ithaca, N.Y.

Novaco, R. W. 1975. *Anger Control: The Development and Evaluation of an Experimental Treatment.* Lexington, Mass.

Nussbaum, M. 1993. "Poetry and the Passions: Two Stoic Views." In Brunschwig & Nussbaum 1993, 97–149.

———. 1994. *The Therapy of Desire: Theory and Practice in Hellenistic Ethics.* Princeton.

Nutton, V. 1999. "Healers and the Healing Act in Classical Greece." *European Review* vii, 27–35.

Oakley, J. 1992. *Morality and the Emotions.* London & New York.

Oatley, K. 1993a. "Social Construction in Emotions." In Lewis & Haviland 1993, 341–352.

———. 1993b. "Those to Whom Evil Is Done." In R. S. Wyer & T. K. Srull (eds.), *Perspectives on Anger and Emotion.* Advances in Social Cognition 6. Hillsdale, N.J. 159–165.

———. 1997. Rev. of M. Nussbaum, *The Therapy of Desire* (1994) and *Poetic Justice* (1995). *Cognition and Emotion* xi, 307–330.

Oatley, K., and J. M. Jenkins. 1996. *Understanding Emotions.* Oxford.

Obbink, D. 1991. Rev. of G. Indelli's edition of Philodemus, *De ira. Bulletin of the American Society of Papyrologists* xxxviii, 79–89.

Ober, J. 1989. *Mass and Elite in Democratic Athens.* Princeton.

Opp, K.-D. 1983. *Die Entstehung sozialer Normen.* Tübingen.

Ortony, A., G. L. Clore & A. Collins. 1988. *The Cognitive Structure of Emotions.* Cambridge.

Ortony, A., & T. J. Turner. 1990. "What's Basic about Basic Emotions?" *Psychological Review* xcvii, 315–331.

Owen, G. E. L. 1960. "Logic and Metaphysics in Some Earlier Works of Aristotle." In I. Düring & G. E. L. Owen (eds.), *Aristotle and Plato in the Mid-Fourth Century.* Gothenburg. 163–190. Repr. in Barnes, Schofield & Sorabji 1979, III:13–32, and in Owen, *Logic, Science and Dialectic: Collected Papers in Greek Philosophy* (London, 1986), 180–199.

Padel, R. 1992. *In and Out of Mind: Greek Images of the Tragic Self.* Princeton.

Page, D. 1955. *Sappho and Alcaeus: An Introduction to the Study of Ancient Lesbian Poetry.* Oxford.

Pagels, E. 1988. *Adam, Eve, and the Serpent.* New York.

————. 1993. "The Rage of Angels." In Glick & Roose 1993, 235–244.

Paolucci, M. 1955. "Note sulla datazione del περὶ τοῦ καθ' Ὅμηρον ἀγαθοῦ βασιλέως." *Aevum* xxix, 201–209.

Parke, H. W., & D. E. W. Wormell. 1956. *The Delphic Oracle*, 2 vols. Oxford.

Parker, R. 1983. *Miasma: Pollution and Purification in Early Greek Religion*. Oxford.

Parkin, T. G. 1992. *Demography and Roman Society*. Baltimore & London.

Patterson, C. B. 1998. *The Family in Greek History*. Cambridge, Mass.

Pearcy, L. T. 1984. "Melancholy Rhetoricians and Melancholy Rhetoric: 'Black Bile' as a Rhetorical and Medical Term in the Second Century A.D." *Journal of the History of Medicine and Allied Sciences* xxxix, 446–456.

Pédech, P. 1964. *La méthode historique de Polybe*. Paris.

Peek, W. 1941. *Kerameikos: Ergebnisse der Ausgrabungen* III. Berlin.

Perret, J. 1967. "Optimisme et tragédie dans l'*Énéide*." *Revue des Études Latines* xlv, 342–362.

Pigeaud, J. 1981. *La maladie de l'âme: Étude sur la relation de l'âme et du corps dans la tradition médico-philosophique antique*. Paris.

Plutchik, R. 1980. *Emotion: A Psychoevolutionary Synthesis*. New York.

————. 1991. *The Emotions*, rev. ed. Lanham, Md.

Pohlenz, M. 1896. "Über Plutarchs Schrift περὶ ἀοργησίας." *Hermes* xxxi, 321–338.

————. 1906. "Das dritte und vierte Buch der Tusculanen." *Hermes* xli, 321–355.

————. 1909. *Vom Zorne Gottes: Eine Studie über den Einfluss der griechischen Philosophie auf das alte Christentum*. Göttingen.

————. 1948–49. *Die Stoa*, 2 vols. Göttingen.

————. 1966. *Freedom in Greek Life and Thought: The History of an Ideal*, trans. C. Lofmark. Dordrecht & New York. (Original ed.: *Griechische Freiheit*, Heidelberg, 1955.)

Pollock, L. A. 1983. *Forgotten Children: Parent-Child Relations from 1500 to 1900*. Cambridge.

Pomeroy, S. B. 1997. *Families in Classical and Hellenistic Greece: Representations and Realities*. Oxford.

Price, S. R. F. 1984. *Rituals and Power: The Roman Imperial Power in Asia Minor*. Cambridge.

Procopé, J. 1993. "Epicureans on Anger." In *Philanthropia kai eusebeia: Festschrift für Albrecht Dihle zum 70. Geburtstag*. Göttingen. 363–386. Repr. in Sihvola & Engberg-Pedersen 1998, 171–196.

Purcell, N. 1994. "The City of Rome and the *plebs urbana* in the Late Republic." In *Cambridge Ancient History* IX, 2nd ed. 644–688.

Putnam, M. 1990. "Anger, Blindness and Insight in Virgil's *Aeneid.*" *Apeiron* xxiii, 7–40.

Quasten, J. 1930. *Musik und Gesang in den Kulten der heidnischen Antike und christlichen Frühzeit.* Münster.

Quint, D. 1984. "Repetition and Ideology in the Aeneid." *Materiali e discussioni* xxiii, 9–54.

———. 1993. *Epic and Empire: Politics and Generic Form from Virgil to Milton.* Princeton.

Raaflaub, K. 1979. "Beute, Vergeltung, Freiheit? Zur Zielsetzung des Delisch-Attischen Seebundes." *Chiron* ix, 1–22.

———. 1989. "Die Anfänge des politischen Denkens bei den Griechen." *Historische Zeitschrift* ccxlviii, 1–31.

Rabbow, P. 1914. *Antike Schriften über Seelenheilung und Seelenleitung: I. Die Therapie des Zorns.* Leipzig & Berlin.

Rabel, R. J. 1997. *Plot and Point of View in the Iliad.* Ann Arbor, Mich.

Rakoczy, T. 1996. *Böser Blick, Macht des Auges und Neid der Götter.* Tübingen.

Ramondetti, P. 1996. *Struttura di Seneca,* De ira, *II–III: Una proposta d'interpretazione.* Bologna.

Rapaport, D. 1953. "On the Psycho-analytic Theory of Affects." *International Journal of Psycho-analysis* xxxiv, 177–198. Repr. in his *Collected Papers* (New York & London, 1967), 476–512.

Rather, L. J. 1965. *Mind and Body in Eighteenth-Century Medicine: A Study Based on Jerome Gaub's* De regimine mentis. London.

Rawson, E. 1970. "Family and Fatherland in Euripides' *Phoenissae.*" *Greek, Roman, and Byzantine Studies* xi, 109–127.

———. 1985. *Intellectual Life in the Late Roman Republic.* London.

———. 1989. "Roman Rulers and the Philosophic Adviser." In M. Griffin & J. Barnes (eds.), *Philosophia Togata: Essays on Philosophy and Roman Society.* Oxford. 233–257.

Reckford, K. J. 1976. "Father-Beating in Aristophanes' *Clouds.*" In S. Bertman (ed.), *The Conflict of Generations in Ancient Greece and Rome.* Amsterdam. 89–118.

Reddy, W. M. 1997. "Against Constructionism: The Historical Ethnography of the Emotions." *Current Anthropology* xxxviii, 327–351.

Redfield, J. R. 1975/1994. *Nature and Culture in the* Iliad: *The Tragedy of Hector.* Chicago; expanded ed. Durham, N.C., & London.

Reeve, M. D. 1972. "Euripides, *Medea* 1021–1080." *Classical Quarterly* xxii, 51–61.

Regenbogen, O. 1940. "Theophrastos." In *RE* Supplementband VII, cols. 1354–1562.

Renehan, R. 1963. "Aristotle's Definition of Anger." *Philologus* cvii, 61–76.

Retzinger, S. M. 1991. *Violent Emotions: Shame and Rage in Marital Quarrels.* Newbury Park, Calif.

Richardson, N. J. 1975. "Homeric Professors in the Age of the Sophists." *Proceedings of the Cambridge Philological Society* cci, 65–81.

———. 1992. "Aristotle's Reading of Homer and Its Background." In Lamberton & Keaney 1992, 30–40.

Riedel, M. 1969. *Studien zu Hegels Rechtsphilosophie.* Frankfurt am Main.

Riedinger, J.-C. 1976. "Remarques sur la τιμή chez Homère." *Revue des Études Grecques* lxxxix, 244–264.

Rieks, R. 1989. *Affekte und Strukturen als ein Form- und Wirkprinzip von Vergils Aeneis.* Munich.

Riginos, A. S. 1976. *Platonica.* Leiden.

Ringeltaube, H. 1913. *Quaestiones ad veterum de affectibus doctrinam pertinentes.* Göttingen.

Rist, J. M. 1969. *Stoic Philosophy.* Cambridge.

———. 1994. *Augustine.* Cambridge.

———. 1996. *Man, Soul and Body.* Aldershot.

Robinson, R. J. 1987. "The Civilizing Process: Some Remarks on Elias's Social History." *Sociology* xxi, 1–17.

Robinson, T. M. 1970. *Plato's Psychology.* Toronto.

Rosaldo, M. Z. 1980. *Knowledge and Passion: Ilongot Notions of Self and Social Life.* Cambridge.

Rosenberg, D. V. 1990. "Language in the Discourse of the Emotions." In C. A. Lutz & L. Abu-Lughod, *Language and the Politics of Emotion.* Cambridge. 162–185.

Rosenmeyer, T. G. 1988. *Deina ta polla.* Buffalo.

Rosenthal, F. 1975. *The Classical Heritage in Islam.* Berkeley & Los Angeles. (Original ed.: *Das Fortleben der Antike im Islam,* Zürich, 1965.)

Rosenwein, B. H. 1998. "Controlling Paradigms." In Rosenwein (ed). 1998, 233–247.

——— (ed.). 1998. *Anger's Past: The Social Uses of an Emotion in the Middle Ages.* Ithaca, N.Y., & London.

Rothenberg, A. 1971–72. "On Anger." *American Journal of Psychiatry* cxxviii, 454–460.

Rudich, V. 1997. *Dissidence and Literature under Nero: The Price of Rhetoricization.* London & New York.

Rütten, T. 1992. *Demokrit—lachender Philosoph und sanguinischer Melancholiker.* Leiden.

Runciman, W. 1982. "Origins of States: The Case of Archaic Greece." *Comparative Studies in Society and History* xxiv, 351–377.

Russell, D. A. 1983. *Greek Declamation.* Cambridge.

Russell, J. A. 1991. "Culture and the Categorization of Emotions." *Psychological Bulletin* cx, 426–450.

Said, S. 1984. "La tragédie de la vengeance." In Verdier & Poly 1984, IV:47–90.

———. 1993. "Couples fraternels chez Sophocle." In A. Machin & L. Pernée, *Sophocle: Le texte, les personnages*. Aix-en-Provence. 299–328.

Saller, R. P. 1994. *Patriarchy, Property, and Death in the Roman Family*. Cambridge.

Sandbach, F. H. 1985. *Aristotle and the Stoics*. Cambridge.

Saunders, T. J. 1991. *Plato's Penal Code: Tradition, Controversy and Reform in Greek Penology*. Oxford.

Schadewaldt, W. 1926. *Monolog und Selbstgespräch*. Berlin.

Schieffelin, B. B., K. A. Woolard & P. Kroskrity (eds.). 1998. *Language Ideologies: Practice and Theory*. New York & Oxford.

Schieffelin, E.L 1983. "Anger and Shame in the Tropical Forest: On Affect as a Cultural System in Papua New Guinea." *Ethos* xi, 181–191.

———. 1985. "Anger, Grief, and Shame: Toward a Kaluli Ethnopsychology." In White & Kirkpatrick 1985, 168–182.

Schimmel, S. 1979. "Anger and Its Control in Graeco-Roman and Modern Psychology." *Psychiatry* xlii, 320–337.

Schmidt, J. H. H. 1876–1886. *Synonymik der griechischen Sprache*, 4 vols. Leipzig.

Schmidt, M. 1992. "Medeia." In *LIMC* VI. Zurich & Munich. 386–398.

Schofield, M., & G. Striker (eds.). 1986. *The Norms of Nature: Studies in Hellenistic Ethics*. Paris & Cambridge.

Schröder, S. 1996. "Die Lebensdaten Menanders." *Zeitschrift für Papyrologie und Epigraphik* cxiii, 35–48.

Schubart, W. 1937. "Das hellenistische Königsideal nach Inschriften und Papyri." *Archiv für Papyrusforschung* xii, 1–26. Repr. in H. Kloft (ed.), *Ideologie und Herrschaft in der Antike* (Darmstadt, 1979), 90–122.

Schwyzer, E. 1931. "Drei griechische Wörter." *Rheinisches Museum* lxx, 209–217.

Scully, S. 1981. "The Polis in Homer: A Definition and Interpretation." *Ramus* x, 1–34.

———. 1984. "The Language of Achilles: The ὀχθήσας Formulas." *Transactions of the American Philological Association* cxiv, 11–27.

Seaford, R. 1994. *Reciprocity and Ritual: Homer and Tragedy in the Developing City State*. Oxford.

Sedley, D. 1973. "Epicurus, *On Nature* Book XXVIII." *Cronache Ercolanesi* iii, 5–83.

———. 1976. "Epicurus and His Professional Rivals." *Cahiers de philologie publiés par le Centre de Recherche de l'Université de Lille* i, 121–159.

Segal, C. 1992. "Bard and Audience in Homer." In Lamberton & Keaney 1992, 3–29.

Servan-Schreiber, D., & W. M. Perlstein. 1998. "Selective Limbic Activation and Its Relevance to Emotional Disorders." *Cognition and Emotion* xii, 331–352.

Setaioli, A. 1988. *Seneca e i greci: Citazioni e traduzioni nelle opere filosofiche.* Bologna.

Shaver, P. R., S. Wu & J. C. Schwartz. 1992. "Cross-Cultural Similarities and Differences in Emotion and Its Representation." In M. S. Clark 1992, 175–212.

Shaw, B. D. 1985. "The Divine Economy: Stoicism as Ideology." *Latomus* xliv, 16–54.

———. 1987. "The Family in Late Antiquity: The Experience of Augustine." *Past and Present* cxv, 3–51.

Sherman, N. 1989. *The Fabric of Character: Aristotle's Theory of Virtue.* Oxford.

Siegman, A. W., & T. W. Smith (eds.). 1994. *Anger, Hostility and the Heart.* Hillsdale, N.J.

Sihvola, J., & T. Engberg-Pedersen (eds.). 1998. *The Emotions in Hellenistic Philosophy.* Dordrecht, Boston, & London, 1998).

Simon, A. K. H. 1938. *Comicae Tabellae.* Emsdetten.

Simon, B. 1978. *Mind and Madness in Ancient Greece: The Classical Roots of Modern Psychiatry.* Ithaca, N.Y., & London.

———. 1988. *Tragic Drama and the Family: Psychoanalytic Studies from Aeschylus to Beckett.* New Haven & London.

Singer, J. L. (ed.). 1990. *Repression and Dissociation.* Chicago.

Smith, C. A., & P. C. Ellsworth. 1985. "Patterns of Cognitive Appraisal in Emotion." *Journal of Personality and Social Psychology* xlviii, 813–838.

Snell, B. 1953. *The Discovery of the Mind,* trans. T. G. Rosenmeyer. Cambridge, Mass. (Original ed.: *Die Entdeckung des Geistes,* Hamburg, 1948.)

Snodgrass, A. 1986. "La formazione dello stato greco." *Opus* v, 7–21.

Sodano, A. R. 1991. "Porfirio 'gnomologo': Contributo alla tradizione e alla critica testuale delle sillogi gnomiche." *Sileno* xvii, 5–41.

Solmsen, F. 1938. "Aristotle and Cicero on the Orator's Playing upon the Feelings." *Classical Philology* xxxiii, 390–404.

Solomon, R. C. 1984. "Getting Angry: The Jamesian Theory of Emotion in Anthropology." In R. A. Shweder & R. A. LeVine (eds.), *Culture Theory: Essays on Mind, Self, and Emotion.* Cambridge. 238–254.

———. 1993. "The Philosophy of Emotions." In Lewis & Haviland 1993, 3–15.

Sommers, S. 1988. "Understanding Emotions: Some Interdisciplinary Considerations." In C. Z., & P. N. Stearns (eds.), *Emotion and Social Change: Towards a New Psychohistory.* New York & London. 23–38.

Sorabji, R. 1997. "Is Stoic Philosophy Helpful as Psychotherapy?" In Sorabji (ed.) 1997, 197–209.

———. 2000. *Emotion and Peace of Mind: From Stoic Agitation to Christian Temptation.* Oxford.

——— (ed.). 1997. *Aristotle and After.* London.

Sourvinou-Inwood, C. 1989. "Assumptions and the Creation of Meaning: Reading Sophocles' *Antigone.*" *Journal of Hellenic Studies* cix, 134–148.

Spelman, E. V. 1989. "Anger and Insubordination." In A. Garry & M. Pearsall (eds.), *Women, Knowledge and Reality: Explorations in Feminist Philosophy.* Boston. 263–273.

Spiegel, G. M. 1990. "History, Historicism, and the Social Logic of the Text." *Speculum* lxv, 59–86.

Stahl, H. P. 1990. "The Death of Turnus: Augustan Vergil and the Political Rival." In K. A. Raaflaub & M. Toher (eds.), *Between Republic and Empire: Interpretations of Augustus and His Principate.* Berkeley & Los Angeles. 174–211.

Stanford, W. B. 1983. *Greek Tragedy and the Emotions.* London.

Starr, C. G. 1986. *Individual and Community: The Rise of the Polis 800–500 B.C.* New York & Oxford.

Stearns, C. Z., & P. N. Stearns. 1986. *Anger: The Struggle for Emotional Control in America's History.* Chicago & London.

———. 1990. "Introducing the History of Emotion." *Psychohistory Review* xviii, 263–291.

Stearns, P. N. 1992. "Gender and Emotion: A Twentieth-Century Transition." In *Social Perspectives on Emotion* i, 127–160.

———. 1993. "History of Emotions: The Issue of Change." In Lewis & Haviland 1993, 17–28.

Stewart, A. F. 1977. *Skopas of Paros.* Park Ridge, N.J.

Stewart, C. 2000. "Evagrius Ponticus on Prayer and Anger." In Valantasis 2000, 65–81.

Stocker, M. 1996. With E. Hegeman. *Valuing Emotions.* Cambridge.

Stone, L. 1983. "Interpersonal Violence in English Society." *Past and Present* ci, 22–33.

Stoney, C. M., & T. O. Engebretson. 1994. "Anger and Hostility: Potential Mediators of the Gender Difference in Coronary Heart Disease." In Siegman & Smith 1994, 215–237.

Strauss, B. 1993. *Fathers and Sons in Athens.* Princeton.

Striker, G. 1991. "Following Nature: A Study in Stoic Ethics." *Oxford Studies in Ancient Philosophy* ix, 1–73.

———. 1999. Rev. of M. Erler et al. *Grundriss der Geschichte der Philosophie,* vol. IV. *Gnomon* lxxi, 101–105.

Stroheker, K. F. 1953–54. "Zu den Anfängen der monarchischen Theorie in der Sophistik." *Historia* ii, 381–412.

Sullivan, S. D. 1993. "Person and θυμός in the Poetry of Hesiod." *Emerita* lxi, 15–40.

———. 1999. *Sophocles' Use of Psychological Terminology.* Ottawa.

Sutton, R. F. 1981. "The Interaction between Men and Women Portrayed on Attic Red-Figure Pottery." Ph.D. diss., University of North Carolina, 1981.

———. 1992. "Pornography and Persuasion in Attic Potery." In A. Richlin (ed.), *Pornography and Representation in Greece and Rome.* Oxford. 3–35.

Svenbro, J. 1984. "Vengeance et société en Grèce archaïque: À propos de la fin de l'Odyssée." In Verdier & Poly 1984, III:47–63.

Syme, R. 1939. *The Roman Revolution.* Oxford.

———. 1958. *Tacitus,* 2 vols. Oxford.

———. 1978. *History in Ovid.* Oxford.

Tafrate, R. C. 1995. "Evaluation of Treatment Strategies for Adult Anger Disorders." In Kassinove 1995, 109–129.

Tangney, J. P., et al. 1996. "Assessing Individual Differences in Constructive versus Destructive Responses to Anger across the Life Span." *Journal of Personality and Social Psychology* lxx, 780–796.

Tarkow, T. A. 1982. "Achilles and the Ghost of Aeschylus in Aristophanes' 'Frogs.'" *Traditio* xxxviii, 1–16.

Tarn, W. W. 1952. *Hellenistic Civilization,* 3rd ed. London.

Tcherikover, V. 1958. "The Ideology of the Letter of Aristeas." *Harvard Theological Review* li, 59–85.

Temoshok, L., et al. (eds.). 1983. *Emotions in Health and Illness: Theoretical and Research Foundations.* New York.

Thalmann, W. G. 1986. "Aeschylus' Physiology of the Emotions." *American Journal of Philology* cvii, 89–111.

Thériault, G. 1996. *Le culte d'homonoia dans les cités grecques.* Lyon.

Thesleff, H. (ed.). 1965. *The Pythagorean Texts of the Hellenistic Period.* Åbo.

Thomas, S. P. 1990. "Theoretical and Empirical Perspectives on Anger." *Issues in Mental Health Nursing* xi, 203–216.

Thomas, Y. 1984. "Se venger au forum: Solidarité familiale et procès criminel à Rome (premier siècle av.–deuxième siècle ap. J. C.." In Verdier & Poly 1984, III:65–100.

Thome, J. 1995. *Psychotherapeutische Aspekte in der Philosophie Platons.* Hildesheim.

Thompson, J. B. 1984. *Studies in the Theory of Ideology.* Berkeley & Los Angeles.

Thornton, A. 1984. *Homer's Iliad: Its Composition and the Motif of Supplication.* Göttingen.

Tobin, J. 1997. *Herodes Attikos and the City of Athens.* Amsterdam.

Toohey, P. 1990. "Some Ancient Histories of Literary Melancholia." *Illinois Classical Studies* xv, 143–161.

Treggiari, S. 1991. *Roman Marriage:* iusti coniuges *from the Time of Cicero to the Time of Ulpian.* Oxford.

Trevett, J. 1992. *Apollodorus the Son of Pasion.* Oxford.

Urmson, J. O. 1973. "Aristotle's Doctrine of the Mean." *American Philosophical Quarterly* x, 223–230. Repr. in A. O. Rorty (ed.), *Explaining Emotions* (Berkeley & Los Angeles, 1980), 157–170.

Valantasis, R. (ed.). 2000. *Religions of Late Antiquity in Practice.* Princeton.

Valette-Cagnac, E. 1997. *La lecture à Rome.* Paris.

Van Bennekom, R. 1991. "θυμὸς." In *LFE* II, cols. 1077–1090.

van Krieken, R. 1989. "Violence, Self-Discipline, and Modernity: Beyond the 'Civilising Process.'" *Sociological Review* xxxvii, 193–218.

Van Wees, H. 1992. *Status Warriors: War, Violence and Society in Homer and History.* Amsterdam.

——. 1997. Rev. of Ø. Andersen & M. Dickie (eds.), *Homer's World: Fiction, Tradition, Reality. Journal of Hellenic Studies* cxvii, 216–217.

Vegetti, M. 1995. "Passioni antiche: L'io collerico." In S. Vegetti Finzi (ed.), *Storia delle passioni.* Bari & Rome. 39–73.

Verdenius, W. J. 1970. *Homer, the Educator of the Greeks.* Mededelingen der Koninklijke Nederlandse Akademie van Wetenschappen 33.5. Amsterdam & London.

Verdier, R., & J.-P. Poly (eds.). 1984. *La vengeance: Études d'ethnologie, d'histoire et de philosophie,* 4 vols. Paris.

Vérilhac, A.-M., & C. Vial. 1998. *Le mariage grec du VIe siècle av. J.-C. à l'époque d'Auguste. Bulletin de Correspondance Hellénique* Suppl. 32. Athens.

Vernant, J.-P. 1970. "Greek Tragedy: Problems of Interpretation." In R. Macksey & E. Donato (eds.), *The Structuralist Controversy: The Languages of Criticism and the Sciences of Man.* Baltimore. 273–289.

Versnel, H. S. 1985. "'May He Not Be Able to Sacrifice . . .': Concerning a Curious Formula in Greek and Latin Curses." *Zeitschrift für Papyrologie und Epigraphik* lviii, 247–269.

——. 1991. "Beyond Cursing: The Appeal to Justice in Judicial Prayers." In C. A. Faraone & D. Obbink (eds.), *Magika Hiera: Ancient Greek Magic and Religion.* New York & Oxford. 60–116.

——. 1998. "καὶ εἴ τι λ[οιπόν]. . . : An Essay on Anatomical Curses." In *Ansichten griechischer Rituale: Geburtstag-Symposium für Walter Burkert.* Stuttgart & Leipzig. 217–267.

Veyne, P. 1976. *Le pain et le cirque: Sociologie historique d'un pluralisme politique.* Paris.

————. 1978. "La famille et l'amour sous le Haut-empire romain." *Annales ESC* xxxiii, 35–63.

————. 1987. "The Roman Empire." In P. Veyne (ed.), *A History of Private Life* I. Cambridge, Mass. (Original ed.: *Histoire de la vie privée* I, Paris, 1985).

————. 1993. Introduction to translations of Seneca, *Entretiens*. Paris.

————. 1999. "Païens et chrétiens devant la gladiature." *Mélanges de l'École Française de Rome: Antiquité* cxi, 883–917.

Viljoen, G. 1959. "Plato and Aristotle on the Exposure of Infants at Athens." *Acta Classica* ii, 58–69.

Vlastos, G. 1991. *Socrates, Ironist and Moral Philosopher.* Ithaca, N.Y.

Vögtle, A. 1950. "Affekte Gottes." *Reallexikon für Antike und Christentum* I, cols. 165–173.

————. 1993. "Zorn, I: Schrift und Umwelt." *Lexikon für Theologie und Kirche* X. Freiburg. Cols. 1403–1404.

Voelke, A.-J. 1993. *La philosophie comme thérapie de l'âme: Études de philosophie hellénistique.* Paris.

Voigtländer, H.-D. 1957. "Spätere Überarbeitungen im grossen Medeamonolog." *Philologus* ci, 217–237.

Wade-Gery, H. T. 1952. *The Poet of the Iliad.* Cambridge.

Walbank, F. W. 1972. *Polybius.* Berkeley & Los Angeles.

————. 1984. "Monarchies and Monarchic Ideas." In *Cambridge Ancient History* VII, 2nd ed. 62–100.

Wallace, R. W. 1994. "The Athenian Laws against Slander." In G. Thür (ed.), *Symposion 1993: Vorträge zur griechischen und hellenistischen Rechtsgeschichte.* Cologne, Weimar & Vienna, 109–124.

Wallace-Hadrill, A. W. 1981. "The Emperor and His Virtues." *Historia* xxx, 298–323.

Walsh, P. G. 1963. *Livy: His Historical Aims and Methods.* Cambridge.

Ward, L. G., & R. Throop. 1992. "Emotional Experience in Dewey and Mead: Notes for the Social Psychology of Emotion." *Social Perspectives on Emotion* i, 61–94.

Waters, K. H. 1971. *Herodotus on Tyrants and Despots: A Study in Objectivity. Historia* Einzelschriften 15. Wiesbaden.

Watson, A. 1987. *Roman Slave Law.* Baltimore & London.

Watson-Gegeo, K. A., & G. M. White (eds.). 1990. *Disentangling: Conflict Discourse in Pacific Societies.* Stanford.

Weinstock, S. 1971. *Divus Julius.* Oxford.

Welwei, K.-W. 1963. *Könige und Königtum im Urteil des Polybios.* Cologne.

West, M. L. 1990. *Studies in Aeschylus.* Stuttgart.

———. 1992a. "Analecta musica." *Zeitschrift für Papyrologie und Epigraphik* xcii, 1–54.

———. 1992b. *Ancient Greek Music*. Oxford.

———. 1995. "The Date of the *Iliad*." *Museum Helveticum* lii, 203–219.

———. 1997. *The East Face of Helicon*. Oxford.

Westermann, W. L. 1955. *Slave Systems of Greek and Roman Antiquity*. Philadelphia.

White, G. M., & J. Kirkpatrick (eds.). 1985. *Person, Self, and Experience*. Berkeley & Los Angeles.

White, S. D. 1998. "The Politics of Anger." In Rosenwein (ed.) 1998, 127–152.

Whitehorn, J. C. 1939. "Physiological Changes in Emotional States." In *The Inter-Relationship of Mind and Body: Proceedings of the Association for Research on Nervous and Mental Disease*. Baltimore. 256–270.

Whittaker, J. 1979. "Christianity and Morality in the Roman Empire." *Vigiliae Christianae* xxxiii, 209–225. Repr. in E. Ferguson (ed.), *Christian Life: Ethics, Morality, and Discipline in the Early Church* (New York & London, 1993), 19–35.

Wibbing, S. 1959. *Die Tugend- und Lasterkataloge im Neuen Testament*. Berlin.

Wiedemann, T. 1981. *Greek and Roman Slavery*. London.

———. 1989. *Adults and Children in the Roman Empire*, London.

Wiemer, H.-U. 1995. *Libanios und Julian: Studien zum Verhältnis von Rhetorik und Politik im vierten Jahrhundert n. Chr.* Munich.

Wierzbicka, A. 1992. *Semantics, Culture and Cognition: Universal Human Concepts in Culture-Specific Configurations*. New York.

———. 1994. "Emotions, Language, and Cultural Scripts." In S. Kitayama & H. R. Markus (eds.), *Emotion and Culture: Empirical Studies of Mutual Influence*. Washington, D.C. 133–196.

Williams, B. 1973. "The Analogy of the City and the Soul in Plato's *Republic*." In *Exegesis and Argument: Studies in Greek Philosophy Presented to Gregory Vlastos*. Assen. 196–206.

———. 1997. "Stoic Philosophy and the Emotions: Reply to Richard Sorabji." In Sorabji (ed.) 1997, 211–213.

Williams, C. A. 1999. *Roman Homosexuality: Ideologies of Masculinity in Classical Antiquity*. Oxford & New York.

Wilson, S. 1988. *Feuding, Conflict and Banditry in Nineteenth-Century Corsica*. Cambridge.

Winnington-Ingram, R. P. 1980. *Sophocles: An Interpretation* Cambridge.

Wiseman, T. P. 1995. *Remus: A Roman Myth*. Cambridge.

Wood, S. 1986. *Roman Portrait Sculpture, 217–260 A.D.* Leiden.

Wright, M. R. 1997. *"Ferox virtus:* Anger in Virgil's *Aeneid."* In Braund & Gill 1997, 169–184.

Yavetz, Z. 1996. "Caligula, Imperial Madness and Modern Historiography." *Klio* lxxviii, 105–129.

Zanker, G. 1987. *Realism in Alexandrian Poetry: A Literature and Its Audience.* London.

Commentaries

The following are the commentaries referred to in the footnotes.

Accius, fragments: J. Dangel (Paris, 1995).

Aeschylus, *Eumenides:* A. H. Sommerstein (Cambridge, 1989); *Persae:* H. G. Broadhead (Cambridge, 1960); *Septem:* G. O. Hutchinson (Oxford, 1985); [Aesch.] *PV:* P. Groeneboom (Groningen, 1928), M. Griffith (Cambridge, 1983).

Aristophanes, *Birds:* N. Dunbar (Oxford, 1995); *Ecclesiazousae:* R. G. Ussher (Oxford, 1973).

Aristotle, *Nicomachean Ethics:* F. Dirlmeier (Berlin, 1983).

[Aristotle], *Constitution of Athens:* P. J. Rhodes (Oxford, 1981).

Cicero, *Ad Atticum:* D. R. Shackleton Bailey (Cambridge, 1965–1968); *Ad Quintum Fratrem:* D. R. Shackleton Bailey (Cambridge, 1980).

Demosthenes, *Against Meidias* (XXI): D. M. MacDowell (Oxford, 1990).

Empedocles: J. Bollack (Paris, 1965–1969), M. R. Wright (New Haven & London, 1981).

Euripides, *Andromache:* P. T. Stevens (Oxford, 1971); *Bacchae:* E. R. Dodds (2nd ed., Oxford, 1960); *Heracles:* G. W. Bond (Oxford, 1981); *Orestes:* C. W. Willink (Oxford, 1986).

Greek Anthology, Garland of Philip: A. S. F. Gow and D. L. Page (Cambridge, 1968).

Gregory of Nazianzus, *De ira:* M. Oberhaus (Paderborn, 1991).

Heraclitus, fragments: C. H. Kahn (Cambridge, 1979).

Herodas, *Mimiambi:* I. C. Cunningham (Oxford, 1971).

Herodotus III: D. Asheri (Milan, 1990).

Hesiod, *Works and Days:* M. L. West (Oxford, 1978).

Homer, *Iliad* I–IV: G. S. Kirk (Cambridge, 1985); IX–XII: B. Hainsworth (Cambridge, 1993); XIII–XVI: R. Janko (Cambridge, 1992).

Homer, *Odyssey:* A. Heubeck, S. West, J. Russo et al. (Oxford, 1988).

Homeric Hymn to Demeter: N.J. Richardson (Oxford, 1974).

Horace, *Odes* I: R. G. M. Nisbet & M. Hubbard (Oxford, 1970).

Juvenal: E. Courtney (London, 1980).

Lactantius, *De ira dei:* C. Ingremeau (Paris, 1982).

Laudatio Turiae: M. Durry & S. Lancel (*Éloge funèbre d'une matrone romaine,* Paris, 1992).

Menander Rhetor: D. A. Russell & N. G. Wilson (Oxford, 1981).

Nag Hammadi Codex VII: B. A. Pearson et al. (Leiden, 1996).

Philodemus, *De bono rege secundum Homerum:* T. Dorandi (Naples, 1982); *De ira:* G. Indelli (Naples, 1988); *De musica* IV: A. J. Neubecker (Naples, 1986).

Plato, *Gorgias:* E. R. Dodds (Oxford, 1959); *Protagoras:* C. C. W. Taylor (revised ed., Oxford, 1991).

Pliny, *Letters:* A. N. Sherwin-White (Oxford, 1966); *Panegyricus:* M. Durry (Paris, 1938).

Plutarch, *Coniugalia praecepta:* S. B. Pomeroy et al. (Oxford, 1999); *De cohibenda ira:* R. Laurenti & G. Indelli (Naples, 1988); *Pericles:* P. A. Stadter (Chapel Hill, 1989).

Polybius: F. W. Walbank (Oxford, 1957–1979); Book V: P. Pédech (Paris, 1977).

Poseidonius: I. G. Kidd (Cambridge, 1988).

Seneca, *Dialogi* I–V: G. Viansino (Milan, 1988); *De ira* II–III: R. Malchow (Erlangen, 1987).

Sophocles, *Ajax:* R. C. Jebb (London, 1898).

Tacitus, *Dialogus:* A. Gudeman (2nd ed., Leipzig & Berlin, 1914).

Thucydides: J. Classen, revised by J. Steup (Berlin, 1892–1922); A. W. Gomme, A. Andrewes & K. J. Dover (Oxford, 1945–1981); J. De Romilly (Paris, 1953–1972); S. Hornblower (Oxford, 1991–).

Index

absolute opposition to anger, 4, 18, 26, 31, 48–49, 63, 68, 102, 105–108, 109, 110–112, 112–114, 116–120, 121–122, 123, 125, 210, 377, 380–382, 399, 403

accidie, akēdia, 17, 21–22n

Accius, 202–203

Achilles, 51, 64, 65, 76, 77, 105, 117, 124, 131–135, 136, 137, 140–143, 147, 149, 150, 151–152, 153, 203, 215, 235, 238n, 340–341, 344, 412

adaptive utility of anger, supposed, 46, 414

adultery, 184n, 219

Aelius Aristides, 225

Aemilius Scaurus, M., 322

Aeneas, 149, 265; his killing of Turnus in the *Aeneid,* 217–218, 246–247

Aeschines, 186

Aeschylus, 53n, 76n, 137, 163, 167; *Agamemnon,* 65, 161; *Choephori,* 167; *Eumenides,* 161–162, 297, 344; *Myrmidons,* 163n; *Oresteia,* 74–75, 161, 162, 168, 352; *Persians,* 160, 167, 171; *Seven against Thebes,* 160–161, 299; *Supplices,* 161. See also *Prometheus Bound*

Aesop, and slavery, 335

Aetolians, 198

Agamemnon, 131–133, 136, 140, 141, 152, 153, 278–279

aganaktein, 53, 123

aidōs, 36, 80

Ajax, 64, 150, 174, 210

alastōr, 65

Alcaeus, 153, 154

Alcibiades, 119n, 232

Alcoholics Anonymous, 382

Alexander of Macedon, 41–42, 195, 235–237, 240, 251, 362, 412

Alexandria, Alexandrians, 198, 245, 250–251, 269–270

Alice in Wonderland, 41n

altruistic anger, 41, 61n

ambition, intellectual, 358

Ambrose, 262

American critiques of anger, 7–8, 23, 44; anger therapy, 367–368. *See also* United States

Ammianus Marcellinus, 261

amygdala, 37

Anaxarchus of Abdera, 237

Andronicus of Rhodes, Ps.-, 128

anger: definitions of, 24–25, 32–33, 40–42, 114; terms for, untranslatability of, 35; "bottling up", 44; contemporary pleas in favour of, 45–47; of crowds, 41; dangers of, 409–410 and *passim;* displaced, 41n; possible duration of, 40–42; feminist, 44; hidden, 65, 278, 379; cannot be hidden, 65–66; compared to honey and to smoke, 132; said to be involuntary, 412; judgemental, 39; just, 161, 218, 251; anger and madness, 63–64, 121, 344–345; medical disadvantages of failure to control, 47; as mitigation or excuse, 62, 65, 219, 220; moral indifference of some,

457